ISBN 978-0-260-03435-9
PIBN 11027487

1 MONTH OF
FREE
READING

at

www.ForgottenBooks.com

By purchasing this book you are eligible for one month membership to ForgottenBooks.com, giving you unlimited access to our entire collection of over 1,000,000 titles via our web site and mobile apps.

To claim your free month visit:

www.forgottenbooks.com/free1027487

REPORTS OF CASES

ARGUED AND DETERMINED

IN THE

𝕰nglish 𝕮ourts of 𝕮ommon 𝕷aw.

WITH

TABLES OF THE CASES AND PRINCIPAL MATTERS.

EDITED BY

HON. GEORGE SHARSWOOD.

VOL. XC.

CONTAINING

THE CASES DETERMINED IN PART OF MICHAELMAS TERM, 1856, HILARY
TERM AND VACATION, EASTER TERM AND TRINITY TERM, 1857,
XX. VICTORIA.

PHILADELPHIA:

T. & J. W. JOHNSON & CO., LAW BOOKSELLERS,

NO. 535 CHESTNUT STREET.

1871.

359696

REPORTS

OF

CASES

ARGUED AND DETERMINED IN THE

COURT OF QUEEN'S BENCH,

AND THE

COURT OF EXCHEQUER CHAMBER

ON ERROR FROM THE COURT OF QUEEN'S BENCH.

WITH TABLES OF THE NAMES OF THE CASES ARGUED AND CITED, AND THE
PRINCIPAL MATTERS.

BY
THOMAS FLOWER ELLIS, OF THE MIDDLE TEMPLE,
AND
COLIN BLACKBURN, OF THE INNER TEMPLE,
ESQRS., BARRISTERS AT LAW.

VOL. VII.

CONTAINING THE CASES DETERMINED IN PART OF MICHAELMAS TERM, 1856,
HILARY TERM AND VACATION, EASTER TERM AND TRINITY TERM, 1857,
XX. VICTORIA.

PHILADELPHIA:
T. & J. W. JOHNSON & CO., LAW BOOKSELLERS,
NO. 535 CHESTNUT STREET.
1871.

JUDGES

OF

THE COURT OF QUEEN'S BENCH,

DURING THE PERIOD OF THESE REPORTS.

The Right Hon. JOHN Lord CAMPBELL, Chief Justice.

Sir JOHN TAYLOR COLERIDGE, Knt.
Sir WILLIAM WIGHTMAN, Knt.
Sir WILLIAM ERLE, Knt.
Sir CHARLES CROMPTON, Knt.

ATTORNEYS-GENERAL.

Sir ALEXANDER JAMES EDMUND COCKBURN, Knt.
Sir RICHARD BETHELL, Knt.

SOLICITORS-GENERAL.

Sir RICHARD BETHELL, Knt.
The Right Hon. JAMES STUART WORTLEY.
Sir HENRY SINGER KEATING, Knt.

A

TABLE

OF

THE NAMES OF THE CASES

REPORTED IN THIS VOLUME.

TABLE OF CASES CITED.

D.

R.

S.

T.

CASES

ARGUED AND DETERMINED

IN

THE QUEEN'S BENCH,

IN

𝔐𝔦𝔠𝔥𝔞𝔢𝔩𝔪𝔞𝔰 𝔗𝔢𝔯𝔪,

XX VICTORIA. 1856.

(MICHAELMAS TERM CONTINUED FROM VOL. VI.)

MARTIN v. ANDREWS. *Nov. 22.*

An action is maintainable for money had and received to recover back conduct-money paid to a party, under stat. 5 Eliz. c. 9, s. 12, upon a subpœna to attend a trial as witness where, in consequence of the cause being settled, no trial takes place and the party incurs no expense and does no act in consequence of the subpœna.

It makes no difference that the party paying the money has had the sum allowed on taxation of costs, if, in fact, he has not obtained it. At any rate, such a defence cannot be raised under a plea of Nunquam indebitatus.

DECLARATION for money had and received. Plea: Never indebted. Issue thereon.

On the trial, before the under-sheriff of Middlesex, in Middlesex, on 12th June, 1856, it appeared that the defendant was an attorney residing at Dorchester. He had acted as attorney for a person named Cosserat in an action brought by the present plaintiff against Cosserat, *in which action notice of trial in London was given for 27th June, 1855. The plaintiff subpœnaed the present defendant to give evidence on the trial of that cause, served the subpœna upon him at Dorchester, and placed in his hands 6*l.* for expenses. It was admitted that Dorchester was 140 miles distant from London. The present defendant came up to London on 25th June, and, on 26th June, attended a meeting with the attorney of the plaintiff, and joined in settling the action of Martin v. Cosserat, upon the terms of judgment for a certain

[*2

sum, with costs, being entered against Cosserat. The agreement was
carried into effect; and the cause of Martin *v.* Cosserat was therefore
never tried. The plaintiff afterwards demanded back the 6*l.* from the
defendant, and, upon its not being repaid, brought the present action.
It appeared that the 6*l.* had been allowed in the taxation of costs in
Martin *v.* Cosserat, being included in the affidavit of increase. Sir
Archer Croft, the taxing Master in that cause, stated, on the trial of
the present cause, that he had allowed the 6*l.* on the supposition that
the plaintiff had attempted to get it back; and Mr. Walton, the Master
of the Court of Exchequer, stated that, when the sum paid for conduct-
money is reasonable, and no trial takes place, and the party praying
the money cannot recover it back, it is customary to allow it on taxation. A fi. fa. had issued in Martin *v.* Cosserat; and execution had
been levied; but the sum levied was not nearly sufficient to meet the
judgment debt and costs.

The under-sheriff directed a nonsuit, but suspended execution, reserving leave to move to enter a verdict for the plaintiff for 6*l.* In this
Term, *D. Power* obtained a rule Nisi accordingly.

*3]   *Prentice* now showed cause.—The plaintiff has had the 6*l.*
already allowed him in the taxation : and he may yet recover it
from the defendant in Martin *v.* Cosserat by a further levy. There
has been no failure of consideration. Where money is given to a witness, under stat. 5 Eliz. c. 9, s. 12, it is paid for the witness being
compellable to attend. The party serving the subpœna has then,
under the statute, the compulsory power over the witness : the witness
is immediately subjected to a liability, which renders it necessary for
him to make arrangements enabling him to attend. The money thenceforward is the money of the witness. This is not affected by the circumstance that, in the event, the witness is not required actually to
give evidence. Crompton *v.* Hutton, 3 Taunt. 230, is an authority
against this claim.

D. Power, contrà.—The defendant has no right to insist on the
taxation, which is merely as between the parties to the former action.
[Lord CAMPBELL, C. J.—Do you say that the plaintiff, after getting
the money by the execution, could come upon this defendant for it?]
It is not necessary to contend for that: and the plaintiff is ready to
allow the 6*l.* to be struck off the allocatur, or will hold it as trustee
for the defendant in the former action. The plaintiff now is in truth
carrying out the condition impliedly imposed by the taxation. [Lord
CAMPBELL, C. J.—The defendant pleads only Never indebted : the
allowance in the taxation, at any rate, cannot prevent him from having
once been indebted. ERLE, J.—Will Mr. *Prentice* now suggest, ore
*4]   *tenus, a plea which will raise this defence ?] (*D. Power* was then
stopped by the Court.)

Lord CAMPBELL, C. J.—The declaration is for money had and re ceived; and the only plea is Nunquam indebitatus. It appears that the defendant received 6*l*. as conduct-money: and, on the evidence, he did nothing in pursuance of the subpœna: he only attended, as attorney for one of the parties, to settle the cause. We have therefore to consider the general question whether money so paid to a party on a subpœna is, or is not, recoverable as money had and received. I think it is. The consideration has failed. The money is paid for the purpose of defraying the expenses of the witness's journey: if there is no journey there is no expense, and the consideration fails; and then an action lies for money had and received. There is indeed no express authority: but the general principles upon which that action is maintained are applicable. Had this been a summary application for the exercise of our jurisdiction, I incline to think that we could not have ordered the defendant to refund the money, the plaintiff having included the sum in the judgment. But we must here look at the record. The only plea is Nunquam indebitatus; and it is clear that, before the taxation, the defendant was indebted to the plaintiff. Even if what took place before the Master raised a defence, Mr. *Prentice* was unable to suggest to us, ore tenus, a plea under which such defence could be shown.

COLERIDGE, J.—I am entirely of the same opinion; and I have nothing to add.

(WIGHTMAN, J., was absent.)

*ERLE, J.—I have only to add that here the money was not [*5 paid under a contract that the defendant should attend: the plaintiff was obliged by the law to give the conduct-money. If he had not given it, and the defendant had incurred expense, the plaintiff would have been liable to the defendant; and, if the defendant, not being paid, had not attended, and the plaintiff had sued him for such non-attendance, there must have been a nonsuit.   Rule absolute.

The QUEEN *v.* INGHAM. *Nov.* 22.

Under the General Highway Act, 5 & 6 W. 4, c. 50, s. 18, a board was elected, on 26th March, 1855, to serve the office of surveyors of the highways in a parish for the year ensuing. On 23d November, 1855, they made a highway-rate. In August, 1855, The Metropolis Local Management Act (18 & 19 Vict. c. 120), passed; and, by sect. 251, it came into operation on 1st January, 1856. On 28th November, 1855, under sects. 31, 32, a District Board of Works was elected for the district comprehending the parish, which was included in Part L of Schedule (B).

After 25th March, 1856, application was made, on the part of the late Highway Board, to a party rated to the said highway-rate, for payment of arrears of the rate, under sect. 97 of stat. 18 & 19 Vict. c. 120. Payment not having been made, a summons was taken out against the party; but the magistrate refused to issue a warrant for levying. Afterwards the party paid the arrear to the District Board of Works.

A rule having been obtained for an order directing the magistrate to issue the warrant, this Court discharged the rule, on the ground that the collection of such arrears was not, under sect. 97, to be made by the late Highway Board.

WELSBY, on 18th November, in this Term, had obtained a rule calling on James Taylor Ingham, Esq., one of the magistrates of the Metropolis, sitting at Wandsworth Police Court in Surrey, and Henry Knapp, and the Guardians of the Poor of The Wandsworth and Clapham Union in the said county, to show cause why the said J. T. Ingham should not issue his warrant, directing the proper officer to levy on the goods and chattels of the said H. Knapp, or the said Guardians, the

*6]   sum of 37*l.* 1*s.* 8*d.*, being the sum at *which the Wandsworth and Clapham Union and Infirmary, in the said county, is rated to a highway-rate made for the parish of Battersea in the said county, by the Highway Board of the said parish, on 23d November, 1855.

From the affidavits on which the rule was obtained it appeared that the repair of the highways of the parish of Battersea in Surrey had, since 1845, been under the management of a board serving the office of surveyors, elected in conformity with stat. 5 & 6 W. 4, c. 50, s. 18.

On 26th March, 1855, certain persons were elected to constitute such board. On 23d November, 1855, the Board made a highway-rate, in which "Knapp and others" were assessed at 37*l.* 1*s.* 8*d.* in respect of the Wandsworth and Clapham Workhouse and Infirmary, situate in the parish of Battersea, Knapp being the master and occupier. The rate was duly allowed and published. The same not having been paid on demand, information, on the part of the Board, was, on 25th August, 1856, laid before Mr. Ingham, sitting at the Police Court at Wandsworth within the Metropolitan Police District, the parish of Battersea being within the district. Mr. Ingham issued a summons calling upon Knapp and the other parties so assessed to show cause why the sum should not be levied on the goods and chattels of Knapp. The summons was heard before Mr. Ingham on 3d September last, and opposed by the Guardians of the Poor of the Wandsworth and Clapham Union ; when Mr. Ingham refused to issue the warrant for levying, on the ground that the Board had no authority, after 25th March, 1856, to levy or collect the rate.

*7]   From the affidavits in answer it appeared that the *parish of Battersea is included in the Wandsworth District mentioned in Schedule (B.)(*a*) of stat. 18 & 19 Vict. c. 120, " For the better local management of the Metropolis ;" and that a Board of Works for such District was duly elected on 28th November, 1855,(*b*) which held its first meeting on the Wednesday in the week following, and ever since had continued to act in execution of the statute. The District Board of Works, on 1st January, 1856, called on the vestry clerks of the parishes comprised in the District for a statement of the balances in the hands of any of the officers of such parishes, in respect of highway and lighting rates, requesting payment thereof to the treasurer of The District Board,. a statement of the sums, if any, not collected, and

(*a*) Part. 1.   (*b*) Stat. 18 & 19 Vict. c. 120, sect. 31, et seq.

particulars of the liabilities payable out of the rates.   The vestry clerk of Battersea sent in an account containing as follows.

"St Mary Battersea.

"Highways.

	£
"Rate made 23d November, 1855, 10*d*. in the pound .	2000
"Collected	620
"Uncollected, empty, &c.	1380
"Liabilities	800"

On 22d February, 1856, The District Board resolved that the late Board for repair of the Highways in the parish of Battersea (and others) be respectively required to get in forthwith all arrears of rates made by them, *and to make up their accounts to 31st December last, and submit them to The District Board, on 2d April then [*8 next, and pay and deliver over all moneys, books, &c., in their possession, which, by virtue of the Metropolitan Management Act, were to be accounted for and handed over to The District Board.   On 13th November, 1856, the Board of Guardians of the Wandsworth and Clapham Union paid the 37*l*. 1*s*. 8*d*. to The District Board of Works; and notice of this was given to the attorney of the late Board for the repair of the highways, who were applicants for the present rule, by the clerk to the Board of Guardians on 14th November, 1856.

Bovill and *Corner* now showed cause.—The late Board for the repair of the highways had power, under sect. 18 of stat. 5 & 6 W. 4, c. 50, to appoint a collector and treasurer of the highway-rate.   But the question is, to whom the arrear of a rate made by the late Board is to be paid.   Stat. 18 & 19 Vict. c. 120, came into operation, by sect. 251, on 1st January, 1856.   By sect. 90, " all the duties, powers, and authorities for or in relation to the paving, lighting, watering, cleansing, or improving of any parish included in any district mentioned in Schedule (B.) to this Act" (which comprehends the parish of Battersea), " or any part of such parish, now vested in any commissioners, vestry, or other body, or in any officer of any commissioners or other body, and all other duties, powers, and authorities in any wise relating to the regulation, government, or concerns of any such parish, or part, or of the inhabitants thereof (except such duties, powers, and authorities as relate to the affairs of the church, or the management or relief of the poor, or the administration of any money or other *property [*9 applicable to the relief of the poor, so far as such duties, powers, and authorities relate thereto), now vested under any local Act of

Parliament in any commissioners," &c., "shall cease to be so vested, and shall, save as herein otherwise provided, become vested in and be performed and exercised by the Board of Works for such District." This shows the general intention of the Legislature to put an end to all local bodies. Sect. 96 contains the provision as to highways in particular. "Every vestry and district board shall, within their parish or district (exclusively of any other persons whatsoever), execute the office of and be surveyor of highways, and have all such powers, authorities, and duties, and be subject to all such liabilities, as any surveyor of highways in England is now or may hereafter be invested with or liable to by virtue of his office, under the laws for the time being in force, so far as such powers, authorities, duties, and liabilities are not inconsistent with this Act; but all expenses which under any such law ought to be defrayed by highway-rates shall be defrayed by means of the rates to be raised under this Act, and all moneys which would be applicable in aid of such highway-rates shall be applied in aid of the said rates to be raised under this Act." In the present instance, the powers, &c., are lodged in a district board, not in a vestry. Then, inasmuch as sect. 96 would apply only to moneys raised by rates under this Act, sect. 97 further provides : " That all rates made previously to the commencement of this Act for defraying the expenses of executing any duties, powers, and authorities hereby transferred to any vestry or district board, and all highway-rates made previously to such commence- *10] ment, or so much of such respective rates as *may not have been levied and paid, shall be levied and collected as if this Act had not been passed, and subject to the payment or retainer thereout of any sum or expenses lawfully payable out of such respective rates, shall, where such rates are levied in a parish mentioned in Schedule (A.) to this Act, be accounted for and paid over to the vestry of such parish, and shall, where levied in any other parish, be accounted for and paid over to the board of works for the district in which such parish is comprised, and shall in every case be applied in aid of the rates to be raised for the like purposes under this Act in the particular parish or part in which the said rates so made previously to the commencement of this Act are levied." On the other side, it will be said that the words " as if this Act had not been passed" mean that the same body is to levy the rates as that which did so before the Act. But, as the highway board is put an end to by the Act, and as the late Highway Board expired on 25th March, 1856, that construction is inadmissible; and the words will be satisfied by the substituted authority, The District Board of Works, collecting the rate as the extinct body would have collected it. Sect. 180 provides for the existing liabilities of the bodies which are abolished. Under the General Highway Act, 5 & 6 W. 4, c. 50, s. 34, the surveyor had the same powers for collecting the highway-rate as overseers have for collecting the poor-rate.

Now, under stat. 43 Eliz. c. 2, s. 4, and 17 G. 2, c. 38, s. 11, if over-seers during their year of office leave any portion of the rate uncol-lected, their successors may collect it. So therefore might the surveyor, in the case of highway-rates left uncollected by his predecessor ; and so therefore may The District Board of Works, which exercises *the authority of surveyor, collect rates left unpaid by their pre-decessors, the Highway Board. [*11

Pashley and *Welsby*, contrà.—The Highway Board has been under the necessity of making this application because, in the supposed doubt as to the authority for receiving the uncollected arrear, a very large number of persons rated have refused payment. The money must ulti-mately be accounted for to The District Board of Works ; but it seems that it must be got in by the Highway Board, which, for the purpose of collecting, must be considered as still in existence, though they could no longer lay a rate. The surveyor of highways is to act till his suc-cessor is appointed ; stat. 5 & 6 W. 4, c. 50, s. 6 ; here the Highway Board is the surveyor. [COLERIDGE, J.—But has not the Legislature here provided a successor ?] Not for the purpose of collecting. The District Board of Works now collects by the overseers. [COLERIDGE, J.—Then where is the difficulty ? Why cannot the overseers collect these arrears ?] The persons who collect the arrears, or for whom the arrears are collected in the first instance, are, by sect. 97 of stat. 18 & 19 Vict. c. 120, to retain expenses payable out of such rates. The party retaining cannot be the same as the party to whom the balance is to be paid. [ERLE, J.—Show me anything in respect of which the late Highway Board could be entitled to retain a shilling.] Suppose any party assessed had refused payment, and had been compelled to pay through legal proceedings instituted by the Highway Board, the expense of such proceedings might be retained out of the arrears col-lected under sect. 97. The arrears are to be "accounted for and paid over to The Board of Works." The party to *collect must be the party to account and pay over : but The District Board of Works cannot account and pay over to themselves. The arrears are to "be levied and collected as if this Act had not been passed ;" but "ac-counted for and paid over to the Board of Works." Here the levying and collecting is studiously opposed to the accounting and paying over. If the Act had not been passed, the last-elected surveyor would have levied and collected. Sects. 90 and 180, which have been referred to on the other side, relate only to boards or commissioners under local Acts. [*12

Lord CAMPBELL, C. J.—If a party in the parish disputed his liability to pay, it would be fit that we should see that payment should be enforced. The statute expressly provides that rates already made shall remain in force, and outstanding arrears be paid. Here, however, the parties rated have paid. And I cannot see the object of this application, besides that of setting wrongheaded persons right, if indeed they can be set right. The only dispute, a very idle one, is whether the arrears are to be collected directly by the new District Board of Works, or indirectly by the old Highway Board. There can be no object, that I can see, in the Legislature keeping up the old Board, when the new Board has full powers and adequate officers. It would require strong language to show that the Legislature meant to keep the old Board alive for the mere purpose of collecting arrears. I find words in sect. 97 which clearly admit of the construction suggested, that the intention was merely to put a stop to any notion that arrears were no longer payable, and to provide that they should still be levied and collected as if the Act had not *passed. No attempt has been made to meet the difficulty as to what was to be done after the 25th March, 1856, when the Highway Board would be extinct. There is no provision for keeping it alive. I think the order ought not to have been applied for.

*13]

(WIGHTMAN, J., was absent.)

ERLE, J.—I also am of opinion that this rule should be discharged. Stat. 18 & 19 Vict. c. 120 is, by sect. 251, to come into operation on 1st January, 1856. Its general effect is to transfer to the District Board of Works all the authorities of former boards, &c. Sects. 96, 97, make provisions especially applicable to highways. The District Board of Works is to have all the authorities of the surveyor of highways, an office in this parish performed by a highway board. Then, the powers of this Highway Board having been put an end to, there might arise a doubt whether the arrears of rates made by such Board were payable : and therefore sect. 97 makes a provision showing that the old rates are still to be collected, and to what they are to be applied. The rate-payers become liable to suffer the collection, and the surveyor is accountable to The District Board of Works for all that he has done : that is what I give as the meaning of the words " as if this Act had not been passed." The only difference is that formerly the collector for the Highway Board would have had to apply for the arrears, and now the overseers are to do so. To maintain this rule, we should have to hold that the Board which expired on 25th March, 1856, was to have a contingent existence for the purpose of levying arrears. Sect. 95 is strong to show that, the *Act passing in August, 1855, but not coming into operation till 1st January, 1856, all authorities which would expire in the interval should continue in force till the Act came into operation ; and the inference is that the intention was not to allow to existing authorities a prolonged existence after that time.

*14]

Lord CAMPBELL, C. J.—My brother Coleridge, who was called away at the close of the argument, authorizes me to say that he concurs in our view.   Rule discharged.

The QUEEN *v.* The Justices of the WEST RIDING of YORK SHIRE. *Nov.* 24.

Two justices made an order, adjudging the settlement of a lunatic, who had been sent to an asylum, to be in the township of H. in the union of H., addressed to the overseers of the township and the guardians of the union, and ordering the guardians to pay the expenses. The overseers and the guardians separately appealed. At the first Sessions the appeal of the guardians was entered and respited, that of the overseers was called on. The Sessions refused to hear it on the ground that the overseers had no locus standi.

Held: that the Sessions might in their discretion regulate the time of hearing the two appeals so as to secure that they should be heard together and justice done; but that they were bound, under stat. 16 & 17 Vict. c. 97, s. 108, to hear the appeal of the overseers of the township, to whom at all events the statute gave an appeal. And a rule for a mandamus to enter continuances and hear the appeal was made absolute.

HUGH HILL, in this Term, obtained a rule Nisi for a mandamus commanding the justices of the West Riding of Yorkshire to enter continuances and hear the appeal of the overseers of the poor of the township of Halifax, appellants, and the overseers of the poor of the township of Leeds, respondents, touching the last legal settlement of Hannah Levi, a pauper lunatic.

From the affidavits on both sides it appeared that Leeds is a township, not included in any union. Halifax is one of twenty townships, each maintaining its own *poor and having its own overseers, which form the poor law Union of Halifax. Hannah Levi, a pauper lunatic, having, at the instance of the overseers of Leeds, been sent by two justices of the West Riding from that township to a lunatic asylum, the two justices made an order addressed " To the guardians and overseers of the poor of the township or place of Halifax in the county of York in a certain union, formed according to law, called the Halifax Union, and to the guardians of the poor of the same union, and each and every of them." By this order the justices adjudged the last legal settlement of the lunatic to be in the township of Halifax, and ordered the guardians of the union of Halifax to pay to the overseers of Leeds the expenses already incurred in respect of the removal of the lunatic, and to pay to the treasurer of the asylum the future expenses of her maintenance. Notice of this order was sent by the overseers of Leeds both to the overseers of the township of Halifax and to the guardians of the Halifax Union. Both appealed against it, to the Sessions for the West Riding. At the next Sessions, which were those holden in October, the appeal of the guardians of the Halifax Union was entered and respited; that of the overseers of the township of Halifax was called on. The counsel for the township of Leeds objected that the overseers of the township of Halifax had no locus standi, the right of appeal being given only to the guardians of the union. The Sessions, being of that opinion, refused to hear the appeal. Nothing appeared on the affidavits as to the appeal by the guardians of the Union beyond the fact that it was entered and respited.

[*15

*16]   *Robert Hall* and *H. W. West* now showed cause.—*The question depends on the construction of The Lunatic Asylums Act, 1853 (16 & 17 Vict. c. 97). By sect. 108, " if the guardians of any union or parish, or the overseers of any parish, feel aggrieved by any such order," that is an order under sect. 97, they may appeal. It is clear therefore that the guardians may appeal; and, as it can hardly be supposed that there was to be a double appeal, " the overseers of any parish" must mean of any parish not in a union. And this appears by sect. 97, by which the justices are to order " the guardians of the union to which the parish in which such lunatic is adjudged to be settled belongs, or of such parish in case such parish be in a union or be under a board of guardians, and if not, then the overseers of such parish, to pay to the guardians of any union or parish, or the overseers of any parish," the expenses. [ERLE, J.—It does not seem to me that this is intended to affect the appeal. The expenses may have been disbursed by the guardians of the union, if the lunatic has been sent to the asylum from a union, or by the guardians of a parish under guardians, if sent from that parish, or by the overseers of a common parish if sent thence. The Act says, in each of the three cases, the payment is to be made to the party disbursing; and a similar triple arrangement is made as to the party in the first instance to repay the money. But, though, if the settlement is in a parish comprised in a union, the guardians of the union are to repay the expenses, that repayment will ultimately be charged on the parish. The guardians repay as trustees for the parish; and the parish is the party aggrieved by the order if it be wrong.] The appeal is not given to the party aggrieved, but to those on whom the order is made; that is in one case the *overseers, in the other
*17]   the guardians. It could not be intended to give a double appeal: that might lead to opposite decisions in the different appeals which might be tried at different Sessions and on different evidence. At all events this Court in its discretion will not grant a mandamus to compel the hearing of two appeals. [Lord CAMPBELL, C. J.—If the matter can be as conveniently tried in one appeal we certainly should not interfere. But is that admitted to be the fact? *H. Hill.*—All that is desired by the appellants is that the question should be really tried, the management of the appeal being by the overseers of the township, who are the parties really interested. There is no suggestion in the affidavits that the opposition of the respondents is founded on any fear of the double appeal, or that, if this appeal by the township be got rid off, they will not dispute the locus standi of the guardians also. Lord CAMPBELL, C. J.—The proper and rational course would be to arrange that the respited appeal should abide the event of this, and that this appeal should be tried upon the merits. If, however, the respondents refuse to accede to such an arrangement, they have a right to require us to construe the Act. If it has pleased the Legislature to give the

appeal not to the party interested, we are bound by it.] The guardians of the Union, being trustees for the parish whom they ultimately debit, may well conduct the appeal against a foreign parish. It is true they cannot so well do it when the dispute is between two parishes in the same union; in such a case the remedy would probably be by appeal against the auditor's accounts, as seems to be intimated in Regina v. East Ardsley, 14 Q. B. 793 (E. C. L. R. vol. 68): but that question does not arise in this case.

*Hugh Hill was not called upon to argue in support of the rule. [*18

Lord CAMPBELL, C. J.—The question is, whether the overseers of the township of Halifax, having regularly entered an appeal against the order of two justices, adjudging the last settlement of a pauper lunatic to be in their township, which order had been served upon them, have a locus standi to support their appeal. I am of opinion that they have. It would be unjust if they had not; for it is on them that the burthen imposed by the order will fall; and they have more interest in it than the guardians. But, though justice requires that they should be allowed to appeal, the Act might have been so framed as to give the appeal to the guardians of the union alone. But here sect. 108 in express words gives the appeal to the overseers; and what is there to take away this appeal? There are no words to do so; and I can see no object for doing so except the inconvenience of the double appeal, which might lead to contradictory decisions. That inconvenience I think may be obviated by the Sessions so moulding the hearing of th appeals as to secure that justice is done. I have no doubt it would have been within the power of the Sessions to have respited the appeal of the overseers to the Epiphany Sessions, so that it might come on at the same Sessions as the appeal of the guardians, awarding costs as justice might require; and the Epiphany Sessions, having both appeals before them, could do justice. The rule must be absolute.

COLERIDGE, J.—The overseers of the township, feeling aggrieved by the order, appeal. The Sessions have *decided that they have no right to do so. Now sect. 108 in its literal words gives an [*19 appeal to the overseers if they feel aggrieved. Whoever else may appeal, the overseers may. But in sect. 97 the provision is that the order for payment is to be on the guardians of the union if the parish be in a union, and, if not, on the overseers; and there is a similar restriction in sect. 99. No doubt, if you construe sect. 108 by refer-ence to those sections, the overseers here are not in that specific state; they are not overseers of a parish not in a union. But I do not think the restriction in sects. 97, 99, is to be imported into sect. 108, and restrict the general language there. The sections are not even next each other. Sect. 107, if any section, gives the key to the meaning of sect. 108. Now in sect. 107 I find that the Legislature drops the restriction contained in sects. 97, 99. The notice is not to be sent to the guardians of the union if the parish be in a union, and, if not, to the overseers or guardians of the parish; but in all cases to the overseers or guardians of the parish. The object of sending notice to these parties can be only because they are to have power to appeal. If we held that they had not, they, though really interested, might lose their appeal.

WIGHTMAN, J.—I am of the same opinion: indeed I have had some difficulty in seeing what was supposed to take the case of these overseers out of the express words of sect. 108. It seems reasonable that they, being aggrieved, should have power to appeal; and the Act says they may. I am struck by what has been urged by Mr. *West*, that, if there be two appeals heard at different Sessions, there may be contrary
*20]   decisions: but that may *be avoided in the manner pointed out
by my Lord. The terms of the Act embrace this case; and the obvious intention of the Legislature was that the party aggrieved, whether guardians or overseers or both, should appeal.

ERLE, J.—I think it perfectly clear that the Legislature have given the overseers an appeal. If there is any doubt it is whether, looking at sect. 107, the appeal is given in this case to the guardians of the union. The guardians of a union are the more prominent persons; it is on them the order to pay is made; and in some cases, as when the lunatic is irremovable being in the nature of casual poor chargeable upon the union, the payment is borne by the union fund. When that is the case, the guardians of the union, and they only, are aggrieved; and they have the appeal: but in the ordinary case of a settlement order, though the payment is in the first instance by the treasurer of the union, it is ultimately debited to the parish and borne by it. I think sect. 108 is to be construed reddendo singula singulis. The guardians may appeal if they are aggrieved, the overseers if they are aggrieved. In this I rely much on sect. 107, showing that the Legislature intended that the overseers of the parish, from whose pockets the money would ultimately come, were to have the notice of the order, and the particulars requisite to enable them to determine whether there shall be an appeal or not. In this section the Legislature drops the triple arrangement in sect. 97. The notices are not to be sent to the guardians of the union, or of the parish if in a union or under a board of guardians, and if not to the overseers, but in all cases to the indivi-
*21]   dual parish ultimately *charged. Then the very next section
gives the appeal, at all events, to the overseers. If both they and the guardians prosecute their appeals, it will clearly in my opinion be the duty of the Sessions to see that they are tried together.

                                                    Rule absolute.

The QUEEN v. The GUARDIANS of the Poor of the WEST WARD UNION. *Nov. 25.*

Pauper having resided five years in A., a parish in an union, was removed without an order to the workhouse of the union, where he remained twelve months. A. paid the Union a small sum; afterwards M., another parish in the Union, paid the Union for the maintenance, by consent of the guardian for M. at the board of the Union, on the supposition that pauper was settled in M. Pauper became lunatic, and was removed to an asylum by an order describing him to be from A.; it did not appear that either A. or M. interfered in this removal. Afterwards stat. 9 & 10 Vict. c. 66, passed. M. paid for pauper's maintenance in the asylum for many years after his removal thither, and after the passing of that statute, and of stat. 16 & 17 Vict. c. 97.

Held that, under stat. 16 & 17 Vict. c. 97, s. 102, the Union was properly chargeable for the expenses in the lunatic asylum, as the pauper, at the time of his removal thither, would, but for such removal, have been exempt from removal from A. under stat. 9 & 10 Vict. c. 66, inasmuch as neither the removal to the workhouse without an order, nor the removal to the lunatic asylum, interrupted the residence in A., by stat. 12 & 13 Vict. c. 103, s. 4 (though the time spent in the workhouse and lunatic asylum was excluded from the computation of time of residence).

Stat. 7 & 8 Vict. c. 101, passed before the removal to the workhouse. Held that, so far as regarded irremovability under stat. 9 & 10 Vict. c. 66, sect. 56 of stat. 7 & 8 Vict. c. 101, did not (though it made the workhouse part of the parish of settlement, and though M. had made payments on the supposition of the settlement being in M.) break the residence in A.

And, further, that the payment by M., if evidence of settlement there, was such evidence as might be rebutted.

PASHLEY, in last Term, obtained a rule, on reading the affidavits filed on the motion for the writ of certiorari in this prosecution, and the return to the said writ, calling on the prosecutors to show cause why the surcharge made by John Bell, Esquire, auditor, at the audit of the accounts of the West Ward Poor Law Union in Westmoreland, for the half year ending Michaelmas, 1855, upon the common fund of the said union of *the sum of 13l. 13s. for the lodging, maintenance, [*22 medicine, clothing, and care in Dunstan Lodge Lunatic Asylum, at or near Gateshead, in the county of Durham, of Henry Wilson, a pauper lunatic, belonging to the township of Morland, comprised in the said union, should not be quashed. Upon notice to John Bell, and the overseers and guardians of the poor of the township of Morland,

In this Term(a) *Overend* and *Thomas Jones* (of the Northern Circuit) showed cause, and *Pashley* was heard in support of the rule. The facts and the line of argument will appear fully from the judgment.

In the course of the argument, reference was made to Hartfield v. Rotherfield, 17 Q. B. 746 (E. C. L. R. vol. 79), Regina v. Leaden Roothing, 12 Q. B. 181 (E. C. L. R. vol. 64), Regina v. Christchurch, 12 Q. B. 149 (E. C. L. R. vol. 64), Regina v. Hatfield Peverel, 14 Q. B. 298 (E. C. L. R. vol. 68).   *Cur. adv. vult.*

Lord CAMPBELL, C. J., now delivered the judgment of the Court.

In this case we are of opinion that the decision of the auditor was right.

(a) November 8th. Before Lord Campbell, C. J., Coleridge Wightman, and Erle, Js.

The material facts are as follows.

Before October, 1844, the pauper had resided in Askham for more than five years, and was then taken therefrom, without an order of removal, to the workhouse of the Union in which Askham was situate, he being in a state which ended in lunacy : and a small sum was charged to Askham, by the Union, and paid on account of this removal.   Mor-

*23] land was a parish in *the same Union : and the guardian for Morland, at the Board of Guardians for the Union, appears to have consented that Morland should be charged with the maintenance of the pauper by reason of the settlement being supposed by him to be in that parish.   After twelve months in the workhouse, the pauper was removed(a) by the relieving officer of the Union, under an order of a justice, who was chairman of the Board of Guardians of the Union, to Haydock Asylum ; and he was afterwards removed to Dunstan Asylum : and on both occasions he was described to be from Askham: but there is no evidence that any officer for either parish interfered about this removal.   For several years Morland was charged with and paid the maintenance in the asylum, as if he had been settled therein.

It thus appears that the pauper lunatic was removed to an asylum, having so resided in Askham as to be entitled to the status of irremovability therein, which was afterwards created by stat. 9 & 10 Vict. c. 66 :(b) and he remained therein a pauper lunatic after the status had been so created during the legislation on the subject which followed ; viz., stat. 11 & 12 Vict. c. 110, s. 3, imposing the expense of an irremovable pauper on the funds of the Union, if the parish of residence was in an union ; and stat. 12 & 13 Vict. c. 103, s. 5, imposing it in the case of a pauper lunatic on the funds of the Union in which the parish of residence was in case the lunatic was irremovable when sent to the asylum ; and stat. 16 & 17 Vict. c. 97, s. 102, imposing it under the same circumstances either on the funds of the union, if the parish

*24] of residence was in an union, *and, if not, on the funds of that parish.   The last enactment is made to apply to lunatics removed as well before as after the Act passed, and extends to the pauper in question.

This course of legislation has been directed towards relieving the parish of settlement, and fixing the parish of residence with the maintenance both of paupers and of pauper lunatics who had resided long enough to acquire irremovability at the time they were sent to an asylum : and those enactments appear to us to make the union fund liable for the pauper in question, as he had resided so long in Askham when he was removed to the workhouse as would have made him irremovable there after the passing of stat. 9 & 10 Vict. c. 66.

Stat. 12 & 13 Vict. c. 103, s. 4, enacts that the removal of any

(a) In October, 1845.
(b) Royal Assent, 26th August, 1846.

lunatic pauper to an asylum, and the removal of any pauper, otherwise than under an order of removal, from his place of abode in any parish of a union to the workhouse of such union, shall not be deemed to be an interruption of the residence of such pauper in respect of stat. 9 & 10 Vict. c. 66; but the time spent in such lunatic asylum or workhouse shall be wholly excluded from the computation of the time of residence which, according to that statute, will exempt a person from being removed.

Then stat. 16 & 17 Vict. c. 97, s. 102, imposes the maintenance of a pauper lunatic on the union of the parish of residence, if at the time of his being conveyed to such asylum he would have been exempt from removal to his parish of settlement under stat. 9 & 10 Vict. c. 66. At the time this pauper was conveyed from the workhouse to the asylum, the removal to the workhouse was no interruption of the residence in Askham: *and, as the time passed in the workhouse is to be struck out of the computation, he had the status of irremovability in [*25 Askham; and so the union fund was chargeable.

Against this it was contended that, by stat. 7 & 8 Vict. c. 101, s. 56,(a) " for the purposes of relief, settlement, and removal," " the workhouse of any union" " shall be considered as situate in the parish to which each poor person respectively to be relieved," or " removed," " is or has been chargeable :" that Morland paid for the maintenance of the pauper during the time he was in the workhouse; and so he was chargeable to Morland; and so he was residing in Morland, and not at Askham, at the time he was conveyed from the workhouse to the asylum.

To this it appears to us a sufficient answer that stat. 7 & 8 Vict. c. 101, passed before the status of irremovability had been created; and it had no reference thereto: but stat. 12 & 13 Vict. c. 103, s. 4, expressly relates to that status, and was passed for the purpose of regulating liabilities as between parishes of residence and parishes of settlement; and it appears to apply directly to the case before us, and prevent the technical residence, if it may be so expressed, in Morland under the former statute from defeating the liability of Askham in respect of actual residence.

If we look at the effect of the affidavits on both sides, there seems abundant reason why the parish of settlement should be held not to have lost its exemption under these statutes. After the removal to the workhouse without an order, the consent of the guardians for Morland to charge the maintenance to that parish seems *to have been [*26 given most improvidently, on no sufficient grounds, and without any sufficient inquiry, by a guardian who is stated to have been curate only, and therefore probably not a permanent rate-payer. If the payment of the maintenance is any evidence of admission, it is such

(a) Royal Assent, 9th August, 1844.

evidence as admits of being rebutted; and the circumstances stated in the affidavits are very strong to rebut the effect of it, and to exempt the parish from being prejudiced thereby.

Thus the auditor's construction of the statute seems to us to have been correct; and his application of that construction to the facts before him supports the substantial right according to the intention of the Legislature.   Rule discharged with costs.

———◆———

ROBERT BOWMAN v. BLYTH. *Nov.* 25.

If a clerk to justices demands and receives a fee for the taking of recognisances, as for a principal and two sureties, there being in fact only one surety, he is not guilty of an offence or liable to a forfeiture under stat. 26 G. 2, c. 14, s. 2, if he actually believed that there were two sureties. By the Court of Q. B.

A table of fees to be taken by the clerks of justices was made at the June Quarter Sessions, and submitted for approval to the next October Quarter Sessions; when the further consideration thereof was adjourned to the next Epiphany Sessions; and at these last-mentioned Sessions the table (with some alterations) was approved of; and the same was afterwards ratified and confirmed by the Judges at the next following Assizes. Held: that the table was not duly approved, ratified, and confirmed, under stat. 26 G. 2, c. 14, s. 1, as the approval ought to have been given at the October Sessions, and such Sessions had no power to adjourn the consideration thereof. By the Court of Exch. Ch., affirming the judgment of the Court of Q. B.

THE first count alleged that a certain table of the fees to be taken by the clerks of justices of the peace within and for the county of Norfolk, whereby it was, among other things, directed and appointed that the fees to be taken by the clerk of any justice of the peace *27] within and for the said county for every recognisance *to prosecute, appear and give evidence, or for any other purpose, should be the sum of 1*s.* 6*d.*, and for notice thereof, over and above the fee of 1*s.* for filing the same when necessary, the sum of 1*s.*, was, pursuant to an Act passed, &c. (stat. 26 G. 8, c. 14, " For the settling and ascertaining the fees to be taken by clerks to justices of the peace"), made and settled by the justices of the peace for the said county, at a certain general Quarter Sessions of the peace in and for the said county, and was afterwards, pursuant to the said Act, approved by the justices of the peace for the said county, at the general Quarter Sessions of the peace in and for the said county next succeeding the general Quarter Sessions of the peace at which the same was so made and settled as aforesaid, and afterwards, on the 5th April, 1838, at the Assizes holden in and for the said county next after the said general Quarter Sessions of the peace at which the same was so approved as aforesaid, was, pursuant to the said Act, laid before, and approved, ratified and confirmed by, Sir James Parke, Knight, and Sir William Bolland, Knight, the Judges of our Lady the Queen assigned to hold the said Assizes, and then became and was of validity and effect within the said county. And that, after the space of three calendar months from the time that such table of fees had been so ratified and confirmed as aforesaid, whilst the same was of validity and effect within the said county, after the commencement and taking effect of the Act, &c. (stat. 11 & 12 Vict. c. 42, " To facilitate the performance of the duties of justices of the peace out of Sessions within England and Wales with · respect to persons charged with indictable offences"), and within three calendar months next before the commencement of this suit, the *defendant, he then being and acting within the said county as [*28 clerk to John Calthrop, Esq., and Charles Neville Rolfe, Esq., two justices of the peace in and for the said county, under the pretence of a certain matter or thing done or performed by the said justices in the execution of their offices, to wit, the taking and acknowledging of a certain recognisance taken and acknowledged before the said justices at Docking, within the said county, on 23d January, 1856, by the plaintiff and one Rayner Bowman as his surety, in the sum of 20l. each, conditioned for the appearance of the plaintiff before the said justices on 11th February, 1856, at Snettisham, in the said county, or before such other justice or justices of the peace for the same county as might then be there, to answer further to a charge of felony, to wit, a charge of having feloniously stolen three sheep, the property of one William Wright, made against the said plaintiff on the said 23d January before the said justices, and to be further dealt with according to law, demanded and received of plaintiff the sum of 7s. 6d. as and for the fee due and payable by plaintiff to defendant for the said taking and acknowledging of such recognisance ; which said sum of 7s. 6d. was and is another or greater fee than, at the time of such demanding and receiving, was ascertained, ratified, and confirmed in manner directed by the statute first above mentioned. Whereby, and by force of the statute first above mentioned, defendant forfeited and became liable to pay to plaintiff for his said offence the sum of 20l.

2d Count. That, the said table of fees in the first count mentioned having been so as therein is mentioned made and settled, approved, ratified and confirmed, defendant, after the space of three calendar months from *the time that such table of fees had been so ratified [*29 and confirmed as aforesaid, whilst the same was of validity and effect within the said county, after the commencement and taking effect of the said Act in the first count mentioned (11 & 12 Vict. c. 42), and within three calendar months next before the commencement of this suit, he then being and acting within the said county as clerk to John Davy, Esq., and Charles Francis Neville Rolfe, Esq., two justices of the peace in and for the said county, under pretence of a certain matter or thing done or performed by the said justices in the execution of their offices, to wit, the taking and acknowledging of a certain recognisance taken and acknowledged before the said justices at Snettisham,

within the said county, on 11th February, 1856, by plaintiff and Rayner
Bowman and John Bowman as his sureties, in the sum of 20*l.* each,
conditioned that the plaintiff should personally appear at the next Court
of General Quarter Sessions of the peace to be holden by adjournment
at Little Walsingham in and for the said county, and then and there
answer what should be objected against him for the said felony in the
first count mentioned, and not depart the Court without leave, and
the giving notice of the said recognisance and the filing the same,
demanded and received of plaintiff the sum of 7*s.* 6*d.* as and for the
fee due and payable by plaintiff to defendant for the said taking and
acknowledging, and giving notice of, the said recognisance, which said
sum of 7*s.* 6*d.* is another or greater fee than was, at the time of such
demanding and receiving, ascertained, ratified, and confirmed in manner
directed by the statute firstly in the first count above mentioned.
Whereby defendant forfeited, &c., 20*l.*

Plea 1.   Not guilty.

*30]   *2. To 1st count : That the sum demanded was not another or
greater fee than, at the time of such demanding and receiving,
was ascertained, ratified, and confirmed by the said statute as alleged.

3. To 2d count, a similar plea, mutatis mutandis.

4. To the whole declaration : That the said table of fees was not
made, settled, approved, ratified, and confirmed as alleged.

Issue joined on all the pleas.

On the trial, before Lord Campbell, C. J., at the Norfolk Summer
Assizes, 1856, the following facts appeared.

At the general quarter sessions of the peace holden in and for the
county of Norfolk in June, 1837, a table of fees to be taken by the
clerks of the justices of peace for the said county was made by the
justices so in quarter sessions assembled. And it was thereupon resolved by the said justices that the said table of fees should be printed
and laid before the justices at the General Quarter Sessions of the
peace to be holden in the month of October then next following. At
the General Quarter Sessions of the peace in and for the said county
holden in October, 1837, being the next General Quarter Sessions after
the Sessions at which the justices had made the said table of fees as
aforesaid, the table of fees was taken into consideration by the justices
of the said county, then and there assembled. And it was resolved
that the said table should be taken into further consideration at the
General Quarter Sessions to be holden in and for the said county in
January then next following. At the General Quarter Sessions of the
peace holden in and for the said county in January, 1838, being the

*31]   second quarter sessions after *the Quarter Sessions first mentioned,
some alterations were made in the table of fees by the justices
then and there assembled : and the same, with the said alterations, was
then and there approved by the said justices, and ordered to be laid for

ratification and confirmation before the Judge of Assize at the next Assizes to be holden in and for the said county. At the Assizes holden in and for the said county next after the Sessions last mentioned, the table of fees which had been so approved was laid before Parke, B., and Bolland, B., the Judges of Assize, pursuant to stat. 26 G. 2, c. 14, and was by the said Judges, on 5th April, 1838, approved. No other table of the fees to be taken by the clerks of the peace for the said county has since been made, approved, and confirmed under the said statute. The said table of fees was headed as follows.

"Norfolk, } At the General Quarter Session of the Peace of our to wit. } Lady the Queen, holden at the castle of Norwich, in the Shire House there, in the said county of Norfolk, for the same county, on Wednesday, the 3d day of January, in the 1st year of the reign of our Sovereign Lady Victoria, by the Grace," &c., "and in the year 1838, before," &c., "justices of our said Lady the Queen, assigned," &c.

"A book of fees to be taken by the clerks of the justices of the peace for this county having been made at the Quarter Sessions held in June last, and taken into consideration at the Quarter Sessions held in October last, when the further consideration thereof was adjourned to this Session.

"*Resolved*—That the following table of fees be, and the same is accordingly, approved by this Court:—"

*Then followed the items, among which was the following.   [*32

"*Recognisance.*   .

"For every recognisance to prosecute, appear, and give evidence, or for any other purpose 1 6

"For notice thereof over and above the fee of 1s. for filing same when necessary .   .   .   .   .   .   1 0"

"The clerks to provide all necessary legal books and stationery, and to record all proceedings in a book to be kept for that purpose."

Then followed an order that the table should be laid before the judges.   "By the Court,

COPEMAN,

Clerk of the Peace."

"Approved 5th April, 1838.

J. PARKE.

W. BOLLAND."

On 23d January, 1856, plaintiff and two other persons were brought before Charles Francis Neville Rolfe and John Calthrop, Esquires, two of the justices of the peace for the said county, at Docking, in the said county, on a charge of sheep-stealing. The said justices remanded the plaintiff and one of the other persons so charged to 11th February next following, and discharged the third person so charged; and they also consented to admit plaintiff and the other person so remanded to

bail.   Thereupon plaintiff and one Rayner Bowman as his surety
entered into recognisances before the said justices, in the sum of 20*l.*
each, conditioned for the *appearance of the plaintiff at Snettisham on the said 11th February, to answer further to the said
charge.

*33]

The recognisance was as follows.

" Robert Bowman, of," &c., acknowledges himself to be indebted to
our Sovereign Lady the Queen in the sum of 20*l.*   Rayner Bowman,
of," &c., " acknowledges himself to be indebted to our Sovereign Lady
the Queen in the sum of 20*l.*"

" Norfolk, to wit.   Upon condition that the said Robert Bowman do
personally appear," &c. : " then this recognisance to be void, or else to
remain in full force.

" Taken and acknowledged the 11th day of February, 1856, before
us, two of Her Majesty's justices of the peace, now being sitting," &c.
                                   " J. DAVY.   C. F. N. ROLFE."
Endorsed : " ROBERT BOWMAN, 20*l.*
                   " RAYNER BOWMAN, 20*l.*
" For the appearance of Robert Bowman," &c.

Upon that plaintiff was discharged.   On the said 23d January the
defendant was and still is the clerk to the said justices ; but he was
absent when the plaintiff and the said other persons were so enlarged
on bail.   In absence of the defendant, one of the justices present (Mr.
Rolfe) offered to write out the notices of the recognisance ; but the
attorney for the plaintiff waived the notices.   No fee was then demanded
or received from the plaintiff or his surety.   And afterwards, and
before the hereinafter demanding and receiving by the defendant of the
fee hereinafter mentioned under pretence of the said recognisances,
Mr. Rolfe sent to the defendant a memorandum in writing, which was
as follows.

*34]   *" Memorandum.   Docking, 23d January, 1856.
                     " Bowman and Groom.   Felony.
          " Bail to Snettisham.   Sitting, Monday 11th February.
" Groom,   ⎫
  Bowman,   ⎬ in 20*l.* each, to appear.
Rayner Bowman, ⎫ in 20*l.* each as sureties.
John Lee,   ⎬   " C. F. N. ROLFE."
The practice of the said justice, and of other justices in the same
petty session and division, to whom the defendant is also clerk, is to
require two sureties in cases of felony.

On 11th February, 1856, the plaintiff appeared at Snettisham in
discharge of his said recognisance, and was ordered by the said C. F.
N. Rolfe and John Davy, Esquires, the justices of the peace for the
said county then and there present, to be committed for trial on the
said charge.   The said justices, however, discharged the plaintiff on his

ertering into a recognisance, with two sureties in 20*l.* each, conditioned for his appearing at the next general quarter sessions of the peace to be holden by adjournment at Little Walsingham in and for the said county, there to answer what should be objected against him for the said felony.   Thereupon the plaintiff, the said Rayner Bowman, and one John Bowman, entered into recognisances before the last-named two justices in the sum of 20*l.* each, conditioned for the appearance of the plaintiff at the said Quarter Sessions, there to answer as aforesaid.

The recognisance was in the same form as that taken on the former occasion, and before set out, except as to the difference of the condition, and the addition of the name of John Bowman, as surety in 20*l.*   The defendant *was present and acted as clerk to the last-named jus- [*35 tices at the taking of the said recognisances on 11th February: and he then demanded and received of plaintiff, in respect of the last-mentioned recognisances, the sum of 7*s.* 6*d.*, that is to say the sum of 1*s.* 6*d.* in respect of each recognisor, and the sum of 1*s.* in respect of the notice of each recognisance.   The defendant also then demanded and received of the plaintiff another sum of 7*s.* 6*d.* in respect of the recognisances entered into at Docking on 23d January as aforesaid, that is to say, a sum of 1*s.* 6*d.* in respect of each of the actual recognisors, and a sum of 1*s.* in respect of notice to each actual recognisor; and a further sum of 1*s.* 6*d.* in respect of the supposed entering into his recognisance by the supposed second surety, and a further sum of 1*s.* in respect of a supposed notice to such supposed second surety.   Notice of the recognisances at Snettisham was actually given   The plaintiff subsequently surrendered in discharge of his recognisances, and was tried and acquitted.

At the trial of the present cause, it was contended for the defendant that the table of fees was not made, settled, approved, ratified, and confirmed pursuant to the statute, because it had not been approved, as it ought to have been, at the October Session in 1837.   Secondly, that the table of fees authorized the taking from each recognisor a fee of 2*s.* 6*d.*, composed of 1*s.* 6*d.* for the recognisance and 1*s.* for notice thereof. And, thirdly, that, as to the sum demanded and received in respect of the recognisances taken and acknowledged at Docking, the defendant demanded and received the same under a misapprehension that two sureties had entered into the recognisances with the plaintiff for the *plaintiff's appearance at Snettisham.   For the plaintiff, it was [*36 contended that the table of fees had been well made, settled, approved, ratified, and confirmed pursuant to the statute, because the October Sessions had either power to adjourn the consideration of the table made at the June Sessions, and to give the January Sessions jurisdiction to approve of the table, or else itself was, and must be deemed to be, for the purpose of the inquiry into the validity of the table, the first or making sessions.   Secondly, that the table directed one fee only to be taken in respect of the recognisance, whatever might be the number of recognisors. Thirdly, that the statute prohibited absolutely the taking a greater fee than ascertained by the table, and not merely the taking such greater fee with a corrupt intention.

The Lord Chief Justice left to the jury the questions: Whether, at the remand at Docking, on 23d January, there were two sureties and recognisances, or only one; and whether the defendant knew that there was only one or believed that there were two, and that the notices had been given. The jury found that there was only one surety, and that the defendant thought there were two. A verdict was thereupon entered for the plaintiff, on both counts of the declaration, leave being reserved to move as after mentioned.

In this Term, *Byles*, Serjt., obtained a rule to show cause why a verdict should not be entered for defendant, " on the grounds: that the charges were correct; that the statute does not apply to charges made erroneously under a misapprehension of fact; that the alleged erroneous charges were not other or greater fees than the statute authorizes; that the table of fees was not approved at the proper sessions; that the table was not *a legal table; that the defendant committed no offence under the Act." Afterwards, in this Term,(a)

*37]

O'Malley and *Keane* showed cause.—First, the table of fees was properly made, settled, approved, ratified, and confirmed. Stat. 26 G. 2, c. 14, s. 1, provides that the justices of the peace, at their General Quarter Sessions to be held next after 24th June, 1753, shall make and settle a table of the fees which shall be taken by clerks to justices of peace; and such tables, being approved by the justices of the peace at the next succeeding General Sessions of the peace, with such alterations as such justices so assembled shall think proper, shall be laid before the judges at the next assizes, and the said judges are authorized and required to ratify and confirm such tables, in such manner and form as the same shall be made, settled, and approved of by the said justices, or with such alterations, additions, or abatements as to such judges shall appear just and reasonable. It then authorizes the " justices of peace, in their respective quarter sessions assembled, from time to time to make any other table of fees to be taken, instead of the fees contained in the table which shall have been ratified and confirmed by the judges of assize; and after the same shall have been approved by the justices of the peace at the next succeeding general quarter sessions, in manner as aforesaid, to lay such new table of fees before the judges at the next asssizes," " who are hereby empowered and authorized to approve and ratify the same in manner as aforesaid, if they think fit; but no table of fees to be made and settled by the said *respective justices of peace, shall be of any validity or effect whatsoever

*38]

(a) The argument was heard on November 17th, 18th, and 20th. Before Lord Campbell, C J., Coleridge, Wightman, and Erle, Js.

until the same shall be ratified and confirmed by the said judges." It is objected that here the table, having been made at the Midsummer Sessions, 1837, ought to have been approved at the next sessions, that is the Michaelmas Sessions, 1837, whereas the approval did not take place till the Epiphany Sessions, 1838, the consideration having been adjourned over from the Michaelmas Sessions to the Epiphany Sessions. But the enactment as to the time is directory only. In the case In the matter of a Coroner for Stafford, 2 Russ. 475, 483, Lord Tenterden said: "Where the object of an Act of Parliament is to ordain that something shall be done, which was not done before, and it goes on to enact, that that thing shall be done within a time mentioned,—it has been held in some cases, which might have been referred to, that the provisions as to time are directory only; and that the thing, though not done within the prescribed time, may be done afterwards. And it has been so held for this reason,—that, if the thing, not having been done within the time limited, be not allowed to be done afterwards, the primary object of the Legislature, which was, that the thing should be done, would be disappointed." [Lord CAMPBELL, C. J.—A mandamus might go directing the election of corporate officers after the proper day of election had passed.(a) COLERIDGE, J.—There the body which ought to have elected is called on to elect: here the Sessions are not the same. ERLE, J.—Where a particular sessions ought to begin, no other can begin: here the proper Sessions did begin, and adjourned.] Supposing the enactment *to be more than directory, then, if no table of fees had been made at the sessions [*39 first held after June, 1753, none could have been made at all. The statute does not confer a privilege on the justices, but imposes a duty. It is held that the enactment of stat. 54 G. 3, c. 84, s. 1, which expressly enacts that the Michaelmas quarter sessions shall be held in a particular week, is still only directory: Rex v. The Justices of Leicester, 7 B. & C. 6 (E. C. L. R. vol. 14). At any rate, the October Sessions had here power to adjourn. That is incident to every court of quarter sessions, in default of express enactment to the contrary: Rex v. The Justices of Wilts, 13 East, 352. That case was said, by Patteson, J., in Rex v. Kimbolton, 6 A. & E. 603, 611 (E. C. L. R. vol. 33), to go perhaps too far under the particular statute on which it was discussed: but he upheld the general rule, that there is "a power necessarily incident to the sessions to adjourn the consideration of an appeal properly lodged before them:" and the same rule must apply in every case where a sessions once had properly cognisance of any matter. There may indeed be words taking away the general power, as in stat. 9 G. 4, c. 61, where sect. 27 provides that the appeal shall be to a particular session, "and not afterwards," and that the Court "at such session" shall hear and determine the appeal: Regina v. Belton, 11 Q. B. 379

(a) See stats. 11 G. 1, c. 4, 7 W. 4 & 1 Vict. c. 78, s. 26.

(E. C. L. R. vol. 68).   Of course, also, if the application be made in
the first instance to the wrong sessions, no adjournment can give jurisdiction.   But, further, if the second (October) Sessions had no power
to adjourn the approval, it may be considered that that sessions was
itself the sessions at which the table was, properly speaking, made;
*40] and then the Epiphany Sessions was the proper *sessions for the
       approval.   The circumstance that, at the Midsummer Sessions, a
table was made, and brought for approval to the October Sessions, did
not preclude the October Sessions from making the table, as an original
act then done, instead of approving what had been done before.   In
Regina *v.* Coles, 8 Q. B. 75, 88 (E. C. L. R. vol. 55), Coleridge, J.,
remarked upon stat. 57 G. 3, c. 91, s. 1 (which provides for settling the
fees to be taken by the clerk of the peace, and the provisions of which
closely resemble those of stat. 26 G. 2, c. 14, s. 1), that the object was
to ascertain and settle the fees in the most deliberate manner.   One
court may comprehend more magistrates conversant with the subject,
another fewer: it is desirable that there should be the means of dis-
posing of the matter at the court best fitted for doing so.   [Lord CAMP-
BELL, C. J.—Or at one sessions the court might find themselves equally
divided.]·   And the only evil in the delay is that the table of fees, previously ratified and confirmed, remains unaltered for another quarter.
Next, assuming the table to be well framed, the charge is in violation
of the table, there being, properly speaking, only one recognisance
taken on each occasion.   (The argument on this point is omitted.)
Lastly, even if the view for which the defendant contends is correct,
he is liable on the first count, because at any rate there were but two
recognisances, that of the principal and that of the surety, whereas the
charge is for three.   In answer, it is said that the defendant is entitled
to a verdict on the plea of Not guilty, so far as regards the first count,
on the ground that he thought there were two sureties, although in fact
*41] there was only *one; and so the jury have found.   Sect. 2 of
       stat. 26 G. 2, c. 14, enacts that any clerk who shall, "under pre-
tence of any matter or thing done," &c., by the justice or the clerk,
demand or receive a fee greater than that ascertained, &c., as aforesaid,
"shall for every such offence forfeit" 20*l.*   To constitute the "offence"
it is not necessary that the clerk should know that he has made a
demand too large under the actual facts: the offence consists in his
making the demand without having ascertained the facts accurately.
"Pretence" does not mean the making of a representation knowingly
false, but the holding out or putting forward a fact as true.   The maxim
"mens facit reum" applies to moral responsibility, no doubt: but it is
not always applicable in the case of penal statutes.   In Herbert *v.*
Paget, 1 Lev. 64, a majority of the Judges of this Court held that the
keeper of the writs and records of this Court was liable to an action by

a party who was injured by an improper alteration of a record, "though here appeared no neglect or want of care in the defendant."

Byles, Serjt., and *Couch*, contrà.—It is true that the Sessions has a general power to adjourn; and that, in Rex *v.* The Justices of Wilts, 13 East, 352, Lord Ellenborough thought that the statute there in question fell within the general rule. Afterwards, as has been pointed out on the other side, a doubt was expressed by Patteson, J., in Rex *v.* Kimbolton, 6 A. & E. 611 (E. C. L. R. vol. 33), whether in the case first mentioned the application of the rule had not been carried too far. In Regina *v.* Belton, 11 A. & E. 379 (E. C. L. R. vol. 39), Lord Denman seems to adopt the view of Patteson, J.; and there this Court held that there was no power of adjournment under stat. 9 G. 4, *c. [*42 61, s. 27, where the provision, so far as the present question is concerned, was very much like that of 26 G. 2, c. 14, s. 1; for the words "and not afterwards," in stat. 9 G. 4, c. 61, s. 27, apply only to the bringing the appeal; and the decision turned upon the words "at such session," which apply to the determination of the appeal, and are not stronger than the express words of sect. 1 of stat. 26 G. 2, c. 14, "approved by the justices of the peace of the next succeeding General Quarter Sessions." The table is to be affirmed and ratified by the Judges "at the next Assizes" after the approval; it surely could not be contended that this ratification could be made at the next Assizes but one after the approval, or at any subsequent Assizes. The power to adjourn exists either in cases which are properly criminal, as in Keen *v.* The Queen, 10 Q. B. 928 (E. C. L. R. vol. 59), or in civil cases, where the sessions have jurisdiction by statute. The act of the justices who are to approve would seem to be rather ministerial than judicial: it does not appear that they are to hear any parties. It is not so much the act of the Court as of the individual justices there assembled. The suggestion that the October Sessions may be considered as the Sessions first making the order, is inconsistent with the heading of the table, which states the table to have been "made at the Quarter Sessions held in June last, and taken into consideration at the Quarter Session held in October last, when the further consideration thereof was adjourned to this Session," that is, the Epiphany Sessions. (They then argued the question as to the proper amount of fees.) Lastly, as to the mistake made with respect to the number of sureties, it is clear that there was no "pretence." In Rex *v.* Dobson, 7 East, 218, the defendants were *informed against for having, "by colour and pretence" of [*43 their being collectors, demanded and exacted certain duties. It turned out that their appointment had been irregular. Lord Ellenborough said: "By colour and pretence must be understood what the parties knew at the time of the receipt to be colour and pretence;" and, it appearing that the defendants had no reason to believe that they were not properly appointed, it was held that they were not so chargeable.

Lord CAMPBELL, C. J.—As to the questions of the power to adjourn, and the proper interpretation of the fee table, I should like to take time for consideration. But, on the point whether an offence has been committed by the defendant acting in ignorance of the fact, I am clearly of opinion that the complaint fails. Actus non facit reum nisi mens sit rea. Here the defendant, very reasonably believing that there were two sureties bound, besides the principal, has not, by making a charge in pursuance of his belief, incurred the forfeiture : the language of the statute is "for every such offence." If therefore the table allowed him to charge for three recognisances when there are a principal and two sureties, he has not committed an offence under the Act. Rex *v.* Dobson, 7 East, 218, is an express authority, if authority were required. On this point, therefore, I feel no doubt in giving judgment for the defendant.

COLERIDGE, WIGHTMAN, and ERLE, Js., concurred.

On the other points :   *Cur. adv. vult.*

*44]   *Lord CAMPBELL, C. J., now delivered the judgment of the Court.

In this case, which was tried before me at Norwich, a verdict passed for the plaintiff, subject to leave to move to enter the verdict for the defendant. It was an action for penalties against the clerk to the justices for demanding and taking greater fees than were authorized to be taken by the table of fees ascertained, approved, and confirmed for the county of Norfolk, according to the provisions of stat. 26 G. 2, c. 14. One plea was, that there was no such table validly made; on which there was an issue.

Now, it appeared that there was a table of fees in use in the county of Norfolk, which had been made at the Midsummer General Quarter Sessions of the peace for Norfolk, in 1837. That table was submitted for approval to the · justices at the ensuing Michaelmas Sessions ; but that Sessions did not then approve of it, but adjourned the consideration of it to the next Sessions. At the ensuing Epiphany Sessions the table was considered and approved by the justices ; and at the ensuing Assizes it was laid before the Judges, and by them confirmed.

The question therefore was, Whether this table was approved of as required by stat. 26 G. 2, c. 14. That again depends upon Whether the Michaelmas Sessions had power to adjourn the consideration of the table to the ensuing Epiphany Sessions.

Now it is clear, on the authority of decided cases, Rex *v.* Justices of Wilts, 13 East, 852, and Regina *v.* Belton, 11 A. & E. 379 (E. C. L. R. vol. 39), that in general the Sessions have power to adjourn the con
*45]   sideration of any matter before them, as justice may *require, unless the Legislature has required that there should be an act

done by a particular sessions. In that case there is a limited power given to that particular sessions; and the act must be done by it alone. Now then we look at the statute in this case; and we find that the Legislature have given a limited power of approval to one particular sessions only, viz., that next holden after the making of the table of fees. Stat. 26 G. 2, c. 14, s. 1, after providing for the first making and settling the table in 1753, the approving it by the justices "at the next succeeding general Quarter Sessions," and the ratifying and confirming it by the Judges of Assize, enacts that "it shall and may be lawful for the said justices of peace, in their respective Quarter Sessions assembled, from time to time to make any other table of fees to be taken instead of the fees contained in the table which shall have been ratified and confirmed by the Judges of Assize;" that provides for the making of the table, which was rightly made here. "And after the same shall have been approved by the justices of the peace at the next succeeding General Quarter Sessions, in manner as aforesaid, to lay such new table of fees before the Judges at the next Assizes, or at the great Sessions for the principality of Wales and counties palatine of Chester, Lancaster, and Durham, who are hereby empowered and authorized to approve and ratify the same in manner as aforesaid, if they think fit; but no table of fees to be made and settled by the said respective justices of peace, shall be of any validity or effect whatsoever until the same shall be ratified and confirmed by the said Judges."

Now the powers of approval here, and that of altering the table, are not given to the justices generally, but to *those of a particular [*46 sessions; we think the approval was an act to be done at that particular sessions, which must be completed and done by that sessions only; and here it was not completed by them but adjourned to the next sessions. We think that, notwithstanding the general power of sessions to adjourn, which we are anxious to preserve, the Legislature have prescribed that the approval should be completed by that sessions only; a limitation of the power of adjournment which is not disputed by the Judges who decided Rex v. Justices of Wilts, 18 East, 852, and Regina v. Belton, 11 A. & E. 879 (E. C. L. R. vol. 89). This table was not so approved; and therefore we think that it is not in force, and that no action lies for taking fees contrary to it. This disposes of the whole case, as the verdict must be entered for the defendant.

The result is that there is no table of fees now in force in Norfolk; and a new one must be made. We hope that those whose duty it is to frame it will take care to avoid the ambiguity which exists in the language of the present table, and will say in explicit and distinct language whether a fee is to be taken in respect of each cognisor who enters into a recognisance, or whether only one fee is to be taken when one record is made of several cognisances made at the same time, and subject to the same condition.

At present we can only direct that the rule be made absolute to enter a verdict for the defendant.   Rule absolute.

---

*47]   *IN THE EXCHEQUER CHAMBER.

BOWMAN *v.* BLYTH. [*June* 15, 1857.]

(On Appeal.)

THE plaintiff having appealed, on a case stating the same facts as are stated above, the case was now argued.

Keane, for the appellant, plaintiff below, used the same arguments, and cited the same authorities, used in the Court below, with the addition of Rex *v.* The Mayor of Norwich, 1 B. & Ad. 310 (E. C. L. R. vol. 20).

Couch, for the respondent, defendant below, was not called upon to argue.

COCKBURN, C. J.—We are unanimous in thinking that the decision of the Court of Queen's Bench in this case ought to be affirmed. Their judgment proceeds on the ground that, though the Court of Quarter Sessions have in general power of adjournment, yet, when an Act giving any particular jurisdiction plainly intimates an intention that such particular jurisdiction is to be exercised by one particular sessions, that sessions cannot adjourn it to another. Here the Legislature provides that a table of fees being made by one sessions, " after the same shall have been approved by the justices of the peace at the next succeeding General Quarter Sessions," may be ratified by the Judges at the next Assizes, and become valid. I quite concur in the opinion of the Court below, that the language of the Legislature, " next *succeeding General Quarter Sessions," cannot be interpreted to *48] extend to any subsequent sessions. It was contended in the argument that these words were only directory; and cases have been cited; and it has been argued that in all Acts the object of the Legislature is to be looked at in order to see whether words are directory or not. Even if we were to adopt that test, I think there would be very good reason for supposing in this case that the Legislature intended that the table of fees should be considered by the Quarter Sessions immediately following that at which it was made; for there are many obvious reasons why it should have been an object to have the confirmation as soon as possible after the first making. But, be that as it may, the language is clear; and, if we did not give it effect, I see nothing to prevent the table of fees from remaining undealt with for any number of sessions after it was made, and yet being taken up and approved of by any subsequent sessions. I do not think we should desire to put such a construction on the Act. Even if it was desirable so to do, I think when I find the positive language, "next succeeding" Sessions, that we should not be justified in doing so.

CRESSWELL, J., concurred.

MARTIN, B.—I will only add that, though I do not question that, in construing Acts, language seemingly positive may sometimes be read as directory, yet such a construction is not to bo lightly adopted; and never when, as in this case, it would really be to make a new law instead of that made by the Legislature.

WATSON, B., and CHANNELL, B., concurred.

Judgment affirmed.

———————

*GIBSON v. WILLIAM VARLEY and SAMUEL VAR- [*49
LEY. *Nov. 25.*

Plaintiff took out a writ of summons against J. Afterwards, and before service, having disco-vered that the real defendant was W., he altered the writ, had it resealed, and then served it, for the first time, retaining the original teste. Held that this might be done, although, before the resealing, but after the date of the teste, defendant had made a tender; it appearing that the plaintiff had acted bonâ fide, and had been misled as to the name of the defendant by the defendant's attorney.

LUSH, in this Term, obtained a rule calling on the plaintiff to show cause why the writ of summons issued herein, and all subsequent proceedings thereon, should not be set aside for irregularity, or why the writ of summons should not be amended by altering the date of the teste to the day of resealing, and why the plaintiff should not pay the costs of this application.

The rule was obtained on the affidavit of the attorney for the defendants. He deposed that, in July, 1856, defendants purchased of plaintiff wool exceeding the value of 600l.; immediately after which defendants sent to plaintiff a check for 600l. on account, and which plaintiff cashed. That plaintiff claimed a balance of 28l.; but defendants contended that the balance was only 16l. On 25th July defendants remitted to plaintiff a check upon the same bankers, for 16l. Plaintiff's attorney acknowledged the receipt thereof, by letter of 31st July, in the words following: "A check has come to Mr. Gibson's hands; but you must please understand he does not accept it in payment." Defendants' attorney afterwards wrote to plaintiff's attorney to the effect that "the said defendants" considered that nothing was owing to the plaintiff "by the defendants," "they having paid the sum of 616l.;" and that the writer would give an undertaking to appear to any process plaintiff's *attorney might issue, if plaintiff made further claim. On 20th [*50
August, defendants' attorney received a letter from plaintiff's attorney (containing a writ dated 8th August, addressed to John Varley, and the check sent on 25th July) in the words following: "I enclose

writ, on which please endorse undertaking to appear. I also return check or draft for 16*l.* 0*s.* 0*d.*, which I gave you notice on the 31st ult. would not be received in payment." That defendants' attorney wrote to plaintiff's attorney, stating that John Varley, the father of the said defendants, was dead, and that the business was carried on by his two sons. That John Varley the father died in June 1855; and his death might have been ascertained without difficulty; "but, as I verily believe, the said plaintiff or his attorney made no inquiry whatever, but issued the said writ notwithstanding the receipt of the said check, and returned the said check for 16*l.*, having retained the same nearly a fortnight, entirely for the purpose of saddling the said defendants with the costs of the said writ, and, as I believe, without any intention of recovering more than the sum of 16*l.* previously paid by the said check." On 11th August, defendants' attorney caused the sum of 16*l.* to be tendered to plaintiff in sovereigns, which he refused to accept: "and his said attorney has since resealed the said writ, but has not altered the date thereof, in the hope that he may saddle the said defendants with the costs thereof, even if his client should not recover more than the sum of 16*l.* in the said action actually paid by check before the first issue of the said writ."

It further appeared that the writ of summons was originally issued on 8th August, against John Varley, *and not against William Varley and Samuel Varley; that the writ was resealed on 19th August, having had the names of William Varley and Samuel Varley substituted therein as defendants for John Varley, since the said original issuing.

[*51]

In answer, the plaintiff's attorney deposed that, on 25th July, 1856, he directed a letter to "Mr. John Varley," requesting payment of 35*l.* 12*s.*: he received a letter signed John Varley, disputing the claim, and referring him to the writer's solicitor, the deponent first mentioned. On 28th July, plaintiff's attorney wrote to defendants' attorney a letter, commencing, "Mr. John Varley refers me to you as his legal adviser," and discussing the claim. On 30th July, defendants' attorney replied that he had received no instructions from Mr. Varley. On 31st July, plaintiff's attorney wrote to defendants' attorney, requesting Mr. Varley's decision by the following Monday, and informing him that a check had come to plaintiff's hands, but would not be accepted in payment: and he deposed that, hoping that the dispute might be settled without resort to legal proceedings, he considered it best to retain the check till he received the determination of the defendants' attorney. On 6th August, defendant's attorney wrote to plaintiff's: "I am instructed by Mr. Varley to state that Mr. Gibson has no claim against him; and, in case you issue any process, I will appear." And deponent added: "Such letter not referring to any defendants, as would be inferred from the affidavit of the said John Taylor" (attorney of the defendants), "but to one person only, which person I considered to be John Varley. Having been led to believe, from the correspondence *above set forth, that the actual defendant was John Varley, and having not the slightest reason to believe otherwise, I sent a writ [*52 on the 9th August last, in which the said Francis Johnson Gibson was plaintiff and John Varley defendant, to the said John Taylor, requesting him to endorse undertaking to appear: and I at the same time returned the check before referred to, there being an end of any friendly settlement. I received a letter from the said John Taylor, in reply, dated 12th August, 1856, in the words following: ' There is no Mr. John Varley: he died twelve months ago; and the business is carried on by his sons;' this being the first intimation I had that John Varley was not the actual defendant. That the said John Taylor and the said defendants (if their intentions had been correct) ought in the first instance to have informed me that the business was not carried on by John Varley; and that they misled me by their correspondence; and that, if I had any intention or wish to saddle the said defendant with costs, I should have issued a writ immediately on being instructed in the matter." The clerk of the last deponent deposed that, about 15th or 16th August, he called on the defendants' agents in London, and inquired of their managing clerk if he would undertake to appear to the writ, which he declined to do, stating that there was no such person as John Varley; that the names of the defendants were William and Samuel Varley; and that he, if deponent would issue a new writ, would undertake to appear for them. Deponent observed that there would be no occasion to issue a fresh writ, as he could amend the present one by inserting the correct names, the same not having been served; to which the *managing clerk made no objection. That [*53 deponent amended the writ accordingly, and took it with a copy thereof to defendants' agents on 22d August; when the managing clerk refused to endorse an undertaking, saying that he was instructed by defendants' attorney not to do anything further. That defendants applied at Chambers to set aside the writ; when Bramwell, B., referred the application to this Court. That his Lordship had required a clerk from the writ office of this Court to be brought before him, to state the practice of the office as regards amendments or alterations in writs of summons. " That a clerk from the writ office did accordingly attend before his Lordship, and then stated that such alterations as had been made in the writ in this action were always allowed, and were constantly made any time before service of the writ, but not afterwards; and that the teste or date of such altered or amended writs was never altered, but always remained the same as when the writ first issued. That I believe the object of the defendants' attorney is to deprive the plaintiff of any costs; as I have been informed and believe that, between the teste of the writ and the amendment and resealing thereof, a tender was made on behalf of the defendants of a certain sum in discharge of the plaintiff's claim; and, should the plaintiff recover no more than such sum so tendered, and the writ should be either set aside or the teste altered to the date of the amendment thereof, the action would not have been commenced at the time such tender was made."

On an earlier day in this Term,(a)

*54] *Finlason showed cause.—The defendant subject that the writ should have been tested after the resealing. In Durden v. Hammond, 1 B. & C. 111 (E. C. L. R. vol. 8), under the old practice, it was held that the return day in a writ might be altered, and the writ resealed, without a new stamp, provided that the new return day was not beyond the time at which it might have been made returnable at first. Now, by the writ given in the Common Law Procedure Act, 1852 (15 & 16 Vict. c. 76), Schedule (A.) No. 1, the appearance is to be within eight days of the service: no alteration, therefore, made before the service can prejudice a defendant. Further, it was held, under the old practice, that a writ against four defendants, describing three of them accurately and the fourth inaccurately, might be served on the three, and the name of the fourth might be altered, and the writ resealed; and that it would then be good against all: Anonymous (b) case in Chitty's Reports. It is true that in Knight v. Warren, 7 Dowl. P. C. 663, it was held, by Coleridge, J., that a defective writ, having been altered and resealed, should be dated on the day of resealing. But there the writ, which had a wrong party named as plaintiff, had been served, and an appearance entered, before the alteration: the writ had done its work in its original form; and the altered writ was in effect a new writ. [COLERIDGE, J.—It is said, in 1 Chitt. Archb. Pr. 186 (9th ed.), that "a writ may be altered and restamped before it is served, but not afterwards, without any order allowing an amendment. If, after being altered, it be restamped on a different day to the original *55] teste, the teste must be altered to make *it correspond with the time of resealing, for it will be considered as having issued at that time." Knight v. Warren is cited. Look also at Ashburton v. Sykes, 1 D. & L. 133.] That was the case of a writ of trial. [COLERIDGE, J. —It is there said, generally, that, when a writ is resealed, "it becomes a new writ, from the day of resealing to the new day of return."] In Siggers v. Sansom, 3 Moore & S. 194 (E. C. L. R. vol. 30), proceedings were set aside because the writ of summons had been altered, as to the county, without being resealed: but it seems that, if it had been resealed before service, the writ would have been valid. [COLERIDGE, J., referred to Braithwaite v. Lord Montford, 2 Cr. & M. 408.†] That case is a strong authority against the present rule. It is only by express

(a) November 18th. Before Coleridge, Wightman, and Erle, Js. Lord Campbell, C. J., was present during a part of the argument.
(b) Note (a) to Tomlin v. Preston, 1 Chitt. R. 398.

enactment (sect. 11 of The Common Law Procedure Act, 1852) that, in the case of writs not served, the resealing is dated. That is only for the purpose there contemplated.

Prentice, contrà.—If the argument on the other side be correct, the Statute of Limitations might always be defeated by taking a writ out, and afterwards altering it. [COLERIDGE, J.—Why should that not be so, if the writ was originally meant for the same defendant?] That is not so here, as the affidavit shows. The general rule is that "every writ of summons shall bear date on the day on which the same shall be issued;" sect. 5 of The Common Law Procedure Act, 1852. The issuing is now only the getting the writ sealed at the office. And therefore, if there be an alteration and a new sealing, there is a new writ. The language of the Judges is to *that effect. In Knight v. [*56 Warren, 7 Dowl. P. C. 663, Coleridge, J., said, "This writ must be considered as having issued, in fact, when it was resealed." In Ashburton v. Sykes, 1 D. & L. 133, the language was similar, as has been pointed out. [ERLE, J.—Surely it is quite idle to say that all resealing is creating a new writ.] That, of course, will not be the effect where the resealing is by order of the Court.

Lord CAMPBELL, C. J.—As I heard only a part of the argument, I shall give no opinion. *Cur. adv. vult.*

COLERIDGE, J., now delivered the judgment of the Court.

Upon reading the affidavits in this case, it appears that the plaintiff's attorney is entirely exculpated from any imputation of a desire to make costs and prevent the effect of a tender before action. There was no hurry in suing out the writ; the check which had been sent to the plaintiff was not returned because it was a check, but because the amount was considered insufficient. It is clear, too, that, as to the mistake in the defendants' name, the plaintiff's attorney was led into it by one of the defendants himself, and their attorney. Down to the issuing of the writ the defendants' attorney described his client as John Varley; letters were addressed to him; and he was described in letters, received by him or his attorney, as John Varley; and in the answers the mistake was not pointed out: and, until the defendants' attorney knew that the writ had been *sued out, it is clear that the plain- [*57 tiff's attorney thought there was but one defendant, and that his name was John Varley.

This application, therefore, must stand or fall strictly upon the practice: and the question is, whether a plaintiff is or is not at liberty before service of a writ of summons to correct a mistake in the name of the defendant or the number of the defendants against whom he has sued it out, without altering the teste of it. If the answer to this is to depend on what is stated for the plaintiff, without any counter allegation on the other side, it will be in the affirmative: an officer of our Court appears to have certified to the Judge at Chambers, who applied to him on the subject, that this was permitted in our Court. According to the authorities cited in the argument, the balance is clearly in favour of this practice; the writ, under the circumstances, not being made a new writ by the alteration, but remaining the same. And the reason of the thing appears to us to be the same way. It was admitted, in the argument, that, before the service of the writ, and while it was in the plaintiff's possession, it was in his power to make it perfect for the purpose for which he first sued it out, by correcting any mistake into which he had fallen as to the name or address of the person against whom he had originally sued it out. If he may do this, and is not driven for every such correction to sue out a new writ, the consequence surely is that the corrected writ is still the old writ; else the power to amend means nothing at all. But, if it remains the old writ, the original teste is the proper one to be continued. And no injustice flows from this. Whatever advantage the plaintiff can derive from the time *58] at which the writ *issued*, he ought *not to be deprived of because he has made a mistake in the name or address of the defendant, and afterwards corrected it before the defendant has even any knowledge of the writ. Whatever consequences depend on the *service* of the writ will remain exactly the same after the alteration as before.

This rule must therefore be discharged, and, having been moved with costs, with costs.   Rule discharged, with costs.

SPRYE v. PORTER. *Nov. 25.*

The first count of a declaration stated that plaintiff was in possession of documents and information which would prove defendant entitled to property not then in defendant's possession, and of which defendant was not aware: that, by written agreement, after reciting as above, and that plaintiff proposed to give defendant all the documents in plaintiff's possession on defendant agreeing to pay plaintiff one-fifth of the value of the property if it should come into his possession, to which defendant agreed, defendant, in consideration of the premises, agreed that, if by the documents and information defendant should become possessed of any property not then in his possession or that he did not know of, he would pay to plaintiff one-fifth of the value of the said property "to be recovered and possessed by the defendant as aforesaid;" and it was agreed that "defendant should not be compelled, for the purposes of that agreement, to take any proceedings at law or in equity to recover the said property or any part thereof;" provided that, if defendant did not become possessed of any property, he should not be called upon to pay any money whatever, and that, if he "did not think proper to proceed to recover the property," he would return the papers, and the agreement should be cancelled. Averment that plaintiff gave defendant the documents and information; and defendant, upon the documents and information, took "proceedings in equity and law to recover, and did proceed to recover, and by the said documents and information did actually recover, and did actually become possessed of," property which at the time of the agreement was not in his possession and which he then did not know of. Breach, that defendant had not paid the fifth of the value.

On demurrer to plea, held that the agreement as stated in this count did not disclose champerty or maintenance, and that the count was good.

Plea, that T. died a bachelor and intestate, possessed of personal property, without any known relation, and administration was granted to the solicitor of the Treasury as nominee of the Queen. That, at the time of the unlawful agreement after mentioned, defendant had no know-

ledge that he was next of kin to T. or entitled to the property : and plaintiff represented to
defendant that plaintiff would give such information and evidence, if it became necessary for
defendant to institute proceedings in law or equity for the recovery of the property, that by
means of such information and evidence defendant should recover the property, provided he
would enter into an agreement with plaintiff to pay plaintiff one-fifth of the property which
defendant should so recover.   That thereupon it was unlawfully agreed by plaintiff and defendant that plaintiff should give such information and evidence, &c. (as before), and that, if by
means of such information and evidence defendant should recover the property, defendant
should pay plaintiff one-fifth of the property so to be recovered.   That, in and for the purpose
of carrying out the agreement, and in order to secure to plaintiff one-fifth of the property so
to be recovered, defendant entered into the agreement mentioned in the first count.   That
proceedings were taken in Chancery and Q. B. by defendant for recovering the property ; and
information and evidence was given by plaintiff in pursuance of the agreement, and defendant
recovered the property as next of kin to T., which was the property mentioned in the first
count.   That plaintiff was not interested in any of the property save under the agreement.
And so the agreement was void.
Held, on demurrer, that the plea showed maintenance and was good.
There were also counts for work and labour, for the price of documents delivered by plaintiff to
defendant, for money paid, and on accounts stated.
Plea to these counts, stating the facts and the agreement as in the preceding plea, and that the
claim of defendant was for work and labour performed, for documents delivered and for money
paid, in carrying the agreement into effect, and for accounts stated in respect of documents
delivered and money paid in so doing.
Held, on demurrer, a good plea, as showing maintenance.
Plea to 1st count, and to so much of the claim in the other counts as related to any matter happening before the vesting order after mentioned, imprisonment of plaintiff for debt, and petition by him to the Insolvent Court, after the promise in the first count, and after the accruing
of the causes of action in the other counts pleaded to, and a vesting order by that Court before
the commencement of the suit.   There was no allegation that the assignee had interfered.
On demurrer, held that the interest in the contract stated in the first count was part of the insolvent's estate and vested in the assignee, and that the plea to the first count was good : it was
admitted to be a good plea as to the rest of the claim pleaded to.

THE first count of the declaration alleged that the plaintiff and one
Francois Rosaz, before and at the *time of the making of the [*59
agreement next mentioned, alleged they were, and they in fact
then were, in possession of certain documents and information which
would prove that the defendant was entitled to certain property not
then in the defendant's possession or control, nor which he was then
aware of ; and they proposed to give the defendant all the documents
and information in their possession on the defendant agreeing to pay
them each one-fifth of the value of the property if the same should
actually come in the defendant's possession ; to which proposal the
defendant had agreed.   And thereupon, on 4th November, 1852, by
an agreement in writing made between the plaintiff, therein described
as a genealogist, and the said F. Rosaz, of the one part, and the defendant of the other part, after reciting that the plaintiff and F. Rosaz
alleged that they were in possession of certain documents and information which would prove that the defendant was entitled to certain
*property not then in his possession and control, nor which he [*60
was aware of, and that they had proposed to give defendant all
the documents in their possession on the defendant agreeing to pay
them each one-fifth of the value of the property if the same should
actually come into his possession, to which proposal the defendant

agreed : defendant therefore, in consideration of the premises, agreed
that, if by the said documents and information of the plaintiff and F.
Rosaz the defendant should actually become possessed of any property
not then in his possession or control or that he did not know of, he,
defendant, would pay to each of them, plaintiff and F. Rosaz, one-fifth
of the value of the said property to be recovered and possessed by
defendant as aforesaid.   And it was thereby agreed that defendant
should not be compelled, for the purposes of that agreement, to take
any proceedings at law or in equity to recover the said property or
any part thereof; and that any information defendant should obtain
he should not nor would make known the said documents or information to any person whatsoever without the consent in writing of the
parties of the first part; and the defendant thereby agreed, if the said
property should be recovered by him, to execute all proper documents
at the proper time to vest in each of them, plaintiff and F. Rosaz, one-
fifth as aforesaid provided, and it was thereby understood and agreed
that, if defendant did not become possessed of any property, he should
not be called upon to pay any money whatsoever, and that, if defendant did not think proper to proceed to recover the property, he would
return the papers, and that the said agreement should thereon be cancelled.   Averment, that plaintiff and F. Rosaz did, upon the making
*61]   of the *said agreement, duly give to defendant all the said docu-
ments and information mentioned and referred to in the said
agreement, and so in their possession at the time of the making thereof;
and that defendant, upon the said documents and information so as
aforesaid given to him, did afterwards take certain proceedings in
equity and at law to recover, and did proceed to recover, and by the
said documents and information did actually recover, and did actually
become possessed of, certain property, to wit, a sum of 52,012*l*. 1*s*. 6*d*.,
which, at the time of the making of the said agreement, was not in his,
defendant's, possession or control, and which he then did not know of.
Averment, that plaintiff has always been ready and willing to do and
did do all things on his part which it was necessary he should be ready
and willing to do, and should do, and all conditions precedent have
been performed, and all things and events have happened, and taken
place, to entitle the plaintiff to be paid by defendant one-fifth of the
value of the said property, to wit, the said sum of 52,012*l*. 1*s*. 6*d*., so
by defendant recovered, and so by him actually become possessed of
as aforesaid, and to have executed by defendant all proper documents
to vest in plaintiff one-fifth of the value of the said property or sum so
by defendant recovered and become possessed of as aforesaid, and to
have the said agreement performed by defendant on his part; and the
time for so doing has elapsed : yet that defendant has made default in
paying and has not paid to the plaintiff one-fifth of the value of the
property, to wit, the said sum of 52,012*l*. 1*s*. 6*d*., so by defendant

recovered, &c., by the means aforesaid; and the said one-fifth of the value, &c., amounting *(to wit) to 10,402*l*. 8*s*. 3*d*., is still due in arrear and unpaid to plaintiff, contrary to the said agreement: [*62 that defendant has made default in executing, and has not executed, to plaintiff all or any proper document to vest in the plaintiff one-fifth, &c., but has wholly neglected and refused so to do: and that defendant further broke the said agreement in this, to wit, that he, without the consent in writing of plaintiff and the said F. Rosaz, did wrongfully make known the said documents and information, so given to him as aforesaid, to divers persons, in violation of the said agreement.

Counts for work and labour; for the price and value of various documents and writings furnished and delivered by plaintiff to defendant at his request; for money and materials by plaintiff disbursed and provided in and about the said work and labour; for money paid; for money found due from defendant to plaintiff on accounts stated.

Plea 7. To first count. That, before the making of the unlawful agreement hereinafter mentioned, The Reverend William Townley departed this life intestate, and at the time of his death was possessed of and entitled to large personal property, to wit, goods, chattels, and credits of great value. That, after his death, certain proceedings were had in the Prerogative Court of Canterbury in that behalf wherein it was alleged that the said W. T. died a bachelor, intestate without parent, brother, sister, uncle, aunt, nephew, niece, cousin german, or any known relation: and that Her Majesty, by warrant under Her Royal Sign Manual, countersigned by, &c., three commissioners of Her Treasury, had appointed George Maule, Esquire, her nominee, for the *purpose of obtaining letters of administration of all and singular [*63 the goods, &c., of the said deceased W. T. for Her Majesty's use. And such proceedings were therefore had that afterwards, to wit, on 29th April, 1848, it was decreed by the said Court that letters of administration of the goods of the said W. T., so dying a bachelor intestate, without parent, &c., or any known relation, should be committed and granted, to wit, to the said G. Maule, as the nominee and for the use of Her said Majesty. That, no person or persons, as next of kin or otherwise entitled to have any right, title, or interest in or to the personal estate of the said W. T., having appeared or claimed to be entitled thereto or to the administration thereof as against the right and title of Her said Majesty or the said G. M. as the nominee of Her said Majesty, thereupon, and before the making of the said unlawful agreement, to wit, on 8th August, 1848, administration of all, &c., which were of the said W. T. deceased at the time of his death, who died intestate, by the Archbishop of Canterbury was granted, to wit, to the said G. Maule, as and being the nominee, &c., for the use and benefit of Her said Majesty. That, G. Maule having afterwards died, thereupon afterwards, and after the death of the said G. Maule and before

the making of the said agreement, and upon the passing of a certain
act, &c. (15 & 16 Vict. c. 3, " To provide for the administration of personal estates of intestates and others to which Her Majesty may be
entitled in right of her prerogative or in right of her Duchy of Lancaster"), the said administration, &c., did, by virtue and under and in
pursuance of the said Act, devolve upon and become vested in the
*64] Solicitor for the affairs of Her said Majesty's Treasury *for the
time being, to wit, one Henry Revell Reynolds, whereof plaintiff
had notice.   That afterwards, and before and at the time of the making
of the said unlawful agreement hereinafter mentioned, defendant had
no knowledge that he was next of kin or one of the next of kin of the
said W. T., or that he was in any way entitled to the said property or
personal estate of the said W. T. deceased, or to any part thereof:
and plaintiff and the said Francois Rosaz represented and stated to the
defendant that they would supply and give such information and evidence, in case it should be or become necessary that proceedings should
be had and taken by the defendant, to wit, at law or in equity, for the
recovery of the said property vested in the said H. R. Reynolds as such
administrator as aforesaid, that through and by means of such information and evidence defendant should and might successfully recover the
said property, provided defendant would enter into an agreement with
plaintiff and the said F. Rosaz to pay each of them part, to wit, one-
fifth part, of the amount of the property the defendant should or might
so recover in that behalf.   That it was thereupon wrongfully and unlawfully agreed by and between plaintiff, the said F. Rosaz, and defendant,
that plaintiff and the said F. Rosaz should give and supply such information and evidence, in case it should be or become necessary that proceedings should be had and taken by the defendant, to wit, at law or in
equity, for the recovery of the said property, that, through and by
means of such information and evidence the defendant should and
might successfully recover the said property; and that, if by and
*65] through the means of such information and *evidence, defendant
should actually recover the said property, that defendant should
pay to each of them, the plaintiff and the said F. Rosaz, one-fifth of
the said property so to be recovered by defendant.   That, in and about
and for the purpose of carrying the said unlawful and corrupt agreement into effect and execution, and for the purpose of securing and in
order to secure to plaintiff and the said F. Rosaz respectively the said
one-fifth part of the said property so to be recovered as aforesaid,
defendant made and entered into the alleged agreement in the first
count of the declaration mentioned.   That thereupon proceedings, to
wit, in Her Majesty's High Court of Chancery and in Her Majesty's
Court of Queen's Bench at Westminster, were had and taken by defend
ant for the recovery of the said property, and that information and
evidence was given and supplied, to wit, by plaintiff and the said F.

Rosaz, in the said proceedings under and by virtue and in pursuance of the said unlawful agreement; and that defendant recovered the said property, to wit, as being the next of kin of the said W. T. deceased. That the said property in the first count alleged to have been recovered by and to have actually become possessed of by defendant was and is the same identical property recovered by defendant as in this plea mentioned. That the plaintiff and the said F. Rosaz were not, nor was either of them, entitled to or interested in any of the said property so recovered as aforesaid, save as under the said unlawful agreement. And so the defendant saith that the said agreement and promise in the said first count mentioned was and is void in law.

Plea 8. To the plaintiff's claim in respect of the money counts. Averments as in the 7th plea, down *to and including the allega- [*66 tion of the recovery by defendant and the negation of the inter- est of plaintiff and F. Rosaz. Further averments: That the said claim of plaintiff in the declaration mentioned, so far as relates to the said money counts, was and is in respect of work, labour, care, diligence, journeys, and attendances of plaintiff respectively done, performed, given and bestowed in and about and in respect of the carrying into execution and effect the said last-mentioned unlawful agreement, and in respect of the price and value of documents and writings respectively furnished and delivered in and about and in respect of the performing and carrying into execution and effect the said last-mentioned unlawful agreement, and for and in respect of money and materials disbursed, provided, and paid in and about and in respect of the performing, carrying into execution and effect, the said last-mentioned unlawful agreement, and in respect of accounts stated of and concerning the price and value of the documents and writings so furnished and delivered, and of and concerning the money disbursed and paid in and about and in respect of the performing and carrying into execution and effect the said last-mentioned unlawful agreement as aforesaid respectively, and not otherwise or in respect of any other matter or thing whatsoever.

Plea 9. To the plaintiff's claim in respect of the money counts. That the solicitor for the affairs of Her Majesty's Treasury for the time being, to wit, the said H. R. Reynolds, having, under and by virtue of the provisions of the said Act in the 7th plea mentioned, become and being such administrator as in the 7th plea mentioned, certain proceedings were instituted and had *against him, as such adminis- [*67 trator, in Her Majesty's High Court of Chancery by certain per- sons claiming to be next of kin to the said W. T. deceased, for the purpose of obtaining such and so much of the said estate or property in the said 7th plea mentioned as was vested in the said H. R. Rey- nolds, as such administrator as aforesaid, as the said persons so claiming to be next of kin as aforesaid might be entitled in that behalf. And in such proceedings the now defendant claimed also to be next of kin to the said W. T. and, as such, entitled to the said estate and property. That it was thereupon wrongfully and unlawfully agreed, to. wit, by and between the now plaintiff and the now defendant, that plaintiff should maintain, support, and uphold the now defendant in the said proceedings, and in the now defendant's said claim therein as such next of kin, to wit, by information, evidence, and documents in that behalf, and that, in case of the now defendant recovering such property as such next of kin, the now defendant should pay to the now plaintiff one-fifth of the property so to be recovered. That the said now plaintiff was not interested in or entitled to the said property or any part thereof, save as under the said last-mentioned unlawful agreement. That the claim of the plaintiffs in the declaration mentioned, so far as relates to the said money counts, was and is in respect of work, &c. : allegations, as in plea 8, referring to the agreement in this plea alleged, *mutatis mutandis.*

Plea 11. To the first count, and to so much of plaintiff's claim in that behalf as relates thereto, and as to so much and such part of plaintiff's claim under the money counts as relates to any matters happening before the making of the vesting order hereinafter mentioned, *68] *that, after the making of the promise in the 1st count mentioned, and after the accruing of the causes of action in the indebitatus counts to which this plea is pleaded, and before the commencement of this suit, to wit, on 13th December, 1853, plaintiff, then being a prisoner in actual custody within the walls of a certain prison in England, to wit, in Lancaster Castle, in the county of Lancaster, upon process at the suit of one of his creditors, to wit, one John Basterfield, for the recovery of a debt then due from plaintiff to the said creditor, did, within fourteen days next after the commencement of the said actual custody of plaintiff, to wit, on the day and year last aforesaid, duly and according to the direction and provisions of a certain statute passed, &c. (1 & 2 Vict. c. 110, " For abolishing arrest on mesne process in civil actions, except in certain cases; for extending the remedies of creditors against the property of debtors; and for amending the laws for the relief of insolvent debtors in England"), apply by a petition, &c., in a summary way to the Court for relief of Insolvent Debtors, &c. (stating the effect and prayer of the petition, filed on 19th December, 1853, in the usual form), and that, on the filing of the said petition and before the commencement of this suit, to wit, on 20th December, 1853, the said Court, then having jurisdiction in that behalf, in pursuance of and according to the said statute, ordered that all the real and personal estate and effects of the now plaintiff, both within this realm and abroad (except the wearing apparel, &c.), and also all the future estate, right, title, interest, and trust of such prisoner in or to any real and personal estate and effects within this realm or abroad, which the now plaintiff might purchase or which might revert, descend, or be *devised or bequeathed or come, to him before he should become [*69 entitled to his final discharge in pursuance of the said Act, according to the adjudication made in that behalf, or in case the now plaintiff should obtain his full discharge from custody without any adjudication being made by the said Court, then before the now plaintiff should be so fully discharged from custody, and all debts due or growing due to the now plaintiff to be due to him before such discharge as aforesaid, should be vested in one Samuel Sturgis, &c. (then and still provisional assignee): to have and hold, receive and take all and every the said estate and effects of the now plaintiff, real and personal, in possession, reversion, remainder, or expectancy, of every nature and kind whatsoever (except as aforesaid), and all and every of the said estates and effects which should be so purchased by the now plaintiff, or which should so revert, descend, be devised, bequeathed, or come to him as aforesaid, in possession, reversion, remainder, or expectancy, of any nature and kind whatsoever, with their and every of their rights, members, and appurtenances, unto the said S. Sturgis, his successors and assigns, according to the respective natures, properties, and tenures thereof, in trust, &c. (for the creditors), and to and for such other uses, intents, and purposes, and in such manner and form, as are in and by the said Act expressed of and concerning the same. That the order was entered of record and notice duly published, according to the directions of the said Court. By virtue of which order, and of the said statute, that part and so much of the plaintiff's claim as to which this plea is pleaded became and was vested in the said S. Sturgis, as assignee as aforesaid of the now plaintiff. That, after the making of the said vesting order, *and before the commencement of this suit, to wit, on [*70 20th January, 1854, one Charles Robert Thompson was duly appointed by the said Court assignee of the estate and effects of the said now plaintiff for the purpose of the said Act, and then accepted, and signified to the Court his acceptance of, the appointment; and the appointment and acceptance were then respectively duly entered of record of the said Court according to the provisions of the said Act. And thereupon, by virtue of the said appointment, and the said acceptance thereof by the said C. R. Thompson, and by virtue of the said statute, that part and so much of the plaintiff's claim as to which this plea is pleaded became, and was and now is, vested in the said C. R. Thompson, as such assignee as aforesaid.

Demurrers to the 7th, 8th, 9th, and 11th pleas. Joinder. .

The demurrers were argued on an earlier day in this Term.(a)

Bovill, for the plaintiff.—First, as to the declaration. It will be contended that the contract is illegal, as amounting to champerty or maintenance. The question may be considered as arising on the

(a) November 18th. Before Lord Campbell, C. J., Coleridge, Wightman, and Erle, Js.

common law, as well as on the early statutes which, it has been said,
are in affirmance of the common law.   Manutenentia curialis is said
by Lord Coke to be pendente placito, and is thus defined in Co. Lit.
368 b : " First, to maintain to have part of the land, or anything
out of the land, or part of the debt, or other thing in plea or suit;
and this is called cambipartia, champerty.   The second is, when one
*71]   *maintaineth the one side, without having any part of the thing
in plea, or suit." He also mentions a third sort, embracery,
which is not here in question.   Now in the present case no suit is
maintained at all by the plaintiff; there is no plea pending.   In Wilkinson v. Oliveira, 1 New Ca. 490 (E. C. L. R. vol. 27), the declaration recited that disputes had arisen between defendant and others as
to defendant's right to the effects of D., deceased; that it was necessary for defendant, for the termination of the disputes in his favour, to
prove that D. was an alien when he made his will; that plaintiff was
lawfully possessed of a paper showing this; that plaintiff, at defendant's request, gave the letter to defendant to be used for the purpose
of such proof; that defendant used it for the proof, and by means
thereof was enabled to and did cause the disputes to be determined in
his favour, and acquired a large portion of the effects; and, in consideration thereof, and that plaintiff, at defendant's request, had given
defendant the letter, defendant promised to give plaintiff 1000l., but
had refused to do so.   On demurrer, the declaration was held good.
In 2 Inst. 208, champerty and maintenance are explained as in the
passage above cited from Co. Litt.; they are spoken of as being committed pendente lite; and Bracton, fol. 117, lib. 3, tract. 1, c. 1, s. 3,
and The Mirrour, c. 1, s. 5, are referred to.   Maintenance and champerty were offences at common law.   The statutes are also confined to
cases where there is a suit.   The statute of Westminster the First (3
Ed. 1, c. 25) was especially directed against the King's ministers and
the officers of his Courts.   In the Articuli super chartas (3 stat. 28 Ed.
1, c. 11), the prohibition of champerty was extended to all persons;
*72]   there the words *are, "nor any other (for to have part of the
thing in plea) shall not take upon him the business that is in
suit;" 2 Inst. 563.   By the Statute of Champerty (3 stat. 33 Ed. 1),
reciting the enactments against bargains for maintaining "any manner
of suit or plea," three years' imprisonment with fine is inflicted on
those who "shall be attainted of such emprises, suits, or bargains;"
and they are called "conspirators, inventors, and maintenors of false
quarrels, and partakers thereof, and brokers of debates."   Then stat.
32 H. 8, c. 9, entitled "The bill of bracery and buying of titles,"
appears, by sect. 3, to be also directed against maintenance "in any
action, demand, suit, or complaint in any of the King's Courts."   It
appears thus that the illegality consists, not in the contract to receive
part of the thing which may be recovered, but in supporting an exist-

ing suit. The agreement here expressly leaves it open to the defendant to institute legal proceedings or not, as he chooses: but, if by any means he acquires the property, he is to pay one-fifth of its value to the parties who give him the documents. The necessity of an existing suit, to constitute the offence, appears also from Hawk. Pl. Cr. Book I., c. 83, s. 38,(a) vol. 2, p. 403 (7th ed). In Hartley v. Russell, 2 Sim. & St. 244, a creditor who had sued a debtor agreed to abandon the proceedings in consideration of the debtor giving him a lien upon deeds in the hands of one Collins, with authority to sue for the recovery of the deeds, and agreeing to assist him in so suing : on the creditor filing a bill against the debtor for specific performance, it was held that this agreement was not champerty : and Sir J. Leach, V. C., said : "There is here, therefore, no bargain, or colour of bargain, that Hartley" (the creditor) *"shall maintain the suit instituted by Russell" (the debtor) "against Collins, in consideration of sharing in the profits to be derived to Russell from the success of that suit, which is essential to constitute champerty." The contract will, if possible, be so interpreted as not to imply criminality; per Rolfe, B., in Findon v. Parker, 11 M. & W. 675, 684.† In Harrington v. Long, 2 M. & K. 590,(b) there was an assignment by one plaintiff to another of a debt said to be owing by the testator of the defendant, which had been the subject of a suit; and the defendant swore that she believed the assignment to have been made solely for the purpose of prosecuting this suit. Yet Sir John Leach, M. R., said : "There is no principle which prevents a person from assigning his interest in a debt after the institution of a suit for its recovery. Maintenance is where there is an agreement by which one party gives to a stranger the benefit of a suit, upon condition that he prosecutes it." And he refers to Wood v. Downes, 18 Ves. 120, and Hartley v. Russell, 2 Sim. & St. 244. In Cockell v. Taylor, 15 Beav. 103, money was advanced on the mortgage of a fund which was the subject of a suit, for the very purpose of enabling the mortgagor to carry on the suit; and this was held not to be void for champerty. On the other side reliance will be placed on Wood v. Downes. In that case there was an actual suit; and the attorney stipulated for a share of the proceeds : this was held by Lord Eldon, C., to be champerty. Again, in Stanley v. Jones, 7 Bing. 369 (E. C. L. R. vol. 20), there was not, as here, an agreement to hand over a document absolutely, but an agreement that the plaintiff should have an eighth part of the money *to be recovered in a suit by means of evidence to be furnished or procured by the plaintiff. So in Stevens v. Bagwell, 15 Ves. 189. there was direct maintenance of an existing suit. In Strange v. Brennan, 15 Sim. 346, the contract was for a per

[*73]

[*74]

(a) See also c. 84.
(b) Affirmed on appeal before Brougham, C., 2 M. & K. 595.

centage on a sum to be obtained by proceedings in Chancery. These cases are clearly distinguishable from that before the Court.

Next, as to the 7th plea. There is no averment that an actual suit existed: and, on this plea, the question arises whether the chance of litigation is sufficient to make the agreement unlawful.

The 8th plea raises the same point as the 7th plea.

The 9th plea, if supported in fact, must be admitted to be an answer to the declaration, so far as the money counts are concerned.

As to the 11th plea. There was no complete or ascertained debt at the time of the vesting order: and, therefore, no debt passed to the assignee: Skelton v. Mott, 5 Exch. 231.† And debts accruing after do not vest in the assignee till he interferes, which it is not averred that he has done here: Jackson v. Burnham, 8 Exch. 173,† Herbert v. Sayer, 5 Q. B. 965 (E. C. L. R. vol. 48).(a)

Hugh Hill, contrà.—The general principle is that, though a bond debt, or a specific interest in a fund in Court, may be assigned, and a power of attorney given to use the name of the assignor (which is conceding more than is warranted by some of the earlier authorities), yet, where a party has made a claim, it is illegal for a stranger to strive to obtain an interest in such claim, by bargain, and especially so if he is
*75] to furnish evidence in *aid of the claim. In order to establish this, it is unnecessary to go into the old authorities; Stanley v. Jones, 7 Bing. 369 (E. C. L. R. vol. 20), is sufficient to establish the principle. There Tindal, C. J., said: " Besides the ordinary objection, that a stranger to the controversy has acquired an interest to carry on the litigation to the uttermost extent, by every influence and means in his power, the bargain to furnish and to procure evidence for the consideration of a money payment in proportion to the effect produced by such evidence, has a direct and manifest tendency to pervert the course of justice." [Lord CAMPBELL, C. J.—There a litigation was distinctly contemplated: but is the declaration here impeachable upon any ground which would not make it illegal to sell information as to unclaimed dividends?] The expression in the declaration is " property to be recovered." If that does not mean " recovered by law," the 7th and 8th pleas clearly contemplate litigation. [ERLE, J.—The plaintiff bargains for a given fraction of the sum to be recovered.] He does so ; and that circumstance distinguishes this case from Wilkinson v. Oliveira, 1 New Ca. 490 (E. C. L. R. vol. 27), where the defendant purchased the information for a specified sum from the plaintiff, who had no interest in the success of any litigation. In Evans v. Jones, 5 M. & W. 77,† where a wager on the event of a prosecution was held to be illegal, Lord Abinger said: " No man has a right to acquire by his own act an interest in interfering with the proceedings of Courts of justice." " Here the party had acquired by the wager a direct in-

terest in procuring the conviction of the prisoner ; and although it is
impossible to say in what precise manner an improper bias may be
exerted, or whether it will have any effect *or not, yet the very [*76
tendency of his mind to act in such a way as to prevent the
course of justice, is a sufficient foundation for the illegality of such
wagers." Wood v. Downes, 18 Ves. 120, is in point. Lord Eldon,
C., there said that, if the party had not been the attorney, it would
still have been impossible for a Court of Equity to permit the deal to
have any effect. [Lord CAMPBELL, C. J.—There can be no difference
between setting litigation in motion, and joining in it when already
commenced.] In Bell v. Smith, 5 B. & C. 188 (E. C. L. R. vol. 11),
an action was brought on a policy of assurance by the party who had
effected the policy ; and the interest was averred in A. A., being
called as a witness for the plaintiff, was objected to as incompetent : in
answer, an indenture was produced whereby A., in consideration of L.
indemnifying the plaintiff for costs, assigned to him all A.'s interest in
the policy and all moneys to be recovered in the action. It was held
that this did not do away with A.'s interest in the event: but, further,
Bayley and Holroyd, Js., held the assignment unlawful on the ground
of maintenance. A contract much like that now in question, to which
the present plaintiff was a party, was before the Lords Justices Knight
Bruce and Lord Cranworth, in the case of Reynell v. Sprye, 1 Du G.
M. & G. 660 ;(a) and they held that, whether or not the contract amounted
to champerty or maintenance, it was against the policy of the law, and
would be relieved against in a Court of Equity. This view of the
case is illustrated by Mr. Smith's note (1 Lea. Ca. 278 (4th ed.)) on
Collins v. Blantern, 2 Wils. 341, and by Cholmondeley v. Clinton, 4
Bligh, 1, and *Strachan v. Brander, 1 Eden, 303. The declara- [*77
ration here shows that the contract contemplates that a suit may
be instituted; else why should there be a clause to the effect that the
defendant shall not be compelled to institute proceedings? [Lord
CAMPBELL, C. J.—You cannot put it higher than probability.] At any
rate the clause affords an inference as to the sense in which the word
"recover" is used. But the 7th plea removes any doubt: and it is an
unquestionable rule that illegality may be shown by averments dehors
the written agreement. For instance, to a declaration on a written
contract of sale, good on its face, it might be pleaded that the sale was
a colourable mode of effecting an usurious transaction.

As to the 11th plea. The vesting order appears to have been made
after the cause of action in the indebitatus counts, which is pleaded to,
had arisen. [Bovill.—The plea is good as an answer so far.] As to
the first count, if it shows only a legal sale of the document, the plea
shows that the vesting order was subsequent to such. But, if it shows
a bargain for a sum to be paid, contingently upon the event of a law-

(a) Affirming the decision of Wigram, V. C., in Reynell v. Sprye, 8 Hare, 222.

suit, in proportion to the sum recovered, it discloses illegality. Therefore the plea answers the declaration upon the only construction which
makes the declaration good.   The cases are collected in Beckham *v.*
Drake, 2 H. L. Ca. 579.(*a*)

   Bovill was heard in reply.   *Cur. adv. vult.*

*78]   *Lord CAMPBELL, C. J., now delivered the judgment of the
       Court.

   In this case we must begin by considering the validity of the first
count of the declaration.   The defendant contends that the agreement
on which it is framed is illegal, as being contrary to public policy and
the laws against champerty and maintenance.   But we are of opinion
that nothing appears on the face of the declaration to support this
objection.

   The plaintiff alleges that Rosaz and he were in possession of certain
documents and information to prove that the defendant was entitled to
certain property of which the defendant was not aware, and proposed
to give him all the documents and information in their possession, on
defendant's agreeing to pay them each one-fifth of the value of the
property if it should actually come into his possession ; to which the
defendant assented : that thereupon a written agreement was signed by
the parties, whereby the defendant, in consideration of the premises,
agreed that, if by the said documents and information he should
actually become possessed of any property, not then in his possession
or control and that he did not know of, he would pay to each of the
plaintiff and Rosaz one-fifth of the value of the said property to be
recovered and possessed by the defendant : that the defendant should
not be compelled, for the purposes of that agreement, to take any proceedings at law or in equity to recover the said property : that the
defendant would not make known to any person the documents or
information so communicated to him, without the consent of plaintiff in
writing : that defendant should execute all necessary deeds for assigning
*79]   the one-fifth of the property so *recovered : that, if defendant
       did not become possessed of any property, he should not be called
upon to pay anything ; and that, if the defendant did not think proper
to proceed to recover the property, he would return the papers, and
thereupon the agreement should be cancelled.

   No statute, nor decided case, nor dictum, was cited at the bar,
showing that there is any illegality in this agreement.   No suit was
depending ; and there is no stipulation for the commencement of any
suit for the recovery of this property.   The plaintiff and Rosaz were
merely to communicate certain documents and information then in their
possession to the defendant ; and, having done so, they were to do no
more.   The documents and information must be presumed to be genuine

and sincere. The property might well be recovered without any litigation, the documents and information communicated making out a clear and conclusive title in the defendant to recover it. At any rate, the defendant was not to be forced into litigation; and, if he did resort to litigation, the plaintiff and Rosaz were not to furnish him with money to carry it on, or to provide him with any further evidence, or in any way to assist or to countenance him. There seems abundant consideration for the defendant's promise, both in what the plaintiff and Rosaz did, and in the advantage which the defendant was to derive therefrom. And his promise was merely to make over a portion of that which was his own. We therefore do not think that the agreement at all savours of maintenance or champerty, or is in any way contrary to public policy. It does not resemble any of the cases relied upon, in which agreements have been held illegal; and there seems to be no occasion *for our going over those cases and distinguishing the present from them. [*80

But, when we come to the pleas demurred to, we think it equally clear that, giving credit to their allegations, they show the agreement to be illegal. There can be no doubt that the defendant is at liberty to allege that the written agreement declared upon was merely colourable, and to disclose, as a defence, the real nature of the transaction. Accordingly the 7th plea, after stating the death of Townley possessed of personal property, intestate and without kindred, the grant of administration to the solicitor to the treasury, for the benefit of the Queen, and the defendant's ignorance of his being related to Townley or in any way entitled to the property, goes on to allege that the plaintiff and Rosaz represented to the defendant that they would supply and give such information and evidence, in case it should become necessary that proceedings should be had and taken by the defendant at law or in equity for the recovery of the property, *that, through and by means of such information and evidence, the defendant should and might successfully recover the property*, provided the defendant would enter into an agreement with the plaintiff and Rosaz to pay each of them one-fifth of the property so recovered: and it was thereupon unlawfully agreed between the parties that the plaintiff and Rosaz should give and supply such information and evidence, in case of proceedings being taken at law or in equity for the recovery of the property, that, by means of such information and evidence, the defendant should successfully recover the property; and that, if by means of such information and evidence the defendant should actually recover the property, he would pay each of *them one-fifth of the amount. The plea then goes on to allege that, for the purpose of carrying this illegal agree- [*81 ment into effect, the parties entered into the supposed agreement set out in the first count of the declaration, and shows that it was under the illegal agreement that the property actually was recovered. Here we have *maintenance* in its worst aspect. The plaintiff and Rosaz, entire strangers to the property which they say the defendant has a title to, but which is in the possession of another claiming title to it, agree with him that legal proceedings shall be instituted in his name for the recovery of it, and that they will supply him, not with any specified or definite documents or information, but with evidence that should be sufficient to enable him successfully to recover the property. Each of them is to have one-fifth of the property, when so recovered; and, unless the evidence with which they supply him is sufficient for this purpose, they are to receive nothing. They are not to employ the attorney or to advance money to carry on the litigation; but they are to supply that upon which the event of the suit must depend, *evidence:* and they are to supply it of such a nature and in such quantity as to insure success. The plaintiff purchases an interest in the property in dispute, bargains for litigation to recover it, and undertakes to maintain the defendant in the suit in a manner of all others the most likely to lead to perjury and to a perversion of justice. Upon principle such an agreement is clearly illegal: and Stanley v. Jones, 7 Bing. 369 (E. C. L. R. vol. 20), is an express authority to that effect.

*82]   The 8th plea, pleaded to the money counts, is *substantially the same as the 7th, and is, we think, equally a bar.

The 9th plea is still a little stronger, and is allowed by the plaintiff's counsel to be sufficient.

We have therefore only further to deal with the 11th plea, which is pleaded to the plaintiff's title to sue, supposing the defendant to be liable. In as far as this plea applies to the money counts, it is allowed to be good: but the plaintiff's counsel contends that it is no bar to the first count, as the right of action thereby disclosed would not vest in the assignees under the insolvency, and that it remains in the insolvent till the assignee interposes and claims the money. We are of opinion, however, that the 11th plea is a bar to the first count, as well as the other parts of the declaration to which it is pleaded. This plea, admitting all the allegations in the first count, avers that, after the making of the promise in that count mentioned, and before the commencement of this suit, the plaintiff petitioned the Insolvent Debtors' Court under the Insolvent Debtors' Act, and that all his property vested in the assignee. The plea certainly does not show that the plaintiff had a complete cause of action before the vesting order; but it does show that, for an executed valuable consideration, the defendant had promised to pay the plaintiff a sum of money upon a contingency. We conceive that the interest in this contract is valuable property which would vest in the assignee, and that, when the money becomes payable by the property being recovered, it is part of the estate of the insolvent to be distributed among his creditors. This is not money which he has earned since the vesting order or since his discharge, for which he might sue till the *assignee interferes. If, before petitioning the Insolvent Court, the insolvent

*83]

had entered into a contract under which he paid a sum of money to another, who, in consideration thereof, was upon a contingency to pay him a larger sum of money or to deliver goods to him, surely, on the happening of the contingency after his discharge, the assignee, and not the insolvent, would be entitled to sue for the money or the goods. In Herbert *v.* Sayer, 5 Q. B. 965 (E. C. L. R. vol. 48), the cause of action had arisen subsequently to the bankruptcy of the uncertified bankrupt ; and therefore the Court of error held that, till the assignees interfered, the right of action was in the bankrupt. In Skelton *v.* Mott, 5 Exch. 231,† the question was, how far a discharge under the Insolvent Debtors' Act was a defence to an action brought against the insolvent, and does not appear to apply to a case like the present, where the question is, whether a right of action, which has accrued and does subsist, be in the insolvent or in his assignee. Therefore, on the demurrer to the 11th plea, we think there ought to be judgment for the defendant.

Judgment for defendant on all the demurrers.(*a)*

(a) See the next case.

Champerty is the unlawful maintenance of a suit in consideration of an agreement to have some part of the thing in dispute or some profit out of it. Such an agreement cannot be supported either at law or in equity : Arden *v.* Patterson, 5 Johnson's Ch. Rep. 44 ; Thurston *v.* Percival, 1 Pick. 416 ; Key *v.* Vattier, 1 Ham. 132 ; Brown *v.* Beauchamp, 5 Monroe, 416. It is not essential that there be a suit commenced at the time the agreement is made : Rust *v.* Larue, 4 Litt. 417. The laws against champerty are intended to prevent the interference of strangers, having no pretence of right in the subject of the suit, and standing in no relation of duty to the suitor : Thallhimer *v.* Brinckerhoff, 3 Cowen, 624. The relation of landlord and tenant, master and servant, acts of charity to the poor, the exercise of the legal profession, and where there is consanguinity or affinity between the suitor and him who gives aid to the suit, are cases in which it is not unlawful to maintain : Ibid ; Campbell *v.* Jones, 4 Wendell, 306 ; Perine *v.* Dunn, 3 Johns. Ch. Rep. 508. That the legal profession, however, are not excepted from the consequences of champerty, see Holloway *v.* Lowe, 7 Porter, 488 ; Caldwell *v.* Shepherd, 6 Monroe, 389 ; Dumas *v.* Smith, 17 Alabama, 305 ; Weeden *v.* Wallace, Meigs, 286 Satterlee *v.* Frazer, 2 Sandf. Sup. Ct. 141.

See also Wilhite *v.* Roberts, 4 Dana, 172 ; Evans *v.* Bell, 6 Dana, 479 ; Bayard *v.* M'Lane, 3 Harrington, 139 ; Walker *v.* Cuthbert, 10 Alabama, 213 ; Shirley *v.* Riggs, 11 Humphreys, 53 ; Ex parte Plitt et al., 2 Wallace, Jr., Rep. 453.

It is not maintenance for a person to promote a suit or a defence, in which he has, or believes that he has, a legal interest : M'Call *v.* Capehart, 20 Alabama, 521.

END OF MICHAELMAS TERM.

The Court of Queen's Bench did not sit in banc during the Vacation following this Term.

CASES

ARGUED AND DETERMINED

IN

THE QUEEN'S BENCH,

Hilary Term,

XX. VICTORIA. 1857.

The Judges who usually sat in Banc in this Term, were,—

Lord CAMPBELL, C. J.,	WIGHTMAN, J.,
COLERIDGE, J.,	CROMPTON, J.

SIMPSON and Another *v.* LAMB.

An attorney conducting a cause for the plaintiff, though not the attorney on the record, after verdict, but before judgment, bonâ fide purchased from his client the benefit of his verdict, and gave notice of this to the defendant. Afterwards the same plaintiff became nonsuited in another action against the same defendants. A rule having been obtained to set off the one judgment against the other:

Held, that the set-off was subject not only to the lien for costs, but to any equitable rights acquired in the judgment.

Held, also, that the transaction, being a purchase of the subject-matter of a suit by the attorney, was void as against the policy of the law, and that it made no difference that the purchaser was not attorney on the record. *Semble*, that such a purchase by a stranger to the suit would have been valid.

BADELEY, in Trinity Term, 1856, obtained, on behalf of the defendant, a rule calling on the plaintiffs to show cause why, upon payment to them of the sum of 14*l.* 2*s.* 6*d.*, parcel of the sum of 85*l.* 4*s.* *paid into Court by the defendant, they should not enter up satisfaction on the judgment obtained by them in this cause; and why, upon defendant entering up satisfaction on the judgment obtained by him against the plaintiffs in the Court of Common Pleas, the residue of the sum of 85*l.* 4*s.* should not be paid out of this Court to the defendant.

From the affidavits the following appeared to be the material facts. The writ in this action was sued out, on 22d December, 1854, by John

Scott as the plaintiffs' attorney. On 22d February, 1855, Scott transferred the cause to another attorney, William Shaen, who thenceforth took the management of the cause as attorney for the plaintiffs, instead of Scott, though the latter continued the attorney on the record. On 26th February, 1855, after Shaen, though not attorney on the record, had taken up the conduct of the cause as attorney for the plaintiffs, a verdict was obtained for the plaintiffs for 50*l.* On the 27th February, 1855, Shaen advanced to the plaintiffs 50*l.* on the security of the judgment to be signed on this verdict, and on the same day gave notice to the defendant and his attorney that he, Shaen, had a claim upon the whole amount to be recovered in the action, and that no part was to be paid to any one else than himself, or Scott on his behalf. On the 23d March, 1855, after this notice, the plaintiffs commenced an action in the Common Pleas against the defendant. Shaen had no concern in the action in the Common Pleas, and was not aware of it till afterwards. On 28th March, 1855, judgment was signed for the plaintiffs in the action in this Court for 85*l.* 4*s.*, viz.: 50*l.* damages and 35*l.* 4*s.* taxed costs. The plaintiffs' costs between them and their attorney were not taxed; but it was agreed that the costs between attorney and client did not amount to *70*l.* On 5th July, 1855, the plaintiffs were non-suited in the action in the Common Pleas. A rule to set aside [*86 that nonsuit was obtained and afterwards discharged: and on 21st January, 1856, judgment of nonsuit was signed in the Common Pleas for 71*l.* 1*s.* 6*d.* costs. On 26th February, 1856, an order to change the plaintiffs' attorney in the action in the Queen's Bench was obtained; and from that time Shaen was attorney on the record in this cause. On 9th April, 1856, the defendant having been taken in execution at the suit of a third person, a detainer in the cause in this Court was lodged. On 21st April, 1856, a summons was taken out in this Court to show cause why the defendant should not be discharged out of custody, upon payment of 14*l.* 2*s.* 6*d.*, being the balance of debt and costs in this cause, after giving credit for the amount of the judgment obtained by the defendant against the plaintiffs in the Common Pleas. Williams, J., endorsed the summons: "No order, except that the defendant may be discharged on payment of 85*l.* 4*s.* into Court. I recommend the defendant to go to the Court so that cause may be shown in the first instance." In deference to this suggestion *Quain* appeared and showed cause in the first instance, when the present rule was applied for;(*a*) but, he being taken by surprise by an objection founded on the statutes of champerty, the Court directed that only a rule Nisi should issue, and cause be shown afterwards.

Quain, in last Michaelmas Term,(*b*) showed cause.—There is no legal set-off between cross judgments; but the Court, in the exercise of its

(*a*) June 12th, 1856. Before Lord Campbell, C. J., Coleridge, Erle, and Crompton, Js.
(*b*) November 21st, 1856. Before Lord Campbell, C. J., Coleridge, Wightman, and Erle, Js.

*87] equitable jurisdiction, *sets off one against the other, subject to the attorney's lien for costs.(a) But, it being an equitable set-off, the beneficial interests are to be looked to : Bristowe v. Needham, 7 M. & G. 648 (E. C. L. R. vol. 49). In this case the assignment to Shaen of the interest in the judgment was perfect in equity, as soon as notice was given, which was on the 27th February, 1855, before the action in the Common Pleas commenced, if that date be material. There is no pretence here that the assignment was not a security for money bonâ fide lent; but it is said that, though bonâ fide, it is illegal, either because the assignor and assignee stood in the relation of client and attorney, or because it was an assignment of the subject-matter of a suit before judgment, and so within the prohibitions in the statutes against champerty. No doubt, though Shaen was not attorney on the record, the relation of attorney and client existed ; and, if the fiduciary relation was in any way abused, the client might set aside the trans-action. Perhaps, as against the client, the onus would be on the attorney to show that the transaction was such as could be supported ; but this is the application of a stranger; and, as against him, the relation between the assignor and assignee was immaterial. Then as to champerty : the assignment, pendente lite, is not illegal per se, though if there were any agreement to maintain the action it would be : Har-rington v. Long, 2 M. & K. 590.(b) Lord Coke (2 Inst. 484) in com-menting on Stat. West. 2 (1 stat. 13 Ed. 1), c. 49, says, " And it is to be observed, that neither the chancellor, treasurer, any of the justices, or any of the King's council, nor any clerk herein mentioned, nor any
*88] of the King's house of the clergy or *laity shall (hanging the plea) receive any advowson, land, or tenement, by gift, purchase, or farm, either for champerty or otherwise ; so as none of these persons here prohibited can acquire any advowson, land, or tenement, depending the plea, though it be bonâ fide, and not for champerty or maintenance ; partly in respect of their greatness, and partly in respect of their places, both in King's Court, and in the Courts of justice ; so as the very countenance and places of these men, when they become interested in the land (eo ipso) are apparent hindrances of the due and indifferent proceeding of law and justice. An excellent law and worthy to be known, and most necessary to be put in execution ; so as true it is, that if any other person purchase bonâ fide, depending the suit, he is not in danger of champerty : but these persons here prohibited cannot pur-chase at all, neither for champerty nor otherwise, depending the plea. But these persons here prohibited must be charged upon this Act, and not for champerty, unless they maintain. And this is a great addition to the statute of W. 1, cap. 25, which extended only where the pur-chaser (pendente placito) did maintain."

(a) Reg. Gen. Hil. 16 Vict. 1853, r. 63; 1 E. & B. xiii. (E. C. L. R. vol. 72).
(b) See Spry v. Porter, ante, p. 53.

Badeley, in support of the rule.—First: the right of set-off between cross judgments is an incident to them, and cannot be prevented by any arrangement of the judgment-creditor. [Lord CAMPBELL, C. J.— Your proposition would lead to this result, that, if a judgment-debt were publicly sold by auction, and the sale notified to every one, the purchaser might at any period, before satisfaction, be deprived of the fruits of his judgment.] He is liable to be so defeated by writ of error or auditâ querelâ; and there is no decision that he is not so liable by set-off.

*Secondly: a purchase by an attorney from his client of the [*89 subject-matter of the suit is void as against public policy : Wood *v.* Downes, 18 Ves, 120. [Lord CAMPBELL, C. J.—That was on the application of the client.] The reasons given by Lord Eldon, C., seems to go on general policy. At all events it is void as being against the statutes against champerty. 15 Vin. Abr. 149, *Maintenance* (B. 2), collects the old statutes on the point. It is immaterial whether it be bonâ fide or not, if it amount to maintenance.

Lord CAMPBELL, C. J.—I feel no difficulty as to two of the points made. This is an application to the Court in the exercise of its equitable jurisdiction to order a set-off between the two judgments. There is no strict right to such a set-off; and the proposition that the Court is bound to order it, whatever may have intervened between the one judgment and the other, is wholly untenable. Secondly, whatever may be the general rule as between solicitor and client, as to invalidating purchases by the former for the latter, the rule as between solicitor and client does not apply in favour of a third person. On the rest of the case we will take time to consider what our judgment should be.

COLERIDGE, J.—Mr. *Badeley* says that it is a legal incident to a judgment that it is subject to set-off if at any time thereafter there should be a judgment between the same parties; so that any assignment of a judgment must always be liable to this infirmity. I never heard this doctrine stated before; and I cannot accede to it *now. The [*90 set-off always is by order of the Court, in the exercise of their equitable jurisdiction, and is subject to equitable considerations. One is well known and is recognised by a general rule of Court, I mean the lien of solicitors. The rule that the set-off is subject to such a lien is quite inconsistent with Mr. *Badeley's* principle.

WIGHTMAN, J.—I am of the same opinion. The set-off is not a legal right, but is allowed by the Courts in furtherance of justice. If the two suits had been running together, something might have been said against the justice of depriving the party of the security, on which he might rely, by an assignment; but that is not the case here.

ERLE, J.—I think it clear that the set-off is on equitable grounds, and subject to equitable considerations. And it is clear that the assignee of a chose in action, who has perfected his equitable title

according to the rules of equity, has an equitable right of which a
Court of law will for this purpose take notice. The set-off therefore
must be subject to such rights.

As to the rest of the case, time is taken to consider.

Cur. adv. vult.

Quain referred the Court to 1 Chitty's Statutes, 422 (ed. 2.), note
(*b*), and to Cockell *v.* Taylor, 15 Beav. 103.

Lord CAMPBELL, C. J., in this Term (January 13th), delivered judgment.

*91]   The facts of this case, as they appear upon the *affidavits, are
as follows.   In December, 1854, Mr. John Scott, as attorney for
the plaintiffs, commenced an action at their suit in the Court of Queen's
Bench against the defendant.   The cause was tried on 26th of February,
1855; and the plaintiffs had a verdict for 50*l.* damages: and on the
28th of March, 1855, judgment was signed for the damages and taxed
costs, which together amounted to 85*l.* 4*s.*   All the proceedings, down
to final judgment inclusively, were carried on in the name of Mr. Scott,
as attorney for the plaintiffs: but it appears that, a day or two before
the trial, some private arrangement was made between Mr. Scott and
Mr. Shaen, another attorney, that from that time Mr. Shaen should
have the conduct of the proceedings, as if he were the plaintiffs' attorney,
but, on account of the expense, without any order to change the
attorney: and the proceedings were accordingly carried on by Mr.
Shaen in the name of Scott, until the 26th of February, 1856, when
an order to change the attorneys was made by consent, and Mr. Shaen
was substituted for Mr. Scott as the plaintiffs' attorney.   In the mean
time, it appears that on the 27th of February, 1855, the day after
the trial, and of course before judgment, Mr. Shaen purchased the
interest of the plaintiffs in the verdict for the sum of 50*l.*, the amount
of the damages which they had recovered: and, on the same day, Shaen
gave notice to the defendant's attorney that he had a claim upon the
sum recovered to the full amount, and requesting that the damages so
recovered might be paid only to him, or to Mr. Scott.

In July, 1855, the plaintiffs were nonsuited in another action which
they brought in the Common Pleas against the defendant; and on the
*92]   21st of January, 1856, *judgment of nonsuit, with 71*l.* 1*s.* 6*d.*
costs, was signed against the plaintiffs; and the defendant now
claims to be entitled to set off that sum against the damages and costs
in the action in the Queen's Bench, in which the plaintiffs were successful.

There is no doubt, since the Rule of Court of Hilary Term, 2 W. 4,
I. 93, 3 B. & Ad. 888 (E. C. L. R. vol. 23),(*a*) that the plaintiffs'
attorneys have a lien upon the judgment obtained by them for their
costs in that particular suit, and that no set-off can be allowed to the

(a) See Reg. Gen., Hil. 16 Vict. 1853, r. 63; 1 E. & B. xiii.

prejudice of that lien: but, as it is agreed that their costs in that suit amount to less than 85*l*. 4*s*., for which judgment was signed, the question for us to determine is, whether Mr. Shaen's claim as purchaser of the damages is to be allowed: for, if it is valid, there can be no set-off in this case. The purchase of the damages, immediately after the verdict and before judgment, was a purchase of the matter in suit *pendente lite;* and it may be very material to consider in what relation Shaen stood to the plaintiffs at the time of the purchase. It appears by the affidavits of Shaen and Scott that, although Scott was nominally the attorney for the plaintiffs down to a time long subsequent to the final judgment, Shaen became before the trial really and substantially the attorney for the plaintiffs in the management and conduct of the suit; and it appears to us that, for the purpose of the question before us, Shaen is to be considered as the attorney having the management of the cause for the plaintiffs, and that the purchase was in effect a purchase by the attorney in the cause of the subject-matter of it *pendente lite*, not for the purpose of enabling them to carry on the suit, but because they *wanted the money. Independently of the statutes referred [*93 to upon the argument, restraining the purchase of property in suit, particularly by persons concerned in the administration of justice (1st Statute of Westminster, c. 25; 2d Statute of Westminster, c. 49, and 3 stat. 28 Ed. 1, c. 11, commented upon in the 2d Institute, 484), it has been held, in several cases, that no attorney can be permitted to purchase anything in litigation, of which litigation he has the management (Hall *v*. Hallet, 1 Cox, 134, Wood *v*. Downes, 18 Ves. 120, and the authorities therein cited), and considering the relation in which the attorney and client stand to each other, it would seem, as was said in Hall *v*. Hallet, to be against the policy of the law to permit such a dealing by an attorney with the subject of a suit of which he has the conduct as the attorney, whilst the case is still undetermined by judgment, as that which is now in question before us, whatever might have been the case had the purchase been by a stranger.

We are therefore of opinion that the rule must be absolute for setting off one judgment against the other without reference to Mr. Shaen's claim as purchaser, but subject to the lien of the plaintiffs' attorney for his costs in the action. *Order accordingly.*

See note at p. 83, ante. An agreement between client and attorney made after a judgment is recovered, that the attorney shall have part of the judgment when collected, is not void: Floyd *v*. Goodwin, 8 Yerger, 484.

*94] *FREDERICK HATTON *v.* HENRY ENGLISH and
GEORGE WILLIAMS. *Jan. 12th.*

Under stat. 17 & 18 Vict. c. 36, s. 1, a bill of sale is void against creditors unless a description
of the residence and occupation of the person granting it be filed along with the bill of sale.
It is not sufficient that the bill of sale, which is filed, itself contains a description of his resi
dence and occupation.

ISSUE, under which plaintiff affirmed and defendants denied that
certain goods seized by the sheriff of Middlesex, under a fi. fa. against
the goods of Joseph Hare, at the suit of defendants, were, at the time
of the delivery of the writ, the goods of the plaintiff.

On the trial, before Lord Campbell, C. J., at the Sittings at Westminster after last Term, it appeared that the writ was delivered on 24th
October, 1856. The execution-debtor, Joseph Hare, had, on 18th July,
1856, executed a bill of sale conveying the goods in question to the
plaintiff by way of security. This bill of sale was, within twenty-one
days, filed along with an affidavit of the time when it was executed.
The bill of sale was expressed to be made between " Joseph Hare of
No. 11, Clarges Street, Piccadilly, in the county of Middlesex, lodging-
house keeper, of the one part," and the plaintiff of the other ; but the
affidavit accompanying it contained no description of the occupation
of Joseph Hare ; nor was there any other description of his occupation
filed, except that in the bill of sale itself. It was objected that the
provisions of stat. 17 & 18 Vict. c. 36, s. 1, had not been complied
with. The Lord Chief Justice, on this objection, directed a verdict
for the defendants, with leave to move to enter a verdict for the
plaintiff.

*95] *Montagu Chambers*, in the ensuing term, moved for a rule nisi
pursuant to the leave reserved.—The description of the occupation
here given is sufficient ; the case is not like that of Allen *v.* Thompson, 1
H. & N. 15,† where no occupation at all was stated. The object of the
Legislature was to furnish the officer materials for making the proper
entries in the book to be kept under sect. 3. [Lord CAMPBELL, C. J.—
The question is whether the Legislature did not intend that those
materials should be supplied by something extraneous to the bill of sale,
something filed along with it.] It is immaterial, for the purpose of the
Act, how the description is given if it be supplied. [WIGHTMAN, J.—
In the interval between the execution of the bill of sale and the filing,
the residence and occupation may have changed, and the description at the
time when the bill of sale was executed is not what the Legislature want.]

COLERIDGE, J.—I think there should be no rule. The words of the
Act are too strong to bear any doubt. The bill of sale contained a
description of the residence and occupation ; and it was filed together
with an affidavit which contained no such description ; and no more was
filed. Now the enactment is that the bill of sale, " or a true copy

thereof, and of every attestation of the execution thereof, shall, together with an affidavit of the time of such bill of sale being made or given, and a description of the residence and occupation of the person making or giving the same, or, in case the same shall be made or given by any person under or *in the execution of any process, then a descrip- [*96 tion of the residence and occupation of the person against whom such process shall have issued, and of every attesting witness to such bill of sale, be filed" within twenty-one days after the making of the bill of sale; otherwise it shall be void against creditors. Now it is impossible to say, in this case, that the enactment has been complied with, or that any description has been filed together with the bill of sale.

WIGHTMAN, J.—The terms of the Act do not require that the bill of sale itself should contain any description, and do require that a description should be filed together with the bill of sale.

CROMPTON, J.—I entertain no doubt that the intention of the Legislature was that the affidavit should contain the descriptions required.

Lord CAMPBELL, C. J.—At the trial I thought the point very clear, but reserved it on account of its general importance. My opinion formed at the trial is confirmed by what has passed.   No rule.

---

*The Mayor, Aldermen, and Burgesses of the Borough of CLIF- [*97 TON DARTMOUTH HARDNESS *v.* THOMAS SILLY.

A bond executed before the passing of stat. 6 & 7 Vict. c. 89, by the sureties of P., treasurer of a borough, was subject to a condition by which, after reciting that P. had been elected treasurer under stat. 5 & 6 W. 4, c. 76, it was provided that the bond should be void if P. should account for moneys that might come to his hands as treasurer "(whether by virtue of his present or any subsequent appointment to the said office), according to the directions and true intent and meaning of the said statute, and in every other respect act in strict conformance with the same, and all other laws and regulations now or hereafter to be in force touching the said office of treasurer, or the person or persons performing or liable to perform the duties thereof."

Held, that the sureties were liable for misconduct of P. after the tenure of the office had been altered by stat. 6 & 7 Vict. c. 89, from an annual office to an office held during pleasure.

COUNT for 500*l.*, the penalty of a bond. The only plea which it is necessary to notice was plea 2, which set out the bond and condition verbatim. It was the joint and several bond of Solomon Pentecost, William Follett, and the defendant, and was dated 8th October, 1839. The condition was as follows. "Whereas the above bounden Solomon Pentecost hath been appointed by the council of the said borough to be the treasurer thereof, under an Act," 5 & 6 W. 4, c. 76, "and the said William Follett and Thomas Silly have agreed to join with the said Solomon Pentecost in the above written obligation as his sureties, with such condition for making void the same as hereunder ir written; now the condition of the above written obligation is such that, if the said Solomon Pentecost, his executors or administrators, shall, from time to time and at all times hereafter, duly and faithfully account for, apply and pay, all and every the sum and sums of money, matters and things which hath come or shall come to his hands or under his order or control, as treasurer of the borough aforesaid (whether by virtue of his present *98] or any subsequent appointment to the *said office), according to the directions and true intent and meaning of the said statute, and in every other respect act in strict conformance with the same, and all other laws and regulations now or hereafter to be in force touching the said office of treasurer, or the person or persons performing or liable to perform the duties thereof: then this obligation to be void, else to remain in full force." Averment of performance of the condition by Pentecost " as long as he continued such treasurer by virtue of any appointment under the said statute."

Replication 1 to plea 2, that Pentecost continued treasurer under successive annual appointments, the last of which was on 9th November, 1842, up to the passing of stat. 6 & 7 Vict. c. 89: assignment of breaches during that time. Replication 2 to plea 2, that, after the passing of stat. 6 & 7 Vict. c. 89, on 9th November, 1843, Pentecost was appointed treasurer, and continued such till 1852; assignment of breaches subsequent to 9th November, 1843. Issue was taken on these and several other pleadings.

There were demurrers respectively to plea 2, and to the replication 2 to plea 2. Joinder thereon.

Before argument of the demurrers the case went down for trial of the issues of fact, and assessment of contingent damages on the demurrers. A verdict was taken subject to the award of a barrister, to whom the whole was referred. He made his award, finding performance up to the passing of stat. 6 & 7 Vict. c. 89, and breaches subsequently. He disposed of the other issues of fact in favour of the plaintiffs, and directed judgment to be entered for them on the demurrers, subject to the provision thereinafter contained, that is to say, " If the Court of Queen's Bench shall be of opinion, upon the pleadings in the *99] said cause, that, according to the *condition of the bond therein mentioned, the liability of the defendant as surety, under the said bond, is limited to the appointment of the said Solomon Pentecost to be the treasurer of the said borough under the Act in the said bond mentioned, and does not extend to the appointment of the said Solomon Pentecost to be the treasurer of the said borough under the Act," 6 & 7 Vict. c. 89, " which point I submit for the opinion of the said Court at the request of the parties respectively to the said cause :" then judgment on the demurrers to be entered for the defendant.

The order of Nisi Prius having been made a rule of Court, *T. K. Kingdon,* on behalf of the defendant, in Hilary Term, 1855, obtained a rule to show cause why judgment should not be entered for the defendant on the point submitted by the arbitrator to the Court.

The rule was enlarged from Term to Term to await the final decision of Oswald v. Mayor, &c., of Berwick, then pending in the House of Lords. In last Michaelmas Term (November 24) *Butt* showed cause,(a) and *Collier* and *T. K. Kingdon* were heard in support of the rule. The only point argued was as to the application of Oswald v. Mayor, Aldermen, and Burgesses, of Berwick-upon-Tweed, 5 H. L. Ca. 856,(b) to the terms of this condition. *Cur. adv. vult.*

Lord CAMPBELL, C. J., in this term (January 13th), delivered judgment.

The question which we have to determine in this case is, Whether the bond entered into on the 8th of October, 1839, by Solomon Pentecost and his sureties for his proper execution of the duties of the office of treasurer of the borough of Dartmouth, remained in force after the passing of stat. 6 & 7 Vict. c. 89,(c) which enacted that the treasurer of a borough, instead of being annually elected as under stat. 5 & 6 W. 4, c. 76,(d) should " thenceforth hold his office during the pleasure of the council for the time being." Unless there be words in the condition of the bond to continue the obligation after such a change in the tenure of the office, there can be no doubt that it would be extinguished, both as to principal and sureties. The condition recites that the appointment to the office of treasurer was under stat. 5 & 6 W. 4, c. 76; and without any such recital parties to such a bond are always supposed to contract according to the existing state of the law, and in the belief that the law will continue unchanged if they make no provision for the contingency of a change in the law. But, as observed by Maule, J., in Mayor of Berwick v. Oswald, 3 E. & B. 653, 665 (E. C. L. R. vol. 77), there is nothing " to prevent parties, if they choose by apt words to express an intention so to do, from binding themselves by a contract as to any future state of the law. Supposing that the parties to this bond had contemplated that some alterations might be made by law in the office of treasurer, there would have been nothing illegal in the sureties binding themselves to be answerable though the nature, and tenure, and duties of the office were changed." Now, looking to the whole of the condition of the present bond, we think that it is framed with this view, and that it contains language more potent for this purpose than any to *be found in the instrument adjudicated upon in the Mayor of Berwick v. Oswald, 3 E. & B. 653 (E. C. L. R. vol. 77). The first part of the condition, even when speaking of "any subsequent appointment," expressly

[*100

[*101

(a) Before Lord Campbell, C. J., Coleridge, Wightman, and Erle, Js.
(b) Affirming the judgment of the Exch. Ch. in Mayor of Berwick v. Oswald, 3 E. & B. 653 (E. C. L. R. vol. 77); which affirmed the judgment of the Queen's Bench in Mayor of Berwick v. Oswald, 1 E. & B. 295 (E. C. L. R. vol. 72).
(c) Sect. 6.   (d) Sect. 58.

refers to the office as regulated by stat. 5 & 6 W. 4, c. 76; but it goes on to say that Pentecost, as treasurer, should "in every other respect act in strict conformance with the same, *and all other laws and regulations now or hereafter to be in force touching the said office of treasurer, or the person or persons performing or liable to perform the duties thereof.* Therefore, should there be any change of the law by Act of parliament extending the duties of the treasurer and increasing the perils of the sureties, the bond remains in force if the change touches "the said office of treasurer or the person or persons performing or liable to perform the duties thereof." We think that these words apply to a discharge of the duties of the office under the new tenure of holding during pleasure, whether this change may be considered either as increasing or diminishing the risk of the sureties. There were no such words in the instrument to be construed in Oswald *v.* Mayor, Aldermen, and Burgesses of Berwick-upon-Tweed, 5 H. L. Ca. 856, 8 E. & B. 653 (E. C. L. R. vol. 77), 1 E. & B. 295 (E. C. L. R. vol. 72); and therefore, to show the continuing liability, it was necessary to rely on the words "annual *or other future* election" "to the said office." But, by the condition of the present bond, an alteration in the office by future legislation was manifestly contemplated; and the intention, as expressed, appears to have been that the obligors should remain liable for the due discharge by Pentecost of the duties of the office, while its identity

*102] substantially remained, whatever change might take place *touching its duties or its incidents. Stat. 6 & 7 Vict. c. 89, only regulates the office; and no one can contend that its identity is destroyed by its being held during pleasure instead of being held for a year, all its duties remaining unchanged. Such we think was the intention of the parties when they executed the bond, and continued to be their belief till this action was commenced. We therefore pronounce judgment for the plaintiffs.   Judgment for the plaintiffs.

CHRISTOPHER FRANCIS O'TOOLE and EDWARD STEVENSON *v.* JOHN MONGER POTT.

A verdict was taken in Vacation, subject to the award of an arbitrator, to whom the cause and all matters in difference were referred. The award was made directing a verdict in favour of the plaintiff. Before next Term, but more than fourteen days after the publication of the award, the plaintiff signed judgment. A summons having been obtained to set aside the judgment, the matter was referred to the Court.

Held, that the judgment was regular, and that it was not necessary, before signing judgment, to wait till the time for moving to set aside the award had elapsed.

HAWKINS, in last Michaelmas Term, obtained a rule Nisi to set aside the judgment signed in this cause.

From the affidavits it appeared that the cause stood for trial at the

London sittings after last Trinity Term, when a verdict was taken by consent, on 9th July, 1856, subject to the award of a barrister to whom the cause and all matters in difference between the parties were referred, with all the usual powers. On 18th July, 1856, the arbitrator published his award, that the verdict should stand for 548*l.* 17*s.*, that the plaintiffs were indebted on the matters in difference to the defendant in 202*l.* 13*s.*, and that the defendant should pay the difference between those sums, viz., 346*l.* 4*s.*, and the costs. On 8th August the plaintiffs signed judgment, and applied to *have their costs taxed. [*103 On 22d August a summons to set aside the judgment was heard before Crowder, J., who referred the matter to the Court, on the terms of the defendant giving security for the amount of the judgment.

Mellish, in last Michaelmas Term, showed cause.(*a*)—The Common Law Procedure Act, 1852 (15 & 16 Vict. c. 76), sect. 120, enacts, that "a plaintiff or defendant, having obtained a verdict in a cause tried out of Term, shall be entitled to issue execution in fourteen days, unless the Judge who tries the cause, or some other Judge, or the Court, shall order execution to issue at an earlier or later period, with or without terms." The power to issue execution necessarily involves the signing of a judgment; and the question here is, Whether, when the verdict is subject to an award, there is an implied exception, and the successful party is not to issue execution till the time for moving to set aside the award has elapsed, that is till the fifth day of the ensuing term if the reference be of the cause only, and till the end of the term if it be a reference of the cause and all matters in difference. There is no object in such a delay; for the arbitrator always has the powers of the Judge, and may order a stay of execution; or, if he does not, a Judge has power to do so, and will exercise it if there be plausible ground for moving to set aside the award. By the general rules of practice of Hilary Term, 16 Vict., rule 170, 1 E. & B. xxviii. (E. C. L. R. vol. 72), "costs may be taxed on an award, notwithstanding the time for setting aside the award has not *elapsed." That cannot be done when [*104 the award directs a verdict, unless the judgment be signed. The award may be enforced by attachment; Hare *v.* Fleay, 2 L. M. & P. 392; and in every way except execution, if that be an exception. Jones *v.* Ives, 10 Com. B. 429 (E. C. L. R. vol. 70), was relied on in moving the rule; but that proceeded on the old practice and law, which have since been changed. Even under the old practice the verdict entered under a certificate did not differ from a verdict found by the jury: Cromer *v.* Churt, 15 M. & W. 810.†

Hawkins, in support of his rule.—This is an award as to all matters in difference between the parties. If it had been a mere certificate the judgment might have been regular; the rule 170 of Hilary Term, 16 Vict., 1 E. C. L. R. vol. 72), was meant to apply only

(*a*) November 25th. Before Lord Campbell, C. J., Coleridge, Wightman, and Erle, Js.

to such a case. [ERLE, J.—It is general in its terms, and was intended to be general in its application, founded on the analogy to taxation of costs on a judgment which is not delayed till the time for bringing error has elapsed.] Jones v. Ives, 10 Com. B. 429 (E. C. L. R. vol. 70), is expressly in point.

Cur. adv. vult.

Lord CAMPBLLL, C. J., in this Term (January 14th), delivered judgment.

Upon a rule for setting aside a judgment, it appeared that a cause and all matters in difference between the parties had been referred at Nisi Prius on the common terms. The award was that the verdict should stand for the plaintiff for 500*l.*, and that the plaintiff was indebted to the defendant in 160*l.* upon a matter in difference, not in the cause: and the plaintiff had signed judgment for the 500*l.*, after
*105] fourteen days from the *making of the award, by analogy to the time allowed for signing judgment after a verdict by a jury.

The defendant contended that, upon a reference, where no cause existed, no proceeding could be taken to enforce the award till the Term had elapsed in which a party might move to set it aside, that is till the end of the term next after making the award; and that upon a reference of a cause together with all matters in difference between the parties the same time must elapse before any step can be taken to enforce any part of the award. He relied upon an expression of Maule, J., in Hobdell v. Miller, 2 Scott N. R. 168, asking how a proceeding to enforce an award could be taken when it was doubtful whether the award would stand: and also on the judgment of the Common Pleas in Jones v. Ives, 10 Com. B. 429 (E. C. L. R. vol. 70), allowing proceedings to be taken upon an award made in a reference of a cause, distinguishing that from other references, and so, by implication, recognising the rule now contended for. But we are of opinion that there is no ground for the defendant's contention. No reason has been suggested why a creditor who has established his right should be thus delayed in enforcing it. The limitation of the time for moving to set aside an award was intended to aid the successful party, and make his title secure after that time, but was not intended to give insecurity in favour of a debtor who had been adjudged to be liable. The award is to be taken to be valid until a competent tribunal has questioned its validity and stayed proceedings upon it. In respect of verdicts subject to a reference, they
*106] are not considered verdicts *till the award has been made; and the practice in respect of such verdicts has been to give the same time for moving against the award as there would have been for moving against a verdict of a jury given at that time: in respect of such awards they give only an inchoate right till that time has elapsed; and Maule, J., in Hare v. Fleay, 2 L. M. & P. 392, says that his question in Hobdell v. Miller, 2 Scott N. R. 168, related to this class of awards, not to awards out of a cause; and he then explains that the moving to set

aside awards made on a reference without any cause is analogous to bringing a writ of error; and that, as the power to bring a writ of error is no stay of execution until error brought, so the power of moving to set aside the award ought to be no stay of proceedings thereon until motion made. The rule, under the Common Law Procedure Act, that the successful party in a reference might proceed forthwith to tax his costs on taking up the award, is a declaration that the party is not bound to wait till a Term has elapsed before taking proceedings on the award. Therefore we think that the judgment was regular, and that this rule must be discharged with costs. **Rule discharged.**

---

*JAMES CUNNINGHAM, Appellant, v. The Local Board of [*107 Health of the Borough of WOLVERHAMPTON, Respondents.

A local Board of Health required the owners of property adjoining a street, not being a highway, to level it; and, they having made default, the Local Board caused the work to be done by contract. Before making the contract, no estimate was made of the annual expense of repairing the work when done; nor was any report obtained as to whether it would be more advantageous to contract only for the execution of the work, or for the execution and maintenance thereof. In other respects the directions of sect. 85 of the Public Health Act, 1848 (11 & 12 Vict. c. 63), were followed. On a special case:

Held, that, as the work when complete would not be repaired and maintained under the Act, or out of the rates, no such estimate or report was required; and that the Local Board might enforce payment of the expenses from the owners, notwithstanding the absence of the estimate and report.

NOTICE of appeal against an adjudication or order of two justices of the peace in and for the borough of Wolverhampton, made under sect. 69 of "The Public Health Act, 1848," having been given, a case was stated for the opinion of this Court, in substance as follows.

In the year 1852, the provisions of The Public Health Act, 1848 (11 & 12 Vict. c. 63), were, by an order of Her Majesty in council, duly applied to and put in force within the borough of Wolverhampton: and the Mayor, aldermen, and burgesses of the borough, by the council of such borough, became and were The Local Board of Health within and for the district of the borough under the Act. The appellant is the owner of certain houses situate in a street called York Street, within the district of the said Local Board of Health, the said street not being a highway. Early in the year 1854, the said street and other adjoining streets, which together formed a district called Commercial Road district, required levelling, paving, flagging, and channelling: and, by notices in writing, The Local Board of Health required the appellant, and upwards of a hundred other persons, *being the owners or [*108 occupiers of houses and premises fronting, adjoining, or abutting upon York Street and the said other adjoining streets, to level, pave, flag, and channel the said streets within a time specified in such notice, as provided by sect. 69 of the Public Health Act, 1848. The appellant and the said several other owners or occupiers failed to level, pave, flag, and channel the said streets, or any part thereof, in the manner and within the time required; and, upon such default, The Local Board of Health, under the provisions contained in sect. 85 of The Public Health Act, 1848, contracted, in writing under the seal of The Local Board, with certain persons as contractors, for executing at the expense of The Local Board of Health the works specified in the notices, and then necessary for the levelling, paving, flagging, and channelling the said streets; and the said necessary works were afterwards executed and fully completed by the said contractors, according to the terms of the said contract, and within the time specified by such contract. Previous to and at the time of giving the notices and entering into the contract, Thomas Fiddes Meyrick had been duly appointed to the office of surveyor of the district by The Local Board for the purposes of The Public Health Act, 1848, and then continued to act as such surveyor. By sect. 85 of The Public Health Act, 1848, it is, amongst other things, provided " that before contracting for the execution of any works under the provisions of this Act, the said Local Board shall obtain from the surveyor an estimate in writing, as well of the probable expense of executing the work in a substantial manner as of the annual expense of repairing the same, also a report as to the most advantageous mode of *109]   *contracting, that is to say, whether by contracting only for the execution of the work, or for execution and also maintaining the same in repair during a term of years, or otherwise." Before entering into the contract for the execution of the said works as aforesaid, The Local Board obtained from the surveyor an estimate in writing of the probable expense of executing the works in a substantial manner, and also a report, to the effect that the most advantageous mode of executing the works was by contracting for the execution of the same according to certain specifications prepared by the surveyor; but The Local Board did not, before entering into the contract, obtain from the surveyor any report as to whether it was at the time better or more advantageous to contract only for the execution of the works, or to contract for executing and also for maintaining the said works in repair during a term of years or otherwise. The surveyor, when he made the before-mentioned estimate of the probable expense of executing the works in a substantial manner, as also the report that the most advantageous mode of executing the said works was by contracting for the execution of the same according to the plans, had no reference whatever to the repair at any time of the said works; nor had the surveyor, before or at the time of making the estimate and report, at all considered or had in his contemplation the subject of the after repair of the said works. The expense incurred by The Local Board for the works executed under the said contract amounted to about 200l.; and the proportion of that sum, as settled by the surveyor to be paid by the appellant, was 41*l*. 16*s*. 9*d*. On the 8th January, 1856, the order or adjudication appealed against was made under The Public Health *Act, 1848. [*110 It recites that complaint had been made by the collector of rates under The Public Health Act for the said district, that certain expenses had been incurred by the Local Board in levelling, paving, flagging, and channelling the street called York Street, fronting, adjoining, or abutting on certain premises belonging to the appellant, and that the proportion of the expenses which the appellant was liable to pay was 41*l*. 16*s*. 9½*d*., and that he had neglected to pay the said sum. It further recites that the appellant had been duly summoned to answer the said complaint, and had appeared, and then states that the justices making the said order or adjudication had heard the complaint and the evidence, and, having ascertained the said complaint to be true, thereby adjudged the appellant to pay the said collector the said sum of 41*l*. 16*s*. 9*d*., with costs.

The questions for the opinion of the Court are: First, Whether, before contracting for the execution of the said works necessary for levelling, paving, flagging, and channelling the said street, the said Local Board had obtained from the surveyor an estimate and report as required by the provision in the 85th section of The Public Health Act, 1848; Secondly, Whether the said Local Board were bound to obtain the estimate and report of the surveyor required by the provision in the said 85th section before contracting for the execution of the said works; and, Whether, if they have omitted to comply with such provision, The Local Board can, under the said order or adjudication, enforce payment by the appellant of a proportion of the expenses incurred in executing the said works.

If the Court shall be of opinion that The Local Board have not complied with the said provision in the 85th *section of The Public [*111 Health Act, 1848, and that by reason of such non-compliance the said Local Board cannot enforce payment by the appellant of a proportion of the expense of executing the said work, the said order or adjudication is to be quashed. But, if the Court shall be of opinion that the said Local Board have complied with the said provision, or that the omission to comply with the said provision does not affect the right of the said Local Board to enforce the said payment by the appellant, then the said order or adjudication is to be confirmed. And it is agreed that a judgment in conformity with the decision of the said Court shall be entered at the sessions next or next but one after such decision.

J W. Huddleston, in support of the order.—The provisions of sect. 85 are only directory: Nowell *v.* Mayor, &c., of Worcester, 9 Exch. 457.† [Lord CAMPBELL, C. J.—In determining whether anything is a condition precedent, it is necessary to consider between what parties the question arises. Nowell *v.* Mayor, &c., of Worcester, was between a contractor and the Local Board of Health ; the only question there· fore was if the contract was illegal. Here the question is between the Local Board and the owners, who are sought to be charged with the expenses.] At all events, the justices had jurisdiction. [Lord CAMP- BELL, C. J.—We are not asked the question whether they had juris- diction or not, but whether the Local Board have a right to enforce the payment. In other words, whether it was the intention of the Legis- lature that the owners and occupiers might be charged, though there was no further estimate than in this case.]

*112]   *Scotland*, contrà.—In Nowell *v.* Mayor, &c., of Worcester. Parke, B., states the question to be, " Whether the directions in the 85th section are formal conditions to the validity of obligations by boards of health under the Act, or whether they are only directions to them, with which they are bound to comply, under the penalty, in case of non-compliance, of being deprived of all remedy of reimbursement against their constituents." The question here is, whether there is a remedy for reimbursement against their constituents. The only object of the Legislature in enforcing these conditions must have been to pro- vide a safeguard against improper taxation or undue expenditure. [ERLE, J.—Where the work, when completed, is to be kept in repair out of the rates, there is an intelligible reason for requiring an estimate of the annual expense of the same : but is such an estimate to be made when the work is done once for all ; as, for instance, when a sewer is set right for a private house, under sect. 54 ? Lord CAMPBELL, C. J.— Perhaps the estimate of the annual expense of the repair might induce the board to make the sewer on a different plan, so as not to cast upon the owner the burthen of such repairs.] As the Local Board have power under sect. 70 to convert the private street into a public one, the estimate of the cost of repairs may be very material. And the pro- viso is entire.

J. W. Huddleston, in reply.—The owner of the houses may put his own private street into good order in any way he pleases : it is only on *113]   his default that the board are *to interfere. The mode of repair in future also is at his option. The intention of the Legislature was to require estimates only when the expenditure was to be out of the rates.   *Cur. adv. vult.*

Lord CAMPBELL, C. J., in this Term (January 14), delivered judg- ment.

In this case, the Board of Health had entered into a contract for paving, &c., in front of the appellant's premises, in a street which was not a highway, under sect. 69 of The Public Health Act, 1848. This work the board was authorized to do, only in case the owners failed to do it after notice ; and, after doing it, the board was not authorized to keep it in repair. The board made a contract for doing the work, according to all the provisions of sect. 85, except that no estimate had been made as to the annual expense of repairing the same, and no report had been made of the most advantageous mode of contracting, that is to say, whether only by contracting for the execution of the work or for executing and also for maintaining the same in repair during a term of years or otherwise. The appellant contended that this proviso in sect. 85 was a condition for the validity of every contract for work, as between the board and their constituents to be charged thereby, and that, therefore, this contract was void as against the constituents, and so the appellant was not liable to be charged with any payment in respect thereof. But we are of opinion that the part of the proviso relating to repair has no application to any contract for a work which the board is not authorized to repair. It seems inconsistent to require a surveyor to estimate repairs and *to compare the advantage [*114 of contracting to repair when no repairs can be done, *in carrying the Act into execution;* and we think the section can properly be construed without coming to such a result. The section begins by enabling the board to enter into all such contracts as may be necessary *for carrying the Act into execution.* If no repairs are authorized, no contract comprising repairs would be within the Act, as necessary for carrying it into execution; and the proviso for the estimate and report is confined to works *under the provisions of the Act.* If a work may be both executed and repaired under the provisions of the Act, there must be an estimate and report on the execution and the repair; but, if the work may be only executed or only repaired according to the provisions of the Act, the estimate and report need not extend to a work not within the provisions of the Act, and not necessary for carrying it into execution.

In case of a contract for repairing an existing road, an estimate and report relating to executing the work of making that road originally would be absurd, and equally so would be the estimate and report on repair where none can be done. It follows that the order must be confirmed.

Order confirmed.

*115]   *INGRAM v. BARNES.

The plaintiff, an illiterate labouring man, attached his mark to a written contract with defendant, by which he engaged to make as many bricks as defendant required in defendant's brick
field, finding all labour, the defendant finding the materials.   Payment to be 10s. 6d. per
thousand for the bricks when complete.   Plaintiff, assisted by others, made bricks, having
worked at them personally; in payment he accepted tickets for goods.   Afterwards he sued
for the full price, contending that he was an artificer within the Truck Act (1 & 2 W. 4, c. 37),
and that, consequently, the payment by tickets was void.
Held, by Lord Campbell, C. J., and Coleridge, J., in the Queen's Bench, that, though if the
matter were res integra they might have come to a contrary conclusion, they were concluded
by authority from holding him an artificer, as he was not bound by the contract to do any
part of the work personally.   Erle, J , dissentiente.
Held, by Cockburn, C. J., Cresswell, Williams, and Willes, Js , Martin, Bramwell, and Channell,
Bs., in the Exchequer Chamber, affirming the judgment of the Queen's Bench, that the plaintiff, not being bound by his contract to do any part of the work personally, was not an artificer within the Truck Act.
And quære, per Cockburn, C. J., and Bramwell, B., whether, if the plaintiff had been bound to
labour personally, but was at liberty to hire labourers to assist him, he would have been within
the Act.

DECLARATION for money payable for work done by the plaintiff for
defendant at his request, for money paid, and for money found due
from defendant to plaintiff on accounts stated.
    Plea : Satisfaction and discharge of claim, before action, by payment.
Issue thereon.
    The particulars of demand were as follows.
    This action is brought to recover 74l. 17s. 8d., the balance due to
the plaintiff upon the following items of account.   £   s.   d.
For work done and money paid from the 12th March,
    1855, till the close of the same month by the plaintiff
    for the defendant 12 10 6
For work done and money paid by the plaintiff for the
    defendant from the month of April to the month of
    November, 1855, both inclusive   317   2 0
April 11th. Building two kilns   15   0 0
        16th. Repairing hacks   2   0 0
May 15th. Setting and burning sands .   .   .   0 19 6
        17th. Burning and sorting bricks .   .   .   0 19 0
                                                   _____
                                            £348 11 0

*116]   *On the trial, before Lord Campbell, C. J., at the Sittings in
London after last Trinity Term, the following facts appeared.
    On the 2d of April, 1855, an agreement was entered into between
the plaintiff and the defendant, of which the following is a copy.
                                            " Leigham Court.
" To Mr. Richard Barnes.
    " Sir, I, the undersigned Thomas Ingram, do hereby agree to make
as many bricks as you may require me to make on the upper ground

in your brick field adjoining the railway; to be dried and burnt according to the following conditions, viz.: to take the clay in its present state, and to find all labour required in turning the clay, and mixing it with ashes, breeze, and sand; to mould, set, and burn the bricks in kilns, and deliver the same into the trucks, or stack them on the ground when properly burnt, finding all labour for drying the bricks and protecting them from the weather and other damage. Mr. R. Barnes to find all materials for the same: but all labour of every description to be found by me for the sum of 10s. 6d. per thousand, for the bricks when finished and complete. Payments to be made on account, as the work proceeds, at the rate of 7s. 6d. per thousand when in hacks, and 2s. 6d. while they are being burnt, and the remaining 6d. when the contract is performed. To proceed with the work as fast as possible, and as may be directed by the said Mr. Barnes. The work to be done under the direction of Mr. Barnes, and to his entire satisfaction. If I, Thomas Ingram, fail to carry out or do not proceed to Mr. Barnes' satisfaction and the contract, 6d. left per thousand in hand to be forfeited; and all damages for any neglect or *inconve- [*117 nience that I may put him to. And I, the said Richard Barnes, hereby agree and accept the above contract and conditions.

RICHARD BARNES.

"Witness, Edward Mace.
"Witness my hand, this second day of April, 1855.
"THOMAS INGRAM + his mark."

The said agreement was executed by both plaintiff and defendant. The former executed it by making a +, he being unable to write his name.

Before and at the time of making the said agreement, the plaintiff was a brickmaker, and, assisted by other brickmakers engaged and paid by him for the purpose, turned the clay for, and made, a large number of bricks under the said agreement; for which he was entitled, by virtue of the said agreement, to be paid at the rate of 10s. 6d. per thousand.

The plaintiff himself worked at the said brickmaking along with the said other persons.

The plaintiff accepted of the defendant, from time to time, in part payment of the bricks which were so made, tickets which were exchangeable, and which were exchanged by the plaintiff, for goods supplied to him by the defendant at a shop which was kept by the defendant near the place where the said bricks were made. The following is the form of the ticket and the endorsement thereon: "Good for   ." And, on the back: "This ticket is issued to the bearer, by request, for his accommodation, and is not compulsory."

It was proved that, on 1st December, 1855, the plaintiff received of defendant a sum of 5*l.* 7*s.* in money, and gave a receipt, of which the following is a copy:

*118]   *"1856.   December 1.

"Received of Mr. Richard Barnes the sum of 5*l.* 7*s.*, being the final balance for work done at the railway works at Streatham, including clay-turning, brickmaking, kiln-building, clay work, and all other work, and in full of all demands. 5*l.* 7*s.* 0*d.*   THOS. INGRAM + 5*l.* 7*s.* 0*d.* his mark.   EDWARD MACE."

Nothing further was due to the plaintiff, unless he was entitled to recover anything in respect of a portion of his claim as having been discharged by tickets instead of in money, as next mentioned.

It was proved that a portion of the other part of the plaintiff's claim had been discharged, by the defendant giving, and the plaintiff accepting, tickets from time to time in the above form, for goods to be exchanged as aforesaid.

It was contended, at the trial, on the part of the plaintiff, that the giving and taking tickets as above, was contrary to and void by stat. 1 & 2 W. 4, c. 87, and that the plaintiff was entitled to recover the amount of the said tickets, notwithstanding they had been so accepted by him as aforesaid. The Lord Chief Justice directed the verdict to be entered for the plaintiff for the sum of 35*l.*, being one-third of the amount of the said tickets; but which, it was agreed by both parties, should be taken to be the sum due to the plaintiff if entitled to recover anything. And his Lordship, by consent of plaintiff, reserved leave for defendant to enter a verdict for him if the Court of Queen's Bench should be of opinion that he was entitled thereto.

In last Term, *Collier* obtained a rule, calling on the plaintiff to *119] show cause why a verdict should not be *entered for the defendant: "on the ground that the statute, 1 & 2 W. 4, c. 87, did not apply to the payments to the plaintiff by way of goods under the circumstances."

In last Term,(*a*)

Manisty and *C. Warner Lewis* showed cause.—The alleged payment by the tickets constituted no discharge, but was illegal, null, and void under stat. 1 & 2 W. 4, c. 87, s. 8. Sect. 1 of that statute recites that "it is necessary to prohibit the payment, in certain trades, of wages in goods, or otherwise than in the current coin of the realm;" and it enacts "that in all contracts hereafter to be made for the hiring of any artificer in any of the trades hereinafter enumerated, or for the performance by any artificer of any labour in any of the said trades, the wages of such artificer shall be made payable in the current coin of this realm only, and not otherwise; and that if in any such contract the whole or any part of the wages" be made payable otherwise, the contracts shall be illegal, null, and void. Sect. 2 avoids the contract, if it

(*a*) November 14th, 1856. Before Lord Campbell, C. J., and Coleridge and Erle, Js.

contain any provision as to the place where, the manner in which, or the person with whom, all or any part of the wages is to be expended. Then sect. 3 enacts: "That the entire amount of the wages earned by or payable to any artificer in any of the trades hereinafter enumerated, in respect of any labour by him done in any such trade, shall be actually paid to such artificer in the current coin of this realm, and not otherwise; and every payment made to any such artificer by his employer, of *or in respect of any such wages, by the delivering [*120 . to him of goods, or otherwise than in the current coin aforesaid, except as hereinafter mentioned, shall be and is hereby declared illegal, null, and void." Then sect. 19 enumerates the trades, by excluding from the operation of the Act every artificer, &c., "excepting only artificers, workmen, labourers, and other persons employed in the several manufactures, trades, and occupations following: (that is to say), in or about," &c.; "or in the making or preparing of salt, bricks, tiles, or quarries." The interpretation clause, sect. 25, enacts and declares: "That in the meaning and for the purposes of this Act, all workmen, labourers, and other persons in any manner engaged in the performance of any work, employment, or operation, of what nature soever, in or about the several trades and occupations aforesaid, shall be and be deemed 'artificers';" "and that within the meaning and for the purposes of this Act, any money or other thing had or contracted to be paid, delivered, or given as a recompense, reward, or remuneration for any labour done or to be done, whether within a certain time or to a certain amount, or for a time or an amount uncertain, shall be deemed and taken to be the 'wages' of such labour." If these interpretations be substituted in sect. 3 for the words interpreted, it is plain that the case is thus within the letter of the statute. And, according to the authorities, it makes no difference that the contract contemplates that the labourer may have the assistance of others. In Bowers v. Lovekin, 6 E. & B. 584 (E. C. L. R. vol. 88), it was held that butty colliers were artificers within the Act, it appearing that they were bound to work *personally, though they also employed others. There Erle, J., [*121 said: "I take the true construction of the Act to be that it applies to contracts for artificers' work to be paid for by the piece, whenever it was intended that the contractor should personally do all or part of the work as a workman, so as to make him one of the class of artificers." And this agrees with Weaver v. Floyd, 21 L. J. N. S. Q. B. (County Court appeal, before two Judges), 151. Those cases, and the present, are distinguishable from Riley v. Warden, 2 Exch. 59,† where the party was a sub-contractor under the defendants, and performed the work by means of others, and was not bound to work personally. The Court there sustained the ruling of Coleridge, J., at Nisi Prius, who told the jury that he was "of opinion that the plaintiff was not a labourer or contractor within the Act, which he thought did not apply as between contractor and sub-contractor, and that the mere fact of the plaintiff joining in the work did not make any difference." In Sharman v. Sanders, 13 Com. B. 166 (E. C. L. R. vol. 76), a similar decision was given, principally upon the authority of Riley v. Warden. The present plaintiff clearly belongs to the class to which, as pointed out by Parke, B., in Riley v. Warden, the Act was intended to apply, "such men as earn their bread by the sweat of their brow, and who are, for the most part, an unprovided(a) class." Lowther v. The Earl of Radnor, 8 East, 113, decided on the Masters' and Servants' Act, 20 G. 2, c. 19, s. 1, illustrates the present question, and furnishes an analogy in favour of the plaintiff.

*122] *Collier and Needham, contrà.—The test, as appears from the authorites cited, and as is indeed admitted on the other side, is, whether the plaintiff, by the contract, was bound to bestow his personal labour upon making the bricks. If he was not, the statute is inapplicable. [Lord CAMPBELL, C. J.—Is it not enough if it was in the contemplation of both parties that he should do so?] That must appear from the contract itself. [Lord CAMPBELL, C. J.—May we not look at the facts?] They may not be in all cases inadmissible: but here it is plain that it was in the plaintiff's choice whether he would work at all himself, or would find labour by the hands of others. In fact, he did both; and that was the case also in Riley v. Warden, 2 Exch. 59.† But he would not have broken his contract if he had merely employed others. [Lord CAMBPELL, C. J.—We must look at his antecedent status.] That may be looked at, for some purposes: but the only safe guide is the language of the contract. [Lord CAMPBELL, C. J.—We must keep in view the circumstances under which it is made. Suppose he were a day labourer.] There is nothing to bind him to continue so. There was no evidence of any surrounding circumstances modifying or explaining the contract. The statute itself, as was remarked by Maule, J., in Sharman v. Sanders, 13 Com. B. 166 (E. C. L. R. vol. 76), departs from the general principle of allowing parties to contract as they please for themselves: and therefore it will not be extended by construction. If the plaintiff here failed to perform the contract, the remedy would be, not by turning him out of the employment, but by suing him on the breach of contract. [COLERIDGE, *123] J.—Are you not *forgetting the interpretation clause?] That was brought fully before the Court in Sharman v. Sanders, 13 Com. B. 166 (E. C. L. R. vol. 76). The object of the contract here is to secure the general supervision by the plaintiff: in some parts of the work, as, for instance, in the burning, judgment and experience are required.   *Cur. adv. vult.*

In this Term (January 13th), the learned Judges, not being unanimous, delivered their opinions seriatim.

(a) Quære, "improvident," or "unprotected?" See 13 Com. B. 173, note (a).

Lord CAMPBELL, C. J.—My brother Coleridge agrees with me in the judgment which I am about to pronounce. My brother Erle differs from us, and will deliver his own judgment.

If this were *res integra*, I should be inclined to hold that the plaintiff was an artificer within the Truck Act, 1 & 2 W. 4, c. 37. Although regard is to be had to the original contract under which the work is done, and a person who works under a contract which is a mere speculation in the labour market clearly is not such an artificer, I should have thought that, if his personal labour was in the contemplation of both parties when the contract was entered into, his personal labour under the contract would make him such artificer, although, if the work stipulated for by the contract were perfectly done, he would not be liable to an action for omitting to do any part of it with his own hands. The 25th section of the Act says: that " all workmen, labourers, and other persons in any manner engaged in the performance of any work, employment, or operation, of *what nature soever, in or about the" enumerated " trades and occupations," " shall be and be deemed ' artificers :' " and that " any money" " given as a recompense,. reward, or remuneration for any labour" " shall be deemed and taken to be the ' wages' of such labour." It appeared, at the trial, that the plaintiff, an illiterate labouring man, entered into the contract with the intention of working under it himself, as he actually did; and that the money earned by him really was a recompense and remuneration for his own labour, although he was to pay a part of the money as a recompense and reward to his fellow labourers. [*124

But a different view appears to have been taken of the statute by the Judges of the Court of Exchequer and of the Court of Common Pleas, in Riley *v.* Warden, 2 Exch. 59,† and Sharman *v.* Sanders, 13 Com. B. 166 (E. C. L. R. vol. 76), and in this Court, by Patteson, J., in Weaver *v.* Floyd.(a) Perhaps these decisions might all be supported without the narrow construction of the statute which will exclude from its protection many of that class who, the Legislature seems to have thought, required to be protected from the frauds of their employers in the payment of their wages. But the Judges to whom I have referred consider the criterion to be, whether the workman who did work with his own hands in performance of the contract was absolutely bound by the terms of the contract so to do. And I do not feel myself at liberty, sitting here, to say that they were wrong.

Adopting this criterion, it appears to me that the plaintiff was not an artificer within the meaning of the *statute. I think it was in the contemplation of both parties that he should work under the contract, as he did; and that his personal labour may in some sense be considered an ingredient in the contract; but, if by the labour of others the bricks had been made in all respects according to the con- [*125

(a) 21 L. J. N. S. Q. B. (County Court appeal before two Judges), 151.

tract, I cannot say that the plaintiff would have been liable to an action if he had not worked at the making of them himself, or even personally superintended the operation.

In construing the statute, I do not think that I ought to be in the slightest degree influenced by the vituperation passed upon it as an improper obstruction to the freedom of trade, or by the panegyric that it is a laudable instance of the state interfering with the dealings of individuals to prevent fraud and oppression. I am only to try to discover what the Legislature meant to enact, and to give force to the enactment. I must look, however, to the construction put upon it judicially by Judges of co-ordinate jurisdiction: and, doing so, I say that the plaintiff was not an artificer as he alleges. The consequence is that credit is to be given for the payments made to him in goods, and that there ought to be judgment for the defendant.

ERLE, J.—In an action for wages for work done, a plea of set-off for goods sold(a) has raised the question whether the plaintiff's claim is within the protection of the Truck Act. The plaintiff contracted to make bricks, and find all labour, for 10s. 6d. per thousand: he was in the class of labourers: he was engaged in the performance of the work; that is, in personally labouring at the *brick-making; and *126] the labour and the wages in question were legally his as against the defendant, his employer, although he had hired and paid for assistance in the work. The plaintiff was clearly an artificer; and the wages claimed were clearly a remuneration for labour within the definition given in sect. 25, brick-making being one of the occupations comprised within sect. 19.

The plaintiff, therefore, under sect. 4, had a right to be paid in current coin; and the defendant, under sect. 5, was prohibited from the set-off. If the letter and the spirit of the Act are alone consulted, there is no doubt about judgment for the plaintiff.

But the defendant contends that the Court of Exchequer decided, in Riley v. Warden, 2 Exch. 59,† that the statute must be construed as if it contained a proviso that no claim for wages should be within its provision unless, in the contract of hiring, there was a stipulation that the party should serve personally; and that this decision was confirmed by the Common Pleas in Sharman v. Sanders, 13 Com. B. 166 (E. C. L. R. vol. 76). Now, conceding, for this argument, that the plaintiff's contract contains no such stipulation, still I am of opinion that the decision of the Court in Riley v. Warden contains no such general proposition as is above supposed, and that the true principle of that decision is not opposed to judgment for the plaintiff in this case. There Warden had a contract to make a line of railway; and Riley contracted with him to make a part of that line, and personally did some work under his contract, and, in cutting, moved some clay which was kept

(a) It appears from the record that the only plea was satisfaction by payment.

for bricks; and so he claimed to be working clay within the Act. This claim, as to the clay, though *very doubtful, was conceded for the argument; and still it was held that the plaintiff failed, on [*127 the ground that the Act comprised contracts for labour for wages in the common meaning of those words, for the sake of protecting the poor, the weak, and the ignorant, and that it did not extend to contracts of great magnitude and value where the contractor would serve more by superintending labour than by labouring, and would need no protection. Baron Rolfe specifies a contract for twenty miles of line, Baron Parke for 100,000*l*., and Baron Platt a great building where the master merely puts a finishing touch, as contracts to which the Act does not extend. Magnitude and value are matters of degree. They say the line must be drawn somewhere; and they consider the plaintiff's contract there beyond the line of the Act. To this principle, and its application thus far, there has been no objection. Baron Alderson's judgment is on the totally distinct ground that the plaintiff ought not to complain of receiving truck from the employer, because he gave truck to those whom he employed. The notion, that no claim of wages is protected by the Act unless the contract of hiring binds the party to do the work personally, seems to have originated from an observation of Alderson, B., in the argument in p. 67, saying "Would not the plaintiff have equally performed his contract if he had not worked himself! He did not enter into an agreement to do the work personally." And the learned Baron asks how it could be called his wages, and his labour, if not so done. This notion is adopted by Parke, B., in his judgment, who says the statute is applicable to those persons only who strictly contract as labourers; that is, to such as enter into a contract to employ their personal *services and to receive pay- [*128 ment for that service in wages. These are the two passages on which the doctrine rests. Baron Alderson in his judgment does not allude to it. Neither does Baron Rolfe or Baron Platt: and the rest of the judgment of Baron Parke is on the ground that the magnitude and value of a contract may place it beyond the statute. But that the form of the contract was the principle of the decision in Riley *v.* Warden, 2 Exch. 59,† is assumed in Sharman *v.* Sanders, 13 Com. B. 166 (E. C. L. R. vol. 76). Talfourd, J., had so ruled: and his ruling is upheld on that authority by the four Judges in Banco; Cresswell and Williams, J., on that ground simply; Jervis, C. J., adds his exposition of the Act thus. "To be an 'artificer' within the meaning of the statute, the party must be personally engaged in the performance of labour for which he is to receive wages, and that must have reference to the original contract." I submit, from these words, that the Chief Justice thought the case to be within the statute if it was consistent with the contract that the party should work personally, and he actually did so. Maule, J., says, that some expressions in Riley *v.* Warden may

be open to criticism, but that " the substance of the decision is clearly
right, viz. that the intention of the 1 & 2 W. 4, c. 37, was, to afford
protection to a class of persons not very able to protect themselves."
" The persons the Act was meant to benefit are those who hire themselves to labour with their hands for daily or weekly wages. More
people, no doubt, are comprehended within it than that ; but it is that
sort of people to whom the Act was intended to apply. I do not think
it was at all designed for the protection of persons taking contracts
*129] *for labour to be done by others,—persons who speculate on the
state of the labour market." Thus far he has distinguished
between contracts of hiring of labourers and contracts of magnitude and
value with superintendence of labour : he applies that distinction to the
case before him, adding that the contract there in question was of the
latter class, and that the plaintiff there, although he had done something,
had not been engaged in the performance of any work within the
statute. Then follows the passage which supports Mr. Justice Talfourd's ruling : " The whole context shows it was only intended to apply
to those who are actually and personally engaged or employed to do
the work. And, when the procuring work to be done by the hands of
others comprehends the whole of what a man contracts for, the circumstance of his doing some portion of the work himself, does not bring
him within the statute. There must be a contract by which he binds
himself to do it." This passage contains the ground of the learned
Judge's opinion, that no contract is within the Act unless it stipulates
for personal service. But I submit, with deference, that the statute not
only does not require any form of contract, but on the contrary excludes
any reference to the form of the contract. By sect. 25, the statute
applies if the party has been actually engaged in the performance of
the work, that is, has worked and has become thereby entitled to be
remunerated ; and that section goes on to exclude reference to the form
of the contract by enacting that, within the meaning and for the
purpose of the Act, any agreement, understanding, device, contrivance,
collusion, or arrangement whatsoever on the subject of wages, whether
*130] written or oral, whether direct *or indirect, to which the em-
ployer and artificer are parties or are assenting, or by which they
are mutually bound to each other, or whereby either of them shall have
endeavoured to impose an obligation on the other of them, shall be and
shall be deemed a contract. And I do not see how it is possible, without self contradiction, to hold that a contract for payment of wages by
the piece is not a contract within this clause, although it does not expressly stipulate for personal service.

I also submit that procuring labourers is not the whole of a contract
to do work by the piece. The party contracting must do the work ; and,
although he may have the option to do it by himself or some others, the
contract is within the Act ; but the *performance* is not, unless he has
actually worked himself.

Upon this review of the two cases, it seems to me that the majority of the Judges did not express assent to the supposed principle in the judgments in Riley *v.* Warden, 2 Exch. 59,† and that Sharman *v.* Sanders, 13 Com. B. 166 (E. C. L. R. vol. 76), rests only on the assumption that they had done so; and that the judgment of the Chief Justice there does not support that principle.

I also submit that the Judges who originated the doctrine meant that the labourer, to be within the Act, must have personally done all the work in respect of which the wages are claimed. Alderson, B., assumes that to be the meaning of *his wages for his labour;* and Parke, B., concurs. Now it has been decided that the labourer may be within the Act although he has had assistance in doing the work, and has not personally *done the whole himself. It is so expressly [*131 adjudged in Weaver *v.* Floyd, 21 L. J. N. S. Q. B. 151,(a) and in Bowers *v.* Lovekin, 6 E. & B. 584 (E. C. L. R. vol. 88): and the necessity of a winder to assist a weaver of gloves was recognised in Chawner *v.* Cummings, 8 Q. B. 311 (E. C. L. R. vol. 55). Two of these cases must be overruled if the doctrine is affirmed as just laid down in Riley *v.* Warden, 2 Exch. 59,† viz. that the labourer must have himself done the whole of the work. Also, if the doctrine is affirmed, the statute is virtually repealed as to contracts to work by the piece; as none has been cited which contains a stipulation inconsistent with the party obtaining assistance; and it would afford a ready mode of evading the statute by framing contracts without the stipulation to serve personally.

In reality, the contracts in those two cases relied on by the defendant were decided to be not within the statute on account of the magnitude, and value, and nature of service there contracted for. Tried by that test, the present contract would be within the statute, both in respect of its subject-matter and of the status of the plaintiff, who is a labouring man hiring out his labour. On that ground I think that judgment may be given for him, without conflicting with those decisions. They may well stand, to exclude from the protection of the statute such contracts as they refer to, and may leave it to apply to such a contract as that of the present plaintiff.

According to this view, the application of the statute will depend on an affirmative answer to three questions. 1. Is the subject-matter of the contract such as the *statute intended both in kind and [*132 degree? 2. Was it consistent with the contract that the party should work? 3. And has he actually done substantial work? My answer to these questions is in the affirmative in this case. It follows that, in my opinion, judgment should be for the plaintiff.

Judgment for the defendant.

(a) County Court appeal, before two Judges.

IN THE EXCHEQUER CHAMBER.

June 16.

For syllabus, see ante, p. 115.

THE plaintiff appealed against this judgment on a case stating the facts as before set out.(a)

Manisty, for the appellant (plaintiff below).—This is an appeal against the judgment of the Court of Queen's Bench, the majority of the Judges of which Court felt themselves bound by the decision of the Court of Exchequer in Riley *v.* Warden, 2 Exch. 59,† though, as is intimated in the judgment, had the matter been res integra their decision would have been different. This Court is not so bound, but will look at the statute. The preamble and first section of the Act show the object of the Legislature. [CRESSWELL, J.—The Legislature speaks of the wages of any artificer. Must not you show the plaintiff to be an artificer and the remuneration to be his wages?] The words are defined in sect. 25; and within that definition this case falls: the plaintiff is a labourer *183] engaged in the performance of work; the *payment here is a remuneration for labour done. [COCKBURN, C. J.—Do you contend that the plaintiff here was bound to do the work himself? Whatever may be the effect of that fact, would it have been a breach of this contract if the plaintiff had supplied bricks made by others?] Not on the written contract: but the Court, looking at the status of the parties, can have little doubt that it was so intended. If the plaintiff had not worked himself so as to give the employers the benefit of his skill, the work would have been instantly stopped. It is not a contract for any fixed period or quantity of bricks, but terminable at pleasure. The words of sect. 25 are "in any manner engaged in the performance" of work in the specified trades. [MARTIN, B.—Sect. 4 provides that every artificer may recover his wages before a justice. Assuming the plaintiff to make a thousand bricks by the aid of others whom he hired, what do you say would be the wages he could so recover? The whole 10*s.* 6*d.* ?] Probably only the part of it which remained after he had paid his assistants: but, even in that case, he is not the less a labourer because other labourers assist him. [CRESSWELL, J.—Supposing that one of those assistants negligently injured a third person: who would be answerable for his negligence, the plaintiff or the defendant? Surely the plaintiff, and that because these assistants are the plaintiff's servants, not the defendant's. BRAMWELL, B.—Or take it that by their unskilfulness a lot of bricks were spoiled in the making: the defendant would not have to pay for them. The plaintiff would bear the loss in either of those cases; and the 10*s.* 6*d.* is, at least in part, in consideration of his running these risks, and is therefore, at least, not entirely wages. I do not look to the words *of the [*134 contract, but the substance. It is one thing for a man to engage as one of several labourers to work at a job, being paid for his personal work; and quite a distinct kind of thing to engage to be responsible for the due execution of the whole work for a stipulated remuneration.] The Act cannot be evaded by causing an illiterate man to sign a written contract in which there is no express engagement to work personally. The circumstances show that the primary intention here was that the plaintiff should labour personally; and that the employment was but an incident. If that be so the case is within the Act. (He cited and commented on Riley v. Warden, 2 Exch. 59,† Weaver v. Floyd, 21 L. J. N. S. Q. B. 151,(a) Sharman v. Sanders, 13 Com. B. 166, and Bowers v. Lovekin, 6 E. & B. 584 (E. C. L. R. vol. 88), and relied much on the reasoning in the judgment of Erle, J., in the case below, ante p. 125.)

Needham was not called upon to argue.

COCKBURN, C. J.—We are all of opinion that the judgment of the majority of the Court of Queen's Bench must be affirmed. Speaking for myself, I wish in doing so to affirm it, subject to a remark upon the judgment delivered, which I will make presently. I am of opinion that the law as to the construction of this Act has been correctly laid down by the Judges in the earlier cases. I agree in what I find stated by Parke, B., in Riley v. Warden; and I concur in what is stated by Maule, J., in Sharman v. Sanders, that the Act was not designed for the protection of persons *taking contracts for labour to be [*135 done by others, persons who speculate upon the state of the labour market; that the whole context of the Act shows that the term artificer was intended only to apply to those who are actually and personally engaged or employed to do the work, and that, "when the procuring work to be done by the hands of others comprehends the whole of what a man contracts for, the circumstance of his doing some portion of the work himself, does not bring him within the statute. There must be a contract by which he binds himself to do it." Now, applying this language to the present case, it is clear that, according to it, the plaintiff is not an artificer. I am aware that in the judgment in the Queen's Bench Lord Campbell says that, if this were res integra, he should be inclined to come to a different decision. It is on this that I wish to remark that I do not concur in this doubt. If this were the first time of construing the statute, my opinion would be that it bears the meaning put upon it in Riley v. Warden, 2 Exch. 59.† When we look at the provisions of the Act, it seems to me clear that the Legislature intended to protect only labourers, not what are commonly called contractors. The language shows it. In sect. 1 the wages of the artificer are spoken of; in sect. 3 the provision is as to the wages earned

(a) County Court appeal, before two Judges.

by the artificer "in respect of any labour by him done;" sect. 5 speaks of "the wages of his labour:" all evidently referring to contracts in which a man engages to furnish his personal labour, for personal wages; not to those contracts in which he engages to have the work
*186] performed for a consideration which *is not personal wages. It was the class where personal labour is given for wages that the Legislature intended to protect. If the plaintiff be an artificer, then, as my brother Martin points out, he is entitled under sect. 4 to go before a justice and enforce payment of his wages; but what portion of the 10*s.* 6*d.* was wages? There is an essential distinction between the profits of fulfilling a contract and the wages of labour. Mr. *Manisty* was obliged to say that the wages recoverable before the justice would only be the surplus remaining after deducting the remuneration to his assistants; but that surplus is profit, quite a different thing from wages. Again, in what relation did these assistants stand to the defendant? Clearly they were not his servants, but the plaintiff's, showing that the plaintiff was not a servant but a contractor. I cannot think that it makes any difference whatever, if it be a contract to get the work performed, that by accident it happens that the contracting party is a labouring man. In Weaver *v.* Floyd, 21 L. J. N. S. Q. B. 151, the two Judges seem to have been of opinion that, if the agreement was that the contractor should in fact do the work by his own labour, the case was within the Act. It is not necessary to review that opinion now; it may require serious consideration hereafter how far such a case is within the Act: but both agreed that, to make a man an artificer within the Act, it is not enough that he is at liberty to work personally, but that he must be bound to do so. In the present case it is clear that, though the plaintiff was at liberty to work, he was not bound to do so; and therefore that decision is an authority for the defendant.

*187]   *CRESSWELL, J.—I also think the judgment of the majority of the Queen's Bench right; and I think the reason assigned in that judgment, namely, that the point had been decided by Courts of coordinate jurisdiction, was a good reason for it. But that is not a good reason for affirming the judgment here in a Court of error. I ground my judgment on this: that, if this were res integra, I should be convinced that the statute applied only to cases where, by the contract, personal service was to be given for wages. That was the view taken in all the cases up to this. It was so held in Riley *v.* Warden, 2 Exch. 59.† In Sharman *v.* Sanders, 13 Com. B. 166 (E. C. L. R. vol. 76), the Judges did not, as my brother Erle seems to suppose, proceed merely in deference to the authority of Riley *v.* Warden. Each Judge expressed his full approbation of that decision. The Chief Justice did so; my brother Maule puts it very clearly; and I also expressed my concurrence in it. In Bowers *v.* Lovekin, 6 E. & B. 584 (E. C. L. R. vol. 88), I find the same doctrine acted upon. The ground of the decision upholding the judgment of the county court was, as stated by Lord Campbell, C. J., in his judgment, that "it is found as a fact that the defendants were bound to give their personal labour like any other workmen." It was an oral contract; and the county court judge found that such was the contract; and, on his finding, the judgment proceeded. I think the judgment below right, and the doubt expressed unfounded.

WILLIAMS, J.—I entirely concur, and will only add that in Sharman *v.* Sanders I did not simply defer to the authority of Riley *v.* Warden, but approved of it.

*MARTIN, B.—I think this case undistinguishable from Sharman *v.* Sanders, 13 Com. 166 (E. C. L. R. vol. 76), which I [*138 think rightly decided. Looking at the Act, I have no doubt about it. Sect. 9 imposes a penalty on any one making any contract declared illegal by the Act, the third offence being a misdemeanour, punishable by fine. I think it clear that the Legislature, giving power to justices to convict for such an offence, must have meant the words of the Act to be construed in a popular sense: and, when the statute prohibits the payment of wages otherwise than in money, it applies to what is popularly called wages, the hire of a man who personally labours: and I think this is clearly shown by sect. 4; for it seems absurd to suppose that the justices who would have no jurisdiction as to the payment, if the contract were fulfilled in one way, should have jurisdiction over it if it were fulfilled in another. I think, therefore, that the Act is confined to cases of master and labourer. Mr. *Manisty* was obliged to admit that this contract would not be within the Act if the man were not in the position of a labourer. So that, according to his argument, when one of those great contractors, who began as labourers, was getting up in the world, there would come a time when no one would know whether a contract made with him was within the Act or not.

WILLES, J., concurred.

BRAMWELL, B.—But for the respect which I entertain for my brother Erle's judgment, I should think this a very clear case. It is no part of a Judge's duty to criticise the policy of the Legislature: but I may observe that in this Act sect. 5 holds forth a direct temptation to a man *to be dishonest: it may well be that this evil is accompanied [*139 by more than counterbalancing good; but it seems to me a good reason for not extending the Act beyond its apparent meaning. Now, as to the construction of the Act, I concur in every word uttered by Maule, J., in Sharman *v.* Sanders, 13 Com. B. 166 (E. C. L. R. vol. 76); and I shall not attempt to improve upon his language. I must say, however, that I am strongly inclined to think that a man, whether he is to work personally as an upper workman or not, who contracts to get work done by the hands of others whom he is to employ, if he is speculating on making a profit out of the labour market even to the extent of hiring one man to help him, is not an artificer within the Act. It seems to me that, extend the definition of wages as widely as you may, a portion of what such a person gets is the profit from employing others; and, if a portion of the renumeration is not wages, I think the case cannot be within the Act.

CHANNELL, B.—The construction of this contract is for the Court: and I arrive at the conclusion that this plaintiff is not bound by it to do any part of the work personally. Coming to that conclusion, the case is not distinguishable from Riley *v.* Warden, 2 Exch. 59,† and Sharman *v.* Sanders: and I entirely agree in the reasoning on which the judgments in those cases proceed. As to the cases of Bowers *v.* Lovekin, 6 E. & B. 584 (E. C. L. R. vol. 88) and Weaver *v.* Floyd, in which the Court proceeded on the ground that there was an engagement personally to do part of the work at least, our decision does not clash with them.   Judgment affirmed.

------

*140] *The QUEEN *v.* WILLIAM HENRY JEWELL and WILLIAM PERCIVALL. *Jan.* 13.

Two defendants being indicted jointly in the Central Criminal Court for conspiracy, one of them applied to a Judge for a certiorari, who granted it on such defendant entering into a recognisance for the payment of prosecutor's costs in case either defendant should be convicted. Held, that such terms were reasonable, and within the discretion of the Judge; and that stat. 16 & 17 Vict. c. 30, s. 5, made no difference in this respect.

C. W. WOOD, on behalf of the defendant, Jewell, moved for a rule to show cause why an order of Coleridge, J., should not be rescinded. The following facts appeared on the affidavit of Jewell's attorney.

On 26th November, 1856, the following notice was served upon Jewell:

          " Central Criminal Court.

" Mr. William Henry Jewell. Sir, Take notice that the Grand Jury at the Old Bailey have this day found a true bill against you and one William Percivall, for conspiracy, &c. And that the Court has ordered that you do forthwith enter into your own recognisances in the sum of 1000*l.* with two sureties of 500*l.* each, or that a warrant will be issued for your apprehension. The Court has further ordered that forty-eight hours' notice of bail be given to me. Dated this 26th day of November, 1856. Yours, &c., SAMUEL B. ABRAHAMS, 27 Bloomsbury Square."

The deponent on the same day inquired at the Central Criminal Court, was informed that the notice was true, and saw the indictment, which appeared to him to be of about one hundred and fifty folios. On

27th November, 1856, Erle, J., granted a fiat for a certiorari. The deponent, on the application, stated that he applied on behalf of Jewell only, and informed the Judge of the amount of bail named: when the Judge fixed the *same amount: and the recognisances were en- [*141 tered into accordingly, conditioned for Jewell's appearance, "and for payment of the prosecutor's costs after removal of indictment in case he should be convicted." On the 8th December, 1856, the deponent received a letter from Mr. Abrahams, who was attorney for the prosecution, stating that the costs of the prosecutor against Percivall should have been included. After some correspondence between the attorneys, a summons was taken out, calling on Jewell to show cause why a procedendo should not issue to take back the indictment into the Central Criminal Court, or why he should not give security for the prosecutor's costs by recognisance in the event of either of the defendants being convicted. The summons was attended before Coleridge, J., on the 23d December, and was, as the deponent stated, opposed on behalf of Jewell. The learned Judge made the following order :

"Upon hearing," &c., " and by consent, I do order that the defendant Jewell do give security for the prosecutor's costs, by recognisance, in the event of either of the defendants being convicted."

Afterwards Coleridge, J., issued a summons to show cause why his order should not be rescinded. The summons was attended before Erle, J., on 7th January, 1857 ; when his Lordship referred the application to this Court.

C. W. Wood, in support of the application.—The order by Coleridge, J., was not made "by consent": these words have been inserted by mistake. As to the merits: by the terms of the condition, as imposed by the Judge who granted the certiorari, the security was confined *to the event of the prosecution succeeding against Jewell only: [*142 and it was within his discretion so to limit the condition; Regina v. Wilks, 5 E. & B. 690 (E.C. L. R. vol. 85). No subsequent order of another Judge could vary this. [ERLE, J.—I thought that Jewell ought to give recognisances in respect of both defendants.] If so, the question is whether such recognisances can be required. It is manifestly a hardship that a party removing should be compelled to give security for costs although he himself should be acquitted : an innocent man might thus be always harassed by a prosecutor joining him with a guilty man. This condition of the recognisance originated in stat. 16 & 17 Vict. c. 30, s. 5, where the words prescribing the recognisance are: "that the defendant or defendants, in case he or they shall be convicted, shall pay to the prosecutor his costs incurred subsequent to the removal of such indictment." That must be read reddendo singula singulis. [Lord CAMPBELL, C. J.—The Judge might refuse the certiorari altogether : cannot he prescribe the conditions of granting it?] The Judge might refuse to grant the certiorari; but, if he does grant it, he must do so on the statutory terms. The practice before 16 & 17 Vict c. 30 appears in Corner's Practice on the Crown Side of the Court of Queen's Bench, pp. 50, 51. Stat. 5 & 6 W. 4, c. 33, s. 2, required the conditions to be in the terms required by stat. 5 & 6 W. & M. c. 11, s. 2 (made perpetual by stat. 8 & 9 W. 3, c. 33, s. 1), namely, "at the return of such writ to appear and plead to the said indictment or presentment in the said Court of King's Bench, and at his or their own costs and charges to cause and procure the issue that

*143] shall be joined upon the said indictment or presentment, *or any plea relating thereunto, to be tried at the next assizes," &c. [COLERIDGE, J.—In Regina v. Foulkes, 1 L. M. & P. 720, Patteson, J., allowed the recognisances to be conditioned in respect of all the defendants, though it appeared that there was no precedent.] That was done by consent, and before stat. 16 & 17 Vict. c. 30, which introduced the condition as to the costs of the prosecutor.

Lord CAMPBELL, C. J.—We are all of opinion that such terms would have been reasonable before that statute, and that the statute does not make any alteration as to this.

COLERIDGE, J.—There would be great inconvenience in any other rule.

WIGHTMAN and ERLE, Js., concurred.   Rule refused.

C. W. Wood then applied to be allowed to deposit a sum of money, in lieu of security, to the satisfaction of the Coroner and Attorney of this Court.

Lord CAMPBELL, C. J.—That is reasonable.

"Ordered that the defendant, William Henry Jewell, be at liberty to lodge in the hands of the Coroner and Attorney of this Court, within a fortnight, such sum of money as the said Coroner and Attorney shall direct, as security for the payment of the prosecutor's costs in this prosecution in case the defendant, William Percivall, shall be convicted, in lieu of giving security for the said costs by recognisance, as by the said order" (of Coleridge, J.) "directed."

---

*144]   *KNOWLES v. TRAFFORD and KENNEDY.

A lunatic having a settlement in I., but having the status of irremovability from M., was, in 1851, sent to an asylum from M., which was not comprised in any union; and an order for the expenses was made on I. Stat. 16 & 17 Vict. c. 97, having afterwards passed, I. refused to pay any expenses incurred subsequently to 29th September, 1853. Two justices issued a distress warrant to levy the arrears, under which the goods of one of the overseers of I. were seized. A writ being issued by him, against the justices, a case was stated for the Queen's Bench.

Held, by the Exchequer Chamber, reversing the judgment of the Queen's Bench, that the justices had no jurisdiction to issue the warrant; the order on I. being by implication annulled by stat. 16 & 17 Vict. c. 97, and there being no obligation on I. to take any steps to get rid of it.

A SUMMONS having issued at the suit of the plaintiff against the defendants, the following case was, by consent and order of Coleridge J., stated for the opinion of the Court under sect. 46 of The Common Law Precedure Act, 1852 (15 & 16 Vict. c. 76).

On the 3d January, 1851, one Sarah Wilson, residing in the township of Manchester, in the county of Lancaster, having become lunatic and chargeable to the said township, was, by an order of a justice of the peace of the said county, sent to the county lunatic asylum at Prestwich in the said county. Manchester was then, and is still, a township maintaining its own poor, and not comprised in any union. And S. Wilson, at the time of the application for the said order, had been a resident in the said township for upwards of five years, and was exempt from being removed from it by any warrant or order of removal to the place of her last legal settlement by virtue of stat. 9 & 10 Vict. c. 66, s. 1.

On 11th September, 1851, two justices of the peace for the county of Lancaster, namely, Henry Leigh Trafford, the defendant, and Samuel Ashton, Esquires, made an order directed to the overseers of the poor of the township of Ince within Mackerfield, in the county of Lancaster, wherein, after reciting that the said S. Wilson, a pauper lunatic, was then confined in the county *lunatic asylum situated at Prest- [*145 wich in the county of Lancaster, and that they, the said justices, had, on the day and year last aforesaid, inquired into the last legal settlement of the said S. Wilson, and had obtained satisfactory evidence as to the settlement of ·the said S. Wilson, they, the said justices, did find and adjudge that the last legal settlement of the said S. Wilson was in the township of Ince. And, by another order, of the same date, and directed to the said overseers, the said justices, after reciting the said first mentioned order and that by virtue thereof the said S. Wilson was removed to the county lunatic asylum at Prestwich aforesaid, and was received into the said asylum, and had ever been, and then was, confined therein, the said justices, by their said last mentioned order, did order and direct the overseers of Ince (in which township the said S. Wilson had been adjudged to be settled as aforesaid) to pay unto the overseers of the township of Manchester certain sums of money for expenses incurred by them in and about the examination of the said lunatic, and in and about the conveying of her to the said lunatic asylum; and also did further order the overseers of Ince to pay to the overseers of Manchester a certain sum of money, which the said overseers of Manchester had paid to the superintendent of the asylum for the reasonable charges, for the lodging, &c., of the lunatic in the asylum. And the said justices, by their said order, did further order and direct the overseers of Ince to pay to the treasurer of the asylum, weekly and every week, the sum of 7s. 7d., and such other weekly sum as the existing justices of the said asylum should from time to time

direct, so long as the said S. Wilson should remain and be confined in
*the asylum. The oversers of Ince did not appeal against the
last mentioned order, but, in obedience thereto, duly paid to the
overseers of Manchester the said several sums so expended by them as
aforesaid, and paid unto the treasurer of the asylum (as by the order
directed) the sum of 7*s.* 7*d.* weekly and every week, from the date of the
order up to and inclusive of 29th September, 1853; the said sum of
7*s.* 7*d.*, being the weekly sum which, during all that time, was fixed by
the visiting justices of the asylum to be paid for the lodging, &c., of
the lunatic in the asylum.

    By stat. 16 & 17 Vict. c. 97 (which came into operation the 1st day
of November, 1853, (a)) it was provided, by sect. 102, 'that all expenses incurred since 29th September, 1853, for the maintenance, &c.,
in an asylum of any lunatic who, at the time of his removal to it, was
irremovable to the place of his settlement by reason of some provision
in stat. 9 & 10 Vict. c. 66, should be paid by the overseers of the poor
of the parish in which he had acquired such exemption. The overseers
of Ince, having paid the said weekly sum for the maintenance, &c., of
the lunatic in the asylum up to and including the 29th day of September, 1853, as aforesaid, conceived that, by force of the said stat. 16 &
17 Vict. c. 97, s. 102, the last mentioned order ceased to be any further obligatory upon them; and they ceased to pay any further sums
to the treasurer of the asylum for the maintenance, &c., of the lunatic:
and the payments thereafter directed by the order then became in arrear.
And afterwards, on 11th April, 1855, when the said arrears from 29th
September, 1853, to that time amounted to 29*l.* 12*s.* 8*d.*, *the
treasurer of the lunatic asylum made a complaint unto the defendant, H. L. Trafford, then sitting as a justice of the peace of and
for the county of Lancaster, at Salford in the said county, that the said
weekly sums, to the amount of 29*l.* 12*s.* 8*d.* as aforesaid, were then in
arrear and unpaid: whereupon the defendant, H. L. Trafford, then issued his summons to Richard Boardman, Thomas Knowles (the plaintiff
in this case) and Henry Frith, the then overseers of the poor of the
township of Ince, commanding them in Her Majesty's name to be and
appear, on the 17th May then next, at Salford, in the county as aforesaid, before such justices of the county as might then be there, to answer to the complaint, &c. The case then stated that the three overseers
accordingly attended before the said H. L. Trafford and John Lawrence
Kennedy (the defendants in this case), justices of Lancashire, then
sitting as such justices at Salford. And, in answer to the said complaint, showed to the said justices the said stat. 16 & 17 Vict. c. 97,
s. 102, and contended, before them, that the said provision exempted
them as overseers of Ince from payment of the said weekly sum
of 7*s.* 7*d.* for the maintenance of the lunatic since 29th September,

1853, and that the township of Manchester, being that in which the lunatic had acquired exemption from removal as hereinbefore is mentioned, was, by the terms of the said statute, the township by the overseers of which all expenses incurred, since 29th September, 1853, for the maintenance, &c., of the pauper ought to be paid. However, the last mentioned justices then overruled the defence so set up by the overseers of Ince to the said complaint, and afterwards, on 9th July, 1855, the said sum of 29*l*. 12*s*. 8*d*. still continuing wholly unpaid and unsatisfied to the treasurer, they, the *said justices, issued their warrant of distress against the overseers for the recovery of the [*148 said sum of 29*l*. 12*s*. 8*d*., together with costs. (The case set out the warrant of distress, upon the form of which nothing turned.)

Under this warrant, a constable of the county of Lancaster, on 18th July, 1855, entered the house of the plaintiff, Thomas Knowles, then one of the overseers of the poor of the township of Ince, and seized and distrained his goods and chattels: and the said Thomas Knowles, in order to prevent the same from being sold, as in the said warrant was directed, was obliged to pay, and did pay, unto the said constable the said sum of 29*l*. 12*s*. 8*d*. and the sum of 1*l*. 6*s*. 6*d*. for costs.

The questions for the opinion of the Court are:

1. Whether the defendants, as such justices, had by law any right or jurisdiction to issue the warrant of distress on the overseers of the township of Ince for recovery of the sums incurred for the maintenance &c., of the lunatic since the 29th September, 1853.

2. Whether the overseers of Ince are liable to pay such sums or any part thereof.

If the Court shall be of opinion in the negative, then it is agreed, by and between the said plaintiff and the said defendants, that the judgment of the Court may be entered for the said plaintiff for 1*l*., with costs, to be taxed as in ordinary cases. But, if the Court shall be of opinion in the affirmative, then it is agreed, between the said parties, that the judgment of the Court shall be entered for the defendants with costs.

The case was argued in last Michaelmas Term,(*a*) by *Pashley* for the plaintiff and *Robert Hall* for the *defendant; and *Archbold* [*149 (in the absence of *Pashley*) was heard in reply.

It is considered sufficient to state the judgment of this Court and of the Court of Exchequer Chamber.   *Cur. adv. vult.*

Lord CAMPBELL, C. J., in this Term (January 14th), delivered the judgment of the Court.

In this action of trespass the question is raised, whether the justices had jurisdiction to issue the warrant of distress against the plaintiff. The material facts are: that a pauper lunatic was sent to an asylum from Manchester, and, in September, 1851, an order for maintenance

(*a*) November 11th, 1856. Before Lord Campbell, C. J., Coleridge, Wightman, and Erle, Js.

was made on Ince, the parish of settlement, under stat. 8 & 9 Vict. c. 126, s. 62. This order had been obeyed down to September, 1853: but further payment thereunder to the treasurer of the asylum had been refused, on the suggestion, by Ince, that the pauper at the time of being sent away was irremovable from Manchester by reason of five years' residence therein, and that, from September, 1853, the cost of main-tenance was cast on Manchester by stat. 16 & 17 Vict. c. 97. s. 102, which provides that from September, 1853, all the expenses of the re-moval and maintenance of a pauper lunatic who was irremovable when sent to the asylum should be borne by the parish of residence if not in any union; and Manchester is not in any union. The treasurer of the asylum then applied to the justices to compel the overseers of Ince to make further payments under the order of 1851, by distress; and so the warrant in question was issued.

The plaintiff contends that there was no jurisdiction, because the order for maintenance on the parish of *settlement, made in 1851, \
*150] was annulled by stat. 16 & 17 Vict. c. 97, s. 102, together with the fact of irremovability in Manchester, which in this case, between this plaintiff and this defendant, is found as a fact.

But we are of opinion that the order of 1851 is not annulled until the fact of irremovability has been found against Manchester, either by admission or by judicial decision; and that the order of 1851 against Ince remains in force until Ince has substituted the liability of Man-chester to the treasurer, and so, by implication, has become released itself.

The maintenance of a pauper lunatic was imposed by stat. 8 & 9 Vict. c. 126,(a) on the parish sending him to the asylum: and this parish was enabled to transfer it, by obtaining an order on the parish of settle-ment, if that could be found, and, if not, on the county.(b)

Stat. 9 & 10 Vict. c. 66, created irremovability by five years' resi-dence. Stat. 10 & 11 Vict. c. 110, s. 1; charged the burden of irre-movable paupers on the union fund if the parish was in an union: and subsequent legislation has attempted to make an analogous provision for the maintenance of pauper lunatics who had the status of irremova-bility. Stat. 12 & 13 Vict. c. 103,(c) cast it on the union of the par-ish of residence, if that parish was in an union. See Overseers of Wigton v. Overseers of Snaith, 16 Q. B. 496 (E. C. L. R. vol. 71). And, finally, stat. 16 & 17 Vict. c. 97, s. 102, provided that, from Septem-ber, 1853, it should be cast upon the union fund of the parish of resi-dence, if it should be in an union, and, if not in an union, then on the fund of the parish itself; and it is made to apply to paupers \
*151] *removed before as well as after the Act was passed. Under this clause, Manchester is liable if it was the parish of residence. In respect of paupers sent from the parish of residence after this Act passed,

(a) Sect. 61.   (b) Sects. 58, 59, 62, 63.   (c) Sect. 5.

the order must be made on that parish as the parish sending, under sect. 95. But the legislation seems defective in making no provision for adjudicating how and when the liability of the parish of settlement, under orders made for the maintenance of paupers removed before the Act passed, is to be determined by being transferred to the parish of residence. If an order has been made on a county, and a settlement is afterwards discovered, provision is made, enabling the county to obtain an order on the parish of settlement, cancelling the order on the county, and so ending its liability; sect. 99.

In sect. 102 any order on the parish of settlement is prohibited for the future in all cases where the parish of residence is made liable; but no power is given to make an order substituting the parish of residence for the parish of settlement in respect of orders made before the Act passed. It is probable, therefore, that the remedy by mandamus or action would be applicable: and the practical question is, Upon whom is the duty cast of taking proceedings to effectuate the transfer. Is it on the treasurer of the asylum or on the parish of settlement?

The plaintiff contends that it is cast on the treasurer in all cases where the parish of settlement suggests that a parish of residence was liable by reason of the required residence therein, and offers to prove such suggestion. But we are of the contrary opinion. The necessary proof is proof good against Manchester. If Ince proved irremovability in Manchester, as against the treasurer, *that would be of no effect [*152 against Manchester; and the same proof in a contest between the treasurer and Manchester might be so met as to fail: and the treasurer ought not to be forced into such litigation for money which is clearly due to him, and due from Ince, until Manchester is fixed. The interested parties are Ince and Manchester, and the litigation ought to be by them. The liability of Ince under the order of 1851 is expressly continued by sect. 121. Notwithstanding the repeal of the statute under which it was made, that liability gave the magistrates jurisdiction to enter upon the inquiry, and made it their duty to issue the distress warrant in question against Ince, whose liability has not been determined, by being transferred to Manchester, conclusively, either by its own admission or by adjudication against it.

Our judgment therefore is for the defendant.

Judgment for defendant.

IN THE EXCHEQUER CHAMBER.

June 15.

For syllabus, see ante, p. 141.

ERROR was brought upon the decision of the Court of Queen's Bench.

Archbold now argued for the appellant, and *Knowles* for the respondent. The effect of the arguments used sufficiently appears from the judgment.

Archbold was not called upon to reply.

*153] *COCKBURN, C. J.—We are all of opinion that in this case the judgment of the Queen's Bench must be reversed. The question depends upon a series of enactments. First, by stat. 8 & 9 Vict. c. 126, s. 62, the expenses of the maintenance of a lunatic sent to an asylum were to be borne by the parish in which the lunatic was settled. Then came stat. 9 & 10 Vict. c. 66, rendering a pauper irremovable after five years' residence. That was followed by stat. 12 & 13 Vict. c. 103, s. 5, casting the burthen of payment of the expenses of a lunatic, who had the status of irremovability in another parish, on the union containing that parish. But that enactment was applicable only when that parish happened to be in a union. Then came stat. 16 & 17 Vict. c. 97, s. 102, extending the enactment and casting the burthen of all expenses, incurred since 29th September, 1853, on the union containing the parish of residence, or on the parish itself, when it is not in a union. By sect. 96 of the same Act, justices may make an order on the parish from which any lunatic is or has been sent. Now, the effect of these provisions seems to be this, to relieve the parish of settlement: under stat. 12 & 13 Vict. c. 103, at the expense of the union in which the residence was; and under stat. 16 & 17 Vict. c. 97, at the expense of the union, if the parish of residence is in a union, and, if it is not, at the expense of the parish of residence itself. And it seems to me that the effect of the Acts must be the same, whether there was an existing order on the parish of settlement or not: for, if that order is to be enforced, it would be in direct contravention of the intention of the Legislature that the burthen should not be on the parish of settlement. The

*154] Legislature could not intend such an *anomaly as to leave such orders capable of being enforced. It is true that stat. 16 & 17 Vict. c. 97, is silent as to previous orders: but, as it could not be intended to make the liability different in one case from another, I think the only legitimate inference from that silence is, that the provision, that the parish of settlement should not be liable, by implication deprived all orders to the contrary of force. It seems to me that light is thrown upon stat. 16 & 17 Vict. c. 97, s. 102, by stat. 12 & 13 Vict. c. 103, s. 5. The two enactments are in pari materiâ: and it seems absurd to suppose that the former order should be left in force under the one and not under the other. The contention, however, is, that it is incumbent on Ince to get rid of the previous order on it. I do not find that the Act casts on it any such obligation; but, if I could see any mode in which Ince could get rid of that order, I might give more weight to the argument. But I find none. The Act does not authorize the parish of settlement to apply to the justices to annul the order; nor does it empower the justices to hear them, and on their application to annul the order: all that it does is to authorize the justices to make an order in favour of the treasurer on the parish of removal. That should have been done here. The liability being transferred by the Legislature, the previous order is annulled by implication.

CRESSWELL, J., WILLIAMS, J., MARTIN, B., WILLES, J., BRAMWELL, B., WATSON, B. and CHANNELL, B., concurred.   Judgment reversed.

---

*The QUEEN v. PARKER and others.   Jan. 15.   [*155

Under stat. 41 G. 3, c. 23; if a rate be appealed against and reduced, but the party rated has during the appeal paid on the unreduced assessment, the parish officers may, in subsequent rates, credit him for the excess paid, without an order of Sessions.

A. R. ADAMS, in last term, obtained a rule calling on William Parker, Esquire, and four others, five justices of Warwickshire, to show cause why a mandamus should not issue commanding them or some of them to issue a warrant or warrants of distress against the goods of the London and Northwestern Railway Company, to levy the several sums of 12l. 8s. 9d. and 18l. 5s. 7½d. imposed upon them by two several rates or assessments for the relief of the poor of the parish of Kenilworth in the said county, made respectively on the 10th day of November, 1855, and the 8th day of March, 1856.

The following facts appeared from the affidavits in support of and opposition to the rule.

In November, 1853, The London and North-western Railway Company were assessed to a rate for the relief of the poor of the parish of Kenilworth, Warwickshire, at 787l. 10s., for land occupied by them as a railway in that parish. Against this they appealed to the Quarter Sessions holden at Warwick in January, 1854. This appeal was duly respited. Another rate was made in February, 1854, by which the Company was assessed at the same amount, and against which they appealed to the Quarter Sessions held at Warwick in April, 1854. At the last-mentioned Sessions it was ordered that the appeal of November, 1853, should be referred to the arbitration of John Lewis Hornblower, upon certain terms; *one of which was, that the decision [*156 as to that rate should be binding on all rates made or to be made before the date of the award, provided such award should be made before 31st December, 1855.   Seven subsequent rates were afterwards made, the last in November, 1855, in each of which the Company was assessed at the same sum of 787*l.* 10*s.*; against all of which appeals were entered.   On 18th December, 1855, the arbitrator made his award, by which he reduced the assessment of 787*l.* 10*s.* to 262*l.* 10*s.* While the appeals were pending, the Company paid all the rates, except that of November, 1855, on the original assessment, on the understanding that, in case of the assessment being reduced, the amount paid by the Company in excess of the amount which they would have paid, had they originally been assessed at the lower amount, should be repaid to them, or credited to them on account of future rates.   At the Quarter Sessions held at Warwick on 31st December, 1855, the award was confirmed : but, in consequence of such understanding as aforesaid, no order for repayment was applied for, though, at that time, 175*l.* was due to the Company in respect of their payments in excess: and no such order was made.   The parish officers of Kenilworth had always expressed their willingness to repay or give credit for the excess, and actually made a rate for the purpose of repayment: but the auditor of the district intimated to them that he would not allow such repayment. The assessment in the rate of November, 1855, was reduced to 262*l.* 10*s.*, in respect of which and of the assessment on other property, not disputed, 12*l.* 3*s.* 9*d.* would be payable.   Another rate was made on 8th March, 1856, in which the Company were assessed at the 262*l.* 10*s.*, *157]* and in respect *of which, and of the other property, 18*l.* 5*s.* 7½*d.* was payable.   The parish officers demanded of the Company these two sums of 12*l.* 3*s.* 9*d.*, and 18*l.* 5*s.* 7½*d.*, and were requested to pay themselves the same out of the 175*l.* due to the Company: but this the auditor would not permit: and at his instance the parish officers applied to the five defendants, sitting in petty Sessions, for warrants of distress to levy the sums upon the goods of the Company.   The magistrates refused to grant such warrants.   The auditor then informed the parish officers that, unless they applied for a mandamus against the justices, he should surcharge them at the next audit.   The parish officers accordingly applied for and obtained the above rule.

Bittleson now showed cause, and contended that, as the parish officers had already in their hands money of the Company more than sufficient to satisfy the rate, no levy ought to be made ; and that it was unnecessary to get an express order of Sessions.

A. R. Adams, contrà.—It is true that the payments of the rate, which now turns out to be excessive, ought, under stat. 41 G. 3, c. 23, s. 1, to be taken as payment on account of the subsequent rates: and the whole question is one of form.   The auditor seems to have considered that, under sect. 8, an express order of Sessions was necessary to authorise the repayment.   Possibly, in the case of disallowance and surcharge, as threatened by the auditor, the Commissioners, under stat. 11 & 12 Vict. c. 91, s. 4, might grant equitable relief: but the parish officers cannot act upon that probability, and are compelled to apply for the warrant in conformity with the intimation *of the auditor. Per- [*158 haps the best course would be to allow the rule to stand over till Trinity Term, the Court now stating their view of the law.

Lord CAMPBELL, C. J.—Let that be so: and you have the authority of all of us that the want of an express order of the Sessions is immaterial, and that the money should be refunded.

(COLERIDGE, J., was absent.)

WIGHTMAN and ERLE, Js., concurred.

The rule stood over accordingly.

In the following Trinity Term(a) Sir *F. Kelly* showed cause, and *Hayes*, Serjt., was heard in support of the rule.

Per CURIAM.—It is out of the question that we should, in the exercise of our discretion, grant a mandamus for the purpose of doing manifest injustice. The rule is discharged. We think that the parish officers will do well to allow to the Company the sum paid in excess, and that they will run no risk in doing so. Rule discharged.

(a) June 11th, 1857. Before Lord Campbell, C. J., Coleridge, Erle, and Crompton, Js.

---

*JOHN IVENS v. WILLIAM JONES BUTLER and ANN BUTLER, his wife. *Jan.* 15. [*159

Where judgment is obtained against a husband and wife for the debt of the wife dum sola, and the wife is taken in execution, the Court, in its discretion, will discharge the wife from custody, unless it is shown that she has separate property which may be applied to the satisfaction of the debt.

Although the husband has not been and cannot be taken, he having obtained final protection from the Court of Insolvent Debtors.

It is not sufficient, in order to prevent this exercise of the discretion of the Court, that the wife's property was, before her marriage, assigned to trustees for her creditors, and the trustees had power, if they thought fit, to make her an allowance, and were to make over to her any surplus which might remain after the creditors should be satisfied.

FORTESCUE moved for a rule to show cause why the defendant, Ann Butler, should not be discharged out of the custody of the sheriff of Surrey as to this action.

From the affidavits in support of the rule it appeared that Ann Butler, while single, before 31st July, 1854, carried on business as a wheelwright in Middlesex, and had become indebted to the plaintiff in 70l. 15s. On that day she executed an assignment of the whole of her estate and effects to trustees for the benefit of all her creditors who should assent before 1st November following. The trusts of the deed were that the trustees should carry on the business for the benefit of the creditors, and might pay to her such a sum as they might think fit

for the maintenance of herself and family, not exceeding 100*l.* for the
first year and 200*l.* for any succeeding year; and they were to reas-
sign to her what surplus might remain after the performance of the
trusts. They had power to sell the effects, if they found the business
not profitable, and to apply the purchase-money to the said trusts. It
was deposed that the estate and effects were very valuable, and that
the trustees, or one of them, had continued to carry on the business
*160] under *the trusts. The plaintiff had not executed the deed of
assignment.   On 7th September, 1854, the defendant, Ann,
intermarried with the other defendant. On 9th October, 1856, plaintiff issued a summons against the defendants to recover the 70*l.* 16*s.*
Afterwards the defendant, William Jones Butler, filed his petition in
the Court for the relief of Insolvent Debtors; and on 20th December,
1856, he obtained his final order for protection. Ann Butler deposed
that she had no separate property wherewith to discharge the debt.
She was arrested on 5th January, 1857, at the suit of plaintiff in this
action.

From the affidavit in answer it appeared that final judgment was
signed on 8th Nov., 1856. That W. J. Butler had not been arrested, nor
had any of his effects been taken in execution; and that the judgment
remained unsatisfied, except by the arrest and detention of Ann Butler.
That the trustees, since the assignment, had paid to her out of the
estate money to a considerable amount; and that their solicitor had expressed his intention of advising the trustees to continue such payments
to her notwithstanding the insolvency of her husband.

Fortescue, in support of the motion.—The wife is entitled to be
discharged, though the husband has not been arrested, she having no
separate property. This principle was acted upon in Edwards *v.* Martin,
17 Q. B. 693 (E. C. L. R. vol. 79), where the authorities are collected;
among others Larkin *v.* Maskell, 4 Exch. 804,† where the husband,
having obtained protection from the Court of Bankruptcy, was not
*161] arrested, and the Court of Exchequer refused to *discharge the
wife from arrest, though it appeared that she had no separate
property; but Lord Campbell, in reference to that case, said that the
circumstance of the husband being or not being arrested could make
no difference.   Larkin *v.* Marshall, 4 Exch. 804,† may perhaps be supported on another ground: the action there was for an assault committed by the wife. [Lord CAMPBELL, C. J.—You say she was the
*im*meritorious cause of the action.] Yes: and the same principle was
acted upon in the case of an infant, against whom, as defendant, there
had been found a verdict in an action for slander, and the Court of
Common Pleas refused to discharge him from custody under execution, referring at the same time to the case of a feme covert; Defries
v. Davis, 1 New Ca. 692 (E. C. L. R. vol. 27).(*a*) In Lockwood *v.*

(*a*) See S. C., 3 Dowl. P. C. 629.

Salter, 5 B. & Ad. 303 (E. C. L. R. vol. 27), it was held to be a good plea in bar, to an action brought against husband and wife on a covenant made by the wife dum sola, that the husband had been discharged by The Insolvent Debtors' Court. If it be said that here the wife has separate property by reason of her interest in the possible surplus of the trust fund, the answer is that no such surplus is shown to exist. Here the plaintiff, not having chosen to come in pari passu with the other creditors, attempts to obtain his debt by detaining in custody the wife.

Garth showed cause in the first instance.—In Edwards v. Martin, 17 Q. B. 693 (E. C. L. R. vol. 79), the discharge was allowed, not as of right, but in the exercise of the discretion of the Court, it appearing that the wife had no separate property. Now here it appears that the trustees will continue to pay to *her an allowance. [ERLE, J.— [*162 All due to her will be due to the husband. Lord CAMPBELL, C. J.—We can hardly act upon an interest so shadowy.] The wife is not without remedy; she may, under stat. 1 & 2 Vict. c. 110, s. 101, apply for a discharge to the Insolvent Debtors' Court. In Larkin v. Marshall, 4 Exch. 804,† Parke, B., puts the practice of discharging the wife expressly upon the ground of precedent, and said that the Court would act only in cases similar to those where there had been such a discharge granted : and he pointed out that, though the wife had no separate property, her friends might come forward. Here the trustees may come forward.

Lord CAMPBELL, C. J.—According to all the authorities, it is clear that, when wife and husband are taken in execution for the debt of the wife, the wife is entitled to be discharged unless she has separate property from which she can pay the debt. She has not indeed an absolute right, not a right which she can enforce by habeas corpus. But, according to the practice long established in Westminster Hall, she will be discharged by the Court in such a case. According to the view which is said to have been taken by the Court of Exchequer in Larkin v. Marshall, 4 Exch. 804,† this will be done only where the husband has been arrested. I cannot accede to that: under such a rule, the creditor, by omitting to arrest the husband, might inflict perpetual imprisonment on the wife, unless she could obtain a discharge from the Court of Insolvent Debtors. The question, therefore, here is whether the creditor can *point out a separate property from which the wife [*163 can satisfy the debt: if he can, the wife must remain in gaol till she pays. But there is not a scintilla of such interest. All her property was assigned before marriage; and she cannot enforce from the trustees any allowance: and, if they made such allowance, it would belong to the husband and would not enable her to satisfy the debt. That being so, we ought according to the rule which guides our discretion, order the discharge.

[COLERIDGE, J., was absent.]

WIGHTMAN, J.—The circumstances under which the Court will exercise the discretion which it undoubtedly possesses are clearly settled in
Edwards *v.* Martyn, 17 Q. B. 693 (E. C. L. R. vol. 79). Then, is it
here shown that the wife has any separate property? Before marriage
she assigned away the whole of the property: under the trusts, she has
only a contingent interest in what would in effect be at the husband's
disposal. The only contingency upon which it would be at her disposal
would be that of her surviving her husband. Even if this case be not
directly within Edwards *v.* Martyn, we ought to exercise our discretion
in favour of the wife where it is not affirmatively shown that she has
separate property.

ERLE, J.—It is clear that the wife ought to be discharged if she has
no separate property. The law gives all her property to her husband;
and it is he that should be made to pay her debts. If she has no
*164] means, she *should be discharged. Now, before her marriage,
she assigned all her property to trustees: I presume the trustees
will do their duty, and not make a large allowance till the creditors are
satisfied. The plaintiff might have come in as a creditor: but he tries
to get an advantage by inducing some one to pity her distress when she
is imprisoned.   Rule absolute.

———◆———

GEORGE ALDHAM and HENRY BARDSLEY *v.* JOHN BROWN.
Jan. 16.

Covenant by the trustees named in a deed, being the ordinary Parliamentary subscription contract required before applying for an Act to make a railway. The contract contained a clause
that the provisional directors might abandon the application. Averment that the provisional
directors called upon the defendant, who had executed the deed, to pay money in pursuance
of a covenant so to do. Breach, non-payment. Plea 2, on equitable grounds, that the scheme
was abandoned. Plea 4, that the plaintiffs sued as trustees for the Company, which was not
provisionally registered at the time of the suit. Plea 5, that the Company was not completely
registered, and that the action was for the purpose of enforcing payment of a call. On demurrer: Held, that all the pleas were bad: the object of the Parliamentary subscription contract
being to provide means for paying preliminary expenses in case the scheme should be abandoned, and such object not being rendered illegal by any enactment.

COUNT: that, by an indenture made 1st December, 1854, between
the defendant and the several other persons whose names and seals
were thereunto respectively subscribed and affixed in the schedule thereto, being subscribers to the undertaking thereinafter mentioned, of the
first part, and the plaintiffs, trustees named and appointed for the
purpose of enforcing and giving effect to the covenants thereinafter contained, of the second part, each of them, the defendant and the said
several other persons, parties thereto of the first part, did respectively,
but to the extent only of the sum or amount of subscription set opposite
to his or her name in the said schedule thereto, covenant with the

*plaintiffs that each of them had subscribed and did thereby sub- [*165
scribe the sum set opposite to his or her name in the said schedule thereto, for the purpose of establishing a Company to be called
The Swansea Docks and Mineral Vallies Railway Company, or such
other name as the provisional directors or committee of management of
the said Company might direct or appoint, and for enabling such Company to make the railways and works thereinafter mentioned. And
the parties of the first part did thereby authorize and empower the said
provisional directors or committee of management for the time being, to
fix, alter, and vary the capital necessary to be raised, and " to abandon
or defer, if they should think fit, the application to Parliament in
respect of all or any part or parts of the said proposed undertaking, and
from time to time to renew such application as they might think pı ɔper
in case the said application should be suspended, deferred, or interrupted in the next session of Parliament." And defendant thereby covenanted with the plaintiffs that he "would pay the full amount so subscribed by him, or such part thereof as should not have been paid by
him at the time of the execution of the said indenture, in such sums, and
at such place or places," and at such time or times, as should, from time
to time, be required or appointed by the said provisional directors or
committee of management, until the passing of the said Act to be
obtained as aforesaid; and, after the passing thereof, as should be
required or directed by the said Act, or as the directors or others
authorized by such Act should direct or appoint; it being the express
meaning and intention of each of them the parties thereto of the first
part, that the amount so subscribed by him or her should be *re- [*166
coverable from him or her, his or her heirs, executors, and administrators, by the parties thereto of the second part, or the survivor
of them, his executor or administrators, by action atlaw in case default
were made in the payment thereof. Averments that the sum set opposite to the defendant's name in the schedule and subscribed by him was
400l.; that, after the making and executing of the indenture, and before
the passing of the said Act, the provisional directors required the
defendant to pay the sum of 50l., parcel of the said sum of 400l. so
subscribed by him and set opposite his name as aforesaid, at The Commercial Bank of London, in Lothbury, in the city of London, on 21st
March, 1856. General averment of performance. Breach: non-payment of the 50l.

Plea 2, for defence on equitable grounds: That the Company in the
declaration mentioned was a Company provisionally registered under
the provisions of the Act of Parliament (7 & 8 Vict. c. 110); and the
said deed in the declaration mentioned is the subscription contract, made
and entered into in pursuance of the standing orders of the Houses of
Parliament, for the purpose of obtaining an Act of Parliament to
enable the said Company to carry into execution the purposes and

objects in the said declaration mentioned, and for no other purpose whatsoever, and which could not be carried into execution without the authority of Parliament; that the said sum of 50*l.* was and is claimed to be due in respect of a certain deposit to be paid on certain shares in a certain projected undertaking, to be called The Swansea Docks and Mineral Vallies Railway, and not otherwise; and that, after the making of the said contract in the declaration mentioned, and before payment *167]* of the said *deposit, or any part thereof, was claimed or required of the defendant as in the declaration alleged, and before the passing of any Act of Parliament as in the said contract mentioned, and before the making of the said railways, works, stations, and conveniences in the said contract mentioned, or any part thereof, and before the commencement of this suit, the said projected undertaking and every part thereof, and the intention to apply for the said Act of Parliament, was wholly abandoned, as abortive, by the provisional directors and promoters of the said projected undertaking; and at the time of the payment of the said deposit being claimed and required of the defendant, and at the commencement of this suit, the said projected undertaking and every part thereof was and remained, and the same and every part thereof still is and remains, wholly abandoned as aforesaid. Averment that this action is brought and prosecuted by the plaintiffs as the trustees of and for the sole benefit of the said Company, and of the provisional directors, and not otherwise.

Plea 4. That the said Company in the declaration mentioned was a company within the meaning of stat. 7 & 8 Vict. c. 110, and was promoted and set on foot for the purposes in the said declaration mentioned, and which could not be carried into execution without the authority of Parliament; and that at the time of the commencement of this suit the Company was not provisionally or completely registered, according to the provisions of the said Act of Parliament: that this action was brought and prosecuted by the plaintiffs as the trustees of and for the sole benefit of the said Company and the said directors in the said declaration mentioned, and not otherwise, and in order to *168]* enforce payment *from the defendant of a deposit on certain shares in the capital of the said intended Company subscribed for by the defendant as in the said declaration mentioned, and not otherwise, contrary to the statute in the case made and provided.

Plea 5. That the Company was a company within the meaning of the said statute, and never obtained a certificate of complete registration, and was instituted for the purpose of carrying into execution the purposes in the said declaration mentioned, and which could not be carried into execution without the authority of Parliament: that the deed in the declaration mentioned is the subscription contract entered into in pursuance of the standing orders of the Houses of Parliament, for the purpose of applying for the said Act of Parliament in the declaration mentioned : that the action is brought and prosecuted by the plaintiffs as trustees for and for the sole benefit of the said Company, and of the said provisional directors, and for the purpose of making and enforcing the payment from the defendant of a call in respect of the said sum subscribed by him as in the said deed mentioned, that is to say, a call of 2l. 10s. per share on twenty shares of twenty pounds each, in the capital in the said intended Company, contrary tc the statute in that case made and provided.

Demurrer to the 2d, 4th, and 5th pleas. Joinder.

Lush, in support of the demurrer.—Stat. 7 & 8 Vict. c. 110, s. 2, provides that the Act shall not extend to any company for executing works which cannot be carried into execution without the authority of Parliament, except as thereinafter specially provided. Sect. 9 enacts that such a company may obtain a certificate of *complete regis- [*169 stration if the subscription contracts have been duly executed. Sect. 23 enacts what companies provisionally registered may do, and may not do. They may receive deposits ; but they may not make calls. Now here the action is not by the Company, but by trustees for them ; and it is not for a call, but in respect of a covenant in the subscription contract to contribute to the preliminary expenses. The question is, whether such a covenant can be enforced. The plea on equitable grounds might be good if it averred that there was an intention to apply the money when recovered to some purpose in fraud of the original subscription ; but it is not so averred. Neither are the legal pleas good.

Quain, in support of the pleas.—The second plea is good on equi- table grounds. [Lord CAMPBELL, C. J.—Before such a sheme is aban- doned, there may be preliminary expenses incurred in the attempt to carry it on. How are those to be paid ?] They are to be borne by the promoters, who cannot abandon the scheme without consent. [Lord CAMPBELL, C. J.—There is an express provision in this contract that the directors may abandon the undertaking if they see fit, and an express covenant with the plaintiffs to pay the money. CROMPTON, J.—The very object of requiring a subscription contract is to have security for the payment of preliminary expenses.] It does not appear here that there were any such incurred. Plea 4 is good. The Company cannot receive deposits, not being provisionally or completely registered. [WIGHTMAN, J.—But this plea is not that the Company were not pro- visionally or completely registered when the contract was made, [*170 *but when the suit was instituted. If the action had been com- menced the day before the certificate of provisional registration expired, this plea could not have been pleaded. Why should not the trustees sue afterwards ?] Plea 5 at all events is good. The Company, not being completely registered, are, by sect. 23, forbidden to receive calls. Sect. 25 expressly mentions receiving instalments in respect of shares not paid up, as one of the things which may be done by a Company when completely registered.

Lush, in reply.—Sect. 25 is applicable to companies not within sect. 9, and therefore having no subscription contract.

Lord CAMPBELL, C. J.—I am of opinion that the plaintiffs are entitled to judgment on all three demurrers.

The second plea is on equitable grounds. I have no doubt that, if after the abandonment of the scheme an attempt were made to enforce payment with a view to carry on the undertaking, a Court of equity would grant a perpetual injunction. But it cannot be supposed that an injunction would be granted against an action on an express covenant to contribute to pay the preliminary expenses incurred before abandonment, thus preventing the performance of a lawful contract. On this record we must take it that the action is for the purpose of enforcing payment of preliminary expenses properly incurred before abandonment, in which case equity would not interfere. To the 4th plea there is an answer in a few words. Though the Company was not provisionally *171] registered when the action was brought, that *does not avoid the deed, made when the Company was provisionally registered. And this action is on a covenant in that deed by the covenantee. As to the last plea, I think the provision as to not making calls was intended to protect allottees against calls, and not to discharge those who have executed a contract binding themselves to pay preliminary expenses. The provision does not apply to a subscription contract at at all.

COLERIDGE, J.—I am entirely of the same opinion. The pleas are founded on sections not applicable to such a case.

WIGHTMAN, J.—It is nowhere averred that the object of the plaintiffs is to apply the money to carrying on the abandoned undertaking, or to any other improper purpose: that disposes of the plea on equitable grounds. As for the others, I agree with my Lord that the enactments relied on do not apply to this case. There is nothing in the Act to forbid parties from binding themselves to pay money for purposes not prohibited.

CROMPTON, J., concurred.   Judgment for plaintiffs.

*GEORGE THOMPSON *v.* J. REYNOLDS. *Jan.* 16. [*172

A ship, the M., was insured, "including the risk of running down or doing damage to any other vessel, the same as the Indemnity Company's policy," valued at 3000*l.* The Indemnity Company's running down clause is, that, if the ship, by negligence, shall run down any other vessel, "and the assured shall thereby become liable to pay, and shall pay, any sum not exceeding the value of the said ship or vessel" (assured) "and her freight, by or in pursuance of the judgment of any Court of law or equity," the insurers shall pay "such proportion of three-fourths of the sum so paid as aforesaid as the sum" "hereby assured shall bear to the value of the said ship or vessel hereby assured and her freight."

The M., through negligence, ran down another vessel. The M. was sold under a decree of the Court of Admiralty, and the proceeds paid over for satisfying the damage. On a demurrer, upon pleadings in which it was admitted that the insured lost his ship, which was of the value of 3000*l.* and upwards, it being sold against his will, but that the proceeds which were paid over were only 2110*l.* :

Held, that the under writers were bound to make good three-fourths of the proceeds actually paid, viz. 2110*l.*, and not three-fourths of the value of the ship.

COUNT against an underwriter of 100*l.* on a policy which was set out in the count. It was a time policy on the ship Margaret, valued at 3000*l.*, "including the risk of running down or doing damage to any other ship or vessel, the same as the Indemnity Company's Policy." The rest of the policy was in the ordinary form. Averment that the Indemnity Company's clause is as follows: " And we, for ourselves and each of us, do covenant and agree that, in case the said ship shall, by accident or negligence of the master and crew, run down or damage any other ship or vessel, and the assured shall thereby become liable to pay, and shall pay, any sum not exceeding the value of the said ship or vessel   and her freight, by or in pursuance of the judgment of any court of law or equity, or by or in pursuance of any award made upon any reference entered into by the assured with the concurrence of two of the directors for the time being of the said Company, the capital stock and funds of the said Company shall and will bear and pay such proportion of three-fourth parts of the sum so paid as aforesaid as the sum of   *l.* hereby assured shall *bear to the value of the said ship or vessel [*173 hereby assured and her freight." Averment that, during the insurance, the Margaret, by negligence of the master and crew, ran down and damaged another ship; and the plaintiff, being possessed of the Margaret, and the master and crew being the plaintiff's, the plaintiff thereby " became liable to pay, and did pay, for the said running down and damage, a sum not exceeding the value of the said ship the Margaret and her freight, to wit, 3000*l.*, by and in pursuance of a decree and judgment of the High Court of Admiralty, the said ship the Margaret having been, under and by virtue of the said decree and judgment, sold for the purpose of discharging and satisfying, and the proceeds of the said sale having been paid over for satisfying, the said damage ;" and thereby defendant became liable to pay 75 per cent. of his subscription of 100*l.*

Plea, as to 52*l.* 15*s.*, payment into court. And, as to the residue,

" that the sum which the assured became liable to pay under the decree of the High Court of Admiralty in the declaration mentioned was 2110*l.* and no more; and that the assured did not at any time pay more than the said sum of 2110*l.* in respect of the said running down or damage; and that the proportion of three-fourths of the sum so paid, which defendant as underwriter for 100*l.* should contribute, is 52*l.* 15*s.* and no more."

Replication to the plea to the residue: that the sum which the assured. became liable to pay for the said running down and damage far exceeded the sum of 2110*l.*; and that for payment thereof the said High Court of Admiralty by the said decree ordered the said ship to be sold, and plaintiff's ship was accordingly sold, under and by virtue of the said *174] decree, without his *consent and against his will; and that, by means of the premises and of such decree and sale, he lost and was deprived of his ship, which at the time of the sale was of the value of 3000*l.* and upwards. And so the plaintiff says that he became liable to pay and did pay, within the meaning of the said policy, for the said running down and damage, to a sum exceeding the said sum of 2110*l.*, to wit, 3000*l.*; and that the proportion of three-fourth parts of the said sum so paid, which the defendant as an underwriter for 100*l.* was liable to contribute, far exceeded 52*l.* 15*s.* Demurrer. Joinder.

Blackburn, in support of the demurrer.—Collision is one of the perils of the sea; and for its direct consequences the underwriters on an ordinary policy are responsible. But they are not bound to make good the liability which the owners of the ship may incur in consequence of such collision. It is too remote a consequence of the peril of the sea; De Vaux *v.* Salvador, 4 A. & E. 420 (E. C. L. R. vol. 31). In this case the parties have made a special bargain by reference to that in the Indemnity Company's clause; and no doubt each underwriter takes upon himself to make good personally the same proportion of his subscription as the Indemnity Company's funds would be liable to make good under that clause. Now, when the position of the parties is looked to, the meaning of the clause is clear. The ship-owner may be personally in fault; in which case he is not able to recover against his underwriters at all; Thompson *v.* Hopper, 6 E. & B. 172 (E. C. L. R. vol. 88): if he is not personally in fault, his responsibility is limited to the value of the ship and freight; The Merchant Shipping Act, 1854 (17 & 18 Vict. *175] c. 104), sects. 504, 514. To protect *themselves, the underwriters stipulate that the assured shall stand his own insurer for one-fourth; and, to provide against the possible case of his colluding with the other side, they bargain that they shall only be answerable for three-fourths of what has been both found to be due by a competent court, and actually paid. If judgment were signed on a verdict for 5000*l.*, and under a fi. fa. the ship were sold, the sum paid would be, neither the 5000*l.* nor the value of the ship, but the proceeds which the judgment-creditor received. In this case it is admitted on the record that the proceeds paid over were 2110l. and no more.

Manisty, contra.—The ship by this policy is to be taken, for every purpose between these parties, to be of the value of 3000l.; and that ship the plaintiffs have lost. Had it been delivered to the owners of the injured ship in satisfaction, it would have been payment. [CROMPTON, J.—Possibly, if the owners of the injured ship had accepted the Margaret in satisfaction of 3000l., it might have been payment of so much. But in this case they did not accept it, and probably would be surprised if told they had been paid more than 2110l.]

Blackburn was not called upon to reply.

Lord CAMPBELL, C. J.—It is clear that the underwriters are liable only by virtue of the special clause. Their liability must be limited by its terms; and these are that they are to make good "three-fourth parts of the sum so paid." The sum paid is here the amount of the damages which have been satisfied to the damaged party.

*(COLERIDGE, J., had left the court.)

WIGHTMAN, J.—If the owners of a damaged ship had taken [*176 the Margaret in satisfaction of their claim, there would have been more ground for Mr. *Manisty's* argument: as it is, there is none.

CROMPTON, J.—The underwriters limit their liability by using the word *paid*. No more than 2110l. is here paid.

Judgment for the defendants.

———◆———

CHARLES BROCKLEHURST and JOHN LOWE *v.* ROBERT LAWE. *Jan. 16.*

The goods of a trader on premises of which he was tenant were mortgaged for more than their value. The mortgagee entered and took possession. Then the tenant became bankrupt, owing more than a year's rent. Held, that the landlord might make his distress upon those goods available for the whole rent due; sect. 129, of the Bankrupt Law Consolidation Act, 1849, protecting only the interest of the assignees of the bankrupt, and not that of his mortgagee.

The assignees of the bankrupt, being ordered to elect whether they would accept or decline the tenancy, declined it. No formal notice was given to the bankrupt; and nothing was done. Then, a fresh quarter having elapsed: Held, that the tenancy continued, and that the landlord might distrain on the goods of the mortgagee for the quarter's rent thus accruing.

THIS was a special case, without pleadings, in substance as follows.

The plaintiffs are seised in fee simple of a cotton mill in Stockport. In the year 1852, plaintiffs demised it to Mr. Joseph Wright as tenant from year to year at the yearly rent of 1400l., payable quarterly on 16th January, 16th April, 16th July, and 16th October in every year; and he took possession of the mill as tenant to the plaintiffs, and continued in the actual occupation thereof as such tenant until 11th July, 1856, the day of the

*177] seizure *hereinafter mentioned. There was no lease or agreement in writing, but only a demise by word of mouth. On 21st May, 1855, an indenture, to which Wright and the defendant were parties, was executed: and by that indenture, for the purpose of securing to the defendant the repayment of the sum of 14,900l., Wright and some former mortgagees assigned to the defendant, his executors, &c., all and singular the spinning, weaving and other machinery, implements, goods, chattels and effects, whatsoever and wheresoever, and whether fixed or movable, of the said Wright, then standing and being in, upon and about the said mill; the particulars whereof were set forth in the first schedule thereunder written or thereunto annexed; and also all and singular other (if any) the spinning, weaving and other machinery, wheel, mill gear, plant, chattels, and effects, whether fixed or movable, of or belonging to Wright, which then were, or which, at any time during the continuance of the security intended to be thereby made, should be, in or about the said mill, and premises; together with all and singular the rights, members and appurtenances thereto belonging or in anywise appertaining: to have and to hold in trust as a mortgage security with powers of entry and sale. Wright, after the execution of the deed, continued in possession of the machinery, implements, goods, chattels, and effects assigned by the deed, and from time to time sold some of the said machinery, implements, goods, and chattels, and brought other machinery, implements, utensils, mill whells, mill gear, plant, chattels, and effects upon the said mill and premises. On 11th July last, the defendant served Wright with a written demand of the payment of the balance then remaining unpaid of the said sum of 14,900l.: and, Wright having
*178] failed *to pay, the defendant on 11th July last, under the power contained in the deed, entered into the mill and took possession of all the machinery, goods, chattels, and effects, which he was entitled to take possession of under the powers of the said deed, and which consisted partly of machinery, goods and chattels mentioned in the inventory annexed to the said deed, and partly of other machinery, goods and chattels which had been subsequently brought upon the mill by Wright, and which the defendant was entitled to take possession of under the provisions of the deed. From that time, the whole of the machinery, goods and chattels continued in the mill in the possession of the defendant, until the same were sold as hereinafter mentioned. After the defendant had so taken possession, Wright committed an act of bankruptcy: and, on 17th July last, a petition for adjudication of bankruptcy was filed against him, upon which he was on the same day duly adjudged a bankrupt; and assignees of his estate and effects were afterwards duly appointed. The machinery, goods, and chattels of which the defendant so took possession have been valued by a sworn appraiser for the defendant at the sum of 10,325l. 11s. 3d., if sold to a person who could use them in the mill. The defendant has however been unable to sell them

in that way: and they have since, during the month of December, 1856, been sold by him in lots by auction for the sum of 5300*l*. A sum exceeding 14,000*l*. still remains due from Wright to the defendant on the mortgage; and the defendant has no security for the said sum except the said machinery, goods, and chattels. The assignees of Wright have not interfered with the machinery, chattels, and effects. The rent which became from Wright *to the plaintiffs was not [*179 regularly paid: but Wright, at the request of the plaintiffs, made from time to time a variety of payments to third persons on account of the plaintiffs. Wright kept an account with the plaintiffs in his ledger, in which each quarter's instalment of rent, and certain other sums received by him on account of the plaintiffs, were entered on one side, and the payments by him on the other side; and the plaintiffs assented to this mode of keeping the account: and at the time when Wright became a bankrupt the sum of 2100*l*. 6*s*. 10*d*. was due from Wright to the plaintiffs on the balance of the account; of which sum, the sum of 1948*l*. 5*s*. 11*d*. was due for rent of the mill, including the quarter's rent. which became due on 16th July, 1856. Wright used from time to time, before he became bankrupt, to pay the income tax due in respect of the mill, and used to enter such payments when he made them to the debit of the plaintiffs in his account with them. The last payment by Wright on account of income tax on the mill was made on 24th January, 1856, and amounted to the sum of 93*l*. 6*s*. 8*d*., and was the income tax which was payable in respect of the said mill for the year commencing 5th of April, 1855, and was entered by Wright in the account to the debit of the plaintiffs at the time the payment was made. After Wright had so become bankrupt, and whilst the said machinery, goods, and chattels remained in the said mill in the possession of the defendant, the plaintiffs gave notice to the defendant that they intended to distrain the said goods and chattels for the sum of 1948*l*. 5*s*. 11*d*.: and thereupon, for the purpose of preventing such distress being put in, the defendant agreed to pay the plaintiffs the sum for which in point of law the plaintiffs *were entitled to distrain upon the said goods and [*180 chattels. The defendant however contended that the plaintiffs in point of law were only entitled to distrain for one year's rent, after deducting therefrom the sum of 93*l*. 6*s*. 8*d*., for one year's income tax. The plaintiffs on the other hand contended that they were entitled to distrain for the whole 1948*l*. 5*s*. 11*d*.: and that, even if the plaintiffs were only entitled to distrain for one year's rent, still that the said sum of 93*l*. 6*s*. 8*d*. ought not to be deducted therefrom. The defendant has paid the plaintiffs the sum of 1306*l*. 13*s*. 4*d*., being the amount for which he admits the plaintiffs were entitled to distrain.

Since the last mentioned payment was made, the defendant has paid to the Queen the sum of 46*l*. 13*s*. 4*d*., being one-half of the income tax for the mill for the year commencing 1856. On the 5th September,

1856, cne of the Commissioners of the Court of Bankruptcy, upon an application made to him by the plaintiffs, ordered the assignees of Wright to elect whether they would accept or decline the bankrupt's tenancy of the mill and premises; and thereupon the assignees declined to accept the said tenancy.   No formal notice was given to Wright that his assignees had declined to accept the tenancy.   Neither Wright, nor the defendant, nor the assignees, have ever offered to surrender the possession of the mill to the plaintiffs: and the defendant continued in possession of the mill and of the said machinery, goods and chattels until the same were sold as aforesaid.   After 16th October, 1856, the plaintiffs gave notice to the defendant that they should distrain the goods and chattels which so as aforesaid still remained in the said mill, in the possession of the defendant, for the quarter's rent which they allege became due on 16th October.   The defendant denied that the plaintiffs were entitled to distrain the said goods and chattels for the said quarter's rent, but agreed with the plaintiffs, for the purpose of preventing the said distress, that, if the plaintiffs were in point of law entitled to distrain the said goods and chattels for the said quarter's rent, he would pay the amount of the said quarter's rent to the plaintiffs, deducting the said sum of 46*l.* 13*s.* 4*d.*

The questions for the opinion of the Court are: First, Were the plaintiffs, after Joseph Wright become bankrupt, and before 16th October, 1856, entitled to distrain the said goods and chattels for any sum exceeding the said sum of 1806*l.* 13*s.* 4*d.*; and, if they were, What was the sum for which they were entitled to distrain the said goods and chattels in addition to the said sum of 1806*l.* 14*s.* 4*d.*? Secondly, Were the plaintiffs, after the said 16th October, entitled to distrain the said goods and chattels for the quarter's rent, which they allege became due on the said 16th October, deducting the said sum of 46*l.* 13*s.* 4*d.*?

If the Court is of opinion that the plaintiffs were entitled to distrain for all or any of the sums in dispute, the judgment of the Court is to be entered for the plaintiffs for the sum for which the Court may think they were entitled to distrain; but, if the Court should think that the plaintiffs were not entitled to distrain the said goods and chattels for any of the sums in dispute, the judgment of the Court is to be entered for the defendant.

The Court is to be at liberty to draw any inference of fact which a jury might and ought to draw.

*182]   *Atherton*, for the plaintiffs.—If there had been no *bankruptcy, the plaintiffs would have had a right to distrain for all the rent due to them; they still have it, except in so far as that right is limited by the Bankrupt Law Consolidation Act, 1849 (12 & 13 Vict. c. 106).   As far as regards the first question, the whole turns on sect. 129, "that no distress for rent made and levied after an act of bankruptcy upon the goods or effects of any bankrupt, whether before or after the issuing of the fiat or the filing of the petition for adjudication of bankruptcy, shall be available for more than one year's rent accrued prior to the date of the fiat or the day of the filing of such petition, but the landlord or person to whom the rent shall be due shall be allowed to come in as a creditor for the overplus of the rent due, and for which the distress shall not be available." But, when Lawe entered and seized the goods under the power in the deed, they became his . goods, not those of Wright: Hope v. Hayley, 5 E. & B. 830 (E. C. L. R. vol. 85). If they had been of greater value than the sum for which they were mortgaged, Wright till his bankruptcy, and the assignees after it, would, in equity, have been entitled to the surplus : but there was no surplus ; and so nothing vested in the assignees: Dangerfield v. Thomas, 9 A. & E. 292 (E. C. L. R. vol. 36). It is quite immaterial, as regards the assignees and the general body of creditors, whether the landlords make these goods satisfy so much of their rent, or the mortgagees make them satisfy so much of their debt ; either way the surplus of the rent and debt is provable. The words of sect. 129, "upon the goods or effects of any bankrupt" (which must mean "belonging to the assignees of any bankrupt,") show that the intention was to prevent the landlord making *his distress available to the prejudice of [*188 the general body of the creditors. A similar interpretation was put upon the Insolvent Debtors' Act: Congreve v. Evetts, 10 Exch. 298.† It is not necessary to inquire whether the income tax should be deducted from the year's rent, unless the landlord's right to mak the distress available is limited to that amount. Then, as to the second question, it depends upon sect. 145, by which, if the assignees decline to take to a lease, "the bankrupt shall not be liable if, within fourteen days after he shall have had notice that the assignees have declined," he shall give up the lease. It may be that, no formal notice having been given to Wright, so as to call on him to give up the lease, he is not personally liable: but there is nothing to determine the tenancy ; and, whilst it exists, the landlord's right to distrain for rent, accruing after the filing of the petition, is not affected: Briggs v. Sowry, 8 M. & W. 729,† Newton v. Scott, 10 M.ˢ & W. 471,†(a) Phillips v. Shervill, 6 Q. B. 944 (E. C. L. R. vol. 51).

Montague Smith, contrà.—The hardship is great on a third party if his goods may be made available for the landlord's rent, as it does not appear how he could prove against the estate for what he loses. [Lord ᴶ CAMPBELL, C. J.—If Mr. *Atherton's* argument is right, your client is but left as he would be if there were no such enactment as that in sect. 129. What sense do you put on the words "upon the goods or effects of any bankrupt?' Remembering that it is a section for the benefit of the estate.] In sect. 184 the same language is used when speaking

(a) In Exch. Ch., affirming the judgment of Exch. in Newton v. Scott, 9 M. & W. 434.†

*184] of *securities; that shows that the equity of redemption in goods pledged is included, in this Act, under that phrase. It cannot alter the case, whether the lien on the goods is for much or little. [CROMPTON, J.—This is not a case of lien; the property passed subject to the equity of redemption. If there had been a surplus, it would have vested in the assignees; and then it may be that the landlord could make his distress available only for a year's rent as far as regarded their interest, which is protected, and for his whole rent as far as regarded the mortgagees, whose interest is not protected. But here there never was any surplus; so nothing vested in the assignees; and that question does not arise.] Then, as to the quarter's rent, the landlord was bound to give notice to the bankrupt that he might give up the lease.

Atherton was not called upon to reply.

Lord CAMPBELL, C. J.—I am of opinion that both questions must be answered in favour of the plaintiffs; the landlord still has his right to distrain. The policy of the legislature was to prevent him from using that right to an unlimited extent, so as to sweep away the whole estate, leaving nothing for the general creditors; and, to protect them, this very salutary enactment was framed. But there was no intention to protect any individual creditor against another; the intention was that the landlord's right should be curtailed, so far as was necessary for the benefit of the general body. Then language is used apt to express that intention. The distress on the "goods or effects of any bankrupt" is not to be made available. Here, in fact, the bankrupt had no inter-
*185] est in the goods; neither was the interest of the *general body of the creditors at all affected if the landlord exercised his rights at common law to the utmost. There are neither words to deprive him of his rights, nor is it within the policy of the enactment. Then as to the other point: the assignees declining to take the term, and nothing being done, the term continues in the bankrupt. The law says that he continues tenant, and the rent still runs. It may be he is not personally liable; but that is not the question here.

WIGHTMAN, J.—These were not the goods of the bankrupt within the meaning of sect. 129. They had been assigned to Lawe, who had made his title complete by entry; and they were legally his property. If there had been any surplus, that would have belonged to the assignees: but, looking at the facts, it is clear there never was anything available for the assignees; and it made no difference to them whether the proceeds of the goods went to the landlord or the mortgagee. The Act was never meant to favour the mortgagee at the expense of the landlord. As to the second point, the tenancy continues. The bankrupt may be protected; but the tenancy is not determined: and there is nothing to deprive the landlord of his right at common law to distrain on the goods of a stranger on the premises.

CROMPTON, J.—The object of sect. 129 was to protect the estate; the assignees here had no interest in these goods. The case is within neither the words nor spirit of sect. 129. Judgment for plaintiffs.

---

*The QUEEN v. MARIA CLARKE. Jan. 21. [*186

(In the matter of ALICIA RACE.)

An infant of the age of ten years being brought up from a school, on habeas corpus, at the instance of the mother, who was guardian for nurture, the father being dead, and there being no testamentary guardian, although it was deposed that the child was of intelligence and wished on religious grounds to remain in the school, this Court refused to examine the child and ascertain its intelligence, holding that a guardian for nurture has a legal right to the custody of the ward, irrespective of the wishes of the ward, unless it be shown that the custody is sought for improper objects, or that the application is not bonâ fide, or that the guardian making the application is grossly immoral. And, in this case, no more appearing than that the father had been a Protestant, and that the mother was a Catholic, and intended to educate the child in her own persuasion, the Court ordered the child to be given to its mother.

A WRIT of habeas corpus ad subjiciendum, returnable at Chambers, to bring up the body of Alicia Race, an infant, issued by order of Coleridge, J., on 2d January, 1857, at the instance of Alicia Race, the mother of the infant. It was addressed to Maria Clarke. The return was, that the child was placed under the care of Miss Clarke by the Commissioners of the Royal Patriotic Fund; and that she did not detain, and never had detained, the child against its will. Crompton, J., at Chambers, referred the matter to the full Court.

Affidavits on both sides were used. By these it appeared that the child was born in July, 1846, and was therefore now between the age of ten and eleven. She was the daughter of Lanman Race, a sergeant in the Marines, who fell in the action at Petropaulowski in 1854, leaving a widow and two children, this girl and a boy. In 1855, the widow and orphans were selected as objects for the bounty of the Royal Patriotic Fund. The mother received an allowance; and the children were sent to school. The rule of the Commissioners is, in general, to send children to schools conducted by *persons of the same religious persuasion [*187 as the parents of the children. In this case the father had been a Protestant, and the mother was a Roman Catholic; the children had been baptized, and during the father's lifetime had gone to church, as members of the Church of England. This being so, they were sent by the Commissioners to Protestant schools, with the full concurrence of the mother, who at the time stated that her late husband had been a Protestant, and that she was one of those who thought there were as good Protestants as Catholics. Subsequently, in the latter part of 1856, she sought to take away the children for the avowed purpose of having them educated as Roman Catholics. It was suggested on the affidavits that this was really done by a priest in her name, and that the application was only colourably hers; but this was

distinctly denied by her on affidavit; and the Court acted on the belief
that in fact the application was really the mother's. The Commissioners
of the Royal Patriotic Fund, on the application being made, took the
matter into consideration, and consulted the wishes of the children.
The boy was desirous of returning to his mother; and she was permitted to remove him.   The girl expressed great repugnance to leaving
her present school, assigning as her reasons that, much as she loved her
mother, she would not go to a school where she would be taught idola-
trous worship of the Virgin and Saints.   There were numerous affidavits showing the belief of respectable persons that this wish of the child
was the unbiassed result of an intelligent religious conviction, and that
she was of intelligence beyond her years.   The Commissioners and
Miss Clarke, the schoolmistress, refused, under those circumstances,
*188]   *to give the girl to her mother.   This writ was obtained to com-
          pel them to do so.   It appeared, by the affidavits on which it
was obtained, that the father appointed no testamentary guardian, and
gave no directions in his will as to the manner in which his children
should be brought up.   He appointed his wife sole executrix of his
will in the following terms:—"I do hereby nominate, constitute, and
appoint my wife, Alicia Race, executor of this my last will and testament, feeling confident that she will do justice to my two children as a
wife and mother."   The following letter, received after the husband's
death, was also set out in the affidavits:

"H. M. S. Pique, at Sea, 25th August, 1854.

"My dear wife and children,—I now sit down to write a few lines to
you previous to going into action.   When you receive this I shall be no
more, as it will not be sent to you if I survive.   I hope you are all
quite well, as I am at the present time.   My dears, I write to bid you
an eternal farewell, if such be God's will that I am cut off: but I trust
in Providence, and hope I may be spared to meet you again: but, as we
cannot all expect to survive to tell the tale, and I may be one that is
doomed to die in defence of my Queen and country, therefore, my dear
wife, it will be a consolation that I died in defence of liberty, and done
my best as in duty bound by my oath when I took to the profession of
arms.   My dear Alicia, I have made my will to you; and I trust you
will carry it out according to my wish.   I wish, my dear, that you will
remain a widow until the children are capable of taking care of them-
*189]   selves.   I *hope, my dear, that you will not disregard this my
          last wish, as I should not die happy if I thought a stepfather
would be over my babes; but I feel confident that you will not forget
my last wish.   My dear wife, I have not received any letter from you
or any one else since I left England; I should feel very happy to hear
from you before I am called into eternity: but the Lord's will be done.
We must bow to His commands.   My dear Ally, I am but ill prepared
to meet my Maker face to face; but I trust He will have mercy on my

poor soul, and forgive me my transgressions as I forgive all men that have done me any wrong. Before I die I have settled all my worldly affairs as far as I can. My dear wife, kiss my dear children for me as a last embrace from a loving father, and tell them that his last thoughts were for them, and bring them up in the fear of the Lord. My dear wife, I think I see poor Alicia, by turns weeping for the loss of her poor old man, and then I see her rejoicing at his return; but, alas, such dreams! My dear, I have written a farewell letter to my mother, brothers, and sisters, and all friends and relations, and I trust you will not be forgotten by them. My dearest wife, give my dying love to your mother and sister, and all your friends that may befriend you or my dear children. May we all meet in Heaven is the last prayer of one that you know how to prize, although he will be in eternity when you receive this last letter he ever wrote, as we are only waiting for the morning dawn to go into Petropaulowski, and commence the work of destruction. It is a Russian colony; and we are about to take it or die in the attempt. My dear wife and children, it is late; and I require some rest before I commence the work of carnage that to-morrow may bring forth. My *dear, I have not set my foot on shore but [*190 twice since I left England, and then only for a few hours on duty. The last from your affectionate and loving husband, LANMAN RACE '

Nothing further appeared to indicate what the wishes of the father as to the education of his children had been, except that, as already stated, he habitually took them with him to the Established Church, and, on the other hand, that the mother taught them Roman Catholic prayers, without his making any objection. Counsel in opposition to the application argued, from the first of those facts, that he must have intended them to be Protestants; the mother's counsel argued from the other that he would not have approved of the misocatholic opinions indicated by the reasons assigned by the girl for her refusal to go home, and which had been, it was suggested, instilled into her in the process of unteaching these prayers, affording, it was said, a sufficient motive for the mother's interference. The judgment of the court, however, as will be seen, proceeded on grounds independent of either view. In this Term,(a)

Shee, Serjt., and *Finlason*, appeared for the mother, and submitted that, the child being under fourteen, the proper order for the court to make was, that the child should be delivered to the custody of her guardian for nurture, in this case the mother.

O'Malley and *Lush* for the schoolmistress, and *Bovill* for the Commissioners of the Patriotic Fund, contended that the wishes of the child should be respected.

The Court(a) expressed their opinion to be, that, if the wishes of a

(a) January 17th. Before Lord Campbell, C. J., Wightman and Crompton, Js.

*191]   child of that age, however intelligent, *could affect the rights of
the guardian by nurture, the court must, in each case, ascertain
whether there was sufficient intelligence by a personal examination of
the child: and they desired the counsel, in the first instance, to confine
their argument to the single question, whether the guardian for nurture
had a legal right to the custody of the ward, though against the wishes
of the ward, however intelligent; or whether the court was bound to
examine her.   On this point counsel were heard at length.

O'Malley and Bovill then further argued that, assuming that the
mother, as guardian for nurture, had a primâ facie right to the custody
of the child, in this case the custody was sought for an object improper
in itself, namely, to bring up the child in a faith different from that of
its deceased parent; and that this was not the bonâ fide application of
the mother; and therefore that the court would not assist the applicant.
Shee, Serjt., was heard in reply.

The arguments and authorities are so fully stated in the judgment as
to render a more detailed report unnecessary.   Cur. adv. vult.

Lord CAMPBELL, C. J., now delivered judgment.

In this case we are to determine what directions ought to be given by
the court respecting Alicia Race, an infant of the age of ten years and
a few months, brought up under a writ of habeas corpus granted at the
instance of her mother.   On the one side, it is contended that we ought
at once to order the child to be delivered to the mother; and, on the
other, that we should ask the child to make her election, whether to
*192]   go home with *her mother or to return to the school from which
her mother wishes to remove her.   It is not disputed that, the
father being dead without appointing a guardian, the mother is now
guardian for nurture: and it is laid down, Ratcliff's Case, 3 Rep. 37 a,
38 b, that guardianship for nurture continues till the child attains the
age of fourteen.   An observation was made that the commissioners of
the school are in loco parentis; but this was little relied upon, and is
wholly untenable.   As a general rule it is admitted that, if a child
under the age of seven years is so brought up, the court ought at once
to order the child to be delivered to the guardian.   But the contention
is that, between the ages of seven and fourteen, the court ought to
examine the child and ascertain whether it has mental capacity to
be competent to make a choice, and, according to the degree of mental
capacity which it is found to possess, to hand it over to the guardian,
or to liberate it and to desire it to go where it pleases.   With regard to
the maintenance of the poor, a rule has been introduced, that while a
child is under seven it shall not be separated from the mother for the
purpose of being maintained by the parish in which it is settled.   Again,
by Serjeant Talfourd's Act (2 & 3 Vict. c. 54, s. 1), it is enacted that,
where infants under the age of seven are in the sole custody or control
of the father, the Lord Chancellor or the Master of the Rolls may make

an order that such infants shall be delivered to and remain in the custody of the mother until they attain the age of seven years. Under seven is sometimes called the *age of nurture;* but this is the peculiar nurture required by a child from its mother, and is entirely different from *guardianship for nurture, which belongs to the father in his lifetime, even from the birth of the child. We can find [*193 no distinction in the books as to the rights and incidents of this species of guardianship from the time when it commences till the time when it expires. One of these incidents is that the guardian shall be entitled to the custody of the person of the child. Without such right he could not possibly perform the duties cast upon him as guardian. He is to *nurture* the child; the legal sense of this word is its natural and common sense in the English language, which, Dr. Johnson says, is "to educate; to train; to bring up." Accordingly, from the case to be found in the Year Book(*a*) to the present time, it has ever been considered that the father, or whoever else on his death may be the guardian for nurture, has by law a right to the custody of the child, and shall maintain an action of trespass against a stranger who takes the child. See the authorities, Com. Dig. *Gardian* (D.).

The question then arises, whether a habeas corpus be the proper remedy for the guardian to recover the custody of the child, of which he has been improperly deprived. Certainly the great use of this writ, the boast of English jurisprudence, is to set at liberty any of the Queen's subjects unlawfully imprisoned; and, when an adult is brought up under a habeas corpus, and found to be unlawfully imprisoned, he is to have his unfettered choice to go where he pleases. But, with respect to a child under guardianship for nurture, the child is supposed to be unlawfully imprisoned when unlawfully detained from the custody of the guardian; and when *delivered to him the child is sup- [*194 posed to be set at liberty. Rex *v.* De Manneville, 5 East, 221, clearly proves that such is the fit mode of proceeding if the child is under seven. Is there any reason for following a different course between seven and fourteen? The intellectual faculties of the child may be considerably developed in this interval; and the child may now have a very strong inclination to leave the home of the guardian, and, from religious as well as frivolous motives, to be educated at a different school from that which the guardian has selected. But the consequences which would follow from allowing such a choice are most alarming. We must lay down a rule which will be generally beneficial, although it may operate harshly in particular instances. If the proposed choice were given to the child, the relation of guardian and ward would still subsist; the guardian might retake the child wherever he finds it; and he might maintain an action against the person who, contrary to his wishes, takes or detains the child. Then, how could *nurture* be carried on with such

(*a*) Yearb. Mich. 8 Ed. 4, fol. 7 B. pl. 2.

a doctrine, which, if established, would apply to every father of a family in the kingdom, in respect of all his children, male and female, above the age of seven years? If a father wishes to take his son when ten years old from a private school where flogging is not practised, and send him to Eton, and the boy refuses to come home, and is brought up by habeas corpus, is he to be permitted to say that, on consideration, he is of opinion that the private school is preferable to any public school where flogging is permitted, and therefore he makes his choice to return to the private school, the master being willing to receive him? Or *195] *suppose that a Protestant mother, guardian for nurture of a daughter seven years of age, sends her to a boarding school professing to be a Protestant seminary; in a short time she finds that attempts have been successfully made by teachers there to convert the girl to the Roman Catholic faith; the girl refuses to come home, saying, in analogy to the language used by Alicia Race, "I will not go home to my own mother; I will stay here where I may pray to the Mother of God;" she is in consequence brought up by habeas corpus. Are we to examine her, and, finding her of quick parts and professing to be a sincere convert to the Roman Catholic faith, to tell her that, in spite of the wishes of her mother, she is at liberty to return to the school where she has been converted? Such a doctrine seems wholly inconsistent with parental authority, which both reason and revelation teach us to respect as essential for the welfare of the human race. Indeed, allusions were made during the argument at the bar to the workings of *prevenient grace,* and to the words of our Lord,(a) "Suffer little children, and forbid them not, to come unto me; for of such is the Kingdom of Heaven." It must be enough merely to say that the parental authority is in no degree weakened by such sacred doctrines or precepts; for it is impossible, without irreverence, to show more fully how irrelevant they are. This suggests the extreme inconvenience which would arise from the proposed examination of the child. If there is to be an examination, it ought to be conducted before all the Judges who are to take part in the adjudication; and, after testing her mental *196] acumen, we ought to ascertain whether it is upon *due investigation that she has imbibed a preference to Protestantism and such an aversion to the Roman Catholic faith.

When we look into our law books, although we do not find the exact age defined within which the Court, on a habeas corpus, will order the child to be delivered up to the parent or guardian without examination, we do find cases where this course has been adopted, the child being above seven years of age; and we find nothing to indicate that the rights of the guardian for nurture are in any respect impaired during the period of guardianship. In Rex *v.* Johnson, 1 Str. 579, 2 Ld. Raym. 1333, a female child, nine years old, was brought up by habeas

(a) Ev. Mat. xix. 14.

corpus in the custody of her nurse, having a testamentary guardian appointed by the father. The Court at first doubted whether they should go any farther than to see that the child was not under any illegal restraint; but afterwards declared that, this being the case of a young child who had no judgment of her own, they ought to deliver her to her guardian, although she was very unwilling to be taken from Mrs. Johnson, her nurse, who was her near relation and had cared for her very tenderly and disinterestedly. It was afterwards said, in Rex v. Smith, 2 Str. 982, that Lord Raymond, who had been a party to this judgment, repented of what he had done. But in his own report of the case he throws no discredit upon it; and Lord Mansfield afterwards expressed strong approbation of the case, and said that, if Lord Raymond had changed his mind, his first judgment was clearly the right one: Rex v. Delaval, 1 Sir W. Bl. 410, 418. It is unnecessary to travel through *the cases seriatim, as they are all reviewed [*197 in Rex v. Greenhill, 4 A. & E. 624 (E. C. L. R. vol. 31), where the Court laid down the rule that, where a young person under twenty-one years of age is brought before the Court by habeas corpus, if he be of an *age* to exercise a choice, the Court leaves the infant to elect where he will go, but, if he be not of that *age*, the Court must make an order for his being placed in the proper custody. Lord Denman, Littledale, J., Williams, J., and Coleridge, J., all make *age* the criterion, and not *mental* capacity, to be ascertained by examination. They certainly do not expressly specify the age: but they cannot refer to seven as the criterion; and there is no intervening age marking the rights or responsibility of an infant till fourteen, when guardianship for nurture ceases, upon the supposition that the infant has now reached the years of discretion.

When we attend to the authorities cited by the counsel for the commissioners, we find some vague dicta, and even some decisions, which, at first sight, give a colour to the doctrine of examination and choice under fourteen, but which admit of an explanation entirely consistent with the claim of the guardian. In Rex v. Smith, 2 Str. 982, Rex v. Johnson, 1 Str. 579, 2 Ld. Raym. 1333, is said to have been overruled, because a boy who had not completed his fourteenth year, being brought up by habeas corpus at the suit of the father, from the custody of an aunt with whom he wished to live, was set at liberty instead of being delivered up to his father, and was allowed to return to his aunt: but Lord Mansfield, in commenting upon this case, gives the true *ratio decidendi* upon which, *and upon which alone, it can be sup- [*198 ported. That case was determined right; "for the Court were certainly right in refusing to deliver the infant to the father; of whose design in applying for the custody of his child, they had a bad opinion;" Rex v. Delaval, 3 Burr. 1434, 1436. There is an admitted qualification on the right of the father or guardian, if he be grossly immoral, or if he wishes to have the child for any unlawful purpose.

The counsel for the commissioners relied much upon the case of In re Lloyd, 3 M. & G. 547 (E. C. L. R. vol. 42), where, the mother of an illegitimate child between eleven and twelve years of age having obtained a habeas corpus directed to the putative father to bring it up, the Court refused to order it to be delivered to the mother, and declared that it might use its own discretion; and, the child being unwilling to go with the mother, the Court would not allow the mother to take it by force. But Maule, J., there asked, "How does the mother of an illegitimate child differ from a stranger?" And, although the relation of the mother to her illegitimate child is recognised for some purposes, it is clear that she has not over it all the rights of guardian for nurture. From what was said by Lord Ellenborough, in Rex v. Hopkins, 7 East, 579, it would appear that it is only while an illegitimate child is under seven (an age during which the law of nature and the law of the land both say that the child, whether legitimate or illegitimate, ought not be separated from the mother) that the Courts will interfere to protect the custody of the mother. In In re Lloyd, 3 M. & G. 547, the child was considerably

*199] above that age. The only other decision much *relied upon as to the right of the parent or guardian on a habeas corpus was In re Preston, 5 D. & L. 233, where a most distinguished Judge refused to grant a writ of habeas corpus to bring up a legitimate child, above the age of seven, on the alleged application of the mother who had become guardian for nurture, the father being dead. But the application was made under a power of attorney, the mother remaining in the East Indies, so that the child could not have been delivered to her. The real opinion of my brother Patteson, upon this subject, we have fortunately an opportunity of knowing from a note of Sir Erskine Perry, late Chief Justice of Bombay, in a very interesting collection of "Oriental Cases" decided and published by him. A Parsee family having detained an infant child from its father, a Parsee, on the ground that the father had embraced the Christian religion, on a habeas corpus the Court had ordered the child to be given up to the father. In another case the Court, on habeas corpus, had ordered a Hindu boy, of twelve years of age, who professed to have embraced Christianity, to be delivered up to his father, who adhered to the Hindu religion; and the Judges refused to examine the boy as to his capacity and knowledge of the Christian religion. In similar cases the Supreme Court at Calcutta had followed a different course. There being no appeal in such matters to a higher Court, Sir Erskine Perry, for his subsequent guidance, very properly submitted the question to my brother Patteson, whose response was as follows: "I cannot doubt that you were quite right in holding that the father was entitled to the custody of his child, and enforcing it by writ of habeas corpus.   *The general law is [*200 clearly so, and even after the age of fourteen ; whereas this boy (Shripat) was only twelve.   The right may indeed be forfeited by mis- conduct of a very gross nature, but nothing of that kind appears to have been brought forward.   It may have been an act of imprudence ori- ginally in the father to place his boys with persons who were likely to bring them up in religious opinions and faith contrary to their father ; I suppose he made some stipulation for avoiding this ; but whether he did or not, I do not think that the law would be affected thereby.   Even if he had changed his mind on that subject, as well as on the education of his boys in other respects, I know of no law which forbids him to do so, or binds him to the arrangement which he had at first made."(a) For these reasons, and on these authorities, we are of opinion, in the present case, that primâ facie the mother is entitled as guardian for nurture to have her child delivered over to her.   Still she may have forfeited her right by prior immoral conduct, or by proof that she does not make the application bonâ fide, or by having some illegal act in view when she has obtained possession of the child.   According to Rex v. Greenhill, 4 A. & E. 624 (E. C. L. R. vol. 31), the immorality, to extinguish the right of the parent or guardian to the custody of the child, must be of a gross nature, so that the child would be in serious danger of contamination by living with him.   But here no immorality whatever is imputed to Mrs. Race ; and she seems to have been a virtu- ous woman, well deserving the ardent affection which her husband felt for her.   An attempt is made to show that in applying for this writ *she is a mere tool in the hands of others.   But, on carefully [*201 looking through the affidavits, we do not see that this charge is at all substantiated ; and we think that we are bound to give credit to what she swears as to the purity and sincerity of her motives.   In wish- ing to take her two children from these Protestant schools, she may act conscientiously although not prudently ; and, when the boy was allowed to go, she might not unnaturally desire to have the girl also that they might be educated together.   The answer to this application, if there be any, we think must rest upon the ground that the mother was under a legal obligation to educate her children in the Protestant faith, and that she now seeks to get possession of the daughter, with intention of following a course with her which the law forbids.   Had she been a testamentary guardian, and the will had directed that the children should be educated as Protestants, we should not have ordered the girl to be delivered up to the guardian—she intending to send the girl to a Roman Catholic seminary.   But she is guardian for nurture, with all the rights belonging to a mother as surviving parent.   The husband certainly was a Protestant ; his children had been baptized in the Anglican Church ; and he probably expected that they would be

(a) Regina v. Nesbitt, Perry's Cases illustrative of Oriental Life, &c., p. 103.   See p. 109.

brought up as Protestants. But his will is entirely silent upon this subject; and, in his most beautiful and affecting letter of 25th August, 1854 (showing him to have been a model of a Christian soldier), he appears to have had unbounded confidence in her, and to have left the education of the children entirely in her discretion. Indeed, by marrying a Roman Catholic, and by permitting the children in his lifetime to join in Roman Catholic prayers, he does not seem to have had the *horror of popery felt by many pious Protestants. Still, if the, proposition laid down can be supported, that it was her duty as guardian for nurture, from the simple fact of the father having been a Protestant, to educate the children as Protestants, she would be contemplating what the law forbids by wishing to remove the children from a Protestant to a Roman Catholic school. But no sufficient authority has been cited in support of this proposition; and, the mother becoming guardian for nurture on the death of the father, no provision to the contrary being made by will, she appears to us to have in all respects the same parental authority which might have been exercised by the father had he survived the mother. As the law stands, since the repeal of the statutes for persecuting papists, the question must be the same under the actual circumstances of this case as if the father had died a Roman Catholic, and the mother surviving had been a Protestant: would it, in that case, have been unlawful for the mother to have brought up the children as Protestants? The cases of Villareal *v.* Mellish, 2 Swanst. 533, and Talbot *v.* The Earl of Shrewsbury, 4 Myl. & Cr. 672, show that in such matters the Courts know of no distinction between different religions, and will not interfere with the discretion of guardians as to the faith in which they educate their wards. The authority relied upon, to show that the ward must invariably be educated in the religion of the father, is In re Arabella Frances North, 11 Jurist, 7, before Vice Chancellor Knight Bruce. That case arising jointly on a return to a habeas corpus, and on a petition for the appointment of a guardian to children as wards of the Court of Chancery, it is difficult to *distinguish what was done or said by the Vice Chancellor as a common law and as an equity Judge. He cannot be alleged to have *decided* anything upon this point; and he had only to consider it with a view of determining whether the children should for a few days, till a guardian was appointed, be in the custody of a Roman Catholic or of a Protestant nurse. He certainly does draw an inference of fact that the father died a Protestant, although, for some time before his death, he had conformed to the worship of the Roman Catholic church, and when dying he would not permit the ministration of a Protestant clergyman; and his Honour does express an opinion that, although the wife had been formally admitted into the Roman Catholic church, the children must be educated in the Protestant faith, the father having given no directions upon the subject by will. But this

*202]

*203]

doctrine, if well founded, would only apply to the education of wards of the Court of Chancery, respecting whom an equity Judge, representing the Queen, as *parens patriæ*, has a very large discretion, and may give directions beyond the scope of the duties of a guardian for nurture under the common law. Therefore, without venturing to question the dictum of so eminent a Judge (although it seems not altogether to accord with what was said by Lord Cottenham, C., in Talbot *v*. The Earl of Shrewsbury, 4 M. & C. 672, we do not think it enough to show that the mother of this infant, as guardian for nurture, was legally bound to educate the children as Protestants, or that she can be charged with an illegal purpose when intending to send them to a Roman Catholic school. The commissioners in detaining this *girl from her [*204 mother have no doubt acted from the most laudable motives; but they are wrong in point of law, in supposing that the mother, by committing the child to their care to be educated, has lost all right over her. In the case cited from the Year Books,(*a*) it was held that, "if a guardian, by reason of nurture, delivers the infant to another for instruction, he may afterwards retake the infant:" and this is vouched for good law by Lord Chief Baron Comyns in his Digest.

It might be every way much better for this child to remain in the school at Hampstead, which appears to be in all respects so admirably conducted; and we may individually deplore her removal from it; but upon this matter, as there is nothing contrary to law in contemplation, we have no jurisdiction to determine: and we think that we are bound, in the discharge of our official duty, to order that the infant, Alicia Race, be now delivered up to her mother. We trust that she will ever be treated by her mother with the affection and tenderness anticipated by her father in the letter which he wrote, when he foresaw that he was soon to fall in defence of his country.   Ordered accordingly.

(*a*) Yearb. Mich. 8 Ed. 4, fol. 7 B. pl. 2.

A child brought up on *habeas corpus* was ordered to be delivered to the mother where the return of the defendants stated that the child was put to them with the mother's consent, to live and remain with them until of full age, and that she wished to remain: The State *v*. Clover, 1 Harrison, 419.

*205]   *The QUEEN v. The Inhabitants of SAINT GILES IN
          THE FIELDS. *Jan.* 21.

By a local Act (11 G. 4 & 1 W. 4, c. x.), the landlords of houses in the parish of G., instead of
the occupiers, are to be rated to the relief of the poor if the assessable value of the house be
assessed at less than 30*l.* per annum. G. is within a borough. The occupier of a house in G.,
assessed at less than 30*l.*, claimed under the Reform Act to be rated, and was rated, and paid
the rates for three successive years; he did not during that period occupy the entire house.
Held, that he had acquired a settlement, under stat. 3 W. & M. c. 11, s. 6, by being charged with
the rates and paying them.

On appeal against an order of a Metropolitan police magistrate
removing Eliza Rushforth and her children from the parish of St.
Andrew Holborn to the parish of Saint Giles in the Fields, the Sessions
confirmed the rate, subject to a case of which the material facts are as
follows. The pauper Eliza Rushforth is the wife of one George Rushforth, who, in the year 1835, rented a tenement, being a separate and
distinct dwelling-house in the parish of Saint Giles in the Fields, at the
yearly rent of 44*l.* free of all rates and taxes, and rated at the yearly
value of 26*l.*, of one Spencer John Henry Hammond, the owner thereof,
which tenement the said George Rushforth occupied for a period of three
years, and paid the rent for the same during such period. He underlet
a portion of the tenement during all the time he so occupied it, and
therefore gained no settlement by renting a tenement: but the respondents relied upon a settlement, which they alleged George Rushforth
had gained by being charged with the poor's rate of the said parish of
Saint Giles in the Fields, in respect of the premises, during the years
1835, 1836, 1837, and 1838. It appeared that in 1835 a rate
was made in pursuance of the provisions of stat. 11 G. 4 & 1 W.
4, c. x.(a)

(a) Local and personal, public. "For the better regulation of the affairs of the joint parishes
of Saint Giles in the Fields and Saint George Bloomsbury, in the county of Middlesex, and of
the separate parishes of Saint Giles in the Fields and Saint George Bloomsbury in the same
county."

The following sections were referred to in the argument.

Section 86 empowers the vestry to make poor-rates "upon the several tenants or occupiers of
all lands, houses, buildings, tenements, and hereditaments within the said parishes or either of
them."

Sect. 88. "That all rates made by authority of this Act shall be paid by the tenant or occupier rated for the several lands, houses, buildings, tenements, or hereditaments," and in case of
non-payment may be levied by distress on the goods of the party neglecting to pay.

Sect. 89. In default of distress, the person liable to pay may be committed for three months.

Sect. 92. "That the several lessors, landlords, and owners of all lands, houses, tenements,
buildings, or hereditaments within the said parishes, or either of them, the yearly assessment
or valuation whereof respectively shall be less than 30*l.*, or which, whatever the yearly assessment or valuation may be, shall be let to weekly or monthly tenants," "shall and may from time
to time and at all times hereafter, be rated towards all rates to be made by authority of this Act,
for or in respect of such lands, houses, buildings, tenements, and hereditaments respectively,
instead of the actual occupiers thereof; and the persons so rated, whether the lessors, landlords,
or owners, or the occupiers thereof, shall from time to time pay" the rates.

Sect. 95. Provided "that the goods and chattels of all persons occupying any house," &c.,
"whereon the lessor, landlord, or owner thereof is hereby made liable as aforesaid, although the
person or persons occupying any such house or other premises or any part thereof, be not rated

*The following is an extract from the rate book.   [*206

No. of House.	Persons Rated.	Assessment or Valuation.	Amount due.	No. of Receipt.	Received up to Lady Day.	Remarks.
15	George Rushforth. Spencer John Henry Hammond.	£26	£1. 6s.	620	£1. 6s.	George Rushforth claims to be rated under the Reform Act, 7th February, 1835

In the two following rates, bearing date 6th November, 1835, and 7th April, 1836, both names were inserted in like manner, as appears by the following extracts from the rate books.

Name of Person rated.	Description of Premises for which they are rated.	Assessment or annual Value.	Sum Assessed.	No. of Receipt.	Received up to Michaelmas.	Midsummer.
Rushforth George Spencer John Henry Hammond	No. 15 Great White Lion Street.	£26	£1. 6s.	622	£1. 6s.	£— 1s.

Name of Person rated.	Description of Premises for which they are rated.	Assessment or annual Value.	Sum Assessed.	No. of Receipt.	Received up to Lady Day.
Spencer John Henry Hammond Rushforth Geo.	Premises situate No. 15 White Lion Street.	£26	£1. 3s. 10d.	619	£1. 3s. 10d.

*In all the subsequent rates during the occupation of the said [*207 George Rushforth, namely in those bearing date the 5th November, 1836, 28th April, 1837, 10th November, 1837, 12th May, 1838, and 9th November, 1838, the name of Rushforth did not appear, and the name of the owner was alone inserted. At the several times of making the rates from which extracts are above given, Spencer John Henry Hammond was owner, and George Rushforth was his tenant, and occupier of the house in respect of which the assessments were made. The reason why the name of George Rushforth was inserted in each of the rates in which such name appears *was that he had made a claim [*208 under the Reform Act, as mentioned under the head " remarks"

under or by virtue of this Act, shall be at all times liable to be distrained" "for any rate which may have accrued or become due during the term of the occupancy of such persons," and costs ; " but no such person shall be liable to the payment of a greater sum for or towards the discharge of the said rates and expenses, or any of them, than the amount of rent actually due and payable by such persons to the lessor," &c. ; and such payments may be deducted from the rent.

in the first rate. George Rushforth paid each of the above rates: and, if, by such insertion of his name in each or either of such rates, he was charged with the same, he paid the same and did every other act necessary to acquire a settlement by being so charged. The appellants contended that the said George Rushforth was not charged by such entry of his name, and that under the provisions of stat. 11 G. 4 & 1 W. 4, c. x., s. 92, which Act is to be taken as part of this case, the owner alone could by law be charged with the payment of such rates; the same being imposed in respect of property under the annual value of 30*l.* : that such owner was in fact the only person charged in and by them, and legally liable to pay the same. The Court of Quarter Sessions confirmed the said order, subject to the opinion of this court.

The question for the opinion of this court is : Whether, under the circumstances above stated, · the said George Rushforth was legally charged with his share of the public rates of the said parish of Saint Giles so as thereby to gain a settlement in such parish? If this court should decide the question in the affirmative, the order of Sessions confirming the order of removal is to be confirmed; if in the negative, both the said orders are to be quashed : and, by consent of the appellants and respondents, in either event no costs are to be paid by either party to the other.

Huddleston, in support of the order of Sessions.—The local Act (11 G. 4 & 1 W. 4, c. x.) permits the vestry to rate the landlord in such cases as the present ; but it does not make it imperative on them not ***209]** to rate the occupier : *but it is not necessary to inquire how that is ; for the Reform Act (2 & 3 W. 4, c. 45), sect. 30, enacts that the occupier of any building within a borough may claim to be rated in respect of it, " whether the landlord shall or shall not be liable to be rated to the relief of the poor in respect thereof:" and that on such claim he shall be so rated : with the proviso that in such cases as the present the landlord shall remain liable to pay the rates in case the tenant makes default. The occupier here was actually rated ; and he actually paid : it is not material whether he was rated under the provisions of the one Act or the other. Under the local Act, sect. 95, the goods of the occupier, though not rated, might be taken under a distress ; so that, independently of the Reform Act, he was charged with and paid the rates ; and that is all that is required by stat. 3 W. & M. c. 11, s. 6 ; Regina *v.* Marylebone, 15 Q. B. 399 (E. C. L. R. vol. 69).

Clerk, contrà.—The local Act makes it imperative in such cases as the present to rate the landlord : and, though, by sect. 95, the goods of the occupier may be distrained, it is only to the extent of the rent due to the landlord ; so that the landlord, and not the occupier, is the person charged. And the Reform Act was not intended to affect the settlements, but only the franchise. [Lord CAMPBELL, C. J.—That might be the object of the Legislature; but still the enactment makes the rating of the occupier compulsory.]

Lord CAMPBELL, C. J.—My opinion is that Rushforth was charged with the rate. I think that the local Act *gives no option; [*210 and that, whilst it was the only Act regulating the matter, the occupier of such premises could not be rated. But the Reform Act gave the occupier a right to be rated; he claimed to be so; and he was rated. And, being so, he was charged.

WIGHTMAN, J.—The Reform Act, in express terms, made it compulsory to rate the occupier on his claim to be rated. And, though, by a proviso, the landlord is not free from liability to pay the rates on default of the occupier, I find nothing to exempt the occupier from the payment of the rates enforced against him as against any other person rated. But I give no opinion as to that; for it is not necessary. I think it enough that he was rated, and so charged, and that, being charged, he paid the rates.

ERLE, J., concurred.

(CROMPTON, J., was absent.)

GEORGE PEMBERTON, Executor of SARAH SHUTER, v. JOHN CHAPMAN, Public Officer of the Union Bank of London. *Jan. 22.*

Payment, by a debtor of a testator, and delivery of chattels bailed by the testator, by the bailee, to a feme covert who is appointed executrix, are valid as against the co-executor, though the husband of the executrix never assented to his wife acting as executrix, and, subsequently to the payment, refused to allow her to act, and although on that ground probate was refused to her; if the payment and delivery were made bonâ fide at the request of the executrix as such, without knowledge of the dissent of the husband, though with knowledge that she was a feme covert.

THE first count was in the ordinary form by the plaintiff as executor for money had and received, and lent to the copartnership, in the life of the testatrix. *There was also a count in trover by the plain- [*211 tiff, as executor, for bonds and securities for money, converted by the bank since the death of the testatrix.

Plea 3, to the first count: That Sarah Shuter by her last will constituted and appointed one Sarah McGill and the plaintiff executrix and executor thereof, and that, after the death of the testatrix, the said Sarah McGill " took upon herself the burthen of the execution thereof; and, afterwards and before action, the said copartnership satisfied and discharged the plaintiff's claim, in respect of the matters herein pleaded to, by payment to the said Sarah McGill as such executrix, at her request."

Plea 6, to the whole declaration, averred the appointment of Sarah

McGill as executrix, and her taking upon herself the burthen of the execution of the will, as in plea 3, and then proceeded: "and, afterwards and before action, the said copartnership satisfied and discharged the plaintiff's claim in respect of the first count, by payment to the said Sarah McGill as such executrix, at her request, and delivered to her as such executrix, and at her request, the said bonds and securities for money in the last count mentioned, which is the supposed conversion thereof in the last count mentioned, and all which moneys so paid to her by the said copartnership, and bonds and securities for money so delivered to her by the said copartnership, the said Sarah McGill hath duly administered."

Replication 2, to plea 3: That, before and at the time of the making of the last will of the testatrix, and from thence hitherto, the said Sarah McGill was the wife of one Peter McGill, who is still alive; that she was appointed executrix without the knowledge or consent of the said Peter McGill, and that he never took upon himself, or on Sarah, his *212] wife, the execution of the will; and never *in any way consented to Sarah, his wife, taking on herself, or him, the execution of the said will, and wholly departed therefrom. That Peter McGill never in any manner administered, or consented to Sarah, his wife, ever in any manner administering, any of the goods and chattels which were of the testatrix to be administered. That, after the death of the testatrix, probate was granted by the Archbishop of Canterbury to the plaintiff alone; that it was always refused to Sarah McGill, although she applied to be joined in the probate; and that the payment by the copartnership was voluntarily made to the said Sarah McGill, without the knowledge or consent of Peter McGill and of the plaintiff, or either of them, the copartnership, at the time the payment was made, well knowing that Sarah McGill was a married woman.

Replication 1, to so much of plea 6 as relates to count 1: Similar to replication 2 to plea 3, with the additional averment that Sarah McGill had not duly administered as in the sixth plea alleged.

Replication 2, to so much of plea 6 as relates to the count in trover, similar to the replication to the first part of that plea, except that an averment that the bonds were delivered voluntarily, and with notice of the coverture, was substituted for the averment that the payment was so made.

Demurrers to each of these three replications.   Joinders.

The case was argued in last Michaelmas Term.(a)

Rochfort Clarke, for the defendants.—On this record it is admitted *213] that Sarah McGill, who was appointed *executrix, acted as such; and that the payment and delivery by the copartnership was to her as executrix.   It is true that, where an executrix, as in this case,

(a) Friday, November 7th, 1856. Before Lord Campbell, C. J., Coleridge, Wightman, and Erle, Js.

is a feme covert, she ought not to administer without her husband's assent. But, if she does so administer in fact, the husband and wife are estopped from pleading that she is not executrix; 1 Williams on Executors (4th ed.), p. 190, note (a), where many authorities are collected. In addition to those, the same doctrine is laid down in Com. Dig. *Administration* (D), *Baron and Feme* (P 3). [Lord CAMPBELL, C. J.—All these appear to be cases against the husband and wife, showing that there was an estoppel against them: not cases between the personal representative and a debtor.] The objection to a feme covert proving a will without her husband's assent is personal to the husband; if he is estopped, it is disposed of. The co-executor has no right to set up the dissent of the husband against the will of the testatrix, who intended the wife to be executrix. It appears on this record that everything concurs to make her personal representative, except that after she acted probate was refused to her. But " the executor has the right immediately on the death of the testator, and the right draws after it a constructive possession. The probate is a mere ceremony, but, when passed, the executor does not derive his title under the probate, but under the will: the probate is only evidence of his right, and is necessary to enable him to sue; but he may release, &c., before probate:" Smith v. Milles, 1 T. R. 475, 480. If the executor be himself a debtor to the estate and die before probate, after taking on himself the burthen of the execution, the *debt is discharged: Wankford v. Wank- [*214 ford, 1 Salk. 299. It is sufficient for the decision of this case to say that the feme covert was executrix till her husband dissented; if this were not so there would be great inconvenience. Lord Denman, C. J., said, delivering judgment in Whitehead v. Taylor, 10 A. & E. 210 (E. C. L. R. vol. 37): " the law knows no interval between the testator's death and the vesting of the right in his representative:" but, if the husband were in Australia, a long interval might elapse before it was known whether he would or would not assent to his wife acting. In that interval the Statute of Limitations would continue to run; yet no payment could be safely made to the wife till he assented: and she might be the sole executrix: and this could not be supplied by a grant of letters of administration, which, when there is a will, cannot be granted, at least not till there has been a refusal by the executrix: Venables v. East India Company, 2 Exch. 633, 647.† If the co-executrix had been joined as plaintiff, the pleas would have been clearly good, and the replication no answer. Perhaps she should have been joined: Hensloe's Case, 9 Rep. 36 b; Creswick v. Woodhead, 4 M. & G. 811 (E. C. L. R. vol. 43).

H. Hill, contrà.—The authorities cited show clearly that a person appointed executor, if sui juris, is executor before probate. But the law is accurately stated in 1 Williams on Executors (4th ed.), p. 190: " A married woman may be appointed an executrix, and according to

the canon law (in which there is no distinction between women married
and unmarried, but the wife may sue and be sued alone), she may take
*215] upon her *the probate without the assent of her husband. But
by the law of England, husband and wife are considered but as
one person, and as having one mind, which is placed in the husband, as
most capable to rule and govern the affairs of the family; and therefore
the wife can do no act which may prejudice the husband, without his
consent: consequently, the wife cannot, by our law, take upon her the
office of executrix, without the consent of the husband." And the
distinction between the law of England and the canon law, in this
respect, is fully proved by the authorities. Godolphin, Orphan's
Legacy, Part 2, c. 10, s. 2, says: "As a wife named or appointed
executrix in a will, may not be compelled unto the execution thereof,
without her own and her husband's consent; so neither shall she assume
or accept such executorship, without her husband's consent and approbation, because it is in his power to oppose and hinder it." If probate
had been taken out by the wife, it must have been presumed to have
been taken out with his assent: Adair *v.* Shaw, 1 Sch. & Lefroy, 243,
266. The author of The Office of Executor, p. 377, 8 (14th ed.),
thinks that this would be conclusively presumed, and that the husband
would be estopped from showing the contrary. But in the present case
there was no probate: the wife took the assets; but it is stated on the
record that the husband did not know, and did not assent to her doing
so. There is no principle on which the husband should be estopped on
such a ground. The only authority for it is a passage in The Office of
Executor (14th ed.), p. 378, where it is said: "And I doubt whether
the wife administering without the husband's privity and assent, though
the will be not proved, do not conclude her husband as well as herself
*216] from saying after, in any suit against them, that she *neither
was executor, nor did ever administer as executor. Yet perhaps
this administration by the wife, against her husband's mind, will (as
against him) be as a void act; else I cannot see how Brian's opinion
before cited, viz., that the wife shall not be executor without or against
her husband's mind, can be law." The opinion of Brian referred to is
in the Year Book,(a) and is as follows: "Semble, that the action does
not lie. For a wife cannot be executrix without the assent of her husband during the coverture; and for the same reason that she cannot be
executrix without his assent, she cannot dispose of the assets without
assent of her husband. And if it so were that a *devastaverunt* were
returned, the goods of the husband would be taken in execution: Ergo,
she cannot any single thing do, &c. And a wife cannot give an acquittance without her husband: but in the law spiritual she can be executrix
without assent of her husband, and for the same reason she can perform the legacies and spiritual things without the assent of her husband."

(a) Year Book, 2 H. 7, fol. 15 B. pl. 23.

The opinion of Brian, that the wife cannot give an acquittance without her husband's assent, is precisely in point. The same doctrine is repeated in Wankford v. Wankford, 1 Salk. 299, 306, and Thrustout dem. Levick v. Coppin, 2 W. Bl. 801. [ERLE, J.—Though the wife might not be able to make her husband liable without his assent by taking payment from the testator's debtor, does it follow that the debtor may be made to pay twice?] If not, the estate of the testator is prejudiced; for the wife cannot be made to account for what she has taken, without joining the husband.

R. *Clarke* was heard in reply.   *Cur. adv. vult.*

*Lord CAMPBELL, C. J., now delivered judgment.   [*217

As far as the facts of this case appear upon the pleadings, it is to be assumed that the plaintiff was appointed executor, and Mrs. McGill (a married woman) executrix, of the will of the testatrix, without the knowledge and assent of Mrs. McGill's husband, who never administered himself nor consented to her administering; that she endeavoured to obtain probate, but was refused, and probate was granted to the plaintiff; and that the debt was paid, and the securities delivered voluntarily, by the defendant to Mrs. McGill, at her request as executrix, they knowing that she was a married woman. It is also to be assumed, as far as the sixth plea is concerned, that Mrs. McGill has not duly administered the debt or securities paid and delivered to her by the defendants; but it is also to be assumed that the payment and delivery was made by the defendants to Mrs. McGill as executrix, before her husband dissented from her administering, and before probate was refused to her and obtained by the plaintiff, and without any knowledge by the defendants that the husband had dissented, or that probate had been refused to her.

Under these circumstances the question is, Whether the defendants can successfully resist the claim of the plaintiff, who has alone obtained probate, on the ground of having paid and delivered the debt and securities to an executrix appointed by the will, before probate and without the assent of her husband?

The right of an executor to the personal estate of the testator is derived from the will; and the property in the personal goods and chattels of the testator is vested in him immediately upon the testator's death: and he is deemed to be in legal possession of them from that *time, though before probate granted; Smith v. Milles, 1 T. R. [*218 480, Plowd. 281, 2 Inst. 398; and he may pay and receive debts, and commence actions, before probate: and, if there are several executors appointed by the will, they ought all to join in such actions, though some do not prove the will before declaring, or even refuse to do so; for they may come in and prove at any time: Brookes v. Stroud, 1 Salk. 3, Hensloe's Case, 9 Rep. 36 b.

There is no doubt but that a married woman may be appointed an

executrix during coverture; and, immediately upon the death of the
testator, the property in his personal goods would be vested in her.
And it is said by Swinburne (Treatise of Testaments, &c., Part VI. s.
3, p. 417, 6th ed.; vol. 2, p. 751, 7th ed.) that, though a feme covert
executrix cannot sue alone without her husband, she may do an act
extrajudicial, as receive a debt due to the testator; but it is also said
that, by common law, she cannot administer or take upon herself the
duties of an executrix without the assent of her husband, as he must
be joined in all actions by or against her, and she cannot without his
assent do an act which may make him liable for a devastavit: Office of
Executor, 381 (14th ed.). And accordingly, in Taylor *v.* Allen, 2 Atk.
213, a feme covert executrix, whose husband was abroad, was retained
by the Court of Chancery from getting in the assets, and a receiver
with power to sue was appointed. But, though a feme covert executrix
cannot maintain an action without her husband, nor obtain probate, nor
take upon herself the general administration of the estate, without the
*219] assent of her *husband, yet as she may do all these with the
assent of her husband, and the testator's personal estate is immediately upon his death vested in her, and the husband may, at any time,
assent to her acting as executrix (which assent, if given, would have
relation back), there is no authority or principle of law, of which we
are aware, to warrant the conclusion that the bonâ fide payment of a
debt to a feme covert executrix, at her request as such, before probate,
and without any knowledge by the debtor of non-assent by the husband,
is void as against a co-executor of the feme covert, who has subsequently obtained probate without her, or that it is voidable at *his* election, though the payment to her might be made good at any time by
the husband's subsequent assent, and her obtaining probate.

It is settled that the devastavit of one of several executors does not
affect the others who took no part in the receipt of the assets: and the
plaintiff, in the present case, would not incur any liability in consequence of the receipt of the debt from the defendants by Mrs. McGill
(the executrix), even if she were guilty of a devastavit, which does not
appear to have been the case, it being only alleged that she has "not
duly administered," which would be fulfilled by proof of assets in her
hands unadministered.

The defendants, when they paid the debt and delivered the securities
to the executrix, at her request as such, might well presume that she
had the assent of the husband: and, if the present plaintiff could, under
the circumstances as they appear upon the pleadings, maintain this
action, the defendants might be obliged to pay the same debt twice to
the personal representatives of the testator, as the first payment to the
*220] executrix might *be affirmed by the assent of the husband and
her taking out probate.

Upon the whole, we are of opinion that judgment should be entered for the defendants upon the special replications to the 3d and 6th pleas which have been demurred to.   Judgment accordingly.

———◆———

The QUEEN v. DUNN, GRAHAM, and SAMPSON. *Jan.* 22.

Under stat. 3 & 4 W. 4, c. 90, a meeting of the rated inhabitants of the parish of H. was held, to determine whether the provisions of the Act should be applied to the parish. The assent of as much as two-thirds of the voters was not given. Within a year, a meeting was held of the rated inhabitants of a district of the parish, to determine whether the Act should be applied to that district; when two-thirds of the voters assented. A rate was laid upon the district in conformity with this.

S., one of the parties so rated, having refused to pay the rate, was summoned before the justices, when he objected that, the latter meeting having been held within a year of the former, the proceedings were void by sect. 16, and the rate invalid. The parties agreed that the question was whether the two meetings were substantially the same. The justices decided in the affirmative, and refused a warrant for levying.

Held, that the question was properly put before the magistrates, and that, they having determined it, the Court could not, on a rule to order the justices to issue a distress warrant, review their decision.

Although S. had, before he was aware of the objection, paid a rate.

PASHLEY, in this Term, obtained a rule calling on John Roberts Dunn and Reginald John Graham, Esquires, two justices of Sussex, and Richard King Sampson, to show cause why the said two justices should not issue their warrant to levy by distress and sale of the goods and chattels of the said R. K. Sampson, an inhabitant rate-payer of the parish of Hailsham in the said county, the several sums of 1*l.* 12*s.* 5½*d.* and 1*l.* 10*s.* 0½*d.*, assessed upon him by two several rates, allowed, respectively, the 5th September, 1855, and the 17th September, 1856, under and by virtue of stat. 3 & 4 W. 4, c. 90, for the purposes of carrying into effect so much of the *provisions of the said Act as   [*221 relates to lighting part of the said parish.

The following facts appeared from the affidavit on which the rule was obtained.

On 11th November, 1853, a meeting of the rate-payers of the parish of Hailsham was held, in pursuance of due notice, for the purpose of determining whether so much of the provisions as relate to lighting contained in stat. 3 & 4 W. 4, c. 90, (" to repeal An Act of the eleventh year of His late Majesty King George the Fourth, for the lighting and watching of parishes in England and Wales, and to make other provisions in lieu thereof") should be adopted and carried into execution in the parish of Hailsham. At this meeting, the consent of two-thirds of the rate-payers for the adoption of the provisions of the Act was not obtained. On 18th November, 1853, there was delivered to one of the churchwardens of the parish a notice addressed to the two churchwardens, dated 17th November, 1853, and signed by three inhabitant rate-payers of the aftermentioned part of the parish, to the effect that the undersigned "do hereby request that you will appoint and

notify, pursuant to the statute 3 & 4 W. 4, c. 90, ss. 5 and 73, or one of
them, a time and place for a public meeting of the rate-payers and rated
inhabitants of that part of the said parish of Hailsham comprised in a
circle of half a mile on every side of the centre of the Market Square
of Hailsham, as drawn on the Hailsham parish map, from the centre
of the said Market Square, for the purpose of determining whether so
much of the provisions as relate to lighting contained in a certain Act"
&c., (3 & 4 W. 4, c. 90), "shall be adopted and carried into execution
*222] in the said part of the said parish." The two *churchwardens
signed a notice, dated 19th November, 1853, reciting the above
application, and stating that they appointed " a public meeting of the
rate-payers and rated inhabitants of the said part of the said parish to
be held at The George Inn in Hailsham, on Thursday the 1st day of
December, at six o'clock in the evening, for the purpose of determining
whether," &c. (as in the application).   One of these notices was affixed
to the principal door in the only parish church in Hailsham, on Sunday,
20th November, 1853.   A meeting of the rate-payers and rated inhabitants of that part of the parish was held at the time and place assigned:
when the chairman read over the requisition at the meeting, and "required the persons assembled thereat to determine, by a majority of
votes, whether so much of the provisions of the said Act as relate to
lighting should, or should not, be adopted and acted upon within the
said part of the said parish." Thirty-three (including two persons named
Thomas Colbron and Philip Piper) of the persons present at the meeting voted in the affirmative ; three, including a person named George
Fears, in the negative; the chairman not voting either way.   And it
was deposed, on belief, that no other person was present at the meeting entitled to vote who did not vote. Three inspectors were appointed
unanimously.   It was then carried, by a majority of forty-two to two,
that the total amount which the inspectors should have power to call
for in the succeeding year should be 60*l*.   The affidavits then asserted
the qualifications of all the voters, and of the inspectors, except that
Thomas Colbron had not been rated to the poor-rate, and Philip Piper
and George Fears had not paid all the highway-rates which had become
*223] due more than six months before the meeting.   *The church-
wardens signed a notice, dated 3d December, 1853, announcing
the resolutions passed; and a copy thereof was affixed to the door of
the church within ten days of the date.   On 16th December, 1853, the
inspectors appointed a treasurer, who gave security for the due execution of his office.   On 21st December, 1853, the inspectors, by written
notice, required the overseers to collect the sum of 60*l*., and pay it to
the treasurer ; and a rate was made accordingly, and afterwards allowed
by two justices, and notice thereof given. In this rate R. K. Sampson was
assessed; and he paid the rate accordingly.   Afterwards, in pursuance
of notices duly given, the accounts of the said inspectors were examined

and passed at a meeting of the rated inhabitants of the said part of the parish, held on 1st December, 1854; when also inspectors were appointed for the year following, and it was determined that the inspectors should have power to call for 60*l.* Afterwards, in pursuance of this, and by order of the inspectors, a rate was made on the said part of the parish, which was allowed; and notice thereof given, and duly affixed to the church. In this rate R. K. Sampson was assessed; and the sum due from him in respect of the rate would be 1*l.* 12*s.* 5½*d.*: he had not appealed. Similar proceedings took place in the year commencing 1st December, 1855; and a rate was made, in respect of which the sum due from R. K. Sampson would be 1*l.* 10*s.* 0½*d.* He had not appealed against this rate. He refused to pay either the 1*l.* 12*s.* 5½*d.* or the 1*l.* 10*s.* 0½*d.* The assistant overseer summoned him before the justices of the county for non-payment. It was deposed that the whole parish of Hailsham contains about 5283 acres of land, and that, in November, 1853, the parties rateable to the poor-rate in the parish were *about 210, and the rateable [*224 value of the property in the parish was about 7117*l.*; but that the part of the parish in question contains about 503 acres; and, in November, 1853, the parties rated were about 96, and the rateable value of property was about 1646*l.* That the said part comprises the whole of the town of Hailsham, and a small portion of the land surrounding the town; and the residue of the parish consists almost entirely of farms and marsh land. The summons was attended on 10th December, 1856, before Mr. Dunn and Mr. Graham only, and was then partly heard, and was adjourned to 24th December; on which day the hearing was resumed before the same justices only. The attorney for R. K. Sampson then " objected that the said rates sought to be recovered against the said R. K. Sampson were illegal and void, and that the meeting of the part of the said parish held on the said 1st day of December, 1853, was illegal, on account of a meeting of the whole parish having been held on the 11th day of November in the same year, as hereinbefore mentioned. Whereupon evidence was produced, on behalf of the overseers of the said parish, showing the difference, in the respects above mentioned, between the whole of the said parish and the said part of the said parish (except as to the number of acres of the whole of the said parish and of the said part of the said parish, evidence whereof could have been given; but the said justices intimated it was unnecessary to go into any further evidence); and the said justices were informed that the said R. K. Sampson had paid the amount of the first rate to which he had been assessed, as hereinbefore mentioned. The said justices, however, dismissed the said summons, and stated they did so because they considered that the last meeting was void *on account of [*225 having been held within a year of the first meeting."

In answer, James George Langham deposed that he appeared on both occasions before the justices as the attorney of R. K. Sampson, and that Henry Charles Sinnock appeared as attorney for the assistant overseer. That evidence of the different meetings was given. That Langham asked Stephen Breads, a witness called on behalf of the assistant overseer, "whether the circle of half a mile on every side of the centre of the Market Square of Hailsham did not comprise the great bulk of the inhabitants of the said parish of Hailsham, to which the said Stephen Breads replied that it did. And thereupon I submitted to the said justices that the question for them to consider was, whether the persons convened to the meeting of the 11th day of November, 1853, and those convened to the meeting of the 1st day of December, 1853, were substantially the same body; and that, if they should be of opinion that they were, then I submitted that the said meeting of the first day of December, 1853, was illegal, and the proceedings thereat void. Whereupon the said H. C. Sinnock agreed that the question to be decided by the said justices was, whether the said two meetings were substantially the same or not; and he contended that they were substantially different: and he proceeded to adduce evidence to show the rateable value of the entire property comprised in the said parish, as compared with the rateable value of the property comprised within the said circle of half a mile, and also to show the number of persons rated to the poor in respect of property comprised within the said parish, and within the said circle *respectively. Whereupon *226] some of the said witnesses stated that several of the persons who were rated in respect of property situate within the said parish, but beyond the said circle, were not inhabitants of the said parish, but resided elsewhere. And the said justices, after some time spent in considering the said question, gave their decision, which was recorded by their clerk in writing, and signed by the said justices: and the following is a copy of such decision.

" ' The justices are of opinion that the meeting held on the 11th November, 1853, and the meeting held 1st December, 1853, are substantially the same, and consider that the second meeting, being held within twelve months of the first meeting, is therefore contrary to the Act of Parliament; and consequently void. And the summons is therefore dismissed. J. ROBERTS DUNN, REGINALD J. GRAHAM.' "

The affidavits in opposition also stated some other facts inconsistent with or qualifying the affidavits on the other side: and R. K. Sampson deposed that he had paid the first rate in ignorance of the Act not having been properly adopted; adding statements to show that he derived no benefit from the lighting.

Lush now showed cause.—By sect. 16 of stat. 3 & 4 W. 4, c. 90, where a meeting has refused to adopt the Act, "it shall not be lawful for the inhabitants to meet again in less than one year from the period at which such meeting shall have been so convened as aforesaid." The question therefore is, whether the second meeting was a meeting substantially of the same body as that which met before ; and this is a question of fact ; as was *ruled at Nisi Prius by Cresswell, J., [*227 in a case reported in The Law Times, Wilkinson *v.* Grey.(a) Then the question, being one of fact, was for the justices to decide : and the Court will not review the decision. It is clear that the provision might be evaded, by calling a second meeting colourably different from the first.

The Court then called on

Pashley, contrà.—The question was, properly, not on the identity of the two meetings, but on the identity of the two areas to which the proposals related. The two questions discussed at the two meetings were entirely different : the same person might consistently have voted against the adoption of the Act on one occasion, and in favour of it on the other. It is as if the meetings had been held in respect of distinct townships. The first meeting could not have authorized the application of the Act in the limited district only. It is said that the magistrates have decided the question of fact : but it appears that they could not have had the real question before them. [WIGHTMAN, J.—But the affidavits show that both parties agreed as to what the question was.] The case is not to be decided as between party and party : if it be, then Sampson, having paid a rate, is estopped from disputing the authority.

Lord CAMPBELL, C. J.—If the fact had come out that the party had paid the rate with full knowledge, I should have felt a strong inclination to make the rule absolute. But we cannot do so, consistently with the rule of law *which prevails in this class of cases. Could we [*228 have granted a mandamus to compel the magistrates to issue their warrant, when they, in the exercise of their jurisdiction, had found a fact which makes the rate bad ?

COLERIDGE, J.—I am of the same opinion. The impression upon my mind at present is that the decision to which the magistrates have come upon the question of fact is wrong ; but we cannot interfere. The question was rightly put to them, whether the two bodies were substantially the same ? It is possible that they may have taken this in the wrong sense : but we cannot disturb what has been done. When magistrates refuse to hear, we may compel them to proceed : but, when they have heard, we cannot entertain the question whether they have decided wrongly.

WIGHTMAN, J.—The magistrates have clearly heard that which the parties agreed to be the question : and they have acted within their jurisdiction, even if their decision is wrong, which I would not now say.

(CROMPTON, J., was absent.)

Lord CAMPBELL, C. J.—Mr. *Pashley's* clients are not precluded from applying to other magistrates.   Rule discharged.

(a) 1 Law Times, 598.

*229]   *JOSEPH DAVISON *v.* WILLIAM ELLIOTT DUNCAN
                    and Another.   *Jan.* 23.

The publication of matter defamatory of an individual is not privileged because the libel is contained in a fair report in a newspaper of what passed at a public meeting.

COUNT for a libel on the plaintiff published in the Durham County Advertiser.   The libel was set out.   It commenced "West Hartlepool Improvement Commission.   At a meeting of the commissioners held 7th October, Present," &c.: it then purported to give an account of the proceedings of the meeting, in the course of which a license from the Bishop of Durham to a gentleman, as chaplain of the West Hartlepool Cemetery, was laid before the commissioners.   Various commissioners commented on this, and in so doing used injurious expressions regarding the plaintiff, who, it appeared, had been the late bishop's secretary, and whom they accused of procuring the license by misrepresentations to the present bishop.

Plea: "That, before the printing or publishing of the said supposed libel, the said meeting of the West Hartlepool Improvement Commissioners in the said libel mentioned was held as therein stated, and the same was a public meeting of the commissioners, acting under the powers of the West Hartlepool Improvement Act, 1854, and was held for the purpose of putting that Act into execution; and the facts, matters, circumstances, and things in the said libel stated and alleged to have taken place and happened at that meeting did take place and happen as therein so stated and alleged; and the said libel contains, and is, a
*230]   just, true, faithful, *correct, and accurate report and account of the proceedings, facts, circumstances, matters, and things which occurred and took place at the said meeting; and there was no malice on the defendants' part in printing and publishing; and therefore, they printed and published the same."   Demurrer.   Joinder.

Manisty, in support of the demurrer.—It is to be taken on this record that the dialogue took place, and imputations were made by the speakers injurious to the plaintiff: and, as there is no justification on the ground of truth, it is to be taken that their imputations were without foundation.   Is it open to a newspaper to give extended currency to such unfounded imputations?   The cases have never gone further than to privilege the publication of a fair report of proceedings in a court of justice not being ex parte: Hoare *v.* Silverlock, 9 Com. B. 20 (E. C. L. R. vol. 67).   This meeting is not in the nature of a judicial proceeding.

Unthank, contrà.—The meeting is averred to be a public meeting under the West Hartlepool Improvement Act.   That Act incorporates the Commissioners Clauses Act, and the Cemeteries Clauses Act; so that it appears that the subject-matter of the discussion was relevant to the powers of the meeting. And the public of Hartlepool and its vicinity have an interest in knowing what passes at such meeting.

Manisty was not called upon to reply.

Lord CAMPBELL, C. J.—I am of opinion that, as the *law now stands, the plea is bad. A fair account of what takes place in a court of justice is privileged. The reason is, that the balance of public benefit from the publicity is great. It is of great consequence that the public should know what takes place in court; and the proceedings are under the control of the Judges. The inconvenience therefore arising from the chance of the injury to private character is infinitesimally small as compared to the convenience of publicity. But it has never yet been contended that such a privilege extends to a report of what takes place at all public meetings. Even if confined to a report of what was relevant to the object of the meeting, it would extend the privilege to an alarming extent. If this plea is good, a fair account of what takes place may be published, whatever harm the publication may do to private character, provided it take place at a meeting of a public nature,—a wide description, embracing all kinds of meetings, from a county meeting to a parish meeting. At such meetings things may well be said very relevant to the subject in hand, yet very calumnious. In what an unhappy situation the calumniated person would be if the calumny might be published and yet he could not bring an action and challenge the publishers to prove its truth! The Legislature may think fit to extend the privilege of publication beyond the limits to which it now goes. If it does, it can impose such restrictions on the extension as it thinks fit. We, in a court of law, can only say how the law now stands; and, according to that, it is clear the action lies and the plea is bad. [*231

COLERIDGE, J.—There is no difference in law whether the publication is by the proprietor of a newspaper or *by some one else. [*232 There is no legal duty on either to publish what is injurious to another; and, if any person does do so, he must defend himself on some legal ground. Now, if the publication be a fair account of a proceeding, not ex parte, in a court of justice, it is privileged. The principle on which that proceeds is, as my Lord says, that the balance of advantage in having such proceedings public is great. But that principle does not extend to this case; and it never has been laid down that whatever is said at any meeting held for a public purpose, however injurious to an individual, is public property, and may be repeated with impunity.

WIGHTMAN, J.—Primâ facie it is actionable to publish a repetition of what is injurious to another, unless justified by truth, or by its being a fair report of what has been said in a public judicial proceeding, not ex parte, or it may be, in Parliament. The only foundation of the exception is the superior benefit of the publicity of judicial proceedings which counterbalances the injury to individuals, though that at times may be great. So it may be in a case of a Parliamentary proceeding. But, where a member of Parliament volunteered to publish a corrected edition of his speech, it was held in Rex *v.* Creevey, 1 M. & S. 273 (E. C. L. R. vol. 28), not to be privileged; so that even the privilege of making a report of what took place in Parliament is limited. It would, I think, be very dangerous if any public meeting might be made an opportunity for publishing, innocently it may be, what is injurious to individuals, and false.

*233]　　*CROMPTON, J.—I am of the same opinion, and for the same reasons.

Lord CAMPBELL, C. J.—As Rex *v.* Creevey has been mentioned, I will add that, though I perfectly concur in the doctrine of Rex *v.* Lord Abingdon, 1 Esp. N. P. C. 226, that a malicious publication of his speech by a member of either house of the Legislature is not privileged, I should think a publication of a report of his speech by a member of the House of Commons, bonâ fide addressed to his constituents, would be privileged.

WIGHTMAN, J.—I did not intend to express any opinion that it would not.

CROMPTON, J.—The privilege in such a case would arise because the publication was as a communication between a member and his constituents, and not because it was a true report of what took place in Parliament.　　　　　　　　　　　Judgment for the plaintiff.

It is no justification that the defendant signed the libellous paper as chairman of a public meeting of citizens convened for the purpose of deciding on a proper candidate for the office of governor, at an approaching election, and that it was published by order of such meeting: Lewis *v.* Few, 5 Johns. 1.

———◆———

*234]　*JESSE BRANDON, SAMUEL HOLBERT ELLIS, and HAIM GUEDALLA, *v.* SAMUEL SCOTT and CHARLES ROBINSON. *Jan.* 23.

Action by J. and two other plaintiffs on a contract, on the deposit of goods by the three plaintiffs with defendant, not to give them up without the joint order of the three plaintiffs. Breach, that they were given up without the joint order. Plea, that they were given up to J., one of the present plaintiffs, at his request. On demurrer:

Held a good plea; for J., being disabled from suing for what he himself procured, could not at law sue, though joining other plaintiffs with him.

COUNT. That defendants, at their request, "held possession of and were intrusted with the custody of a box, containing bonds and securities, on the terms and undertaking by defendants that they would safely and securely keep the same, and would not deliver up or part with the possession or custody thereof, except on the joint order or request of the plaintiffs.'' Breach: that they parted with the possession '' without any such joint order, authority, or request of the plaintiffs.''

Plea 1. That defendants, at the request and by the order of the plaintiff Jesse Brandon, delivered the box to one Alexander Brandon.

Plea 6. That they delivered them to the plaintiff Jesse Brandon.

Plea 7. That the papers were deposited in the joint names of the plaintiffs, but on no special terms, and were delivered to the order of the plaintiff Jesse Brandon.

Plea 9. Leave and license from '' the plaintiffs or some or one of them.''

To each plea there was a demurrer and joinder.

Petersdorff, for the plaintiffs.—On this record it is confessed that the defendants have broken the special contract not to deliver the papers without a joint order. *The seventh plea denies that there was [*235. a special contract; but that is immaterial, as the duty is implied from a joint bailment: May v. Harvey, 13 East, 197. [Lord CAMPBELL, C. J.—The bailees were not bound to give up the property without a joint demand. And you may assume that it was a breach of contract to do so. But can Jesse Brandon sue for that act which he himself procured? If all the rest were dead, could Brandon, as survivor, sue alone for this?] It would seem he could, though perhaps he could not recover more than nominal damages. It does not appear that the plaintiffs are partners; and, unless they are, the delivery to one is not a delivery to the others. In Innes v. Stevenson, 1 Moo. & R. 145, Lord Tenterden held that bankers were not discharged by paying checks drawn by one of two joint depositors, who were not partners. His ruling was similar in Stone v. Marsh, R. & Moo. 364 (E. C. L. R. vol. 21). The defendants cannot use as an answer to the action their own breach of contract.

Sir *F. Thesiger*, contrà.—The question is whether a person who has procured an act to be done can sue as one of several co-plaintiffs for that very act. It is correctly admitted that if he can he could equally sue, supposing the other co-contractors dead and the consenting party the sole plaintiff. There is no doubt that the defendants might, under the circumstances stated on the record, have refused to deliver the box without a joint order; but it does not lie in Jessee Brandon's mouth to complain of their having trusted him; and, as he is a necessary plaintiff in an action at law, the remedy, if any, must be *in equity: [*236 Jones v. Yates, 9 B. & C. 532 (E. C. L. R. vol. 17); Wallace v. Kelsall, 7 M. & W. 264, 273.† In the latter case, in delivering his judgment, Parke, B., says of Jones v. Yates: '' The principle of the decision is, that if one of the plaintiffs is barred, he cannot recover by joining other plaintiffs in an action to undo his own act. And Wallace *v.* Kelsall was approved and followed by the Court of Common Pleas in Smith *v.* Lovell, 10 Com. B. 6, 23 (E. C. L. R. vol. 70). In Innes *v.* Stephenson, 1 Moo. & R. 145, and Stone *v.* Marsh, R. & Moo. 364 (E. C. L. R. vol. 21), the parties consenting to the irregular payments were not plaintiffs. In both cases they were dead; and the actions were by the innocent survivors. It may be also that there is a peculiar relation between banker and customer in such cases; it is so suggested by Maule, J., in Husband *v.* Davis, 10 Com. B. 645, 650 (E. C. L. R. vol. 70).

Petersdorff was heard in reply.

Lord CAMPBELL, C. J.—The defence in substance is, that the goods bailed by the plaintiffs have been delivered to one of them. It is said that this is no defence, because the contract of bailment was not to deliver them except to the plaintiffs jointly. But, as, in fact, one of the plaintiffs has got the goods, the question arises whether he can sue the defendants for giving them to himself. It would be contrary to all principle, and the cases cited clearly show that it would be contrary to all decisions, if he could. I do not think an action at law could be maintained against bankers in this position more than against others; but it is not to be supposed they could therefore with impunity deliver up to *237] one *securities deposited with them to hold for several. I think in such a case they would stand in the relation of trustees for all the joint bailees; and there would be a clear remedy in equity for the breach of trust in delivering the joint property to one only of the cestui que trusts.

COLERIDGE, J., concurred.

WIGHTMAN, J.—I think the case is exactly as if Jesse Brandon sued alone; it is clear he could not then recover.

CROMPTON, J.—The principle is, that several cannot sue at law jointly, unless each one is in a position to sue. The decisions cited establish that, where a person is disabled from suing alone, he cannot enable himself to sue by joining others as co-plaintiffs.

Judgment for the defendants.

MARTIN and COLES, Executors of JOHN JENKINS MAT-
THEWS, *v.* ROBERT ROE, Clerk.   *Jan.* 24.

A rector erected in the garden of the rectory, apart from the rectory house, hothouses about 70 feet long and between 10 and 20 feet high. They consisted of a frame and glass work, resting on brick walls about 2 feet high, and embedded in mortar on these walls.
Held that he, or his executors in a reasonable time after his death, were entitled to remove them, without incurring any liability as for either dilapidations or waste.

THIS was a special case, stated for the opinion of the Court without pleadings, by order of Coleridge, J.

The Rev. John Jenkins Matthews, deceased, was, for *some [*238 years prior to and up to the time of his death, rector of Melbury Osmond, in Dorsetshire. He died on 17th October, 1855. The plaintiffs are, and sue as, his executors. The defendant succeeded Mr. Matthews as rector on 17th December, 1855, and is entitled to all the rights and benefits attached to the office of rector.

Mr. Matthews, while he was rector, erected at his own expense, at a cost of about 600*l.*, two hothouses, in the rectory garden, a short distance from and unconnected with the rectory-house or any other building.

The walls of the hothouses consisted of brick about two feet high from the ground. Over these, and resting on the brick walls, was the frame and glass work about ten feet high above the brick; and this frame and glass was bedded in mortar in the brick walls. The glass work was made to slide up and down, and was worked by pullies, and was in no way fixed.

The plaintiffs, claiming the frame work and glass work, removed it from the mortar in which it was bedded on the brick wall, therein doing no damage except that which was necessarily done to the mortar in removal. The defendant took the same out of their possession, and claimed and claims it as belonging to him as rector.

(Plans were annexed to, and were to be taken as part of, the case.)(*a*)

The value of the property is agreed, as between the parties, to be 300*l.*

The question for the opinion of the Court is, Whether the plaintiffs were, or the defendant was, entitled to the property. If the former, judgment is to be entered up for them for 300*l.* : if the latter, a nolle prosequi is to *be entered. The judgment to be for costs to [*239 the successful party.

The case was argued in last Term.(*b*)

Barstow, for the plaintiffs.—The erection is no part of the rectory house, any more than it would be if it were a mile distant from the house. The principle upon which questions of this kind are to be determined between successive incumbents is laid down in Huntley *v.* Russell, 13 Q. B. 572 (E. C. L. R. vol. 66): "The incumbent of a rectory is not precisely in the situation of a particular tenant, because there is no person who has the inheritance in reversion; but, the fee simple of the glebe being in abeyance, the incumbent is in truth but tenant for life, and he or his executors are no doubt liable for any waste committed. But, to constitute waste there must be either, first, a diminishing of the value of the estate, or, secondly, an increasing the burthen upon it, or, thirdly, an impairing the evidence of title." Here the deceased rector

(*a*) See post, p. 243, note (*a*).
(*b*) November 14th, 1856. Before Lord Campbell, C. J., Coleridge, Wightman, and Erle, Js.

could, during his life, have removed the frame without being guilty of
waste.   If the defendant were entitled to retain the frame, he would
also be bound to keep it in repair : it cannot be that he is to adopt it
or not as he pleases, thus leaving a burthen to his successor.   Now it
has been decided that an incumbent is not bound to repair a merely
ornamental structure which he finds in the rectory : Wise *v.* Metcalfe,
10 B. & C. 299 (E. C. L. R. vol. 21): but that he must keep up what
is part of the old rectory, and restore and rebuild, if necessary.   The
building here is a mere luxury.   [COLERIDGE, J.—Is it not somewhere
said that, if an *incumbent puts up an expensive building, he
may be procceded against ?   ERLE, J.—I had that notion certainly, and that the succeeding rector might clear such a building away
and charge the expenses, as dilapidations, against the executors of his
predecessor.   COLERIDGE, J.—I recollect a case of an incumbent who
was so careful as to build a large library room in such a way that it
might be easily removable : and, late in life, he sold off his books that
he might take the room down.]   It is true that the plaintiffs, if they
had done any injury in the course of the removal, would be liable; but
this is negatived in fact.   In 4 Burn's Ecc. L. 413 (9th ed.), title
Wills, VI., it is said : " If an incumbent enter upon a parsonage house
in which are hangings, grates, iron backs to chimneys, and such like,
not put there by the last incumbent, but which have gone from successor to successor, the executor of the last incumbent shall not have
them, but it seemeth that they shall continue in the nature of heir-
looms ; but if the last incumbent fixed them there only for his own convenience, it seemeth they shall be deemed as furniture, or household
goods, and shall go to his executor."   [Lord CAMPBELL, C. J.—What
do you say as to the brickwork ?]   If it be inconvenient to the defendant, he may perhaps have a ground of complaint : perhaps, if it be an
irremovable fixture as between landlord and tenant, it could not be
removed.   [Lord CAMPBELL, C. J.—It might be a structure removable
only during the tenancy.]   In Culling *v.* Tuffnal, Bul. N. P. 34, it was
held that a barn erected by a tenant upon timber not fixed into the
ground might be removed by him, if the custom of the country were
in conformity with such *practice : and Buller, J., considers
that it might be removed without a special custom : and such was
clearly the opinion of this Court in Wiltshear *v.* Cottrell, 1 E. & B. 674
(E. C. L. R. vol. 72).   So it is, though the movable structure rests on a
foundation of brick or stone let into the ground : Wansbrough *v.* Maton,
4 A. & E. 884 (E. C. L. R. vol. 31), Rex *v.* Londonthorpe, 6 T. R.
377, Rex *v.* Otley, 1 B. & Ad. 161 (E. C. L. R. vol. 20).   In Buckland
v. Butterfield, 2 Br. & B. 54 (E. C. L. R. vol. 6), it was held that a conservatory placed on a brick foundation could not be removed by a tenant for years who had erected it : but there the conservatory opened
into the dwelling-house, which, upon the removal, was exposed to the

*240]

[*241

weather. The very slight injury here done to the mortar, in the removal, is immaterial to the question, as appears by Grymes v. Boweren, 6 Bing. 437 (E. C. L. R. vol. 19). It is no more than if so much glue had been broken. But, even if such removal as this were illegal as between tenant for life and remainder-man, it would not follow that it is so as between successive incumbents, though, if it be legal in the former case, it must be so in the latter.

Petersdorff, contrà.—The whole building passed with the soil, and was irremovable. The law as between successive incumbents is much like that between tenant for life and remainder-man: Amos and Ferard on Fixtures p. 145 (2d ed.). Now it seems quite clear that a tenant could no more remove such a structure than he could remove the wall on which it stands and of which it in effect forms part. [WIGHTMAN, J.—If it be attached to the freehold, and be in fact *damnosa hæreditas*, would it be a dilapidation to leave it unrepaired?] That *could [*242 not be maintained. [Lord CAMPBELL, C. J.—Can we presume that a hothouse is for the advantage of the incumbent?] It is not here found to be otherwise. [Lord CAMPBELL, C. J.—Is the question to turn on the fact whether the growing of the grapes is found to answer? COLERIDGE, J.—It is only by custom that executors of an incumbent are liable for dilapidations; and the custom is confined to what is a beneficial part of the rectory. Can you claim to retain what you would not be bound to keep up for your successor, as the domos et ædificia belonging to the living? Lord CAMPBELL, C. J.—Is there such a thing as a faculty for putting up buildings? I heard that said by a clerical man; but I have not found it in my reading. *Barstow.*—That was said in Huntley v. Russell, 13 Q. B. 589 (E. C. L. R. vol. 66); but the Court seemed to consider this unnecessary where for an old building another equally beneficial was substituted.] It is true that, if the succeeding incumbent is entitled to this structure, he is bound to keep it up. Buckland v. Butterfield, 2 Br. & B. 54 (E. C. L. R. vol. 6), is decisive, if the analogy of tenant for life and remainder-man applies. From B. Moore's report of that case, 4 B. Moore, 440, 443 (E. C. L. R. vol. 16), it appears that Blosset, Serjt., there cited a MS. case of The Marquis of Townsend v. ——, "where it was determined, that glasses and frames, resting on brick work in a nursery ground, were not removable." The true definition of a tenement (which, for the present question, is identical with an irremovable structure) is that given by Parke, J., in Rex v. Otley, 1 B. & Ad. 166 (E. C. L. R. vol. 20): "To constitute a tenement, it is necessary that the structure should be affixed to the soil, or to something annexed to *the soil. Here the windmill rested [*243 merely upon the brick foundation, without being annexed to it by cement."

Barstow, in reply.—It is true that a tenant for years must exercise his right of removing fixtures within the term. But "in the case of a

tenant for life, or in tail, his executor must, it should seem, remove the
fixtures to which he is entitled within a reasonable time after the death
of the testator :" Williams on Executors, Part II., B. II., Ch. II., s. 3,
(vol. 1, p. 631, 4th ed.).   The case of an incumbent is certainly much
nearer to that of a tenant for life than to that of a tenant for years:
and here it does not appear that there was unreasonable delay.

                                                    Cur. adv. vult.

Lord CAMPBELL, C. J., now delivered the judgment of the Court.

In this case the testator Matthew, being an incumbent of Milbury
Osmond, erected in the rectory garden, on a spot entirely detached from
the parsonage house, two hothouses, respectively 22ft. 10 and 47 ft. in
length, by 14 ft. 9 and 17 ft. 6 in depth,(a) consisting of low brick walls
on which mortar was spread, and bedded into this mortar wooden frames
and glass work, the glass work sliding up and down on pullies, and not
fixed.   The plaintiffs, after his death, removed this frame and glass
work, taking it from the mortar in which it was bedded, doing no damage thereby, except what was unavoidable to the mortar.   The defendant, who has succeeded as rector, afterwards took these materials from
*244]   *the possession of the plaintiffs, claiming them as belonging to
him as such rector.   And we are called on to decide, simply and
without any question as to the time or manner of the first removal by
the plaintiffs, in which of the two parties was the property in the materials so removed.

In considering which question, we treat the removal by the plaintiffs
as having been in fact effected without injury to the freehold.   In
all cases of this kind, injury to the freehold must be spoken of with less
than literal strictness.   A screw or a nail can scarcely be drawn without
some attrition: and, when all the harm done is that which is unavoidable to the mortar laid on the brick walls, this is so trifling that the
law, which is reasonable, will regard it as none.   Upon any other principle the criterion of injury to the freehold would be idle.

We have found no decision nor authority of any text book precisely
governing this case; and we consider it therefore on principle.

In the first place, it seems clear that, had the testator in his lifetime
done what the plaintiffs have done since his death, the defendant could
not have sued them for dilapidations.   The character of the building
would have justified the incumbent in the removal of the whole of it:
only he must have restored the garden to its former condition, if in the
removal he had occasioned any injury to it amounting to waste.   For
the duty of a *present* and the right of a *succeeding* incumbent, *as such*,
are correlative.   Any matter of needless expense, or luxury, or ornament, in which the present incumbent, to gratify his own taste, has
indulged himself (blameably or not is immaterial), he is not only not
bound, but he ought not, to transmit to his successor.   If the successor

(a) These measurements were taken from the plans.

*may recover damages from the executor because such things [*245 have been removed by their testator, there can be no doubt he, in his turn, must maintain them; and what he must maintain he must also restore and rebuild when decayed by his fault; and so the benefice will become permanently saddled with a useless burthen, and an indefinite, it may be ruinous, expense. Hothouses, pineries, and conservatories do not, in this respect, differ from observatories, menageries, or aviaries: they are equally what, in a provincial constitution of 1236, 21 H. 3, cited in Wise v. Metcalfe, 10 B. & C. 314 (E. C. L. R. vol. 20),(a) are called impensæ voluptuosæ, as distinguished from necessariæ. The parsonage and the glebe are for the decent and suitable residence and sustenance of the incumbent, and are to be maintained, according to the intention of the law, out of the revenues of the benefice. This parsonage and glebe the succeeding incumbent is entitled to receive from his predecessor: the former of such convenience and character as *he* found it, and in good condition, properly repaired, or even rebuilt, if by *his* neglect that has become necessary; the latter in good repair and order, with its buildings and fences. Whatever he is so entitled to receive he must transmit: and the extent to which, in any particular case, this reciprocal right and duty will go must be determined by a liberal and sensible consideration of the circumstances. It is impossible, from the nature of the thing, to lay down a more precise rule. Therefore cases may occur which are near the dividing line, and so present a practical difficulty. But what we have now to deal with, [*246 *namely hothouses nearly seventy feet in length, present none.

The testator did an unnecessary, probably a very unwise and unsuitable act, in erecting them; and, when he had done so, there was a locus pœnitentiæ. Nothing prevented him from removing at once all that was mere fixture: and this is all that we need decide now: though, as we have already intimated our opinion, we should have no difficulty in deciding, if necessary, that he might have removed the whole erection.

Thus far we have been upon the strict law of dilapidations, in which the deceased incumbent is always supposed to have committed a wrong for which, from the peculiar nature of his holding and of the property, there was no one who could sue *him*, but for which, by the custom and contrary to the general rule of law, an action lay against his personal representative. And it is only with reference to this law of dilapidations that our previous remarks must be considered as made.

It is of course a different, and perhaps a more difficult, question, whether, if the incumbent at his death leave entire on the glebe and in good repair an erection which he might have himself removed, the executor may, within a reasonable time after his death, remove such

(a) The words appear to be taken from Lyndwood's commentary on the constitution, *Provinciale*, lib. III. tit. 27, p. 250 (ed. 1679), not. *s.*

parts of it as are in their nature fixtures and capable of removal
without injury to the freehold. The case now supposed is that of an
erection, which if the deceased had left out of repair, the successor
could not have maintained any action for dilapidation, which he himself
therefore will not be bound to keep in repair, which imposes no burthen
on him, which he may remove. For it would be unreasonable to hold
that he might not remove, however useless or unsuitable to the living or
*247] *even inconvenient to the occupation of the parsonage or glebe,
that which, for any one of those reasons, he was not bound to
keep in repair.

The question, thus stated, clearly stands apart from the peculiar law
of dilapidations: it has no reference to the character of the testator as
incumbent of a benefice, or to the relation between him and the defendant as predecessor and successor in the same incumbency. The testator
has committed no waste, either voluntary or permissive : he has left on
the glebe that which he might have removed, and which, being left,
imposes no duty on the successor: it is that which, if he had himself
severed it from the freehold, would clearly have reverted to his personal
estate and gone to his personal representative. Then has he, by leaving them so united to the freehold as the case states, annexed them
inseparably to it, so that they are no longer part of his personal
estate ?

Messrs. Amos and Ferard, in their excellent book on The Law of
Fixtures (part 1, ch. 3, s. 4, p. 146, 2d ed.), say : "It may therefore,
it is conceived, be laid down, that an incumbent or his executor will,
in general, be entitled to fixtures of a same description as those which
form part of the personal estate of the deceased tenant for life." It
may be worth observing that there is this distinction between an incumbent and ordinary tenant for life: that the former has at no time any
reversioner with any present interests or rights, whereas, when the
latter annexes anything to the freehold or in any way meddles with it,
he annexes to or meddles with that in which some other person or persons has or have at the moment an existing interest which may be
*248] increased or decreased in value by what he does, and *which the
law will protect. But neither the patron of the benefice nor the
future unknown successor has any such interest in the parsonage or
glebe: if any one can interfere it is the Ordinary; and he not in
respect of any interest vested in him, but to advance the general
public object of endowments to the clergy. This seems a reason for
enlarging the rule as between the executor and successor, where the
subject-matter in dispute is not of a kind that can be considered as
inalienably attached to the benefice, as in such case there would be no
ground even for the interference of the Ordinary. Suppose the case
of an observatory, which an incumbent, having built, should take down
again : it would be absurd to talk of the Ordinary interfering to prevent

him. When, however, the cases between the executor of tenant for life and remainder-man are looked into, they will be found to turn each on its peculiar circumstances; the character, the use, the mode of attachment, the facility of severance, the injury to the freehold ,by severance. In regard to an ecclesiastical benefice, the character and object of the building to which the chattel is attached, and for which it has been so attached, seem of very great consequence in determining whether there was any intention to separate it permanently and irrevocably from the personal estate. Here then is an erection, in itself, purely matter of luxury and ornament, which the testator might have pulled down, but which he probably wished to enjoy so long as he lived in the benefice, and therefore did not remove. To this, and for the purpose of completing that luxurious and ornamental creation, a chattel is so attached that it may be detached without injury to the freehold. We think the inference is that it never ceased to be a chattel during the testator's life, *that it continued to be so at the moment of [*249 his death, and therefore passed as part of the personal estate to the executors. Had this chattel been merely screwed, or had it been, as a telescope in an observatory, strongly secured, as such instruments commonly are, to what is part of the building itself, we think no question would have been made. And this seems to us to present no substantial difference in principle.

Our judgment therefore will be for the plaintiffs.

Judgment for plaintiffs.

The QUEEN v. The Council of the Borough of BRIGHTON.
Jan. 24.

After the passing of stat. 5 & 6 Vict. c. 111, the corporate borough of B. was created by charter, not containing a non intremittant clause. Its area was a part of the county of S. A grant of a Court of Quarter Sessions was made, and the council appointed a clerk of the peace for the borough.

Held, that the clerk of the peace of the county of S. was not entitled to compensation under sect. 66 of stat. 5 & 6 W. 4, c. 76, he not having been removed nor his office abolished, although the profits were diminished.

MANDAMUS. The writ suggested that, by Royal letters patent or charter of incorporation, dated 1st April, 1854, whereby the inhabitants of Brighton in Sussex were incorporated, the Queen, by the advice of Her Privy Council, extended to the inhabitants within the district therein set forth, in the said county of Sussex, the powers and provisions of stat. 5 & 6 W. 4, c. 76 (" To provide for the regulation of Municipal Corporations in England and Wales;"), and by letters patent, dated 16th December, 1854, " did grant that a separate court of quarter sessions of the peace should be held for and be holden in and for the said

borough of Brighton, pursuant to the provisions of the said Act. In
virtue whereof you, the said council," "duly, in *pursuance of
the provisions of the said Act, appointed Ewen Evershed to be,
and the said E. Evershed has thenceforth been, and still is, the clerk
of the peace of the said borough." "That William Vidler Langridge,
of," &c., "before and at the respective dates of Our said charter of
incorporation and of Our said grant, was an officer of the said county
of Sussex wherein the said borough is situated, holding an office of profit therein, that is to say the office of clerk of the peace for the said
county, and entitled to certain fees and emoluments pertaining to his
said office for business arising within that part of the said county which
is now the said borough of Brighton. And that, by virtue of our aforesaid grant and the appointment of the said E. Evershed as aforesaid,
the said office, so held by the said W. V. Langridge as aforesaid, was
abolished, and the said W. V. Langridge was removed therefrom in and
so far as regards that part of the said county of Sussex which is now
the borough of Brighton. And the said W. V. Langridge has been
deprived of part of the fees and emoluments of his before-mentioned
office, and thereby become and is entitled to compensation under the
provisions of the statute in that behalf." "That the said W. V. Langridge, being entitled as aforesaid, duly claimed of you, the said council,
such compensation, and presented to the town council of your said
borough such statement, as by the first-mentioned Act is required in that
behalf; and that you, the said council, took the same into consideration, and admitted in part the claim of the said W. V. Langridge, and
disallowed the same in part, and admitted and determined that he was
entitled to, and awarded that he should receive, as and for such compensation as aforesaid, during the period of *his natural life, an
annuity or yearly sum of 7l. 12s. from the said 16th day of December, 1854, and delivered to the said W. V. Langridge such notice
in that behalf as by the said statute is required." "That the said W.
V. Langridge, thinking himself aggrieved by such determination as
aforesaid, duly, and according to the provisions of the said Act, appealed to the Lords Commissioners of Our Treasury, who thereupon,
by order duly made and signed as by law is required, and bearing date
the 20th day of October, in the year of Our Lord 1856, ordered and
determined that the said W. V. Langridge was entitled to, and should
receive from you, the said council, as and for such compensation as
aforesaid, the sum of 143l. per annum, to commence from the said 16th
day of December, 1854, to continue for and during his life, subject to
a deduction from the said annuity of the net amount of the fees and
emoluments which he had, at the date of the said order, actually
received since the said 16th day of December, 1854, for business arising
within the said borough of Brighton." "That the amount of the fees
and emoluments actually received by the said W. V. Langridge, since

*250]

*251]

the said 16th day of December, 1854, for business arising within the said borough, and to be deducted from the said annuity, was and is the sum of 12*l.* 15*s.* 11*d.* Of all which you had long ago due notice. And that the said W. V. Langridge has required you, the said council, to prepare and execute, under the common seal of the said borough, and deliver to the said W. V. Langridge, a bond in sufficient penalty, conditioned for the payment to the said W. V. Langridge, during his life, of the said annuity, commencing from the said 16th day of December, 1854, subject to such deduction as aforesaid:" but that [*252 *the council had refused so to do. The writ then required the council to prepare, execute, and deliver such bond.

Return. That the said office, so held by the said W. V. Langridge, as in the said writ mentioned, was not abolished, nor was the said W. V. Langridge removed therefrom, as in the said writ mentioned. That the said charter of incorporation, and the said letters patent granting a separate Court of quarter sessions, as in the said writ mentioned, were respectively made after the passing of an Act, &c. (5 & 6 Vict. c. 111, "To confirm the incorporation of certain boroughs, and to indemnify such persons as have sustained loss thereby"). And that the said office, so held by W. V. Langridge, at the respective times of the granting of the said charter and the said letters patent, was not at any time or in any manner abolished; nor was W. V. Langridge at any time or in any manner removed therefrom, otherwise than by the deprivation of W. V. Langridge, as such clerk of the peace of the county of Sussex, by reason of the said grant of the said separate Court of Quarter Sessions, and of the appointment of a clerk of the peace for the said borough, of certain fees and emoluments pertaining to his said office for business arising within that part of the said county which is now in the said borough of Brighton. That the said compensation claimed by W. V. Langridge from said Council of the said borough was in respect only of the loss of such last-mentioned fees and emoluments; and that the said determination by the Council was made under the supposition that the loss of such fees and emoluments by reason of the said grant of a separate Court of Quarter Sessions for the borough and of the appointment *of a clerk of the peace for such borough consti- [*253 tuted a valid claim on the part of W. V. Langridge upon the said Council for compensation, under the statutes in such case made and provided.

Demurrer. Joinder.

M. Chambers, for the Crown.—The prosecutor is entitled to compensation under sect. 66 of the first Municipal Corporation Act, 5 & 6 W. 4, c. 76. His office has been abolished within the meaning of that section; for the office which he now holds is not, nor is any office, identical with the former office of which the duties extended over the whole county of Sussex. The appointment of the clerk of the peace of the borough, under sect. 103, supersedes, so far as respects the area of the borough comprehended within the county, the functions of the clerk of the peace of the county.   The provisions of that Act, by stat. 16 & 17 Vict. c. 79, s. 2, apply to the new borough of Brighton: stat. 5 & 6 Vict. c. 111, s. 2, had applied the compensation clauses to the new boroughs incorporated before the passing of that Act.   It is enough, to bring a case within stat. 5 & 6 W. 4, c. 76, s. 66, that any part of the remuneration incidental to the office should be taken away: Rex v. The Mayor, &c., of Bridgewater, 6 A. & E. 339 (E. C. L. R. vol. 33): it is not even necessary that the office should be a chartered one: Regina v. The Mayor, &c., of Carmarthen, 11 A. & E. 9 (E. C. L. R. vol. 39). The words in sect. 66 of stat. 5 & 6 W. 4, c. 76, are "every officer of any borough or county": the office of an officer of a county could be abolished, under the Corporation Acts, in no other way than by that

*254] which has occurred here: no officer of a *county had duties confined to the area of any old or new borough.   [COLERIDGE, J.— In some boroughs the jurisdiction was formerly much larger than it is since the Municipal Corporation Act; for instance, in some cases there was a capital jurisdiction.   Has compensation been given to the old officers in such cases?]   Probably not: but there the office has not been abolished nor the officer removed.

Phipson, contrà.—An office is abolished, within the meaning of sect. 66 of stat. 5 & 6 W. 4, c. 76, only when it ceases to exist.   The word "county" was probably inserted with a view to cities which were counties of themselves.   [*M. Chambers.*—That would not be necessary: sect. 142 includes all such.   CROMPTON, J., as to stat. 5 & 6 Vict. c. 111, referred to in Regina v. Council of Manchester, 9 Q. B. 458 (E. C. L. R. vol. 58 (a).]   It is observable that, in sect. 2 of stat. 5 & 6 Vict. c. 111, the words "or who shall have been deprived of any part of the fees and emoluments of his office," are inserted: these words are not in sect. 66 of stat. 5 & 6 W. 4, c. 76; which suggests the inference that the section last named did not include such a case as the present. Now stat. 5 & 6 Vict. c. 111, does not apply to corporations created, like Brighton, after that Act passed.   The office of the clerk of the peace of the county is still exercised within the area of the new borough: there is no non intromittant clause: the county magistrates may still commit for an offence committed within the borough.   There is no clerk of the peace of the county except the prosecutor.   [WIGHT-

*255] MAN, J.—Is not the prosecutor at any rate entitled to the *7l. 12s. which the Corporation has allowed?   Regina v. The Mayor, &c., of Sandwich, 2 Q. B. 895 (E. C. L. R. vol. 64).]   It should seem not: but the question does not arise on this demurrer.   The 2d and 3d sections of stat. 16 & 17 Vict. c. 79, are not very intelligibly worded: but they appear to be confined, in their provisions, to boroughs mentioned in the Schedule to stat. 5 & 6 W. 4, c. 76, and to boroughs created subsequently to that Act, but before stat. 16 & 17 Vict. c. 79. That stat. 5 & 6 Vict. c. 111, does not apply to Brighton appears from stat. 18 & 19 Vict. c. 31, confirming the incorporation of Brighton, which, had stat. 5 & 6 Vict. c. 111 been applicable, would have been unnecessary.

M. Chambers, in reply.—The office is abolished by what has taken place, just as that of county coroner is abolished by the appointment of a borough coroner under stat. 5 & 6 W. 4, c. 76, s. 62.

Lord CAMPBELL, C. J.—I am of opinion that the prosecutor is not entitled to compensation. I regret that we must so decide; because he certainly has suffered a material diminution of profits. But we have no power, beyond what the legislature has given, to award compensation. I agree that a liberal construction is to be put on the statute, and this not merely from my own inclination, but because I am convinced that it has always been the intention of the legislature to compensate for private loss. The question turns on sect. 66 of stat. 5 & 6 W. 4, c. 76; for I think stat. 16 & 17 Vict. c. 79 neither hurts nor aids the case of the prosecutor. *M. Chambers* says the office has been abolished; it *certainly is not a case of removal from office. [*256 But how can we say that the office has been abolished? The prosecutor was long ago appointed clerk of the peace for the county; and he is so still. But it is said that the office is abolished, quoad the area of the Corporation of Brighton. That, however, is not so; he has duties to perform in Brighton. Thus, in respect of the list of county voters having their property in Brighton, he has the same duties to perform as before. The office therefore is not abolished; and the case resolves itself clearly into a case of diminution of profits. We do find a provision for compensation in respect of such diminution in stat. 5 & 6 Vict. c. 111, s. 2: but that statute is inapplicable to Brighton; and no such provision is to be found in stat. 5 & 6 W. 4, c. 76.

COLERIDGE, J.—I am of the same opinion. The language of sect. 66 of stat. 5 & 6 W. 4, c. 76, is "every officer of any borough or county," "whose office shall be abolished, or who shall be removed from his office." Before we can act upon this, we must see that all the particulars are made out. If anything had happened which took the district altogether out of the county, I am not prepared to say that we might not apply a liberal interpretation to such a case: it is not necessary to pronounce an opinion as to this: but I do agree with the view taken by this Court in Rex v. The Mayor, &c., of Bridgewater, 6 A. & E. 339 (E. C. L. R. vol. 33), that the statute ought to be interpreted liberally, in order that no injustice should be done to an individual for the public benefit. But here the prosecutor was clerk of the peace for the whole county, Brighton included. That office is not abolished;

*257] *it is affected so far only that another party is entitled to take a portion of the profits: "abolition" means putting an end to an existing office: and I think that we cannot, without absurdity, say that this office is abolished.

WIGHTMAN, J.—The prosecutor still remains generally in the same office. On the other side, it is said that the office is abolished, because the duties are lessened. They are so certainly: he is deprived of the profits of a certain part of the business arising in the borough. But such a diminution of profits is not an abolition of the office.

CROMPTON, J.—I am entirely of the same opinion. We must look at the statutes. I am much inclined to agree with Mr. *Phipson* as to stat. 16 & 17 Vict. c. 79. I think sects. 2 and 3 inapplicable to corporations created after the Act. But, even if that were otherwise, I am clearly of opinion that this office has not been abolished within the meaning of sect. 66 of stat. 5 & 6 W. 4, c. 76. It seems to be argued that the county is changed for the purposes of this Act, for that no clerk of the peace or coroner, not being an officer of the borough, can act within the borough. I do not know that that is so: and I do not see that there might not be a county coroner acting within the district, as an inspector of weights and measures. The case here clearly resolves itself into one of diminution of profits, not of the abolition of office. The office is not abolished either wholly or partially: and sect. 66 of stat. 5 & 6 W. 4, c. 76, is therefore inapplicable.

Judgment for defendants.

---

*258] *The Guardians and Overseers of LEEDS v. The Guardians of the Poor of The WAKEFIELD Union and The Overseers of the Poor of the Township of WAKEFIELD. *Jan. 24.*

A pauper, having the status of irremovability in L. by virtue of stat. 9 & 10 Vict. c. 66, while she was in W. for a temporary purpose not such as to break the status, became lunatic, and was removed by a justice's order to a lunatic asylum. She was settled in T.

Held that, under The Lunatic Asylums Act, 1853 (16 & 17 Vict. c. 97), sect. 102, justices had power to make an order on L. for payment of expenses incurred since 29th September, 1853, in the examination, removal, maintenance, &c.

THIS was a case stated by consent, under stat. 12 & 13 Vict. c. 45, s. 11, upon an appeal by The Guardians of the Poor and The Overseers of the Poor of the township of Leeds, in the West Riding of Yorkshire, against an order under the hands of two justices of the same Riding.

On 7th July, 1856, Bessy Thorpe was at the house of her sister in the township of Wakefield, in the Wakefield Poor Law Union (in the West Riding of Yorkshire), and was then of unsound mind. In consequence thereof she became chargeable to the township of Wakefield, and, on the last-mentioned day, was taken as a pauper lunatic, under an order of a justice of the peace made in pursuance of The Lunatic Asylums Act, 1853, from the township of Wakefield to the Lunatic Asylum of the West Riding of Yorkshire, wherein she has remained ever since under the same order. She was, when so sent to the said Asylum, and still is, of unsound mind, and a proper person to be taken charge of and detained under care and treatment.

The expenses of examination, bringing before the justice, convey-ance to the Asylum, and of subsequent maintenance therein, have been incurred by the board of guardians of the Wakefield Union on behalf of the *township of Wakefield, the said expenses for mainte- [*259 nance having been paid pursuant to an order of a justice of the peace made in conformity with The Lunatic Asylums Act, 1853.

When sent to the Asylum, as aforesaid, the lunatic was the wife of James Thorpe, and had several children by him then living. On 21st July (two weeks after his wife was so sent to the Asylum) James Thorpe died in the township of Leeds. His settlement throughout his life was in the township of Thorne in Yorkshire.

For many years next before and at the time when his wife was sent to the Asylum, the said James Thorpe was tenant of a dwelling-house in the township of Leeds : and he then resided there with his children He had in fact resided in that township, without interruption, for above forty years and immediately preceding his death (exclusive of all time coming within the first proviso of sect. 1 of stat. 9.& 10 Vict. c. 66), and was, when his wife was sent to the Asylum as aforesaid, exempt from removal to the place of his settlement, and had acquired such exemp-tion in the township of Leeds.

From the time of their marriage, which took place about the year 1836, until within about a fortnight prior to her removal to the Asylum, the lunatic resided with her husband in the said township of Leeds. She had been ill for several weeks next preceding the said removal ; and, in consequence thereof, she, for the benefit of her health, went from their home in the township of Leeds to visit her sister, who resided at Wakefield : and, whilst there, namely when she had stayed there for about a fortnight, she become insane ; and it was found neces-sary to confine her in the Asylum. *She was not taken back [*260 to Leeds, where her husband and children then resided ; but, the relieving officer of the Wakefield Union having administered relief, she was sent directly from the said township of Wakefield to the Asylum as a lunatic chargeable to the Wakefield Union.

The township of Leeds is subject to a separate board of guardians of the poor.

The guardians of the poor of the Wakefield Union and the overseers of the poor of the Wakefield township, on 29th September, 1856, obtained an order of two justices of the peace of the said West Riding upon the guardians and overseers of the poor of the township of Leeds, adjudging that the lunatic was settled in Thorne, but that, at the time of her conveyance to the Asylum, she was exempt from removal to the place of her settlement, or the country of her birth, by reason of a provision of stat. 9 & 10 Vict. c. 66; and that the place wherein she had acquired such exemption was the said township of Leeds, from which township she was then irremovable; and therefore ordering the guardians of the poor of that township to pay the expenses of examining, bringing before a justice, and conveyance to the asylum, of the lunatic and of her maintenance therein, to the date of the order, and also to pay a weekly sum for her future maintenance in the Asylum. The grounds of adjudication accompanying the order allege " that James Thorpe, the husband of the lunatic, was, at the time of her conveyance to the Asylum, exempt from removal to the place of his settlement or country of his birth, by reason of a provision of the said Act 9th and 10th Victoria, chapter 66 (namely), by reason of his having resided

*261] in that township for *above five years then immediately preceding. Also that the lunatic, having then resided for above five years within the meaning of the last-mentioned Act, with her husband in the same township, and having no other settlement than his, was removable or irremovable only when he was; and that she then was legally domiciled in the township of Leeds, and only temporarily residing in Wakefield: and, being exempt from removal as aforesaid, the expenses of her examination, bringing before a justice, conveyance to the Asylum, and maintenance therein, ought to be paid by the guardians of the poor of the township of Leeds, the township wherein she then had acquired such exemption as aforesaid."

Against the order the guardians and overseers of the poor of Leeds have appealed, alleging, in their grounds of appeal, amongst other grounds:

" That the lunatic, when sent to the Asylum, was not exempt from removal as aforesaid, and was not then legally domiciled in the township of Leeds, but was residing and inhabiting in, and was a bonâ. fide resident in, and an inhabitant of, the said township of Wakefield."

" That, after her conveyance to the Asylum, but before the making the order appealed against, her husband died: whereupon she ceased to have or follow his residence, but became a resident and inhabitant in the township of Wakefield in her own right."

" That the expenses, before mentioned, of examination, bringing before a justice, and conveyance to the Asylum, and maintenance therein, ought not to be paid by the said township of Leeds; but the order ought to have been made on the said township of Thorne, the place of settlement."

*262] *" That the justices making the order had not, for the reasons set forth in the grounds of appeal, jurisdiction to make the same; and that the said order is illegal."

If the Court should be of opinion that the lunatic, when sent to the Asylum as aforesaid, was not exempt from removal to the place of her settlement, and that the said order of the 29th day of September, 1856, for her maintenance in the Asylum ought to have been made upon the place of her settlement, and not upon the township of Leeds, then the said order is to be quashed : if otherwise, it is to be confirmed.

Pickering, for the respondents.—The order was properly made on Leeds, under The Lunatic Asylums Act, 1853 (16 & 17 Vict. c. 97). By sect. 102 of that Act, the expenses incurred since 29th September, 1853, in respect of the examination, &c., " of a pauper lunatic heretofore or hereafter removed to an asylum," &c., "under the authority of this or any other Act, who would, at the time of his being conveyed to such asylum," &c., "have been exempt from removal to the parish of his settlement or the country of his birth by reason of some provision in" stat. 9 & 10 Vict. c. 66, "shall be paid by the guardians of the parish wherein such lunatic shall have acquired such exemption if such parish be subject to a separate board of guardians," &c., or the overseers of such parish, or the union in which it is comprised, where there is no such board ; "and no order shall be made under any provision contained in this or any other Act upon the parish of the settlement in respect of any such lunatic pauper during the time that the above-mentioned charges are to be paid and charged as herein provided :" and sect. 5 of stat. *12 & 13 Vict. c. 103, is repealed. Sect. [*263 95 had imposed the liability on the parish from which the removal takes place, till otherwise adjudged ; sect. 97 on the parish of settlement, upon adjudication of settlement ; and here it is adjudged that the settlement is in Thorne. But neither of these sections takes effect in the case of a pauper lunatic who has the status of irremovability. The case is not varied by the pauper having been casually at Wakefield : she had not gone thither to settle : had she not been a lunatic, relief given to her in Wakefield would have been given as relief to casual poor, not therefore justifying a removal to the place of settlement : and the lunacy makes no difference. The residence in Leeds was never broken, either by the temporary visit to Wakefield or the removal to the Lunatic Asylum. The facts of this case are like those in Regina *v.* St. Leonard's, Shoreditch, 14 Q. B. 340 (E. C. L. R. vol. 68), where a casual absence from the parish of settlement, with animus revertendi, did not relieve the parish from the expense to which it was subjected under stat. 8 & 9 Vict. c. 126, s. 62 : and the same principle must apply to the provisions of stat. 16 & 17 Vict. c. 97, s. 102.

R. Hall, contrà.—The exemption from removal, imposed by stat. 9 & 10 Vict. c. 66, is an exemption from physical removal. Had the pauper been resident at Wakefield, she would have been removable thence to Thorne, if permanently chargeable. Now the lunacy produces a permanent chargeability. At the time of the removal from Wakefield, the pauper was neither removable nor irremovable from Leeds, not being there in fact; *and sect. 102 of stat. 16 & 17

*264]   Vict. c. 97, has no application. That section is in the nature of a proviso on the earlier sections. Sect. 95 makes the parish from which the removal takes place chargeable, unless there is an adjudication of settlement, or a failure to ascertain it; sect. 97 imposes the chargeability on the parish of settlement upon such adjudication; sect. 98 imposes it on the county when it is shown that the settlement cannot be ascertained. Where a pauper has no known settlement, and thus is irremovable, the consequences annexed by stat. 11 & 12 Vict. c. 110, s. 3, to the statutory irremovability under stat. 9 & 10 Vict. c. 96, do not apply, though the pauper has a five years' residence; Regina *v.* Bennett, 3 E. & B. 341 (E. C. L. R. vol. 77): and the same must be true of the substituted provisions of stat. 16 & 17 Vict. c. 97, s. 102. There are no words expressly giving the power to make such an order as this, as there are in the cases under sects. 95, 97, and 98: no mandamus could issue to compel the making of such an order: sect. 102 merely abridges the power under the earlier sections. But, when there is a statutory irremovability from the parish whence the actual removal is made, the order must be made upon that parish, by sects. 95, 96, sects. 97 and 98 becoming inoperative by sect. 102: so that this construction satisfies every case; for, in every other case, the question will arise only between the removing parish and the parish of settlement and the county; and then there are express words authorizing the order.

Lord CAMPBELL, C. J.—We all agree that these expenses must be

*265]   borne by Leeds. The words of sect. 102 *show that, when the pauper cannot be removed to the parish of settlement, the expenses are thrown upon the parish in which he has a status of irremovability. That impliedly gives justices the power to make the order on such parish. Had this pauper been at Leeds when it became necessary to send her to the Asylum, that would clearly have been so: and her temporary visit to Wakefield can make no difference.

COLERIDGE, J.—I take sect. 102 as a proviso applying to a set of cases not comprehended in the previous sections. Those previous sections do not comprehend the case where the settlement is known, but a status of irremovability has been acquired elsewhere. That is the present case: the pauper was exempt from removal from Leeds; and the parish whence the removal in fact took place, and that of the settlement, are both exempt from the expense. There are no express words in sect. 102 giving power to the magistrates to make such an order; but the power is clearly implied.

WIGHTMAN, J., concurred.

CROMPTON, J.—It is quite clear upon whom the charge is thrown by the Legislature: and it is lucky that we can so interpret the provision as to enforce the liability. No express words are used: but it is enacted that no order shall be made on the parish of settlement; and that clearly implies that the order must be made on the parish from which the pauper is irremovable. Judgment for respondents.

———◆———

*CHARLES HUMFREY *v.* HENRY COURTHORN DALE, WILLIAM HENRY MORGAN, and THOMAS MOR- [*266 GAN. *Jan.* 26.

Defendant, a broker, being employed by S. to purchase oil, signed a note as follows: "Sold this day, for Messrs. T.," plaintiff's broker, "to our principals, ten tons of linseed oil," &c.; "quarter per cent. brokerage to" defendant. This note defendant delivered to Messrs. T. Defendant did not disclose the name of his principal, S., who became insolvent and did not accept the oil. Plaintiff then sued defendant for not accepting the oil, laying the sale as by himself to defendant. Defendant denied the contract.
On the trial, plaintiff proved a custom in the trade that, when a broker purchased without disclosing the name of his principal, he was liable to be looked to as purchaser.
Held: that evidence of the custom was admissible, as not contradicting the written instrument but explaining its terms, or adding a tacitly implied incident; and that the action lay.

THE declaration alleged that defendants bargained for and bought of the plaintiff, who at the request of the defendants sold to them, a large quantity, to wit, ten tons, of linseed oil, at and for a certain price, to wit, 44*l.* per ton, real tare and usual draft, to be free delivered during the last fourteen days of February, A. D. 1856, and to be paid for in ready money, allowing 2½ per cent. discount. And, although the time for the delivery and acceptance of the said goods, pursuant to the said contract, had elapsed before the commencement of this suit, and the plaintiff was ready and willing and offered to deliver the said goods to the defendants, pursuant to the said contract, and duly performed all conditions, &c., yet defendants did not nor would accept or pay for the said goods, or any part thereof, pursuant to the said contract, but wholly neglected, &c:

Plea: That defendants did not bargain for and buy of plaintiff the said linseed oil, or make the said contract as alleged. Issue thereon.

On the trial, before Coleridge, J., at the London Sittings in Easter Term, 1857, the following facts appeared, as stated in the judgment afterwards delivered, *post*, p. 272.

*"The action was for the price of linseed oil, alleged to be [*267 bargained and sold by the plaintiff to the defendants, and not accepted by them. The plea denied the bargain and sale.

"The plaintiff had employed Thomas & Moore, brokers, to sell the oil for him. One Shenk was a buyer of oils, and had employed the defendants, who were brokers, to buy for him. The dealing in question was between the brokers: and, after proof of the facts now stated, in order to prove the specific contract, the plaintiff put in the two following notes.   First:

‘75 Old Broad Street.

‘London, 14th August, 1855.

‘Sold this day, for Messrs. Thomas & Moore to our principals, 10 tons of linseed oil, of merchantable quality, at 44*l.* per ton, real tare and usual draft: to be free delivered during the last 14 days February next, and paid for in ready money, allowing 2½ per cent. discount.

‘DALE, MORGAN & Co., brokers.

‘Quarter per cent. brokerage to D. M. & Co.’

“This note was signed as above, and sent by the defendants to Thomas & Moore.

“Second: ‘London, 14th August, 1855.

‘Sold to Dale, Morgan & Co., for account of Mr. Charles Humfrey, 10 tons of linseed oil of merchantable quality, at 44*l.* per ton, real tare and usual draft: to be free delivered during the last 14 days February next, and paid for in ready money, allowing 2½ per cent. discount.   ‘THOMAS & MOORE, brokers.

‘Quarter per cent. brokerage to D. M. & Co.; a half to us.’

*268]   “And the plaintiff further gave in evidence, without *objection, that, according to the usage of the trade, whenever a broker purchased without disclosing the name of his principal, he was liable to be looked to as the purchaser.   In this case the defendants had not disclosed their principal's name till an unreasonable time after the contract made, and when he had become insolvent.”

On this evidence, the counsel for the defendants contended that the contract between the parties, as laid in the declaration, was not proved. A verdict was taken for the plaintiff, leave being reserved to move for a nonsuit.

In the same Term *Manisty* obtained a rule Nisi for a nonsuit on the following grounds: “First, that there was no evidence of the alleged contract of sale and purchase; Second, that evidence of alleged custom not admissible:” or for a new trial on the ground of surprise; which was not insisted upon in argument.

In last Term,(*a*)

Pigott, Serjt., and *Kemplay*, showed cause.—There was evidence making the defendants liable as purchasers.   The note signed by them, indeed, describes them as selling for Thomas & Moore; but it goes on to state the sale to be made “to our principals:” they are therefore, on the face of the note, agents for undisclosed principals, who are the purchasers: and this renders them personally liable, though the principals might also be sued: Thomson *v.* Davenport, 9 B. & C. 78 (E.

(*a*) November 4th, 1857. Before Lord Campbell, C. J., Coleridge, Wightman, and Erle, JJ.

C. L. R. vol. 17), and Smith's note on that case, 2 Lea. Ca. 297 (4th ed.); Story's Commentaries on the Law of Agency, *sect. 267. [*269 And that this is consistent with the form of the document appears from Pennell v. Alexander, 3 E. & B. 283 (E. C. L. R. vol. 77). If this be not enough, on general principles, to fix the liability on the defendants, at any rate the usage does so. ~An objection is now made to the admissibility of the evidence of the usage. But it was given, not to contradict the terms of the contract, but to interpret its meaning as between the parties. Mr. Smith, in his note on Thomson v. Davenport,(a) says : " Some difficulty has been thought to surround the subject-matter of this note (namely, the creditor's right of election), arising out of that inflexible rule of the law of evidence, commented on in Wigglesworth v. Dallison, 1 E. & B., 1 Lea. Ca. 460 (4th ed.), 1 Doug. 201, viz., that the terms of a written contract cannot be qualified, or contradicted, by parol testimony. It has been said, if A. contract in writing without naming his principal, so that he appears upon the writing to be himself the principal, does not a creditor who seeks to show, that while thus professedly contracting for himself, he *really* contracted for a principal, endeavour to infringe this rule of evidence, by adding to the written contract a new term at variance with the written terms? This question, it is however apprehended, must receive different answers upon different occasions, answers varying according to the object with which it is sought to introduce the parol testimony, which, it is submitted, never can be heard for the purpose of discharging the agent, but may always be so for that of charging the principal." That view is fully confirmed by the judgment in Higgins v. Senior, 8 M. & W. 834,† where Smith's note is *referred to. Trueman v. Loder, 11 A. [*270 & E. 589 (E. C. L. R. vol. 89), may be cited as opposed to this. The marginal note there states that " evidence was ~offered, by defendant, of a custom in the tallow trade that, on such contracts as the above, ' a party might reject the undisclosed principal, and look to the broker for the completion of the contract.' Held inadmissible, as varying a written contract." There the broker, acting for both parties, signed a bought note beginning " bought for T.," the plaintiff, and a sold note beginning " sold for H.," who represented the defendant, " to my principals," not named ; and the attempt was to get rid of the liability of the defendant, as principal vendor ; it was held that this could not be done ; but it is here contended only that the evidence may be given to fix the principal, which accords with Mr. Smith's rule, and does not contradict Trueman v. Loder. So in Magee v. Atkinson, 2 M. & W. 440,† where the broker was held liable, the evidence rejected was not of a custom charging the agent. In Carr v. Jackson, 7 Exch. 382,† it was held that evidence might be given to show that a party, describing himself in a written contract as agent, was in fact a principal. So, conversely, in Schmaltz v. Avery, 16 Q. B. 655 (E. C. L. R. vol. 71),

(a) 2 Lea. Ca. 303 (4th ed.).

it was held that a party, who had signed a written contract expressing
that he acted for another, might still prove himself to be principal. The
defendants, therefore, are here liable; and they are liable to the
plaintiff, who has a right to sue on the contract made by his broker,
if the state of accounts between the other parties be not disturbed
thereby.

Manisty, contrà.—The note signed by the defendants is, at any
rate, not in the ordinary form of a contract between *themselves
*271]   and the plaintiff: and it has been found necessary, in the argu-
ment on the other side, to treat it as a contract, not for sale for Thomas
& Moore, but for purchasing on behalf of the unnamed principals. But,
so understood, it is not a contract of purchase by or sale to the defendants. If the statement of the sale to the principals be untrue, the
defendants are liable to an action. [COLERIDGE, J.—By "principals"
must we not understand the principals in this particular contract?] If
evidence may be given, as no doubt it may, as to who the principals
are, that shows with whom the contract was made: if it could not, no
contract at all would be proved. It is true that a party who takes the
broker as the contractor, intending so to do, cannot afterwards look to
the principal: but here the intention appears to have been to treat the
contract as made, not between the plaintiff and the defendants, but as
between Thomas & Moore and the principals of the defendants. In
Thomson *v.* Davenport, 9 B. & C. 78 (E. C. L. R. vol. 17), and other
cases of that class, the question was as to resorting to the principal,
which, it was held, the other party to the contract was entitled to do.
Here the principals are the parties expressly made liable. The evidence of the custom, if admissible, would show a different contract, and
would contradict the language of the written instrument. If the contract was with the defendants as purchasers, it was a contract not shown
by any memorandum in writing; and therefore, by the Statute of
Frauds, it cannot be enforced.   *Cur. adv. vult.*

Lord CAMPBELL, C. J., now delivered the judgment of the Court.
*This was a rule to enter a nonsuit: and the facts, upon
*272]   which the question to be decided arises, appear to be the follow-
ing. (His Lordship then stated the facts as ante, p. 267.)

It was then objected that, upon this state of facts, there was no evidence of any contract; but, if of any, that it was of a contract between
Thomas & Moore and the defendants, not of a contract between the
plaintiff and them. And, upon the argument, the admissibility of the
evidence of usage was debated; upon which therefore it will be necessary for us to express our opinion.

Upon consideration, we think that there is no foundation for either
objection. Parol evidence was clearly admissible to show the circumstances under which the contract was made, and the relation of the
plaintiff and defendants to it, and to each other, in respect of it. It

was shown then, without the help of usage, that the plaintiff was the owner of the oil, and that Thomas & Moore were employed by him to sell it. By the note first stated, the defendants, signing as brokers, say that *they have sold* for Thomas & Moore to their own principals, whom they do not name, but for whom they, by necessary implication, say that they have bought. It cannot be doubted that, although they say in the note that they have sold for Thomas & Moore, the plaintiff might show that Thomas & Moore were only his agents, and that he was in fact the principal for whom the defendants sold, and with whom, if with any one, as the seller, the contract was made. But the defendants also state that they have bought; for they say they have sold to a person who is their principal, which must mean their principal as buyer in that transaction. Whether they had authority from him, so as to bind him by their *signature, is not now the question as against him, but [*273 as against themselves; and they cannot deny that they have made such purchase as they themselves state. We have, then, as the case now stands, clear evidence of a contract of bargain and sale between the plaintiff as the seller and the undisclosed principal of the defendants.

The only remaining question is, Having stated a purchase for a third person as principal, is there evidence on which they themselves can be made liable? Now neither collateral evidence nor the evidence of a usage of trade is receivable to prove anything which contradicts the tenor of a written contract: but, subject to this condition, both may be received for certain purposes. To use the language of Mr. Phillipps (Phillipps and Arnold on the Law of Evidence, vol. 2, p. 415, 10th ed.): "Evidence of usage has been admitted in the foregoing instances of contracts relating to transactions of commerce, trade, farming, or other business,—for the purpose of defining what would otherwise be indefinite, or to interpret a peculiar term, or to explain what was obscure, or to ascertain what was equivocal, or to annex particulars and incidents which, although not mentioned in the contracts, were connected with them, or with the relations growing out of them; and the evidence in such cases is admitted, with the view of giving effect, as far as can be done, to the presumed intention of the parties." Now here the plaintiff did not seek, by the evidence of usage, to contradict what the tenor of the note primarily imports, namely, that this was a contract which the defendants made as brokers. The evidence, indeed, is based on this: the usage can have no operation except on the assumption of their having so acted, and of there having been a *contract made with [*274 their principal. But the plaintiff, by the evidence, seeks to show that, according to the usage of the trade and as those concerned in the trade understand the words used, they imported something more: namely, that, if the buying broker did not disclose the name of his principal, it might become a contract with him if the seller pleased. Supposing this incident had been expressed on the face of the note, there would have been no objection to it as affecting the validity of the contract; for the effect of it would only have been that the sale might be treated by the vendor as a sale to the broker unless he disclosed the name of his principal: if he did, that it remained a sale to the principal, assuming of course the broker's authority to bind him. The case would then be analogous to that of the delivery of goods on a contract of "sale or return," where the goods pass only conditionally, that is, unless the buyer, within the limited or a reasonable time if none be limited, exercises the option of returning them; if he does, the contract falls to the ground, and is defeated, as if it had never been; if he does not, it takes effect from the time when it was made.

Whether this evidence be treated as explaining the language used, or adding a tacitly implied incident to the contract beyond those which are expressed, is not material. In either point of view, it will be admissible unless it labours under the objection of introducing something repugnant to or inconsistent with the tenor of the written instrument. And, upon consideration of the sense in which that objection must be understood with reference to this question, we think it does not.

In a certain sense every material incident which is added to a written *275] contract varies it, makes it different *from what it appeared to be, and so far is inconsistent with it. If, by the side of the written contract *without*, you write the same contract *with* the added incident, the two would seem to import different obligations, and be different contracts. To take a familiar instance by way of illustration: on the face of a bill of exchange at three months after date the acceptor would be taken to bind himself to the payment precisely at the end of the three months; but, by the custom, he is only bound to do so at the end of the days of grace, which vary, according to the country in which the bill is made payable, from three up to fifteen. The truth is that the principle on which the evidence is admissible is that the parties have not set down on paper the whole of their contract in all its terms, but those only which were necessary to be determined in the particular case by specific agreement, and which of course might vary infinitely, leaving to implication and tacit understanding all those general and unvarying incidents which a uniform usage would annex, and according to which they must in reason be understood to contract unless they expressly exclude them. To fall within the exception, therefore, of repugnancy, the incident must be such as *if expressed in the written contract* would make it insensible or inconsistent. Thus, to warrant bacon to be "prime singed," adding "that is to say slightly tainted," Yates *v.* Pym, 6 Taunt. 446 (E. C. L. R. vol. 1), or to insure all the boats of a ship and add, "that is to say all not slung in the quarter," Blackett *v.* Royal Exchange Assurance Company, 2 C. & J. 244,† and other cases of the same sort scattered through the books, would be instances of contracts in which both the two *parts could not have full effect given to [*276 them if written down; and therefore, when one part only is expressed, it would be unreasonable to suppose that the parties intended to include the other also. Without repeating ourselves, it will be found that the same reasoning applies where the evidence is used to explain a latent ambiguity of language.

But here, if all that the plaintiff contends for had been expressed, the defendants would have contracted thus: " We buy for our principal; but, if we do not disclose his name within a reasonable time, we agree that you may treat us as the purchasers." And it cannot be said that the latter branch is inconsistent with the former, any more than the power to return, subject to which the goods pass, is inconsistent with their passing. There is a case of Bywater v. Richardson, 1 A. & E. 508 (E. C. L. R. vol. 28), which illustrates this. It was an action of deceit for the breach of a warranty of soundness in the sale of a horse: the warranty was in writing, absolute and unconditional in its form; and the horse was unsound. Yet it was held an available defence to show that, by a rule of the repository at which the horse was sold, known to the plaintiff, all warranties there given were to be in force only until twelve at noon on the day following the sale, unless meantime a notice of the unsoundness, with a certificate from a surgeon, was delivered at the office. Here the rule known to the parties is exactly analogous to the usage of trade: the warranty did not in its terms import that it was binding for all time exclusively of the rule; it was not therefore inconsistent with those terms to import a limitation of time; and, by virtue of the rule, it was held that the parties had implicitly imported it. *Brown v. Byrne, 3 E. & B. 703 (E. C. L. R. vol. 77), has been so [*277 lately decided by us, and we there expressed ourselves so fully on this point, that we need do no more than refer to it. But our brother *Pigott*, in showing cause against the rule, cited, for the purpose of distinguishing it, the case of Trueman v. Loder, 11 A. & E. 589 (E. C. L. R. vol. 39): and it is certainly a difficulty in his way, not as to the decision itself, which is quite consistent with our present observations, but in respect of a collateral matter there said to have been determined. That was an action for non-delivery of tallow; the sale was effected by a broker, one Woolner, acting for both parties, and signing both the bought and sold notes; in the former, the purchase was described to be for Trueman & Cooke, the plaintiffs; in the latter, the sale was expressed to be " for Mr. Edward Higginbotham to my principals:" and the main struggle in the case was to make the defendant liable as trading under the name and through the instrumentality of Higginbotham: and there could be no doubt as to the soundness of the principle on which that might be done if the facts bore it out. But, in the judgment, it is stated that the defendant on the trial sought to put this question, " whether it was not a custom in the tallow trade that under such contracts a party may reject the undisclosed principal, and look to the broker for the completion of the contract," and that this question was not allowed to be put; which ruling the Court confirms. How this question could have any bearing on the matter in issue, where the contract apparently disclosed both principals, and where the plaintiff was seeking to enforce it against a disclosed principal (for such, as to the present point,

*278]   *Loder must be taken to have been under another name), it is certainly difficult to see: and this difficulty is pointed out in the judgment. In it the same principle was admitted on which the plaintiff here relies: but it was thought, in the application of that principle, that the term in question sought to be annexed to the contract would be inconsistent with its tenor. We do not cite Hodgson *v.* Davies, 2 Camp. 530, as a legal decision to be opposed to this. Lord Denman dealt with it in the judgment in question, and showed how little it can be supposed to carry with it of the weight of Lord Ellenborough's opinion. But we refer to it in connexion with Trueman *v.* Loder, 11 A. & E. 589 (E. C. L. R. vol. 28), because both cases, we think, disclose how entirely the minds of lawyers are under a different influence from that which, in spite of them, will always influence the practice of traders; which practice creates the usages of trade. The former desire certainty, and would have a written contract express all its terms, and desire that no parol evidence beyond it should be receivable. But merchants and traders, with a multiplicity of transactions pressing on them, and moving in a narrow circle, and meeting each other daily, desire to write little, and leave unwritten what they take for granted in every contract. In spite of the lamentations of Judges, they will continue to do so; and in a vast majority of cases, of which Courts of law hear nothing, they do so without loss or inconvenience; and, upon the whole, they find this mode of dealing advantageous even at the risk of occasional litigation. It is the business of Courts reasonably so to shape their rules of evi-

*279]   dence as to make them suitable to the habits *of mankind, and such as are not likely to exclude the actual facts of the dealings between parties when they are to determine on the controversies which grow out of them. It cannot be doubted, in the present case, that *in fact* this contract was made with the usage understood to be a term in it: to exclude the usage is to exclude a material term of the contract, and must lead to an unjust decision.

Of course this could be no reason for a decision contrary to authority: but we think any one who reads the judgment of the Court in Trueman *v.* Loder, 11 A. & E. 589 (E. C. L. R. vol. 28), with attention, will perceive how much it was influenced by a feeling of the supposed inconvenience of receiving any parol evidence in the case of a written contract. And, as it was not necessary to the decision of the case then before the Court, we are not bound by it now; and we did not hold ourselves bound by it in the case of Brown *v.* Byrne, 3 E. & B. 703 (E. C. L. R. vol. 77), when it was brought to our notice.

For the reasons we have given, we are of opinion that the evidence was receivable, and that the rule to enter a nonsuit should be discharged.

Rule discharged.

The true office of a usage or custom of trade is to interpret the otherwise indeterminate intentions of parties, and to ascertain the nature and extent of their contracts, arising not from express stipulation, but from mere implications and presumptions and acts of a doubtful or equivocal character, or to ascertain the true meaning of particular words in an instrument where those words have various senses. Per Story, J., The Reeside, 2 Sumner, 569; Winthrop *v.* Union Ins. Co., 2 W. C. C. 7; Gordon *v.* Little, 8 S. & R. 533; Snowden *v.* Warden, 3 Rawle, 101; Thompson *v.* Hamilton, 12 Pick. 425; Astor *v.* Union Ins. Co., 7 Cowen, 202; Cooper *v.* Kane, 19 Wend. 386; Shaw *v.* Mitchell, 2 Metc. 65; Leach *v.* Beardslee, 22 Conn. 404.

A usage of an individual, which is known to the person who deals with him, may be given in evidence, as tending to prove what was the contract between them: Loring *v.* Gurney, 5 Pick. 15. A usage or custom of trade to be a guide in the construction of contracts, must be certain, uniform, reasonable, and sufficiently ancient to be generally known: Kendall *v.* Russell, 5 Dana, 501; The Paragon, Ware, 322. The usage or custom of a particular

port, in a particular trade, is not such a usage or custom as will in contemplation of law limit, control, or qualify the language of contracts of insurance. It must be some known general usage or custom in the trade, both applicable and applied to all parts of the state, and so notorious as to afford a presumption that all contracts of insurance in that trade are made with reference to it as a part of the policy: Rogers *v.* Mechanics' Ins. Co., 1 Story 603. The clear and explicit language of a contract may not be enlarged or restricted by proof of a custom or usage; George *v.* Bartlett, 2 Foster 496; Wadsworth *v.* Allcott, 2 Selden, 64; yet in applying the contract to its subject-matter, or bringing it to bear on any particular object, the customs and usages of trade are admissible to ascertain what subjects were within and what were excluded from its operation: Hone *v.* Mutual Safety Ins. Co., 1 Sandf. S. C. Rep. 137. A usage governing a question of legal right cannot be proved by isolated instances, but should be so certain, uniform, and notorious that it must probably have been understood by the parties as entering into the contract: Cope *v.* Dodd, 1 Harris, 83; Dixon *v.* Dunbar, 14 Illinois, 324.

---

*Ex parte BASSETT. Jan. 27. [*280

Under The Nuisances Removal Act for England, 1855 (18 & 19 Vict. c. 121), the sanitary inspector for The Local Authority of a district obtained an order of justices for the abatement of a nuisance. The Local Authority were requested by the party aggrieved to take steps for enforcing the order, but did not do so. This court refused an application by the party aggrieved, for a mandamus to compel the Local Authority to enforce the order.

BOVILL moved for a mandamus ordering The Local Board of Health

for the parish of Ham in the county of Surrey to take steps for enforcing an order of justices.   From the affidavits on which the motion was
founded the following facts appeared :

On 2d August, 1856, two justices of Surrey, upon complaint of John
Doddrell on behalf of The Local Authority (Local Board of Health) of
Ham, made an order on John Parsons, occupier of premises within the
district, to cleanse a drain upon the premises, proved to the satisfaction
of the justices to be a nuisance caused by his act or default, within
fourteen days from the service of the order, and to cease from draining
into the same, and to pay 10s. costs : and, if the order for abatement
should not be complied with, the justices authorized and required Doddrell, from time to time, to enter upon the premises, and to do all such
works, matters, and things as might be necessary for carrying the order
into full execution according to The Nuisances Removal Act for
England, 1855 (18 & 19 Vict. c. 121).   Alfred Bassett, the party on
behalf of whom the present motion was made, was interested in the
removal of the nuisance, as the drain ran past his premises, and was
injurious to health.   Doddrell was sanitary inspector to The Local
Authority.   Doddrell was afterwards requested to serve this order on
Parsons, which he refused to do ; and on 18th November, 1855, at the
request of Bassett, the clerk *to the justices caused a copy of
the order to be served upon Parsons ; and Parsons had not
appealed.   On 2d January, 1857, Bassett served a notice on Doddrell,
containing a copy of the order, and a statement of its having been
served upon Parsons, and that no steps had been taken by Parsons to
abate the nuisance or comply with the order ; and adding : "I have
therefore to request, as a party interested in the removal of the said
nuisance, that you will forthwith enforce the said order, and put in execution the provisions of the above Act against the said John Parsons."
A similar order was, on the same day, served by Bassett upon the
chairman of The Local Authority.   On 17th January, Bassett served
another notice on Doddrell, referring to the former notice, and stating
that the nuisance still existed, and that no steps had been taken by Parsons to abate it, or comply with the order ; and adding : "I therefore
again request, as a party interested in the removal of such nuisance, that
you will, within seven days from the service hereof, enforce the said order,
and put in execution the provisions of the above Act against the said
John Parsons : and, in default of your compliance with this request, I
hereby give you notice that I shall apply to the Court of Queen's
Bench for a writ of mandamus against you, and take such other proceedings as I may be advised."   On the same day Bassett served a
similar notice on the chairman of The Local Authority.   Bassett now
deposed that the nuisance still existed ; that no step had been taken by
Parsons to abate it or obey the order ; nor had The Local Authority, or
any person on their behalf, or any person whosoever, taken any step to

abate the nuisance or enforce the order; that Parsons was still occupier, and was also one of the committee of The Local Authority.

Bovill, in support of his motion.—It is the duty of The Local [*282 Board to proceed. Under sect. 10 of The Nuisances Removal Act for England, 1855, any person aggrieved by a nuisance may give notice to The Local Authority; and that has been done by Bassett. Then, under sect. 12, The Local Authority is to apply for the order of the justices, and, under sect. 14, The Local Authority is to enforce the order of the justices for abatement and prohibition, charging the costs to the person on whom the order is made, who is liable to penalties for his default or disobedience to the prohibition. [Lord CAMPBELL, C. J.— Has not The Local Authority a discretion?] There must be some means of enforcing the Act on behalf of an aggrieved party: it does not appear what means there are except through the action of The Local Authority, which, by sect. 38, is to recover the penalties and apply them.

Lord CAMPBELL, C. J.—But this is not obligatory on The Local Authority; and therefore we cannot grant a mandamus. There will be no rule.

COLERIDGE, J., concurred.

(WIGHTMAN, J., was absent.)

CROMPTON, J., concurred.   Rule refused.

———◆———

*CURLEWIS v. The Earl of MORNINGTON, Administrator [*283 of JAMES FITZROY HENRY TYLNEY LONG WEL- LESLEY. *Jan. 27.*

Plaintiff sued defendant, administrator of W., for money due from intestate in his lifetime.

Plea: that the cause of action did not accrue within six years before the suit.

Replication: that plaintiff, in the lifetime of W., commenced an action against W. within six years after the cause of action against W. accrued, and W. was never served or appeared to the writ, and plaintiff never appeared for him, and no declaration was filed or delivered, and no proceedings to outlawry taken; and the suit was continued up to the death of W., which occurred on a day named, within six years before the commencement of the present suit; whereby the first action abated: that W. died intestate; and defendant became his administrator; and thereupon plaintiff commenced the present suit against defendant within a reasonable time after the death of W., and within a reasonable time after defendant became administrator, and within one year after defendant became administrator, and within one year next after the time when it first became possible to issue any writ against any personal representative of W.

Rejoinder: that, after the death of W., at the time mentioned, plaintiff, as a creditor of W., on a day named (more than four years after W.'s death), no administration having been granted, caused defendant, as sole next of kin of W., to be served with a citation to accept or refuse administration, or show cause why administration should not be granted to plaintiff as creditor; and, in consequence, on a day named (between two and three months from service of citation), administration was granted to W., and the suit was not commenced until a day named (more than four years from the death).

On demurrer to the rejoinder:

Held, that the plaintiff was entitled to judgment, no laches appearing on his part, and he having a reasonable time (not necessarily limited to a year) for bringing his action, within the equity of sect. 4 of stat. 21 Ja. 1, c. 16.

FIRST count: For money payable by the intestate in his lifetime for goods sold and delivered to him, work and labour done for him, money lent to him and paid for him, interest for moneys owing from him, and for money due on an account stated.

Second count: Upon a bill of exchange for 100*l.* at three months, drawn by plaintiff and accepted by the intestate.

Plea (2), to 1st and 2d count: That the alleged causes of action did not, nor did any of them, accrue within six years next before this suit.,

Replication (2), to plea 2 : That, in the lifetime of the said J. F. H. T. L. Wellesley (the intestate), and after the accruing of the causes of *284] action in the first *and second counts mentioned, and while the money claimed in the declaration in respect of the causes of action in the said first and second counts mentioned was due and payable from the said J. F. H. T. L. Wellesley to plaintiff, plaintiff, for the recovery of the money so claimed in respect of the causes of action in the said first and second counts mentioned, by Oliver Richards, his attorney, sued and prosecuted, and caused to be issued, out of the Court of Queen's Bench a summons dated 22d of February, 1851, the day on which it was issued, commanding the intestate, within eight days after service, inclusive of the day of service, to cause an appearance to be entered in an action of debt at the suit of plaintiff, with notice that, in default of his so doing, plaintiff might cause an appearance to be entered, &c. That the writ was issued within six years next after the accruing of the causes of action in the first and second counts mentioned. That on 16th July, 1851, being within one calendar month next after the expiration of the said writ, including the day of expiration, the writ was in due form, &c., returned by O. Richards, plaintiff's attorney, *Non est inventus,* and, on the same day, entered of record: that on the same day, being within one calendar month, &c., and during the lifetime of J. F. H. T. L. Wellesley, plaintiff, for the recovery of the said money claimed in the declaration in respect of the causes of action in the first and second counts mentioned, by O. R., his attorney, sued, &c., in due form, &c., in continuation of the first-mentioned writ, another writ of summons, dated 16th July, 1851, the day on which it was issued, commanding and giving notice (as before), containing a memorandum, endorsed thereon, specifying the date of the first-*285] mentioned writ and of its *return. That J. F. H. T. L. Wellesley was never served with, and never appeared to, either of the writs; and plaintiff never appeared for him; and no declaration was ever filed or delivered in either of the said actions; and no proceedings to outlawry were taken in either of them. That the writs "were so issued, and such proceedings were thereupon had, as, according to law and the statutes in that behalf, was, at the times of the issuing of the said writs and of such proceedings being had respectively, requisite and necessary for the purpose of preventing the operation of the statutes for limiting the commencement of actions; and that the said writs were so issued, and such proceedings had thereon, as by the statute," &c. (2 & 3 W. 4, c. 39), " is enacted to be necessary and requisite for the purpose of rendering a first writ available to prevent the operation of any statute whereby the time for the commencement of an action may be limited in cases where the defendant is not arrested on such writ, or served therewith, or proceedings to or towards outlawry had thereon." " That, up to and at the time of the death of the said J. F. H. T. L. Wellesley, the said first-mentioned writ was, according to the practice of the said Court and in due form of law, continued and depending and undetermined in the said Court." That, on 23d October, 1851, " being after the issuing of the said secondly mentioned writ, and before the lapse of four calendar months from the date and issuing thereof respectively, and within six years next before the commencement of this suit, the said J. F. H. T. L. Wellesley died; and thereupon the said first and secondly mentioned writs abated; and the said action so begun was ended and determined." " That the said J. F. H. T. L. *Wellesley died intestate; and that after the death of the said J. F. [*286 H. T. L. Wellesley the defendant became such administrator," &c., " of the said J. F. H. T. L. Wellesley, deceased, as in the declaration mentioned. And thereupon the plaintiff commenced this suit against the defendant, as such administrator, amongst other things for the recovery of the money claimed in the declaration in respect of the causes of action in the said first and second counts of the declaration mentioned." " That this suit was commenced within a reasonable time in that behalf after the death of the said J. F. H. T. L. Wellesley, and within a reasonable time in that behalf after the defendant became such administrator as aforesaid, and within the space of one year next after the defendant became such administrator as aforesaid, and within the space of one year next after the time when it first became possible to issue any writ against any personal representative of the said J. F. H. T. L. Wellesley."

Rejoinder: That " after the death of the said J. F. H. T. L. Wellesley at the time in the said second replication to the second plea mentioned, the plaintiff, as a creditor of the said J. F. H. T. L. Wellesley, deceased, on" 30th April, 1856, "(no administration of the goods, chattels, and credits of the said J. F. H. T. L. Wellesley having been granted) did cause the defendant, as sole next of kin of the said J. F. H. T. L. Wellesley, deceased, to be served with a citation issued out of the Prerogative Court of Canterbury, for the defendant, as such next of kin, to accept or refuse letters of administration to the goods, chattels, and credits which were of the said J. F. H. T. L. Wellesley, deceased, or show cause why administration should not be granted to the plaintiff as *such creditor: and such proceedings were had, upon and in [*287 consequence of the said citation, that, on" 3d July, 1855, " administration of the said goods, chattels, and credits of the said J. F. H.

T. L. Wellesley, deceased, was in due form of law granted to the defendant. And, for a further rejoinder to the said second replication to the second plea, the defendant says that this suit was not commenced until the 17th of November, 1855."

Demurrer. Joinder.

Hugh Hill, for the plaintiff.—The plaintiff relies upon tne equitable extension of stat. 21 Ja. 1, c. 16, s. 4, which is explained in note (6) to Hodsden *v.* Harridge, 2 Wms. Saund. 64 a: "where a person brings an action before the expiration of six years, and dies before judgment, the six years being then expired, it has been held that his executor or administrator may within the equity of the fourth section bring a new action;" "provided he does it *recently*, or within a reasonable time.' The analogy of journeys accounts applies, the action against the intestate having been abated by the act of God; and the only question is, whether the last writ has been issued in reasonable time: of that the Court is to judge: Spencer's Case, 6 Rep. 9 b 11 a, Com. Dig. *Abatement* (P). Now it is alleged on this record that the writ was sued out within a reasonable time after the defendant became administrator, and within a year after the time when it first became possible to issue any writ against any personal representative of the intestate. The defendant sets out the dates, and must contend that from them it appears that
*288] the time was not reasonable, and that the writ ought to *have been sued out within a year after the death of the intestate. In Wilcocks *v.* Huggins, 2 Str. 907, S. C. Fitzgib. 170, 289, it was held that an interval of four years from the death of the first plaintiff (an executor) to the commencement of the second action was unreasonably long: and it was said by the Court "that the most that had ever been allowed was a year, and that within the equity of the proviso in the statute, which gives the plaintiff a year to commence a new action, where the judgment is arrested or reversed: but they said they would not go a moment farther, for it would let in all the inconveniences which the statute was made to avoid." It is, however, added: "Indeed if the second executor has been retarded by suits about the will or administration, and he had shown that in pleading, it would have been otherwise, because then the neglect would have been accounted for." That is so here: the defendant abstained from taking out administration till cited by the plaintiff; but that delay could not legally have the effect of defeating creditors: and, after administration was taken out, there was no unreasonable delay.

Hayes, Serjt., contrà.—The utmost time which will be allowed, beyond the six years, after the time has once begun to run, is to the end of one year from the death of the intestate. Supposing the rule to be, as contended on the other side, that a reasonable time is to be allowed, then the dates show that more than a reasonable time elapsed before the commencement of this action. It is for the plaintiff to show on the record that the time is reasonable. It was not till more than *four years had elapsed from the death of the intestate [*289 that the plaintiff served the citation on the defendant: this might have been done immediately after the death; and then the administration, which was in fact granted in less than three months from the service of the citation, would have been in full time to have enabled the plaintiff to commence this suit within a year of the death of the intestate. If the defendant had refused to take out administration, the plaintiff might have done so himself, as creditor. But for the 4th section of the Statute of Limitations, 21 Jac. 1, c. 16, it is clear that the words "and not after," in sect. 3, would have barred the action. But the equity of sect. 4 does not reach such a case as this. In Rhodes v. Smethurst, 6 M. & W. 351,†(a) it was held to be no answer to a plea of the Statute of Limitations that, after the statute had begun to run, but before the six years had expired the debtor died, and that, by reason of litigation as to the right of probate, an executor was not appointed till after the expiration of the six years, and that the suit was commenced within a reasonable time after the grant of probate. In that case, the plaintiff relied upon Murray v. The East India Company, 5 B. & Ald. 204 (E. C. L. R. vol. 7), where the six years were held to run from the time of the grant of letters of administration, because, till then, the right of action had not accrued, there having never been a person liable. But there the right of action had never existed at all; on which ground the cases were distinguished. [Lord CAMPBELL, C. J.—You do not contend that here *the right of [*290 action was barred at the expiration of the six years.] No: the equity of sect. 4 preserves the right for a reasonable time after the intestate's death, the extreme limit of which is one year. [Lord CAMPBELL, C. J.—But it will be contended that the year must reckon from the grant of the letters of administration. Suppose there had been more than five years between the death and the grant: could the year have been reckoned from the death?] That is really the case of Rhodes v. Smethurst. [Lord CAMPBELL, C. J.—That case is not very closely applicable: no action there had been commenced within the six years.] In Kinsey v. Heyward, 1 Ld. Raym. 432, S. C. 1 Lutw. 256, it is said that the reasonable time is a year from the abatement, that is, from the death: the decision, however, was reversed on a collateral point. It is to be observed that, in sect. 4, the time limited is a year from the judgment reversed, or judgment given against the plaintiff in arrest of judgment, or outlawry reversed, "and not after:" the time is not reckoned from the time at which there is a party who can sue or be sued: yet often in fact the course of events might deprive the party of the benefit of the year, as if the plaintiff died two days after the reversal. By analogy, therefore, the time under the equity of the sta-

(a) In Exch. Ch., affirming the judgment of Exch. in Rhodes v. Smethurst, 4 M. & W. 42.†

tute must be a year from the death itself.   The loss of the benefit of
the whole year is no more contrary to the principle of the law than the
loss of a part of the six years when the statute has begun to run.
[CROMPTON, J.—Can we say that a year is always a reasonable time
without reference *to the circumstances?]   In Gargrave *v.*
*291]
Every, 1 Lutw. 261,(*a*) the equity of sect. 4 was held not applicable, although the Court admitted that it was a hard case for the plaintiff.   Wilcocks *v.* Huggins, 2 Str. 907, S. C. Fitzgib. 170, 289, is an
authority that not more than a year from the death will be allowed.
In Adam *v.* The Inhabitants of Bristol, 2 A. & E. 389 (E. C. L. R.
vol. 29), this Court refused to apply such an equity to stat. 7 & 8 G.
4, c. 31, s. 3, which limits the time for commencing actions against the
hundred.

Hugh Hill, in reply.—That was a decision on a statute different from
that now in question, and, as the Court thought, not subject to the same
rules.   But in Lethbridge *v.* Chapman(*b*) fourteen months were allowed
in a case like the present; and it was said in Wilcocks *v.* Huggins,
Fitzgib. 290, that "what is, or is not a recent prosecution in a case of
this nature, is to be determined by the Court from the circumstances
of the case: but generally the year in the statute is a good direction."

Lord CAMPBELL, C. J.—I am of opinion that the plaintiff is entitled
to recover.   The original action was commenced within the six years,
which distinguishes the case from Rhodes *v.* Smethurst, 6 M. & W. 351.†(*c*)
After the *abatement, by the death of the defendant, of an
*292]
action so commenced, a reasonable time is allowed for commencing a fresh action.   If I had now to construe the statute for the
first time, I might feel some difficulty; but the authorities clearly are
in favour of the plaintiff.   It is argued, for the defendant, that a year
is the utmost time that can be allowed.   Is that year to commence from
the death or from the grant of administration?   If from the death, the
privilege would often be illusory: till there is a representative, no
action can be brought.   After that, a year seems the least that can be
allowed for a reasonable time; the representative should have so long
for looking about him.   It is said that the plaintiff might have used
more expedition, and have made the defendant a representative sooner:
but no case has been cited showing that this is laches on the part of the
plaintiff.

(COLERIDGE, J., was absent.

WIGHTMAN, J.—The plaintiff commenced his suit in the lifetime of
the intestate, and long before the statute had run.   Then the intestate
died; and the writ in the present suit issued.   The plaintiff seeks to
avail himself of an equitable construction of sect. 4 of stat. 21 Ja. 1, c.

(*a*) Cited in note to 15 Vin. Abr. 103, 4, *Limitation* (A), pl. 8.   See note (*e*) to Adam *v.* The
Inhabitants of Bristol, 2 A. & E. 399 (E. C. L. R. vol. 29).
(*b*) Cited in Fitzgib. 171, 289; 15 Vin. Abr. 103, *Limitation* (A). pl. 8.
(*c*) In Exch. Ch., affirming the judgment of Exch. in Rhodes *v.* Smethurst, 4 M. & W. 42.†

16, as having brought the action as soon as he reasonably could. Sect. 4 contemplates a case where the same parties exist as were parties to the first suit, and where there is no cause for the plaintiff not commencing his second action in a year. But such a permission would be illusory if applied to a case like this: numberless cases may occur in which it would *be impossible to bring the action within the time. The creditor himself is not primâ facie entitled to take out [*293 administration: the next of kin is so entitled, and has never in this case repudiated. Is not that a reasonable excuse for the delay? It is said that the plaintiff is bound by the precise term named in sect. 4; but there are many cases in which a different construction has been given to the equitable application of the Act, and a reasonable analogy to the law of journeys accounts has been applied. In Wilcocks v. Huggins, 2 Str. 907, S. C. Fitzgib. 170, 289, the Court expressly take that ground. They say that a year may be a reasonable time under ordinary circumstances, and that, if it appear in pleading that there has been a retardation by suits about the will or administration, it would be otherwise. That distinction has been adverted to in many other cases: there are expressions of Mr. Baron Alderson to that effect.(a) I think therefore that the plaintiff was here entitled to judgment, having commenced his action in a reasonable time after he was in a situation to do so.

CROMPTON, J.—I think the plaintiff entitled to recover, whether we consider the case with reference to the old action of journeys accounts, or with reference to an equitable construction of sect. 4 of stat. 21 Jac. 1, c. 16. The plaintiff was not to lose the remedy on account of the death of the testator. It is impossible for us to doubt what the established doctrine is. I look upon the construction of old statutes as law not to be *interfered with; it has been acted upon; and the [*294 Legislature has taken it for granted. We are therefore to abide by the old decisions. It is said that the time has been limited to a year. But that is a year during which it is possible to commence an action. It would be strange to say that a man is to commence an action during a year in which he has no power to sue at all. This would be my view if we had no decisions. But, when I hear the cases that have been decided, I find it laid down that a party is not so limited. If he has not used due diligence he is bound to the year; but, if he does use due diligence, he is not bound to the year. That would be the rule where the executor's probate was delayed. It is here said that the defendant was forced to take the administration on himself, and therefore, such force being practicable, it was the fault of the plaintiff not to have used it earlier. But it seems not reasonable to say that the plaintiff was bound to do so, when the alternative was that he must take out administration himself, which might be onerous, as there might be

(a) Rhodes v. Smethurst, 4 M. & W. 64.†

no funds. I think, therefore, that no laches appears, and that there ought to be judgment for the plaintiff.   Judgment for plaintiff.

An action abated by the death of one of the parties, if recommenced within a reasonable time, is not affected by the statute of limitations: Hunter *v.* Glenn, 1 Bailey, 542. The act of limitations was held no bar, where a suit, seasonably brought, had abated by the death of the defendant; and no letters testamentary being taken on his estate until after the expiration of the time of limitation, the plaintiff brought a new suit without delay against the executor: Parker *v.* Fassit, 1 Har. & John. 337; Allen *v.* Rountree, 1 Speers, 80.

When a suit has been commenced within the period of the statute, and abated by the death of the plaintiff, the operation of the statute will be prevented if the suit is recommenced within a reasonable time; but in no case has more than one year been allowed for this purpose: Martin *v.* Anker, 3 Hill S. C. 211. A defendant having pleaded a partnership in abatement, the plaintiff commenced a suit within a year and a day after the writ was quashed, process in which was served upon the original defendant alone. Held that the statute did not run after the commencement of the original action: Downing *v.* Lindsay, 2 Barr, 382.

---

*295]   *JAMES GOOD *v.* SARAH GOOD and RICHARD BATES. *Jan.* 27.

Devise of land to G., his heirs lawfully begotten, for ever, gives G. an estate tail.
Although there is no limitation over.
And although the devise is made subject to G.'s making payments of specific pecuniary legacies out of the land.

EJECTMENT for land situate at Carlton in Moorland, in Lincolnshire. The following case was stated for the opinion of the Court under sect. 46 of The Common Law Procedure Act, 1852.

William Good, at the time of making his will, and thence until and at his death, was seised in fee of the land for which this action has been brought: he was seised of no other real estate.

William Good was twice married. By his first wife he had one only child, viz., a son, James Good: by his second marriage he had two sons, Joseph Banks Good, the eldest son, and John Beasley Good, the second son; also two daughters, Ann Beasley Good and Sarah Good. The above-mentioned children were alive at the time William Good's will was made as hereinafter mentioned, except Sarah Good, who was born after the will was made, and is referred to in the will as the child the wife was then pregnant with. She is one of the defendants in this action.

On 26th October, 1822, William Good, being seised of the said land, made his will, which was duly executed so as to pass real estate. The following is a copy of the will.

"This is the last will and testament of me, William Good, of," &c.
"I give and devise unto my dear wife, *Mary Good, all my estate, [*296 lands, tenements, and hereditaments in Carlton in Moorland, in the said county of Lincoln; to hold the same unto her, my said wife, and her assigns for and during the term of her natural life, if my said wife remain my widow. And, from and after her decease, I give and devise all my estate, lands, tenements, and hereditaments in Carlton in Moorland aforesaid unto my son, John Beasley Good, to hold the same unto him, the said John Beasley Good, his heirs (lawfully begotten), for ever, subject to his paying the following sums: that is to say, to James Good, Joseph Banks Good, and to Ann Beasley Good, 40l. to each of them, which said legacies I give and bequeath accordingly, but not to be paid till the death of my said wife: I give and bequeath to the child which my said wife is pregnant with at this time the sum of 40l., to be paid by my son, John Beasley Good, out of my said estate at Carlton in Moorland." Then followed bequests of personalty.

On 29th October, 1822, the testator William Good died, seised as aforesaid, without having altered or revoked his said will. On the testator's death, his wife, the said Mary Good, entered into possession of the said land under the said will. She never married again, and continued in possession, or in receipt of the rents and profits, of the said land until her death on 3d August, 1855.

In 1837, John Beasley Good, the devisee in remainder mentioned in the said will, died under the age of twenty-one years, leaving his brother of the whole blood, Joseph Banks Good, his heir at law.

In 1839, Ann Beasley Good died a minor, and unmarried: and, in 1847, James Good, the only son of *William Good by his first [*297 marriage, died, leaving the now plaintiff James Good his only son and heir at law.

On 30th September, 1848, Joseph Banks Good, the eldest son of the second marriage, made his will, which was duly executed so as to pass real estate: and he thereby gave and devised all his real and personal estate, property, and effects whatsoever and wheresoever, and whether in possession, reversion, remainder or expectancy, to his said sister, the defendant Sarah Good, her heirs, executors, administrators, and assigns.

The testator Joseph Banks Good died on the 3d of December, 1848; and he had done nothing to divest himself of the estate or interest (if any) in the said land which descended to him on the death of his brother the aforesaid John Beasley Good.

On the death of the widow Mary Good, in August, 1855, as before mentioned, the defendant Richard Bates was in possession of the said land as tenant to Mary Good at the annual rent of 12l.; and he has since continued, and still continues, in possession thereof: but he has, since the decease of Mary Good, paid the rent to the defendant Sarah

Good, who, as well as the plaintiff, claims to be entitled to the said land.

The question for the opinion of the Court is: Whether the plaintiff James Good is, under the circumstances aforesaid, entitled to the said land. If the Court should decide that he is so entitled, then judgment is to be given for the plaintiff against the defendants, without costs: but, if the Court shall decide that the plaintiff is not so entitled, then judgment is to be given for the defendants against the plaintiff, without costs.

*298] *Hayes,* Serjt., for the plaintiff.—If John Beasley Good *took a remainder in fee simple under the will, the defendants are entitled to judgment, Sarah Good being devisee of his heir at law: but, if he took only a remainder in fee tail, the plaintiff is entitled to judgment, being heir at law of the donor who was reversioner expectant upon the determination of the estate tail which was extinct by the death of John Beasley Good without issue. The latter is the true construction of the devise. If the direct words of limitation have that effect, such effect will not be controlled by the charge on the estate: such charges may convert what would otherwise be a life estate into a fee; but they do not convert an estate tail into a fee. [CROMPTON, J., referred to Denn dem. Slater. *v.* Slater, 5 T. R. 335.] That case is in point; and so is the case there mentioned, Doe dem. Hanson *v.* Fyldes, 2 Cowp. 833. The question therefore arises simply on the words of limitation, "unto him, the said John Beasley Good, his heirs (lawfully begotten), for ever." In Com. Dig. *Devise* (N 5) it is laid down that an estate tail is created by the words in a will "to A. and his heirs legitimè procreatis," for which Church *v.* Wyat, Moore, 637, is cited; and that case seems to be also cited by Lord Hale in note (2) to Co. Lit. 20 b. In Nanfan *v.* Legh, 7 Taunt. 85 (E. C. L. R. vol. 2), an attempt was made to impeach these authorities; but the decision was in conformity with them. The law is also recognised in Mathews *v.* Gardiner, 17 Beav. 254. An attempt was there made to extend the principle: and it was contended that "lawful heirs" meant other than "heirs;" and this was not allowed: but the doctrine that "heirs lawfully begotten" means, in a *299] devise, heirs of the body, *was not impeached. In 2 Jarman on Wills, ch. 35 (p. 267, 2d ed.), Church *v.* Wyat, Moore, 637, is referred to, and is stated to be recognised in Nanfan *v.* Legh, 7 Taunt. 85.

J. Gray, contrà.—It is not intended to dispute the authorities which have been cited. But it appears that the decisions have proceeded on the ground that there were limitations over in remainder expectant upon the estate created: here are no such limitations. [Lord CAMPBELL, C. J.—You would not deny that the words "heirs of his body," without any limitation over, give an estate tail.] No; for they are the words appropriated to such an estate. But the question is as to "heirs," followed by the words "lawfully begotten." Every heir must be lawfully begotten: where such words are followed by a limitation over, it is implied that the whole fee is not disposed of by the first words; and therefore an estate tail is implied; and that appears to have been the reasoning in Beresford's Case, 7 Rep. 41 a, 42 a,(a) and of Lord Langdale, M. R., in Simpson v. Ashworth, 6 Beav. 412, where the words of the devise were only "lawful heirs," but they were followed by limitations in the event of the devisee dying without lawful heirs: and the remainder over was clearly in part the foundation of the judgment in Church v. Wyat. [CROMPTON, J.—In Mortimer v. Hartley, 6 Exch. 47, 59,† the Court of Exchequer consider the point for which the plaintiff contends so clear that they reason from it.] In Nanfan v. Legh there were remainders over; and upon this the counsel arguing in support of *the estate tail insists; and he comments [*300 upon Comyns having overlooked the limitation over in Church v. Wyat, and having thus founded on the case a more general proposition than it really established. It is to be observed that the present case is not among those enumerated by Lord Coke, Co. Lit. 20 b, in which an estate tail will be created without naming the "body." In endeavouring so to interpret this will as to give effect to the whole, the circumstance of the charges being made on the estate is not immaterial.

Hayes, Serjt., was not called on to reply.

Lord CAMPBELL, C. J.—Mr. *Gray* has taken the only possible ground: that in some of the cases, where words like these in a will have been held to create an estate tail, there have been limitations over, and that here are none. But the devisor has clearly used apt words for giving an estate tail, by limiting the land to a man and his heirs lawfully begotten.

(COLERIDGE, J., was absent.)

WIGHTMAN, J.—It is true that in some cases the additional reason to which Mr. *Gray* calls our attention has been given for the decision; but there are none which throw doubt on the law as it would stand independently of such reason.

CROMPTON, J.—There has been no doubt in my mind for a moment. The words of the first limitation have *always been considered [*301 to give, in a will, an estate tail; and that is clearly assumed by the Court of Exchequer in Mortimer v. Hartley, 6 Exch. 47, 59.† As to the charges, in appears from Denn dem. Slater v. Slater, 5 T. R. 335, and Doe dem. Hanson v. Fyldes, 2 Cowp. 833, that, though they would have the effect of giving the implication of an inheritance in preference to that of a life estate, they do not introduce any distinction between different inheritances.   Judgment for plaintiff.

(a) See Willes, C. J., in Goodright dem. Goodridge v. Goodridge, Willes, 369, 374.

COLLEN v. MARY WRIGHT, ROBERT JOHN WRIGHT, and
ADAM TAYLOR the Younger, Executrix and Executors of
ROBERT WRIGHT. *Jan. 27.*

W. signed a written agreement, describing himself in the signature as agent to G., whereby he
agreed with C. that a lease should be granted to C. of a farm belonging to G. C. and W. both
believed that W. had authority from G. to make the agreement; in fact W. had no such
authority. G. refusing to grant the lease, C. filed a bill against G. for specific performance;
and, after G. had put in his answer, denying W.'s authority, C. gave notice to W. of the suit
and ground of defence, and that C. would proceed with the suit at W.'s expense, unless W.
gave him notice not further to proceed; and that C. would bring an action against W. for
damages in the event, either of the bill being dismissed on the ground of defence set up, or
of W. requiring C. not further to proceed. W. answered, repudiating his liability to C. The
bill was dismissed on the ground of defence set up.
On a case, stating the above circumstances, with liberty to the court to draw inferences of fact:
Held :
1. That C. was entitled to maintain an action against W. as for breach of a promise that W. had
   the authority.
2. That C. might recover in such action damages for the expense of the Chancery proceedings,
   it not appearing that he had instituted them incautiously, and they being therefore damages
   naturally resulting from the misrepresentation made by W.

THIS was an action brought to recover damages. By consent, and
by order of Coleridge, J., a case, in substance as follows, was stated for
the opinion of the Court, under The Common Law Procedure Act, 1852,
sect. 46.

*302] *In the beginning of the year 1853, the plaintiff was desirous
of obtaining a lease of a farm situated in Soham Fen in the
county of Cambridge, belonging to William Dunn Gardner, of Fordham
Abbey, in the county of Cambridge, Esquire, then about to become
unoccupied. Robert Wright, the testator, was a land agent and valuer
residing at Norwich; and, up to within a short time before the plaintiff's application to him hereinafter mentioned, had had the management of the property of the said W. D. Gardner in and near Soham.
The plaintiff, believing the testator Wright still to have the management of the said property, and to be the general agent of Gardner for
the letting of the same, including the said farm in Soham Fen, applied
to the testator Wright, as the supposed agent of Gardner, for a lease
thereof. And, after some negotiation between them, on 21st April,
1853, an agreement in writing was prepared by the testator Wright, and
signed by him as the agent of Gardner, and by the plaintiff; and which
agreement is as follows.

"Terms for letting a farm on Soham Fen, containing," &c. "Term
12½ years from Lady Day last; rent 350l. to be paid quarterly; landlord to pay the tithe rent-charge and drainage taxes; landlord to put
buildings, gates, and posts in repair; and tenant afterwards to keep
them in repair, being allowed rough timber; tenant to pay for the
muck and straw upon the farm by valuation. All the other conditions
to be the same as on the lease under which John Hazlewood Burgess
now holds the said farm. Landlord to allow tenant 25l. of the first

half year's rent. We agree to the above conditions, this 21st of April, 1853. ROBERT WRIGHT, agent to William Dunn Gardner, Esquire. JOHN COLLEN.''

*It was further agreed, between the plaintiff and the testator [*303 Wright, that an agreement, stating in detail the terms referred to in the above agreement, should be prepared without delay, and be signed by the parties. And, on 22d April, 1853, the plaintiff, on the faith of the signature of the said agreement by the testator Wright, as above set forth, took possession of the farm in question.

On 31st May, 1853, the plaintiff met testator Robert Wright by the appointment of the latter. And an agreement in writing, which the testator Wright had brought with him, was then produced by him, and was signed by him and the plaintiff, and is as follows (omitting such parts as relate only to the mode of cultivating the farm, and the repairs to be done to the premises): "Proposals for letting a farm situate in the parish of Soham," &c. (description of premises). "Lease to be for twelve and a half years from the 25th day of March, 1853, at the yearly rent of 350*l.* with usual exceptions, and with usual clause of re-entry on non-payment of rent, bankruptcy, insolvency, non-perform-ance of covenants, or on parting with the possession of the premises without lessor's consent; and other usual and proper covenants. Lessee is to covenant to pay the rent quarterly, to pay all parochial and other rates and taxes, except the land tax, landlord's property tax, tithe rent-charge, and drainage taxes. And it is also hereby agreed, by the said parties, that a lease and unstamped copy thereof shall be forthwith prepared of these premises, agreeably to these proposals, by lessor's attorney, at their joint expense, and to execute the same when ten-dered for that purpose. Witness our hands, this 31st day of May, 1853. ROBERT WRIGHT, agent to *William Dunn Gardner, Esquire, [*304 lessor. JOHN COLLEN. Witness, THOMAS HUSTWICK.''

The said agreement was signed by the testator Wright in the manner above set forth.

On 1st June, 1853, a valuation of the straw and muck on the farm was made in accordance with the said agreement; and the amount thereof was paid by plaintiff to Robert John Wright, the son and partner of the testator Wright, and was by the said Robert John Wright paid into the bank of Messrs. Eaton & Hammond, the bankers of Gardner, to the credit of Gardner's account there. The plaintiff, after he took possession of the farm, and before September, 1853, relying upon the said agreement, and believing that the testator Wright had authority to make and sign the same as agent of Gardner, and that the lease would be granted in accordance therewith, expended a considera-ble sum of money in the cultivation and improvement of the farm.

On 16th November, 1853, plaintiff was informed, as was the fact, that Gardner refused to sign the said lease on the ground that the testator

Wright was not authorized to let the farm' for 12½ years or on the terms set forth in the said agreement. And plaintiff, shortly afterwards, believing that the testator Wright was duly authorized by Gardner to sign the said agreement as his agent, and on his behalf, instituted a suit in the Court of Chancery against Gardner for the specific performance of the said contract, and for a decree that Gardner might execute and deliver to plaintiff a lease according to the terms thereof; which suit came on to be heard on 29th February, 1856, before the Master of the Rolls; and judgment was pronounced therein that plaintiff's bill should *305] be dismissed without costs, upon the ground *that the testator Wright had no authority from Gardner to sign the said agreement as his agent, or on his behalf.

After the suit had been commenced, and Gardner had put in his answers to the plaintiff's bill therein, from which it appeared that Gardner defended the suit upon the ground that the testator Wright had no authority from him to sign the said agreements as his agent, the plaintiff on 7th April, 1855, and before the hearing of the said suit, caused the testator Wright to be served with a notice of which the following is a copy.

" To Mr. Robert Wright, of Norwich, Land Agent.

" Whereas you, assuming to act as agent for William Dunn Gardner, Esq., on the 21st day of April and the 31st day of May, in the year of our Lord 1853, signed two several agreements with Mr. John Collen, dated respectively on the above-named days, for letting to the said John Collen a certain farm situate in," &c., " belonging to the said W. D. Gardner, for the term of twelve years and a half, from Lady Day, 1853, at the rent of 350*l.*; and whereas the said W. D. Gardner has refused to execute a lease of the said farm for the said term of twelve years and a half, pursuant to the said agreement, and the said John Collen has instituted a suit in the Court of Chancery against the said W. D. Gardner to compel a specific performance of the said agreements, and which the said W. D. Gardner defends upon the ground that you had no authority whatever from him, the said W. D. Gardner, to sign the said agreements as his agent: Now, therefore, take notice that the said John Collen will proceed with the said suit at your risk and expense, unless *306] within one week from *the receipt hereof, you require the said John Collen, by writing under your hand, not further to proceed with the same. And, further, take notice that, in the event of the bill in the said suit being dismissed on the ground of your not having had authority to sign the said agreements or to let the said farm for the term of years therein mentioned, or of your requiring the said John Collen not further to proceed with the said suit, the said John Collen will commence an action against you to recover from you the damages sustained or to be sustained by him by reason of your not having had authority to sign the said agreements as agent for the said W. D. Gardner, and also the costs and charges sustained and incurred by the said John Collen in prosecuting the said suit.

"Dated this seventh day of April, 1855.

"THOMAS HUSTWICK,
Attorney for the above-named John Collen."

The said Thomas Hustwick, in answer to the said notice, received the following letter.

"Sir, We beg on the part of Mr. Wright, who has consulted us relative to the notice which you served upon him on Saturday last, to apprise you, on behalf of Mr. Collen, that Mr. Wright will resist any attempt on the part of Mr. Collen to saddle him with the risk and expense of the suit in Chancery mentioned in such notice. The suit was instituted by Mr. Collen at his own risk and expense, and for his own purposes, without Mr. Wright's privity or sanction: and it has been carried on by Mr. Collen's solicitor without Mr. Wright's consent or concurrence. We have also to inform you that Mr. Wright will defend all actions, if any, which Mr. Collen *may bring against him [*307 for the purposes mentioned in said notice.

"We are, Sir, yours obediently, ADAM CLEMT. TAYLOR.

"Norwich, April 11th, 1855.

"Thomas Hustwick, Esq., Solr., Soham."

For the purposes of this action it is to be taken as admitted that the testator Wright was not authorized by Gardner to sign the said agreements, or either of them, as his agent or on his behalf, or to let the said farm for the period or on the terms specified in the said agreements; and that neither of the said agreements was in law binding upon Gardner. The testator Wright, however, bonâ fide believed, at the time when he signed the said agreements, that he was so authorized. The plaintiff has always been willing to perform the said contract on his part, and has done all things which it was necessary for him to do in order to entitle him to have the same performed.

The testator Wright died in January, 1856, leaving the defendants his executrix and executors. And, on or about 22d March, 1856, plaintiff received from Gardner a notice to quit the said farm on 29th September next, or at the expiration of the current year of his tenancy. And the plaintiff has since quitted the said farm in pursuance of such notice.

It is agreed that the Court shall be at liberty to draw such inferences from the facts above stated as a jury might have drawn; and that, in the event of the opinion of the Court upon the first of the questions raised being in the plaintiff's favour, the amount of the damages to be received by him shall be ascertained, in accordance with the judgment of the Court upon the second question, by an arbitrator, to be named by the parties, or, in *default of their agreeing, to be named [*308 by one of the Judges of the Court.

The questions for the opinion of the Court are :

1st. Whether the plaintiff is entitled to maintain an action against the defendants, as executrix and executors of the said Robert Wright, to recover damages.

2d. Whether, if so, the whole of the damages sustained by the plaintiff, including his costs of the said suit in Chancery, can be recovered, or, if some of such damages and costs only can be recovered, which of them, and to what extent, without regard, however, to the exact amount.

If the Court shall be of opinion upon the first question in the affirmative, judgment is to be entered up for the plaintiff for such amount of damages as shall be awarded by the arbitrator in accordance with the decision of the Court upon the second question, with costs of suit. If the Court shall be of opinion upon the first question in the negative, judgment of nolle prosequi, with costs of defence, shall be entered up for the defendants.

O'Malley, for the plaintiff.—The testator was liable, although he acted with perfect bona fides ; the facts were within his knowledge. There is clearly no remedy against the alleged principle : and it is reasonable that the party making the mistake should answer for the consequences. The agent cannot indeed be treated exactly as principal in the contract itself; Lewis *v.* Nicholson, 18 Q. B. 503 (E. C. L. R. vol. 83) ; any more than a man undertaking that J. S. should marry A. would be liable to an action for not himself marrying A. if J. S. had not authorized the *undertaking. But in the case cited Lord Campbell, C. J., expressed his opinion that the agents were " personally contracting that they had authority to make a contract binding the assignees" (the alleged principals). And Wightman, J., said : " I am strongly inclined to think that there is in such cases an implied undertaking by the agent that he has the authority to bind his principal which he assumes to have. Certainly, if there is fraud, he would be answerable personally in an action on the case ; if there is such an implied undertaking, he is liable personally in an action of assumpsit whether there be fraud or not." [Lord CAMPBELL, C. J.—And, in addition to this, you are perhaps entitled to insist on the principle that, the representation of the testator having been acted on, he was not entitled to deny its truth.] In Randall *v.* Trimen, 18 Com. B. 786 (E. C. L. R. vol. 86), the declaration alleged that defendant falsely and fraudulently represented that he was authorized to make a contract for A., upon which representation plaintiffs acted, and furnished materials ; and A. refused to pay ; and plaintiffs, suing A., failed and had to pay A.'s costs : the Judge told the jury that, if the defendant made the representation and it was untrue, the plaintiffs were entitled to recover from him the price of the materials and the costs of the action ; and the Court of Common Pleas discharged a rule for a new trial, holding that the defendant was liable though he believed the representation to be true. Then as to the damages. The case last cited is decisive in favour of the plaintiff, so far as regards the costs of the Chancery suit. [CROMPTON, J.—It seems to be a question *for the jury, whether it was reasonable for the plaintiff to institute the suit.] The Court here has the functions of a jury. The case is not like Malden *v.* Fyson, 11 Q. B. 292 (E. C. L. R. vol. 63), where the Court of Chancery gave no costs to the plaintiff in a suit where the bill was dismissed on the ground that the defendant was unable to comply with the contract, of which plaintiff claimed the specific performance, the plaintiff himself having insisted on the inability. As to the loss of the bargain: in Robinson *v.* Harman, 1 Exch. 850,† it was held that a party, who engaged to grant a valid lease, having full knowledge that he could not do so, was liable to answer for the value of the bargain. There Parke, B., said: " the rule of the common law is, that where a party sustains a loss by reason of a breach of contract, he is, so far as money can do it, to be placed in the same situation, with respect to damages, as if the contract had been performed." The sale of real estate is indeed, as there pointed out, an exception to this rule, because the contract for the sale is merely conditional on the vendor having a good title. There can be no question as to the plaintiff's right to be reimbursed the money which he laid out in consequence of his being misled by the testator.

Horace Lloyd, contrà.—Randall *v.* Trimen, 18 Com. B. 786 (E. C. L. R. vol. 86), does not really militate against the defendants. It was common to bring an action for a false representation fraudulently made. Then it was held that the action also lay where there was no bad motive. But, from *Polhill *v.* Walter, 3 B. & Ad. 114 (E. C. L. R. vol. 23), downwards, including Collins *v.* Evans, 5 Q. B. 820,(*a*) and Ormrod *v.* Huth, 14 M. & W. 651,† it has been held that, where the party making the representation bonâ fide and reasonably believed in its truth, no action lies. [CROMPTON, J.—I was counsel for the defendants in Ormrod *v.* Huth, and was in much dread that the jury might be asked whether the defendant had actually promised, which I believe the jury would have found.] Can the testator here be said to have contracted for any fact but that of his own belief? [CROMPTON, J.—He would hardly have made a representation of his mere belief to the plaintiff.] That is as natural an inference, from his conduct in acting as agent, as an inference of his actually undertaking that he was so. Then, as to the damages, assuming the liability. [The Court suggested that the plaintiff should abandon the claim of damages in respect of the loss of the bargain, and that the defendants should admit, on the assumption of their liability, the claim of damages in respect of the money laid out : the counsel assented to this.] The question then is as to the expenses of the Chancery suit. [CROMPTON, J.—Is not that a question for us,

[*310

[*311

(*a*) In Exch. Ch., reversing the judgment of Q. B. in Evans *v.* Collins, 5 Q. B. 804 (E. C. L. R. vol. 48).

as jurymen, whether those expenses were a natural consequence of the misrepresentation ?]

Lord CAMPBELL, C. J.—There can be no doubt that the testator asserted that he had authority to let the property on the terms to which he agreed. That is a promise and a warranty. Might he not then *812] have been *sued on the warranty, although he believed it to be true ? If he induced the plaintiff to act upon it, he was bound. It is broken, since the testator had not authority. A lawful promise, having been broken, why should there not be an action upon it, although there has been no bad faith? I should clearly be of opinion that such action lay, even without the authority of Randell *v.* Trimen, 18 Com. B. 786 (E. C. L. R. vol. 86). But that case is an express authority. There the question which the Court had to decide was, Whether the action was maintainable in the absence of fraud ? I always thought the notion of suing the agent as principal absurd: the illustration, which Mr. *O'Malley* suggested, of a promise that an alleged principal should marry shows this. But, if a man describes himself as agent, when he is not so, he must pay for the damage occasioned by the breach of warranty. Whether the plaintiff could recover against the testator all that he might have recovered against the principal had there been the alleged authority, I do not say. Mr. *O'Malley* having abandoned one claim and Mr. *Lloyd* having admitted another, we are to consider whether the plaintiff is entitled to recover in respect of the expenses of the Chancery suit. I think he is. He acted as a reasonable man would who gave faith to the representation that a contract had been made by the alleged principal ; he required that that contract should be specifically performed. The case cannot differ from that of a sale of goods by a party alleging himself to be broker. The purchaser says that the alleged broker's contract is broken, because he had no authority to sell. If, *813] before the action was brought, *the alleged broker had explained the mistake, the purchaser could not have recovered damages incurred by subsequently prosecuting the action. But, if the assertion was made and never retracted, I could not blame him for bringing the action. If the purchaser could not know that the alleged broker had no authority to make the contract, the loss arising from the action seems to me naturally to result from the allegation. I cannot distinguish the case of such an action from the case of a bill for specific performance filed in the belief that the contract was authorized on the part of the alleged principal.

(COLERIDGE, J., was absent.)

WIGHTMAN, J.—If a man makes a contract as agent he does promise that he is what he represents himself to be, and he must answer for any damage which directly results from confidence being given to the representation. There can be no doubt that in the present case the testator did represent himself to be agent for William Dunn Gardner: he thought he had Gardner's authority for making the lease; but he had not. He became answerable for the consequences. As to the amount of the damages: no doubt, if the action lies at all, the testator would be liable to the expenses which the plaintiff incurred in the management of the farm. I own that some question may be made as to the Chancery suit. It may be a question whether the plaintiff ought not to have given notice that he was going to commence the suit, and that this would be at the risk of the expense falling upon the property of the testator. But I assume that the testator did persist in asserting his authority to the last; *and then it was reasonable that the plaintiff, believing the assertion, should claim a specific performance. [*314

CROMPTON, J.—I am of the same opinion. The first question is, Whether an action lies on the contract of a person representing himself to have authority, there being good consideration for such contract. When the contract is written, the question is for the Court; when it is not written, the question is for the jury. Here we have a written document in which the testator states himself to be agent. It never was doubted that an action would lie on such contract. I agree that an action for deceit would not lie, since there is no mala fides: all the cases agree as to that. But there clearly was a contract on which the action would lie: and this reduces the question to one of amount of damages. As to the money laid out on the farm, it is conceded that this is recoverable. As to the loss of the bargain, the plaintiff's counsel did not insist upon damage for that, and wisely; it is too vague a claim. I have most doubt as to the Chancery suit. The plaintiff, supposing the bargain duly made, would have a right to bring an action for its non-performance, or to institute a suit for specific performance: and the damage resulting from such proceedings seems not too remote. Yet circumstances vary so much that it may often be rash to commence proceedings without warning to the party who is said to be ultimately liable to the expense in case of failure. Still I do not think it can be said that the complaining party is always bound to go, in the first instance, to the alleged agent to inquire: nor would this have been of any use in the present case, where the alleged agent did not know that he had not authority. *The facts that we have before us do not appear to me to show want of caution: so I should say as a juryman; and I should give damages accordingly. [*315

> Judgment for the plaintiff, for the damages incurred in the cultivation of the farm and the prosecution of the Chancery suit.(a)

(a) See Mr. Smith's note, in 2 Lea. Ca. 297 (4th ed.), to Thomas v. Davenport, 9 B. & C. 78 (E. C. L. R. vol. 17).

The QUEEN *v.* Sir JOHN DODSON, Knight, Official Principal of the Arches Court of CANTERBURY.   *Jan.* 28.

In a proceeding under the Church Discipline Act (3 & 4 Vict. c. 86), the accused party holding preferment in the gift of the Bishop of the Diocese, the Archbishop of the Province (under sect. 24) sat and heard the cause in the diocese, and there pronounced judgment of deprivation. The accused appealed to the Court of Appeal of the Province.   The Judge of that court refused to hear the appeal, on the ground that he had no jurisdiction to entertain an appeal from the Archbishop.   On a rule for a mandamus to hear the appeal,

Held : that the proceeding was in a court of the nature of a Diocesan Court, in which the Archbishop sat as representing the Bishop ; and that the appeal under sect. 15 of the Act lay to the Court of Appeal of the Province.   Rule absolute.

H. HILL, on behalf of Archdeacon Denison, obtained a rule nisi for a mandamus to a Judge of the Arches Court to hear an appeal from the sentence pronounced by the Archbishop of Canterbury in a proceeding instituted against the Archdeacon by the Rev. J. Ditcher, under The Church Discipline Act (3 & 4 Vict. c. 86).   From the affidavits it appeared that a Court was held at Bath, within the diocese of Bath and Wells, before the Archbishop of Canterbury, and three assessors, of whom one (Dr. Lushington, Judge of the Admiralty) was an advocate of five years' standing in the Court of the Archbishop, and
*316]   another was the Dean of *Wells; and such proceedings were there taken that sentence of deprivation was pronounced against Archdeacon Denison.   From this sentence he appealed in due form to Sir John Dodson, Judge of the Arches Court, as Judge of the Court of Appeal of the Province of Canterbury; the Judge of the Arches Court refused to entertain the appeal.

The proceeding was one instituted by the Rev. J. Ditcher under stat. 3 & 4 Vict. c. 86, against Archdeacon Denison, for offences alleged to have been committed within the diocese of Bath and Wells.   As the preferments held by Archdeacon Denison were in the gift of the Bishop of Bath and Wells, the Archbishop of Canterbury acted in place of the bishop, as directed by sect. 24.   The Court was held at Bath in obedience to a peremptory mandamus from this Court.   See Regina *v.* Archbishop of Canterbury, 6 E. & B. 546 (E. C. L. R. vol. 88), where the nature of the proceeding is stated in more detail.

No case was shown on behalf of the Judge of the Arches Court.

Dr. *Bayford* and *Fortescue,* for the promoter, Mr. Ditcher, now showed cause.—The intention of the legislature could not be to give an appeal from the Archbishop to his own officer; the appeal from his decision, if there is any, must be direct from the Privy Council.   At all events there is no need for a mandamus, as, if the decision of the Judge of the Arches Court was wrong, there is another remedy; for an appeal will lie to the Privy Council against the judgment refusing to hear the appeal.

*H. Hill, Dr. Phillimore, and J. D. Coleridge, in support of the rule, were not called upon to argue.   [*317

Lord CAMPBELL, C. J.—If this were merely a doubtful case it would be our duty to grant the mandamus, so that the opinion of a Superior Court might be taken on the law. But I am of opinion that it is not really a doubtful question. It seems to me, looking to the Act of Parliament, that there is an appeal to Sir John Dodson as Judge of the Arches Court; and, with the most sincere and profound respect for his opinion, I think it quite clear that he was wrong in deciding that he had no jurisdiction. This seems to me to follow as a legitimate consequence from the decision of this Court, in Regina v. Archbishop of Canterbury, 6 E. & B. 546 (E. C. L. R. vol. 88), that the trial must take place within the diocese of Bath and Wells. I was not a party to that decision; but, on consideration, I entirely concur in it. The principle of that decision was that, under this Act, though the Archbishop of Canterbury sat upon this trial, he did so not as Archbishop, but as locum tenens for the Bishop of Bath and Wells. The Court was in the nature of a Diocesan Court, and not of a Provincial Court, though the individual who was for the time Archbishop of Canterbury sat instead of the Bishop of Bath and Wells. I shall in a few words give my reasons for this opinion. Sect. 15 gives the appeal. Now it seems to me clear that, where the trial takes place before a Bishop sitting in person, the appeal is not to the Archbishop personally but to the Arches Court. The appeal " shall be to the Archbishop, and shall be heard before the Judge of the Court of Appeal *of the Province."   [*318 The Judge of the Court of Appeal of the Province is the Official Principal of the Arches Court, not his Grace the Archbishop. That being the course of appeal where the trial takes place before the Bishop of the Diocese, he not being interested, we are to see what is to be done if he be interested. That is provided for by sect. 24. That when any act " is to be done or any authority to be exercised by a Bishop under this Act, such act shall be done or authority exercised by the Archbishop of the Province in all cases where the Bishop who would otherwise do the act or exercise the authority is the patron of any preferment held by the party accused." Therefore, when the party accused holds preferment in the gift of the Bishop, the Archbishop is to do the act which the Bishop would otherwise have done. Is not that plainly saying that, pro hâc vice, the Archbishop is to act as Diocesan? The case is to proceed accordingly under the same machinery. It is not to be referred to the Arches Court, but is to be tried before that special tribunal created by this Act of Parliament for the trial of charges against clerks. That tribunal so constituted is to be presided over, pro hâc vice, by the individual who happens to be Archbishop of the Province for the time being, not as Metropolitan, but as substitute for the Bishop of the Diocese. By way of illustration, if it so happened that I myself were interested in a cause in this Court, and I were to ask, as I might now do, the Lord Chief Baron to sit for me, and the cause were to be tried by him, still it would be a trial in the Court of Queen's Bench and not in the Court of Exchequer. That being so, the appeal is not an appeal ab eodem ad eundem, nor from the superior to his officer. It is an

*319] appeal from a court presided over by the person *who happens to be Archbishop of Canterbury to one presided over by the person who is the Judge of the Arches Court for the time being; but it is an appeal from a Diocesan Court of Bath and Wells, in which, under sect. 24, the Archbishop is merely substituted for the Bishop. When my brothers unanimously held, in Regina v. Archbishop of Canterbury, 6 E. & B. 546 (E. C. L. R. vol. 88), that the trial must be within the diocese of Bath and Wells, they decided that it was a Diocesan Court. All the rest follows. If it is a proceeding in a Diocesan Court, then under sect. 15 there is an appeal to the Arches Court over which Sir John Dodson so worthily presides. It has been argued that we ought not to interfere by mandamus, because there is an appeal from the decision of Sir John Dodson, denying his jurisdiction, to the Judicial Committee of the Privy Council. There might be such an appeal; and I have no doubt that, if it came before the Judicial Committee, they would decide as we are now doing. What would be the consequence? They would not remit it to the Arches Court; but they would immediately act as a Court of appeal; and the appellant would lose entirely the benefit which the Legislature has intended he should enjoy by the intermediate appeal to the Arches Court. I see no reason, therefore, assigned why the mandamus ought not to go; and I am of opinion that the rule ought to be made absolute.

COLERIDGE, J.—With great respect for the opinion of Sir John Dodson, I also must say that I think, on looking at the Act, that this is a clear point. It is common learning that from a statutable tribunal

*320] no appeal lies *unless given by statute; and the enactment giving the appeal gives its limits. Here sect. 15 gives the appeal: and on the words of that enactment it is plain that there are two courts and no more, to which an appeal from the judgment pronounced in the first instance is given. "Such appeal shall be to the Archbishop, and shall be heard before the judge of the Court of appeal of the province, when the cause shall have been heard and determined in the first instance by the Bishop;" "and the appeal shall be to the Queen in council, and shall be heard before the judicial committee of the Privy Council when the cause shall have been heard and determined in the first instance in the Court of the Archbishop." The appeal must be to one or other of these courts, or else there is no appeal given. It was contended that this cause was not determined before the Bishop; if so, as it clearly was not determined in the Court of the Archbishop, no appeal lies. But it is clear that the intention of the Legislature was that there should

be an appeal from every judgment in the first instance: and we should
be reluctant to put a construction on the Act which should make this,
which is a judgment in the first instance, be without appeal. The point
really rises on the construction of sect. 24. If, on looking at that, we
found that where the Bishop was interested the Court was changed, it
might be different; but it is not so. It provides that, if there is a personal objection to the Bishop, another person is to be substituted for
him. Any act to be done or any authority to be exercised by the
Bishop shall, where the Bishop is interested, be done and exercised by
the Archbishop of the Province. There are many subordinate acts, such
as the issuing of the monition, to be done by the Bishop *besides [*321
sitting in judgment. The natural remedy, where there is a personal objection to the Bishop, is that the Archbishop, taking his place,
should do these acts merely as an individual substituted for the Bishop.
It seems to me clear that such is the construction of the Act. If so,
the Archbishop sat merely as Bishop of Bath and Wells. The appeal
is not from the Archbishop to himself, but from the Bishop of Bath and
Wells, acting by his Grace, to the Arches Court.

WIGHTMAN, J.—If the Bishop of Bath and Wells had not been interested, he would have had two courses open to him. He might at once
have sent the cause by letters of request to the Arches Court, or he
might have sat in person. If he did the latter, there would be an
appeal given by sect. 15; and that appeal "shall be to the Archbishop,
and shall be heard before the Judge of the Court of Appeal of the
Province." The whole difficulty arises from the words "to the Archbishop:" but it is plain that the meaning is to give an appeal to the
Court of Appeal of the Province, and that all proceedings on that
appeal would be the same as if the cause had been originally sent there
by letters of request. And it is not disputed that, if the Bishop had
sat in person, the appeal must have been heard by Sir John Dodson, as
Judge of the Court of Appeal of the Province. But it happens, in this
case, that the Bishop of Bath and Wells has a personal interest as being
patron of the preferments of the accused. Therefore, under sect. 24,
the Archbishop acted instead of the Bishop; and the question now is,
Did he so act as Provincial or as Diocesan? The object of the statute
was to substitute for the Bishop, if he was interested, *a disin- [*322
terested person. It might be difficult on each occasion to select
a proper substitute; and therefore the statute designates the particular
person, him who at the time is the Archbishop. But it seems to me
clear that he is to be taken as sitting in lieu of the Diocesan, and that
the proceedings before him are subject to the same incidents, as to appeal
and otherwise, as if held before the Bishop in person.

CROMPTON, J.—If there were no more than a probable primâ facie
case, it would be our duty to make the rule absolute; for by doing so
we enable the parties to have our judgment reviewed, whilst by dis-

charging the rule we should determine the case finally, which we ought not to do if anything like a probable primâ facie case is made out. But in this case I agree with the rest of the Court in entertaining a very strong opinion on the construction of the Act. I heard the argument in the case of Regina *v.* Archbishop of Canterbury, 6 E. & B. 546 (E. C. L. R. vol. 88); and I then concurred with the rest of the Court in thinking that the construction of the Act was such that, though there was a change of one individual for another, the change did not vary the nature of the Court, which was still a special Diocesan Court, and that the substitution of the Archbishop for the Bishop did not affect the place at which that Court was to be held. And I also hold a very decided opinion that the substitution does not vary the nature of the Court so as to affect the appeal, which I think lies to the Arches Court. It was said that the mandamus was not required, for that an appeal lay *323] to the privy counsel from Sir John Dodson's *judgment that the appeal did not lie to him. But I do not agree that this is an equally efficient mode of enforcing Archdeacon Denison's legal right. He is by law entitled to have the judgment of the Arches Court, to go before it and there to be heard; and it is no answer to say that he may have another right, the exercise of which may, perhaps, not be so beneficial to him.

Rule absolute.

EDWARD ROBERTS *v.* ROBERT BELL, Public Officer of the National Provincial Bank of ENGLAND. *Jan.* 28.

A., being in possession of a house, deposited the title deeds with a bank as a security for a loan. Amongst them was what purported to be a grant to B., deceased, in fee. A. died. B.'s heir demanded the grant from the bank, claiming it as his property. A.'s heir, who was in possession of the house, paid off the advance, and demanded the deeds deposited. The bank gave up all but the grant claimed by B.'s heir, which they refused to give to either party. B.'s heir brought trover against the bank; A.'s heir threatened to sue the bank. On a rule under the Interpleader Act, this court relieved the bank, though in the relation of bailee to the person represented by the claimant: Crompton, J., hesitante.

WILDE, on behalf of the defendant, in this Term, obtained a rule calling on the plaintiff and Thomas Evans to appear in this Court and there state the nature and particulars of their claims to the deed, the subject of this action, and maintain or else relinquish the same, and to show cause why the Court should not make such order touching the same, as the said Court should think fit.

From the affidavit on which the rule was obtained, it appeared that the action was commenced on 26th August, 1856, and the defendant had appeared. The declaration was delivered, containing a count in trover, and another in detinue, for a deed. The defendant had not *324] *pleaded. That, in December, 1855, the deed, purporting to be a grant from the Crown to Mrs. Ann Evans, in fee, of a piece of ground which was an encroachment on a lordship belonging to the Crown, was deposited with the manager of the Wrexham branch of the defendant's bank by Edward Evans, as collateral security for an advance of 76*l*. 11*s*. 4*d*.   On 10th July, 1856, the bank was served with a notice from the plaintiff's solicitors demanding this deed as his property.   In this notice, the plaintiff claimed as assignee from the heir at law of Ann Evans, who, after having married Robert Pearce, had died.   The affidavit stated that the advance of 76*l*. 11*s*. 4*d*. was paid off before the action.   It did not on any of the affidavits appear distinctly when this payment was made; but it was apparently after this claim by the plaintiff.   The affidavit stated that in consequence of this notice the bank did not know to whom the deed belonged.   That the deed was claimed by Thomas Evans, the eldest son and heir at law of Edward Evans, who had died since the deposit; and that it was expected he would bring an action.   The defendants disclaimed all interest in the deed.

From the affidavit of Thomas Evans, the claimant, it appeared that, in 1842, John Evans purchased a piece of land, which was the same land as that said to be an encroachment on the property of the Crown, and built on it an inn called the Foresters' Arms.   In 1843, he died childless, bequeathing all his personal estate to his wife, Ann Evans, but intestate as to his real estate.   Edward Evans, his brother and heir at law, took possession of the real estate, but permitted the widow, Ann Evans, to occupy the Foresters' Arms for her life, she paying him a nominal acknowledgment of 5*s*. per annum.   Ann *Evans [*325 afterwards married Robert Pearce, and died in May, 1855, childless.   On her death Edward Evans resumed possession of the Foresters' Arms; and Robert Pearce gave over to him the title deeds relating to the property.   Edward Evans continued in possession of the premises till his death in May, 1856, when the claimant, Thomas Evans, his eldest son and heir at law, entered into possession, which he still retained. The title deeds of the property were deposited by Edward Evans, in his lifetime, with the defendant's bank to secure an advance which since his decease had been paid off by Thomas Evans, the claimant. Amongst them was the deed in question.   The claimant deposed to information and belief, that, when Ann Evans was in possession as tenant to his father, Edward Evans, she falsely and fraudulently represented to the Commissioners of the Woods and Forests that she had purchased the fee simple of the piece of land which was an encroachment on the property of the Crown, and thereby she obtained a grant of Her Majesty's interest therein; and that this was without the knowledge of, and in fraud of Edward Evans.   The claimant had demanded back his title deeds, and had offered to give the bank an indemnity, and to defend the action in their name, but had been refused.

No affidavit was used on the part of the plaintiff: but, throughout the discussion, it was assumed that his claim was made bonâ fide. The case had been before Erle, J., at chambers, where Smith *v.* Wheeler, 1 Gale, 15, 163,(*a*) was relied on by the plaintiff. Erle, J., referred the matter to the Court.

*326] *Horace Lloyd*, for the claimant Evans.—The bank, *being bailees of Edward Evans, are bound to give up the deed to his representative, the claimant. [COLERIDGE, J.—If they do so, the claimant will be subject to an action precisely similar to that in which the bailees are now sued; and whatever is a defence for you would be a defence for them. I do not see what hardship the claimant would suffer by being substituted as defendant.] He has all along been willing to be so, and to indemnify the now defendants. It is the bank that insist on an interpleader. But the case is not one for an interpleader: Horton *v.* Earl of Devon, 4 Exch. 497;† Crawshay *v.* Thornton, 2 Myl. & C. 1. [Lord CAMPBELL, C. J.—Has it been decided in equity that, where there is precisely the same claim against the depositee that there would be against the depositor, there can be no interpleader when the proposal is merely to substitute the depositor for the depositee in the action? By doing so, the depositee is relieved, and no burthen is cast upon the depositor beyond what he must bear if the chattel is given up to him, and the claimant sues him. If no more is asked than that the action should be defended by you, it should be done.] At least the claimant should have costs.

Tomlinson, for the plaintiff in the action.—The bank have at least acted improvidently, and are not entitled to relief: Belcher *v.* Smith, 9 Bing. 82 (E. C. L. R. vol. 23). [Lord CAMPBELL, C. J.—We cannot consider that a general rule. CROMPTON, J.—It may be hard upon the plaintiff if, finding property in the hands of a solvent party, which he has a legal right to have given up to him, he is obliged to abandon *327] his claim against the solvent defendant, and sue one who *may be insolvent.] Besides, trover for title deeds is not within the Interpleader Act: Smith *v.* Wheeler, 1 Gale, 15, 163. [WIGHTMAN, J.—If the deed is to be considered as realty, trover would not lie for it.] At all events, the deed should not be put into the claimant's hands. It should be deposited with the master. [CROMPTON, J.—The best course would be to let the action go on, the claimant having the conduct of the defence, but giving the bank an indemnity to the satisfaction of the master.]

Wilde, for the defendants.—The bank do not desire to be liable for the costs, and rely on an indemnity. They are entitled to this relief, and ought to have costs. [CROMPTON, J.—It would be very dangerous if, in cases where bankers are pledgees of available property, such as bills of lading, or bills of exchange, they could deprive the pledgor of the use of his property by keeping it on account of a claim. I now feel

(*a*) Before Parke, B., at Chambers.

some fear of that consequence being supposed to follow, from what we have already done for you.]

Lord CAMPBELL, C. J.—On the whole, I think the ends of justice will in this case be answered by directing that the action be proceeded with, but that the claimant, Evans, be substituted for the defendant on the terms that he admits a conversion, and pleads to title only. But the bank ought to have no costs, as they are benefited by the indemnity.

Per CURIAM.(a)   Order accordingly.

(a) Lord Campbell, C. J., Coleridge, Wightman, and Crompton, Js.

---

*The QUEEN v. THOMAS PAYNTER, Esq.   Jan. 29.   [*328

A district board of works, under sects. 109 and 227 of The Metropolis Local Management Act (18 & 19 Vict. c. 120), and stat. 11 & 12 Vict. c. 43, summoned a gas company before a justice for opening ground without the consent of the Board. The Company defended the proceeding on the ground that, under their charter and certain Local Acts, they were justified. The justice stated that he considered the answer valid, and that the summons ought to be dismissed; but, at the request of the Board, he refused to adjudicate, stating that he did so in order that the opinion of this Court might be obtained. The Company insisted on his dismissing the summons.

A rule having been obtained by the Board for an order directing the justice to adjudicate and convict, this Court discharged the rule, refused to give any opinion upon the question, holding that the justice must act upon his own view, and could not by this proceeding obtain the opinion of the Court; and that the Board, having requested him to refuse to adjudicate, were not entitled to an order compelling him to do so.

Stat. 11 & 12 Vict. c. 44, s. 5, is inapplicable to such a case.

HAYES, Serjt., in last Term, obtained a rule calling upon Thomas Paynter, Esq., one of the magistrates of the Police Courts of the Metropolis, and The Gas Light and Coke Company, to show cause why he, the said magistrate, " should not adjudicate upon a summons issued by him," on 1st July, 1856, against The Gas Light and Coke Company for unlawfully breaking up and opening the pavement and soil in a certain street within the Westminster District, for the purpose of laying down new mains of pipes, without the consent in writing of The Board of Works for the said Westminster District; " and why he should not convict the said Gas Light & Coke Company in a sum not exceeding 5l. for such offence."

The following facts appeared from the affidavits in support of and opposition to the rule.

The Company, which was created by charter of 52 G. 3, granted in pursuance of stat. 50 G. 3, *c. clxiii.,(a) and which   [*329

(a) Local and personal, public: "For granting certain powers and authorities to a company to be incorporated by charter to be called, 'The Gas Light and Coke Company,' for making inflammable air for the lighting of the streets of the metropolis, and for procuring coke, oil, tar, pitch, asphaltum, ammoniacal liquor, and essential oil, from coal, and for other purposes relating thereto." (Printed at length in the Statutes at Large.)

had its powers enlarged by stats. 54 G. 3, c. cxvi.,(a) 56 G. 3, c. lxxxvii.,(b) 59 G. 3, c. xx.,(c) and 4 G. 4, c. cxix.(d), applied, under sect. 109 of The Metropolis Local Management Act, 18 & 19 Vict. c. 120, to The District Board for the Westminster District, for their consent to the Company opening the ground for the purpose of laying certain mains for the conveyance of gas. The District Board refused their consent. The Company however, after notice to The District Board, proceeded to break up the pavements. The District Board then caused the Company to be summoned before Mr. Paynter, and required him to ·adjudge a forfeiture, in pursuance of the section last mentioned. The Company, in answer, insisted that they had the right to perform the work without the consent of the Board, inasmuch as they had, before the passing of stat. 18 & 19 Vict. c. 120, contracted *830] for the performance by them of the works with The *Commissioners for paving and lighting the Parishes of St. Margaret and St. John, Westminster, who, before the last-mentioned Act passed, acted under stat. 5 & 6 W. 4, c. xviii. :(e) and they referred to sect. 41 of the Act last mentioned, and to sect. 1 of stat. 50 G. 3, c. clxiii. Mr. Paynter took time for consideration, and, on 28th July, 1856, delivered a written judgment (dated 8th July) of considerable length, in which he stated that he considered the answer to the complaint valid. But he concluded his judgment as follows: " Such being the conclusion I have come to, the summons must be dismissed: but I am ready to put my decision in any shape that will best enable the parties to obtain the judgment of a superior Court." He then adjourned the meeting, that the parties might agree upon the course of proceeding. The parties attended Mr. Paynter on 10th October, 1856, and again, upon adjournment, on 24th October. The counsel for the Board requested him either to convict the Company or to refuse to adjudicate: the solicitor for the Company objected to either course being taken, on the ground that the Company were entitled, upon the magistrate's view, to have the summons dismissed, and that stat. 11 & 12 Vict. c. 44, s. 5, was inapplicable to such a case. Mr. Paynter, however, said: " I

(a) Local and personal, public: " For enlarging the powers of an Act of His present Majesty for granting certain powers and authorities to The Gas Light and Coke Company." (Printed at length in the Statutes at Large.)

(b) Local and personal, public: " To alter and enlarge the powers of two Acts of His present Majesty, for granting certain powers to The Gas Light and Coke Company." (Printed at length in the Statutes at Large.)

(c) Local and personal, public: " To alter and enlarge the powers of The Gas Light and Coke Company, and to amend three Acts of His present Majesty relating to the said Company."

(d) Local and personal, public: " To enlarge the powers of The Gas Light and Coke Company, and to amend several Acts passed in the reign of His late Majesty relating to the said Company."

(e) Local and personal, public: " For paving, cleansing, lighting, and regulating the several parishes of St. Margaret, St. John the Evangelist, and St. James, within the liberty of Westminster in the county of Middlesex, and the precinct of the Savoy, and also part of the liberty of Saffron Hill, Hatton Garden, and Ely Rents, within the same county; and for the purposes therein mentioned."

refuse to adjudicate upon this complaint, because the point is beyond a Court of this jurisdiction: and I do so in order that, upon my refusal to adjudicate, The District Board may apply to the Court of Queen's *Bench under the 11 & 12 Victoria, cap. 44, section 5, and [*331 obtain the decision of the Court on this important question."

There were also affidavits as to the merits.

Bovill and *J. W. Huddleston* now showed cause.—The question arose before the magistrate under the Metropolis Local Management Act, 18 & 19 Vict. c. 120, s. 109. The Company, having broken up the pavement without the consent in writing of The District Board, was summoned before the magistrate for the purpose of enforcing the forfeiture of a sum not exceeding 5*l.*; sect. 227 giving to the magistrate the jurisdiction, by reference to stat. 11 & 12 Vict. c. 48. He has heard the case; and, exercising a deliberate judgment upon it, he has pronounced that the summons should be dismissed. That is final. It is true that he has offered to put the case in any shape which shall enable the parties to bring the question before this Court; and, with that view, he formally refused to adjudicate. But he had in fact adjudicated. Even supposing this not to be so, the present application must be refused. If the Court make absolute the latter part of the rule, they will be directing the magistrate what judgment he is to give; and no such power is vested in this Court. If the first part of the rule is made absolute, the magistrate can only act upon his own judgment; and then he will, as before, dismiss the summons. The applicants called upon him either to convict or to refuse to adjudicate. He could not convict, because he thought the complaint was answered: in form, he refused to adjudicate: and how can the applicants now object to his having done so upon their application? They rely upon *stat. 11 & 12 Vict. [*332 c. 44, s. 5. But that enactment was made with a totally different object: it was to facilitate the protection of magistrates required to do an act which they were previously unable to do safely without a mandamus. The Act in such cases substitutes an order for a mandamus. It is confined to cases in which a mandamus would be granted. Now in this case the Court certainly never could have granted a mandamus ordering the justice to do that which would be perfectly useless, and which the applicants had asked him not to do. He did not "refuse to do any act relating to the duties of his" "office as such justice." The Act does not apply to a refusal to convict, whether erroneous or not: Regina *v.* Justices of Bristol.(a)

Hayes, Serjt., and *Clerk,* contrà.—The magistrate has suspended his formal judgment in order that he may obtain the opinion of the Court: and, if the Court make the order for him to adjudicate, at the same time intimating their opinion upon the question, which is purely one of law, he will adjudicate in conformity with that view. That course

(a) Note (a) to Regina *v.* Justices of Worcestershire, 3 E. & B. 479 (E. C. L. R. vol. 77).

was sanctioned by Erle, J., in Regina v. Charlesworth, 2 L. M. & P. 117. [Lord CAMPBELL, C. J.—There seems to be a difficulty in our entertaining the question unless we are prepared to act on the second part of the rule. The justice, if we simply directed him to adjudicate, would not be bound by our opinion on the merits: would that be seemly?] It will be a hardship if some such course be not open to the complainants: sect. 231 of the Metropolis Local *Management
*333] Act gives an appeal against a conviction but not against a refusal to convict. [CROMPTON, J.—If you are right in that construction, you are endeavouring to get the effect of an appeal in a case where the statute withholds it.] The latter part of the rule may also be made absolute. In Regina v. Pilkington, 2 E. & B. 546 (E. C. L. R. vol. 75),(a) this Court ordered justices, who made an order of maintenance in bastardy, to enforce it by warrant of distress, though, on an erroneous view of the law, they had refused to do so. In both that case and Regina v. Charlesworth, 2 L. M. & P. 117, the magistrates had expressed an opinion, as here. The protection of the magistrate is only one object of stat. 11 & 12 Vict. c. 44, s. 5: to confine its application to cases where mandamus would be granted is to restrict its operation unduly: the preamble to the section shows that the Legislature intended to devise simple and inexpensive means " by which the legality of any act to be done by such justices might be considered and adjudged by a Court of competent jurisdiction."

Lord CAMPBELL, C. J.—It is impossible to make this rule absolute without sanctioning a practice which might be carried to a most alarming extent. The Petty Sessions might, in all cases, call upon us to adjudicate instead of adjudicating themselves. Such was not the intention of the very useful enactment in stat. 11 & 12 Vict. c. 44, s. 5. The magistrate here did not decline adjudicating from his own spontaneous wish: he did so at the request of one of the parties. We cannot make this rule absolute unless we are prepared to say that a magistrate may,
*334] in *every case which comes before him, follow the same course; and that would make us a Court of appeal in every matter. The suggestion made by my brother *Hayes* would, if adopted, lead to the degradation of the Court. It would come to this: that we should give an opinion upon which the magistrate would be free to act or not as he thought fit. The statute gives us no authority; what is done must still be done by the justice, and must be his act. Suppose we were to offer an opinion and send the case back for the adjudication of the magistrate: it would be monstrous to say that he would be bound to act upon our opinion against his own. No case goes to such a length. In Regina v. Charlesworth, 2 L. M. & P. 117, which comes nearest, the proceeding was voluntary on the part of the magistrate, and the parties

(a) See Regina v. Wood, 5 E. & B. 49 (E. C. L. R. vol. 85).

did not concur. Here we should be allowing an appeal at the instance of one of the parties against the will of the other.

COLERIDGE, J.—I am of the same opinion. No one who knows how the law stood before stat. 11 & 12 Vict. c. 44, can entertain a doubt. It constantly happened that we had to call on a party to indemnify the magistrate before we would issue a mandamus. That was thought unjust; and the Act was introduced, in order that, where magistrates, from a well grounded doubt, refused to act, we might order them to act and they might be protected. I agree that, though this was the intention, we must, if the words of the enactment go further, obey them. But in the present case the magistrate had made up his mind; and it is contended that *we are to compel him to act contrary to the opinion which he has formed after going into the law and the [*335 facts. That is, although the jurisdiction from the first to the last is with the magistrate, and there is no appeal, or only one to an intermediate Court, that of Quarter Sessions, he can always come to us for an opinion. That would be most inconvenient: the Legislature has left the decision to him alone.

WIGHTMAN, J.—The course proposed would make this a Court of Appeal destitute of any means of enforcing its judgment, which would not be binding on a magistrate who did not choose to adopt it. Stat. 11 & 12 Vict. c. 44, s. 5, had the double object of protecting a magistrate and lessening delay and expense; but no more.

CROMPTON, J.—The course suggested would even go further than making this a Court of Appeal: it would be making this a Court of Advice in all cases where magistrates have to act, as, for instance, in questions whether a party should be committed for trial.

Rule discharged. (a)

(a) See Regina v. Dayman, post, (May 8).

---

*GALES v. Lord HOLLAND and BROWNE. Jan. 29. [*386

A plea of payment of money into Court will not be allowed together with pleas denying or justifying the whole cause of action in respect of which the payment is pleaded.
Even on the terms of the defendant consenting, if plaintiff accept the money, to withdraw the other pleas and suffer judgment.
Although the complaint in the declaration appear to be oppressively multifarious.

HANCE, in this Term, obtained a rule calling on the defendants to show cause why so much of an order of Coleridge, J., dated 2d January instant, as allows the defendants to plead a plea of payment of money into Court together with the other pleas mentioned in the abstract referred to in the affidavit on which the rule was obtained should not be rescinded, and why the said plea should not be struck out.

From the affidavit on which the rule was obtained it appeared that

the first count of the declaration charged defendants with breaking
and entering lands, &c., of plaintiff, breaking down and injuring the
hedges, &c., cutting down and converting trees and underwood, digging
holes and pits, trampling down and digging up grass and crops,
making roads and paths over the premises, cutting up and converting
turf and grass and earth, carrying earth, &c., and building materials
over the land, depositing earth, &c., and building materials on the land,
whereby plaintiff's cattle were injured, building buildings and planting
trees and shrubs on the land, causing persons to break and enter the
lands and trespass thereon, digging up, subverting, and spoiling the
dressings and manure and drainage pipes, converting drainage pipes,
hindering plaintiff and his family from going over divers parts of the
lands, making divers unlawful seizures and distresses of plaintiff's cat-
*337] tle and *goods, and impounding them on the land, unlawfully
threatening to make other unlawful seizures, and thereby preventing persons from purchasing, ejecting and expelling plaintiff and
his family from possession of parts of the land and keeping them so
ejected.

The second count was for an excessive distress for alleged rent
arrear, and selling the cattle, &c., distrained without notice to plaintiff,
according to the statute, and for not using due care in selling at the
best price, and for not leaving the overplus in the hands of the sheriff,
&c., according to the statute.

Third count; for converting plaintiff's cattle and goods.

Fourth count; That, after the distress mentioned in the second count,
which was sufficient to satisfy the alleged rent arrear and costs, &c.,
defendants made a second distress for part of the said alleged rent
arrear, and sold the cattle, &c., so secondly distrained without notice to
plaintiff according to the statute.

Fifth count; for converting plaintiff's cattle and goods.

The defendants delivered pleas with the following abstract thereof.

1st. Not guilty, by statute.

2d. To so much of plaintiff's claim as relates to parts of trespasses:
denial of plaintiff's property.

8d. To same: liberum tenementum, in Lord Holland.

4th. To same: That plaintiff was tenant of said lands, &c., to
defendant, Lord Holland; that, by terms of tenancy, said defendant
might enter and take possession of said lands, &c., with said hedges,
&c.; that trespasses complained of were a user by defendant, Lord
*338] Holland, *in own right, and by other defendant by his command,
of right conferred by said terms of tenancy.

5th. To same: accord and satisfaction.

6th. To same: release.

7th. To part of trespasses: justifying under power to distrain off
the land in respect of which the rent became due.

8th. To so much of plaintiff's claim as relates to not leaving an over-plus with sheriff: payment to plaintiff.

9th. To so much of plaintiff's claim as relates to defendants' converting and wrongfully depriving plaintiff of use and possession of goods: that said goods were not plaintiff's.

10th. To so much as relates to making second distress: denial of there being sufficient goods on premises.

11th. To so much as ninth plea is pleaded to: that, at time of the first distress, defendants bonâ fide believed that first distress would have been sufficient, but it proved otherwise.

12th. Leave and license.

13th. Statute of limitations.

14th. Accord and satisfaction.

15th. Payment into Court.

Coleridge, J., at chambers, allowed these pleas, "the defendants hereby undertaking, if plaintiff accepts the money paid into Court in satisfaction, to withdraw all the other pleas and suffer judgment." This was the order mentioned in the rule.

Bovill now showed cause.—The question is, whether the Court will any longer restrain a defendant from pleading two inconsistent pleas. It seems that the *principle has ceased to prevail generally: [*339 Not guilty may be pleaded with a justification. The Court will, unless the rule be peremptory, hesitate to apply it in such a case as this, where the complaints are so multifarious, and are manifestly accumulated for the purpose of embarrassing the defendants.

Hance, in support of the rule, was not called on.

Lord CAMPBELL, C. J.—There may be cases where such a mode of declaring is oppressive: but I do not think this mode of pleading the proper remedy.

COLERIDGE, WIGHTMAN, and CROMPTON, Js., concurred.

Rule absolute.

In the Matter of a Plaint in the County Court of WARWICKSHIRE, holden at BIRMINGHAM, in which JESSE SMITH is Plaintiff, and JOHN PRYSE and others Defendants.

The rules of a Friendly Society had not been enrolled previous to the passing of stat. 18 & 19 Vict. c. 63. Subsequently, a copy of the rules was deposited with the registrar. After this deposit, but before any certificate was obtained, application was made to the judge of the county court to settle a dispute which had arisen before the deposit.

Held, that the county court had no jurisdiction; and a prohibition was awarded.

BITTLESTON, in this Term, obtained a rule Nisi for a prohibition to the judge of the county court from proceeding further in the above plaint. By the affidavit it appeared that Smith was the Secretary of a

Friendly Society called The Good Samaritan Lodge, with printed rules,
*340] which had not been enrolled before *1st August, 1855, when stat.
18 & 19 Vict. c. 63, came into operation. On 12th May, 1856, a
majority of the members, including Pryse and the others joined with
him as defendants in the plaint, directed an application of the funds,
which Smith and others complained of. In the month of June, 1856,
and not before, a copy of the rules was deposited with the registrar.
In December, 1856, this plaint was brought as an application made to.
the county court to settle the dispute that arose on 12th May, 1856.
The defendants objected that the county court had no jurisdiction.
The Judge adjourned the hearing to give time for an application for a
prohibition.

C. R. Kennedy now showed cause.—The question depends upon the
construction of stat. 18 & 19 Vict. c. 63. This was a Friendly Society,
having printed rules; and, as it was not registered before the present
Act came into operation, it was necessary by sect. 26, that a copy of
the rules should be deposited with the registrar and his certificate
obtained. As soon as that was done, the Society and its members
would be subject to all the provisions of the Act. Amongst others, by
sect. 41, disputes would be settled in the county court. The certificate
has not been yet obtained, but by sect. 44, "in the case of any
Friendly Society" "whose rules have not been certified by the registrar, provided a copy of such rules shall have been deposited with the
registrar, every dispute between any member or members of such
Society, and the trustees, treasurer or other officer, or the committee
of such Society, shall be decided in manner hereinbefore provided with
respect to disputes, and the decision thereof, in the case of societies to
*341] be *established under this Act, and the sections in this Act pro-
vided for such decision, and also the section in this Act which
enacts a punishment in case of fraud or imposition by an officer, member, or person, shall be applicable to such uncertified societies: provided always, that nothing herein contained shall be construed to confer
on any such society whose rules shall not have been certified by the
registrar, or any of the members or officers of such society, any of the
powers, exemptions, or facilities of this Act, save and except as in and by
this section is expressly provided." The object of the enactment was
to make the deposit of the rules a condition precedent to the jurisdiction of the county court; but, when once complied with, the jurisdiction is over all dispute. [CROMPTON, J.—If you are right, the deposit
of the rules relates back so as to make acts punishable which were not
punishable before. It is not likely that such was the intention of the
Legislature.] In Yeates *v.* Roberts, 3 Drew. 170, Kindersley, V. C.,
exercised jurisdiction over the trustees in respect of transactions before
registration.

Bittleston, in support of his rule, was stopped by the Court.

Lord CAMPBELL, C. J.—It seems to me that the county court has no jurisdiction except under the Act; and the condition to the jurisdiction given by the Act has not been fulfilled.

COLERIDGE, WIGHTMAN, and CROMPTON, Js., concurred.

Rule absolute for a prohibition.

---

*WILLIAM HALLETT and FREDERICK FRANCIS HAL- [*342
LETT, Appellants, The Churchwardens and Overseers of the
Parish of BRIGHTON, Respondents.

Where part of the land comprehended within a municipal borough has, previously to the coming into operation of stat. 5 & 6 W. 4, c. 76, ss. 84, 92, been subject, under a local Act, to a rate including the expense of watching, and part expressly exempted, the town council, under those sections, may rate so much of the exempt part, for the purposes of watching, as is not more than 200 yards distant from any street or continuous line of houses regularly watched; but they cannot rate parts more distant, if exempt under the local Act.

And, though the council does not lay a watch rate, but defrays the expenses of watching out of the borough fund of which part is raised by a general borough rate to be paid by the parish officers out of the poor-rate, parties cannot be indirectly made to contribute to the expense of watching, in respect of parts so exempt and so distant, by being rated to a poor-rate partly applicable to the borough fund; but such poor-rate, so far as applicable to such expenses, cannot be sustained as against such parties.

THIS was an appeal against a poor-rate. By consent of parties, and order of Coleridge, J., a case was stated for the opinion of the Court, which, so far as regards the decision of the Court, was as follows.

The appellants are the occupiers, as partners, of two farms in the parish of Brighton, known as Black Rock and Scabes Castle, held for long terms of years. The farms consist of arable land, with some meadow and sheep down, and of buildings bonâ fide used for the purpose of agriculture.

By stat. 6 G. 4, c. clxxix., local and personal, public, "For the better regulating, paving, improving, and managing the town of Brighthelmston, in the county of Sussex, and the poor thereof," it is, by sect. 2, enacted that, for the purposes of that Act, the town of Brighton should be deemed and taken and be co-extensive with the parish; and commissioners are appointed for the purpose of carrying the provisions thereof into execution.

*By the 69th section, the commissioners were empowered to [*343
appoint watchmen, beadles, and other officers and persons, for
guarding, watching, and keeping and preserving the peace of, the town.

Under the powers conferred by the Act, the commissioners appointed watchmen who were sworn in as constables, and continued them until the charter of incorporation was granted to the borough as hereinafter appears.

By sect. 133 of the above-mentioned Act, the commissioners were empowered, once in every year after the passing of that Act, or oftener, if they should think it necessary, to make one or more equal rate or rates, assessment or assessments, to be signed as therein provided, upon the tenants or occupiers of all houses, shops, warehouses, coachhouses, cellars, vaults, buildings, gardens, grounds, lands, tenements, or hereditaments whatsoever, within the said town; so as such rate or rates, assessment or assessments, do not exceed in the whole in any one year, to be computed as aforesaid, the sum of 4*s.* in the pound on the scale or rate for the time being on which rates are raised to and for the relief of the poor of the said parish of Brighton; and the money or moneys, so rated or assessed on the said tenants or occupiers, were to be paid by them respectively to the collector or collectors, or other person or persons appointed, or who should or might be appointed by the said commissioners to receive the same. The section then contains a power of distress in case the rates are not paid; and proceeds: "Provided always, that nothing in this Act contained shall extend to charge any barns or other buildings, yards or closes, bonâ fide used for the purposes of agriculture, nor any *arable lands, meadows, or pasture land, or sheep down, within the said parish, nor any owner or occupier thereof, with the said rates or assessments."

*344]

From the date of the passing of the above Act down to the granting of the charter of incorporation, the practice of the commissioners, acting under the said Act, was to make a town rate; out of the proceeds of which they paid all the expenses attending the watching of the town, and also all other expenses incurred under the Act, except the expense of watering the streets.(*a*)   No separate watch-rate was made by them; nor was there any power to make one. The said farms were not rated or assessed to the said town rate, and never contributed in any way towards the expenses of the town under the local Act: but the dwelling-houses thereon were assessed to and paid the town rate.

On 1st April, 1854, a charter of incorporation was granted to the said borough of Brighton, under The Municipal Corporations Acts; and, by the charter, the municipal Borough is declared to be co-extensive with the parish.

A town council was duly elected for the borough: and, on 7th June, 1854, a watch committee was appointed in accordance with the requirements of stat. 5 & 6 W. 4, c. 76, s. 76.   And, on 28th June, 1854, a meeting of the said watch committee was held, the minutes whereof were partly set out in the case, and which included resolutions as to the appointment of certain persons as chief constable, superintendent constables, inspector constables, and constables, at various salaries *and wages.   The said minutes were approved by the council on 25th July, 1854. On 12th July, 1854, the Mayor published a notice,

*345]

(*a*) By sect. 117 the rates, tolls, &c., were to be consolidated into one fund, and be applicable for the general purposes of the Act, except the watering rate, authorized by sect. 60, as to which a separate account was kept.

stating the appointment of the constables, and that they would begin to act on 26th July.

The said constables began to act on the day mentioned in the said notice (being long prior to the rate in question), and acted thenceforth to the time of the making of the rate in question. And, in so acting, the said constables regularly watched by night and by day the whole of the said parish, including the said farms. Parts of the farms are less than two hundred yards distant from streets or continuous lines of houses regularly watched within the borough under stat. 5 & 6 W. 4, c. 76.

The commissioners appointed under the stat. 6 G. 4, c. clxxix., continued to act for all other purposes connected with that Act except the purposes of watching the town, until all their powers were transferred to the town council by The Brighton Commissioners Transfer Act, 1855 (18 & 19 Vict. c. vi., Local and Personal, Public).

No separate watch-rate has been made by the council of the borough; nor has any order been made by the council that the said farms, or either of them, should be rated to the watch-rate in like manner as. other parts of the borough.

The borough fund is insufficient for the purposes of defraying the expenses of the constabulary force of the borough together with the other expenses legally payable out of it. And, at a meeting held on 19th April, 1855, the town council made an order, which was set out in the case, and which, after reciting that it had been *ascertained [*346 by the meeting that the borough fund would not be sufficient for the purposes required by stat. 5 & 6 W. 4, c. 76, proceeded to an estimate, by which it appeared that it would be necessary to raise 9000l. at least for those purposes; and the council, by the authority of the said Act and of stat. 55 G. 3, c. 51, rated the parish of Brighton, wholly within the borough, for the said sum of 9000l., and, under stat. 7 W. 4 & 1 Vict., c. 81, ordered the parish officers of the parish of Brighton to pay the amount out of the poor-rate; and, under stat. 6 & 7 W. 4, c. 104, appointed the chief constable of the borough high constable, and ordered him to demand the sum of the parish officers. On 25th April, 1855, the Mayor issued his precept, commanding the high constable to make the demand on the parish officers and pay the amount to the borough treasurer; which demand the high constable made on the same day, in writing: and the parish officers, on 30th of May, 1855, made a rate accordingly, in which the appellants were rated for the whole of their said farms at 24l. 9s.

The sum which would be raised by the said rate was more than necessary for the ordinary purposes of a poor-rate, and was made for the purpose of (amongst other things) paying part of the said sum of 9000l., and has been, in part, applied towards payment of that sum. A considerable portion of the said sum of 9000l. was required for the purposes of watching.

Against this rate the appellants appealed, on the ground that it was raised for the purpose of paying money required by the council (amongst other things) for watching the borough, and that the lands for which they are rated are not liable to contribute for that purpose.

*347]   *The before referred to Acts of Parliament to form part of the case.

The question for the opinion of this Court is:

Whether the appellants are liable in respect of the farm lands known as Black Rock and Scabes Castle, in their occupation, to contribute towards the expenses of the police of the borough of Brighton.

If the Court should be of opinion that the appellants are not so liable, then the rate is to be amended, so far as regards them, by reducing the sum of 24l. 9s., at which they are now charged, to the sum of 21l.: and the Court are to adjudge the costs of this case to be paid by the respondents. If the Court should be of opinion that the appellants are liable, then the rate is to be confirmed: and the Court are to adjudge the costs of this case to be paid by the appellants.

The case was argued in last Term.(a)

Sir *F. Kelly*, for the respondents.—There may be some technical questions as to the way in which this particular rate is framed; but both the parties wish to waive all such questions, and to obtain the opinion of the Court whether the appellants can, in any way, be rated, in respect of their farms, for the fund which is to be applied to the watching. [*Lush*, for the appellants, assented.] It becomes necessary to decide the question whether it is obligatory on the council to lay a separate watch-rate, under stat. 5 & 6 W. 4, c. 76, s. 92; or may they, if it seems more expedient, pay the expense of the watching out of the general fund raised by the *borough rate? If they may do the latter, which is what in fact they have done here, it seems that no party liable to the general borough rate, as the appellants here unquestionably are, can object to being rated equally with others. [Lord CAMPBELL, C. J.—It cannot be desirable that it should be matter of discretion for the council, whether they will lay the rate so as to include a particular property.] It may be presumed that the general policy of the Legislature meant the whole area to be liable for the expense of the watching which is for the benefit of all. [Lord CAMPBELL, C. J.—No doubt it would be important to protect the sheep on the downs from being stolen.] It is true that, under sect. 133 of the local Act, 6 G. 4, c. clxxix., land used for agriculture or pasture is exempted from the rate which, by sect. 117, is to be applied to the payment of watchmen appointed under sects. 69, &c., of the same Act, the rate being made applicable to every purpose of the Act except the watering. The exemption of the land was reasonable when the Act was

*348]

(a) November 15, 1856. Before Lord Campbell, C. J., and Wightman, J. During the reply, Erle, J., left the Court; and Coleridge, J., heard the remainder of the argument.

passed : many of the purposes of the Act relate only to the town, which was then much less extensive than at present. But this state of things is entirely altered by stat. 5 & 6 W. 4, c. 76, the general Municipal Corporation Act. Sect. 76 authorizes the appointment of a watch committee ; and other sections, down to sect. 83 inclusively, regulate the authority and proceedings of such committee. The committee has been appointed and is in full action, by its constables. Upon notice thereof (which has been given), by sect. 84, from the day specified in . the notice, so much of all Acts previously passed " as relates to the appointment, regulation, powers, and duties, or to the assessment or collection of any rate to provide for the expenses of any *watch- [*349 men, constables, patrol, or police for any place situated within such borough, shall cease and determine ;" and, by stat. 16 & 17 Vict. c. 79, s. 2, these provisions are applicable to municipal corporations created since the passing of stat. 5 & 6 W. 4, c. 76. Then, by sect. 92 of stat. 5 & 6 W. 4, c. 76, the corporation is to apply the borough fund to, among other things, " the payment of the constables ;" and, if the borough fund be not sufficient for all the purposes to which it is applicable, a borough rate is to be ordered by the council, in the nature of a county rate. Such a borough rate has been ordered ; and the appellants now dispute their liability to it. There are, in sect. 92, the following provisoes after the enactments as to the borough rate. " Provided that in every case in which before the passing this Act any rate might be levied in any borough, or in any parish or place made part of any borough under the provisions of this Act, for the purpose of watching solely by day or by night, or for the purpose of watching by day or by night conjointly with any other purpose, it shall be lawful for the council of such borough to levy a watch-rate sufficient to raise any sum not greater than the average yearly sum which during the last seven years, or where such rate shall not have been levied during seven years then during such less number of years as such rate shall have been levied, shall have been expended in the maintenance and establishment of watchmen, constables, patrole, or policemen within the district in which such rate was levied, and for that purpose the council shall have all the powers hereinbefore given to the council in the matter of the borough rate ; and where any part of any borough shall not at the time of the passing of this Act be within the *provisions of the [*350 Act authorizing the levy of such rate for watching as aforesaid it shall be lawful for the council from time to time to order that such part, or so much thereof as to the council shall seem fit, shall be rated to the watch-rate in like manner as other parts of the borough to be specified in such order, and such watch-rate thereupon shall be levied within the part mentioned in such order in like manner as in the other parts of the borough so specified, and all such sums levied in pursuance of such watch-rate shall be paid over to the account of the borough fund: Provided always, that no such order as last aforesaid shall be made for rating to such watch-rate any part of any borough in which at the time of passing this Act such rate as aforesaid shall not be levied, and which is more than two hundred yards distant from any street or continuous line of houses which shall be regularly watched within the borough under the provisions of this Act." No watch-rate has been laid under this clause, which is permissive only: it might have been advisable to act upon the power if the benefit of the watch-rate were confined to a part of the parish; but that is not so; and therefore the constables are paid under the general rate. That the Legislature had in view the conferring such a discretion appears by the power given to include particular parts of the borough not subject to former rates. The local Act, if that is to aid in interpreting this section of the Municipal Corporation Act, exempts the pastures, &c., not specifically from the watch-rate, but from the general rate: therefore it affords no more reason for insisting on an exemption from the borough rate in respect of the expenses of watching than in respect of any other expenses. But, in fact, the *exempting proviso in sect. 92 of stat. 5 & 6 W. 4, c. 76, applies only where a watch-rate has been previously levied: but no watch-rate was so previously levied, only a general rate applicable to the expenses of watching among many others. Stat. 7 W. 4 & 1 Vict. c. 81, does not affect the point now in dispute: it only provides for cases where a borough or watch-rate may be made in any borough, and directs that it shall be paid out of the poor-rate, or by a separate pound-rate if the council choose so to order. This Act is merely permissive; and the same remark applies to stat. 2 & 3 Vict. c. 28, which enables the council to lay a watch-rate upon the occupiers of premises watched by day and night, exempting from such a rate premises exempted by any local Act from the payment of watch-rates, and prohibiting any alteration in the comparative liability of premises to any watch-rate under any local Act.

*351]

Lush, contrà.—The local Act exempted the farms from the rate leviable under that Act; and that rate was, in part, a watch-rate. Therefore, if a separate watch-rate were now laid under stat. 5 & 6 W. 4, c. 76, s. 92, it is clear that such parts of the farms as lie more than two hundred yards from the continuous line of houses could not be liable to such rate. It is true that sect. 84 of stat. 5 & 6 W. 4, c. 76, puts an end to the power of rating under local Acts for watching; but sect. 92 perpetuates exemptions from the liability to the expenses of watching (except within the two hundred yards); and, moreover, it left the other powers possessed by the Commissioners untouched. It is suggested that the exemption in sect. 92 is inapplicable, because there was never any watch-rate in Brighton. But the language, *in the earlier part of the proviso, is: "in every case in which before the passing this Act any rate might be levied in any borough, or in any

*352]

parish or place made part of any borough under the provisions of this
Act, for the purpose of watching," &c. A rate is not the less made for
the purpose of watching because it is made also for other purposes; an
exemption from a rate partly applicable to watching is surely an exemption from a watch-rate. Even as to the parts of the farm within the
two hundred yards, the watch-rate cannot be laid without an express
order of council bringing such parts within the rateable district. No
such order has here been made. Then stat. 7 W. 4 & 1 Vict. c. 81, even _
if the council have a discretion, shows the principle which the Legislature had in view, that of providing a machinery by which exempt property might be separated from property not exempt. Stat. 2 & 3 Vict.
c. 28, clearly recognises the same kind of exemption, and points to the
necessity of a direct order of the council for including property not
before exempted. The proviso is conclusive evidence of the intention
of the Legislature; it would be unintelligible in the view taken by the
respondents; and the prohibition against altering comparative liabilities
gets rid of the argument suggested from there having been previously
no rate exclusively for watching. Further, stat. 8 & 9 Vict. c. 110, s.
6, enacts that, where a part only of a parish is liable to a watch-rate,
the parish officers are not to pay the amount out of the poor-rate, but
are to make a separate rate for the parts liable: this cannot be confined
to the case where the exemption was only from any rate that might be
made exclusively for the purposes of watching.

*Sir *F. Kelly*, in reply.—The objections urged apply only to [*353
that which has not been done: they may show that the council
had no power to lay a watch-rate; but no watch-rate has been or need
be laid. Unless the council are bound in all cases to defray the expense
of watching by a rate which is exclusively a watch-rate, there is a discretion: if there is, the Court will not assume that the discretion has
been improperly exercised. In sect. 92 of stat. 5 & 6 W. 4, c. 76, the
word "required" is used more than once; but it is not used in the part
empowering the council to lay the watch-rate. It is not true that stat.
2 & 3 Vict. c. 28, is unintelligible upon the view of the respondents:
the clause would be applicable to local Acts passed since stat. 5 & 6
Vict. c. 76, giving powers of rating for watching which therefore would
not be repealed by sect. 84 of the last-mentioned Act, or to cases where
no watch committee had been appointed. [Lord CAMPBELL, C. J.—Is
it not imperative to appoint a watch committee?] Taking that to be
so, the enactment would apply in the mean time. Stat. 8 & 9 Vict. c.
110, s. 6, applies to two cases: first, where part of the parish is without the borough, and therefore ought not to be liable to a rate laid for
borough purposes; secondly, to cases where a watch-rate, eo nomine,
is laid, and there is an exemption from such a rate.

Cur. adv. vult.

Lord CAMPBELL, C. J., in this Term (January 13th), delivered the judgment of the Court.

It was agreed, upon the argument of this case, that the question which the parties wished to have determined was, not whether the particular rate could be *supported as far as it related to the property of the appellants, but whether so much of their property within the parish and borough as is more than two hundred yards from streets or continuous lines of houses is liable to be rated in any form or manner to a rate which would include the expense of watching.

*854]

By the 92d section of stat. 5 & 6 W. 4, c. 76, the payment of the constables appointed by the watch committee, under sects. 76 and 84, and of all other expenses necessarily incurred in carrying the provisions of the Act into effect, and not otherwise provided for, are to be made out of the borough fund : and, if the borough fund is not sufficient, the council of the borough may order a borough rate in the nature of a county rate to be made within the borough ; and the sums levied to be paid over to the borough fund.

The 84th section of the Act provides that, upon the appointment of constables under that Act, and notice given as specified (which was given in the present case), all Acts relating to police and watching within the borough shall cease. And it was contended, for the borough, that, under the powers in the enacting part of the 92d section, the council of the borough might make a borough rate which would include the whole of the appellants' property, and apply a sufficient portion of the general fund to the payment of the expenses of watching.

The enacting part of the 92d section is, however, subject to provisoes which, in connexion with some subsequent statutes, show that the appellants' property more than two hundred yards from the streets and continuous lines of houses in the borough could not be included in any rate to be made for defraying in part *the expense of watching and police. By the 92d section of stat. 5 & 6 W. 4, c. 76, it is (amongst other things) provided that, where any part of the borough shall not, at the time of passing the Act, be within the provisions of the Act for authorizing the levying a watch-rate, the council may order such part to be rated to the watch-rate ; but no such part shall be included in the order, if at the time of passing that Act it was more than two hundred yards from a street or continuous line of houses regularly watched.

*855]

The effect of the 84th and 92d sections of stat. 5 & 6 W. 4, c. 76, is to make all property within the borough rateable to the watch-rate, provided it be within two hundred yards of a street or continuous line of houses : and to that extent it supersedes the local Act : but there is no power to rate any property which is more than two hundred yards from a street or continuous line of houses ; and as to so much of the property of the appellants as is beyond that limit, they are not liable to be rated to the watch-rate of the borough. Any difficulty that might arise in consequence of part of the parish not being liable to the watch-rate of the borough is provided for by stat. 8 & 9 Vict. c. 110, s. 1.

The result is, that the town council may make all the property of the appellants within the borough which lies within two hundred yards of a street or continuous line of houses rateable to the watch-rate, but not that part of their property which is beyond the two hundred yards.

Rate to be amended.

----

*HENDERSON v. The ROYAL BRITISH BANK.   *Jan.* 30. [*356

Under stat. 7 & 8 Vict. c. 113, s. 10, if judgment has been obtained against a joint stock bank, and, execution against them being ineffectual, it is sought to charge a shareholder, such shareholder cannot resist the claim on the ground that he was induced to become a shareholder by fraud on the part of the bank, and repudiated the shares after the bank had become bankrupt but as soon as he discovered the fraud, the judgment-creditor being no party to the fraud. The fact that a party charged is a shareholder is (at any rate primâ facie) sufficiently shown by his name appearing on the registered memorial at the time of the judgment being recovered. Although such memorial varies in some particulars from the register prescribed in stat. 7 & 8 Vict. c. 113, s. 16, and Schedules (A.), (B.); as in referring to a wrong Act of Parliament at the head of the memorial, and in signatures not having been affixed at the proper times.

ASPLAND, in this Term, obtained a rule calling on Leonard Morse Goddard to show cause why the plaintiff should not be at liberty to issue execution against the person, property, or effects of the said L. M. Goddard, as a shareholder of The Royal British Bank, for the sum of 131*l.* 3*s.* 11*d.*, remaining due on a judgment recovered by the plain tiff against the said Bank for the sum of 178*l.* 8*s.* 9*d.*

It appeared from the affidavits on which the rule was obtained that The Royal British Bank was incorporated by letters patent under stat. 7 & 8 Vict. c. 113. On 24th September, 1856, under the Joint Stock Companies Winding-Up Act, 1848 (11 & 12 Vict. c. 45), and The Joint Stock Companies Winding-Up Amendment Act, 1849 (12 & 13 Vict. c. 108), an order absolute was made for winding up the Bank; and an official manager had since been appointed. On 9th October, 1856, the Bank had been adjudicated to be bankrupt, and an assignee was then appointed. On 7th November, 1856, plaintiff obtained final judgment against the Bank, by default for want of a plea, for 300*l.* debt and 6*l.* 13*s.* costs; of which debt, as he now deposed, 171*l.* 15*s.* 9*d.* was, at the time of the obtaining the judgment, justly due to *him, and [*357 (together with the said costs) was still due to him. On 13th November, 1856, the plaintiff proved his said debt before the Master, as required by sect. 73 of stat. 11 & 12 Vict. c. 45; and on 14th November he issued a fi. fa. which, on 17th November, was returned Nulla bona. Plaintiff deposed to his belief that there was not, at the

time of the issuing the writ nor afterwards, any property or effects of
the Bank out of which the money could be levied, but the execution
was wholly ineffectual, and that any other execution against its property or effects would be so.   On 5th December, the plaintiff proved
before Mr. Holroyd, Commissioner in the Court of Bankruptcy, for 171*l.*
15*s.* 9*d.*, being the balance of his claim after giving credit to any amount
due from him to the Bank, exhibiting at the time his judgment paper
with a view of proving for the costs; of which last, however, the Commissioner disallowed the proof.

On 20th December, 1856, the registry of the memorial relating to
the Bank, filed at the Stamp Office in London, was examined, and the
name of Leonard Morse Goddard appeared as one of the members of
the Company, with his address; and it was deposed, on behalf, that he
then and still was a member of the Company. (It was stated, and
admitted on argument, though it did not appear on the depositions, that
this memorial was not strictly conformable to the provisions of stat. 7
& 8 Vict. c. 113, s. 16, &c., and schedules (A.) and (B.), the Act being
wrongly described in the heading of the memorial,(*a*) and that the signatures were not made at the proper times.)   On 12th December, 1856,

*358]   notice, on *behalf of the plaintiff, was given to Goddard, that,
in ten days from service, application would be made to a Judge
at Chambers for a summons, calling on Goddard to show cause why
plaintiff should not have execution against Goddard's property and
effects in satisfaction of the judgment.   The summons was obtained
accordingly, and was attended before Coleridge, J., on 24th December,
1856.   The clerk to the plaintiff's attorney deposed that, on the hearing, " it was admitted, on behalf of the said Leonard Morse Goddard,
that he was on the register of shareholders of the said Bank: but it
was contended that an order ought not to be made on the said summons
for execution against him for the debt due to the plaintiff, inasmuch
(as was alleged) the said L. M. Goddard and others had been induced to
accept shares in the said Bank by a fraud: but it was expressly admitted,
on behalf of the said L. M. Goddard, that the plaintiff was in no way
connected with any such fraud; and the fact of a dividend of 5*s.* 6*d.*
in the pound on the debts of the Bank having been declared was referred
to."   Coleridge, J., then ordered that the summons should be adjourned
until the fifth day of the then next Term, Goddard bringing into Court
(in a week) the sum of 125*l.*; otherwise liberty to issue execution: no
objection to be taken on the ground of a dividend to be received.   On
making the order, Coleridge, J., directed that no objection to the rule
to be moved for in Court by plaintiff should be made except in respect
to the matters relied on before him as aforesaid, and that the 125*l.* was
to abide the application to the Court.   Since the making of the order
the plaintiff had received 47*l.* 4*s.* 10*d.*, the amount of the dividend of

(*a*) See note (*a*) to Daniell *v.* Royal British Bank, 1 H. & N. 681.†

5s. 6d. in the pound on the 171*l.* 15*s.* 9*d.*; and 131*l.* 3*s.* 11*d.* was still
due on the *judgment. The 125*l.* had been paid into Court. [*359
The 171*l.* 15*s.* 9*d.*, for which (with costs) judgment was obtained,
was the balance of money deposited by plaintiff with the Bank as his
bankers: and plaintiff deposed that Goddard " was on the register of
shareholders of the said Bank at the time of the accruing of the debt
in which I recovered the said judgment, and also at the time of recovering the said judgment."

From affidavit made by Goddard it appeared that the alleged fraud
by which he was induced to purchase shares consisted in statements, by
the directors, officers, and clerks of the Bank, respecting the state and
prospects of the Bank; including declarations of dividends where there
were no real profits; which statements he first ascertained to be false
(and, as he believed, wilfully so) after the stoppage of the Bank. That
he had repudiated the shares, and had proved in the Court of Bankruptcy against the Bank for 250*l.* for the alleged purchase-money in the
alleged shares, which claim now stood over for consideration. He did
not deny the receipt of dividends on the shares before the repudiation.

On a previous day in this Term,(*a*)

Hugh Hill and *Mellish* showed cause.—The rule is improperly
framed: as the money has been paid into Court, the application should
have been for liberty to the plaintiff to take it out. But the Court will
probably mould the rule, if the plaintiff is entitled to succeed. The
application is made under the 9th and following sections of stat. 7 & 8
Vict. c. 113, the Company having been incorporated under sect. 3.
The execution, by *sect. 10, is to issue against the individual [*360
shareholder if the execution against the Company be ineffectual,
as appears to be the case here: the shareholders for the time being are
first liable: in default of satisfaction being obtained against them, individuals who were shareholders when the cause of action arose; but " no
person having ceased to be a shareholder of the Company shall be liable
for the payment of any debt for which any such judgment, decree, or
order shall have been so obtained, for which he would not have been
liable as a partner in case a suit had been originally brought against
him for the same, or for which judgment shall have been obtained, after
the expiration of three years from the time when he shall have ceased
to be a shareholder of such Company." Here the shareholder has
renounced his shares, and has " ceased to be a shareholder." Under
the Joint Stock Companies Act, 7 & 8 Vict. c. 110, it was held that a
party, sued by a joint stock company for calls, could not defend himself on the ground that he was induced to become a shareholder by the
fraud of the plaintiffs, without showing that he had ceased to be a shareholder, or had, on discovering the fraud, renounced the shares and all
benefit to be derived from them: Deposit Life Assurance *v.* Ayscough,

6 E. & B. 761 (E. C. L. R. vol. 88).   But here Goddard, on discovering the fraud, repudiated his shares.   [Lord CAMPBELL, C. J.—Could he do so after the Bank had stopped?]   He could, if he did so as soon as he discovered the fraud; which is the fact here.   [Lord CAMPBELL, C. J.— But the doctrine of the defence on the ground of fraud is very alarming.] In Ex parte Ginger, 5 Irish Chancery Reports, 174, it was held that a purchase of shares issued in violation of the partnership deed did not *361]   *render the purchaser of such shares, who was induced to become so by a fraudulent report, a proprietor or contributory.   In fact, the principle upon which this application is founded would make a shareholder who was fraudulently induced to become so, and remained so for a week only, and received no profits, liable to all debts for which a judgment might be recovered in three years, and for all debts due before the commencement of the partnership.   This is a much higher liability than that of a partner at common law; and the statute, if relied upon, must be strictly complied with.   The repudiation having taken place before any transfer of the shares, the case is like that of a sale brought about by the fraud of the purchaser, which the vendor may repudiate if the goods have not passed into the hands of a bonâ fide purchaser, as was admitted in White v. Garden, 10 Com. B. 919 (E. C. L. R. vol. 70).   It will be insisted that he is liable, under sect. 21 of stat. 7 & 8 Vict. c. 113, as being on the last delivered memorial.   The memorial is prescribed by sects. 16, 17, which refer to Schedules (A.) (B.).   But the memorial here does not follow those forms: it recites the Act wrongly; nor was it signed at the proper time.   The claim here is founded entirely on the statute.   It may be proved, without the aid of the memorial, that a party is a shareholder under the statute: but no such proof is offered here: the applicant relies entirely on the memorial, and therefore can succeed only if the memorial fulfils the statutory requisitions.   No prejudice to him will arise by his being put to a scire facias.

*362]   Aspland, contrà.—As to the objection to the memorial: *the plaintiff is not to be prejudiced by the Bank having made an informal return to Somerset House.   The corporation exists only under stat. 7 & 8 Vict. c. 113; it is enough that a memorial appears registered on their behalf, including the name of Goddard.   Even where a bank, by its public officer, was plaintiff, under the Bankers' Act, 7 G. 4, c. 46, it was held that strict regularity in the Stamp Office return, in all particulars, was not a condition precedent to the right of action: Armitage v. Hamer, 3 B. & Ad. 793 (E. C. L. R. vol. 23).   As to the other point: fraud, to make it a defence by a party charged as contributory under the Winding-Up Acts, must be the fraud of all interested: In re The Direct London and Exeter Railway Company, Parbury's Case, 3 De G. & Sm. 48.   The fraud relied upon here is partly effected by declaring dividends where there were no profits; it appears, therefore, that Goddard has received a part of the deposit money of the plaintiff: he cannot insist, as against such a creditor, that he himself has become a party by means of a fraud in which the creditor is not involved. In Ellis *v.* Schmæck, 5 Bing. 521 (E. C. L. R. vol. 15), defendants had innocently purchased scrip in a company originating in fraud, after which the plaintiff became a creditor of the company; the defendants afterwards transferred their scrip, having never signed the partnership deed: yet they were held liable to an action brought by the plaintiff after the transfer. Here the only repudiation is the claim in bankruptcy, which is not finally disposed of. Deposit Life Assurance Company *v.* Ayscough, 6 E. & B. 761 (E. C. L. R. vol. 88), is an authority in favour of the plaintiff. In Ex parte Ginger, 5 Irish Chancery Reports, 174, the difference was pointed out *between a [*363 question among shareholders, and a question of a claim by a creditor: the marginal note there states that " the proper test to apply, in considering whether a party should be retained on the list of contributories, under the Joint Stock Companies Winding-Up Acts, is not whether he would be liable to the creditors of the bank, if sued by them, but whether, having regard to the rights of the shareholders *inter se,* he ought to be on the list." That case therefore is inapplicable to the present question. *Cur. adv. vult.*

Lord CAMPBELL, C. J., now delivered the judgment of the Court.

This was an application for leave to take out execution against a shareholder: and the proposed answer to the application was, that the shareholder had been induced by fraud to take the shares. He had remained a shareholder for some time, and received dividends, and acted in all respects as a shareholder until the Royal British Bank stopped payment, and until its bankruptcy; and he then gave notice that he was no longer a shareholder, and, as far as he could, disaffirmed the contract under which he became a shareholder as being induced by the fraud of the directors: he demanded back all the moneys he had paid, and, being a depositor himself, he demanded the deposit and all the advances. The question is, whether, if it were established that this fraud had been practised upon him, it could be an answer to this application. If there were any doubt about it, we should not make this rule absolute; but we should direct a scire facias to issue, so that the question might be raised on the record. We entertained no *doubt on the argument: but, [*364 being informed that similar applications had been made to the Courts of Common Pleas and Exchequer, and that rules were depending in those Courts, we thought that, upon a matter of this sort, it would be well if we had a conference with the other Judges before our judgment was given. That conference has taken place: and the Judges are unanimously of opinion that this can be no answer to the application either upon principle or authority. This is an application by a creditor, who, upon the faith of the party, who then was a shareholder, and who held himself out to the world as a shareholder, and being one, gave credit to the Bank. He has obtained judgment against the Bank. There were no assets of the Bank as a Company. And the application now is that execution may issue against that party individually. It would be monstrous to say that, he having become a partner and a shareholder, and having held himself out to the world as such, and having so remained until the concern stopped payment, could, by repudiating the shares on the ground that he had been defrauded, make himself no longer a shareholder, and thus get rid of his liability to the creditors of the Bank, who had given credit to it on the faith that he was a shareholder. It would be monstrous injustice, and contrary to all principle. Whether he could say that, with regard to other shareholders not privy to the fraud, we need not say; there may be some difficulty about that. But that is not the question we have to determine; which is, simply, whether this is an answer to a creditor who has given trust upon the faith of his being a shareholder. Suppose this were a common partnership, and that there was credit given to the firm: would it be any *answer to an action by the creditor against one of the partners that the defendant was fraudulently induced by the other partners to become a partner? Inter se that might be considered: but, as between the firm and a creditor, it is a matter wholly immaterial. Now the party here admits that he is a shareholder, and acted as such until the Bank stopped payment. His name was placed on the register, and remains on the register. There is some irregularity in that register: but we are of opinion that all that is said in the statutes as to the manner in which the register shall be intituled and made up is only directory and not conditional, and that he was bound, at all events prima facie, by his name appearing on the register, notwithstanding those errors. The rule will therefore be absolute.(a)

"Ordered: That the plaintiff be at liberty to take out of Court, in part satisfaction of his judgment herein, the sum of 125*l*., paid into Court by the said L. M. Goddard; and that the plaintiff be at liberty to issue execution against the person, property, or effects of the said L. M. Goddard, as a shareholder of the Royal British Bank, for so much of the sum of 131*l*. 3*s*. 11*d*. remaining due on a judgment recovered by the plaintiff against the said Bank for the sum of 306*l*. 1*s*. as may not be satisfied by the money so to be taken out of Court by the plaintiff, and the dividend (if any) received by the plaintiff, under the adjudication of bankruptcy against the Bank, and if not already credited by the plaintiff." (Costs of application to be paid by Goddard.)

(a) See Daniell *v.* Royal British Bank, 1 H. & N. 681,† and Powis *v.* Harding, 1 Com. B. N. S. 533, decided on the authority of the case in the text.

*The QUEEN *v.* WILLIAM JOHN LAW, Esquire, Chief [*866
Commissioner of the Court for the Relief of Insolvent
Debtors. *Jan.* 31.

Under stat. 1 & 2 Vict. c. 110, s. 92, which directs that it shall be lawful for the Insolvent
Debtors' Court, if there be a surplus after satisfaction of the debts, to make an order vesting
such surplus in the insolvent, his heirs, executors, administrators, and assigns, that Court acts
judicially and not merely ministerially.
Therefore, where a party claimed such order under an alleged assignment from the insolvent,
and that Court, upon inquiry, held the assignment invalid as against other claimants, this
Court refused to issue a mandamus commanding the Insolvent Debtors' Court to make an
order vesting the property in the alleged assignee.

SIR F. THESIGER, in last Term, obtained a rule calling on the Chief
Commissioner of the Court for the Relief of Insolvent Debtors to show
cause why a writ of mandamus should not issue, commanding him to
make an order for payment of the surplus money in the said Insolvent Court standing to the credit of the estate of George William
Dyson, an insolvent debtor, to Robert Cook, his assignee, and also to
vest all the property, of any kind or description, estate and effects,
whatsoever, of the said G. W. Dyson in the said R. Cook.

The rule was obtained on affidavits of the following facts.

George William Dyson having petitioned the Court for the Relief
of Insolvent Debtors, an order was make, on 1st December, 1849, by
that Court, vesting Dyson's estate and effects in two assignees, one of
whom had since died and the other had been removed by the Court;
and in his stead Samuel Sturgis, provisional assignee of the Court, had
been appointed assignee. The case was in the Court of William John
Law, Esquire, the Chief Commissioner. By indenture, dated 8th
July, 1850, between G. W. Dyson of the first part, Robert Cook of
*the second part, and James Cook (a trustee to bar dower) of [*867
the third part, in consideration of 3000*l.* expressed to be paid
by R. Cook to Dyson, Dyson did bargain, sell, convey, release, and
assign to R. Cook, his heirs, executors, administrators, and assigns, an
undivided third part of the interest, dividends, and annual produce of
and in the residue of certain real and personal estate and effects
bequeathed to Dyson, and of and in other real estates, and all other
the estate and effects of Dyson, subject to the payment of his encum-
brances and debts. The 3000*l.* had been paid or accounted for to
Dyson. On 6th August, 1855, the Chief Commissioner made the following order in the matter of the insolvency.

"Pursuant to the Acts," &c. "Whereas it is now ascertained that the
fund in Court exceeds the amount required to pay all debts and costs,
And whereas it is not the ordinary case of an insolvent claiming a vesting order, but there are various claimants of the surplus, those known
to the Court being Mr. Cook, Messrs. Taylor and Rennison, and the
assignee of a subsequent insolvency: Let those parties attend me on

Mond/ y, 13th August, at 12 o'clock, to exhibit the grounds of their claimr. I do not purpose to go into any discussion on that day." "Mr. Cook will exhibit the original instruments and accounts on which he relies, and will produce a specific account in debtor and creditor form, with dates of all transactions between him and W. Dyson from 14th March, 1850, to 16th March, 1853, verified by affidavit."

The execution of the indenture of 8th July, 1850, had been proved in the Court. There was a large surplus now in Court, amounting to. 4000*l.* Application had been made to Samuel Sturgis for a particular *368] *account thereof, which he had refused to give. On 12th July, 1856, the Chief Commissioner made the following order.

"Pursuant to the Acts," &c. "After paying the debts under the former insolvency, a considerable sum remains in Court. There are three claimants: 1. The. whole is claimed by Mr. Cook, under a deed made to him; 2. By Ch. Taylor and Mr. Rennison, under a deed made to them; 3. By the assignee for the creditors under the latter insolvency of 1853. All parties interested are at liberty to attend the Court in this matter and deliver their claims on Tuesday, the 22d July, instant, at 11 o'clock."

On 22d July R. Cook attended the Court of the Chief Commissioner. And he now deposed that, "after showing the said Commissioner that the said indenture of conveyance to me hereinbefore mentioned was long prior to the second insolvency," he, R. Cook, "again demanded the said vesting order and payment of the money in Court; which the said W. J. Law refused, and also refused to act upon my said deed, and insisted upon inquiring into the validity of my said deed, and the consideration paid for the same, and as to the rights of the said Mr. Taylor and Mr. Rennison under a deed of subsequent date and execution to my deed, and also into the rights of the assignee for the creditors under the second insolvency," in 1853, "and another person of the name of Maclaren, who also claimed under an assignment from the said G. W. Dyson. All of which claims are subsequent to my said deed of the 8th day of July, 1850. That without prejudice I did endeavour to satisfy the said W. J. Law that I had paid the consideration 3000*l.*, and also *369] that the said several other *claims were subsequent in date, and could not possibly have any claim. And I have, on each of the said occasions, protested against the jurisdiction of the said W. J. Law or the said Court for the Relief of Insolvent Debtors to question or try the validity of my said deed; and that, the said W. J. Law still persisting in so doing, I served a written protest." This was set out in the affidavit. It referred to the indenture of 8th July, 1850, and added: "I claim to be entitled to the surplus estate of the said G. W. Dyson under the said deed which has been produced to you. And I hereby give you notice that I object and protest that you have no right and authority to try the validity of the said deed. And I hereby respectfully request you not to part with the said surplus estate to, or vest the same in, any other person than myself."

R. Cook further deposed that the Chief Commissioner, notwithstanding, "insisted upon considering the claims of the said other parties and adjudicating upon my said deed." R. Cook then obtained, on affidavit, from Lord Cranworth, C., the following order, dated 5th August, 1856.

"It is ordered that a writ of prohibition do issue, prohibiting the Court for the relief of Insolvent Debtors in England from adjudicating on, or dealing with, the surplus fund in Court in the said affidavit mentioned or referred to, except so far as is necessary in order, under the Act," &c. (1 & 2 Vict. c. 110, s. 92), "to give effect to the deed of the 8th day of July, 1850, in the said affidavit mentioned."

A copy of this order was served upon the Chief Commissioner; and the writ was issued, and copies of it served upon the proper officers of the Insolvent *Debtors Court. The Chief Commissioner had, [*370 however, on 11th September, 1856, refused to make an order vesting the surplus in R. Cook, or any order whatsoever: and R. Cook deposed that the Chief Commissioner "did state that he would, if the said prohibition had not been granted, have made an order to vest the same in the assignee under the said second insolvency of the said G. W. Dyson. And, by reason of such refusal, I am prevented from obtaining the said surplus estate." No proceeding had since been taken to discharge the order in prohibition, or vest the surplus in any one.

The chief clerk of the Chief Commissioner's Court deposed that Dyson petitioned the Court on 15th March, 1853, and that a vesting order was made on 16th March, 1853, vesting his effects in Samuel Sturgis, the provisional assignee of the Court, in whom they still remained vested, and who, on 22d July, 1856, on the hearing of the claims to the surplus before the Chief Commissioner, claimed it for the benefit of the creditors under the second insolvency, by reason of the assignment to said Robert Cook in the said affidavit mentioned being invalid.

Bovill and *Clerk* now showed cause.—The application is made under stat. 1 & 2 Vict. c. 110, s. 92, which directs that, if the Insolvent Debtors Court be satisfied that all the debts in respect of which the adjudication was made have been discharged, and that there remains property in the possession or control of the assignees, "it shall be lawful for the said Court, on application duly made, to order that all such property so remaining as aforesaid shall be vested in the person whose debts shall have been so discharged or satisfied, or his heirs, executors, administrators, or assigns; and such order *shall have the effect [*371 of vesting the same accordingly." Here the Court is satisfied that the debts are discharged and that there remains a surplus: Cook applies for an order vesting the surplus in him as assign: the Commissioner examines into the matter and thinks it right to refuse such order. The question therefore is whether the Commissioner, on such applica-

tion, is to act judicially or only ministerially : if he is to act judicially
this Court will not interfere.   Sturgis v. Joy, 2 E. & B. 739 (E. C.
L. R. vol. 75), is a strong instance of this principle; for there the
Insolvent Debtors Court was desirous of obtaining the assistance and
advice of this Court; which, however, was not given, because it was
considered that the judicial question was for the Insolvent Debtors
Court.   The Court of Chancery has prohibited the Commissioner from
adjudicating on the surplus, except so far as is necessary to give effect
to the deed of 8th July, 1850 : but that does not compel him to give
effect to the deed.   The application is, in fact, for a mandamus commanding a judicial functionary to come to a particular conclusion.
[CROMPTON, J.—If the Act requires the Commissioner to vest the
surplus in the insolvent's assign, he must surely inquire who the assign
is.]   He must so : and, in so doing, he cannot but act judicially.   If
he considers the deed fraudulent, he cannot treat Cook as assign.
Wearing v. Ellis, 25 L. J. N. S. Chancery, 248, shows that the beneficial interest of a party taking such an assignment may be inquired into.
    Sir F. Thesiger, Montague Smith, Lush, and Gill, contrà.—By sect.
62 the Commissioner has power over the fund in his Court as long as
the creditors are *unsatisfied : he is also the judge, under sect.
*872]   92, on the question whether they are satisfied, as appears from
Sturgis v. Joy.   But, so far, there is no dispute in the present case.
That being so, and the deed not having been impeached in Chancery,
the proper tribunal for setting it aside, he has only the ministerial duty
of giving effect to the deed.   Thus, where a special body is directed by
statute to levy a rate, this Court issues a mandamus commanding them
to levy the rate, not to consider whether they will levy it, treating
them as ministerial only,(a) although they must, in laying the rate,
inquire into several particulars, and so far may be said to act judicially
or with a discretion.   [WIGHTMAN, J.—Here Goddard has to show that
he is assign.   COLERIDGE, J.—Suppose the execution of the deed is
denied.]   The fact of the assignment must of course be ascertained :
but that is not in dispute.   The surplus has ceased to be a part of the
insolvent estate fund.   [Lord CAMPBELL, C. J.—Suppose a deed bearing on the face of it a prior date were produced, or a deed dated on the
same day.]   In such a case, a judicial duty would no doubt arise.   But
that would be confined to ascertaining the priority : that ascertained,
what remains is ministerial.   Thus, if two bills falling due on successive
days were presented to a banker, he would look at them to ascertain
the time of maturity, and, so far, might be said to exercise his judgment.   But, afterwards, he has no discretion; he would as a matter of
routine first pay the one becoming first due, and then, if that exhausted
the drawer's fund, would write "no effects" on the other.

(a) See Regina v. The Select Vestrymen of St. Margaret, Leicester, 8 A. & E. 889 (E. C. I.
R. vol. 35); 10 A. & E. 730 (E. C. L. R. vol. 37).

*Lord CAMPBELL, C. J.—This rule was granted with great [*373 reluctance, and only upon the strong opinion expressed that the duty of the Commissioner could be shown to be purely ministerial. But the learned argument which has been addressed to us in support of the rule has failed to show this. The functions of the Commissioner are clearly judicial, not merely ministerial. The Insolvent Debtors Court has first to dispose of all the property for the satisfaction·of the debts. If it appears that there is a surplus, the Court is to assign this to the insolvent, his heirs, executors, administrators, or assigns. If the surplus consist of real estate, must not the Commissioner determine judicially who is heir? If a party claim it under an alleged assignment from the insolvent, must not the Commissioner determine judicially whether there is an assignment giving such a title? It is admitted that he must inquire into the fact of execution if, for instance, it be suggested that there is a forgery; and that he may inquire which of two deeds has the priority in date. Can he be bound to give effect to a deed ministerially, merely because the deed is shown to him? Surely he must determine whether the party claiming is the party named in the deed. I am very glad to find that our view does not conflict with that of the Lord Chancellor, for which I should feel the greatest respect, though we should not be bound by it. He left it to the Commissioner to decide upon the effect of the deed: we have no authority to inquire what its effect is.

COLERIDGE, J.—I am of the same opinion. The application is for a mandamus commanding the Commissioner to vest property in a particular individual. *That, it is said, is a ministerial duty; and it [*374 is admitted that, if this is not so, we cannot make the rule absolute. That question depends upon the Act of Parliament. I agree that the Commissioner cannot carry the Act into effect without exercising a judicial power. The enactment is not merely that when the surplus arises he is to order it to vest in the insolvent: if that were all, he would unquestionably be bound to make the order without reference to rival claims. But the Act goes further, and, assuming the property to have been once in the insolvent, enumerates all who could have an interest in it. For what purpose is this done? In order that he may ascertain who is the party entitled. During the argument it was asked whether the Commissioner has not to determine if he finds parties with rival claims, as heirs, assigns, and so on. It was admitted that he must do so: and that puts an end to the argument that his duty is ministerial.

WIGHTMAN, J.—I think that, for the purpose of the question before us, the duty of the Commissioner is not merely ministerial, but judicial. That follows from the necessary construction of the Act. The case might have been otherwise if the application could be made only by the insolvent. But the Act goes further: his heirs, executors, administrators, or assigns may claim. Must not that give the Commissioner authority to determine who the heir, &c., is? It is admitted that he has such authority up to a certain point. But surely, if it appeared to the Commissioner that the assignment was void, and the title under it could not be supported, so that there was no assign, he must be invested with the judicial power of determining that, and of acting upon his determination.

*875]   *CROMPTON, J.—I am quite of the same opinion. The Insolvent Debtors Court is to administer the fund, and to determine who are the proper recipients of it. The creditors are to be satisfied if there be sufficient. If there be more than sufficient, what is to be done with the surplus? It is, primâ facie, to be vested in the insolvent, or else in his heirs, executors, administrators, or assigns. That Court must therefore ascertain who these are: we cannot interfere. Some of the surplus may go to the heir, some to the executors, some to an assign: we cannot carry out the enactment. I can conceive that the Insolvent Debtors Court may require powers which we do not possess, in order to enable them to ascertain how they are to exercise the functions vested in them of administering the property. This seems to be admitted to a certain extent; for it was allowed that, if there appeared two deeds of assignment bearing the same date, the Commissioner must hear evidence as to which was first executed. If he can go so far, can he not ascertain whether a deed is valid, and what passes by it? I am therefore of opinion that the writ should not issue.

Rule discharged.

MEMORANDUM.

In this Term Sir Edward Hall Alderson, one of the Barons of the Court of Exchequer, died.

END OF HILARY TERM.

CASES ·

ARGUED AND DETERMINED

IN

𝔅ilary 𝔅acation,

XX. VICTORIA. 1857.(a)

The Judges of the Court of Queen's Bench who generally sat in Banc in this Vacation, were,—

COLERIDGE J., ERLE, J.,
WIGHTMAN, J., CROMPTON, J.

MEMORANDUM.

In this Vacation William Fry Channell, Serjeant at Law, was appointed a Baron of the Court of Exchequer on the vacancy created by the death of the late Mr. Baron Alderson in the Term preceding. Mr. Baron Channell afterwards received the honour of Knighthood.

◆

---

*IN THE EXCHEQUER CHAMBER. [*877

(Error from the Court of Queen's Bench.)

CHARLES SAMUEL TOZER v. ROBERT CHILD and THOMAS HOWARD. Feb. 2.

An action does not lie against a churchwarden presiding (under stat. 18 & 19 Vict. c. 120) at the election of vestrymen and auditors, for refusing the vote of a party entitled to vote for vestrymen and auditors, or for refusing to allow as a candidate a party entitled to be candidate, unless malice be alleged and proved.

IN this case judgment was given for the defendants below. Error was now brought on a bill of exceptions, to the ruling of Lord Campbell, C. J., filed by plaintiff below. The first count of the declaration charged that the first election of vestrymen and auditors of accounts

(a) The Court of Queen's Bench sat in banc on February 2d, 3d, 9th, and 10th, and, for the delivery of judgments only, on 24th.

for the parish of Saint Clement Danes in Middlesex, under stat. 18 &
19 Vict. c. 120, was duly holden: and the plaintiff, being a parishioner
and duly qualified to vote, offered his vote to the defendants, who were
churchwardens presiding at the election: but the defendants, "well
knowing the premises, but contriving and fraudulently and maliciously
intending to injure the plaintiff, and disappoint him of his privilege of
and in the premises, hindered and prevented the plaintiff, so being such
parishioner and qualified and entitled to join and vote in the said election as aforesaid, from joining and voting in the said election, and did
not nor would receive or allow the votes so offered by him as aforesaid:
and divers persons, other than the plaintiff so offered and was desirous
to vote for as aforesaid, were at the said election elected respectively to
*378] be vestrymen and auditors of accounts of the said *parish with-
out any votes of him the plaintiff in that behalf having been
received or allowed. To the great injury," &c.

The second count charged that the election of vestrymen and auditors was holden as mentioned in the first count; and plaintiff, being a
parishioner and a fit and proper person duly qualified in that behalf to
be proposed for and elected to the office of a vestryman, was a candidate for the said office and ready and willing to be elected; and
many persons, entitled to vote, were ready and desirous to vote, and
would have voted, for electing plaintiff; and plaintiff was, before the
defendants, then being churchwardens presiding, &c., to whom it
belonged to receive and allow the proposal of plaintiff for the office,
and submit him for election to the persons entitled to elect, for election to the office, duly proposed; and defendants were requested to
receive the proposal and submit, &c.: yet defendants, "well knowing
the premises, but fraudulently and maliciously intending to injure the
plaintiff and disappoint him of his privilege of and in the premises, did
not nor would receive or allow the said proposal," &c., "or submit,"
&c., for election, but refused to and did not receive or allow votes to be
received for the election of plaintiff, though divers persons entitled
to vote were ready to vote, and would have voted, for plaintiff, if plaintiff had been allowed by defendants to be submitted, &c., as defendants
well knew; and divers persons were elected vestrymen without plaintiff
having been submitted, &c.: whereby, &c., (damage to plaintiff).

Plea 1. Not guilty. Issue thereon.

The 2d and 3d pleas also led to issues of fact, not material to the
*379] present decision. The bill of exceptions *set out the evidence
at length, whereby it appeared that, on the election, a question
arose as to the qualification of plaintiff, it being suggested that he was
disqualified by reason of his non-payment of a certain church-rate, and
that the defendants refused, on that ground, to allow the vote of plaintiff, or submit him as a candidate. The bill of exceptions then proceeded as follows.

"And thereupon the said Lord Chief Justice directed the said jury that the defendants were not necessarily liable in this action, although the plaintiff, notwithstanding his non-payment of the said church-rate, was qualified and entitled to vote, and to be a candidate at the said election, as he alleged: and that it was incumbent on the plaintiff to make out that the acts of the defendants complained of were malicious; and that malice might be proved, not only by evidence of personal hostility or spite, but by evidence of any other corrupt or improper motive: and that, if the defendants committed the acts and grivances in either counts of the declaration complained of bonâ fide, and acting upon advice which they believed sound, the defendants were not guilty as alleged, and that they the said jury ought, as to each of the counts of the declaration, to find and give their verdict for the defendants upon the first issue within joined between the said parties, unless, upon the evidence, they were of opinion that the defendants, in committing and occasioning the acts, grievances, and omissions in such count of the declaration alleged, had acted malâ fide and dishonestly. And with that direction the said Lord Chief Justice left the issues joined between the said parties to the consideration of the said jury. Whereupon the counsel for the plaintiff make their exception to the said direction and opinion *of the said Lord Chief Justice. And the said jury, [*880 upon and with that direction and opinion of the said Lord Chief Justice, gave their verdict for the defendants upon the said first issue and for the plaintiff upon each of the other issues joined between the said parties." The bill then concluded in the usual form.

Shee, Serjt., for the party assigning error (plaintiff below).—The question is whether malice is essential to liability to an action for refusing to allow the vote of a plaintiff entitled to vote or for refusing to admit as a candidate a plaintiff entitled to be a candidate. The principal authority on this point is Ashby *v*. White, 2 Ld. Raym. 938.(*a*) There an action was brought against a returning officer for refusing a good vote: three puisne judges, on motion in arrest of judgment, thought the action not maintainable: Holt, C. J., thought it maintainable; and his opinion was upheld in the House of Lords, which reversed the judgment of the majority of the Queen's Bench. Now, though the declaration there expressly averred knowledge and malice, it is remarkable that Lord Holt laid no stress upon this; and he must have thought it immaterial; otherwise he need not have noticed the point that the defendants were not exercising a judicial function. [CROWDER, J.—I observe that the Court of Queen's Bench, in the argument in this case upon the demurrer to the rejoinder to the replication to one of the pleas,(*b*) held this action maintainable, the knowledge and malice being admitted on the record: but it is there said: "if the churchwardens

(*a*) See note to S. C. in 1 Smith's Lea. Ca. 212 (4th ed.).
(*b*) Tozer *v*. Child, 6 E. & B. 289 (E. C. L. R. vol. 88). See p. 295.

*381]   acted honestly in rejecting the vote, *they are liable to no
action, be the vote good or bad;" and, "If they acted bonâ fide,
although mistakenly, under their plea of Not guilty they have a good
defence." That you dispute.]   Yes: the Lord Chief Justice acted
upon that view, in directing the jury: and the question is as to the correctness of that view: it was not necessary to the judgment on the
demurrer, which is correct, whether or not the existence of malice is
necessary to the maintenance of the action, upon the grounds urged by
Lord Holt.   [*Knowles*, for the defendants.—A fuller report than that
in Lord Raymond of Lord Holt's judgment has been published from a
manuscript,(*a*) under the sanction, as is understood, of the late Lord
Chief Justice, Lord Denman.   From this report it distinctly appears
that Lord Holt did insist on the malice.   He says, referring to the
Statute of Westminster the First (3 Ed. 1, c. 5): "Indeed I do not
find that the defendants did by force of arms drive the plaintiff away
from the election, nor by menaces deter him, but I find they did maliciously hinder him ; and so it is charged by the plaintiff in the declaration, and so found by the jury, that they did it by fraud and malice, and
so the defendants are offenders within the very words of the Statute of
Westminster I."]   There may be a question whether greater weight is
to be attached to this publication than to the reports of Lord Raymond,
which are always considered as of very high authority.   [CRESSWELL,
J.—Certainly they are.]

Knowles, for the party denying error (defendants below), was not
called upon.

*382]   *CRESSWELL, J.—We are all of opinion that the judgment of
the Court below must be affirmed.   My brother *Shee* has brought
before us, as the only apparent solid foundation which he could find for
his argument, the omission of Lord Holt to insist upon malice in his
judgment in Ashby *v.* White, 2 Ld. Raym. 938.   I am aware of no
others; and the report to which Mr. *Knowles* has referred us takes
away that.   Abbott, C. J., in Cullen *v.* Morris, 2 Stark. 577 (E. C. L.
R. vol. 3), held that malice was essential to such an action; and he
there refers to the case of Drewe *v.* Colton,(*b*) where Wilson, J., took
the same view.   Cullen *v.* Morris was an action which arose from a very
violent contest for the city of Westminster; and the Chief Justice, com-
menting upon what Lord Holt was supposed to have said in Ashby *v.*
White, stated that the reports of that case were very imperfect, and
that he himself, if Lord Holt really meant to lay down that malice was
not essential to the action, could not assent to that doctrine; and he
pointed out that in Ashby *v.* White "upon the face of the record the
defendant was charged with malice, and when a writ of error was brought,

(*a*) *The judgment delivered by the Lord Chief Justice Holt in the case of Ashby v. White and
others, and in the case of John Patey and others.*   London, 1837.   See p. 12.
(*b*) Note (F.) (at p. 245) to p. 225 of The Case of the Borough of Saltash, 2 Luders, 107.

the record itself was conclusive as to the malice of the defendant, since the Court would look at nothing beyond the record." He very happily expressed the mischief which might arise from making returning officers responsible beyond this. "The returning officer is to a certain degree a ministerial one, but he is not so to all intents and purposes; neither is he wholly a judicial officer, his duties are neither entirely ministerial nor wholly judicial, *they are of a mixed nature. It cannot be [*383 contended that he is to exercise no judgment, no discretion whatsoever in the admission or rejection of votes; the greatest confusion would prevail if such a discretion were not to be exercised. On the other hand, the officer could not discharge his duty without great peril and apprehension, if, in consequence of a mistake, he became liable to an action." He could not indeed preside at an election without being liable to five hundred actions. A similar principle was applied to the judicial functions of a coroner in Garnett v. Ferrand, 6 B. & C. 611 (E. C. L. R. vol. 13).

(WILLIAMS, J., had left the Court.)

MARTIN, B.—There is a great difference between saying that a man has a right to vote and saying that he has a right to bring an action against the officer who refuses his vote. It is difficult to support an action against a returning officer: if the party claiming the vote has it allowed at any stage he is not deprived of his right. At any rate the officer cannot be liable for merely drawing a wrong conclusion of law.

BRAMWELL, B.—It may be that the only right which the party has is that his claim shall be fairly considered.

WATSON, B., concurred.   Judgment affirmed.

---

*THOMAS RACE v. WILLIAM WARD and Others. *Feb.* 8. [*384

Action for breaking a close. Plea that, by custom, the inhabitants of a township had a right to take water for domestic purposes from a well in the close; that plaintiff choked it up, and justifying the acts complained of as done by inhabitants of the township to clear out the well. Issue thereon.

On the trial it appeared that the inhabitants had, from time immemorial, taken the water from the well. About fifty years before the action the locus in quo was enclosed under a special enclosure Act, incorporating the general Enclosure Act then in force (41 G. 3, c. 109). Neither in the special Act, nor in the award of the Commissioners, was any mention made of this well, or of any access to it. Verdict for defendants, with leave to move.

Held, on a rule to enter the verdict for the plaintiff, that the right to take water from the well was not extinguished by the enclosure; and that, whether the ancient right of access to the well for that purpose was or was not extinguished (and *semble* it was not extinguished), the inhabitants might in other modes legally get access to the well, so that the fifty years' enjoyment de facto since the enclosure might have a legal origin; and the verdict for defendants stood.

FIRST count, for breaking and entering plaintiff's close. Second count, for stopping up a drain therein. Pleas 1 and 2, to each count respectively, justifying under an immemorial custom for the inhabitants of the township of Horbury, in which plaintiff's close was situated, to take water from a well in that close, and carry the same to their houses, to be there used for domestic purposes. The plaintiff demurred to and took issue on each plea. Judgment was given for the defendants on the demurrers in Hilary Term, 1855. See Race *v.* Ward, 4 E. & B. 702 (E. C. L. R. vol. 82), where the pleadings are set out fully.

On the trial of the issues in fact, before Willes, J., at the last Yorkshire Assizes, it appeared that the close in question was a part of a tract of land which was anciently a common, but had been enclosed under an enclosure Act, 49 G. 3, c. 77.(a)

*385]　*The award of the Commissioners was published in 1815. In it three wells, named, with ways to them, were set out for the inhabitants of Horbury. There was no mention in the award of any footpath to the well in the plaintiff's close, nor of that well itself. Evidence was given that there always had been a spring in the plaintiff's close forming a well, and that the water from the well had been constantly taken as of right by the inhabitants, from time immemorial down to the time of the enclosure ; and that, since the enclosure, the water of this well had been de facto enjoyed by the inhabitants crossing the plaintiff's close on foot to get the water, until the plaintiff, in draining his land, laid the well dry. The learned Judge reserved leave to move to enter a verdict for the plaintiff, if the enclosure Act and the award had the effect of extinguishing the custom ; and, subject to that, left the question whether the plea was proved to the jury, who found for the defendants.

Hill, in the ensuing Term, obtained a rule Nisi to enter a verdict for the plaintiff, " on the ground that the effect of the local Act, 49 G. 3, c. 77, the general Enclosure Act (41 G. 3, c. 109), and the award of the commissioners made thereunder, was to extinguish the way to the well of water mentioned in the pleas, and consequently that the custom stated in the pleas was not proved."

Knowles and *Cleasby* now showed cause.—The general Enclosure Act, in force at the time when stat. 49 G. 3, c. 77, passed, was stat. 41 G. 3, c. 109. By sect. 10 of this latter Act the commissioners are empowered in their award to set out and appoint " such private roads, bridle-

*386]　ways, *footways, ditches, drains, watercourses, watering places, quarries, bridges, gates, stiles, mounds, fences, banks, bounds, and landmarks," on the allotments as they think fit. And by sect. 11 " all roads, ways, and paths," over such lands, " which shall not be set out as aforesaid, shall be for ever stopped up and extinguished." But the right of going across land to a well is not such a way as would be

(a) Private. " For enclosing lands in the township of Horbury, in the parish of Wakefield, in the West Riding of the county of York."

stopped up under this section; it is accessary to the right to take water; and, unless that right is gone, access to it is of necessity preserved. It might as well be said that a churchpath was stopped up, by an enclosure, unless it was set out in the award. The nearest analogy is to the continuation across the allotments of a path between old enclosures; the path across the allotments is preserved, because the path over the old enclosures still exists: *Thackrah v. Seymour,* 1 Cr. & M. 18.†

R. Hall, in support of the rule.—Stat. 41 G. 3, c. 109, gave the commissioners no power to affect public ways, except in sect. 8; and that section requires the assistance of justices of the peace. This may explain *Thackrah v. Seymour; Gwyn v. Hardwicke,* 1 H. & N. 49.† But the right of way confined to the inhabitants of a district, however large, is not a public way: *Rex v. Richards,* 8 T. R. 634. The powers which the Commissioners had over private easements is given by sect. 10; and it extends to wells. The word is not used; but "well" is included in "watering places;" and, since this well is not set out, the right to it is extinguished. [CROMPTON, J.—Sect. 10 does not extinguish any rights. Sect. 11 does not extinguish anything but roads, ways, and paths. Under what words do you say this well is extinguished? In sect. 14 no words are *used that could comprise such a right, unless you [*387 call it a right of common, which it would be difficult to maintain.] It is within the words at the end of section 14, "all rights whatsoever, by such Act intended to be extinguished, belonging to or claimed by any person or persons whomsoever, bodies politic or corporate, in, over, or upon such lands or grounds, shall cease, determine, and be for ever extinguished." It is true that in the private enclosure Act in this case no mention is made of the rights of the inhabitants to take water, nor of their rights to dance or play at cricket, or at the local game of knor and spell over the waste; but all such rights, being inconsistent with the enjoyment of the allotments as enclosed for agricultural purposes, are, by implication, intended to be extinguished under every enclosure Act.

COLERIDGE, J.—I am of opinion that this rule ought to be discharged. The ground on which it was moved was that by the effect of the enclosure Acts the access to the well was gone, and therefore the prescriptive right to access to the water broken. It has now, on the argument, been contended that the right to the well itself is directly extinguished. Now it is certain that the right to the well is not taken away in terms or by express words; but it is said to be so by implication. Now, assuming that "well" is included in the term "watering places," on which I express no opinion whatever, sect. 10 is an affirmative section authorizing the Commissioners to set out new watering places, but not extinguishing the old ones. In sect. 11 you do not find that watering places, not set out, are extinguished, but only roads, paths, and ways. But then it is said that sect. 14 extinguishes this right, not expressly

*388] in terms, but by its general clause. *That enactment, however, is limited to such rights as are by the local enclosure Act "intended to be extinguished." After such long-continued usage as was shown in this case, Mr. *Hall* was bound to show conclusively that this right must have been extinguished; now he totally failed in that. All he contended was, that the right to take water from a well must be taken to be by implication extinguished for the sake of agricultural enjoyment; but it is far from being correct to say that it is universally desirable to extinguish such a right. So that the right to the well itself is neither directly nor indirectly extinguished. Taking it that the well remains: then, before the award, the inhabitants had a right of access to that well. Now assume (a matter on which I express no opinion) that such a right of access is a way within the meaning of sect. 11, and that therefore, not being set out, it is extinguished: still for many years the access to the well has existed in fact. I do not see that the defendants are bound to show that all the public have of right a means of access to the well; it is enough if they themselves have; and, after fifty years' enjoyment, if there could be any legal origin to their right we must assume that there was one. Now there are many possible legal origins to such a right.

WIGHTMAN, J.—The inhabitants claim a right by custom to take water from this well. They had such a right; but it is said the right is taken away by the operation of the local enclosure Act, and the general Enclosure Act then in force. Now first: Is it directly taken away by those Acts? It seems to me that it is not: for, even supposing that a well is within sect. 10, and that the Commissioners were *389] authorized to set out *wells, which it may be that they were, it by no means follows that the ancient existing wells, if not set out, are extinguished: for in sect. 11 there is no mention of wells or of watering places as being extinguished if not set out, though, in express terms, ways not set out are extinguished. But then it is urged that by sect. 14 of the general Enclosure Act, "all rights whatsoever" by the local enclosure Act "intended to be extinguished" are put an end to. And it is said that this species of right must be intended to be extinguished. But I do not think that is so. And, therefore, I think this right was not directly extinguished by the Acts. But it is said it was indirectly extinguished, by extinguishing all access to the well. That the customary right of the inhabitants to take water from the well was only to take the water, if they could get at the well. But it is only if it can be shown that it was impossible to obtain access to the well that such an argument can apply. Even if all ancient ways to the well were extinguished, there would be no necessary impossibility of access to the well. In fact, for fifty years since the enclosure, the inhabitants have gone to it: it may be that access was preserved by previous bargain or otherwise; but, at all events, they have had access.

So it by no means conclusively follows, even if the ancient ways were extinguished, that the well was.

ERLE, J.—The question, is whether the right of the inhabitants to use this well has been proved. It is clear that, from time immemorial down to the present time, they have exercised it; but the contention is, that the right was extinguished by stat. 41 G. 3, c. 109, which in sect. 10 authorizes the Commissioners to set out *watering places and [*390 ways; and, by sect. 11, enacts that ways not set out are extinguished. It is said that, as no way to this well was set out, all access to the well, and therefore the well itself, is extinguished. I by no means accede to the proposition that under an extinguishment of all ways such a right of access for the inhabitants to a well would be extinguished; but I do not affirm the contrary. I say that, if the Act had said in terms no one shall have a right to go over the land to this well, still it would not be either illegal or impracticable to exercise the right of getting the water from the well. Then it is said the right is extinguished, as being one of those by implication intended to be extinguished by an enclosure. That proposition does not meet my assent. I do not think that there is in all enclosures an intention to extinguish, for the sake of agriculture, a right which is often of so great importance to the inhabitants as that of drawing water for domestic purposes. Then, not seeing clearly that this right cannot exist, and there having been fifty years' user, the right is to be supported.

CROMPTON, J.—The plea here justifies on the ground that the well was choked up, and that the defendant entered to put it in a proper state to exercise his right to take water. I do not see that this claims a right of access to the well. The issue taken on it puts in issue the right to the well; but I think that is proved. I find no power in the enclosure Act to extinguish wells. In looking at the extinguishing clause (sect. 14) I find mention of rights of common and other rights which I take to mean rights to take the produce of the earth; but nothing else is mentioned there except the rights *intended to [*391 be extinguished by the special Act. If the Commissioners had directly extinguished the right to the well they would, in my opinion, have exceeded their powers. But it is neither directly nor indirectly extinguished. I am not prepared to say that, the right being preserved, a reasonable right of access was not therefore preserved; but it is not necessary to decide that question; for the plea as pleaded is proved.

Rule discharged.

CHAMPION MURGATROYD *v.* ABRAHAM ROBINSON.

Count by the owner of a mill on the river C., which mill of right ought to be supplied with a flow of water from a mill pool on the C. against the owner of works higher up the stream, for placing cinders, &c., at his works, so as to fall into the stream of the C., whence they were carried down into plaintiff's mill pool and filled it up, to the obstruction of his right to water.

Plea : that the occupiers of defendant's works had, for more than twenty years, of right placed cinders, &c., the refuse of their works, on the banks of the stream and in its channel; and that the cinders, &c., complained of were such refuse, so placed. The issue on this plea having been found for the defendant:

Held, that the plea was bad, non obstante veredicto, as not showing that defendant had, during twenty years, of right caused the refuse to go into the plaintiff's pond; as, till the occupiers of the mill sustained some damage from the defendant's user, no right as against them began to be acquired.

FIRST count. That plaintiff was lawfully possessed of a water-mill, water-wheel, head goit, and tail goit, with the appurtenances, near the river Calder; which mill had been and of right ought to have been, and still of right ought to be, supplied with a fall of water for the working thereof, flowing down the river into a certain mill pond or mill pool of the plaintiff, in the river there formed by a weir of the plaintiff across the river, and from the mill pool into the head goit unto the water-wheel *392] of the plaintiff, and from the water-wheel along *the tail goit into a part of the river Calder, belonging to the plaintiff, below the weir and tail goit, which fall of water was of right used and enjoyed by the plaintiff for the working of his mill. And that defendant was possessed of certain mill works, buildings, and premises, near to and upon a certain other river called the Hebble, the water of which last-mentioned river flowed into the river Calder at a point higher up in the stream thereof than the said mill, &c., of the plaintiff. Yet defendant threw, placed, and deposited into and upon the bed and channel of the said river called the Hebble, and upon the banks and sides of the same river, at and near the said mill, &c., of defendant, large quantities of cinders, ashes, scoria, coals, soil, dirt, rubbish, and things, whereby the said cinders, &c., fell and were washed, blown, and carried into the Hebble, and were carried and floated, and passed by and with the water of the last-mentioned river, into the river Calder, and thence down and along the bed and channel thereof, unto and into the said mill pond or mill pool of the plaintiff, and unto and into the said head goit and tail goit of the plaintiff, and unto, into, and upon the plaintiff's said part of the said bed and channel of the said river Calder, below the said weir and tail goit of the plaintiff, and became and were deposited in the said goits and mill pond or mill pool of the plaintiff respectively, and in the plaintiff's said part of the bed and channel of the said river Calder below the said weir and tail goit of the plaintiff, whereby they were choked up.   .

Plea 3. "To so much of the declaration as related to the throwing, placing, and depositing, and causing and permitting to be thrown, placed, and deposited, upon the bed and channel of the river Hebble, and upon·*the banks and sides of the same, the quantities of [*393 cinders," &c., "in the declaration mentioned: that defendant had been and was the occupier of the mill, works, buildings, and premises in the declaration mentioned, situated near to and upon the river Hebble, for more than twenty years before the commencement of this suit, and was the occupier thereof at and'for more than twenty years before the committing of the grievances complained of; and that during all that time large quantities of cinders," &c., "were necessarily produced at the said mill," &c., "being the refuse of the ash pit of the engine by which the same was worked, and the sweepings of the said mill, works, buildings, and premises; and that defendant, "being the occupier of the said mill," &c., for more than twenty years before the commencement of this suit, enjoyed, as of right and without interruption, the privilege and easement of throwing, placing, and depositing upon the bed and channel of the Hebble, and the banks and sides of the same, at and near to his said mill, all such quantities of cinders," &c., "as were produced in the said mill," &c., "being the refuse of the ash pit of the engine by which the same was worked, and the necessary sweepings of the said mill," &c. "And that the said cinders," &c., "in the introductory part of this plea mentioned were cinders," &c., "produced in the said mill," &c., "being the refuse of the ash pit of the engine by which the same was worked, and the necessary sweepings of the said mill," &c.; "and that he committed the grievances in the introductory part of that plea mentioned, in the lawful exercise of the said privilege and easement." Issue thereon. Verdict on this issue for the defendant.

*Knowles, in Michaelmas Term, obtained a rule for judg- [*394 ment non obstante veredicto.

Hill and Cleasby, in this Vacation (February 3d), showed cause;(a) and Knowles and Addison were heard in support of the rule. The main contention on the part of the plaintiff's counsel was, that the right claimed by the defendant was not of such a nature as to be within the meaning of stat. 2 & 3 W. 4, c. 71, s. 2; and that a custom to the extent claimed was destructive of the mill of the plaintiff, and therefore unreasonable and void. The defendant's counsel denied this. As the Court pronounced no opinion upon this point, the arguments are omitted. The following authorities were cited on the part of the defendant: Wright v. Williams, 1 M. & W. 77,† Wood v.Waud, 3 Exch. 748.† The plaintiff's counsel cited Hilton v. Earl Granville, 5 Q. B. 701 (E. C. L. R. vol. 48), Broadbent v. Wilks, Willes, 360,(b) Rogers v. Brenton, 10 Q. B. 26 (E. C. L. R. vol. 59), Tyson v. Smith, 9 A. &

(a) Before Coleridge, Wightman, Erle, and Crompton, Js. Crompton, J., left the Court before the conclusion of the argument.
(b) In C. B., affirmed in error, Wilkes v. Broadbent, 1 Wils. (B .R.) 63.

E. 406 (E. C. L. R. vol. 36),(a) Clayton v. Corby, 5 Q. B. 415 (E. C. L. R. vol. 48), Com. Dig. *Præscription* (E 4).   *Cur. adv. vult.*

COLERIDGE, J., on a subsequent day in this Vacation (February 24th), delivered judgment.

This was a rule for setting aside the verdict which passed for the defendant on the 3d plea, and *notwithstanding such verdict *395] entering judgment for the plaintiff, on two grounds, 1st, that the right claimed in such plea is not an easement within the 2d section of, stat. 2 & 3 W. 4, c. 71; and, 2d, that the prescription relied on is unreasonable. From the declaration it appears that the plaintiff is possessed of a mill on the Calder, and the defendant of a mill on the Hebble, which stream flows into the Calder at a point above the plaintiff's mill. The plaintiff complains that, whereas he is the lawful occupier of a mill and works near to the Calder, which ought to be supplied with a fall of water flowing down the said river, the defendant, before the commencement of the action, threw, placed, and deposited into and upon the bed of the Hebble, and on the bank and side thereof, at and near to his the defendant's mill, works, buildings, and premises, large quantities of cinders, ashes, scoria, coals, soil, dirt, rubbish, and things, whereby they fell, and were washed down and carried, into the Hebble, and so were floated and passed with the water of the Hebble along its bed and channel into the Calder, and unto and into the plaintiff's mill pond, and head goit and tail goit, and unto and into the plaintiff's part of the bed and channel of the Calder, filling them up and obstructing the working of his mill. To this throwing, placing, and depositing, the defendant pleads his occupation of his mill, works, buildings, and premises near to and upon the Hebble for more than twenty years before the committing of the grievances complained of, and that, during all that time, large quantities of cinders, ashes, scoria, and small coal, and coal dust and rubbish were necessarily produced at the said mill, works, buildings, and premises, being the refuse of the ash pit of *396] the engine by which the same was worked, *and the sweepings of the said mill, works, buildings, and premises; and that he, being such occupier for more than twenty years before the commencement of this suit, enjoyed, as of right and without interruption, the privilege and easement of throwing, placing, and depositing upon the bed and channel of the said river Hebble, and the banks and sides of the same, *at* and near to his said mill, all such quantities of cinders, ashes, scoria, small coals and coal dust and rubbish as were produced in the said mill, being the refuse of the ash pit of the engine, by which the same was worked, and the necessary sweepings of the said mill, works, buildings, and premises. The plea then identifies the stuff thrown in and deposited with that complained of, and so justifies.

(a) In error in Exoh. Ch., affirming the judgment of K. B. in Smith v. Tyson, 6 A. & E. 745 (E. C. L. R. vol. 33).

This plea is clearly framed on the 2d section of stat. 2 & 3 W. 4, c. 71. And the first question raised is, whether the facts which it discloses, and which must now be taken to be truly alleged, bring the case within that section. To do so, the plea must disclose a "claim which may be lawfully made at the common law, by custom, prescription, or grant, to any way or other easement, or to any watercourse, or the use of any water, to be enjoyed, or derived upon, over, or from any land or water" of some person other than the party making the claim. This last qualification is clearly necessary from the nature of an easement, and from the language of the section itself. Now the plaintiff states no possession in himself of the bed or banks of the Hebble, neither does the defendant allege any in him; the plaintiff merely states his possession of a mill and works near to the Calder, a right in a part of the bed and channel of that river, and a right to a fall of water down that river for the working of his mill; the defendant claims *nothing [*397 directly in respect of any of these; but he alleges a user as of right for twenty years to throw cinders and scoria into the bed of the Hebble, and to deposit them on the banks of that stream. Only three cases are supposable on the facts alleged. The defendant might, first, claim distinctly the right to the easement of depositing, or suffering to be deposited, the cinders in the bed of the Calder, in that part of it which the plaintiff claims to occupy; but he has not done so; and it is perfectly consistent with the language of his plea, that no cinders or scoria, or none in any such quantity as to occasion the slightest substantial obstruction to the working of the plaintiff's mill, had come on the plaintiff's part of the bed of the Calder during twenty years, or until shortly before the commencement of the action. And if this had been alleged in express terms, the question of law might have arisen which was argued at the bar, whether this was a claim to an easement, or watercourse, or use of water within the meaning of the statute; on which, however, it is not now necessary to express any opinion. Or, secondly, the defendant might claim the banks and bed of the Hebble on and in which the cinders and scoria have been deposited as in his own occupation, in which case the right to deposit them there could be no easement; and the lapse of twenty years during which the deposit had been made would *in itself* have given no right pleadable under the statute, thereby to occasion any injury to the rights and enjoyments of the neighbouring occupier. Or, thirdly, the defendant might claim that the bed and banks, of the Hebble, on and in which the cinders and scoria were deposited, were in the occupation of some third person, as against whom the easement had been enjoyed; but, *even if this [*398 plea could be so understood, and such a right were clearly an easement within the statute, such easement would give no right against the plaintiff. The supposed owner of the bed and banks, whatever rights he might grant as against himself, could impose no servitude by such grant on the plaintiff's land; and, as we have already observed, the plea fails to allege any such user affecting the plaintiff's mill or lands as could be the foundation for presuming any grant from him. In any point of view, therefore, it appears to us that the plea fails to establish or even to allege a claim to. affix any servitude on the plaintiff's part of the bed and channel of the Calder. And, even if it could be maintained that, after verdict, a valid claim to the enjoyment as of right of an easement on the bed and banks of the Hebble is to be taken to have been alleged and proved, and, that being so, the natural consequence, namely the deposit on the bed of the Calder, must be taken as also necessarily established, one answer to this is certain; that, at all events, before any right could be acquired thereby which would support this plea, such consequence must be shown to have attached on the land sought to be burdened with the servitude for the term of years required by the statute. So far from its being necessary that the consequence should follow immediately on the cause in the sense of occasioning any substantial inconvenience, the contrary is far more probable. It was, therefore, incumbent on the defendant to have alleged that he had of right caused the deposit of cinders and scoria on the plaintiff's part of the channel of the Calder in the manner alleged by the plaintiff for the term of twenty years, if he intended to make that a legal justification. But the plea as now framed may be *399] true *in every allegation; and yet no perceptible deposit may have been occasioned for anything like that period of time.

On this ground, therefore, and without expressing any opinion on some of the points mainly argued at the bar, we are of opinion that the plea is bad after verdict, and that judgment notwithstanding the verdict ought to be entered for the plaintiff.   Judgment for plaintiff.

The QUEEN *v.* MORGAN THOMAS.   *Feb.* 10.

On appeal against a conviction for obstructing a highway, the Sessions confirmed the conviction, subject to a case; and it was brought before this Court by certiorari.

Held that this Court could not take notice of any objections to the conviction not stated in the case.

The case showed that the road in question was made by turnpike trustees, under a temporary Turnpike Act, which expired in 1848; but the whole line of turnpike road authorized by the Act was never completed. That the road as made had been used by the public, and had been repaired by the parish, but before and since the expiration of the Act: and the question for the Court was, if there was any evidence that it was a highway compulsorily repairable by the parish.

Held: that there was evidence of a dedication, and of an adoption by the public, and that, though the fact that the road was originally made under the Turnpike Act might explain away such evidence in fact, it did not conclusively in law rebut it.

Held, also, that the General Highway Act (5 & 6 W. 4, c. 50), sect. 23, did not apply to a road made by turnpike trustees; and that, consequently, the absence of a certificate by two justices, &c., as required by that section, did not prevent the road becoming compulsorily repairable by the parish, on a dedication by the owners of the soil in 1848.

ON appeal to the Glamorganshire Sessions against a conviction of Morgan Thomas by two justices of the county of Glamorgan, for obstructing a highway, called the New Mill Road, in the parish of Llantwit Vardre in that county, the Sessions confirmed the conviction, subject to the following case.

By stat. 7 & 8 G. 4, c. xcviii.,(a) which came into full force and effect June 14th, 1827, and was to continue *in full force and effect [*400 for twenty-one years then next following, certain commissioners appointed under the said Act were empowered, amongst other things, to make and maintain a new line of road from or near a place called Wern y Gerwn, in the parish of Eglwysyllan, through the several parishes of Eglwysyllan, Llantwit, Vardre, and Llantrissent, to a place called New Mill, in the parish of Llantrissent, and also a new line of road from or near the Lower Forest Farm, to or near New Bridge, in the parish of Llanwonnan, and which two new lines of road were, by the said Act, declared to be the New Mill district. The above-mentioned Act was repealed by stat. 7 & 8 Vict. c. 91, s. 34; and by sect. 38 it is provided how far the provisions of the general Turnpike Acts are to be applicable. The road from Lower Forest Farm to New Bridge was never made. The road from New Mill to Wern y Gerwn was completed as far as Lower Forest Farm, but was not carried to Wern y Gerwn, in the parish of Eglwysyllan, in the line indicated by the Act of Parliament. It was shown that the river Taff runs between Wern y Gerwn, in the parish of Eglwysyllan, and New Mill. At Lower Forest Farm the road joined a private road about a hundred yards on the New Mill side of the river Taff, leading to a private bridge, belonging to a Mr. James, across the said river. The bridge was erected by Mr. James, at his own expense, some time before the passing of the Act for making the above-mentioned road, and was his private property, and joined, on the Eglwysyllan side of the river, a turnpike road leading to Wern y Gerwn. No rent was paid by the commissioners of the road to Mr. James for the use of the said private road or bridge; but they were used by the public passing along the said *road by the leave and [*401 license of the owners for the time being. Witnesses were called, who proved that, from twenty to twenty-five years since, they had paid toll on the said bridge to a person who rented it of Mr. James; and Mr. Crawshay, the now owner of the bridge, demanded and took toll eight weeks before the hearing of the said appeal. Witnesses were called, who proved that the road in question was the only road between New Mill and Lower Forest Farm; that there were rows and clusters of houses on each side of it; that, since it was made, twenty-eight years ago, it had been used by the public, and the inhabitants of the district through which it passed have been in the habit of passing over it with

(a) Local and Personal, Public: "For the better and more effectually repairing or otherwise improving the roads in the county of Glamorgan."

carts and horses, and some of them daily. No one has, during the above period, been prevented from using the road from New Mill to Lower Forest Farm as a public road, until it was obstructed by the appellant shortly before the conviction. Rates have frequently been made, during the last twenty-eight years, at the parish meetings, for the repair of the portion of the road lying in the respondents' parish, at several of which meetings the appellant has been present, and has on some occasions objected, and others assented, to the rate. The appellant was also present at a parish meeting, at which the following resolution was passed: that Mr. David Thomas, Mr. David Jones, Mr. Morgan David, be appointed with William Thomas to contract for the repairs on the New Mill road. The New Mill road is the road in question: and the road has on many occasions been repaired; and the surveyor has been paid for such repairs: but during such time portions of the road were frequently not kept in sufficient repair. In one part of

*402] the road in the respondents' parish there is a hole *a yard deep in the road, made by persons employed to repair the road in order to obtain materials. Vehicles could pass between that and the hedge. The parish have not attempted to fill it up. There were two or three bars or chains put up shortly after the making of the road, and toll demanded and sometimes refused; but the chain and bars have been removed for more than twelve years. The obstruction complained of in the said recited conviction was on a part of the road where the property on either side belonged to the appellant. The fact of the obstruction is not disputed.

If the Court of Queen's Bench think that there is evidence that the above-mentioned road ever became a highway, compulsorily repairable by the parish, the conviction, as affirmed by the Quarter Sessions, to stand.

If, on the contrary, the Court should think that the road never was a highway compulsorily repairable by the parish, the conviction to be quashed.

The case was accompanied by a map, by which it appeared that the portion of the turnpike road from New Mill to Lower Forest Farm was about six miles and a half in length. The portion of the line of the turnpike authorized to be made, but never in fact made, from Lower Forest Farm to Wern y Gerwn, was rather less than half a mile in length, and the route by the bridge across the Taff, from Lower Forest Farm to Wern y Gerwn, which was used in fact as described in the case, was a little more than half a mile in length.

H. S. Giffard and *F. W. Lloyd*, in support of the order of Sessions. —The question is, whether there is evidence that the road in question

*403] was a highway, compulsorily *repairable by the parish. It might, in point of law, be a highway, even if it stopped at Lower Forest Farm; for it is not essential that a highway should be a thoroughfare:

Bateman *v.* Bluck, 18 Q. B. 870 (E. C. L. R. vol. 83). Then, if it is a highway which the public have used, it is repairable by the parish without any adoption on their part : Rex *v.* Leake, 5 B. & Ad. 469 (E. C. L. R. vol. 27). In that case Littledale, J., says : "If a road has been used by people in the parish, it furnishes evidence pro tanto of its being a way for the rest of the public ; and if the parish have repaired it, it furnishes a strong inference that it is a public highway, or else they would not have been at that expense : but it only raises a strong presumption, and there is no estoppel against a parish in such a case ; the adoption by the parish does not necessarily, as a matter of law, make a road public ; nor does their refusal to adopt it prevent its being so." Evidence of such facts appears to have been before the Sessions in the present case. Then, it is true that the commissioners, acting under the Act which has expired, have not completed the line authorized by that Act ; and therefore it perhaps never was a complete turnpike road ; but it has been used de facto as a public highway, both before the Act expired, and after the Act expired. In Rex *v.* Cumberworth, 3 B. & Ad. 108 (E. C. L. R. vol. 23), and in Rex *v.* Edge Lane, 4 A. & E. 723 (E. C. L. R. vol. 31), there was no statement of user by the public ; but those seeking to charge the parish relied exclusively on the statutable authority of the trustees. As the authority had not been pursued, that proof failed. In the present case there is independent evidence of the road being a highway ; and the utmost effect of the Act can be only in the nature of rebutting evidence to explain that user. *Rex *v.* Cumberworth, so far as it proceeded on the supposition [*40- that adoption is requisite, is overruled by Rex *v.* Leake. There being user in fact, a dedication by whoever could dedicate is to be presumed : Regina *v.* Petrie, 4 E. & B. 737 (E. C. L. R. vol. 82). A highway through a turnpike road is repairable by the parish : Regina *v.* Lordsmere, 15 Q. B. 689 (E. C. L. R. vol. 69).

T. Allen and *Charles E. Coleridge*, contrà.—Before entering on the case, the Court will look at the conviction returned, which, it is submitted, is bad on the face of it. [COLERIDGE, J.—On a case being sent to us can we travel out of it ?] The order is before the Court : and, that being so, the Court can look at it. [*H. S. Giffard.*—Stat. 12 & 13 Vict. c. 45, s. 7, prohibits the taking of objections to any order unless specified in the rule for issuing the certiorari. No objections at all were specified in the rule in this case.] Then on the merits : the road was a turnpike road, made under a temporary Act ; when the Act expired, it ceased to be a highway repairable by the parish : Rex *v.* Mellor, 1 B. & Ad. 32 (E. C. L. R. vol. 20), Rex *v.* St. Benedict, 4 B. & Ald. 447 (E. C. L. R. vol. 6). It is said that there is evidence of dedication and user and repairs, after the expiration of the Act, that is since 1848. But, by the general Highway Act (5 & 6 W. 4, c. 50), sect. 23, "no road or occupation-way made or hereafter to be made by and at the expense of any individual or private person, body politic or corporate, nor any roads already set out or to be hereafter set out as a private driftway or horsepath in any award of commissioners under an enclosure Act, shall be deemed or taken to be a highway which the inhabitants of any parish shall be compellable or liable to repair, unless the person, body *405] *politic or corporate, proposing to dedicate such highway to the use of the public" shall give three months' notice of his intention to the surveyor of highways for the parish, and shall put the road in repair to the satisfaction of the surveyor and of two justices. These preliminaries have not, in this case, been complied with.(a)

COLERIDGE, J.—I am of opinion that this Court has no power to quash this conviction, supposing it to be defective, for any reasons appearing on the face of it. By the General Highway Act (5 & 6 W. 4, c. 50), sect. 107, no conviction is removable by certiorari, "except as herein mentioned." The exception is in sect. 108 (and it is not unimportant that it is in the section next ensuing after sect. 107). " That in any case of appeal the Court of Quarter Sessions before whom the same is heard and determined may, if they think fit, state the facts specially for the determination of His Majesty's Court of King's Bench thereon, in which case it shall be lawful to remove the proceedings, by writ of certiorari or otherwise, into the said Court of King's Bench." The certiorari is taken away; and this Court has no power to quash the conviction, supposing it bad. If any inconvenience arises from this, it must be borne; and it is not increased because a case is stated and brought before us; there is then a certiorari; but it is preserved merely as machinery to bring the case before us; and we can look at nothing but the facts stated. Then let us look at the facts stated here. In substance they seem to be that a turnpike road was to be *406] made *under a temporary Act, but in fact was only partially made. Whilst the Act continued in force, the road was treated as a highway repairable by the parish. Then came the South Wales Turnpike Act (7 & 8 Vict. c. 91). Under sect. 34 the Turnpike Act might have been terminated; but it appears it was not; and it continued in force till it expired, by efflux of time, in 1848. Things then reverted to the state they were in at common law before the Act passed. The owner of the land, which had been taken for the turnpike-road, might resume it; and the parish might decline further to repair it, or the public to use it. But the owner might allow the public to continue to use the road: and, if the public did use it as a highway, the burthen of repair would fall upon the parish, whether they would or not; for after reasonable evidence of dedication and user it is no answer to an indictment against the parish that they have not adopted the highway.

(a) See Roberts v. Hunt, 15 Q. B. 17 (E. C. L. R. vol. 69); Fawcett v. York & North Midland Railway Company, 16 Q. B. 610, 614, note (a) (E. C. L. R. vol. 71); Regina v. Wilson, 18 Q. B 348 (E. C. L. R. vol. 83).

But it is said that, however that might be at common law, sect. 23 of
the Highway Act (5 & 6 W. 4, c. 50), interposes a difficulty; for this
was a road which it was sought to turn into a highway. But this
depends upon whether sect. 23 applies to such a case as the present.
It appears that the Legislature contemplated the case of a private person making a road for the purpose of dedicating it, or setting out a
private driftway under an enclosure Act, and not such a case as this.
Neither do the words of the section embrace such a case. This is not
a road made by any person or body proposing to dedicate it. It was
made by turnpike trustees, who had no power to dedicate it. It was
not a road made so as to bring it within sect. 23, but was left to the
common law. I never heard it laid down that all roads were included
in the enactment in sect. 23. The result *that I come to is, that [*407
there was evidence that this road was a highway repairable by
the parish. The only question asked is, whether there was such evidence; and I answer it in the affirmative.

WIGHTMAN, J.—As to the objection to the form of the order, I am
of opinion that we are precluded from entering into a consideration of
that question. If that had been the only objection the case could not
have come before us on certiorari. But the Quarter Sessions have the
power to reserve questions for the opinion of this Court; and, in order
to bring the case before us, the certiorari, which is taken away as to all
questions of form, has, under the provisions of the statute referred to,
been granted. Therefore we are to consider the certiorari merely as
a means of bringing these questions, reserved by the Quarter Sessions,
before us; and not of enabling the defendant to take objections which
it was the intention of the Legislature to prevent his taking. We
have simply to answer the questions which the Quarter Sessions put
to us.

With respect to the question put to us, I think "that there is evidence" that the way in question "became a highway, compulsorily
repairable by the parish." The road was constructed twenty-eight years
ago under the provisions of a local Act (7 & 8 G. 4, c. cxcviii.), which
expired in 1848, though by another Act, 7 & 8 Vict. c. 91, s. 34, it might
have been made to expire in 1844. The road which was made twenty-
eight years ago has been travelled over continually ever since, and has
from time to time been repaired by the parish, from the time of its first
construction to the time of the conviction, as well subsequently to the
expiration or repeal of the local Act, *as before. There is ample [*408
evidence that the road in question is a public highway, and repairable by the parish. Then does sect. 23 of the Highway Act (5 & 6 W.
4, c. 50), which prescribes that certain formalities shall be observed
before a road can become a highway which the parish shall be liable
to repair, apply to this case? This is not the ordinary case of the
dedication of land by an individual, who may possibly wish,   9

purpose of his own, to create a public road, and throw the burthen of repairing it upon the parish, which was the mischief that would seem to have been contemplated by the statute; but in this case the trustees, under the local Act, took the land for the purpose of the road; and it has remained a public road and been repaired by the parish ever since. Clearly, this is not a case within the contemplation of the Legislature in sect. 23 of stat. 5 & 6 W. 4, c. 50, and therefore is not affected by it. We have not to say on which side the balance of the evidence is, but whether there is any evidence that the road in question became a highway to be repaired by the parish. I think there was abundant evidence. And therefore that the conviction should be affirmed.

CROMPTON, J.—We must confine ourselves to the case and the question asked in it. In doing so we do not affect the order at all; if it is invalid we give it no force, but leave the Sessions to deal with it as they ought. The question we are asked is, whether there was any evidence that the road in question ever became a highway compulsorily repairable by the parish. I find it stated that "rates have frequently been made, during the last twenty-eight years, at the parish meetings, for the
*409] repair of the portion of the road lying in the respondents' *parish, at several of which meetings the appellant has been present, and has on some occasions objected, and others assented, to the rate." And it is said that the road has been accordingly repaired at the expense of the parish; and that the public have used the road down to the present time. That certainly is evidence, unless there is something conclusive to rebut it. Now there is nothing conclusive to rebut it. The owners of the land probably dedicated the road on the expiration of the Turnpike Act; but, as they did not then make the road, the case is not brought within the operation of stat. 5 & 6 W. 4, c. 50, s. 23.

Order of Sessions affirmed.

THE QUEEN *v.* The Overseers of CHRISTCHURCH, MIDDLESEX.

By a local Act, the management of the affairs of a parish was confided to a select vestry, consisting of an indefinite body. The Act provided that the vestry at their meetings, "or the major part of such of them as shall be assembled at such meetings," might do whatever could be done by an ordinary vestry. By a subsequent Act, power was given to the vestry, "or the major part of them," to appoint and dismiss collectors of the poor-rate. B. was appointed a collector of the poor-rate. A charge being brought against him, a meeting of the vestry was duly convened to consider. The vestry then consisted of eighty persons; thirty-five attended the meeting. A motion being made to dismiss B., sixteen voted for it, and eleven voted against it. It was declared to be carried; and B. was dismissed.

Held, by the Court of Exchequer Chamber, affirming the judgment of the Queen's Bench, that though the motion was carried by a majority of those voting, yet, not being carried by a majority of those present, it was not carried by a majority of those assembled; the vestrymen declining to vote not being considered in point of law absent. Consequently, that the dismissal was not effectual.

MANDAMUS directed to the overseers of the Poor of the parish of Christchurch, Middlesex. The writ contained suggestions that, by the statutes after mentioned, the vestry of the parish appointed collectors of *the poor-rate for two divisions, called the Old Division [*410 and the New Division, of the parish: that, by an order of the Poor Law Commissioners of 17th March, 1847, it was ordered, amongst other things, that every collector appointed under the provisions of any Act should, amongst other things, "enter in the rate-book all such particulars of every assessment as he should be directed by such overseers to enter therein." Further suggestions that, from the time of the making of this order till the refusal after mentioned, the overseers of this parish always have delivered to each collector of the New Division the rate-books: "and that, during the continuance of his office, it has been and is the duty of the said collector for the said New Division upon and at the time of receiving any of the said rates to, and during the same period he has, entered the same in the said rate-book:" "and that the said collector, without having such rate-book delivered to him, or in his possession, cannot" fulfil his duty. That one James Baynton was appointed collector for the New Division; and the defendants refused to deliver him the rate-books from 5th April, 1855, to 10th January, 1856, for the purpose of enabling him to fulfil his duty. The mandatory part of the writ commanded them to do so.

Return: that before the refusal Baynton was duly removed from his office; and that the overseers had no control over the books. It contained no denial of the suggestions.

Pleas (so far as material to the questions discussed): 1. That Baynton was wrongfully removed; 7. That the overseers might have delivered the books to Baynton. Issue was taken on these and other pleas which it is not necessary to notice.

*On the trial, before Lord Campbell, C. J., at the Westminster [*411 Sittings after Trinity Term, 1856, a verdict was directed for the Crown subject to a special case.

By the case it appeared that the parish of Christchurch, Middlesex, was made a parish by stat. 2 G. 2, c. 10.(a) Sect. 9 of that Act enacts: "that the rector of the said church, and the churchwardens and overseers for the poor of the said new intended parish for the time being, and all other persons who have served, or paid fines for being excused from serving, the office of churchwarden or overseer of the poor in and for the said hamlet of Spittlefields, or who from time to time hereafter shall serve, or by the vestry be admitted to pay fines for being excused from serving the office of churchwarden or overseer of the poor in or for the said new intended parish, so long as they respectively shall con-

(a) "For making the hamlet of Spittlefields in the parish of Saint Dunstan Stebunheath, alias Stepney, in the county of Middlesex, a distinct parish, and for providing a maintenance for the minister of such new parish."

tinue householders within the said new intended parish, and paying to
the poor's rate, shall be the vestrymen for the time being of the said
new intended parish, and shall meet from time to time, upon public
notice to be openly read and published in the said church by the order
of the rector, churchwardens, and overseers of the poor, or either of
them, on the Lord's Day next preceding, immediately after Divine
Service; and the said vestrymen, or the major part of such of them as
shall be assembled at such meetings, shall and may from time to time
elect and nominate a lecturer or lecturers as also churchwardens, sides-
men, parish clerk, and all other officers for the said parish which were
*412] usually chosen in, *by, and for the said hamlet, and also from
time to time elect and nominate, amove and put out, the sexton,
grave-diggers, and all other officers and servants to be employed in or
about opening the pews, making the graves, or otherwise, in or about
the said church; and shall and may also have and exercise all other the
same powers and authorities as they might or could have done in case
they had been named to be the vestrymen of the said new parish by the
said commissioners, or any five or more of them, with the consent of the
bishop or ordinary of the place, by instrument under their hands and
seals enrolled in the High Court of Chancery according to the said
Act" (10 Anne, c. 11, s. 20); "and which said lecturer or lecturers
so to be chosen as aforesaid, shall be admitted by such rector for the
time being to have the use of the pulpit." Stat. 18 G. 3, c. 74,(a) sect.
14, enacts: "that the said churchwardens, overseers, and vestrymen
of the said parish, or the major part of them may, from time to time,
elect and appoint one or more person or persons to be collector or collectors of the rates to be made in pursuance of this Act, in such manner
as they shall think necessary for the purposes of this Act, at any meeting to be held at the vestry-room of the said parish, of which notice shall
be given in the church on Sunday next preceding such meeting; and
shall and may take such security as they shall think proper from such
collector or collectors so to be elected and appointed as aforesaid, for
*413] the due execution of his *or their said office, and for the true
and faithful accounting for all moneys which shall come to his or
their hands by virtue of this Act; and may likewise, from time to time,
remove such collector or collectors, and elect and appoint others or
another in the room of such collector or collectors as shall be so removed,
or shall die; and also shall and may, from time to time, out of the
moneys to be raised by virtue of this Act, pay or cause to be paid, such
salary or other allowance as they shall judge reasonable to be paid or
made to such collector or collectors so appointed, for and in considera-

(a) "To amend an Act, passed in the twenty-sixth year of King George the Second, more
effectually to enable the parishioners of the parish of Christchurch, in the county of Middlesex,
to purchase, hire, or erect a workhouse, for the employing and maintaining the poor of the said
parish, and for the more effectual support and employment of the poor therein."

tion of his or their office, and to such other person or persons as shall be aiding and assisting in and about the execution of this Act."

The case in substance stated that the parish was afterwards divided into two parts, called the Old Division and the New Division, for the purposes (amongst others) of maintaining its poor and collecting its poor-rates. The parish, in 1837, became part of Whitechapel Union. The case then set out the orders of the Poor Law Commissioners, which prescribed the keeping of rate-books, and the making of monthly returns by the collectors of the poor-rate in the different parishes in that union, and stated that from the time of the making of this order rate-books were kept by the overseers and delivered by them to the collector for the said New Division from time to time to collect the rates; and it has been the practice for such collectors, "at the time of receiving any of the rates, to enter the same in the said rate-books so delivered to him as aforesaid, opposite the name and assessment of the person rated for the property in respect of which the said rates were received; and, without having such rate-books in his *possession, he could not [*414 collect the rates or fill up or use the rate receipt check-book in the said order mentioned, or make out the monthly statement therein mentioned." The case then stated that Baynton was duly elected collector on 20th April, 1848. That he was entitled to a poundage on the rates collected by him; and that he continued in his office till September, 1854. At that time a charge was made against him, which, it was agreed, if substantiated, would have been sufficient to justify his dismissal; and he had notice of it. On 17th September, 1854, notice was affixed on the door of the church, calling a meeting of the vestry on the ensuing Friday, in the vestry-room, to consider the conduct of Mr. Baynton. Of this he had notice, and was requested to attend as one of the vestry. The case then proceeded.

"A meeting was held, in pursuance of this notice, in the vestry-room of the said parish, on the 22d day of September, 1854. At the time of the holding of such meeting, the select vestry of the said parish consisted of eighty vestrymen; and of these only thirty-five members attended and were present at the meeting. The following is a copy of the minutes of such meeting: ' At a vestry held in the vestry-room of the said parish on Friday the 22d day of September, 1854.' " (Here followed thirty-five names, including those of a churchwarden, four overseers, and Mr. Baynton himself.) " ' Complaint having been made, by the overseers of this vestry, of Mr. Baynton's improper conduct, and particularly that his collecting book is much in arrear, mainly on account of his having told some of the ratepayers not to pay the amounts due from them, as the rates were illegal; and in consequence of which the broker's man, who had *been left in possession at Mr. Swinney's, [*415 had been forcibly expelled: It was therefore moved by Mr. Nesbit, and seconded by Mr. Wood, That Mr. James Baynton be, and he is now, removed and dismissed from his situation as collector of the poor-rates of this parish. To which an amendment was moved by Mr. Cavalier and seconded by Mr. Palmer: That the complaint against Mr. Baynton be received, entered on the minutes, a copy given to Mr. Bayn-ton; and that a vestry be called on Thursday, October 6th, 1854, to give the complained against an opportunity to make a reply to the charge. And, on the question being put, there appeared: For the amendment 11; against ditto 18: majority against the amendment 7. On the original motion being put there appeared for it 16; against ditto 11: majority for the original motion 5. Which being carried, Mr. Baynton was therefore dismissed from his situation; and the office is declared vacant accordingly.' It is also admitted, for the purpose of the argument of this case, that, before the original resolution for the dismissal of Mr. Baynton was put and carried, he was distinctly requested to explain his alleged misconduct, and answer the charges made against him, but declined so to do. The practice, since the passing of stat. 2 G. 2, c. 10, has uniformly been, in all parochial matters depending upon the decision of the vestry, for the majority of the vestry assembled to decide the various propositions. At this time he had the July rate-book in his possession, finishing the collection of it; and on the 4th October the balance in his hands and this rate-book was delivered up by him to the said Mr. Nesbit, one of the said overseers, who gave him a receipt for the same, notwithstanding his dismissal. And, although *416] Mr. Root his successor had been appointed and that *person had received the Michaelmas Quarter rate-book for collection, Mr. Baynton persisted in acting as collector, and received altogether from different ratepayers a sum amounting to about 150*l.* After the said motion for the dismissal of the said James Baynton had been carried as aforesaid, that is to say on the 5th day of April, on the 5th day of July, and on 11th day of October, 1855, and on the 10th day of January, 1856, rates were duly made and allowed in and for the said parish, and were respectively recorded in the rate-books for the said New Division and Old Division of the said parish, provided for that purpose by the said vestry-clerk under the first above-mentioned order of the poor law commissioners; and the same respectively were duly signed by the trustees; and the said rate-books respectively were, after and as soon as they had been so signed, in the possession of the overseers of the said parish; and they were then, that is to say on the 14th day of January, 1856, required by the said James Baynton to deliver to him the said rate-books for the said New Division of the said parish; but they were not, nor were any of them, delivered to the said James Bayn-ton, nor has he ever had possession of any of them. Immediately after the dismissal of the said James Baynton, a successor was elected and appointed collector.

It is agreed, between the parties, that the pleadings in this cause on both sides, and the said orders of the Poor Law Commissioners and the schedules thereto, and the statutes 2 G. 2, c. 10, and 18 G. 3, c. 74, shall form part of this special case; and that the Court shall be at liberty to draw such inferences from the facts hereinbefore stated as the jury might have drawn.

The questions for the opinion of the Court are:

*1st. Whether the said James Baynton was properly removed [*417 from his said office of collector of the poor-rates for the said New Division of the said parish of Christchurch? And

2d. Whether, if he was not properly removed, the said rate-books respectively containing the said rates made on the 5th day of April, the 5th day of July, and the 11th day of October, 1855, and the 10th day of January, 1856, or any of the said books, should have been delivered by the overseers of the said parish to the said James Baynton?

And, if the Court shall be of opinion that the said James Baynton was not properly removed from his said office, and that the said rate-books or any of them should have been delivered to the said James Baynton, then the verdict is to be entered for the Crown as aforesaid: but, if the Court shall be of a contrary opinion, then a verdict is to be entered for the defendants.

Hugh Hill, in this Vacation,(a) argued for the Crown.—The dismissal under the circumstances stated is not good. Where power is given to a definite body, it is necessary that a majority of the whole should concur in any act: Blacket v. Blizard, 9 B. & C. 851 (E. C. L. R. vol. 17). Perhaps this vestry is not so constituted as to be a definite body within the meaning of that rule; but at all events the concurrence of the majority of those present at the meeting is required by the very words of the Acts. Now here thirty-five were present, and only sixteen voted for the dismissal. That was a majority, it is true, of those present and voting; *and it probably will be contended that those [*418 present, but not voting, were in contemplation of law not part of the assembly. But such is not the law: Eynsham Case,(b) Regina v. Griffiths, 17 Q. B. 164 (E. C. L. R. vol. 79). Then, if Baynton retains his office, it is both on the record and in the case admitted to be necessary that he should have the rate-books to enable him to discharge his duty; and no reason is shown why the defendants do not hand them over.

Atherton, contrà.—The vestry, as constituted by the Acts, is clearly an indefinite body, at present eighty in number, but from time to time more or fewer according to the state of the parish. The wording of the first Act is that the vestrymen, "or the major part of such of them as shall be assembled at such meetings," shall do all acts. The word-

(a) February 9th and 10th. Before Coleridge, Wightman, Erle, and Crompton, Js. Coleridge, J., did not hear the whole of the argument.

(b) Note (a) to Gosling v. Veley, 12 Q. B. 398 (E. C. L. R. vol. 64).

ing of the second Act is that the vestry, " or the major part of them, may" do these acts " at any meeting to be held" pursuant to notice. In case of an indefinite body the two phrases mean the same thing. Littledale, J., points this out: " There must be present a majority of that number of which the definite body consists, although it is not necessary that there should be a majority of the indefinite body:" Blacket *v.* Blizard, 9 B. & C. 851, 860 (E. C. L. R. vol. 17). The question, therefore, is reduced to this, whether the vestrymen actually at the meeting, but who refused to take any part in the division, are to be considered as part of the meeting. But it is reasonable that, when a division takes place at any meeting, those who do not vote

*419] *should be considered as having withdrawn, whether they actually have left the room or not. Then, even if the dismissal was wrong, the office has been filled up de facto, and the rate-books must be given to the actual collector, not to Baynton.

Hugh Hill was heard in reply. *Cur. adv. vult.*

WIGHTMAN, J., on a subsequent day in this Vacation (February 24th), delivered judgment.

We are of opinion that judgment should in this case be entered for the Crown. The first question is, whether Baynton was properly removed from the office of collector. It is enacted by stat. 18 G. 3, c. 74, that the churchwardens, overseers, and vestrymen of the parish, or the major part of them, may at any meeting to be held in the vestry room, of which notice shall be given in the church on Sunday next preceding the meeting, remove the collector.

Notice was given of a vestry meeting to be held on Friday the 22d of September, 1854, to consider the conduct of Mr. Baynton, one of the collectors; and, in pursuance of the notice, a vestry meeting was held on that day, and was attended by 35 members out of 80 who, at that time, constituted the select vestry of the parish. Mr. Baynton himself attended, having had notice of the meeting and its object, and being himself one of the select vestrymen. Upon a motion being made that Mr. Baynton should be removed from his office, 16 of the vestry voted for his removal, and 11 voted against it, the remaining 8 of the members present taking no part on either side of that question;

*420] *whereupon he was declared to be removed from his office and that the same was vacant.

Upon the argument it was contended on the part of the Crown that, though it might not be necessary that a majority of the whole body of vestrymen should concur in voting for the removal of a collector, it was necessary that a majority of those present at a vestry meeting called for the purpose of considering his conduct should concur in voting for his removal, to render it valid; and that members actually present, but taking no part, could not on that account be considered absent; and consequently that there was not a majority of the vestrymen present at the meeting concurring in the removal of Baynton. We think that this is the right view of the case, and that there was not such a majority of vestrymen concurring in the removal of Baynton as the statute required. The removing the collector is an affirmative act to be done by a majority of the vestrymen present at a vestry meeting.   In the present case, a majority certainly did not concur in that affirmative act; for, of those present, a majority either directly voted against it, or did not vote at all; in either case not concurring in the affirmative act of removal. Suppose that 5 only of the vestrymen present at the meeting had voted for Baynton's removal, and the rest had declined to vote at all: could it reasonably be contended that he had been removed by a majority of the vestrymen at a meeting held pursuant to the notice? We think not; and that the principle of the decision in the Eynsham Case, 12 Q. B. 398, n. (E. C. L. R. vol. 64), applies to this. Being then of opinion that Baynton was not properly removed, the next question arises, whether he is entitled to require possession of the *rate-books or any [*421 of them. It is stated, as a fact in the case, that without having the rate-books in his possession, the collector could not collect the rates nor make out the monthly statement required. It also appears by the case that it has been usual for the overseers to deliver the rate-books to the collector, who has returned them when the purpose for which he required them was fulfilled. It does not appear upon the case that there is any legal impediment to the delivery of the rate-books, for such rates as still remain uncollected, to Baynton for the purpose for which they are required to be temporarily in his hands: and we therefore think that he is entitled to have the possession of them for such purpose. We therefore think that there should be judgment for the Crown.

Judgment for the Crown.

IN THE EXCHEQUER CHAMBER.
June 17.

For syllabus, see ante, p. 409.

ERROR having been brought against the above judgment of the Court of Queen's Bench, the case was now argued.(a)

Atherton argued on the special case to the same effect as in the Court below.

Hugh Hill, contrà, was not called upon to argue on this part of the case.

Atherton also argued that, as this proceeding was, *under the [*422 Common Law Procedure Act, 1854 (17 & 18 Vict. c. 125), sect.

(a) Before Cockburn, C. J., Cresswell, Williams, and Willes, Js., and Martin and Bramwell, Bs.

32, in error, and not on appeal, he was at liberty to contend that the writ was bad: and he argued that it was insufficient. *Hugh Hill* was heard on the question of the sufficiency of the writ. The Court took time to consider of the judgment.

The points made, and the arguments used as to the validity of the writ, sufficiently appear in the judgment of the Court.

Cur. adv. vult.

WILLIAMS, J., on a subsequent day in this Vacation (July 4th), delivered judgment.

This was a mandamus directed to the overseers of Christchurch, Middlesex, commanding them to deliver to the prosecutor, as collector of the poor-rates for the New Division of the parish, the rate-books for the said New Division, from the 5th of April, 1855, to the 10th of January, 1856, for the purpose of enabling him to fulfil his duty as collector.

The defendants are the select vestry, constituted by stat. 18 G. 3, c. 74, to manage the affairs of the poor of the parish of Christchurch, Middlesex, with power, inter alia, to make rates and to appoint and remove collectors. Those powers were conferred by the Act upon them "or the major part of them."

The prosecutor was appointed as a collector under the Act, upon the 20th April, 1848. His remuneration was to consist of a percentage upon the rates collected by him. As to his duty with respect to the rate-books, the following statement is made in the mandamus, viz., that during the continuance of his office it has been and is the duty of the collector, upon and at the time of receiving any of the rates, to enter *423] *the receipts in the rate-books opposite the assessment and name of the person rated for the property in respect of which the said rates were so received; and that the collector, without having such rate-books delivered to him or in his possession, cannot fulfil his said duty, or fill up or use, or keep, the said books, required to be filled up and kept by him under and according to an order of the Poor Law Commissioners, recited in the mandamus, or produce to the auditor the statement thereby required, or otherwise fulfil his duties as such collector.

The defendants in their return set up a dismissal of the prosecutor from his office of collector, before he demanded the rate-books in question.

That dismissal was alleged to have taken place at a meeting duly convened and held upon the 22d of September, 1854, for the purpose of considering the prosecutor's conduct with a view to his dismissal. Thirty-five of the select vestry were present: a motion was made and seconded that the prosecutor should be dismissed. Sixteen voted for and eleven against the motion, the remaining eight being present but not voting.

In this state of things the defendants acted upon the above resolution as a valid dismissal of the prosecutor; he, on the contrary, treated it as invalid, and insisted upon the delivery to him of the rate-books to enable him to continue the performance of his duty as collector.

Thus arises the principal question in the case, namely, Whether, in the meaning of the statute, the major part of the select vestry concurred in his dismissal so as to make it valid? We think not. The body being indefinite in number, the major part of them means the major part of those present for the transaction of business at a meeting duly convened. In the present *case there were thirty-five at [*424 the meeting; and, though eight of the thirty-five did not vote, which indeed they were not bound to do, upon the question of dismissal, they constituted part of the body, the major part of which had power to dismiss: the sixteen who voted for the dismissal were therefore not the major part of that meeting.

Consequently, there was no valid dismissal; and the prosecutor has remained in office notwithstanding the resolution of the 22d September, 1854.

It was, however, further contended for the defendants that, assuming the prosecutor not to have been properly dismissed from his office, yet that the mandamus commanding them to deliver their books to their collector appointed by themselves could not be sustained; and several arguments were advanced on their behalf, and which we proceed to consider.

In the first place, it was said that the statement in the mandamus could not possibly be true, as they were at liberty to collect rates, either by themselves or by any other collector appointed by them. This might have been a good reason for not appointing the prosecutor, or for dismissing him because his services were no longer needed. But the defendants have appointed, and have not dismissed, him. By doing so, they have transferred from themselves to, and imposed upon, him the office of collector. They will effectually, though indirectly, dismiss him if they prevent him from fulfilling the duties of his office. To enable him to fulfil those duties, the possession of the books is alleged by him, and not denied by the defendants, to be necessary. And it is not suggested that anybody else was using or intended to use the books for any other purpose, at the time when the prosecutor asked for them.

But then it was further argued that the prosecutor could *not [*425 require the original books, for that a copy would be equally available to him, and that the Court ought to take notice of this. Assuming it to be so, the answer to the objection is, that there is no duty to make, and therefore no power to compel anybody to make, a copy of the rate-book; and a mandamus to make and deliver a copy would therefore be bad. The primary duty of the defendants was to deliver what was in existence and in their power at the time of the demand. The giving a copy instead of the original must be matter of arrangement between the parties, and not part of the judgment of the Court.

Lastly, it was said that the delivery of the books to the collector for the purpose mentioned in the mandamus would interfere with the right of the public to inspection of the rates under stat. 17 G. 3, c. 3, s. 2. There are several answers to this objection. In some cases the collector must have the rate in his possession in order to fulfil statutory duties: stat. 7 & 8 Vict. c. 101, s. 38. The possession of the rate, even for ordinary collectors, subject to the control of the parish officers, is recognised in the order of the poor law commissioners set out in the mandamus. Stat. 6 & 7 W. 4, c. 96, s. 5, gives a right to inspect the rate in whatever custody it may be. Moreover, the temporary custody of the rate by the collector does not necessarily interfere with its inspection, even in the hands of the defendants, whenever required for that purpose after due notice. Nor is it likely that the prosecutor would raise any unreasonable difficulty, seeing that he may be said to hold his office at the will of the majority of the defendants. And, even if all this were not so, the defendants might prevent every difficulty by making the rates in duplicate.

*426]   *As the matter stands, the prosecutor, by his appointment unrevoked, has a duty of a public character which he cannot perform without the books, of which the defendants have the possession as public officers, and which they will not allow him to have for the purpose of fulfilling his duty. There was not, and is not, any legal impediment to the books being delivered to him by the defendants; and they have been guilty of a breach of duty in withholding them. That duty being of a public nature, and there being no other adequate remedy than a mandamus, its performance may be enforced by that process.

The Court of Queen's Bench were therefore right in giving judgment for the Crown: and we affirm that judgment.   Judgment affirmed.

WARD *v.* LEE and Another. *Feb.* 24.

Defendants, being contractors acting under the authority of the Metropolitan Commissioners of Sewers, and bonâ fide acting for the purpose of executing stat. 11 & 12 Vict. c. 112, by negligence injured the plaintiff's premises.

Held that, under sect. 128, they were exempted from all liability; and a verdict was entered for the defendants on a plea of Not guilty by statute.

ACTION for the injury to plaintiff's reversion in premises, occasioned by the defendants obstructing a sewer so as to occasion a nuisance in the premises.

Plea: Not guilty, by statute. Issue thereon.

On the trial, before Pollock, C. B., at the Guildford Summer Assizes, it appeared that the defendants were contractors acting under the Metropolitan Commissioners of Sewers,(a) and, as such, had, in the autumn of 1855, *altered a sewer into which the drain of the [*427 plaintiff's house led. The effect of this alteration was to cause an accumulation of sewage in the drain of the plaintiff's house; which was a nuisance. The defendants, being applied to, three times cleared out the plaintiff's drain, removing the obstruction; which however constantly accumulated again. The last time that the obstruction was removed was in December, 1855. Notice of action was given in May, 1856, more than six months after the alteration in the sewer, but less than six months after the last clearing out of plaintiff's drain. The jury, in answer to a question left to them by the learned Judge, found that the defendants acted bonâ fide under the directions of the Metropolitan Commissioners of Sewers. The verdict was thereupon entered for the plaintiff, with leave to move to enter a verdict for the defendants, if the defendants either were, under stat. 11 & 12 Vict. c. 112, entitled by sect. 127 to a notice of action given within six months after the alteration in the drain, or were absolutely protected by sect. 128.

M. Chambers, in the ensuing term, obtained a rule nisi accordingly.

Edwin James and *Lush*, in last Hilary Term,(b) showed cause.—As to the first point, there was a cause of action in December, within six months before the notice of action. (As the court pronounced no opinion upon this point, the arguments are omitted.) Then, as to the liability of the contractors, it depends on the *construction of [*428 stat. 11 & 12 Vict. c. 112. Sect. 128 no doubt protects parties carrying the Act into execution from liability: but it was not intended to leave without remedy those who might be injured by some collateral negligence or wrong done by those carrying the Act into execution. The part of the Act, if any, which the defendants were carrying into effect was sect. 38; but in that there is an express proviso "that the discontinuance, closing up, or destruction of any sewer as aforesaid shall be so done as not to create a nuisance." This has been negligently done by those defendants; and the Legislature cannot have intended to leave the plaintiff without redress.

M. Chambers, in support of the rule, on the first point cited Boothby r. Morton, 3 B. & B. 239 (E. C. L. R. vol. 7), and Wordsworth *v.* Harley, 1 B. & Ad. 391 (E. C. L. R. vol. 20). On the second point he relied on the express words of sect. 128. (*Lush*, being called upon by the court to say what effect, according to the plaintiff's contention, that section had, argued that it must be read along with sect. 127, which showed that there were causes of action for which such persons

(a) See stat. 18 & 19 Vict. c. 120, s. 94.
(b) January 26th. Before Lord Campbell, C. J., Coleridge and Wightman, Js.

as defendants were allowed to tender amends, and that the present
cause of action ranged itself among them, though the defendants might
be entitled to be indemnified out of the funds of the Commissioners.)

Cur. adv. vult.

WIGHTMAN, J., now delivered the judgment of the Court.

*429]   This was an action by the plaintiff to recover damages *for an
injury to his reversion, caused by the defendants in so closing
up a sewer as to create a nuisance to the plaintiff's premises. The
defendants were contractors for works, acting under the authority of the
.Metropolitan Commissioners of Sewers ; and upon the trial of the cause
the jury found that what was done by the defendants was done by then
bonâ fide for the purpose of executing the Act, under the direction of
the Commissioners of Sewers. The defendants relied upon the 128th
section of stat. 11 & 12 Vict. c. 112, and the finding of the jury. By
that section it is enacted "that no matter or thing done or contract
entered into by the Commissioners, or by any clerk, surveyor, or other
officer or person whomsoever acting under the direction of the Commissioners, shall, if the matter or thing were done or the contract were
entered into bonâ fide for the purpose of executing this Act, subject
them or any of them personally *to* any *action*, liability, claim, or demand
whatsoever ; and any expense incurred by any such Commissioners,
clerk, surveyor, or other officer or person acting as last aforesaid, shall
be borne and repaid out of the funds under the control of the Commissioners." The plaintiff's counsel did not.dispute the application of the
clause to the case in question, but contended that it had not the effect
of absolving the defendants from liability to an action, and that it only
prevented their personal liability to the consequences of a verdict
against them, and that such is the proper view to be taken of the effect
of that section in connexion with the 127th section which immediately
precedes it. We cannot, however, adopt this construction, and are of

*430]   opinion that the effect of the clause is to absolve from *liability
to an action persons who, acting under the direction of the Commissioners, do some matter or thing bonâ fide which, but for that clause,
would subject them to an action. The object of the Legislature seems
to have been in such a case not to leave the complaining party remedi-
less, but to oblige him to bring his action against the Commissioners as
a body, in the name of their clerk, in which case the liability would not
be personal ; and any damages that might be recovered would be payable out of the funds at their disposal under the provisions of the 125th
section, which provides for the payment of the damages and costs
recovered against the clerk in any such action. The clause at the end
of the 128th section is not for the repayment of "damages" recovered
against a person acting bonâ fide in the execution of the Act, but for the
repayment of his expenses ; which may well be construed, consistently
with our view of the meaning of the section, to be repayment of the

expenses he may have been put to in defending an action brought against him personally, and in which he may have been successful on the ground that he was acting bonâ fide in the execution of the Act, and therefore not liable. The 127th section does not appear to affect the question under the 128th section, as it only provides for notice of action, limitation of actions, venue, powers to plead the general issue and give the special matter in evidence, tender of amends, and payment of money into court. If the plaintiff fulfilled the conditions imposed upon him by that section he might maintain the action, however bonâ fide the conduct of the defendant had been, unless protected by the. provisions of the 128th section. Some *other objections were [*481 raised on the part of the defendants to which we do not think it necessary to avert, as we are of opinion that, upon the objection raised under the 128th section, and the finding of the jury, the defendants are entitled to make the

Rule absolute to enter a nonsuit.

RICHARD POOLEY v. WILLIAM THANG HARRADINE.
Feb. 24.

Action on a promissory note. Plea on equitable grounds, that defendant made the notes jointly with J. for J.'s accommodation, and as surety for J.; and that the notes were delivered to plaintiff and taken by him on an agreement between them that defendant should be liable a surety only, and with notice that he was surety only; and that afterwards plaintiff, without defendant's consent, gave time to J., but for which he might have obtained payment. On demurrer,

Held: that, though the absolute written contract between defendant and plaintiff contained in the note could not be varied by parol in equity any more than at law, yet an equity arose from the relation of surety and principal between defendant and J., and the notice thereof to plaintiff at the time he took the note; and therefore that the plea was good.

Quœre, whether the equity would have existed if the notice had been after the taking of the notes, but before the giving of time.

THE declaration contained three counts on three promissory notes, made by defendant.

Plea, to all three counts, for a defence on equitable grounds:' That he, the said defendant, made the said notes at the request of and for the sole accommodation of John Harradine, jointly with John Thang Harradine and one Thomas Harradine, as the surety only of John Harradine, to secure a debt due to the plaintiff solely from John Harradine; and, save as aforesaid, there never was any value or consideration for the defendant making the said notes or either of them; and the said notes were delivered to the plaintiff, and accepted by him from the defendant, upon an express agreement between them that the defendant should be liable thereon as surety only for John Harradine; and that plaintiff, at the time the said promissory notes were made as afore-

*432]　said, had *notice and knowledge of the same having been so made by defendant as such surety as aforesaid; and that plaintiff, whilst holder of the said notes, without the knowledge or consent of defendant, for a good and valuable consideration in that behalf, agreed to give and gave to John Harradine time for the payment of the said notes respectively, to wit, from the times when the same became due until the commencement of this suit, and forbore to enforce payment of the same during that time, upon and for the consideration aforesaid; and that plaintiff could and might, had he not given such time as aforesaid, have obtained payment from John Harradine of the said notes and all moneys due thereon. And that by means of the premises he the defendant hath been greatly prejudiced and damnified, and hath been and is wholly discharged from all liability to pay the amount due upon the said notes and each of them.

Demurrer. Joinder.

Atherton, in last Hilary Term,(a) argued for the plaintiff, and *O'Malley* for the defendant. The arguments and authorities are so fully stated in the judgment as to render any further report unnecessary.

Cur. adv. vult.

COLERIDGE, J., in this Vacation (February 24th), delivered judgment.

This was an action by the payee against the maker of three promissory notes. The defendant pleaded, by way of equitable defence, that the notes were made by him jointly with John Harradine and Thomas *433]　*Harradine, and that he made them at the request and for the accommodation of John Harradine, as the surety only of John Harradine, and to secure a debt due from John Harradine solely, to the plaintiff, and without value or consideration; and that the notes were delivered to the plaintiff, and accepted by him from the defendant, upon an express agreement between them that the defendant should be liable thereon as surety only for the said John Harradine; and that the plaintiff, at the time the notes were made, had notice and knowledge of the same having been so made by him as such surety. The plea then stated that the plaintiff, whilst holder of the notes, without the knowledge or consent of the defendant, for a good and valuable consideration, agreed to give and did give the said John Harradine time for the payment of the notes, and forbore to enforce them; and that he could and might, had he not given such time, have obtained payment from the said John Harradine. The plaintiff having demurred to this plea, we have to determine whether the facts stated in the plea amount to an equitable defence.

At law it seems to have been thought that the discharge of the surety by such giving time to the principal was founded on a variation of the contract between the creditor and the surety: and, if that be so, it

(a) January 16th. Before Lord Campbell, C. J., Coleridge, Wightman, and Crompton, Js.

necessarily follows (the rule of evidence as to not varying a written contract by parol being the same at law and in equity) that no parol contemporaneous agreement could be allowed to vary the contract in the case of a written instrument. Probably the cases at law would be too strong to make it proper for us, not sitting in a Court of error, to decide contrary to the current of authorities on this subject, were we disposed *so to do, if the case now before us were that of a legal [*434 plea. It is important however for the decision of this case to consider whether, in equity, the doctrine of the discharge of the surety by time given to the principal debtor is confined to cases where the relation of suretyship appears on the original contract between the creditor, the principal, and the alleged surety, or whether an equity does not arise from the relation of the co-obligors or co-promisors inter se, and on the knowledge by the creditor of the existence of that relation. In the case of Hollier v. Eyre, 9 Cl. & F. 1, 45, Lord Cottenham, in delivering his opinion in the House of Lords, laid down the rule of law relied upon by the counsel for the plaintiff in the argument before us, that "the question whether the plaintiff as between himself and the grantees was a principal in the grant of the annuity, or only a surety for the payment of it by another, must be ascertained by the terms of the instruments themselves: no extraneous evidence," said he, "is admissible for that purpose." In this doctrine we entirely concur; and we think that, if the discharge of the surety could only be effected by establishing that there was a different contract as between the creditor and the alleged surety from that apparent on the written contract, as for instance that the latter would be liable, not primarily but collaterally only, on the default of the principal debtor, we should be satisfied that the defence was not made out. It remains, however, to consider whether, assuming the contract, as between the creditor and the parties contracting with him, to be, as apparent on the face of the written document, a primary and not a collateral liability, an equity does not arise from the relationship of the *principal and surety inter se known [*435 to the creditor. The counsel for the defendant on the argument referred us to the observations of Lord Cottenham in Hollier v. Eyre immediately following the passage referred to by the plaintiff's counsel. He proceeds as follows: "But although all the grantors were principals as between them and the grantees, yet as between themselves some of them might be sureties for others; and if it was established that such was the case as between the plaintiff and Lynch, and that the grantees knew that such was the case, they might by their dealing with Lynch have raised an equity in favour of the plaintiff, entitling him to the protection of a Court of equity against the legal consequences of the instruments he joined in executing. This distinction is perfectly well settled, and is the ground of many of the decisions." In page 51 Lord Cottenham says: "I am, however, anxious to explain my views of the

law upon the subject; assuming that the plaintiff was only a surety from the beginning, that is, as between himself and the co-grantors of the annuity; for as between himself and the grantees, I think it quite clear that he was a principal grantor. To affect the grantees in that case with any equities arising from the plaintiff being only a surety, they must have had notice of it at the date of the transaction." From those passages it seems to us that the rule, as laid down by Lord Cottenham in the House of Lords, may be inferred to be that equities such as that which we are discussing may arise, dehors the written agreement, from the relation of the principal and surety inter se if known to the credi-
*436] tor, and that such knowledge may be proved *either from what appears on the face of the written instrument or from evidence aliunde. That learned Lord uses the expression " at the date of the transaction," which the reporters in the marginal note of the case seem to have understood as meaning the date of the original grant; but, from the context and the passages which follow in the same page, we are disposed to understand them as referring to the time of the transaction or dealing alleged to amount to a discharge of the surety. The first part of those observations was under the notice of the Court of Common Pleas in the recent case of Strong *v.* Foster, 17 Com. B. 201 (E. C. L. R. vol. 84), and certainly warranted them in concluding that the rule of law and equity is the same so far as to prevent any alteration in the original contract being set up by parol evidence: but the latter observations seem not to have been before the Court; and it was not ultimately necessary for them to give any judgment upon the validity of the plea, or on the point now before us, as it turned out that the truth of the plea was not established by the evidence: and, although there are strong observations of the learned Judges on the subject of the rule being the same at law and in equity, they distinctly leave the question as to the validity of the plea undecided, and as admitting of great doubt: one of the learned Judges states that he should wish to look into authorities before giving any opinion on that part of the question. They decided the case on the question of evidence, holding that there was no proof of suretyship in the sense used in the plea, and that there was no proof of such a dealing as would discharge a surety. The latter ground would have been sufficient to discharge the rule; but still they seem to
*437] *have thought that the agreement mentioned in the plea was the essential part of the plea, and do not consider whether the fact of the suretyship, as between the principal and the surety, and the knowledge of the creditor was not sufficient. That view of the case not having been presented to them, and they having decided the case on the question of the evidence, we cannot treat the case of Strong *v.* Foster as judicially determining the present question. The Court of Common Pleas in that case referred also to a more recent authority,

the case of Davies *v.* Stainbank,(*a*) before the Lords Justices, as an authority that the rule was the same in equity as at law. Mr. G. R. Clarke, one of the counsel for the plaintiff in equity in that case, has kindly furnished us with the shorthandwriter's notes of the judgments of the Lords Justices in that case, agreeing with the account of the decision which he gave to us as *amicus curiæ*, at the close of the argument in the case at bar : and these judgments, agreeing as they do with the doctrine and principles laid down by Lord Chancellor Cottenham in Hollier *v.* Eyre, throw considerable light on what is the real doctrine of Courts of equity on the subject before us. It appeared in that case that Daniel Davies, the plaintiff in equity, had been sued at law in this Court on two bills of exchange, dated 1847 and 1848, for 1000*l.* each, drawn by Benjamin Davies, his nephew, upon, and accepted by, him in favour of Messrs. Stainbank, the plaintiffs at law and defendants in equity, and, as alleged by him, merely by way of suretyship for the drawer Benjamin Davies, who was *largely indebted to the payees. [*438 The defendant in the action at law had pleaded pleas of satisfaction and set-off, and, having failed in his defence at law, filed a bill in equity, alleging that he had discovered that the Messrs. Stainbank had given time by a binding arrangement to Benjamin Davies, and thereby discharged the plaintiff in equity, the alleged surety. Considerable discussion, we understand, took place on the question as to whether the equitable matter could have been taken advantage of at law; but it appears from the judgment that it became unnecessary for the Court to come to any decision on that point. The surety, however, was released in equity, and, as we understand the case, upon the very ground of equity which we are now discussing. Lord Justice Knight Bruce, after stating the facts of the case, says:(*b*) " We have since considered the whole controversy so far as the judgment at law has not rendered it unnecessary to do so, that judgment having reduced the dispute between the litigants to these points :—First. Did the plaintiff accept the two bills of exchange as a surety of B. Davies? Secondly. Was that known to Messrs. Stainbank when they took the bills? Thirdly. Was the plaintiffs' responsibility to Messrs. Stainbank upon the bills, whether in the nature of a floating guarantee or otherwise, of such a kind as to be liable to be discharged by their giving time—if they should give time—to B. Davies without the consent of the plaintiff, that is, to be so discharged, at least in equity, if not at law also? Fourthly. Did Messrs. Stainbank give time to B. Davies without the plaintiffs' assent, and in such a manner as to discharge him equitably if not legally also? Fifthly. Could the *plaintiff, who did not raise this point by way of plea or defence [*439 in the action, have effectually done so? and Sixthly. Whether

(*a*) Now reported, 6 De G. M. & G. 679.
(*b*) 6 De G. M. & G. 688.

the judgment at law precludes him from equitable relief. The plaintiff maintains the affirmative of the first, second, third, and fourth of these questions, and the negative of the two others. With regard to the first, second, and third, I think that the plaintiff has established his case by the evidence, and is certainly so far right. It seems to me that a creditor who holds a floating guarantee from a surety cannot, without the surety's consent, give time to the principal debtor as to a portion of the debt without reserving the creditor's rights against the surety, and yet hold the surety liable for that portion; the necessary consequence of the act being that, for a period of more or less duration, the principal debtor is protected at once against the creditor and against the surety from a demand for payment of the amount so dealt with." The Lord Justice, after examining the nature of the arrangement made between the creditor and the principal debtor, proceeds as follows :(a) " If, then, this agreement became, as I think it did, binding on Messrs. Stainbank and B. Davies, it had, in my opinion, the effect of discharging the plaintiff, if not both at law and in equity, at least in equity, from responsibility to Messrs. Stainbank on the bills, unless the plaintiff assented to it; for it did not reserve to the creditors liberty to proceed, as they otherwise might have done, against him.   And the conclusion is, I think, inevitable that, upon the assumption of the two bills not having been satisfied (an assumption which the verdict and judgment at law sanction and render necessary), the agreement extended to the debt represented or secured by the two bills; and materially, and to his *prejudice (as he has, I conceive, a right to say), affected his rights, remedies, and position in respect of the bills." The Lord Justice Turner, after stating the nature of the bill in equity and stating some points not necessary now to be mentioned, goes on as follows :(b) " It may also, I think, be taken as a fact both from the verdict of the jury in the action, and from the whole of the evidence before us, that the plaintiff (*whatever may have been his position as to the Stainbanks*) *was, as between him and Benjamin Davies, a surety, merely, upon these bills*; and the evidence establishes, to my entire satisfaction, that the Stainbanks at this time *knew* that the plaintiff claimed to stand in that position.   The letter of the 6th of March, 1848, alone seems to me to be conclusive on that point." After setting out that letter he proceeds: " After that letter, I think it is impossible for the Stainbanks to deny. that in the month of September, 1850, they knew that the defendant claimed to stand in the position of a surety as to these bills." In a later part of his judgment he says :(c) " This court, as I apprehend, has at all times exercised jurisdiction in cases of this nature.   It is, in the eye of this court, a fraud in a creditor to proceed to law against a

*440]

(a) 6 De G. M. & G. 689.
(b) Ibid. 694.
(c) Ibid. 696.

surety, after he has agreed with the principal debtor to enlarge the time for payment of the debt; and this court relieves against the fraud." In this case it should be remembered that the acceptances undoubtedly made Daniel Davies a principal debtor and primarily liable to the payees, and that there seems to have been no trace of any agreement either on the face of or dehors the written instruments, as between the creditors and the acceptor, that he should be as between them in the nature of a surety only. Where *then does the equity arise [*441 except from the relation of suretyship existing between the principal debtor and the surety, and from that relation being known to the creditor? Whether that relation must, according to some of the expressions used by learned Judges, have been known to the principal at the time of the original transaction is immaterial with reference to the plea now before us, as it contains an allegation of knowledge by the creditor at the time of the making and receipt of the notes: but we may remark that there does not appear to have been such knowledge at the date of the original transaction in the case of Stainbank v. Davies, 6 De G. M. & G. 679: and, if the equity does not depend on any contract with the creditor, but on its being unequitable in him knowingly to prejudice the rights of the surety against the principal, the equity would seem to extend to the case of the principal knowing the existence of the relation of suretyship only at the time of his dealing in such a manner with the principal debtor as to prejudice the rights of the surety. We believe the doctrine laid down in the cases we have cited from the courts of equity is well warranted by the authorities in equity, many of which are collected in the report of the case of Strong v. Foster, 17 Com. B. 201 (E. C. L. R. vol. 84): and we think it quite consistent with the principle on which the interfering with the rights of the surety against his principal are founded. The surety, we apprehend, on paying the debt has always a right to require the creditor to sue, or allow him to sue the principal in his the creditor's name: and, if, to use, the words of my brother Williams in Strong v. Foster, 17 Com. B. 201, 269 (E. C. L. R. vol. 84), "the creditor has voluntarily placed himself in such a *position as to be compelled [*442 to say he cannot sue him, he thereby discharges the surety." He has, on this supposition, knowingly and wrongfully interfered with the position and rights of the surety. Now does this right of placing himself as it is said in the shoes of the creditor depend on a prior contract between the creditor and surety, or on an implied duty of the creditor not to injure the surety's rights when he knows of the relation subsisting between him and his principal? We do not see that by the doctrine asserted in courts of equity the primary liability is at all altered. In truth, the defence, either at law or in equity, does not arise by any alteration of the original contract, which indeed it assumes and relies on in its original terms, but that the creditor cannot fairly or equitably sue the surety where, knowing of the existence of the

relation of suretyship, he has voluntarily tied up his hands from proceeding against the principal. We agree that no defence could be set
up by parol which should depend on altering the rights of the creditor
on the contract as between himself and the alleged surety as a primary
debtor; as, for instance, by making him liable only on default of the
principal, or after a request to him; but in truth the surety, in most
of the cases where the suretyship is apparent on the deed or written
instrument, contracts, not as surety collaterally, but as a principal
debtor or covenantor. His being named as surety may operate as proof
of notice or knowledge; but his contract is generally that of primary
liability. Thus, in the case of common money bonds, the liability is
not collateral, but primary, though in bonds and contracts to indemnify
it is generally collateral. In the case of money bonds, where the party
*443] is sued as surety, there is no contract as *between the surety,
obligor, and the obligee of any kind but that which imposes a
primary liability: and it may well be argued that it is immaterial
whether the knowledge proceeds from a recital in the instrument or
from extraneous facts. We conceive that equity would relieve in the
case of a co-obligor in a common money bond being made out to be a
surety by extrinsic evidence only, if time were given in such a way as
to discharge a surety in the ordinary case of principal and surety, when
the relation of suretyship appears on the face of the instrument. It
may be worth remarking that in Laxton *v.* Peat, 2 Camp. 185,(a) one of
the earliest cases on this subject, Lord Ellenborough seems to have proceeded on the ground of the plaintiff having notice of the suretyship when
he gave the time, as the plaintiff was the endorsee of the bill, and there
does not appear to have been evidence of any agreement between him
and the surety. The plaintiff, the endorsee, gave value, but had notice
of the circumstances of the original formation of the bill; and his giving
time, with such knowledge, discharged the surety, although the suretyship, as regarded the endorsee, depended on no agreement with him.

In the more recent cases at law, however, the rule in question has
apparently been treated as arising out of the original contract with the
creditor: and, if this was a plea of a legal defence, we should probably
have felt bound by those authorities, and have left it to a court of error
to consider the whole question, taking into their consideration whether
*444] the same rule in such *matters ought not to exist in courts of
law and equity, and to decide, if there be a difference, what the
rule should be. As we are, however, called upon to deal with this case
as if we were sitting in a court of equity, we think that we ought to
decide it according to what we believe to be the doctrine in courts of
equity. At the same time we shall not regret if this important subject
should now, or on any future occasion, be reviewed in all its bearings
by a court of error.

(a) As to this case, see Fentum *v.* Pocock, 5 Taun. 192 (E. C. L. R. vol. 1), Nichols *v.* Norris,
3 B. & Ad. 41 (E. C. L. R. vol. 23).

We give our judgment for the defendant on the present plea, on the ground that it appears to us sufficiently to state that the relation of principal and surety existed between the defendant and the principal debtor, inter se, and that the plaintiff had knowledge of that fact when the notes were made and received by him, and when he entered into a binding agreement to give time to the principal debtor.

Judgment for the defendant.

If a note be drawn and endorsed for the accommodation of the endorser, the holder does not discharge the maker by giving time to the endorser after the day of payment, though the holder knows, when time is given, that it was a note for the accommodation of the endorser: Bank v. Walker, 9 S. & R. 229. One who sets himself forth in a contract as principal, when he is in reality only surety, is held to be a principal in law: Sprigg v. The Bank, 10 Peters, 257.

The QUEEN v. Inhabitants of WESTBURY ON TRYM. *Feb.* 24.

Under stats. 3 & 4 W. & M. c. 11, s. 6, and 6 G. 4, c. 57, s. 2, a settlement cannot be gained by payment of parochial taxes for a tenement not being the property of the party paying, without an occupation of the tenement by him for a year.

ON appeal against an order of justices removing John Stook and his wife from the parish of Westbury on Trym, in Gloucestershire, to the parish of Pitminster, in Somersetshire, the Sessions quashed the order, subject to the opinion of this court upon the following case.

In 1846 the pauper John Stook agreed to take *possession of a separate and distinct dwelling-house, farm, and lands, in the [*445 appellant parish, which were then in the occupation of Joseph Palmer as tenant to Elizabeth Brown. He agreed with Joseph Palmer to take the crops of him, and to pay the whole rent, from Michaelmas, 1845, to Michaelmas, 1846, to E. Brown. He was accepted as tenant by E. Brown, at a rent of 99l. a year, the rent previously paid by J. Palmer being 105l. a year. The pauper put his son into possession, as his agent, in March, 1846, and went himself personally into occupation of the said dwelling-house, farm, and lands in May in the same year, and occupied the same under such yearly hiring till the November following, and resided there till the end of his occupation. Palmer was in occupation of the farm and premises up to March, 1846.

There were four poor-rates for 1846; and the pauper was assessed to and paid the two last of the said rates, Palmer having been assessed to, and having paid, the two previous rates, which were repaid to him by the pauper. And the pauper continued to reside in the said house for more than forty days subsequently to the payment of one of the said two rates to which the said pauper was assessed as aforesaid, and until November, 1846; when E. Brown put in a distress and received the said whole year's rent of 99l. from the effects of the pauper, who then relinquished the possession.

The Sessions found as a fact that there was a tenancy for a year, but no occupation under it for a year.

If the Court should be of opinion that, under these circumstances, the pauper gained a settlement in the appellant parish by payment of rates, then the order of Sessions is to be quashed and the order of removal *confirmed : if otherwise, the order of Sessions to be confirmed, and the order of removal quashed.

*446]

The case was argued in the preceding Term.(a)

Cripps and *Cleave*, in support of the order of Sessions.—The payment of rates was in this case insufficient to give a settlement without a year's occupation. Sect. 2 of stat. 6 G. 4, c. 57, is express : "No person shall acquire a settlement in any parish or township maintaining its own poor, by or by reason of settling upon, renting, or paying parochial rates for any tenement, not being his or her own property, unless such tenement shall consist of a separate and distinct dwelling-house or building, or of land, or of both, bonâ fide rented by such person, in such parish or township, at and for the sum of ten pounds a year at the least, for the term of one whole year: nor unless such house or building, or land, shall be occupied under such yearly hiring, and the rent for the same, to the amount of ten pounds, actually paid, for the term of one whole year at the least." Apparently, under this clause, the payment of rent is also essential to this settlement by payment of parochial rates; but at any rate the year's occupation is so. The term of a year is prescribed for both occupation and payment. Stat. 4 & 5 W. 4, c. 76, s. 66, adds a further requisite to the settlement by occupation of a tenement, but does not affect the settlement by payment of parochial rates. Stat. 6 G. 4, c. 57, is the only recent statute affecting such settlement. Stat. 59 G. 3, c. 50, was confined to settlement by dwelling for forty days in a rented tenement. Stat. 1 W. 4, c. 18, was *confined to settlement by hiring a dwelling-house, &c. In Regina v. St. Mary Kalendar, 9 A. & E. 626 (E. C. L. R. vol. 36), it was held that the requisites of stat. 4 & 5 W. 4, c. 76, s. 66, were not applicable to a settlement by payment of parochial rates, and that it was enough if those of stat. 6 G. 3, c. 57, s. 2, were fulfilled. In that case there had been a year's occupation : and the Court said : "The settlement would not, indeed, have been complete if the pauper had not occupied the premises for a year." And they referred to Rex v. Great Bentley, 10 B. & C. 520 (E. C. L. R. vol. 21), as showing that there was a sufficient occupation, which would have been quite unnecessary if no occupation had been necessary. [COLERIDGE, J., referred to Rex v. St. Pancras, 2 B. & C. 122 (E. C. L. R. vol. 9.)] That case occurred before the passing of stat. 6 G. 4, c. 57 ; there, no doubt, it was held that the occupation for a year was not essential to a settlement by payment of parochial taxes. [COLERIDGE, J.—Very pro-

*447]

(a) January 24th, 1857. Before Lord Campbell, C. J., Coleridge and Crompton, Js. Wightman, J., was present during the latter part of the argument only.

bably the statute was passed to correct that.] That seems to have been part of the intention. [COLERIDGE, J.—In Rex v. Ringstead, 7 B. & C. 607 (E. C. L. R. vol. 14), it was held that a forty days' residence was necessary, after the statute.] It would be so on any view. The occupation, however, under stat. 6 G. 4, c. 57, s. 2, is not quite the same thing as the residence, which is the foundation of all settlements: the residence may be in any part of the parish: the occupation must be of the particular tenement.

Skinner and *R. Sawyer*, contrà.—It has never been expressly decided that occupation was necessary, under stat. 6 G. 4, c. 57, s. 2, to a settlement by payment of parochial rates: and the words of the statute are *satisfied by referring them to the requisites of the settlement [*448 by settling upon or renting any property, to which they more naturally apply. The distinction, as to the effect of the enactments in the various statutes upon the two kinds of settlement, appears from Rex v. Stoke Damerel, 6 A. & E. 308 (E. C. L. R. vol. 33), and Rex v. Ditcheat, 9 B. & C. 176 (E. C. L. R. vol. 17). [CROMPTON, J.—The question in Rex v. Ditcheat was, what constituted an occupation.] The case illustrates the different view taken by the Legislature as to the requisites in both classes of settlement: and the recital in stat. 1 W. 4, c. 18, shows the doubts that had arisen. It might be argued, further, on the authority of Rex v. Ormesby, 4 B. & Ad. 214 (E. C. L. R. vol. 24), that here was in fact an occupation for a year under stat. 6 G. 4, c. 57, s. 2. The construction applied to stat. 3 & 4 W. & M. c. 11, s. 6, has been very liberal: Regina v. Marylebone, 15 Q. B. 399 (E. C. L. R. vol. 69), is a strong instance where the payment of rates was held to confer a settlement, though not coincident throughout with the year of occupation. The principle on which the payment of parochial taxes has been allowed to confer a settlement is that it is a recognition by the parochial authorities of the residence: Rex v. Llangammarch, 2 T. R. 628, Rex v. Ringstead. *Cur. adv. vult.*

COLERIDGE, J., now delivered the judgment of the Court.

The question in this case was whether, since the passing of stat. 6 G. 4, c. 57, a settlement can be acquired by payment of parochial rates in respect of a tenement, not being the party's own, without a year's *occupation of the tenement: in other words, whether that sta- [*449 tute in such case requires a year's occupation as well as the forty days' residence after the payment of rates, which was always necessary in order to acquire a settlement by parochial rating.

We are of opinion that, on the reasonable construction of the words of the statute, it is necessary, to gain a settlement in such case, that there should be an occupation for a year as well as the forty days' residence. The forty days' residence was required under the earlier law, and is certainly not taken away by any statute. In the case of settlement by rating generally, which is, whether intentionally or not, left untouched by stat. 6 G. 4, c. 57, such residence after payment may be all that is necessary. But that statute, which is confined to the case of a rating in respect of a hired tenement, appears to us clearly to require the occupation for a year in addition to residence.

The case of settlement by taxes not having been touched by stat. 59 G. 3, c. 50, stat. 6 G. 4, c. 57, was passed: and its enactments included the case of settlement by payment of parochial taxes in the case just mentioned. By sect. 2 of that statute, no person is to acquire a settle-. ment by reason of settling upon. renting, or paying parochial rates for, any tenement not being his or her own property, unless the tenement shall consist of a separate and distinct dwelling-house or buildings, or of land, or of both, bonâ fide rented by such person in such parish at the rent of 10l. for one whole year, nor unless " such house or building, or land, shall be occupied under such yearly hiring, and the rent for the same, to the amount of 10l., actually paid, for the term of one whole year at *450] the least." According to *ordinary rules of construction, the words " one whole year at the least" must be applied to the occupation as well as the payment of rent. Indeed, seeing that the payment of 10l., however large the amount of rent reserved may be, is sufficient, these words have a more natural connexion with the occupation than with the payment of rent. And, if they are not so connected, then there is no stipulation for any definite time of occupation, which is clearly contrary to the spirit of the Act. It is certain that by so construing the Act we make the rule apparently different in regard to settlement by rating in respect of a tenement and settlement by rating generally. But the extreme rareness of a claim for settlement on this latter ground made this of no importance, and probably was the cause why it was not provided for in the statute, and why provision was made only for the other mode of so becoming settled.

Several cases were cited in the course of the argument: but in no case has this settlement been held to be gained without the conditions in question having been complied with.

In Rex v. Ringstead, 7 B. & C. 607 (E. C. L. R. vol. 14), a settlement had not been gained by payment of taxes before the passing of stat. 6 G. 4, c. 57, as there had not been forty days' residence before that Act, and no settlement could be gained afterwards, because the conditions required by the Act had not been complied with. There is nothing in that case to show that the occupation was not one of these conditions. In the next case, Rex v. Ditcheat, 9 B. & C. 176 (E. C. L. R. vol. 17), the controversy in the case was on the nature of the *451] occupation required by the statute. All the Court took it *for granted that there must be an occupation under the statute, as well as a residence of forty days under the old law. The case was doubtful as to the fact of the residence, and was sent back to the Sessions to ascertain that fact, which it was necessary to ascertain, although two, the majority of the Court, had decided that the occupation was sufficient. Mr. Justice Parke, after holding that the occupation was sufficient, says expressly: "Then" (that is, if there has been a sufficient occupation) "a settlement has been gained, provided there has a residence of forty days. As to that the case is ambiguous." All the Court treat the occupation as necessary. Mr. Justice Littledale and Mr. Justice Parke held, contrary to the opinion of Mr. Justice Bayley, that the occupation of the tenement was sufficient, although part of it had been underlet.

Stat. 1 W. 4, c. 18, was passed shortly afterwards, probably in consequence of the case of Rex *v.* Ditcheat, with the intention of rectifying the omission in the previous statute, remarked upon in Rex *v.* Ditcheat, of the provision that the occupation should be by the person hiring the tenement. But the enacting part of stat. 1 W. 4, c. 18, does not mention the case of settlement by rates. Then came the case of Rex *v.* Stoke Damerel, 6 A. & E. 308 (E. C. L. R. vol. 33), where all the Court express an opinion that the Legislature had failed to remedy the supposed defect. Lord Denman there treats the occupation as clearly necessary, and points out that the enacting part of stat. 1 W. 4, c. 18, did not apply to the case. He says that, after stat. 6 G. 4, c. 57, there clearly could be a settlement by payment of rates, *provided the occupation* (with other *requisites) were sufficient. "Then stat. 1 W. [*452 4, c. 18, recites all stat. 6 G. 4, c. 57, s. 2, but confines its own enactments to settlement by reason of yearly hiring. How can we apply these enactments to settlement by payment of rates?" Mr. Justice Williams says the Legislature, in stat. 1 W. 4, c. 18, recite the clause of stat. 6 G. 4, c. 57, s. 2, "as to renting and payment of rates, and leave the latter head untouched, providing only for the former." After remarking on the argument, that settlements by rating were intended to be abolished, I am made to remark that the stat. 6 G. 4, c. 57, s. 2, "says that there shall be no settlement by payment of rates, except under the conditions there laid down:" and I add that, though the Legislature, in stat. 1 W. 4, c. 18, "recite two grievances, they leave one untouched."

None of these authorities are inconsistent with the Act of 6 G. 4, c. 57, s. 2, requiring a year's occupation: and, on the contrary, such occupation appears to us to be assumed as a necessary condition of acquiring a settlement in both the cases there provided for.

The Sessions, therefore, having negatived the fact of there having been an occupation, we are of opinion that no settlement was gained, that the order of Sessions was right, and that our judgment ought to be for the appellants.   Order of Sessions confirmed.

*453]   *The QUEEN v. The Mayor, Aldermen, and Citizens of the
City of MANCHESTER.   Feb. 24.

An indictment against a corporation, found at Quarter Sessions, may be removed by certiorari
into this Court, at the instance of the prosecutor, without the prosecutor entering into the
recognisance required by sect. 5 of stat. 16 & 17 Vict. c. 30.

MONK, in Michaelmas Term, 1856, obtained a rule calling on the
prosecutor in this case to show cause why the writ of certiorari, issued
to remove the indictment into this Court, should not be set aside, and
the return made thereto taken off the file of this Court, on the ground
that the prosecutor had not entered into a recognisance, as required by
stat. 16 & 17 Vict. c. 30; or why all further proceedings on the said
indictment should not be stayed until the said prosecutor should have
entered into such recognisance.   From the affidavit on which the rule
was obtained it appeared that, at the Sessions of the city of Manchester
holden in April, 1856, an indictment was preferred and found against
the defendants for non-repair of certain highways within the city. On
21st July, 1856, a writ of certiorari was, at the instance of the prosecutor, awarded and allowed by and issued out of this Court, to remove
the indictment into this Court. The writ was served on the clerk of the
peace for the city of Manchester, who returned the indictment into this
Court.   No recognisance conditioned for the payment to defendants of
their costs, incurred or to be incurred subsequently to the removal or
otherwise howsoever, had been entered into by the prosecutor, or any
other person.   The proceedings had not been instituted, prosecuted, or
awarded by or at the instance of the attorney-general.

*454]   *In last Michaelmas Term,(a)

Atherton, Spinks, and R. A. Cross, showed cause.—The
indictment has been preferred(b) under sect. 95 of stat. 5 & 6 W. 4, c.
50.   But the question arises under stat. 16 & 17 Vict. c. 30.   Sect. 5
of that statute recites that "it is expedient to make further provision
for preventing the vexatious removal of indictments into the Court of
Queen's Bench," and enacts that, when a writ of certiorari to remove
an indictment into the said Court shall be awarded at the instance of the
defendant, the recognisance now by law required to be entered into shall
contain a further provision for payment by the defendant to the prosecutor of the prosecutor's costs incurred subsequent to the removal;
and that, "whenever any such writ of certiorari shall be awarded at the
instance of the prosecutor, the said prosecutor shall enter into a recognisance" conditioned that the prosecutor shall, if the defendant be
acquitted, pay to him the costs incurred subsequent to such removal.
In the present case it cannot be truly said that the removal is at the
instance of the prosecutor: in form he obtained the writ; but he had

(a) November 20th, 1856. Before Lord Campbell, C. J., Coleridge, Wightman, and Erle, J.
(b) This did not appear from the affidavit, but was assumed on both sides in argument.

no discretion in the matter : a corporation can appear only by attorney ; and at Sessions or assizes no appearance by attorney is allowed ; so that the indictment can be tried only by its being removed into this court: Regina *v.* Birmingham and Gloucester Railway Company, 3 Q. B. 223 (E. C. L. R. vol. 43). A removal like this cannot be [*455 *said to be "vexatious," the case contemplated in the preamble of sect. 5. That this case is not pointed to in sect. 5 appears from sect. 7, which directs that, if, before a certiorari be allowed, the recognisance has not been entered into, the court to which the certiorari is directed may proceed to try the indictment. Now that is impossible in the case of a corporation. [ERLE, J.—And, in furtherance of your argument, it appears that the case was not lost sight of by the Legislature ; for, in sect. 4, where the removal of indictments is limited to cases in which a fair trial cannot be had, and to one or two more cases, there is a special exception, " except indictments against bodies corporate not authorized to appear by attorney." That seems to override what follows; so that sect. 5 would apply only to "such writ of certiorari." That is a certiorari not of the excepted class.] That is so, unless indeed the word "such" be referred to the earlier part of sect. 5. [ERLE, J.—The next antecedent is "any writ;" to apply "such" to that seems unmeaning.] Even if that could be done, it appears that the enactment of sect. 5 cannot apply to this case: provision is made for the writ of certiorari, whether awarded at the instance of the defendant or the prosecutor : but here it is difficult to suppose that the Legislature contemplated that an indictment is to be removed by defendants from a court in which they could not be tried. Besides, a corporation cannot enter into recognisances, any more than they could cast an essoign: Case of Mayor of Lincoln, Benl. & D. 121, Anonymus(a) case in Moore ; Com. Dig. *Franchises* (F 14); Burghill *v.* Archbishop of York, 1 Ld. Raym. 79 ; Grant's Practical Treatise on the Law of Corporations, 284. The most obvious mode of [*456 *interpreting the enactment is to hold it applicable only to the cases enumerated at the end of sect. 4, namely, where the writ is granted because a fair trial cannot be had below, because a difficult question of law is likely to arise, or because a view, or a special jury, may be requisite. How can the attachment against the "persons" prescribed by sect. 6 be enforced against a corporation ? Before this Act, the defendant could get no costs on such an indictment as this : the prosecutor had his costs paid by the defendant if the Judge certified that the defence was frivolous: stat. 5 & 6 W. 4, c. 50, s. 98. [COLERIDGE, J.—If that argument be of any weight, it goes beyond the cases where a corporation is a party.]

Monk, contrà.—"Such," in sect. 5, means "any" writ of certiorari, by reference to the last antecedent. [ERLE, J.—It looks as if the first

(a) Moore, 68, pl. 182.

enactment in sect. 5 was general, the second limited.] The words can hardly be interpreted with such nicety. Under stat. 5 & 6 W. 4, c. 50, s. 95, if the surveyor of the parish on summons denied the liability to repair, the complainant was directed by the parties to indict the parish; and, in so directing, the justices acted only ministerially; and, even if the parish was found not liable, the costs of the prosecutor were paid out of the parish highway rate; and the Court could not refuse them: Regina v. Justices of Surrey, Lowndes & M. 70. That has been often complained of; and indeed the enactment seems to have been inadvertently made: it is not improbable that the Legislature, in framing sect. 5 of stat. 16 & 17 Vict. c. 30, had in view to remedy the *457] injustice. As to the *language of that section: the attempt on the other side is to read "any such writ of certiorari" as if it were "any writ of certiorari in a case where a corporation is not a party." Such a construction is inadmissible: the Legislature, had they so meant, could have expressly excepted the case, as they have done in sect. 4, which shows that the case was present to their mind. So, in sect. 8, the case of prosecuting by the attorney-general is expressly excepted: and this shows that the argument derived from the last part of sect. 4 is untenable: if that section limited all the enactments following to the particular cases, there enumerated, in which a certiorari is to be allowed, sect. 8 would have been unnecessary. The preamble of sect. 5 is insisted upon: but that cannot control the plain words of the enactment: a strong instance of this principle is the interpretation put upon stat. 25 G. 2, c. 6, s. 1, in Lees v. Summersgill, 17 Ves. 508. The general policy of the Legislature has latterly been to enlarge the right of the defendants in indictments to recover costs, as in stat. 18 & 19 Vict. c. 90. Regina v. Birmingham and Gloucester Railway Company, 3 Q. B. 223 (E. C. L. R. vol. 43), shows only that the removal by certiorari is proper. If the case suggested, of certiorari obtained by a corporation, were to occur, the difficulty as to recognisances might be got over by the corporation finding sureties.(a) [Lord CAMPBELL, C. J.—The difficulty may come to no more than this, that the corporation, in the character of corporation, cannot enter into the recognisance COLERIDGE, J.—Like the case of a married woman.] That is all.

Cur. adv. vult.

*458]   *COLERIDGE, J., now delivered the judgment of the Court. This was a rule to take a certiorari, issued at the instance of the prosecutor, off the file. And the question which it raises is, whether a prosecutor, at whose instance such a writ has issued to remove an indictment against a corporate body, must enter into a recognisance to pay the defendant's costs in case of an acquittal.

This question depends for its answer on the true construction of stat-

(a) See Cortis v. The Kent Waterworks Company, 7 B. & C. 314, 331, 337 (E. C. L. R. vol. 14).

16 & 17 Vict. c. 30. And, according to the plain words of sect. 5, taken in their literal meaning, it would seem that he must. That section enacts in the most general terms that, "whenever any such writ of certiorari shall be awarded at the instance of the prosecutor, the said prosecutor shall enter into a recognisance" "with the condition following; that is to say, that the said prosecutor shall pay to the defendant or defendants, in case he or they shall be acquitted, his or their costs incurred subsequent to such removal." But then, by sect. 7, the consequence of not entering into the recognisance is enacted to be, that the court to which the writ has been directed "shall and may proceed to the trial of the indictment, as if such writ of certiorari had not been awarded." Now in the case of an indictment against a corporate body this consequence cannot follow; for it cannot appear, in person or by attorney, in the Court below; and therefore no trial can take place there at all. Moreover, in the correlative case, and on the supposition that the corporate body had been the prosecutors removing the indictment, there would have been a difficulty in strictly complying with the statute, because they could not enter into a recognisance, although we are aware that *in practice this is evaded by one or [*459 more members of the body entering into one for them: evaded we say, rather than overcome. These circumstances create a reasonable doubt whether the case of corporations is intended to be included within the large words of sect. 5. And, upon a consideration of all the clauses of the statute relating to this subject, and construing them all together as parts of one whole, which is certainly proper, we think i is not.

These sections extend from the 4th to the 8th section, inclusive of both. It appears that, by the 4th, the Legislature, taking advantage of the establishment of the Court of Criminal Appeal, advances in the policy which may be traced in preceding statutes of restraining removals by certiorari. By this section, both prosecutors and defendants are restrained from such removal unless it shall be made to appear that an impartial trial cannot be had in the court below, or that some question of law of more than usual difficulty and importance is likely to arise upon the trial, or that a view of the premises in respect whereof the indictment is preferred, or a special jury, may be required. But out of this section indictments against bodies corporate are expressly excepted; and the reason is given by implication: it is said "indictments against bodies corporate not authorized to appear by attorney in the court in which the indictment is preferred." In consequence of this, which the framers of the Act seem to have treated as one of invincible necessity, indictments against bodies corporate may still be removed (indeed must be) in cases where none of those specified causes exist, which in other cases are made conditions precedent to removal.

*460] Another *exception is made for a different reason, where the Attorney-General is acting on behalf of the Crown.

Then comes sect. 5, which is prefaced by a separate preamble, that it is expedient to make further provision for preventing the *vexatious removal* of indictments into the Court of Queen's Bench. A removal which, in order to procure *any* trial, the prosecutor is compelled to make can scarcely be called vexatious: and, although no doubt enacting words may often go beyond the language of the preamble, and as a general rule must not on that account be restrained, still in construing these words it is proper to pay attention to the preamble as of great moment to ascertain the intent of the enactment. But the enactments of the section are manifestly in accordance with the intent to be gathered from the preamble. As regards removals by defendants, it adds to the recognisance which was previously required by stat. 5 & 6 W. & M. c. 11, s. 2,(a) (the condition of which did not provide for the prosecutor's costs directly) an additional condition securing the prosecutor his costs subsequent to the removal in case of conviction. As regards removals by prosecutors, it goes beyond stat. 5 & 6 W. 4, c. 33, and, for the first time, imposes the necessity of a recognisance which is to be conditioned for the payment of the defendant's costs after removal in case of acquittal. Sect. 6 provides the mode by which the recognisance is to be made effectual in case of acquittal where the prosecutor has removed, or conviction where defendant has removed. This is

*461] by attachment after personal demand, or by estreating the *recognisance. These are the provisions in case the recognisance be entered into, extremely proper and just ones, putting both parties for the first time on the same footing in all respects if both parties be persons, but entirely failing to do so if one of them be a body corporate. For, if the certiorari be sued out at the instance of such body corporate, it cannot, strictly speaking, enter into a recognisance, nor be subject to attachment; and, if sued out at the instance of an individual as against it, being defendants, the party suing it out, who exercises no election in so doing, and cannot therefore be guilty of any vexation in suing it out, is yet subjected to all the same conditions as if he were. Seeing, too, that in sect. 4 the case of indictments against bodies corporate was present to the minds of the framers of the statute, for the purpose, however, of directly excluding it from the operation of the section, one would have expected that some provision would have been made in sect. 5 to remove these anomalous inequalities, if indictments against corporations were intended to be included. The provisions of the two sections will be complete and just if they be not included: they will not be so if they are included. But then we come to sect. 7, which seems to show conclusively that sect. 5 contemplated cases only in which the party suing out the certiorari had exercised an option, and in which, if no certiorari were sued out, still the trial might

(a) Made perpetual by stat. 8 & 9 W. 3, c. 33.

be had. For the only penalty which it attaches on not entering into the recognisance is that the Court to which the certiorari has been directed shall disregard it, and proceed to the trial of the indictment. Now this is inapplicable to the case of an indictment against a corporation; and no other remedy is provided by the statute. The construction, therefore, which *includes such indictments within the [*462 operation of sect. 5 may lead to a total failure of justice. Such indeed would in the present case be the consequence of our making the present rule absolute. We are asked to take the certiorari off the files of the Court, in a case where we cannot award a writ of procedendo; and this, too, where the prosecutor is no volunteer, but has preferred his bill of indictment by direction of justices of the peace under the general Highway Act, 5 & 6 W. 4, c. 50, s. 95. He has now done all that their direction has in fact imposed on him; and it is clear that they have no power to impose more, or to call on him, by entering into a recognisance, to take on himself the personal responsibility of costs in case of an acquittal.

It has not escaped us that sect. 8 expressly excepts any writ of certiorari awarded at the instance of the attorney-general from the operation of the Act. After the exception in sect. 4, this was perhaps unnecessary : and, had sect. 8 been omitted, it is not easy to see on the one hand how the attorney-general could have been practically brought within the operation of sect. 5, or, on the other, to suppose that it could have been intended in any way to fetter the trial of cases in which the Crown was directly concerned.

On the whole, we are of opinion that this case is not within the operation of sect. 5, and, therefore, that the rule should be discharged.

Rule discharged.

 END OF HILARY VACATION.

CASES

ARGUED AND DETERMINED

THE QUEEN'S BENCH,

Easter Term,

XX. VICTORIA. 1857.

The Judges who usually sat in Banc in this Term were,—

Lord CAMPBELL, C. J.,	ERLE, J.,
WIGHTMAN, J.,	CROMPTON, J.

ALLEN *v.* CARY. *April* 17.

On a trial, where the issue was on defendant who accordingly began, plaintiff, at the end of defendant's case, claimed a verdict on the ground that there was not evidence to support the issue for defendant. The Judge refused to direct a verdict, but gave plaintiff leave to move to enter one. The plaintiff then called evidence; and, on the evidence which followed, the issue for the defendant was proved.

Held: that the plaintiff was not entitled to enter a verdict on the ground that there was no proof for the defendant at the close of the defendant's original case.

ACTION on a promissory note. Plea: Set-off. Issue thereon. There were other issues of fact.

On the trial, before Williams, J., at the last Somersetshire Assizes, the counsel for the plaintiff and defendant respectively abandoned all the issues except the one above particularized; and the defendant's

*464] counsel began. *At the end of the defendant's case, the plaintiff's counsel contended that there was no evidence of the set-off. The learned Judge refused to direct a verdict for the plaintiff, but reserved leave to move to enter one. The plaintiff's counsel then called witnesses; and the defendant gave evidence in reply. The jury, upon the evidence given subsequently to the close of the defendant's original case, considered the set-off to be proved. Verdict for the defendant.

Slade now moved to enter a verdict for the plaintiff, on the ground that the case ought to have been stopped at the close of the original case for the defendant.

Per CURIAM.(*a*)—We will consult the learned Judge who tried the cause.   *Cur. adv. vult.*

Lord CAMPBELL, C. J., on a later day in this Term (April 28th), said that, as the plaintiff's counsel had elected to continue the case after the leave reserved, he was not entitled to object to the subsequent evidence having been taken into consideration.   Rule refused.

(*a*) Lord Campbell, C. J., Wightman, Erle, and Crompton, Js.

---

*THOMAS HARRISON and THOMAS ROGERSON *v.* ELLIS ELLIS. *April 20.*   [*465

A time policy was made on the G. B. "on 15.000*l.* on cargo, valued at 15,000*l.* with liberty to increase the value on the homeward voyage." The body of the policy was in the ordinary printed form, expressing the risk on the goods to be from the loading thereof aboard the ship, including risk of craft, and to endure until discharged and safely landed. On the margin was a memorandum, "with liberty to load, reload, exchange, sell, or barter, all or either, goods or property on the coast of Africa and African islands, and with any vessels, boats, factories, canoes; and to transfer interest from the vessel to any other vessel, or from any other vessels to this vessel, in port and at sea, and in any ports or places she may call at or proceed, without being deemed a deviation."

The G. B. sailed to Africa with a cargo, part of which was landed in a factory for the purposes of barter, and was lying at anchor loading from the factory native produce, when the factory with its contents were destroyed by fire.

Held: that the policy embraced only maritime risks, and did not protect either the goods which had been part of the cargo of the G. B., but had been landed in the factory, nor the produce intended to be her cargo, but still on shore; whether that produce had been obtained by barter of the G. B.'s cargo or otherwise.

COUNT against defendant as underwriter of 200*l.* on a time policy of insurance on the Grand Bonny for twelve months, "with liberty to load, reload, exchange, sell, or barter, all or either, goods or property on the coast of Africa, and African islands, and with any vessels, boats, factories, and canoes, and to transfer interest from this vessel to any other vessel, or from any other vessel to this vessel, in port and at sea, and at any ports or places she might call at or proceed to, without being deemed a deviation." The subject of the insurance to be "valued at part of

> 8,000*l.* on ship valued at 8000*l.*
> 15,000*l.* on cargo valued at 15,000*l.*

> ---

> 23,000*l.*

with liberty to increase the value on homeward cargo."

Averments: that goods were shipped at Liverpool: and that, on the coast of Africa, "divers of the said goods so loaded on board thereof, and divers other goods duly bartered for goods so loaded on board as

*466] aforesaid, *then being in divers factories and boats in conformity with and according to the meaning of the said policy, were" burnt and consumed by fire. The count then contained a claim for a loss on ship, and for a loss of freight.

The pleas set out the policy in hæc verba. Its terms are mentioned afterwards.

Plea 3, as to the goods: that so much of the goods, which were so burnt, " as ever were or had been on board the said ship, had been and were safely landed and on shore before the time when they were so burnt; and that the residue of the said goods never had been on board the said ship, or on board any craft, for the purpose of being taken to or from the said ship; and that all the said goods continued to be and were, at the time when they were so burnt, on shore, and not in the said ship; and that the risk by which they were lost was not a sea risk or a risk of craft." Plea 4: that plaintiffs did not lose, nor were they deprived of, " any goods on board the said ship, or in divers or any factories covered by the said policy by reason of the premises in the declaration mentioned or any of them." Issue was joined on these pleas.

There were other pleas directed to the claim for a loss on ship and on freight, on which the defendants had a verdict which was not questioned in banc. All further mention of these claims is therefore omitted in the report.

The policy was one formed by filling up the usual printed form of a Lombard Street policy. Those portions of the parts after cited which were in writing are printed in italics. It was for 2000*l.*, and expressed, in the ordinary form, that the insurers caused themselves " to be insured, lost or not lost," at and from "*for and during the space*
*467] *of twelve calendar months, commencing on the day of sailing from Liverpool, and ending on the day previous to that twelve-months, both days inclusive, in part and at sea, at all times and in all places, and in all services in the coasting and foreign trades, warranted free from capture and seizure, and all consequences from any attempt thereat.* Upon any kind of goods," &c., proceeding in the usual form to name the ship as the Grand Bonny, " beginning the adventure upon the said goods and merchandises from the loading thereof aboard the said ship *as above, including risk of craft,* upon the said ship, &c., and so shall continue and endure during her abode there upon the said ship, &c.; and further until the said ship, with all her ordnance, tackle, apparel, &c., and goods and merchandises whatsoever, shall be arrived at *as above;* upon the said ship, &c., until she hath moored at anchor twenty-four hours in good safety, and upon the goods and merchandises until the same be there discharged and safely landed. And it shall be lawful for the said ship, &c., in this voyage to proceed and sail to and touch and stay at any ports or places whatsoever *for any purpose* without prejudice to this assurance. The said ship, &c., goods and

merchandises, &c., for as much as concerns the assured by agreement between the assured and assurers in this policy, are and shall be valued

Part of 8,000*l. on ship valued at* 8000*l.*

15,000*l. on cargo* "   " 15,000*l.*

23,000*l.*

with liberty to increase the value on the homeward voyage. For account of Messrs. Harrison & Co., or as agents.

Touching the adventures and perils," &c. The policy *then [*468 contained, without any alteration, the rest of the usual printed form, with the usual printed memoranda. On the margin was the following written memorandum. *" With liberty to load, reload, exchange, sell, or barter, all or either, goods or property on the coast of Africa and African islands, and with any vessels, boats, factories, canoes; and to transfer interest from the vessel to any other vessel, or from any other vessels to this vessel, in port and at sea, and at any ports or places she may call at or proceed, without being deemed a deviation."*

This policy was underwritten by the defendant for 200*l.*

On the trial, before Bramwell, B., at the Liverpool Summer Assizes, 1856, the plaintiffs' counsel, in his opening, stated that the plaintiffs were merchants engaged in the African trade, which, he stated, is carried on entirely by bartering goods sent out from Europe for the native produce, consisting principally, though not exclusively, of palm oil. It is carried on along the coast, but chiefly in the rivers Bonny and Benin. In the Bonny river, ships of great burthen can enter; and there the Europeans remain on board ship, and the barter is carried on with the natives over the side of the ships. At the river Benin there is a bar preventing the entrance of vessels of any size; and there it is necessary to conduct the trade by means of factories or establishments on land up the river, in which the agents of the merchants reside. One of those factories was possessed by the plaintiffs; it was called Fort Harrison, and was situated on the shore of the river, about nine miles above the bar. The anchorage for vessels of too great a size to cross the bar was about five miles outside the bar, and therefore about fourteen miles from the factory. A schooner called the Visitor was employed, as a tender, *to carry the goods from the vessels at anchor to [*469 the factory, and to bring down the native produce from the factory to the vessels. The barter was carried on between the plaintiffs' agents resident in the factory and the natives at the factory. The plaintiffs' counsel stated, as their case, that the course of trade was to exchange the goods brought out by a ship for the produce to be sent home in her, in such a manner as to make the factory a mere substitute for the ship's boat, and contended that, under those circumstances, goods brought out from the ship but not yet actually exchanged for produce intended to be put on board, and also produce destined for the

ship but not yet actually put in motion to go on board her, were protected, under the terms of the marginal memorandum in this policy, whether they were in vessels, boats, factories, or canoes.   In this particular case the Grand Bonny arrived and anchored in the anchorage at the Benin on the 29th February, 1853; at which time there was in the factory a considerable quantity of oil, principally obtained from the barter of the out cargo of the Peru, a vessel of the plaintiffs, which had arrived before the Grand Bonny, and which sailed on the 8th of March, having by that time discharged her out cargo and taken on board a full cargo of produce.   The Visitor made several trips from the factory to the Grand Bonny and back, on each occasion bringing down a load of native produce which was stowed on board of the Grand Bonny, and taking back a load of the Grand Bonny's out cargo, which was landed and warehoused in the factory.   On the 29th March, 1853, some gunpowder stored in the factory caught fire; and the explosion totally destroyed the factory and all its contents.   During the interval between
*470] the arrival of the *Grand Bonny and the fire the barter at the factory had been very active, and almost all the cargo of the Peru had been disposed of, and a large part of the cargo of the Grand Bonny.   There were at the time of the fire in the factory 810 puncheons of palm oil, which would have been shipped on the Grand Bonny; of this about 470 puncheons had been obtained by direct barter of the cargo of the Grand Bonny: and there also still was in the factory a considerable part of the out cargo of the Grand Bonny not yet disposed of.   All this was destroyed; and the question in the cause, so far as regarded the goods, was whether the underwriters on this policy were bound to indemnify the plaintiffs for the whole or any part of this oil, and this undisposed part of the out cargo of the Grand Bonny.

The defendant's counsel admitted the substantial accuracy of the statement of the plaintiffs' counsel, with the exception of that part of it which related to the course of trade.   It was agreed that, in the event of the plaintiffs recovering, the question as to amount should be referred; that the plaintiffs should put in evidence the whole of the depositions of absent witnesses taken in the cause, and also the whole of the correspondence between the plaintiffs and their agent at the factory, and also call such parol evidence as they had as to the course of trade; and that upon this evidence the plaintiffs should have leave to move to enter a verdict on any of the issues, the Court to have power to draw all inferences of fact; the verdict being in the mean time directed for the defendant on all the issues.   On this arrangement several merchants conversant with the trade were called for the plaintiffs.   Their evidence showed that, in this trade, the greater part of the
*471] produce *is procured by a direct exchange of goods for produce; and that, on this account, it is probable that the produce shipped in a vessel would in general be principally procured by the barter of

her own cargo, which would be taken out as the other was put in. But their evidence also showed that, at a well supplied factory, the barter goes on all the year round, whether vessels are there or not; though, as might be anticipated, it is briskest at the time when there has been a fresh arrival of goods: and that it frequently happens that produce enough to furnish an entire cargo for a vessel is lying in the factory waiting for the first vessel. It appeared also that, though the greater part of the barter was in exchange without trust, the natives sometimes deliver produce on credit, taking from the agent what is called 'a book' (which is in the nature of an I. O. U., to be paid in goods); but this is not done to any great extent, the natives generally being too poor to be willing to give trust. On the other hand, the native traders are always anxious to get on credit a stock of goods, with which they may go up into the country and obtain produce, which they undertake to bring back. The resident agents generally have a desire to encourage this system of trust, for the purpose of pushing the trade; the merchants, who dread the risk, have a desire to restrict it; it is carried on to a considerable extent.

The learned Baron directed a verdict for the defendant, with leave to move to enter a verdict for the plaintiffs, according to the arrangement. No question was left to the jury.

Sir *Fitzroy Kelly*, in the ensuing Term, obtained a rule Nisi to enter the verdict for the plaintiffs on the *third and fourth issues, or for judgment non obstante veredicto on the third.(a) [*472

The correspondence and other documentary evidence, which was not read at the trial, but was considered as in evidence, was very voluminous; no abstract of it can conveniently be given in this report. On the argument, the defendant's counsel relied on many passages in different letters of the plaintiffs to their agent at Fort Harrison. The following are instances. Extract from a letter of November 1st, 1852; plaintiffs to their agent at Fort Harrison. "Write to us at every opportunity; and always let us know the prospects of what quantity of oil you are likely to procure for the next three or four months, so that we can make proper arrangements to send out tonnage to fetch it home, and keep you supplied with goods."—Extract from a letter of 23d December, 1852; plaintiffs to their agent at Fort Harrison. "The particular object of this letter is to advise you of the Grand Bonny's sailing next week with cargo for you as per enclosed list. She is to take what oil there is at Benin, both Mr. Day's(b) and your own; and this is to be done with the utmost despatch: and then she is to go to Bonny to be filled up by Mr. Wylie, or, if he cannot fill her, by Cap-

---

(a) By mistake the rule was not so drawn up: but on the argument it was agreed to treat the rule as if it had been so drawn up.

(b) The former agent of the plaintiffs, who had died about three months before this letter was written.

tain Stowe. We fear from the unfortunate detention of the Cleopatra
that there will be a large quantity of oil left at Benin, as Mr. Wylie
would not be able to do anything in Bonny for some time after we last
heard of him, end of September; but we expect you will be able to get
it on board the Grand Bonny without *loss of time." And they
relied on the following passage in the cross-examination of one
of the plaintiffs' traders at Fort Harrison, who, being in this country,
was examined before the Master under a Judge's order. After
describing the factory, which consisted of a hulk drawn up ashore and
banked up with mud so as to convert it into a house, used both as a
residence and a warehouse, which, together with shops and other buildings,
and the yard in which the casks of palm oil lay, occupied in the whole
about an acre of ground, all protected by a stockade, he proceeded:
" We took a cargo out of a vessel when it arrived, as quick as we could,
and put it in the hulk; and we put in the oil and loaded the vessel
again as quick as we could. The course of trade I will give an example
of. Supposing Jerry, the black governor of Benin, sent down his head
man with ten puncheons of oil. We test and see it is not watered, and
the casks are full. If it's all right, we roll the casks into the yard,
and give his head man a book for it in which is written ' Good for ten
puncheons to Jerry,' with the date and Fort Harrison upon it. Jerry
comes with that book when he likes, and gets the goods. There is a
fixed price for some goods; and he can select any of those to the value
of the puncheons. That is the common routine of the trade. Immediately those ten casks might be shipped without waiting for payment.
I believe that, before the Grand Bonny arrived, we had books out which
we expected to pay from her cargo. I have seen three of the Messrs.
Harrison's ships there together; but that was since the fire. We
generally try to get the ships longest out first loaded; but there are
exceptions to that practice. When a ship is loading we put oil in as
convenient: oil is oil without regard to *where it came from, or
how it is paid for. We couldn't know, after a little time, whether
we paid for it by goods from one ship or another, or which was Jerry's
oil, unless we had set it apart, which we never do. We put all our oil
together in a mass; and from that we load whatever is handiest to be
got at."

Other passages were referred to; but these above quoted will show
their nature.

Knowles, *Wilde*, and *Blackburn* now showed cause.—The question
upon the fourth plea is whether goods in the factory, under such circumstances as the present, were covered by this policy. Now, on this
policy, it is clear that what is insured is *cargo*; it may be on board the
ship, or it may be in craft; but it must, at the time of the loss, be *cargo*
of the Grand Bonny. It is said here that the course of trade made
the goods in the factory and the produce in the factory part of the

cargo of the Grand Bonny; but that is not so: the correspondence shows that there was a community of interest in all the plaintiffs' ships, and that the produce obtained in any way might be sent home by any of them. In this very case, part of the produce destroyed had been paid for by bartering the out cargo of the Peru. [Sir *Fitzroy Kelly*, for the plaintiffs, admitted that the plaintiffs were not entitled to recover for any part of the palm oil destroyed except the 470 puncheons obtained by barter of the Grand Bonny's cargo.] On the third plea, the verdict must stand, as the goods clearly were on shore when lost: and the question is whether the plea is good after verdict. The policy defines the beginning of the risk to be "from the loading thereof [*475 *aboard the ship as above, including risk of craft." And the duration of the risk is "until the same be there discharged and safely landed." These terms exclude the risk whilst on shore, whether up the country or in the factory. There is nothing in the terms of the memorandum to extend the risk to terrene risks. The words "without being deemed a deviation" are not perhaps very sensible in a time policy: probably these policies originally were for the voyage out and home, and have been continued unaltered after the practice arose of having a time policy. [CROMPTON, J.—It appeared in the case, tried at Liverpool, before me, that it was quite in the course of business, in this trade, to detain a vessel on the coast, using her as a warehouse for the goods brought out in other vessels and the produce which was afterwards sent home in other vessels. The body of the policy here contemplates only an outward and homeward cargo. It is very probable that the words of the memorandum were framed to extend the protection to goods on board a vessel thus detained on the coast as a warehouse ship.] At all events, the words cannot have the effect of overriding the body of the policy, and making the underwriters in a marine policy answerable for a risk on shore. Pelly *v.* Royal Exchange Assurance Company, 1 Burr. 341, will probably be relied on by the plaintiffs. It was an insurance on a ship and her furniture from London to China and back to London. Part of the furniture was, in the ordinary course of the voyage, put on a banksaul and there destroyed by fire; and it was held that the underwriters were liable. That was perfectly correct. The insurance was on the specific thing; and it protected *it during any part of the [*476 ordinary voyage from London and back to London. The principle is that the ordinary usage of the trade is incorporated in the description of the voyage in the policy: Columbian Insurance Company *v.* Catlett, 12 Wheaton's (Sup. C. U. S.) Rep. 383, Hunter *v.* Leathly, 10 B. & C. 858 (E. C. L. R. vol. 21). But in a policy on goods express words exclude liability till the goods are loaded; and this is strictly construed: Royal Exchange Assurance *v.* M'Swiney, 14 Q. B. 646 (E. C. L. R. vol. 68);(*a*) Halhead *v.* Young, 6 E. & B. 312

(*a*) In Exch. Ch., reversing the judgment of Q. B. in M'Swiney *v.* Royal Exchange Assurance 14 Q. B. 634 (E. C. L. R. vol. 68).

(E. C. L. R. vol. 88).   In a Massachusetts policy there aie no such excluding words.   In Martin *v.* Salem Marine Insurance Company, 2 Tyng's (Massachusetts) Rep. 420, which was on a Massachusetts policy, the policy was on cargo of the Catherine "from Marblehead to one or more ports in the West Indies, for the purpose of selling her outward and purchasing a return cargo, and at and from thence to Marblehead, or her first port of discharge in the United States." The outward cargo was unshipped and put in the care of a factor at Cape François, and, while in his care, was burned. The usage of the trade was shown to be, to use the out cargo as a means of getting a home cargo, much as in the present case; except that the negroes at Cape François understood the value of dollars. The Court, in giving judgment, say: "If the words of this instrument, descriptive of the subject-matter of the insurance, and of the duration of the risk, had been in the usual form of English policies, and instead of the term *cargo,* the description had been *goods laden on board the said schooner,* from the loading thereof *aboard, and to continue until the same be discharged and safely*

*477]   *landed,* it would hardly be pretended that goods landed from the vessel, or goods prepared to be put on board, but lost by the burning of a dwelling-house or warehouse on the shore, were within the words of the policy." "In this contract the schooner Catherine and her cargo are insured; and the risk upon the goods or cargo, as to its commencement and duration, is not distinguished from the risk upon the vessel. By this description the goods insured seem to be as clearly connected with the vessel, as her rigging or furniture; at least their connexion with the vessel is essential to ascertain the goods insured: and any other construction would leave the contract altogether uncertain and indefinite as to the subject of it in this instance. The goods which constituted the outward cargo, when landed from the vessel lost that character, and were no longer protected by the policy. The proceeds of those goods, whether existing in the credit of the factor, in money, or in other goods prepared for a return cargo, were equally without the protection of the policy. These are not within the description of goods insured as the cargo of the vessel; nor can they be understood to be within the intention of the parties; especially if we consider the nature of the perils undertaken by the insurers. These are altogether of the sea, or of a maritime nature, and do not include the credit of a factor, or the security of his dwelling-house or warehouse, or the many distinct perils to which goods upon the shore are liable."

Sir *F. Kelly, Hugh Hill,* and *Aspland,* contrà.—This is a time policy on cargo, and therefore cannot be limited to any particular cargo. [CROMPTON, J.—A time policy on the cargo of a ship would seem to be

*478]   like a policy on *goods on a succession of voyages, in each attaching from the loading to the discharge. Lord CAMPBELL, C. J.—

Can the marine policy be extended to goods on shore without something on the face of the policy so to extend it?] It must be so extended here, or the marginal memorandum is inoperative. The body of the policy covers the cargo from time to time, and includes risk of craft; the out cargo therefore would, without more, be protected till they were put on shore, and the return cargo from the moment they were water-borne. The object of the marginal memorandum must have been to extend the protection to goods on shore in the course of barter. As soon as the native produce is obtained by the barter of the out cargo, and is appropriated for the home cargo of the ship, the policy attaches, whether at that time it is in vessels, boats, factories, or canoes.

Lord CAMPBELL, C. J.—I am of opinion that the verdict was properly entered for the defendant. This is a marine policy; a time policy it is true, not a voyage policy; but still one for a maritime adventure. It has, properly, not been disputed in the argument that, unless there are special clauses overriding the common form of a Lombard Street policy, the underwriters are not liable for the loss of goods on shore. The claim has now been restricted to the 470 puncheons of oil obtained by actual barter of the goods brought out in the Grand Bonny. But I think there is great difficulty in making any distinction. If the claim as to this part is right, I think, as at present advised, the plaintiffs might equally recover in respect of the goods brought out in the Grand Bonny, and not yet bartered away, and also in respect *of the [*479 produce, arising from the barter of goods brought out in the Peru, or otherwise, but intended for the Grand Bonny. I think all are the same in principle, and that for none are the underwriters liable. As the loss was of goods, after they had been safely landed, and of produce not yet loaded or put into craft, the underwriters are exempted from liability unless there are some special provisions to make them liable. What provisions are there here for that purpose? The words relied on are those of the marginal memorandum. My brother Crompton, whose practice at the bar gave him much knowledge of this particular trade, points out a case which this memorandum may be meant to meet, because it is the practice in the trade to detain the ship on the coast and use her as a warehouse. But it is not necessary to inquire what the object of the memorandum is, unless, by giving the words a reasonable construction, we can see that it is intended to make the underwriters liable for a loss on land. Now, I am at a loss to see, whether the words are taken in their strict grammatical sense, or whether there is to be an extended construction put upon them, anything to indicate such an intention. The memorandum begins by giving the insured a license. " With liberty to load, reload, exchange, sell, or barter all or either goods or property on the coast of Africa and African islands, and with any vessels, boats, factories, canoes." Well: how do these words make the underwriters liable for a loss on land, either after the maritime risk has ended, or before it has begun? Where is the language indicating an intention to extend the policy to a terrene risk? Then come the words "and to transfer interest from the vessel to any other vessel, or from any other vessels to this vessel, in port and at sea, and *480] at any ports or places she may call *at or proceed, without being deemed a deviation." I can see, here, no words that can be reasonably extended to cover goods on land; if there were such it might, as was pointed out in the argument, make the underwriters liable for two cargoes at once.

Pelly *v.* Royal Exchange Assurance Company, 1 Burr. 341, was, very properly, not relied upon in argument for the plaintiffs. That was an insurance on ship and furniture; and the only question was, whether the sails were protected when in the banksaul; but the American case, cited for the defendant, seems very nearly in point. In my opinion this memorandum licenses the doing of certain things which, it was supposed, might not be within the scope of the policy, but does not make the underwriters liable for a loss on shore.

(WIGHTMAN, J., was absent.)

ERLE, J.—I am also of opinion that the verdict should stand. I will assume the facts to be that the outward cargo had arrived at the factory, and had been bartered for produce destined for the homeward cargo, which was lying in the factory, on land, when it was destroyed. I look to the policy to see what is the contract between the parties; and I find the words "beginning the adventure upon the said goods and merchandises from the loading thereof aboard the said ship as above, including risk of craft." These words, "including risk of craft," make it begin, not merely when the goods are on board the ship, but as soon as they are afloat. The goods here, when lost, were on land. Then, does the memorandum on the margin alter the time of the commencement of the *481] adventure? I cannot find it. No doubt *I have a difficulty in giving a very definite meaning to the words "without being deemed a deviation" when used in a time policy; but on the face of it this purports to be an alteration of the form ordinarily used in a voyage policy; and in a voyage policy such words would have an important effect. But, supposing these words to be inoperative, we are not to strike out of the policy operative words merely because we find, in a subsequent part of the policy, words the meaning of which we cannot precisely define. It may be the words were inserted pro majore cautelâ. But of this I am clear, that it would be contrary to sound principles of construction to alter the meaning of plain distinct words defining the beginning of the adventure because of words the meaning of which I cannot expressly define.

CROMPTON, J.—We are, in construing this policy, to give the fair construction to the whole instrument. Doing so, I am at a loss to find any words which could extend the policy to cover goods in the factory;

nor do I see any indication of such being the intention of the parties. This is a time policy; and the memorandum is very probably taken from those in use in voyage policies; but its terms are not insensible when used in a time policy. For this policy is on the outward cargo from Liverpool, with liberty to increase the value on the homeward voyage. That contemplates a voyage out and home. The course of this trade is frequently to retain a vessel on the coast, using her as a receiving ship, and from time to time sending home her cargo in other ships. This course of trade as to transshipment was proved very recently before me in a trial at Liverpool, as to a contract for palm oil to arrive. The words of the *memorandum are sensible, as extending the [*482 protection, which in the body of the policy seems confined to the cargo on an out and home voyage, to the cargo of the vessel when employed in such a course of trade; and I have little doubt the memorandum was framed with that object. It is said the object of the merchant is not obtained, and he is not fully protected, unless the goods are covered whilst in the course of barter. But, unless you can introduce into this policy the words "whilst in the factory," the goods, if protected at all whilst on land in the course of barter, must be covered when in the hands of the native traders up the country upon trust. And, if you did introduce such words, you would often make the under- writers liable for two cargoes at once. For it may well be that the Grand Bonny lands her full out cargo at Benin, and, leaving it in the factory, goes to Bonny, and there acts as a receiving ship, till the pro- duce intended as her home cargo is ready at the factory. This would be a legitimate operation; and it would be difficult to deny that the cargo on board was at the risk of the underwriters; and yet, according to the plaintiffs, the cargo in the course of barter in the factory at the same time would also be at their risk. The policy is explained by its being meant to cover the cargo of a vessel which it was contemplated might be detained some time on the coast of Africa; and there are no words in it making the underwriters liable for such a loss as this.

Rule discharged.

---

*JOHN SMITH, Appellant, v. The Guardians, Churchwardens, [*483 and Overseers of the Poor of the Parish of BIRMINGHAM, Respondents. *April* 22.

Houses, the property of a subject, were taken on lease by the Postmaster-General, and occupied as a post office, for the purposes of the post office revenue.

Held, that, the premises being occupied by the servants of the Crown for public purposes, no one was rateable in respect of the occupation of them.

THE appellant having given notice of appeal against a rate for the relief of the poor of the parish of Birmingham, in which he was rated as occupier of property described as "Post office, money order office, house, and premises,'' a case was stated by order of a Judge. It set out the title to the premises in question, by which it appeared that the premises, the property of a subject, and formerly occupied as an hotel, were demised at a rent of 310l. to the Postmaster-General for thirty-two years from 1841. The lease was taken under the powers conferred on the Postmaster-General by stat. 3 & 4 Vict. c. 96, s. 67. The case then proceeded as follows. Soon after the date and execution of the lease, the Postmaster-General took possession of the premises thereby demised, and fitted up and appropriated a part thereof to the purposes of a post office for the town of Birmingham, the cost of which was defrayed out of the post office revenue; and he let off the remainder to the Inland Revenue office at Birmingham. The Inland Revenue department has always been separately assessed to the poor for the part of the premises occupied for the purposes of that department; and the deputy postmistress, who was formerly required by the Post-master-General to reside on the premises for the due performance of the post office duties, and continued to do so until the month of August,

*484] 1855, was assessed to the poor in respect of *that part used as the post office. The rent payable under the lease is paid by the Postmaster-General, out of the post office revenue; and the rates assessed upon the post office were also in fact paid by the Postmaster-General, the same being charged by the Deputy Postmistress, and allowed to her from time to time in her accounts with the post office department until shortly before she resigned her office in 1855, when, various alterations having been made in the management of the post office at Birmingham, the Postmaster-General, conceiving that such premises were not by law liable to be assessed to the poor, declined to pay further poor-rates in respect of the same. In the month of August, 1855, the appellant was appointed the deputy postmaster of Birmingham by the Postmaster-General, under the authority of stat. 7 W. 4 & 1 Vict. c. 33, s. 9, and for the purposes in that act mentioned; and the appellant complied with the conditions imposed by the said Act upon persons appointed to and holding such office; and on such appointment some alteration took place in the arrangement and occupation of the premises. With respect to the premises, they now are and at the time of the making of the rate in question were as follows. On the ground floor of the building there is an office or place in which the general business of the post office is transacted, consisting of a large room having an entrance to it by doors from the street. It is used for sorting all letters which are posted there, or which are sent there by the various inhabitants, whether for delivery at Birmingham or for transmission thence to other places. It is also fitted up with a counter for the transaction of business with the public, (viz.) for paying post letters, for registering post letters, for procuring letters directed to *be left at the post office until called for, and for the procuring [*485 of postage stamps by the public. There is also a wooden screen fronting the counter, which is fitted up with separate open boxes or pigeon holes, called "private boxes." These private boxes are each distinguished by a different number, and are used for the reception of the letters addressed to persons or firms at Birmingham who prefer having their letters sorted into those boxes, and delivered to them or their agents at the post office, instead of having them sorted to and delivered by the letter carriers for them at their respective dwellings or places of business in the ordinary way. Every such person or firm has his letters sorted into one of these boxes (which has its distinguishing number as before mentioned), and has them delivered at the post office upon their being called for there. In addition to this office, there is another large room or office on the ground floor which is used for the issue and payment of money orders, and the management of that branch of the post office. There is an entrance to this office also from the street; and there is an internal communication by means of other rooms between the two rooms or offices before described. Adjoining the first-mentioned office and having an internal communication with it, and also an entrance from an open yard or occupation road leading out of the street, there is another room or office, also upon the ground floor, fitted up for the use of and used by the letter carriers; and there is a cellar under this last-mentioned office, which is used partly as a letter carrier's office and partly for the reception of coals; and there are water closets and other offices near the said cellar, used by the letter carriers. These cellars and offices have no entrance *from the street, but have an external communication with the [*486 open yard or occupation road before mentioned. All the rooms, cellars, and offices before described communicate with each other internally, and comprise that part of the building which is used or occupied for the purposes of the post office; and there is another cellar under the first-mentioned office, which is not used or occupied. The first and second floors of the building comprise altogether nineteen different apartments, and are let off by the Postmaster-General to the Inland Revenue department at an annual rent of 220*l*. None of these apartments are occupied for the purposes of the post office. They are all used as public offices by the Inland Revenue department, and have a separate entrance from the street; and there is no internal communication whatever between the rooms used as the post office and the rooms so let off to the Inland Revenue department. The annual rent of 220*l*. above mentioned is appropriated to the public revenue with other moneys arising from the post office. The appellant pays no rent for the premises appropriated to the post office, neither does he, nor does any other person, reside on any part of them, the business of the post office being carried on each day during the whole twenty-four hours continuously; and the premises are not used or occupied except for the purposes and in the manner above mentioned. There are 226 private boxes in the screen before described, for the use of which, in the manner before mentioned, such of the public as use them pay a gratuity of from one to two guineas each per annum to the post office department. These moneys are likewise appropriated to the public revenue with other moneys arising from the post office, under the provisions of stat.

*487] *7 W. 4 & 1 Vict. c. 33, s. 13. Postage stamps are sold by the appellant on behalf of the post office department to the public at the first-mentioned office; for which the appellant receives from the department a commission or poundage on the amount sold, which is allowed him by the post office department, and which, on an average, amounts to 200*l.* a year; but the amount fluctuates, and depends on the quantity of stamps sold. This allowance, and a fixed annual salary paid to him by the department, form the only remuneration received by the appellant for conducting the business of the post office establishment at Birmingham. The whole of the premises used for the post office purposes are in the possession of the appellant as the deputy and on behalf of the Postmaster-General.

The question for the opinion of this Court is, Whether, under the circumstances above stated, any person is rateable to the relief of the poor in respect of the premises so used as the post office, or any part thereof.

If the Court should be of opinion that no person is so rateable in respect of the occupation of any part of the said premises, then it is agreed that the rate shall be amended by striking out the assessment on the appellant; otherwise the assessment on the appellant is to stand to such extent as the Court shall think right. And, if the parties should differ as to the amount at which the rateable part of the said premises ought to be so assessed, the question of such amount shall be disposed of as the Court shall direct; and it is agreed that judgment shall be entered by the Court of Quarter Sessions accordingly.

*488] *Pashley*, for the respondents.—This is no part of the *hereditary property of the Crown. [Lord CAMPBELL, C. J.—If there is a subject having such beneficial occupation as to be liable to be rated, he is rateable even though it were the hereditary property of the Crown. But the rate cannot be supported unless there is some one liable to be rated in respect of his occupation. Who do you say occupies here?] The Postmaster-General for the time being is the occupier. just as the governor of convicts was considered an occupier of the farm attached to the convict prison in Gambier *v.* Overseers of Lydford, 3 E. & B. 346 (E. C. L. R. vol. 77). In De La Beche *v.* Vestrymen of St. James, 4 E. & B. 385 (E. C. L. R. vol. 82), the property was in the occupation of the Crown. That is not so here. [Lord CAMPBELL, C. J.—The Postmaster-General is obliged, in performance of his public duty, to do what he does. In Gambier *v.* Overseers of Lydford, the Court assumed that the directors of convict prisons acted voluntarily. CROMPTON, J.—The Postmaster-General acts here as the head of a great branch of the public revenue managed by the functionaries of the Crown.] The mode of selling postage stamps, and of using private boxes as described in the case, make this a beneficial occupation.

Wilde, contrà, was not called upon to argue.

Lord CAMPBELL, C. J.—I am of opinion that this rate must be amended. I certainly should be well pleased if it were made part of the general law that whenever property, subject to rates, is taken for a public purpose it should remain subject to the same burthen whilst it is applied to those public purposes. I think this would be but equitable; for the existing law is very *hard upon the occupiers of the [*489 rest of the parish upon whom an increased burthen is thrown. But, as the law now stands, if property is in the occupation of the servants of the Crown for public purposes, it is exempt from rates. It is wholly immaterial whether it be part of the hereditary property of the Crown, or be obtained for this purpose, having before been in the occupation of a subject. No property can be rated, unless there be a subject having a beneficial occupation in respect of which he may be rated. Who is such occupier here? Clearly not the clerks, nor the deputy postmaster at Birmingham. It is said that the Postmaster-General is the occupier; but how? Solely as a public officer of the Crown. This property is in the occupation of the Crown by officers of the Crown; and it is occupied solely for public purposes, which it is the duty of those officers to perform. The case is not distinguishable from that of a jail, or a court of justice, or the offices of the Secretary of State, or other cases in which property is occupied exclusively for public purposes. Mr. *Pashley* relies on Gambier *v.* Overseers of Lydford: but, in that case, the Court distinguished between the prison, which was occupied for the fulfilment of the public duty, and the farm. The Court thought the latter occupied as a voluntary commercial operation of the directors, and therefore rateable. Mr. *Pashley* also refers to the sale of postage stamps, and to the private letter boxes. The stamps are sold in obedience to positive injunctions. The private letter boxes are one mode of delivering letters. The proceeds form part of the public revenue; and no individual derives any benefit from the occupation of *this part of the premises. The whole is [*490 applied exclusively to public purposes.

(WIGHTMAN, J., was absent.)

ERLE, J.—I also am of opinion that land occupied by the servants of the Crown, exclusively for the performance of a public duty, is not rateable. I agree in thinking that it would be just in future to make such land rateable on some equitable principle; but it is the province of the Legislature to alter the law; it is our province to declare the law as it is; and under the existing law such property is exempt. Then is the property in question so occupied as to come within the exemption? To my mind it most clearly is. The sale of stamps and the use of letter boxes for more convenient delivery of letters are clearly within the scope of the duty of the post office, which is to deliver letters and receive the payment for them. The case of Gambier v. Overseers of Lydford, 3 E. & B. 346 (E. C. L. R. vol. 77), has been pressed upon us, where the directors of convict prisons took a farm as an adjunct to the prison. The decision was, that the prison was occupied for the Crown, but that no public duty was cast upon the directors of convict prisons to take a farm. If at some future time an enactment requiring them to take such a farm should be passed, it will be for the consideration of the Court whether, under such a state of law, the Directors would be rateable for its occupation: the principle on which Gambier v. Overseers of Lydford was decided will, under such an altered state of law, be no longer applicable.

*491]   *CROMPTON, J.—I am clearly of opinion that this property is within the rule which exempts from rates property occupied for public purposes. It is said this rule works hardship on the rest of the parish: and this may be, though the Legislature do not seem as yet to be of that opinion. In early canal Acts there often was a provision that property occupied for the canal should be rateable, but at the same rate as if occupied as before. Without some such qualification it might be injurious to make property taken for the Crown rateable in the occupation of its servants. The case of Gambier v. Overseers of Lydford decided that the prison was not rateable, and affirmed the principle on which we now act. The Court distinguish, rightly or wrongly matters not, between the prison and the farm. Probably the distinction was right on the grounds suggested; but, at all events, this distinction was made, and the principle affirmed, that property, occupied exclusively for the performance of a public duty, was not rateable. And, as in the present case the whole is occupied exclusively for the performance of a public duty, it is not rateable.

Rate amended.

———◆———

*492]   *The QUEEN v. THOMAS BEADLE.   April 22.

An officer of the excise having, on behalf of Her Majesty, sued before two justices for a penalty imposed by one of the Excise Acts, and the information being dismissed, appealed on behalf of Her Majesty to the Quarter Sessions, where the Sessions made an order, by which his appeal was dismissed with costs. This Court quashed the order of Quarter Sessions, on the ground that they had no jurisdiction to award costs against the Crown. The provisions of stat. 18 & 19 Vict. c. 90, ss. 1, 2, do not apply to such a case.

WELSBY, in Hilary Term, obtained a rule to show cause why so much of an order of the Recorder of Brighton in Quarter Sessions, dismissing the appeal of Thomas Beadle, an officer of excise, against the adjudication of two justices acquitting Joseph Palmer, upon an information against him for a supposed offence against the excise laws, which order had been brought up by certiorari at the instance of Her Majesty's Attorney-General, as ordered that the said Thomas Beadle do pay the costs of the appeal, be not quashed.

The order of justices appealed against stated that "Thomas Beadle, one of Her Majesty's officers of excise, and who prosecuted for Her Majesty in that behalf," exhibited before them an information, "which information was commenced and prosecuted by order of the Commissioners of Inland Revenue." It was against Palmer for a penalty of 20*l.* for using a stage carriage without a license. Palmer was acquitted. Beadle appealed. The order of Quarter Sessions, after dismissing the appeal, proceeded. "And it is also further ordered and directed by this said Court, before which the said appeal has been brought as aforesaid, that the said Thomas Biddle, officer of excise, the party against whom the said appeal has been and hereby is decided, do pay to Joseph Palmer, the other party thereto, the sum of 12*l.* 4*s.* 2*d.* as and for the reasonable *costs and charges of the said Joseph Palmer in and [*493 concerning the said appeal.

Creasy now showed cause.—Stat. 7 & 8 G. 4, c. 53, s. 82, authorizes the appeal by the officer against an acquittal. He is then a party to an appeal; and stat. 12 & 13 Vict. c. 45, s. 5, authorizes the award of costs against him. [Lord CAMPBELL, C. J.—If it were an appeal between subject and subject, that would be so; but the excise officer, bonâ fide suing for Her Majesty, represents the Sovereign. Now, surely, it is well established law that the Crown is not bound by an Act of Parliament without express words.] That rule is subject to an exception where the words of the statute are large enough to embrace the Crown, and the object of the enactment is the furtherance of justice: Baron de Bode *v.* The Queen, 13 Q. B. 364 (E. C. L. R. vol. 66). But stat. 18 & 19 Vict. c. 90, gives costs to and against the Crown. Sect. 1 enacts: That, "in all informations, actions, suits, and other legal proceedings to be hereafter instituted before any court or tribunal whatever in the United Kingdom of Great Britain and Ireland, by or on behalf of the Crown, against any corporation, or person or persons, in respect of any lands, tenements, or hereditaments, or of any goods or chattels, belonging or accruing to the Crown, the proceeds whereof, or the rents or profits of which said lands, tenements, or hereditaments, by any Act now in force or hereafter to be passed are to be carried to the consolidated fund of Great Britain and Ireland, or in respect of any sum or sums of money due and owing to Her Majesty by virtue of" "any Act of Parliament relating to the public revenue, *Her Majesty's [*494 Attorney-General, or, in Scotland the Lord Advocate, shall be entitled to recover costs for and on behalf of Her Majesty, where judgment shall be given for the Crown, in the same manner, and under the same rules, regulations, and provisions, as are or may be in force touching the payment or receipt of costs in proceedings between subject and subject, and such costs shall be paid into the Exchequer, and shall become part of the consolidated fund." Sect. 2 enacts: That, "if in any such information, action, suit, or other proceeding judgment shall be given against the Crown, the defendant shall be entitled to recover costs, in like manner, and subject to the same rules and provisions, as though such proceeding had been had between subject and subject; and it shall be lawful for the Commissioners of Her Majesty's treasury and they are hereby required to pay such costs out of any moneys which may be hereafter voted by Parliament for that purpose." The words of the latter section are quite large enough to embrace the present case; and it clearly is within the mischief. [CROMPTON, J.—The mode of enforcing the payment of costs given by sect. 2 would be by application to the Commissioners of the Treasury to pay, enforced by mandamus if they refused. The Legislature are not likely to have intended that process to be adopted in respect of every proceeding at petty sessions.]

Wilde and *Welsby*, in support of the rule.—No doubt it seems hard that a defendant, who. has been acquitted of a charge brought against him, and who is therefore to be taken to be innocent, should be left to pay his own costs: but such was the common law; and such still is the law where the Crown is a party, except *where recent legislation [*495] has altered it. Stat. 12 & 13 Vict. c. 45, was passed at a time when in no case had a subject costs against the Crown; and it contains no words to charge the Crown. Then by The Customs Consolidation Act, 1853 (16 & 17 Vict. c. 107), sect. 263, " In all suits or proceedings at the suit of the Crown for the recovery of any duty or penalty, or the enforcement of any forfeiture under this or any Act relating to the customs, the parties thereto shall be entitled to recover costs against each other in the same manner as if such suits or proceedings were conducted and had between subject and subject." That enactment would probably embrace informations for penalties before justices. [CROMPTON, J.—Is there any provision in that Act as to the mode in which the costs are to be obtained from the Crown?] No: the difficulty does not seem to have occurred to those who framed it. But that enactment is applicable only to informations for penalties under Acts relating to the customs. The information in question is one for a penalty imposed by an Act relating to the excise. [Lord CAMPBELL, C. J.—We can only administer the law as the Legislature have framed it; but what reason can there be for making a difference between customs and excise in this respect?] The only other Act is stat. 18 and 19 Vict. c. 90, the words of which have been already cited. Sect. 1 is in terms confined to informations and suits by the Attorney-General in England and the Lord Advocate in Scotland, such as informations of intrusion or informations in the nature of trover or debt, in which the Attorney-General or Lord Advocate, if successful, is to have a judgment which is to carry costs; and sect. 2 provides that, if in such proceedings judgment shall be against *the Crown, the defendant shall be entitled [*496 to recover costs absolutely as an incident to the judgment. But informations before justices are not by the Attorney-General or Lord Advocate; there is not in them, properly speaking, a judgment; and, if the decision on appeal under stat. 12 & 13 Vict. c. 45, s. 5, is to be considered a judgment, costs do not go with it as an incident to the judgment; they are discretionary only.

Lord CAMPBELL, C. J.—I am of opinion that this rule must be made absolute. The law is not in a satisfactory state; and I think it desirable that it should be reviewed, and the excise and customs put upon the same footing. It seems to me that it is desirable that in all such cases costs should be paid and received, as between subject and subject, as otherwise the Crown does not receive costs where it is just that it should receive them; and, on the other hand, the subject does not receive them where it is just that he should. But I regret to be obliged to say that, as yet, there is no enactment applicable to this case, where, on an information for a penalty under an Excise Act, there has been an acquittal, an appeal against that acquittal, and a confirmation of it. It would be becoming that a party thus twice tried, and twice acquitted, should have his costs: but he has them not by common law; and there is no enactment giving them to him. Mr. *Creasy* first relied on stat. 12 & 13 Vict. c. 45, s. 5. I am clearly of opinion that the case does not fall within that Act. It is enough to say that the enactment does not mention the Crown, and, if it applied, the Crown would be made liable to pay money without being named. But stat. 18 & 19 Vict. c. 90, does apply to the Crown. Perhaps *those who framed the [*497 Act had it in contemplation to put excise prosecutions on the same footing as that on which the Legislature had already put customs prosecutions; but, if such was their intention, it has not been expressed: for, looking at sects. 1 and 2, which must be read together, we find them not applicable to any cases except where the Attorney-General or Lord Advocate is a party. Now these officers have nothing to do with informations laid by officers of excise before justices; and, if such informations are not included, the Sessions in this case had no power to give costs, and that part of their order must be quashed.

(WIGHTMAN, J., was absent.)

ERLE, J.—I am of the same opinion. There is no question that sect. 1 is applicable only to informations by the Attorney-General or Lord Advocate. Sect. 2 is more extensive in its terms; but it is co-extensive in its object, and is applied only to "such" informations,

&c., as are mentioned in sect. 1. I think they must not merely be for similar objects, but in the names of the same officer.

CROMPTON, J.—I am clearly of opinion that the Act does not apply to this case. It is confined to suits where the Attorney-General or Lord Advocate sues to recover lands, goods, or money, in suits by them on behalf of Her Majesty. Sect. 1 uses express language applicable to a well-known class of proceedings where the Attorney-General sues the defendant. And the nature of the enactments as to costs, both in sect. 1 and sect. 2, shows this. In both costs are made part of the *498] judgment. By *sect. 1, where the Attorney-General has judgment, it is to be to recover the costs; and that judgment will be enforceable by execution. In sect. 2, if there is judgment against the Crown, the defendant is to have costs; but, as the judgment could not be enforced by execution against the Crown, the section proceeds to give what is equivalent to execution, by making it the duty of the Commissioners of the Treasury to pay the costs; which duty might be enforced by mandamus. So that I think it clear that both sections apply to the same kind of suits, and those only.   Rule absolute.

JOHN GERRARD v. ROBERT TOWNLEY PARKER and Others. *April 22.*

A parish road crossed a turnpike road from P. to W., at a place where there was a toll bar, and then met another turnpike road from P. to C. under the same trust as the first, but not being the same road. A carriage passing along the parish road, crossed the turnpike road from P. to W. at the turnpike, and then, without proceeding further on that turnpike road, followed the parish road, and then went more than one hundred yards on the road from P. to C.
Held, that it was exempted from toll by stat. 3 G. 4, c. 126, s. 32, not having passed over one
. hundred yards on the same turnpike road, though it had passed more than that distance on one in the same trust.

NOTICE of appeal against a conviction, under stat. 4 G. 4, c. 95, s. 30, of John Gerrard, collector of tolls, for taking a greater toll than authorized, having been given, a case was stated for the opinion of this Court. By this case it appeared that, under various turnpike Acts, the Wigan and Preston roads, north of the river Yarrow, are included in one turnpike trust. Amongst those roads were included a road from Preston to Chorley, which passes right through and forms the main street of Chorley, and a road from Preston to Wigan. These roads were shown on a plan, which was to be considered as part of the case. *499] By this it *appeared that the roads from Preston to Chorley and from Preston to Wigan were one for some distance from Preston. They then diverged at a point several miles from Chorley, and ran in a southerly direction nearly parallel to each other; the Chorley road being to the eastward of the Wigan road at a distance of from one to two miles. A public parish road called Euxton Lane runs from Runshaw on the westward of the Preston and Wigan road, across that road, and then for about a mile and a half until it falls into the Preston and Chorley road, at a place near Chorley, called Hartwood Green, where there formerly was a turnpike gate. Under the Chorley Improvement Act, 16 & 17 Vict. c. clxxxi.,(a) the limits of which included Hartwood Green, and stat. 18 & 19 Vict. c. lxxxiii.,(b) s. 21, the toll bar at Hartwood Green was removed, and the turnpike trustees were forbidden in future to levy toll or lay out money in the repair of roads within the limits of the Chorley Improvement Act. The turnpike trustees about the same time erected a new toll bar, called Euxton Bar, on the Wigan and Preston road, where it crosses Euxton Lane. Subsequently to the erection of this bar, Mr. Eccles was travelling in his carriage along Euxton Lane to Chorley, from Runshaw. When he arrived at Euxton Bar he found a side chain across the road. The appellant, who was the toll collector there, demanded from Mr. Eccles whether he was going to Chorley, and, having learned that he was, demanded sixpence for *toll. Mr. [*500 Eccles duly claimed exemption from payment of any toll, under stat. 3 G. 4, c. 126, s. 32, on the ground that he was only crossing the turnpike road : but he paid the toll under protest, and told the appellant he should summon him for taking illegal toll. Mr. Eccles was at the time acting bonâ fide ; but he did at the time intend to go, and he afterwards went, for above 100 yards on that part of the road from Preston to Chorley which lies between the end of Euxton Lane at Hartwood Green and Chorley, within the limits of the Chorley Improvement Act. The appellant was afterwards convicted in the penalty of 2l. 2s. and costs, under stat. 4 G. 4, c. 95, s. 30, for taking this toll under the circumstances ; which is the conviction appealed against.

The question for the opinion of the Court is : whether Mr. Eccles was entitled, under the circumstances, to claim such exemption. A judgment in conformity with the decision of the Court of Queen's Bench, and for such costs as the Court shall direct, may be entered on motion by either party at the Sessions next or next but one after such decision shall have been given.

Hugh Hill now argued for the appellant.(c)—Stat. 3 G. 4, c. 126, s. 32, exempts from toll, inter alia, carriages "which shall only cross any turnpike road, or shall not pass above one hundred yards thereon." Though the trustees are no longer to repair the roads within the limits of the Chorley Improvement Act, still any part of the road within

(a) Local and personal, public: "For the improvement of the parish of Chorley in the county of Lancaster."
(b) Local and personal, public: "To repeal so much of the Act relating to the Wigan and Preston roads as relates to the district of the said roads north of Yarrow, and to make other provisions in lieu thereof."
(c) Before Lord Campbell, C. J., Erle and Crompton, Js.

those limits, which was part of the turnpike road, remains so, and is to
*501] be taken *into account as part of the hundred yards : Bussey *v.*
Storey, 4 B. & Ad. 98 (E. C. L. R. vol. 24), Pope *v.* Lang-
worthy, 5 B. & Ad. 464 (E. C. L. R. vol. 27). And in this case Mr.
Eccles, when he passed the toll bar, intended to go and did go more
than one hundred yards on the road.

Atherton, contrà.—The words of the Act are " shall only cross any
turnpike road, or shall not pass above one hundred yards thereon."
The appellant must contend that this means on any road in the trust ;
for here the Preston and Chorley road and the Preston and Wigan road
are distinct roads in every respect, except that they are under one
trust. The nature of the enactment would seem to require that the
hundred yards should be continuous from the turnpike ; for otherwise
the toll keeper cannot know whether the passenger is bound to pay toll
or not. But, at all events, it must be the same road.

Hugh Hill was heard in reply.

Lord CAMPBELL, C. J.—There seems no doubt that the hundred
yards must be strictly upon the same road as that where the toll is
claimed. We will look into the case to see whether, in this case, there
is identity of road or not.   *Cur. adv. vult.*

Lord CAMPBELL, C. J., on a subsequent day in this Term (April
23d), delivered judgment.

*502]   *We are of opinion that Mr. Eccles was entitled to the exemp-
tion from toll which he claimed. He was called upon to pay
toll for passing a turnpike gate erected upon a turnpike road from
Preston to Wigan. But his carriage only crossed this road : and,
according to sect. 32 of stat. 3 G. 4, c. 126, he was not liable to toll
unless he was to " pass above one hundred yards thereon." The road
over which this passing above one hundred yards is to take place must
be identical with the road on which the turnpike gate is erected. But
Mr. Eccles was immediately to leave this road when he had crossed it,
and to come into Euxton Lane, which is a common parish road, not
under any turnpike trust. After travelling for a considerable distance
along this lane, at right angles to the turnpike road from Preston to
Chorley, and turning into this road, he was to travel upon it above one
hundred yards. This road is under the same turnpike trustees as the
road from Preston to Wigan, where the gate was erected. If the words
of the Act of Parliament referred to had been " or shall not pass above
one hundred yards thereon, *or on any other turnpike road under the
management of the same trustees,*" the exemption could not have been
claimed. But such words cannot be interpolated, and we cannot say
that these two roads are the same ; although they form parts of the
same turnpike trust. To the eye of a stranger they must appear different roads : the plan attached to the special case represents them as
different roads running nearly parallel for a considerable distance ;

they are called by different names in the private Act now regulating them; and the road leading to Chorley, over which Mr. Eccles travelled above one hundred *yards, being within the limits of the Chor- [*503 ley Improvement Act, although still a turnpike road, is in some respects under different regulations from the road from Preston to Wigan where the toll was demanded.

Our judgment therefore is that the conviction be affirmed.

Conviction affirmed.

———◆———

HENRY GREEN v. JOHN SADDINGTON.

Plaintiff and defendant agreed, by word of mouth, that plaintiff should pay 37l. for the interest of the defendant in premises occupied by him as a slaughter-house, and for the fixtures; defendant to return 10l. if plaintiff were refused a license to use the premises as a slaughter-house. The premises and fixtures were transferred to plaintiff; and defendant received the 37l. Subsequently, this action was brought to recover 10l., on an allegation that the license to use the premises had been refused to plaintiff. A nonsuit was directed, on the ground that the contract was for an interest in land, and was void under sect. 4 of the Statute of Frauds. On a rule to set aside the nonsuit:

Held, by Wightman and Erle, Js. (Crompton, J., not concurring), that, the contract being executed as far as regarded the land, and the promise sued on relating wholly to money, the plaintiff might recover, though the contract was not in writing.

THIS was an action in the Court of Record for the trial of civil actions within the city of Manchester.

1st count. That, in consideration that the plaintiff paid to the defendant a certain sum of money, to wit, 37l., as the purchase-money for the tenant right and fixtures of a certain shop and premises, situate in Brook Street, Chorlton upon Medlock, within the said city of Manchester, together with a certain yard and slaughter-house adjoining thereto, upon which said premises the plaintiff was then about to enter and to carry on the trade and business of a butcher, the defendant contracted and agreed with the plaintiff to repay him the sum of 10l., part of the said purchase-money, in case the council of the said city of Manchester should refuse to grant the plaintiff a license for the use and occupation *of the said slaughter-house as a slaughter-house: [*504 and the plaintiff says that, although he the plaintiff accordingly entered on the said premises, and although the council of the said city of Manchester did refuse to grant the plaintiff a license for the use and occupation of the said slaughter-house as a slaughter-house, yet the defendant, although required by the plaintiff, hath wholly neglected and refused to repay the plaintiff the said sum of 10l. or any part thereof. Counts for money received and on accounts stated.

Pleas: 1st, as to first count, denial of the contract: 2d, as to first count, that the council did not refuse the license, but did grant plaintiff a license for the use and occupation of the said slaughter-house as a slaughter-house : 3d, to remainder of declaration, Never indebted. Issues upon the several pleas.

On the trial, before the Recorder, the plaintiff was nonsuited, subject to leave to move, in any of the superior Courts, for a new trial.

Thomas Jones (of the Northern Circuit), in Michaelmas Term, 1856, obtained a rule to show cause why the nonsuit should not be set aside and a new trial granted, on the ground that the plaintiff was entitled to recover notwithstanding the Statute of Frauds.

The following was a transcript of the Recorder's notes at the trial, on reading which the rule was obtained.

" Mr. Ovens for the plaintiff. Mr. Fernley for the defendant. An objection was taken on the part of the defendant that the plaintiff could not recover, inasmuch as the agreement, not being in writing, was void by the Statute of Frauds : and the counsel on both sides agreed to the following facts ; on which I was asked to decide the point.

*505] *" An agreement was made between the plaintiff and the defendant, in the terms of the first count in the declaration, it being part of the agreement, under the word ' tenant right,' that defendant, who then occupied the said premises, should give them up to plaintiff, who was to become tenant in his place. After this agreement was entered into, plaintiff paid the defendant the sum of 37*l.*, and again plaintiff said, ' Recollect you are to repay me 10*l.* of this money, in case the council refuse to grant me a license for the use and occupation of the slaughter-house in question :' to which defendant then agreed. Plaintiff entered upon and occupied the premises according to agreement. Plaintiff proposed to prove that a license was refused. The defendant controverted this, but took this objection, that, however that was, even assuming the license to have been refused, plaintiff could not recover, the contract not being in writing. The plaintiff's counsel stated that he had no evidence to offer applicable to the count in the declaration for accounts stated.

" I held that the contract was void by the Statute of Frauds. The plaintiff was nonsuited, with liberty to move any of the superior Courts for a new trial."

J. A. Russell, in last Hilary Vacation,(*a*) showed cause.—The contract, actually made, was, as appears by the Recorder's note, one entire contract for the purchase of, amongst other things, the plaintiff's interest in the premises. The conversation at the time when the 37*l.* was paid was no fresh contract, but merely a recital of that already existing.

*506] The plaintiff's right to the 10*l.* *therefore depends entirely on that contract : and, in order to recover, ne must prove the contract. But, it being for an interest in lands, the Statute of Frauds prevents his enforcing the contract which was not evidenced by writing ; and the plaintiff was properly nonsuited under the plea denying the contract.

(*a*) February 9th. Before Wightman, Erle, and Crompton, Js.

Neither can the plaintiff recover on the ground of failure of consideration as to 10*l.*; for the contract has been partially executed: Hunt *v.* Silk, 5 East, 449, Blackburn *v.* Smith, 2 Exch. 783.† In Griffith *v.* Young, 12 East, 513, the plaintiff was no party to the contract for the interest in land; she recovered because a sum of money was paid to the defendant by a third person to hand over to her, and it was immaterial what the consideration was which induced that third person to pay it; but Le Blanc, J., says it would have been different if the action had been brought on the contract itself; and so it was held in Cocking *v.* Ward, 1 Com. B. 858 (E. C. L. R. vol. 50).

Rew, in support of the rule.—Cocking *v.* Ward, 1 Com. B. 858 (E. C. L. R. vol. 50), and the more recent case of Smart *v.* Harding, 15 Com. B. 652 (E. C. L. R. vol. 80), were cases in which the seller of the land sought to enforce the payment of the price; he could not do so if the contract was unavailable under stat. 29 C. 2, c. 3, s. 4. But here the defendant, who was in possession of the price, the 37*l.*, says the contract is void; if it be so, the plaintiff is entitled to recover back the whole 37*l.* Hunt *v.* Silk and Blackburn *v.* Smith are authorities that a valid binding contract cannot be rescinded unless there is a total failure of consideration; they are not authorities that a contract may be treated as void, *and yet the money paid under it kept by the repudiating party. Suppose a deposit paid on an auction of [*507 land, and it turns out that the contract is not properly signed; a common case. Could the vendor say the contract was invalid, and that he would not make a title, and yet keep the deposit? [CROMPTON, J.— But, in the present case, the plaintiff has got the defendant's slaughterhouse and his fixtures. He cannot keep those and get back the 37*l.* also.] There is no doubt a difficulty in that. Perhaps, in strict law, the contract being repudiated, the defendant is entitled to have back the land and fixtures, and the plaintiff to have back the whole money. It is difficult to see what defence there would be to an ejectment unless that the whole, as regards the land, is executed, and nothing remains to be done but pay the 10*l.* If that be so, the promise to pay it is a collateral agreement, and the plaintiff may recover on anything collateral, as in Cocking *v.* Ward. *Cur. adv. vult.*

ERLE, J., in this Term (May 5th), delivered judgment.

In this action the question is, whether the contract sued on is within the Statute of Frauds. There was an absolute agreement between the parties that defendant should give up possession of premises to the plaintiff, and the plaintiff should pay to him 37*l.*; and there was an additional contingent promise by the defendant to repay to the plaintiff 10*l.* in case the town council should at a future time refuse a license to the plaintiff. The possession was given by defendant; the 37*l.* was paid by plaintiff; the license has been refused; and the action is for the

*508] 10l. due on the refusal of the *license.   The defendant objects that the whole contract was for a contract or sale of an interest concerning land, and void for the want of writing ; and the objection would prevail if the action was for the land or purchase-money, according to Cocking v. Ward, 1 Com. B. 858 (E. C. L. R. vol. 50).   But the interest in land in this case has passed ; and the purchase-money has been paid.   As far as the land is concerned, the contract is completely executed, and cannot now be rescinded.   In the present action the whole consideration for the promise now sued on was money, viz., 37l. The whole of the promise now sued on is for money, viz., 10l.   It therefore appears to us not to be within the Statute of Frauds ; but, on the contrary, to be within the class of cases where, after the contract directly concerning an interest in land has been executed, the action has been held to lie upon a separate promise to be performed after such execution.   In Griffith v. Young, 12 East, 513, a tenant agreed to pay the landlady 40l. out of 100l., to be received by him from an incoming tenant ; this he was to pay to her for consenting to the assignment by him of his term : the assignment was made and consented to by the plaintiff ; and the 100l. were received by the defendant ; and, in an action by the landlady for 40l., it was held that the action lay without any writing, the contract concerning the interest in land having been executed.   The same reasoning was applied in Poulter v. Killingbeck, 1 Bos. & P. 397, and Seaman v. Price, 2 Bing. 437 (E. C. L. R. vol. 9).   Also the reasoning of Tindal, C. J., in Souch v. Strawbridge, 2 Com. B. 808, 814 (E. C. L. R. vol. 52), that the enactment in section 4 of the Statute of Frauds relating to contracts not to be performed within a year *has no application in an action of indebitatus

*509] assumpsit on an executed consideration, applies equally to the present action of indebitatus assumpsit for money had and received when the defendant seeks to avail himself of the part of the same section relating to land.   On these grounds we think that the rule should be absolute for a new trial.

This is the judgment of my brother Wightman and myself.   My brother Crompton is not prepared to agree in the view we have taken, as he is disposed to think that there was only one indivisible contract ; and he entertains doubts whether the view taken by the learned Recorder at the trial was not the correct one.   Rule absolute.

GEE *v.* WARD.

In 1806 it was referred to the Master in Chancery to report who was the proper person to be committee of G., a lunatic, and to certify who was her next of kin and heir at law, to whom it was directed that notice was to be given. S., maternal grandmother of G., the lunatic, made a deposition before the Master, in which she stated the connexions of the family. In 1854 G. died. In an ejectment in which the question was who was heir at law ex parte paternâ of G., the deposition of S., at that time deceased, was tendered in evidence as a declaration of a deceased relative on a matter of pedigree. No evidence was given either way as to whether, in 1806, there was any real dispute as to who was the heir of G. The evidence was objected to as being post litem motam, but received. On a rule for a new trial,

Held: that the evidence was properly received; the inquiry as to who was heir at law before the Master not being in itself a controversy or lis pendens within the rule, and it being no objection that the declaration was upon oath.

EJECTMENT. On the trial, before Willes, J., at the Liverpool Spring Assizes, 1856, it appeared that the property sought to be recovered had belonged in fee to a woman of the name of Jane Gee, who died intestate and childless in 1854, having been found a lunatic under a commission of lunacy issued in 1805. The *defendant was in [*510 possession. Both plaintiff and defendant claimed to be heir at law to Jane Gee. No dispute appeared to have existed upon the subject before the death of Jane Gee, in 1854. The property had come to her from her father. The plaintiff was the heir at law of John Gee; and he gave evidence of parol declarations of deceased members of the family, according to which they had declared that his ancestor, John Gee, was, after the lunatic, the heir at law of the lunatic's father. The defendant tendered in evidence an affidavit made by Martha Shallcross, now deceased, the maternal grandmother of the lunatic. It appeared that, after Jane Gee had been declared a lunatic, on a petition in Chancery to appoint a committee, it was, in 1806, referred to the Master to inquire who was a fit committee, and to certify who were next of kin, and who heir to the lunatic, to whom notice was to be given. In the course of the inquiry affidavits were used before the Master; amongst others, this affidavit now tendered. In it the deceased grandmother stated the then existing relations and connexions of her grandchild. According to the pedigree stated in this affidavit, an ancestor of the defendant was, in 1806, the next heir; John Gee, the ancestor of the plaintiff, being mentioned as the son of a younger branch of the family. There was no evidence either way as to whether the proceedings before the Master were conducted in a controversial manner, or merely as pro formâ; all that appeared was that there had been a reference to the Master to make these inquiries. The learned Judge admitted the evidence. The defendant had a verdict.

Watson, in the ensuing Term, obtained a rule Nisi for a new trial, on the ground of the improper reception of evidence.

*511]   *Hugh Hill and C. Milward, in Trinity Term 1856, showed
cause.(a)—The declarations of deceased relatives are admissible
in a matter of pedigree, unless made post litem motam. The reason
of this exception is that, after there is a controversy on the point,
suspicion is cast upon the motives of the relatives. This shows that the
lis, to be within the meaning of the rule, must be something of a controversial nature; it is not sufficient, to cast suspicion on the testimony,
that the declaration is made solemnly and in a matter of business, such
as the inquiry for the purpose of appointing a committee; that, in truth,
instead of making the evidence suspicious ought to make it weighty.
Before the Berkeley Peerage Case, 4 Camp. 401, the decisions were
conflicting. The first question in that case supposed that A., claiming
to be the son of J. S., "offered to give in evidence a deposition made
by J. S. in a cause in Chancery, instituted by A. against C. D., in
order to perpetuate testimony to the alleged fact disputed by C. D.,
that he was the legitimate son of J. S., in which character he claimed
an estate in remainder in White Acre, which was also claimed in
remainder by C. D." The Judges, with the exception of Graham, B.,
held it not admissible; and the House of Lords acted upon their opinion:
but the ratio decidendi is that the declaration was after a controversy
on the very point; and the terms of the question show a most distinct
litigation on the very point. In the same case an entry made in a
Bible by T., the deceased father, was unanimously held admissible,
*512]   though, as is stated in the question (the third), it was *proved
"that the said T. had declared 'that he T. had made such entry
for the express purpose of establishing the legitimacy, and the time of
the birth, of his eldest son N., in case the same should be called in
question, in any case or in any cause whatsoever, by any person, after
the death of him the said T.'" This shows that, in the opinion of the
Judges, the mere expectation that the pedigree might be disputed was
not a controversy within the meaning of the rule. In Walker v. Countess
Beauchamp, 6 Car. & P. 552, 561 (E. C. L. R. vol. 25), Alderson, B.,
is reported to have said: "I still think that the commencement of the
controversy must be taken to be the arising of that state of facts on
which the claim is founded, without anything more." According to
that, the lis as to heirship arose as soon as Jane Gee died, not before.
The ruling is said by Alderson, B., in the course of the argument in
Davis v. Lowndes, in error, 6 M. & G. 471, 517, 528 (E. C. L. R. vol.
46), to have been upheld by Lord Cottenham, C. It is, however,
doubted in the judgment of the Exchequer Chamber in the same case;
and in Reilly v. Fitzgerald, 6 Irish Equity Reports, 335, Lord St.
Leonards, after deliberation, held that it was too wide a definition of
lis mota, and that declarations made before there was an actual controversy were admissible. Declarations of deceased persons, as to

(a) June 10th, 1856. Before Lord Campbell, C. J., Coleridge, Erle, and Crompton, Js.

matters of such a public nature that reputation is evidence, are admissible, though made as depositions in a controverted suit, if the point in controversy was not the same: Freeman *v.* Phillipps, 4 M. & S. 486 (E. C. L. R. vol. 30). In reason, declarations of relatives, made to the Master asking for information, are no more open to objection than if they were made in answer to inquiries from any one else.

*Sir *F. Kelly, Watson,* and *Spinks,* contrà.—The deposition, [*513 made for a specific purpose, is not the spontaneous declaration of the relative; it is only when spontaneous that the declarations are admissible, according to Lawrence, J., in the Berkeley Peerage Case, 4 Camp. 409. Lord Eldon, in Whitelocke *v.* Baker, 13 Ves. 511, 514, expresses the same doctrine. They are admitted, he says, on the principle "that they are the natural effusions of a party, who must know the truth; and who speaks upon an occasion, when his mind stands in an even position, without any temptation to exceed or fall short of the truth." And this is cited with approbation by Lord Brougham, C., in Monkton *v.* Attorney-General, 2 Russ. & M. 147, 159. [Lord CAMPBELL, C. J.—Do you say that the inquiry as to who was to be committee was such a lis as to render inadmissible every declaration of relatives made subsequently; or is the objection confined to those declarations made before the Master?] It would seem to be a sufficient controversy to render all inadmissible; the moment Jane Gee became incapable of making a will, it must have been of consequence to know who was her heir at law. [Lord CAMPBELL, C. J.—It does not follow that there was, in 1806, any dispute about it. If the relationship were ever so undisputed, the inquiry before the Master would have been directed, all the same. It is agreed that there was no extraneous evidence given at the trial of any dispute in 1806.] It did not appear that the plaintiff's branch of the family had notice of the proceedings before the Master; which may be the reason why the deposition was allowed to pass uncontradicted. *Cur. adv. vult.*

*Lord CAMPBELL, C. J., in this Term (April 27th), delivered [*514 judgment.

This was an action of ejectment tried before my brother Willes at the Liverpool Assizes. Each party at the trial sought to make out that he was the heir at law of one Jane Gee, a lunatic, who died in 1854. The plaintiff gave primâ facie evidence of his pedigree, according to which one John Gee appeared to have been the son of Nathaniel Gee. According to the defendant's case, John Gee was the son of Newman Gee: and in support of his case he offered in evidence the deposition of Martha Shallcross, a deceased member of the family, made by her in a matter of lunacy in 1806. This was objected to as inadmissible, on the ground of its having been made post litem motam. It appeared that a commission of lunacy had been awarded against Jane Gee in 1806, under which she had been found a lunatic; and, on the

petition of some of her relatives, it had been referred to the Master to
inquire who was or were a proper person or proper persons to be ap
pointed committee or committees of the lunatic, and also who was the
heir at law and next of kin of the lunatic, to whom the order of reference directed notice to be given.   The relations who had petitioned
exhibited a state of facts, and supported that state of facts by certain
depositions, and, amongst others, that of Martha Shallcross.   We must
assume, on the report of the learned Judge, that "no dispute appeared
to have existed upon the subject before the death of Jane Gee in 1854."
The deposition having been received in evidence, and the verdict having
passed for the defendant, a rule for a new trial was obtained, which
has been argued before us, and upon which we have now to give our
opinion.

*515]   *The question is, whether the deposition received at the trial
was admissible as the declaration of a deceased member of the
family, in a case of pedigree.   After great deliberation, we think that
this deposition was properly received in evidence, according to the rule
by which, in cases of pedigree, an exception is made to the common
doctrine of hearsay not being evidence, and the declarations of deceased
members of the family, made ante litem motam, are receivable.

The conditions under which such declarations are said to be receivable are, that they have been made by deceased members of the family,
who, as such, are supposed to have had peculiar means of knowledge,
and that they have been made before the arising of a dispute or controversy on the subject-matter in question.   Such declarations are not
excluded, if made ante litem motam, even though made by a person
expecting that the interest he is speaking about will ultimately vest in
himself.   "If no controversy existed at the time, the principle acted
on is, that such declarations are admissible, though subject to observation;" per Abbott, C. J., in Doe dem. Tilman *v.* Tarver, Ry. & M. 141;
nor is evidence of this nature excluded, if made ante litem motam, by
its being made for the purpose of proof, or of preventing future disputes, as in the common cases of entries made by fathers of families.
Another rule on the subject is that, to exclude testimony of this nature,
the lis or controversy must be on the very point in question; and declarations are not excluded, by reason of lis mota, if made on a collateral point
to that on which the lis exists.   This distinction was recognised in Free-
*516]   man *v.* Phillipps, 4 M. & S. 497 (E. C. L. R. vol. 30), *where Bayley, J., says that, if it were necessary to go into the question of lis
mota, he thinks the distinction correct, that when the declarations are on
the very point they are not evidence, but when the point in controversy
is foreign to that which was before controverted, there never has been a
lis (within the rule), and, consequently, the objection does not apply.   It
has, however, been suggested that depositions taken in suits, from their
very nature and purpose, and from the mode of taking them, are excep-

tions to the general rule, and are not admissible as declarations of deceased members of families in matters of pedigree; and the expressions of some of the Judges in the Berkeley Peerage Case are cited in proof of such an exception. We think, however, that these expressions cannot be taken as authority except with reference to the case, then before the House, of a lis mota on the very point. In that case it had been thought proper, in the assumed state of facts in the questions proposed to the Judges, to state distinctly that *the fact in question was disputed by C. D. in the former suit.* Therefore the case cannot be considered as deciding that depositions are in no case to be received. All the learned Judges who concurred in thinking that the evidence ought to be rejected, point out the lis mota, dispute or controversy, as excluding the evidence. It is true that Mr. Justice Lawrence, after showing the evidence to be excluded by lis mota, proceeds to say that he is likewise of opinion that " no deposition can be received in evidence as a declaration, to prove a fact which it was the object of that deposition to establish." If this means a disputed fact, directly in issue between the parties, it is clearly correct; but if it was meant to apply to any fact *collateral to the fact in dispute, or as to which there was no dispute, it is too large a rule of exclusion, and inconsistent with later authorities. [*517 The learned Judge points out that, besides the general danger arising from there being a lis or dispute on the very point, there was the additional danger of the deposition being prepared with the object of proving the particular fact in dispute; but, in the case before the House, the particular fact had been in dispute in the prior proceeding. The expressions of the learned Judge, and certainly the decision of the House, therefore ought not to be taken as establishing the general doctrine that no deposition or answer on oath is admissible as the declaration of a deceased member of the family. In the Banbury Claim of Peerage, 2 Sel. N. P. 755 (10th ed.), a bill in Chancery *and the depositions* were rejected; and it has been supposed that the Judges in that case intended to say that depositions in a suit in Chancery could not be received as declarations of the deceased members of a family under the rule in question. Besides the remark, however, that the declarations in the prior suit were in that case probably subject to objection, on the ground of the very point having been in dispute in the earlier suit, it will be found on examination that the Judges say no more than that the bill and depositions in question were not evidence either of the facts or as declarations in matters of pedigree, confining themselves very much to the terms of the question put to them; and they proceed to say that the statements in the bill and depositions were no evidence that the deponents were relations of the family. *Some of the depositions in that case were mentioned as not [*518 being the depositions of members of the family; whilst it is stated that some of the deponents stated themselves to be members of the family; and, there not being the necessary evidence *aliunde* of their being members of the family, the Judges were perfectly right in saying that the depositions were not evidence as declarations in a matter of pedigree: and they proceed to say, in answer to a subsequent part of the same question, that the statements in the depositions are not proof of the deponents being relations of the family. The answer appears in effect to be, that neither the bill nor the depositions in question were evidence; and that the depositions, purporting to be made by members of the family, were not made evidence by the deponents stating themselves to be members of the family without proof of that fact aliunde. Accordingly, this case has always been cited as showing the necessity of proof of the relationship aliunde to let in declarations as the declarations of deceased members of the family.

This subject is ably treated by Mr. Phillipps in his book upon Evidence (vol. 1, p. 206, 10th ed., by Phillipps and Arnold): and, after examining his authorities, we concur in the rule which he there lays down. According to this rule the evidence in the present case was admissible; and the verdict for the defendant founded upon it ought not to be disturbed.

Rule discharged.

------

*519]   *WOODLAND, Public Officer of STUCKEY'S BANKING COMPANY, *v.* FEAR.

A joint stock banking Company carried on business by means of branches, at various places amongst others, at G. and B. The Company was one; but each branch kept separate accounts, had separate customers, and in all respects transacted business like a separate bank. Defendant, holder of a check drawn on the G. branch, by a person who kept an account there, got cash for it at the B. branch. The check was without laches forwarded by the B. branch to the G. branch. When it was cashed the balance in the G. branch to the credit of the drawer exceeded the amount of the check; but when it arrived at G. that balance had been paid away, and the check was dishonoured.

The Company having sued for money had and received, on the ground of failure of consideration,

Held: that they were entitled to recover, as the B. branch could not, under the circumstances, be considered as honouring the check, nor as purchasing it, but as taking it from defendant on his credit, as they might have done a check drawn on any other bank: the circumstance that the banks at G. and B. were branches of the same Company being, for this purpose, immaterial.

MONEY had and received. Plea: Never indebted. The case was tried before Channell, Serjt., at the Somerset Summer Assizes, 1856. The following statement of the facts is taken from the judgment of this Court.

" The plaintiff sued as the public officer of a banking Company, called Stuckey's Banking Company, which has banking establishments or branches at many of the principal towns in Somersetshire; among others, at Glastonbury and Bridgwater. The Company is one, and has one public officer; but each establishment has a separate manager, keeps separate accounts with separate customers, and delivers out distinct check books, headed with the name of the place at which it carries on business. One Helyar kept an account with the establishment at Glastonbury, and, having to make a payment to the defendant of 39*l.*, paid him, on the 17th of the month, a check for that amount drawn on the Glastonbury establishment. The defendant, being, at the time of receiving it, in the neighbourhood of Bridgwater, presented it on the same day there: he was known to the *officers there; and they gave him cash for it: the [*520 check was sent by the first post to the Glastonbury establishment, where it was delivered in the course of the 18th; on the morning of that day Helyar had a balance there in his favour of 21*l.*, which had been drawn out before the check arrived; and the check was accordingly refused payment." The learned Judge directed a verdict for the defendant, with leave to move to enter a verdict for the plaintiff for 39*l.*, the amount claimed.

Kinglake, Serjt., in the ensuing Term, obtained a rule Nisi. *Montague Smith* and *F. Edwards*, in Hilary Term, showed cause ;(a) and *Kinglake*, Serjt., and *J. D. Coleridge* were heard in support of the rule. The course of the argument sufficiently appears from the judgment. In addition to the authorities mentioned in the judgment, they referred to Boyd *v.* Emmerson, 2 A. & E. 184 (E. C. L. R. vol. 29), and Bank of England *v.* Newman, 1 Ld. Raym. 442. *Cur. adv. vult.*

Lord CAMPBELL, C. J., in this Term (April 27th), delivered judgment.

This was a rule to enter a verdict for the plaintiff under the following circumstances. [His Lordship then stated the facts as antè, p. 519, and proceeded.]

The action was for money had and received. It was not contended, in the argument before us on behalf of the defendant, that the transaction between the defendant and the establishment at Bridgwater could be considered a sale of the check outright; in which case the [*521 *doctrine of caveat emptor might have applied in the absence of fraud; nor was it contended, on the part of the plaintiff, that, if this were a case of a banker paying a stranger the check of his customer, supposing he had funds, and afterwards finding out that he had not, the banker could recover back the money, there being no fraud in the stranger. This was the case here as contended by the defendant. But the plaintiff insisted that, as regarded the separate customers, the different establishments were in the nature of separate companies; that Helyar kept no account at Bridgwater, could draw no checks on that establishment, and that he and it did not stand in the relation of banker and customer: that the check in question therefore must be considered as having been cashed, not on Helyar's credit, or by his agent, but on the credit of defendant; and that, as there were no laches on the part of the Bridgwater establishment, the case was precisely within the

(a) On January 26th. Before Lord Campbell, C. J., Coleridge and Wightman, Js.

authority of Timmins *v.* Gibbins, 18 Q. B. 722 (E. C. L. R. vol. 83).
It appears to us that this is the true view of the case: the check was
not drawn on the banking Company generally, but on the banking
Company at Glastonbury; and this, coupled with the fact that Helyar
kept his account and his balance only there, shows that the Bridgwater
establishment was not bound to honour his check (even supposing he
had assets at Glastonbury), as a banker, under the same circumstances
as to assets, is bound to honour the check of his customer.   To hold
that the customer of one branch, keeping his cash and account there,
has a right to have his checks paid at all or any of the branches, is to
*522] suppose a state of circumstances so inconsistent *with any safe
dealing on the part of the banker, that it cannot be presumed
without direct evidence of such an agreement; and the giving on the
one hand, and accepting on the other, of a limited check book, seems
intended to guard against such an inference.   The case of Clode *v.*
Bayley, 12 M. & W. 51,† shows that the different branches of the same
establishment may be endorsers from one to the other, and, in case of
dishonour, that notice need not be given direct to the principal establishment branch, but that each branch in succession is entitled to notice.
They are therefore, for certain purposes, distinct.

If, then, Helyar is not to be taken to have drawn the check on the
Company simply, or on the Bridgwater branch separately, and had no
authority to draw on either, so as to enforce payment, we think the
Bridgwater branch cannot be properly considered to have paid the
check as his bankers, or on his credit; and, if so, they must have paid
it on the credit of the defendant, as much as if they had given him
change for a bank note, both parties believing it to be genuine; in
which case, if it turned out to be forged and worthless, an action might
clearly be maintained to recover back the money advanced.   We therefore think the rule should be absolute.   Rule absolute.

———◆———

A case without pleadings, between the insured and the underwriters on a policy on chartered
freight, was stated, on which the following facts appeared.
The ship was chartered to proceed from Liverpool to a foreign port and there load a return
cargo, for freight payable on delivery of the home cargo.   She took on board an outward
cargo and sailed.   She was driven on a bank by a storm near Liverpool; and the cargo was
rescued from her, and carried to Liverpool, and there warehoused; the ship still remaining
ashore in a situation of peril.   Some days afterwards the ship was got off and taken to Liverpool, where she was repaired, and again took the cargo on board and proceeded on her
voyage.
It was agreed between the parties in the case that the freight was to be taken as liable to contribute to general average; and the question for the Court was, only, whether the expenses
incurred after the goods were in Liverpool, in getting the ship off, without which she could
not have proceeded on her voyage or earned the chartered freight, were general average to

which ship, freight, and cargo were to contribute; or were chargeable to ship alone; or were
chargeable on any other principle.

Held: that, as the ship and freight were both in peril and both saved, the freight must contribute
as well as the ship, supposing the cargo not to contribute.

But the Court drew the inference of fact that the whole saving of the cargo and ship was one
continued transaction: and, on that hypothesis,

Held: that the expenses were general average to which ship, freight, and cargo must contribute.

THIS was a special case stated, for the opinion of the Court, without
pleadings, by order of Coleridge, J.

The facts of the case were as follows.

The plaintiff is the sole owner of the ship Tribune, of Saint John,
New Brunswick, which is a large vessel of 1122 tons register.

The defendant is an underwriter in Liverpool.

On 22d May, 1856, plaintiff entered into a charter-party with Messrs.
Anthony Gibbs & Sons, of London, merchants, whereby he chartered
his said ship Tribune to them, to bring home a cargo of guano from The
Chincas, on the coast of Peru.

The terms of this charter-party, so far as they are material to the
present case, are as follows.

The vessel was to proceed in ballast, direct from Liverpool to Callao,
Peru, there to receive orders to load a cargo of guano at The Chinca
Islands. After *completing her loading of guano, and obtaining [*524
the necessary clearance, the vessel was to bring the cargo of
guano to a port in the United Kingdom, calling at Cork for orders,
unless ordered to a port direct at Callao. The freight was to be paid
at the rate of 4l. 10s. per ton. 800l. was to be advanced the master
on account of freight at Callao; and the residue of the freight was to
be paid on the vessel's arrival at her port of discharge. (A copy of
the charter-party accompanied the case.)

On the vessel completing the voyage, the freight under this charter-
party would amount to about 6750l.

With the consent of the charterers, the plaintiff shipped on freight
from other parties a small quantity of goods for Callao, the value of
which was about 600l. And, laden with these goods, and about 800
tons of ballast, the vessel, on 7th July, 1856, set sail from Liverpool to
Callao in performance of the voyage mentioned in the charter-party.
The ballast was intended solely for the outward voyage, and was to be
discharged at The Chinca Islands, so that the vessel might load her
homeward cargo, which did not require any ballast.

On 24th June, 1856, plaintiff, by his agents Messrs. Miller, Houghton
& Company, effected a policy of insurance on freight, in their ordinary
form, for 3500l., at and from Liverpool to The Chinca Islands, and
during thirty days' stay there, with leave to call at Callao for any purpose; on chartered freight valued at 6750l. (A printed copy of this
policy was annexed.) The defendant subscribed this policy as an
underwriter in 200l.

The vessel, shortly after she sailed from Liverpool, and on 7th July, encountered a heavy storm, and was forced to anchor near the East Hoyle Bank, near the entrance *of that port.   To relieve her, the foremast was cut away; but she drove, and got fixed firmly on the bank.   The narrative of what followed is thus given in the average stater's adjustment, which, it is agreed, is accurate in facts.

"The sea made a complete breach over her; and she continued to strike heavily, straining and twisting very much.   At noon on the 8th, she floated and drove further on the bank, and struck very heavily, the decks rising about two feet each time that she struck.   On the 9th, the weather being more moderate, assistance was procured from Liverpool, and men employed saving the wreck from alongside, and the materials of the ship, which, with some goods belonging to the shipowner, which had been intrusted to the master, were all sent in lighters to Liverpool. On the 14th, a stream anchor was carried out; the ship was afterwards scuttled; and about 300 tons of ballast were thrown overboard; and then the ship, being kept free by pumping, floated.   The stream anchor and cable were then shipped; and the vessel was taken in tow by two steamers, and was anchored in the river Mersey.   On her arrival back in that port, the remainder of her ballast was discharged; and she was placed in a graving dock for repairs.   When the repairs were completed, the vessel was again fully ballasted; the goods were reshipped; and she again set sail on her voyage."

The plaintiff submitted the papers to his average adjuster, to apportion the general average amongst the various interests.

This adjustment, it is agreed, is accurate in its facts and figures. (The adjustment was to be in Court; and *either party might refer to it; and, if required, it was to be produced to the Court; but no reference was in fact made to it, all that was material being stated in the case.)

By the adjustment, it appears that the total disbursements were 6334*l.* 16*s.* 7*d.*   Of these, 643*l.* 11*s.* 1*d.* were in respect of expenses incurred, after the goods were discharged, in order to get the ship off. The expenses, exclusive of this sum of 643*l.* 11*s.* 1*d.*, amount to 5691*l.* 5*s.* 6*d.*   In this latter sum of 5691*l.* 5*s.* 6*d.* are included the expenses of repairing the damages done to the vessel arising from the general average act of cutting away the foremast, and those of repairing the damages arising from involuntary casualties, and all the expenses of replacing the ballast thrown into the sea, and of discharging the remainder of the ballast in Liverpool.   The former sum of 643*l.* 11*s.* 1*d.* includes the expenses of repairing the damage occasioned by the scuttling the vessel after the goods were taken out of her, and those of getting the ship off the shoal, including those of discharging the ballast there thrown overboard after the goods were in Liverpool.

In apportioning the loss, the average adjuster has stated that the

*525]

*526]

portion of the sum of 5691*l.* 5*s.* 6*d.*, which is chargeable to general average, amounts to 1528*l.* 1*s.* 7*d.* : and it is not intended, in this case, to raise any question as to the propriety of this part of the adjustment.

With respect to the other sum of 643*l.* 11*s.* 1*d.*, two apportionments have been made in the adjustment. The first has been made on the principle of charging the 643*l.* 11*s.* 1*d.* to general average, so as to make the whole sum, to be made good by general contribution by the *ship, cargo, and freight, be 2197*l.* 17*s.* 8*d.* made up as fol- [*527 lows.

Expenses of adjustment	£26	5	0
	1528	1	7
Together	£1554	6	7
Expenses incurred after the cargo was discharged	643	11	1
Total	£2197	17	8

The other apportionment was made on the principle of charging the sum of 643*l.* 11*s.* 1*d.* to ship and not to general average, so as to make the sum to be made good, by general contribution by the ship, cargo, and freight, be only 1554*l.* 6*s.* 7*d.*

On the first apportionment, the percentage on this policy is 15*l.* 1*s.* 9*d.* per cent. On the second apportionment it is 11*l.* 13*s.* 4½*d.* per cent.

It is admitted that the ship could not have been got off and completed her voyage unless these various expenses had been incurred.

The defendant admits that the freight, under the charter-party referred to, was an insurable interest, and that he is liable to some amount of general average : but he contends that all expenses incurred in getting the ship off the ground after the goods on board the ship were landed and warehoused fall on the ship alone ; and that, as an underwriter on freight only, he is not liable for any part of those expenses.

The question for the opinion of the Court is : Whether the defendant is liable to contribute to the expenses incurred in getting the ship off the ground after the cargo was discharged and safely landed, or any and which of such expenses. If either of the *apportionments [*528 above stated is, in the opinion of the Court, right in principle, the parties have agreed to act upon that. If neither is right in the opinion of this Court, the parties have agreed that the average state-ment shall be readjusted according to the principles to be laid down by the Court, by an average adjuster in Liverpool. (The case then con-tained an agreement as to payment of costs in the several events.)

The case was argued in this Term.(*a*)

Brown, for the plaintiff.—It being admitted that some of the expenses

(*a*) April 21st. Before Lord Campbell, C. J., Wightman, Erle, and Crompton, Js.

are general average to which the freight must contribute, the question
is to how much of the expenses the contribution is to extend, and on
what principle it is to be estimated.   In Job *v.* Langton, 6 E. & B. 779
(E. C. L. R. vol. 88), a cargo was necessarily discharged for the purpose of getting off a ship which had got on shore; and the cargo was
warehoused on land.   Afterwards the ship was got off by the application of fresh means; and (as was taken for the purposes of the case)
the cargo was reshipped in her and forwarded to its destination; it was
held that the cargo was not to contribute to the general average on so
much of the expense of getting the ship off as was incurred after the
cargo was in safety.   There the part of the expenses in question was
incurred separately and distinctly from those incurred in getting out
the cargo, and not at all for the purpose of saving the cargo which had
ceased to be in peril: it was incurred exclusively for the purpose of
saving the ship.   Here the whole is one continuous operation, which
*529] *commenced before the goods were landed, and the expenses in
respect of which cannot therefore be separated into distinct portions.   In such a case the goods must contribute to the general average
upon all the expenses of the preservation, as was decided in the Supreme
Court of Pennsylvania: Bevan *v.* Bank of The United States, 4 Wharton, 301.   No doubt it would be otherwise where the goods were taken
out merely for the purpose of saving them, as was the case in Bedford
Commercial Insurance Company *v.* Parker, 2 Pickering, 1, decided in
the Supreme Court of Massachusetts: that state of things does not
appear on the facts of this case: on the contrary, the object of detach-
ing the goods was to save the whole.   [Lord CAMPBELL, C. J.—Had
the goods remained on board, they would of course have been liable to
contribute to the general average: you will say that these goods virtually were on board.]   It might be so put.   The case shows a series
of connected steps taken to carry out the adventure.   Then, next, it is
clear that the chartered freight was in risk, and must contribute: Williams *v.* The London Assurance Company, 1 M. & S. 318 (E. C. L. R.
vol. 17).   The freight is in fact part of the value saved.   The expense
of getting the ship off the shore is clearly matter of general average:
Molloy De Jure Maritimo, Book II. ch. 6, s. 12.   [Lord CAMPBELL, C.
J.—Do you find any case in the books where there has been a contribution to the general average, no goods being on board?   Setting aside
the insurance, there would be but one interest.]   Supposing the owner
of the ship to be in fact the owner of the goods, there would be only
*530] one interest; yet that could not furnish a defence *for the under-
writer on goods against a claim for general average in respect of
them.   [CROMPTON, J.—It is not then the case of one party suffering
for another.   But perhaps the general average, insured in the policy,
may be taken to include the case where all is in one hand.]

Blackburn, contrà.—The master, in warehousing the goods, must be
taken to have acted for the benefit of the owner of the goods.   After

the warehousing, the owner of the goods ceased to have an interest in the preservation of the ship. It is true that the goods were in fact afterwards reshipped; and it may perhaps be inferred as a fact that the intention, when they were warehoused, was to reship them if possible. But the hypothesis on which Job v. Langton, 6 E. & B. 779 (E. C. L. R. vol. 88), was decided was that the goods were reshipped in the original ship: yet there it was held that they were not to contribute to the general average in respect of expenses incurred after they were landed. The fact that the ship and freight belonged to one person probably makes no difference; an average adjuster in practice always apportions general average between the three items of ship, cargo, and freight, as if the three belonged to three different owners. But it is only by the Rhodian law that general average can be claimed; and by it there can be no general average unless the whole are at risk, and the whole saved. If part of the adventure only is at risk, the parties must stand on the English common law, by which there is no contribution: Mouse's Case, 12 Rep. 63. Here the goods were no longer endangered, though the *adventure was. [*Broun* referred to Dig. Lib. xiv. Tit. ii., "De Lege Rhodiâ de Jactu," sect. 2, § 2. [*531 "Placuit omnes, quorum interfuisset jacturam fieri, conferre oportere, quia tributum observatæ res" [ob servatas res?] "deberent."] The adventure was as much in peril in Job v. Langton as here. What happened after the goods were saved, though necessary to enable the ship to earn freight, was not more so than the repairs of the ship. In Phillips's Treatise On the Law of Insurance, ch. xv. sect. 2, art. 1312, it is said: "The expense of discharging the cargo to get a vessel afloat that has been accidentally stranded, and that of reloading the cargo, and the other expenses requisite to enable the vessel to proceed on the voyage, except those of making repairs, are in practice brought into general average, where the vessel, after being got off, proceeds with the same cargo. But in case the lightening of the vessel does not make her float, and other means are necessarily resorted to for this purpose, such as buoying the vessel with casks, or making a channel, the expenses incurred on the vessel after the cargo is landed are incurred for the benefit of the vessel, that she may be able to earn freight, and are not any more properly the subject of general contribution than the repairs of the vessel."

But, if the Court think that the goods were still so far participators in the adventure as to make the subsequent expenses general average, those interested in the goods ought to contribute to it, and so far diminish the liability of the underwriter on freight.

Broun, in reply.—[Lord CAMPBELL, C. J.—You cannot *say [*532 that there is a general average for contributing to all that is necessary to enable the ship to complete her voyage: where do you draw the line?] The expenses here were extraordinary expenses, to relieve the vessel, cargo, and adventure from peril. Such a case is referred to in Kent's Com. Vol. III. p. 236 (Part v. Lect. 47): " If the expense of the repairs would not have been incurred but for the benefit of the cargo, and might have been deferred with safety to the ship, to a less costly port, such extra expense is general average."

[Lord CAMPBELL, C. J.—So far as respects the liability of the freight to contribute to these expenses, we are prepared to give our opinion now : but as to the cargo we wish to take time for consideration.]

Cur. adv. vult.

Lord CAMPBELL, C. J., now delivered the judgment of the Court.

In this case we never doubted that the defendant, as underwriter on the freight, was liable for a contribution to general average in respect of the sum of 643*l.* 11*s.* 1*d.*, the expenses incurred in order to get the ship off from the bank on which she was stranded, whether the goods were or were not liable to contribute to this portion of the loss. " It is admitted that the ship could not have been got off and completed her voyage unless these various expenses had been incurred." Therefore, without these expenses, there would have been a total loss of the freight, amounting to the sum of 6750*l.* Even if the goods were not liable to contribute, on the ground that they were not exposed to any peril when these expenses were incurred, still the freight, which was *533] then *exposed to peril and has been saved, ought to contribute as if there never had been any goods on board, and the ship had sailed from Liverpool to Callao in ballast. Usually, where there is a general average, ship, freight, and goods all contribute to it : but, if there be no goods on board, and, by a voluntary sacrifice, ship and freight are saved from a common peril, the freight ought rateably to contribute to the loss : and, where there are separate insurances on ship and freight, the calculation must be made as to the amount of the contribution by each, although the whole of the freight which was in peril is to be received by the owner of the ship, and without insurance the whole of the loss would fall upon him.

But the sum for which this defendant is liable will depend, to a certain degree, upon the question, whether, under the circumstances stated, these goods are to contribute in respect of the 643*l.* 11*s.* 1*d.* And, upon this question, likewise, we are bound to give our opinion. The goods had been taken from the ship and put on board a lighter before these expenses were incurred ; and, if this had been a separate operation, by which they were intended to be saved for the benefit of the owner of the goods, we should have thought (as in Job *v.* Langton) that the goods were not liable to contribute to the expenses subsequently incurred. Looking, however, to the facts stated in this special case, it seems to us that the act of putting the goods in the lighter was only part of one continuous operation, viz. getting the ship off the bank on which she was stranded, and sending her to Liverpool, where she might *534] be repaired with a *view to prosecute the original adventure. When she got to Liverpool, the operation of saving her from shipwreck was completed; and the whole expense of the repairs fell upon the owner as owner and must be borne by him in that capacity, or by the underwriters on the ship: but the expenses of this continuous operation, for the common benefit of ship, goods, and freight, are the subject of a general average. In Job v. Langton we considered that the goods had been saved by a distinct and completed operation, and that afterwards a new operation began which could not be properly distinguished from the repairs done to the ship to enable her to pursue the voyage. "The steam tug did no work at the ship," and does not appear to have been engaged," until after the cargo was landed, and the coals and ballast taken out of her." In giving judgment, the Court there observed : "The employment of the steam tug, and the cutting of the channel by which the ship was rescued, cannot, as was contended for, be part of the same operation as the unloading of the cargo." "Under the circumstances stated, after the cargo had been safely discharged and warehoused, it does not even appear that it was for the advantage of the owner of the cargo that The Snowden should be got off the strand and repaired." "The owner of the ship, after the cargo was discharged, appears to us to have done nothing except in the discharge of his ordinary duty as owner, and for the exclusive benefit of the ship." But, in the case on which we have now to adjudicate, the goods were put into a lighter by the master of the ship along with materials of the ship saved from the wreck; and *they remained [*585 in the custody and under the control of the master till the ship was repaired, when they were reloaded in the ship and carried forward, without any interference by the owner of the goods, to their destined port. Unless it had been intended that an operation should be undertaken and completed, by which both ship and goods should be rescued from the peril to which they were exposed, nothing might have been done, and the goods might have perished. Because the goods happened to be saved in the earliest part of the operation, this can be no sufficient reason for saying that they ought not to contribute to all the expenses of the operation which contemplated the benefit of all the interests imperilled by the stranding.

We are glad to find that this distinction (which we had in view in Job v. Langton) is recognised and sanctioned by decisions in the United States of America, which, upon such subjects, we always regard with the highest respect.

The result is that, in our opinion, the first apportionment proposed by the average settler is right, on the principle of charging the 643l. 11s. 1d. to general average, so as to make the whole sum to be contributed by ship, cargo, and freight amount to 2197l. 17s. 8d.

Judgment accordingly.

A vessel bound to Philadelphia, and belonging to the defendants, arrived in having a large sum of specie on board the Bay of Delaware in the month of

December, and after encountering various difficulties, was stranded and ice-bound near Reedy Island, in a situation of imminent peril. The specie was carried over the ice to the shore, and by land to Philadelphia, where it was delivered to the defendants. Some weeks afterwards the vessel reached Philadelphia in safety with the remainder of the cargo, which had been in whole or in part discharged into lighters and afterwards reshipped. Held, that the defendants were liable to contribute to the charges and expenses incurred after the landing of the specie as general average: Bevan v. Bank of the United States, 4 Wharton, 301; Lewis v. Williams, 1 Hall, 430; Columbian Ins. Co. v. Ashby, 13 Porter, 331; Hayligu v. Firemen Ins. Co., 11 Johns. 85.

---

*536]　　　　　　*REGULÆ GENERALES.　April 23.

THE following rules were read in Court on this day.

It is ordered that plaintiffs suing in contract for 20l. or less may, if they claim costs, endorse on the writ of summons the following notice:

"Take notice, that if judgment be signed for default of appearance, the plaintiff will without summons apply to a Judge for his costs of suit, unless before such judgment you shall give notice to him or his attorney that you intend to oppose such application."

And it is further ordered, that if the defendant give such notice, the plaintiff shall proceed by summons and order.

But if the defendant give no such notice, the plaintiff may produce such endorsement to a Judge at Chambers for an order for costs, ex parte, and if the Judge shall sign his name to the endorsement, such signature shall be an order for costs, and the Master may tax them thereon accordingly. In case of any application for costs without such endorsement, the plaintiff shall not be entitled to more costs than if he had made such endorsement, unless a Judge shall otherwise order.

ENTRY OF SATISFACTION ON JUDGMENTS.

*537]　　Upon a satisfaction piece, duly signed and attested *in accordance with the 80th rule of Hilary Term, 1853,(a) being presented to the clerk of the judgments of the Masters in the Court in which the judgment has been signed, he shall file the same and enter satisfaction in the judgment-book against the entry of the said judgment, and no roll shall be required to be carried in for the purpose of entering satisfaction on a judgment.

CAMPBELL.　　　　　　SAMUEL MARTIN.
A. E. COCKBURN.　　　CHARLES CROMPTON.
FRED. POLLOCK.　　　J. WILLES.
W. ERLE.　　　　　　G. BRAMWELL.
E. V. WILLIAMS.　　　W. F. CHANNELL.

April 23d, 1857.

(a) 1 E. & B. xvl.

FELL v. BURCHETT. *April* 23.

A creditor of a banking Company, incorporated under stat. 7 & 8 Vict. c. 113, cannot maintain an action against a shareholder for the debt. His remedy is by action against the corporation, and execution in the statutable mode.

ACTION for money lent. Plea: Never indebted. Issue thereon.

On the trial, before Lord Campbell, C. J.; at the Guildhall sittings after Michaelmas Term, it appeared that the plaintiff was a depositor in the Royal British Bank, incorporated under stat. 7 & 8 Vict. c. 113. The action was for the amount of the balance at his credit. The defendant was a shareholder in the bank. Verdict for the plaintiff, with leave to move to enter a verdict for the defendant.

Phipson, in the ensuing Term, obtained a rule Nisi accord- [*538
ingly.

Lush now showed cause.—Under the former Bank Act (7 Geo. 4, c. 46) banking companies were not incorporated, but were to sue and be sued in the name of a public officer. And it was determined, in Steward *v.* Greaves, 10 M. & W. 711,† that it was obligatory on a creditor to sue in this manner, and that no action lay against the individual shareholders. The Legislature saw fit to· alter this. By stat. 7 & 8 Vict. c. 113, the banking companies are to be incorporated by letters patent, which, by sect. 6, are to incorporate them for a term of years, not exceeding twenty years. Then comes sect. 7: "That notwithstanding such incorporation the several shareholders for the time being in the said banking business, and those who shall have been shareholders therein, and their several executors, administrators, successors, and assigns, shall be and continue liable for all the dealings, covenants. and undertakings, of the said Company, subject to the provisions hereinafter contained, as fully as if the said company were not incorporated." [ERLE, J.—When the Legislature find a decision contrary to what they consider the policy of the law, they frame an enactment applicable to the case. If the Legislature were dissatisfied with the decision in Steward *v.* Greaves it would seem that they would use language very similar to that in sect. 7 to prevent the law from being such in future.] And it was necessary in the new Act to make some such enactment, as the incorporation is for a term of years (sect. 6), and, without some such provision, any creditors *who have not obtained [*539
judgment against the corporation before the end of the term have
no remedy against the shareholders. The meaning of the section cannot be merely that execution may be issued in the manner afterwards specified in sect. 10; for the executors of the shareholder are liable under sect. 7, which is not the case under sect. 10.

Phipson, in support of the rule.—No doubt the Act is not artificially drawn: but it cannot have the construction contended for; otherwise a shareholder, who had ceased to be one for three years, and who, therefore, under sect. 10, is free from all liability, might be answerable on the covenants of the corporation for many years longer. (He was then stopped by the Court.)

Lord CAMPBELL, C. J.—We really are bound, out of respect to the Legislature, if we possibly can do so, to construe this statute so as not to make the individual shareholders liable to be sued; for it would be most iniquitous and foolish to make them so liable; and it would not be respectful to the Legislature to suppose that such could have been their intention.   It is true that section 7 is an ill-penned enactment, like too many others, putting Judges in the embarrassing situation of being bound to make sense of nonsense, and to reconcile what is irreconcileable : yet in this case there is a mode of escaping the absurdity. The earlier part of the Act requires that the banks shall be corporations.   Section 10, and those which follow it, provide machinery by which execution may go against the shareholders, so that they may be personally liable.   All this is consistent.   There is one action and no

*540] more against the corporation, and *one judgment; and yet recourse may be had against each individual.   If, in addition to this, a power were given to sue each individual separately, it would be quite inconsistent with the incorporation of the body : it would be no benefit to the creditors who have already a remedy; and it would allow such vexatious and oppressive proceedings as would be intolerable.   My solution is, thrt the intention was to guard against an inference which, it was apprehended, might be drawn from the incorporation under the letters patent in sect. 6, that the shareholders should not in any way be liable to make satisfaction to the creditors; with this view it was in sect. 7, by way of proviso, enacted that the shareholders, past and present, should be and continue liable, "subject to the provisions hereinafter contained."   Giving effect to those words as meaning that they should be liable, after the corporation had been sued, after its assets had been exhausted, and the other provisions complied with, sect. 7 is made to harmonize with the subsequent sections.   " Subject to the provisions" is not proper language to express this meaning; but, looking to the whole scope of the Act, we are justified in considering "subject" as a word improperly introduced, but meaning " according." By this construction the individual liability is preserved, but the oppressive multiplication of suits is avoided.

(WIGHTMAN, J., was absent.)

ERLE, J.—I am of the same opinion.   The construction of sect. 7 contended for would lead to such extreme inconvenience that it is a caution to us not to read the section in that manner, though at first reading the words seem to bear that meaning.   There are enactments

*541] incorporating the banks; the very object of incorporation *being to prevent multiplicity of suits.   These enactments are followed by sect. 7.   The words of that section are: " That notwithstanding such incorporation the several shareholders for the time being in the said banking business, and those who shall have been shareholders therein, and their several executors, administrators, successors, and assigns, shall be and continue liable for all the dealings, covenants, and undertakings of the said Company." Had the section stopped there, it would be direct legislation that they should be liable simpliciter, as Mr. *Lush* says they are : but it does not stop there ; it proceeds " subject to the provisions hereinafter contained." In section 9 there is precisely the ⌡ same language ; the judgment against the corporation may be enforced against the individuals, " subject to the provisions hereinafter contained." In that section the Legislature clearly intends to express the liability by steps, first having recourse against the assets of the Company, and then, in order, against each set of the shareholders, in the well known mode prescribed in sect. 10. Reading the sections together, sect. 7 means that they shall be liable in that manner.

ᵓ CROMPTON, J.—It may be that the enactment is ill-penned ; but it it has been expressed with sufficient clearness to be understood for thirteen years. It appears to me that there is nothing to express an intention to make the individuals liable to be sued contrary to the common law rule with respect to individuals forming a corporation. The earlier Act made banking joint stock companies only quasi corporations. This Act makes them actual corporations. Some proviso was required to show that, notwithstanding this, the mode of making the individuals liable, provided in the former *Act, should remain. The words [*542 of sect. 7 are not accurately chosen for this purpose ; but the liability is made " subject to the provisions thereinafter contained," that is, to the provisions for execution in sect. 10, for reimbursement in sect. 11, and others, quite inconsistent with direct liability to an action. I have no doubt the intention of the Legislature was to prevent the enormous evil of allowing a multiplicity of suits, and to make the individuals liable only in the statutable method, with statutable remedies for reimbursement. Rule absolute.(*a*)

(*a*) See Harris *v.* Royal British Bank, 2 H. & N. 535.†

SAMUEL STURGIS, Provisional Assignee of the estate and effects
of THEODORE WILLIAMS, an insolvent debtor, *v.* CHARLES
JAMES, Lord Bishop of LONDON.   *April 24.*

D. recovered judgment against a beneficed clergyman, and issued a levari facias, which he
lodged with the deputy registrar of the Ecclesiastical Court, directing that the execution
should be suspended till further orders.   Afterwards the clergyman petitioned the Court of
Insolvent Debtors; and a vesting order was made by that Court.   The assignee, under stat 1
& 2 Vict. c. 110, s. 55, petitioned the bishop for a sequestration.   On the day following. and
before anything had been done, or, according to the Ecclesiastical practice, could have been
done, upon the petition, D., for the first time, applied to the deputy registrar to issue sequestration.

Held, that the sequestration of the assignee was entitled to priority.

THIS case was stated for the opinion of this Court, by consent and
order of a Judge under The Common Law Procedure Act, 1852 (15 &
16 Vict. c. 76, s. 46), and in accordance with a rule of this Court, made
on 24th January, 1856, in a cause in the said Court, in which John
Dawson was plaintiff and the said Theodore Williams was defendant.

*543]   The said Theodore Williams, at the respective times *of the
issuing of the said writs of levari facias at the suit of the said
J. Dawson against the said T. Williams, hereinafter mentioned, was,
and thence hitherto hath been, and still is, a beneficed clergyman: that
is to say vicar of the vicarage of Hendon in the county of Middlesex.
On 22d May, 1847, a writ of levari facias, theretofore issued out of the
said Court of Queen's Bench at the suit of Dawson against Williams,
directed to the said Bishop, and tested on that day, for levying the sum
of 1653*l.* 10*s.* and interest, besides expenses, &c., and being returnable
immediately after the execution thereof, was lodged with the deputy
registrar of the said Bishop at the office of the said Bishop's consistorial
and episcopal Court of London; the same being the proper office in that
behalf.   And, on 3d November, 1847, another writ of levari facias,
before then issued out of the Court of Common Pleas at the suit of
Dawson against Williams, directed to the said Bishop, and tested on
the last-mentioned day, for levying the sum of 11,905*l.* 1*s.* 9*d.* and
interest, besides expenses, &c., and being returnable immediately after
the execution thereof, was lodged with the said registrar at the said
office.   At the time the said writs were respectively lodged, directions
were given by Mr. Day, the attorney of Dawson, duly authorized in
that behalf, to the deputy registrar to suspend the execution of the said
writs for the present until further instructions were given by Day to
the deputy registrar, but with a request that immediate notice should
be given to Day, on the part of Dawson, by the said deputy registrar,
of any subsequent writ being lodged and sequestration applied for in
the office of the deputy registrar; which notice the deputy registrar
promised to give.

*544]   *After the said writs were so lodged, and on 12th March,
1853, Williams, being a prisoner in actual custody within the

walls of the Queen's Bench Prison, upon process at the suit of Samuel Woodburn and Allen Woodburn, for the recovery of a debt due to them from Williams, within fourteen days from the commencement of his imprisonment, according to the statute in that behalf, applied to the Court for the relief of Insolvent Debtors in England (the said prison being within the jurisdiction of that Court) for his discharge from custody according to the provisions of the said Act, by a petition in writing, made and subscribed by Williams pursuant to the said Act, and afterwards filed of record in the said Court, pursuant to the said Act. And the same Court, on the filing of the said petition, and upon evidence in support thereof, made, on the 14th day of the said month of March, the usual vesting order, thereby ordering all the estate and effects of Williams to be vested in the said Samuel Sturgis, then and still being the provisional assignee of the estates and effects of insolvent debtors in England ; which order was duly entered of record in the said Court; and notice thereof was duly published according to the directions of the said Court ; whereby all the estate and effects of Williams became and were, and still are, vested in the said S. Sturgis as being such provisional assignee as aforesaid.

The debts of Williams, due from him to his creditors at the time of filing his said petition, amounted, and still amount, to the sum of 25,000*l.*, including the said debts due to Dawson. S. Sturgis, as such provisional assignee, on the 30th day of the said month of March, which was after the filing and publishing of the said vesting order, applied to the Bishop by petition in *writing, accompanied by a [*545 certified office copy of the vesting order under the seal of the said Court ; and, by the said petition, applied to and petitioned the said Bishop that a sequestration be issued of the profits of the said vicarage and benefice for the payment of the said debts of Williams, with interest and the costs and charges of and incident to the levying of the same, according to the said statute. Which last-mentioned petition, together with the copy of the vesting order, was lodged with the deputy registrar of the Bishop at the said office, the same being the proper office in that behalf, to be executed, and with directions that sequestration thereon should be immediately issued in compliance with the last-mentioned petition.

At the time the said petition and office copy of the said vesting order were so lodged with the deputy registrar at the said office to be executed, no notice or intimation had been or was given by or on behalf of Dawson to the deputy registrar to take any proceedings upon the said writs of levari facias, or either of them. On the said 30th day of March last, after the said petition and copy of the said vesting order were so lodged with the deputy registrar at the office to be executed as aforesaid, the deputy registrar gave notice to Dawson of the lodging of the said petition and application by sequestration. And, on the

31st day of the said month of March, and before any sequestration had been, or according to the ordinary practice of the registrar's office could be, issued upon the said petition of the plaintiff, directions were, for the first time, given on behalf of Dawson to the deputy registrar to issue sequestration upon the said writs of levari facias respectively. The said deputy registrar thereupon afterwards *issued seques-

*546]   trations on the said writs of levari facias, respectively; namely, on that issued out of the Court of Queen's Bench on 13th April, 1853, tested on that day; and on that issued out of the Court of Common Pleas on 18th April, 1853, tested on that day; and caused the former of the said sequestrations to be published on 16th April, 1853, and the latter on 30th April, 1853.

The deputy registrar issued a sequestration on the said petition of S. Sturgis, on 27th April, 1853, tested on that day, and caused the same to be published on 5th May, 1853.

Under the said sequestration, issued on the first-mentioned writ of levari facias, at the suit of Dawson, a sum of 567l. 12s. 4d. was levied by the Bishop out of the profits of the said living: and, after deducting all expenses thereupon, a clear balance of 227l. 8s. 9d. remained and still remains in the hands of the Bishop. The Bishop refused and neglected to levy anything out of the profits of the said living under or upon or in respect of the petition of S. Sturgis.

If the defendant had not given priority to the said writs of levari facias in the manner aforesaid, he might have levied the said sum of 567l. 12s. 4d. under the sequestration issued upon the petition of plaintiff.

If the Court shall be of opinion that the said petition of S. Sturgis was entitled to priority of execution over the said writs of levari facias, so issued at the suit of Dawson, judgment is to be given herein for plaintiff for the said sum of 227l. 8s. 9d., with costs. But, if the Court should be of opinion that the said petition of S. Sturgis was not entitled to priority of execution over the said two writs of levari facias, judgment is to be given herein for the defendant, with costs.

*547]   *Joseph Addison, for the plaintiff.—First: the case is within sect. 16 of the Statute of Frauds, 29 C. 2, c. 3, which enacts that "no writ of fieri facias or other writ of execution shall bind the property of the goods against whom such writ of execution is sued forth, but from the time that such writ shall be delivered to the sheriff, under-sheriff, or coroners, to be executed." A levari facias comes within the words "other writ of execution." Stat. 1 & 2 Vict. c. 110, s. 55, regulates the right of the assignee of a clergyman who is an insolvent debtor over the income of his benefice or curacy. It enacts: "That nothing in this Act contained shall extend to entitle the assignee or assignees of the estate and effects of any such prisoner, being a beneficed clergyman or curate, to the income of such benefice or curacy, for the purposes of this Act: provided always, that it shall be lawful for such assignee or assignees to apply for and obtain a sequestration of the profits of any such benefice, for the payment of the debts of such prisoner; and the order appointing an assignee or assignees of such prisoner, in pursuance of this Act, shall be a sufficient warrant for the granting of such sequestration, without any writ or other proceedings to authorize the same: and such sequestration shall accordingly be issued, as the same might have been issued upon any writ of levari facias, founded upon any judgment against such prisoner." The question is, therefore, what is the law as to the levari facias. It may be argued, on the other side, that, inasmuch as the sheriff, under-sheriff, or coroner would not have anything to do with a levari facias, the enactment in sect. 16 of the Statute of Frauds cannot apply to that writ, but must be confined to a fieri facias. But these officers are named only by way of example. In *3 Bac. Abr. 387 (7th ed.), [*548 *Execution* (C) 4, it is said : " The fieri facias and levari facias are judicial writs which lay at the common law." When the sheriff returns to a fi. fa. that there are no goods or chattels, or lay fee, and that C. D., the defendant, is a beneficed clerk in a diocese named, a writ issues, reciting this, and commanding the bishop: "that of the ecclesiastical goods of the said C. D. in his diocese, he cause to be made the debt," &c. Then the levari facias commands the bishop: "that of the ecclesiastical goods of C. D., clerk, in your diocese, you cause to be levied," &c.(a) This is simply a writ of execution. [Lord CAMPBELL, C. J.—What are ecclesiastical goods?] They may be the crops of glebe. But, whether or not the Statute of Frauds be applicable, the plaintiff, by his petition and application for sequestration, had acquired a priority over the two writs of levari facias. In 3 Bac. Abr. 413 (7th ed.), *Execution* (I), it is said : " As to goods and chattels, the execution at common law had relation to the time of the awarding thereof, and therefore, if after the teste of the writ of execution, the defendant had sold the goods, though *bonâ fide*, and for valuable consideration, yet were they still liable to be taken in execution, into whose hands soever they came"; and it is added that the enactment of sect. 16 of the Statute of Frauds was passed to remedy the inconvenience produced by this rule. Now the two writs of levari facias, as they were delivered with the direction not to execute them till further orders, are of no more effect than if they had remained in the pocket of the attorney. In fact such a direction was a legal fraud, of *which the Court will take notice: it might even be treated as [*549 covinous under stat. 27 Eliz. c. 4, and within the analogy of sect. 5: without such direction the writ is returnable immediate. In Pringle v. Isaac, 11 Price, 445, it was held that a judgment-creditor, who issued a fi. fa., with directions not to execute unless another exe-

---

(a) See Tidd's Practical Forms, ch. XLI. p. 386 (8th ed.).

cution should come in, was to be postponed to a creditor who issued a later writ of execution to be executed forthwith.   There the Court relied on Kempland v. Macauley, 1 Peake's N. P. C. 65, where Lord Kenyon said: "That though in general the sheriff must first levy on the writ which he first receives, yet if the plaintiff in that writ directs it not to be executed before a distant day, and in the mean time another execution comes, the sheriff is not to keep the first writ hanging over the heads of other creditors, but is to levy under the last execution as if no other had ever been delivered to him."   It does not appear that in either of those two cases the Statute of Frauds was relied upon. But in Hunt v. Hooper, 12 M. & W. 664,† a judgment-creditor delivered to the sheriff a fi. fa. with the intent that it should be executed; he, however, before execution, did desire the sheriff to suspend the execution till further orders: and, before the giving of such orders, another judgment-creditor delivered a fi. fa. to the sheriff with orders to execute immediately: and it was held that the direction not to execute was equivalent to a withdrawal of the writ, and the writ was no longer in the sheriff's hands to be executed, within the meaning of sect. 16 of the Statute of Frauds; so that the party issuing the second writ had priority.   In the argument there all the cases are collected.

*550]   *Lush, contrà.—At common law a fi. fa. did not transfer any property, but only enabled the sheriff to sell: and he must have first executed that writ which had the first teste, as the execution had relation to the time of awarding the writ.   In the case of elegits, the lands are bound as from the date of the judgment; and therefore, if the sheriff receive two elegits, he must first execute that which is on the first judgment, whatever be the testes.   Inquiry has been made as to the practice of the Ecclesiastical Courts on writs of levari facias; and the following letter has been received from the deputy registrar of the Consistory Court of London.   "Bishop of London's Registry, 3, Godliman Street, Doctors' Commons, 3d February, 1857.   Sir, In reply to your inquiry as to the practice in this office in issuing sequestrations upon a writ levari facias being lodged here, I have to inform you that, upon such writ being so lodged, the same is submitted to the bishop by me, and his Lordship's directions taken as to the party to be appointed sequestrator, and as to the provision to be made for supplying the cure.   I have then to apply to the party named by the bishop, to ascertain whether he will undertake the office: and, on his assenting thereto, a bond is prepared for the execution of himself and a sufficient surety for the fulfilment of his duties.   On such bond being executed, the sequestration is prepared, and issues under seal; and, on being duly published, the sequestrator is at once authorized to receive the profits of the living.   This is the practice now subsisting: but I think it right to add that it has only been adopted of late years, and that, previously, writs were lodged; and, if accompanied by a written request from the attorney who lodged them, that the issue of the sequestrations was *to be delayed, this request was complied with, until instruc- [*551 tions were given to issue sequestrations, which thereupon went under seal, in the order as to time in which the writs were lodged. I am, Sir, your very obedient Servant," (Signed) "JNO. SHEPHARD." In answer to further inquiry, a letter has been received from the same gentleman, dated 10th February, 1857, of which the following is an extract. "In reply to your letter of the 6th instant, it is somewhat difficult to answer precisely your inquiry 'how long it takes to issue sequestration after a writ levari facias has been lodged in this registry for that purpose.' I have already" (here the effect of the former letter was recited). "These preliminary proceedings, under the most favourable circumstances, are seldom completed in a week, and generally occupy a considerably longer period according to circumstances." The question as to the priority in such cases as the present has not arisen : the levari facias in the common law Courts seems to furnish the nearest analogy : and there the writ with the earliest teste would have the priority. Sect. 16 of the Statute of Frauds applies to writs of fi. fa. only. In 2 Tidd's Practice, p. 1000 (9th ed.), it is said : "At common law, the fieri facias had relation to its teste, and bound the defendant's goods from that time ; so that if the defendant had afterwards sold the goods, though bonâ fide and for a valuable consideration, they were still liable to be taken in execution, into whose hands soever they came." Then reference is made to sect. 16 of the Statute of Frauds, which, as in the passage cited on the other side from Bacon's Abridgment, is said to have been passed to remedy this inconvenience ; and it is added : "But neither before the statute nor since, is the property of goods altered, but continues *in the defendant till executed. The [*552 meaning of those words, that 'no writ of execution shall bind the property, but from the delivery of the writ to the sheriff, &c.,' is, that after the writ is so delivered, if the defendant make an assignment of his goods, unless in market overt, the sheriff may take them in execution." But the levari facias directed to the bishop did not bind till the sequestration was published, so that the injury which occasioned the Statute of Frauds did not exist : the clergyman could not so part with his property as to injure the vendee by the relation. [CROMPTON, J.— Where then is your priority in the present case?] The bishop has in his hand two unexecuted writs : he has therefore only to act on that which has the earliest teste. It is true that Dawson is in no better situation than if he had first delivered his writ at the time when he directed that it should be executed. But, as appears from the letters read as to the practice, the bishop cannot execute the sequestration instanter ; so that it comes to the case of contemporaneous writs. It has sometimes been said that the time of the appointment of the sequestrator is the dividing point : Bennett v. Apperley, 6 B. & C. 630, 634

(E. C. L. R. vol. 13).   In 3 Burn's Ecc. L. 340 (a) tit. *Sequestration.*
it is said that, " where a sequestration was made out and not published
while the writ was in force, but was stayed in the register's hands by
desire of plaintiff's attorney, the Court held that it had no priority as
against other sequestrations, afterwards made out, and duly published,
but that if it had been published, the execution would have taken effect
*553] and must have been first satisfied notwithstanding it *was then
returnable:" and he cites Legassicke v. Bishop of Exeter, 1
Crompt. Pract. 351 (3d ed.)   An elegit has priority over an elegit upon
a later judgment though of an earlier teste.   [Lord CAMPBELL, C.
J.—The judgment binds the land : is that so in the case of a levari
facias?]   The two cases seem to be analogous.   Then, as to the Statute of Elizabeth.   [Lord CAMPBELL, C. J.—I think there is nothing
in that point.]

Joseph Addison, in reply.—It does not appear that any of the steps
which, as the practice of the Ecclesiastical Courts is explained, ought
to be taken for effecting the sequestration have been taken on behalf
of Dawson : there is no reason for supposing that there is even now any
intention of making his levari facias available.   All that was decided
in Bennett v. Apperley was that there need be no publication before
the return of the levari facias.   The passage cited from Burn does not
go to the extent necessary for the defendant's argument : and there is
a note to the passage, " semb. contrà."

Lord CAMPBELL, C. J.—I am of opinion that the plaintiff on his
petition is entitled to priority of execution.   The petition is presented
on 30th March.   Long before that, a levari facias has issued ; but it
has been fraudulently kept back ; nothing was to be done, and nothing
was done, till further order : and such further order was not given till
the 31st of March.   I rely on the maxim " Qui prior est tempore potior
*554] est jure."   The party who first lodges the writ is entitled to the
*sequestration on the levari facias ; and, when there are several
writs of levari facias, the sequestrations upon them are to be in the
same order as the writs.   Mr. *Lush* has laid down a proposition, which.
if it were authorized, would entitle him to our judgment.   It comes to
this : that the bishop is bound to look to the teste of the several writs
and to give priority, not according to the order of delivery, but according to the order of the teste.   But, notwithstanding his great learning
and industry, he has not succeeded in producing any authority for this.
He has suggested the analogy of execution by elegit : and he says. I
dare say truly, that, if there be two elegits, the sheriff must give priority
to that which is on the first judgment.   But that is because the judgment binds the lands : that is not the case with a levari facias, which
bound merely by the delivery of the writ.   Then he suggests the
analogy of a fi. fa.   That is process of a different kind.   It calls on

(a) Ed. 8th (by Tyrwhitt).   The passage is wanting in the last (9th by Phillimore) edition.

the sheriff to make the money out of the goods: but the levari facias orders the bishop to levy from the profits of the living, a totally different proceeding, and bearing no analogy to a fi. fa. There is therefore no authority for contending that the business of the bishop is to look at each teste and give priority to the first. I am very glad that we are able to come to this decision; for there has here been what I must call, in point of law, a most fraudulent proceeding. The writs of levari facias were lodged, not for execution, but for the purpose of obtaining notice. The object evidently was to protect the living from the execution of a bonâ fide creditor. To give effect to this would be to establish a precedent by which all livings would be protected from execution. *I am very glad that we can say that the execution is to be in [*555 the order of delivery, not in that of the teste.

(WIGHTMAN, J., was absent.)

ERLE, J.—I am of the same opinion. The goods of the ecclesiastical creditor are bound by the petition, and the sequestration should issue upon it. If there be a prior writ of levari facias delivered for execution, the bishop is bound to issue a prior sequestration on that. If two writs be delivered to the bishop at different times, is he to give priority according to the date of the delivery or according to that of the teste? The facts of this case show clearly to my mind that it ought to be according to the date of the delivery. For here we have a writ put into the hands of the registrar, with orders to suspend the execution until another writ shall come in; and, the morrow after such other writ has come in, the order is given to execute the first. Therefore, in law, the writ of later date was that which was first delivered. There is stringent reason for so holding, when we look at the course pursued by the party who sets up the defence to this action. An amicable creditor gets a writ which is to be a protection against other creditors. I am told that, in fact, Dawson has not been paid his debt: but it is enough that the proceeding here adopted would generally enable any fraudulent creditor to defeat a real one. I endeavoured, again and again, to find what authority there was for this course: had there been any, we must have given effect to it. But none has been cited to show that the bishop is bound to issue the sequestration in the order of the teste. Then, is there any general rule that writs *are to be so executed? One [*556 analogy suggested is that of writs of elegit. They rest quite on a different ground: the land is bound by the judgment: a levari facias at common law and a fi. fa. used to bind from the date of the teste: it was found that this produced great evil; and it was altered by the Statute of Frauds. We are told that we must assume that there is a close analogy between a levari facias directed to the sheriff and one directed to the bishop. We are here dealing only with a writ issued to make the bishop issue a sequestration which will bind when it goes. The analogy therefore fails. We are therefore without a maxim, or a decision, or a symptom of authority, for the proposition that the writ takes priority in the order of the teste.

CROMPTON, J.—I am of the same opinion.   I do not think that I am entitled to proceed on the ground of fraud, because it seems that Dawson has an unsatisfied debt.   But I cannot help remarking that it is a very bad practice, on the part of bishop's officers, to keep back a writ unexecuted: it is at least not commendable.   I am not prepared to say what would be the rule as to priority of writs of levari facias at common law. But it would be strange if we could apply to ecclesiastical writs of levari facias the doctrine that they are to bind according to the date of the teste.   There is no authority for this: nor can I say to what extent the doctrine is to go, nor that there could be such binding more than in the case of a fi. fa., which does not vest any right by the mere issuing of the writ.   It is not necessary to decide that at present.   I am inclined to think that the plaintiff is entitled to judgment either way.   Sup-
*557]   posing the priority of the teste does not *apply in such a case, then the plaintiff has priority on the ground put by my Lord: if it does, then the case is within the mischief contemplated by sect. 16 of the Statute of Frauds, and will be within the remedy.

Judgment for the plaintiff.

The QUEEN v. JOSEPH HIGHAM.   April 25.

An affiliation summons against H. was served at the house of H.'s father. An attorney appeared to the summons before the justices for the petty sessional division of B. in the county of N., representing himself to be authorized to appear for H.   In fact he was retained and paid by H.'s father. He examined and cross-examined witnesses. An order was drawn up purporting to be made on the complaint of the mother "residing at M. within this county," and to be made as on a contested summons, the defendant appearing by attorney. In fact M. was not only in the county, but in the petty sessional division of B., as was well known to every one; but nothing was said about it. H. deposed that, a few days before the summons was served, he, anticipating annoyance from the woman, left his father's house, which had up to that time been his abode, without any intention to return, and was not informed of the proceedings before the justices. A rule to quash the order having been obtained, on the grounds that the attorney was not authorized to appear and that the order did not mention that M. was within the division,

Held: that the Court would infer in fact that H., leaving his abode avowedly for a temporary motive, did intend to return when the motive ceased, notwithstanding his deposition to the contrary; and that, such being taken to be the fact, the summons was duly served; and that, all proper to be proved in an unopposed summons having in fact appeared before the justices, and the state of proof being such as would justify them in drawing up an order stating M. to be in the division of B., the omissions and mistakes were amendable by this Court under stat. 12 & 13 Vict. c. 45, s. 7.

FIELD, in last Hilary Term, obtained a rule to show cause why an order of justices, brought up on certiorari, adjudging the defendant to be the putative father of a bastard child of which Mary Ann Prestridge was the mother, should not be quashed, "on the grounds: That the attorney, in the order mentioned, was not authorized by the said Joseph

Higham to appear; 2d. That it does not appear upon the order that Mary Ann Prestridge resided within the Petty Sessional Division therein mentioned; 3d. That it does not appear upon the said order that the proof or evidence was taken and *heard in the presence and hearing of the said Joseph Higham or his alleged attorney." [*558

The order, which was in a printed form filled up in manuscript, purported to be "At a petty Session of Her Majesty's Justices of the Peace for the county of Northampton holden in and for the division of Brachley in the said county on 11th August, 1856." It contained recitals, of which the material parts are as follows. "Whereas one Mary Ann Prestridge, single woman, residing at Morton Puckney, within this county, did" apply for an affiliation summons against Joseph Higham to a justice, who issued it; "and whereas the said Joseph Higham, having been duly served with the summons within forty days from this day, and now appearing by attorney in pursuance thereof;" "and it now being proved to us that the said child was, since the passing of an Act," &c., born a bastard on 25th November, 1855. The rest of the order was in the usual form of an order on a contested summons. The rule was obtained on affidavits of Joseph Higham and several members of his family. Joseph Higham denied the paternity. He stated that he was indicted for a rape on Mary Ann Prestridge, tried at the Northamptonshire Summer Assizes, 1855, and acquitted on the merits. That in January, 1856, he was served with an affiliation summons, and did appear before two justices, and, there being no reliable corroborative evidence, the complaint was dismissed. That, a prosecution for perjury against one of the witnesses who gave corroborative evidence in favour of the said Mary Ann Prestridge on such hearing having failed, and the deponent having reason to anticipate further annoyance from her, he determined to leave his said father's residence and obtain *employment in a different part of the country; and he did accordingly, on the 13th July last, leave his father's residence and cease [*559 altogether to reside there; and that he shortly afterwards went to reside with John Letts of Wilden in the county of Bedfordshire, and assisted him in his farm there; and he had not, and has not since had, and has not now, any intention of returning to reside with his said father. The summons, on which the present order was based, was left at deponent's father's residence on 29th July, when the deponent was resident at Wilden. He denied explicitly having heard of it at the time, or having in any way authorized the attorney to appear for him: and some of his family deposed to having of their own motion, and without his knowledge, employed the attorney to appear.

It appeared, by the affidavits in opposition, that the attorney, who, it was deposed, was of great respectability and perfectly solvent, appeared before the justices on the 11th August, 1856, and that, being asked by the justices if he was instructed by Joseph Higham to appear, he pledged himself that he was; and, from the affidavit of the attorney himself, it appeared that, though he got his instructions from Joseph Higham's father, he then and still believed he was authorized to appear for the son. By the affidavit of the clerk to the justices it appeared that the service of the summons, by leaving it at the last known place of Joseph Higham's abode on 29th July, was proved before the justices, and that it was read. This summons purported to be made on the application of "Mary Ann Prestridge, residing at Morton Puckney, in, the Petty Sessional division of Brachley:" which the clerk to the justices stated in his affidavit was the fact, and that the witnesses were *560] then examined and were *cross-examined by the attorney, who did not take any objection to the jurisdiction of the justices, well knowing that Morton Puckney was in the division.

Mundell now showed cause.—The result of this motion must depend upon the first ground stated in the rule: that is, whether the justices had jurisdiction to hear the cause, which they had if the summons was duly served, or if the defendant appeared by attorney. For, by stat. 12 & 13 Vict. c. 45, s. 7, if upon appeal against any order or judgment of justices or "if upon the return to any writ of certiorari any objection shall be made on account of any omission or mistake in the drawing up of such order or judgment, and it shall be shown to the satisfaction of the Court that sufficient grounds were in proof before the justice or justices making such order or giving such judgment to have authorized the drawing up thereof free from the said omission or mistake," the Court may amend the order. Now here, if the attorney was authorized to appear, everything in fact was rightly done, as upon a contested order; if the attorney was not duly authorized, then, if the summons was duly served, everything was rightly done as upon an order made 'in default of appearance. Either way the Court can and will amend. Then as to the principal fact. It appears that the defendant left his father's house, which was his residence, on the 13th July, to avoid an anticipated summons, which was left at that house on the 29th July. An attorney appears before the justices on 11th August, having been instructed and paid by the defendant's family, and bonâ fide believing himself to be authorized by the defendant. The order is *561] made; and it is not credible that the defendant should *be ignorant of that fact: yet he does not appeal or take any step till after the year within which a fresh order could be made has expired. Is it not an obvious juggle to obtain for the defendant the benefit of professional assistance, and yet keep open the question whether the service was proper? [Lord CAMPBELL, C. J.—It seems very likely that the defendant was really cognisant of the employment of the attorney; but we can scarcely act on mere probabilities in the face of the distinct statements in the affidavits.] At all events, the appearance being regular and the attorney solvent, the Court will leave the defendant to his remedy against him: Anonymous, 1 Salk. 86, Anonymous, 1 Salk. 88, Stanhope *v.* Firmin, 3 New Ca. 301 (E. C. L. R. vol. 32). [Lord CAMPBELL, C. J.—But here the defendant is liable to imprisonment.] So is a defendant in a civil cause; but there the Court interferes only when he actually is in custody: Hambidge *v.* De La Croucé, 3 Com. B. 742 (E. C. L. R. vol. 56). At all events, the appearance would be good if the service was regular: Bayly *v.* Buckland, 1 Exch. 1.† And the service was regular; for the residence of the defendant did not cease to be at his father's house until he had acquired a new residence: Reg'.na *v.* Davis, 22 L. J. N. S. M. C. 143.(*a*) Ex parte Jones, 1 L. M. & P. 357, may be relied on: but there the place of service never had been the fixed abode of the putative father: in the present case the defendant had left his abode avowedly for the purpose of keeping out of the way; and when that motive ceased no doubt he would come back. *[Lord CAMPBELL, C. J.—He says he had [*562 no intention of returning: but, in forming my opinion as to what were the facts, I look rather at his conduct than his words; and it seems to me that his father's house continued his abode just as if he had been absent on a visit.]

Field, in support of the rule.—It is true that the house of the defendant's father was his abode up to the 13th July; but after that it ceased to be so. [Lord CAMPBELL, C. J.—Not if he went away with intent to return.] That intention is denied on the affidavits. [Lord CAMPBELL, C. J.—It is averred that the sole motive of his departure was to avoid annoyance from the woman; when that temporary motive ceased at the end of the year from the birth, the inference is that he would return.] If the Court think that in fact the summons was served at his abode, the order may be amended as far as the last objection goes, as the evidence was in fact rightly taken, on that supposition. But there is nothing to justify the amendment as to the residence of the woman. Stat. 12 & 13 Vict. c. 45, s. 7, authorizes amendments only where it is shown that "sufficient grounds were in proof before the justice or justices." Here there was no proof of the fact that Morton Pinkney was in the division. The summons stated it to be so, but is not evidence of the truth of its contents. Neither could the justices take judicial notice of its situation: Brune *v.* Thompson, 2 Q. B. 789 (E. C. L. R. vol. 42).

Lord CAMPBELL, C. J.—The reasonable construction of stat. 12 & 13 Vict. c. 45, s. 7, must be that, when it *is shown that the [*563 state of the case before the justices was such that they would have been justified in drawing up the order with the statement in it, and only omitted to do so through a mistake, the amendment may be made. Was not that the case here? The clerk made a slip in filling up the form of the order. If the justices had noticed it at the time,

(*a*) Bail Court, coram Wightman, J.

might they not, without impropriety, have amended it? I think they might; and, as I think that, in fact, the summons was properly served, the amendments should now be made.

(WIGHTMAN, J., was absent.)

ERLE, J.—I also think both amendments are within the purview of the Act. On all trials much is taken by all parties as assumed, and only those facts really in dispute strictly proved. In such cases what is assumed is in proof. In this case I think the fact that Morton Pinkney was within the petty sessional division was sufficiently in proof; that is, I think the justices had sufficient grounds for inserting the fact in the order.

(CROMPTON, J., was absent.)

> Rule discharged, without costs, on the amendments being made.

------

*564]   *ELIZA ANN EDWARDS *v.* HENRY ENGLISH and GEORGE WILLIAMS. *April 25.*

A bill of sale of goods was bonâ fide made by J. H. to F. H. by way of security, and was filed, but with an affidavit which turned out to be defective. A subsequent bill of sale of the same goods, subject to that to F. H., was bonâ fide made by J. H. to E. by way of security, and was properly filed. A creditor of J. H. suing out execution against him required the sheriff to seize the goods as those of J. H. Two interpleader issues were directed, in which F. H. and E. respectively were plaintiffs, and the creditor defendant; in each of which the issue was whether the goods were the goods of the plaintiff.

In F. H.'s issue defendant had a verdict, on the ground that the bill of sale to F. H. was void as against defendant, a creditor, because not duly filed. In E.'s issue it was urged that, though void against defendant, F. H.'s bill of sale was valid as against E., and that therefore the goods were not the goods of E., and the defendant was entitled to the verdict in that issue.

Held, that the substance of the issue was to inform the Court whether the goods were seizable by the sheriff as against E.; that they were not so seizable, and that therefore the plaintiff was entitled to the verdict.

THIS was an interpleader issue, in which the plaintiff affirmed, and the defendants denied, that the goods and chattels, seized by the sheriff of Middlesex, under a fi. fa. against the goods of Joseph Hare, were, at the time of the delivery of the writ to the sheriff, the goods of the plaintiff.

At the Westminster Sittings after last Michaelmas Term, before Lord Campbell, C. J., a similar interpleader issue between Frederick Hatton, plaintiff, and the present defendants, stood before this issue in the paper, and was tried first. On the trial of that issue it was proved that English was the execution-creditor, and that the execution-debtor, Hare, had, on 18th July, 1856, conveyed the property in question by bill of sale to Hatton, by way of security; that Hatton's bill of sale was made bonâ fide, and was filed within twenty-one days; but that the affidavit accompanying it contained no description of the occupation of Joseph Hare. The defendants in that issue had a verdict, subject to

leave to move to *enter a verdict for the plaintiff.   It was then [*565
agreed that the evidence given in the case of Hatton v. English,
antè, p. 94, should be considered as given in the present issue, and the
further facts be added, that the plaintiff, Edwards, bonâ fide made an
advance to Hare on the security of a bill of sale, conveying the same
goods to her, subject to the prior bill of sale to Hatton, and that the
bill of sale to Edwards was properly registered.   The verdict was
directed in this issue for the plaintiff, with leave to move to enter a
verdict for the defendants.

In the ensuing Term the Court refused a rule in the case of Hatton
v. English, antè, p. 94.

Montague Smith obtained a rule Nisi in this case, pursuant to leave
reserved.

H. Hawkins now showed cause.—The bill of sale to Hatton was
valid as against Hare and as against the present plaintiff; but, not
being duly filed, it was, by stat. 17 & 18 Vict. c. 36, s. 1, void as
against any creditor who should issue process.   The defendant English
was such a person, and has avoided that bill of sale as against Hatton;
he now seeks to treat it as valid as against Edwards: but the instrument is either void or valid; it cannot be sometimes one sometimes
the other as may suit the defendants.   Gadsden v. Barrow, 9 Exch.
514,† was referred to at the trial, but is quite a different case; there
the plaintiff had neither title to nor possession of the goods, which
were vested in a third party by a prior valid conveyance.   Here the
defendant himself has avoided the very conveyance on which he relies.

Montague Smith, in support of the rule.—Under this issue [*566
none but legal rights can be regarded.   [Lord CAMPBELL, C. J.
—Surely if no execution had intervened, and Hatton had been paid
off, the goods would have belonged to Edwards.]   Yes, in equity and
by way of trust, but not at law.   If the plaintiff, on whom the affirmative lies, shows no legal title, the defendant in an interpleader issue
succeeds: Gadsden v. Barrow; Carne v. Brice, 7 M. & W. 183.†
[CROMPTON, J.—The object of an issue is to inform the conscience of
the Court.   It cannot for that purpose be material which party is
made plaintiff.]   The plaintiff's title may be impeached by showing the
jus tertii: Chase v. Gobble, 2 M. & G. 930 (E. C. L. R. vol. 40).
[Lord CAMPBELL, C. J.—The ratio decidendi there was that the proof
showed that the deed, under which the plaintiff claimed, passed
nothing.]

ERLE, J.—In this issue between Edwards and English I think that
Edwards is entitled to succeed.   As between Hatton and Edwards
there had been a valid bill of sale to Hatton; but it was void as against
English, who has availed himself of the statute, and treated it as void,
and, having done so, tries to set it up as valid against Edwards.   But
this issue is tried to inform the Court whether the execution-debtor

Hare had goods liable to be taken in execution by English ; and that is what is really meant by the issue. Both bills of sale were valid as against Hare ; and Edwards's bill of sale as against English. There may no doubt be a question between Hatton and Edwards as to which *567] is to have those goods. I rather think at present Hatton is not *entitled to maintain any claim against Edwards ; but, whether he can do so or not, that in no ways concerns English. I think the principle in Carne *v.* Brice was that the issue, being to inform the Court, is to be construed with that view. Chase *v.* Gobble confirms the principle in Carne *v.* Brice : in that case the proposed evidence would have shown that the plaintiff had nothing whatever in the goods claimed. And Gadsden *v.* Barrow is to the same effect.

CROMPTON, J.—I am of the same opinion. The matter to be inquired into, to satisfy the judgment of the Court, was whether English had a right to order the sheriff to seize these goods under the execution, as Hare's goods. The sheriff could not, for that purpose, set up Hatton's prior bill of sale. It is said, however, that Edwards's interest, being subject to Hatton's, was only equitable. That I doubt : but granting it to be so, I do not think it open to English to rely on that at this stage of the proceeding. The only thing embarrassing is the suggestion that, if the goods are given up to Edwards, Hatton may claim as against her. If so, I think she must have a defence ; if not at law, certainly in equity. But it is impossible to put the construction upon the Act that the existence of a prior bill of sale, void against an execution-creditor because not registered, has the effect of defeating all subsequent bills of sale, though properly registered.

*568] Lord CAMPBELL, C. J.—Upon the issue in this case *the question was whether the creditor had a right to seize the goods. It was quite immaterial which party was plaintiff in the issue : that was the substance of it. Here, had English been plaintiff, and begun and proved a primâ facie case, Edwards would have shown, at least, a primâ facie case in answer by showing a bonâ fide bill of sale to herself, duly registered. In answer to that, the existence of a prior invalid bill of sale might have been shown ; but the very utmost effect of that is to show that no strict legal property was in Edwards, by no means showing that the property was liable to be taken in execution as being Hare's. This fact should therefore be set aside as not material to the substance of the issue, on the principle acted on in Carne *v.* Brice.

Rule discharged.

SIMONS v. PATCHETT. *April* 25.

Action for a breach of implied warranty that the defendant, purchasing a ship in the name of R. from plaintiff, had authority to make the contract for R. It appeared at the trial that, R. having refused to adopt defendant's contract, plaintiff resold the ship at a less price than the contract price. The resale was taken to be reasonably made for the best price that could be obtained: and it was taken that R. was perfectly solvent. A verdict for the plaintiff being taken for the difference between the contract price and that obtained on the resale,

Held, that the damages were properly assessed.

FIRST count on a promise that defendant was authorized by Rostron & Co. to purchase of the plaintiff a screw steamer, then in progress according to a certain specification, to have a range of deck cabins, fitted up according to certain plans pointed out by defendant, *for 6000*l*. Breach: that defendant was not authorized by Rostron & Co.; by reason whereof plaintiff was unable to enforce the contract. 2. Count on a promise that defendant had authority from Rostron & Co. to employ plaintiff to do work for them. Similar breach. [*569

Pleas. Non assumpsit, and a denial of the breaches.

On the trial, before Lord Campbell, C. J., at the Sittings in London after Michaelmas Term, 1856, it appeared that the defendant had made a contract as agent for Rostron & Co. to purchase the steamer in question for 6000*l*., payable on the completion of the vessel and her being fitted with a range of deck cabins as pointed out by the defendant. In fact, the defendant had only a limited authority from Rostron & Co., which he had exceeded; and they refused to be bound by the contract. The plaintiff was informed of this; but, by that time, he had incurred expense in preparing the deck fittings, which was thrown away, as they were not required since Rostron & Co. did not take the ship. The plaintiff then resold the ship in the best manner he could, without these fittings. There was no doubt suggested as to the competency of Rostron & Co., if the contract had been binding on them, to pay the price or any damages for the breach of it. It was agreed that the sum thrown away in consequence of the expense incurred about the fittings should be taken to be 250*l*.; and it was not disputed that this sum might be recovered as damages. It was also agreed that the net price obtained for the ship, without the fittings, should be taken at 5500*l*., and that the verdict should be entered for 500*l*., with leave to move to reduce the damages to 250*l*.

Montague Smith, in the ensuing Term, obtained a rule Nisi accordingly. [*570

Hugh Hill and *C. Milward* now showed cause.—Had the defendant's warranty been complied with, and Rostron & Co. had been bound by the contract, they would either have fulfilled it, or been liable for a breach of it. In the first case the plaintiff would have parted with his ship, as he has, and had 6000*l*. instead of 5500*l*., making a difference of 500*l.* If, on the other hand, they had refused to accept it, the plaintiff might have recovered damages against them in an action for not accepting the ship.   In that action the measure of damages would have been the difference between the contract price and the market price at the time of the breach of contract.   In the present case, the plaintiff having done his best to resell the ship well, the sum he actually received on the resale is a fair criterion of the market price.   Therefore here the plaintiff would have had 500*l.* more than he has.   In Hadley *v.* Baxendale, 9 Exch. 341,† the Court, in delivering judgment, cite with approbation the rule laid down in Alder *v.* Keighley, 15 M. & W. 117,† " that the amount which would have been received if the contract had been kept, is the measure of damages if the contract is broken."   And, though the judgment in that case limits the damages to the consequences of a breach of contract which might be naturally expected, it includes such consequences as might naturally be expected according to the information given at the time of the contract.   [Lord CAMPBELL, C. J.—There is extreme difficulty in laying down a rule of law on the subject.]   Perhaps so : but, *unless the defendant can show some rule of law to prevent the plaintiff from recovering the sum which he would have recovered against Rostron & Co. if the warranty had been complied with, the Court, who are in the position of a jury, will give that sum.

*571]

Montague Smith, in support of his rule.—The agent is not liable as a principal; and the measure of damages is not the same against him as if he were.   [CROMPTON, J.—It is not the same thing to warrant to a man that a supposed principal is bound to fulfil a bargain, and to contract to fulfil it one's self.   Though the principal was bound, the vendor might be no better off, as in the possible case that he was insolvent.   But, when the principal would be able to pay if he were bound to do so, I do not see the difference in the damages.]   The real damage in this case was only that the ship was kept out of commerce during the interval between the making of the bargain and the information to the plaintiff that it was not binding on Rostron & Co.   The rest is but the fancied value of his bargain, which is not recoverable any more than in the case of the sale of real estate.

Lord CAMPBELL, C. J.—I had formed no opinion at the trial: but now, having heard the argument, I come to the conclusion that the verdict should stand as it is, the damages being the loss directly arising from the breach of contract.   What was the contract in this case ?   That the defendant had authority from Rostron & Co., so that the bargain he made in their name was binding on them.   What then has the plaintiff suffered from this bargain not being binding on Rostron & Co. ?   It is not disputed that, if the bargain had been binding, and had not *been fulfilled, the plaintiff would have recovered against Rostron & Co. damages for not fulfilling the contract ; and if they had ful-

*572]

filled the contract, the plaintiff would have had from them the full price. The loss of the damages, therefore, which he would have recovered from Rostron & Co. is the direct consequence of the breach of the defendant's contract. Viewing the matter in another light, the result is much the same. It is not to be disputed that, if direct evidence had been given of a fall in the market price of ships between the time of the making of the supposed bargain and the time at which the plaintiff might reasonably resell the ship, that fall in price would be recoverable. Might not the jury reasonably infer such a fall in price from the difference in price actually obtained in this case? If so, the case would be brought within the general rule as to the measure of damages in an action for not accepting goods. Our attention has most properly been called to the different rule which prevails in the case of sales of real estate. But that rule is rather anomalous.(a) It is a custom long established, supposed to be incorporated in all contracts for the sale of real estate as being universally known, that when the sale goes off for want of title in the vendor, the damages shall be limited to the actual expenses. If the sale goes off because the vendor changes his mind, or otherwise by his fault, the custom does not apply, and full compensation is given. There is, however, no custom that can be set up in such a case as the present; so that the general rule of law prevails. We must look at the contract, and the direct consequences of the breach. It *seems to me that, under the circumstances, 500l. [*573 does no more than place the plaintiff in the same position as if there had been a valid contract with Rostron & Co.

ERLE, J.—I am of the same opinion. The facts I take to be, that the defendant purchased as agent for Rostron & Co. a ship from the plaintiff, and promised that he had authority to bind Rostron & Co. It turns out that he had not such authority, and that the contract was not binding. The question is, what are the damages? There is a sum of 250l. expended on the faith of the contract as to which there is no question raised; but the dispute is as to the loss of 250l. on the resale. The general principle is, that he who has broken a contract is to make good to the plaintiff all the damage which is the direct consequence, in the ordinary course of affairs, of the breach of contract. Now, here the ship was purchased by the defendant in a fair bargain, at what must be taken to be its ordinary value. When resold at a reasonable time after, the contract proved invalid; also in a fair manner, it fetched 250l. less. In the interval, whilst the plaintiff believed he was a vendor to Rostron & Co., he was unable to take any steps to sell his ship, and necessarily, as the direct consequence of the contract, lost opportunities of sale, which cannot be otherwise estimated than by the result. I should be loth to hold an agent liable to unlimited damages from the

(a) See Flureau v. Thornhill, 2 W. Bl. 1078; Parke, B., in Robinson v. Harman, 1 Exch. 850, 855.†

breach of his warranty: but I think these damages are no more than the direct consequences in the ordinary course of affairs of such a breach of contract.

*574]   CROMPTON, J.—We are rather in the situation of a *jury assessing damages, than of Judges laying down the law. I quite assent to what Mr. *Smith* said in argument, that the damages recoverable from an agent for such a breach of warranty are not identical with those which would have been recoverable from the principal for not fulfilling the contract. The damages to be recovered are what was lost to the plaintiff by not having the valid contract which the agent warranted he had. Though, if there had been such a binding contract, the purchaser would have been liable to the plaintiff in damages, yet, if the purchaser was not solvent, the jury would say that the loss in consequence of not having a binding contract was not the sum for which he would in that case have had judgment against the purchaser. But here the supposed purchasers are solvent; and no doubt is raised that, if the contract had been binding, the plaintiff would actually have received whatever sum he could have recovered against them: and, that being so, I am at a loss to see why we, being a jury, should not give the plaintiff the sum which he would have had if the defendant's contract had not been broken. That is the principle on which I go. With respect to contracts for the sale of real estate, there is an anomaly arising from an implied exception that, if the contract goes off from defect of title, there should be no damages for the loss of the bargain. That is a technical rule; and I see no reason why it is to be taken for our guide in this case, more than in a breach of contract for not accepting goods, in which there is no such technical rule, and no such exception.   Rule discharged.(*a*)

(*a*) See Collen *v.* Wright, ante, p. 301. (Judgment of Q. B. affirmed in Exch. Ch., Nov. 30 1857.)

---

*575]   *The QUEEN *v.* ROBERT GLADSTONE and eight others. *April* 27.

In the parish of L., under a local Act, a body called The Select Vestry of L. have the functions of a Board of Guardians. There is also a general Vestry, having the management of the general parochial affairs of L.

Held, that the members of a Burial Board for L., under stats. 16 & 17 Vict. c. 134, s. 7, 15 & 16 Vict. c. 85, ss. 10, 11, 52, were to be elected by the General Vestry having the management of the general parochial affairs, and not by the body created by the local Act.

ASPLAND moved for a rule Nisi for an information in the nature of Quo warranto against the defendants for usurping the office of members of the Burial Board of Liverpool.

He moved upon an affidavit, by which it appeared that in the parish of Liverpool there is a body called The Select Vestry of the Parish of

Liverpool, constituted by stat. 5 & 6 Vict. c. lxxxviii.(a)   Sect. 1 of that statute enacts: "That the rectors, the churchwardens, and the overseers of the poor of the said parish for the time being, together with twenty-one persons to be elected in the manner by this Act directed, shall be the select vestry for carrying into execution the provisions of this Act, and shall be styled ' The Select Vestry of the Parish of Liverpool,' and shall be and shall be deemed to be a Board of Guardians for the relief and management of the poor, and, subject to the rules, orders, and regulations of the Poor Law Commissioners, shall have, exercise, and perform all the same rights, powers, privileges, authorities, duties, immunities, protections, and remedies as are given to or imposed upon guardians of the poor in and by an Act," &c. (5 & 6 W. 4, c. 76).   By sect. 21, as soon as The Select Vestry should hold their *first meeting, the functions of the Board of Guardians were to cease. [*576

Before and since the passing of this Act, a General Vestry has always been held in the parish for the management of the general parochial affairs.   Upon the requisition in writing of more than ten ratepayers, the churchwardens convened a meeting of the General Vestry to determine whether a burial ground should be provided for the parish: it was determined that there should; and the nine defendants were elected by the General Vestry to be the members of the Burial Board; in all respects regularly, if the General Vestry was the proper body to elect.

Aspland, in support of his motion.—Stat. 16 & 17 Vict. c. 134, s. 7, provides for the election of a Burial Board in places beyond the Metropolis, by incorporating by reference the enactments in stat. 15 & 16 Vict. c. 85, as to the election of Burial Boards in places within the Metropolis.   Stat. 15 & 16 Vict. c. 85, ss. 10, 11, requires the elections to be by the vestry.   Sect. 52 defines the vestry to mean "the inhabitants of the parish lawfully assembled in vestry, or for any of the purposes for which vestries are holden, except in those parishes in which there is a select or other vestry elected under" stat. 59 G. 3, c. 12, "or elected under" stat. 1 & 2 W. 4, c. 60, "or elected under the provisions of any local Act of Parliament for the government of any parish by vestries, in which parishes it shall mean such select or other vestry."   The election in Liverpool should therefore have been by the Select Vestry: Regina v. Peters, 6 E. & B. 225 (E. C. L. R. vol. 88).

*Lord CAMPBELL, C. J.—I think it quite clear that the members of the board have been duly elected.   They have been [*577 elected by the vestry which has the government of the parish.   It is important that those who are to tax the inhabitants should be elected by those who have the management of the general affairs of the parish on the inhabitants of which the burthen will fall.   Such is the policy of the Act, which gives the election to the inhabitants assembled in

(a) Local and personal, public: "For the administration of the laws relating to the poor of the parish of Liverpool in the county of Lancaster."

vestry, unless there be a select vestry for the government of the parish. The body here called the Select Vestry are but a Board of Guardians of the Poor, called by a different name. In Regina *v.* Peters the Select Vestry was the only one which governed the parish.

WIGHTMAN, J.—The question is, whether the government of this parish was taken from the General Vestry by the local Act. That Act creates what is called " The Select Vestry," but only for carrying into execution the provisions of the Act. Had it been amongst those provisions that they should be the only vestry for governing the parish, Regina *v.* Peters would have been in point.

(ERLE, J., was absent.)

CROMPTON, J.—If there was any doubt, I should say let a rule be granted, that the matter may be discussed : but I see none. The word " vestry" is defined in sect. 52. The definition seems carefully worded, to show that it is only when there is a select vestry having the govern-
*578] ment of the parish that it shall be substituted *for the general vestry. There cannot be two vestries at the same time governing this parish ; the defendants have been elected by that which has the general government. The other has merely the executive functions of the guardians of the poor. Rule refused.

JOHN HAIGH *v.* JOHN OUSEY and others. *April 27.*

Action by a solicitor to recover the amount in his bill. Plea, No signed bill delivered. A signed bill was proved to have been delivered. It contained items for business done in a cause, without any statement as to what Court the cause was in. The nature of the business was not such as to show conclusively whether the action was in one of the Superior Courts at Westminster or not. The bill contained other items admitted to be unobjectionably described. On a rule to enter a nonsuit, on the ground that this was not a compliance with the statute:
Held that, the description of the business being such as was reasonably sufficient, when coupled with what must have been known to the client, to give information as to the charges, none of the items were objectionable, and the solicitor might recover his whole bill.
Held also that, even if some items had been badly described, the solicitor might, notwithstanding, recover for the items in his bill sufficiently described.

ACTION for work and labour as an attorney. Plea : No signed bill delivered. Issue thereon.

On the trial, before Erle, J., at the sittings at Westminster in last Hilary Term, it appeared that there was a signed bill delivered in due time, which contained charges for business transacted in different suits, the items in which were as usual classed together under different heads. In one of those, which was headed " Yourselves ats. Walker," were charges for the following items. " Attending on the charges of plaintiff's attorneys herein." " Writing for particulars." " Letter to agent, with instructions for settlement." " Instructions to defend." " Agent perusing correspondence, and attending plaintiff's attorneys;

conferring and inspecting original writ; arranging amount of costs; when, under the circumstances, plaintiff's attorneys agreed to accept 19s. 6d. in discharge of debt and costs." There was nothing else in the bill to indicate the nature of this *action. Several of the other actions, in respect of which charges were made, appeared [*579 on the face of the bill to have been actions in the Superior Courts at Westminster. The learned Judge directed a verdict for the plaintiff, with leave to move to enter a verdict for the defendants if on this bill he was entitled to it.

Manisty, in that Term, obtained a rule Nisi accordingly, on the ground that "the plaintiff's bill of costs did not state the Court in which the business charged for was done, and is not in accordance with the statute."

When the rule·was called on for argument, and the notes of the trial read, the Court called on *Manisty*, for the defendants, to point out the items which he considered most objectionable; he selected the charges under the head of "Yourselves ats. Walker" before mentioned, and some others; but, as the objections to those latter items were similar in principle, it is unnecessary for the purposes of this report to state any more particulars of the bill.

Rew now showed cause.—The first question is whether there really is any objection to any of the items. The nature of the business charged for in the suit of Walker v. Ousey and others, coupled with what the defendants themselves must have known, sufficiently indicates that it must have been an action in one of the Superior Courts at Westminster. It is not necessary that the bill should be so worded as to exclude all possibility of ingenious perversion. If it gives reasonable information it is enough: Cook v. Gillard, 1 E. & B. 26 (E. C. L. R. vol. 72). [ERLE, J.—In Roy v. Turner, 26 Law Times, 150, the Court of Exchequer seem to have *treated that decision as [*580 inconsistent with Ivimey v. Marks, 16 M. & W. 843,† and did not follow it. And in Pigot v. Cadman, 1 H. & N. 837,† Ivimey v. Marks was acted upon to its full extent.] In Roy v. Turner, Parke B., in delivering the judgment of the Court of Exchequer, expressed much doubt whether Ivimey v. Marks was rightly decided. Pigot v. Cadman is certainly an authority that any error in the signed bill delivered bars the plaintiff's action altogether: but that is contrary to other decisions; Waller v. Lacy, 1 M. & G. 54 (E. C. L. R. vol. 39), Drew v. Clifford, Ry. & M. 280; in both of which cases the attorney recovered for the good items, though there were defective items in the bill. In Keene v. Ward, 13 Q. B. 515 (E. C. L. R. vol. 66), the principle was stated to be that "the Legislature intended that the client should have sufficient materials for obtaining advice as to taxation," and that, if the Court went beyond this, they "should give facilities to dishonest clients to defeat just claims upon a pretence of a defect of form in respect of which they had no real interest." In such a conflict of authorities this Court may well follow their own decision in Cook *v.* Gillard. As the leave reserved is only to enter a nonsuit, the verdict must stand unless the plaintiff is absolutely barred from recovering anything.

Manisty, in support of the rule.—The doubt, expressed by Parke, B., as to whether Ivimey *v.* Marks was rightly decided, was only as to the necessity of naming which of the Superior Courts the action was *[581]* in. He *did not express any doubt that the bill must give all requisite information for advice as to taxing the bill. [ERLE, J.—All the cases agree in that. The bill must itself give the necessary information. But in Keene *v.* Ward and Cook *v.* Gillard this Court did not think that the client had a right to use astuteness perversely to misunderstand that information.] Supposing this bill were taken to a solicitor of competent skill, and he were asked if the charges in the suit of Walker *v.* Ousey were such as would be allowed on taxation, his answer must be, " I cannot say unless you tell me whether the action was in the Superior Courts at Westminster, or in the Common Pleas at Lancaster. The charges for the agent may exist in either." [CROMPTON, J.—No doubt that is not conclusive, as there are Preston agents as well as London agents, though the client could no doubt tell him pretty well in which Court the suit was. If the principle is, as you must contend, that the bill must, without extrinsic statements, enable a consulted solicitor to say if the charges are right, every charge for conveyancing should specify how many folios were in the conveyance, and every charge for attending and advising should specify what the conference was about, as, without such information, no one can tell whether the charge for such items is excessive or not. Now I think no decision has gone to that extent yet. The true principle would seem to be, that the bill should give such reasonable information as would easily enable the client to ascertain if the charges are right.] Pigot *v.* Cadman is irreconcileable with such a principle.

[582] *Lord CAMPBELL, C. J.—This is an action on an attorney's bill. The only plea is that no signed bill was delivered pursuant to stat. 6 & 7 Vict. c. 73, s. 37; and on that issue has been joined. The plaintiff at the trial gave in evidence a bill of fees and disbursements, signed by himself, and delivered in due time. The only question was whether this was evidence to go to the jury or not under this issue; the verdict was directed for the plaintiff, with leave to move to enter a nonsuit; and a rule has accordingly been obtained. I am of opinion that it ought to be discharged. I think the plaintiff has proved that he delivered such a bill as the statute requires. The statute, it is to be observed, requires the delivery of a bill of fees, charges, and disbursements, but does not specify further what its contents shall be. I agree, however, that the bill must disclose on the face of it sufficient

information as to the nature of the charges. I adopt the rule as to this, laid down in Keene v. Ward, before I was a member of this Court, and in Cook v. Gillard, to which I was a party. The view taken by my brother Patteson in Keene v. Ward seems very sensible. He says: "In requiring the delivery of an attorney's bill the Legislature intended that the client should have sufficient materials for obtaining advice as to taxation : and we think that we fulfil that intention by holding the present bill sufficient within that principle : whereas, if we required in respect of every item a precise exactness of form, we should go beyond the words and meaning of the statute, and should give facilities to dishonest clients to defeat just claims upon a pretence of a defect *of form, in [*583 respect of which they had no real interest." And in Cook v. Gillard we laid down the principle that the Legislature intended, "while it secured the client a right to reasonable information respecting the bill before an action should be brought upon it, at the same time to give the attorney security that the delivery of a bill intended to give and giving all requisite information should be a compliance with the Act, unless the client could show that information which was really wanted had been withheld." Applying this to the present bill, it seems to me to contain all that the Legislature intended to require.

Complaints have sometimes been made that solicitors are not at liberty to recover the fair remuneration for their services as freely as any other persons. It may be necessary to subject them to some regulations; but they have just ground for complaint if those regulations are vexatious, preventing the fair recovery of a just demand. I do not think that the Legislature intended to throw on a solicitor the burthen of preparing a bill such that another solicitor on looking at it should, without any further statement, see on the face of the bill all information requisite to enable him to say if the charges were reasonable. As to business done in Court, I adhere to what was decided in Cook v. Gillard, that, since the scale of costs in the superior Courts has been made uniform, it is immaterial to show in which of the superior Courts the business was, if it be in one of them; and, that being so, the greater part of the items in this bill are free from any objection. But, even if one were defective, is that which is sufficient to be vitiated *by [*584 that which is not? Such a doctrine is not required to protect the client, and would be most unjust to the solicitor. If the omission or misstatement of a single item were to vitiate the whole of a long bill, it would be most unjust: if further information were required as to that item, it would be easy for the client to ask for and obtain it. Still, if the Court of Exchequer had decided that such was the law, and that the client, it may be never having complained of the bill till six years from the time the debt accrued had expired, might then successfully take the objection, and, if that decision stood alone, I, sitting here, should bow to it. But, if I find contrary decisions, I must elect

between them. Now, in the Court of Common Pleas, I find the late
venerable Chief Justice Tindal, in Waller *v.* Lacy, 1 M. & G. 68 (E.
C. L. R. vol. 39), delivers the solemn decision of the Court. He says:
" The first question is, whether the signed bill delivered is sufficient
within the statute of the 2 G. 2, c. 23, s. 23, to enable the plaintiff to
maintain his action for any portion thereof. On that we all agree that
it is sufficient to enable the plaintiff to support an action for some part
of his demand." The same had been the decision of Lord Tenterden
in Drew *v.* Clifford, Ry. & M. 280 (E. C. L. R. vol. 21). The Court
of Exchequer, however, has decided otherwise ; first in Ivimey *v.* Marks,
16 M. & W. 843,† and more recently in Pigot *v.* Cadman, 1 H. & N.
837.† Between those decisions and that in the Common Pleas I must
elect. Courts of co-ordinate jurisdiction are not bound to adhere to
the latest decision. I am of opinion that the doctrine in the Common
Pleas is right; and I am therefore bound to act upon it, and hold that
the attorney may recover for that part of his demand which is properly
*585] *included in his signed bill of fees, charges, and disbursements.
It would be lamentable if we were compelled to facilitate frauds
which, as is pointed out in Cook *v.* Gillard, 1 E. & B. 26 (E. C. L. R.
vol. 72), may be perpetrated if a client, having been indulged till the
Statute of Limitations had become a bar to a fresh action, might raise
a point of this sort as a bar. For these reasons I think that this rule
to enter a nonsuit should be discharged.

WIGHTMAN, J.—The only issue is, whether there was a signed bill;
and the rule is, according to the leave reserved, to enter a nonsuit.
The question therefore is, whether, some out of several items in the
bill, being in actions, as it is said, not sufficiently designated as to the
Court in which the action was, that is enough to disentitle the plaintiff
to recover at all. For on this rule it is necessary only to decide whether
such a defect as to some of the items bars the whole claim. Now on
that point we have the express decision of the Court of Common Pleas
in Waller *v.* Lacy, 1 M. & G. 54 (E. C. L. R. vol. 39), that such a
defect is not enough to disentitle the plaintiff to recover as to the items
properly designated. Mr. *Manisty,* however, relies on the decisions
of the Exchequer in Ivimey *v.* Marks and Pigot *v.* Cadman. It might
be sufficient to say that the Court of Common Pleas, and also the Court
of Queen's Bench, have come to a different conclusion, and that there
is no foundation in justice for the decision of the Exchequer. But
Ivimey *v.* Marks, which was the first of those cases, is distinguished in
the judgment in Keene *v.* Ward, 13 Q. B. 515 (E. C. L. R. vol. 66),
*586] where my brother Patteson pointed *out that, when the facts were
looked at, the case did not lay down the law contended for. He
then states what he considered was the principle ; and I agree in what
he stated. That case was followed by the considered judgment of this
Court in Cook *v.* Gillard, to which I was a party, and in which I wholly

concurred.   So that, even if it should appear that some items were not
sustainable, it would not support this rule to enter a nonsuit, which
cannot be if the plaintiff is entitled to recover for any part of his bill.

ERLE, J.—The application for a nonsuit is on the grounds that some
of the items in the bill delivered are not sufficiently stated to enable
the defendant to obtain advice as to taxation; and that, if any of the
items are insufficiently stated, the whole bill is vitiated.   These are
two points, both to be made out by the defendants: in my opinion they
have established neither.   The principle laid down in Ward v. Keene,
that all that is required is that the bill should supply sufficient materials
for advice, is not, I think, anywhere disputed; but it is said that,
in applying it, we must consider it indispensable that a solicitor on
reading the bill may be able, without asking for further information,
to advise whether the items are overcharged; and that for this purpose, if any of the items are for business in Court, it is indispensable
that the Court should be named.   Now I am sure no bill that contained charges for anything beyond mere steps in a cause ever did
contain this full information.   No person on earth by reading a
bill of costs without further information can tell what is a fair
*charge for such an item as "advising you."   It may have been   [*587
a minute's work; it may have required a week's careful consideration.   No man, unless there were interminable prolixity in the
bill, could tell from the bill alone what is the fair charge for matters
depending on the quantum meruit, that is, for almost everything except
mere steps in a cause.   In looking at the items pointed out in this case
as being the most objectionable, I find none to be of such a nature as
to be dependent for the remuneration on the Court in which Walker's
action was depending.   The fair charge for each would depend, not on
the Court, but upon the nature of the work done.   I think it was a
mistake in fact originally to think that the name of the Court was
requisite to enable any one to decide on the quantum.   Before stat. 6
& 7 Vict. c. 73, the name of the Court was of essential importance;
but I think the decision in Ivimey v. Marks was founded on a mistake
in fact.   In electing amongst conflicting decisions, I do not adhere to
that which I think based on a mistake.   It seems to me that the statute with regard to solicitors' bills ought to be construed on the principle on which we act with regard to particulars of demand.   The bill
should give reasonable information; if the client wants more, he may
demand it.   Formerly, the law has been administered as if it was the
object of the Act to enable a fraudulent client to defeat his solicitor on
a mere matter of form which it would be ludicrous to suppose to have
misled in point of fact.   But in Cook v. Gillard, after an elaborate
review of the law, a rule was laid *down, applying which to this   [*588
bill I find no item insufficient.   But I am further of opinion that,
supposing there was one bad item, it would not prevent the plaintiff

from recovering for the rest.   The doctrine that it would is founded
on what was thrown out in Ivimey v. Marks, that a solicitor applied to
for advice cannot tell whether the sums which he thinks overcharged
form one-sixth of the whole, unless he sees all the items.   It may be
desirable that he should be able to tell this; but the evil arising from
enabling a client to lie in wait with a formal objection, and dispute the
whole bill because of the absence, as to some one item, of information
which he never asked for or needed, greatly outweighs this.   To decide,
that one bad item vitiates the whole bill is to affirm that the Legislature
intended that a fraudulent client might lie in ambush with a technical
point till the moment of trial.   The authorities being in conflict, I choose
those which seem to me the soundest law, not that which is the latest in
date.   If the decision of the Exchequer stood alone, I should defer to
it; as it is, I adhere to the decisions of the Common Pleas and Queen's
Bench.

CROMPTON, J.—I also think that the rule should be discharged. It
cannot be made absolute if the plaintiff is entitled to recover anything.
If the decision of a Court of co-ordinate jurisdiction stood alone on this
point, I should, sitting here, yield to it, whatever might be my own
opinion.   But, in truth, there is a conflict of decisions, the Court of
*589] Exchequer differing from us; *and I must elect which deci-
sions I shall follow.   I am strongly opposed to the idea that the
presence of one bad item vitiates the whole bill: and I cannot well see
the force of the reason for the rule contended for, that the consulted
solicitor must be able to judge, ex facie, and without further information, whether he will advise the reference of the bill to taxation.   No
bill ever gives such information as to items not done in a cause in Court,
and I do not see why more particularity is required in items done in
the course of a cause.   I think it would be a very dangerous rule to
require the description to be such as to enable a person of competent
skill on reading the bill to say, ex facie, whether it is reasonable.   I
think it should be sufficient if it contains such reasonable information
as, coupled with what the client must be able to tell him, would be sufficient to enable him to judge.   Tried by that test this bill is sufficient;
and, in a conflict of authorities, we may well give judgment according
to our own view of what is right.   Rule discharged.

*GEORGE DAVID EVANS, Appellant, WILLIAM MA- [*590
THIAS and JOHN LEWIS, Respondents. *April* 27.

In an action of replevin, brought by E. against M., M. avowed for rent arrear in respect of a
farm V., and E. pleaded in bar denying the tenancy.

M., in support of the avowry, proved that C. had filed a bill against E. and others, in which C.
claimed to be entitled to V. as tenant for life, subject to a term of 1000 years and a later
mortgage for 500 years, and prayed for an account of what was due on the trusts of the term
of 1000 years and the mortgage; and that directions might be given to raise the sums required
for the trusts of the term; that C. might be permitted to redeem the mortgage: that E. and
the mortgagee might be decreed to deliver V. to C.; that the money which C. should pay for
the redemption might be raised by sale of V.; and that a receiver might be appointed of the
rents of V.

M. further proved that the Court of Chancery decreed that V. should be sold, and that out of the
proceeds the sum required for the trusts of the term should be first paid, then the mortgage
debt; that a receiver should be appointed, and that E., who was in possession of V., should
attorn to him for V.

That a receiver was appointed; and E. attorned to him, adding, "such attornment being without
prejudice to my right to appeal against the decree."

That E. paid the rent to the receiver, and afterwards to another receiver appointed on the death
of the first.

That the term of one thousand years was sold to M., and the termor in trust conveyed to M.

Held: that on this evidence, and assuming M. to have a good title under the term, the relation
of landlord and tenant was still not proved to exist between M. and E.

Where a case from a county court was stated by the parties at unnecessary length, the judge
signing it in obedience to the county court rule, this Court, in reversing the judgment of the
county court, refused costs.

APPEAL from the County Court of Cardiganshire held at Cardigan.
The material facts of the case stated were as follows.

This is an action of replevin to try the validity of a distress, made
on plaintiff's goods, on 4th August, 1856, for 40*l*. alleged to be half a
year's rent due to defendant Mathias on 1st June, 1856, in respect of
a farm and lands called Vrochest in Pembrokeshire; the other defendant
being the bailiff employed by him in making the distress. Defendants
made avowry and cognisance for rent arrear (as above). Plaintiff
pleaded: Non demisit; Non tenuit; and Riens in arrear. Judgment
was given for defendants in the county court.

*On the trial, evidence was given by the defendants of a [*591
chancery suit wherein Catherine Mary Jane Evans was plaintiff,
and Jane Martha Jones, George David Evans (the plaintiff in replevin),
Anna Maria Evans, Maria Letitia Evans, William Henry Lewis, David
Arthur Saunders Davis, John Taubman, William James, David Griffith
Evans, and William Thomas Bowen Evans were defendants. The case
described at very great length the equity proceedings, which, so far as
was material to the present decision, were as follows.

The bill was filed 15th December, 1851, and stated that Caleb Evans,
being seised in fee of the farm of Vrochest, executed a lease and release of 23d and 24th June, 1813, between himself and his eldest son
Benjamin Evans of the first part, David Griffith and his daughter Easter
Griffith of the second part, Essex Bowen and John Evans of the third
part, and William Bowen and Thomas Lewis of the fourth part: whereby,

in consideration of an intended marriage (afterwards solemnized) between
Benjamin Evans and Easter Griffith, Caleb Evans and Benjamin Evans
conveyed the farm to Essex Bowen and John Evans, to the use of
Caleb Evans in fee until the solemnization of the marriage, and, after
that, to the use of Benjamin Evans for life, remainder to the use of
Easter Griffith for life or widowhood, remainder to Essex Bowen and
their heirs during the lives of Benjamin Evans and Easter Griffith, and
the survivor, remainder to the use of William Bowen and Thomas
Lewis, their executors, administrators, and assigns, for one thousand
years upon the trusts after declared; and, subject to that term and
its trusts, to the use of the sons of the marriage successively in tail
general, remainder to the daughters in tail with cross remainders,
*592] *remainder to Benjamin Evans in fee: and the trusts of the
term were to levy, by sale or mortgage, 1000l. for the portions
of younger sons and daughters, to be paid at majority or marriage, if
occurring after the decease of Benjamin Evans and Easter Griffith.
otherwise within twelve months after such decease. That the issue of
the marriage were Benjamin Griffith Evans, the eldest son, and George
David Evans (plaintiff in the replevin), and two other younger sons,
and two daughters, defendants in the chancery suit, and a daughter
who died under age and unmarried. That in 1827 Benjamin Evans
assigned his life interest to trustees and their heirs for the benefit of
his creditors; and the trustees in 1828 assigned that life interest to
David Griffith and his heirs, subject to redemption on payment of 1400l.
advanced by David Griffith. That David Griffith died intestate as to
the legal estate, which vested in his heir at law George David Griffith.
That Easter Evans died in 1828. That, on 12th September, 1843,
Benjamin Griffith Evans executed a disentailing deed, in which George
David Griffith joined: by which the estate was conveyed to a trustee in
fee to the use of Jane Martha Jones for five hundred years, in consideration of 1200l. paid by her to George David Griffith, to cease on payment
to her of the 1200l., remainder to Benjamin Evans for life, remainder to
Benjamin Griffith Evans in fee. That default was made in payment
of the 1200l. That, on 19th September, 1843, Benjamin Griffith Evans
married Catherine Mary Jane James, the plaintiff in the chancery suit.
That, by an indenture of 19th September, 1843, the remainder of
Benjamin Griffith Evans was settled to the use of him for life, remainder to his said wife for life, with remainders in favour of their children.
*593] remainder to Benjamin Griffith *Evans in fee. That, by inden-
ture of 4th April, 1844 (endorsed on the indenture of 12th September, 1843), Jane Martha Jones assigned to trustees her interest in
the 1200l., on trusts declared in a deed of settlement bearing even date
therewith, and also assigned to them the farm of Vrochest for the
residue of the five hundred years, subject to such equity of redemption
as was then subsisting. That Benjamin Griffith Evans died in 1845,

there having been no issue of his marriage, intestate, and leaving his father Benjamin Evans his heir at law. That Benjamin Evans died in 1849, having devised hereditaments, including the farm of Vrochest, amongst all his children except George David Evans, as tenants in common. That Thomas Lewis, the trustee for the term of one thousand years, having survived the other trustee William Bowen, died, and that William Henry Lewis was his executor. That David Griffith Evans and other three children of Benjamin Evans, were entitled to the equity of redemption on the farm of Vrochest in remainder, after the death of Catherine Mary Jane Evans. That no part of the 1000*l.* had been raised. That the bill prayed that an account might be taken of what was then due for principal and interest in respect of the 1000*l.* secured by the term of one thousand years, and of what was due to Jane Martha Jones for principal and interest on the mortgage. And that an account might be taken of the rents and profits of the mortgaged hereditaments received by Jane Martha Jones, and that directions might be given for raising and paying the 1000*l.* and interest, and that the complainant might be permitted to redeem the mortgage debt of 1200*l.* And that George David Evans and Jane Martha Jones might be respectively decreed to deliver the *hereditaments to the complainant, [*594 and permit her to receive the rents thereof. That the money which the complainant should pay for such redemption, and her costs of suit, might be raised by sale of the hereditaments. And that (if necessary) a receiver might be appointed of the rents of the mortgaged estates.

The case then set out the answer of George David Evans (the plaintiff in replevin) to the above bill. He therein stated that he could not speak as to the execution of the indentures of 1827, 1828, and 1843, nor as to what remained due to George David Griffith on the mortgage security, nor as to whether Benjamin Griffith Evans died intestate: and he admitted the other allegations of the bill. He submitted to the Court whether the term of one thousand years was still a subsisting term. He further alleged that he, on the death of Benjamin Evans, became entitled in possession to all the hereditaments, and applied to the tenants to attorn, and they accordingly did attorn, to himself; and that he claimed to be entitled to the rents and profits, paramount to the title of Jane Martha Jones.

The case then stated that a replication was filed, and issue joined.

And that, by decree of 1st December, 1853, it was ordered that the farm of Vrochest should be sold, and the money be paid in to the credit of the cause, subject to further order: that the sum of 1000*l.*, charged by the term of one thousand years, should be first paid out of the proceeds of the sale, and the mortgage to Jane Martha Jones; and an account be taken of what was due on the several sums; and that inquiry should be made what children there were of the marriage of

*595] Benjamin Evans and Easter Griffith, their personal *representatives, &c. ; and that a proper person should be appointed receiver of the rents and profits of the mortgaged premises ; and that George David Evans (the plaintiff in replevin) should attorn tenant to the said receiver for such part of the premises as were then in his occupation.

The case then stated the other evidence given in the county court, which established the allegations in the bill; and from which it further appeared that, on 5th June, 1854, Owen Davies was appointed receiver of the estates, including Vrochest.   That the suit was revived in August, 1854, on the marriage of Catherine Mary Jane Evans with William Macaubrey ; and an order was made, in November, 1854, directing an inquiry as to the amount of the occupation rent to be paid by George David Evans (the plaintiff in replevin) for the part of the farm of Vrochest then in his occupation.   The following attornment, signed by the plaintiff in replevin, was also put in.

" Evans *v.* Jones.   I hereby attorn to Owen Davies, the receiver in this case, in respect of the premises called Vrochest, and in my occupation ; such attornment being without prejudice to my right to appeal against the decree made in this cause, dated the 1st day of December, 1853.   Dated this 2d day of November, 1854.   GEO. DAVID EVANS."

That, by order of Court of 15th January, 1855, the occupation rent for that part of the farm of Vrochest in the occupation of George David Evans was fixed at 80*l.*, which, by order of 27th February, 1855, he was ordered to pay to the receiver (deducting for property tax), for rent from 1st December, 1853, to 1st December, 1854 ; and it was *596] ordered that all subsequent payments *should be made half yearly on 1st June and 1st December, as long as he should continue in occupation.   That, on 2d May, 1855, the suit was revived against personal representatives of two of the original defendants.   That Vrochest, with the other estates in question in the chancery suit, was sold by public auction on 7th July, 1855, under the decree, for the residue of the term of one thousand years ; and William Mathias, the defendant in replevin, became purchaser, of which the plaintiff in replevin was informed.   That, by order of 15th December, 1855, it was ordered that William Mathias (defendant in replevin) should be let into possession as from 2d December, 1855, and all proper parties should execute a conveyance to him ; and William Henry Lewis did accordingly assign to him, by indenture of 23d February, 1856, for the residue of one thousand years.   That, on 23d January, 1856, the Master certified that five only of the children of the marriage of Benjamin Evans and Easter Griffith lived to attain a vested interest in the 1000*l.* including the plaintiff in replevin.   That on 2d June, 1855, Owen Davies, the receiver, died ; and David Jones was, by order of 29th December, 1855, appointed receiver in his stead.   That the plaintiff in replevin had paid the rent for Vrochest to the two receivers in succession regularly up to

1st December, 1855. That, on 2d August, 1856, the attorneys of the defendant in replevin, by his order, wrote to the plaintiff in replevin, requiring payment to Mathias of 40*l*., the half year's rent due on 1st June, 1856, "for that portion of the farm of Vrochest which you lately held as tenant to the receiver appointed by the Court of Chancery in the suit of Evans *v.* Jones, and which farm he has purchased under a decree of the said Court;" and the letter threatened a distress in case *of non-payment. That this letter was delivered to the plaintiff [*597 in replevin by David Jones, who then told him that the authority of him, David Jones, as receiver had ceased. That the plaintiff in replevin refused to pay; and, on 4th August, 1856, a distress for 40*l*. was put in.

The case stated that it was contended, at the trial, on behalf of the plaintiff in replevin, that the relationship of landlord and tenant did not subsist between him and the defendant Mathias, and that the attornment to the receiver of the Court of Chancery did not enure to create such tenancy. It was argued, in reply, on behalf of the defendants, that under the foregoing facts such relationship of landlord and tenant did exist; and that the defendant Mathias, as the assignee of W. H. Lewis in whom the legal estate was alleged to be vested, had a right to distrain; and that the attornment to the receiver of the Court of Chancery, and payment of rent to him, was in fact an attornment and payment to W. H. Lewis in whom the legal estate was vested, and who alone was justified in distraining.

The case also set out the grounds of appeal, which, so far as materia to the present decision, substantially agreed with the points urged, as above stated, on behalf of the plaintiff in replevin.

The questions for the opinion of the Court of Queen's Bench are: Whether the plaintiff held as tenant to the defendant William Mathias at a rent payable half yearly of the premises in respect of which he attorned; and whether the said William Mathias had a right to distrain for the rent.

The case was signed by the judge of the county court as follows. "The above case was settled by the *parties themselves. I sub- [*598 scribe it in obedience to the county court rule No. 162." "JOHN JOHNES, judge, &c."

The case was argued in this Term.*(a)*

Lush, for the appellant (the plaintiff in the county court).—The appellant never became tenant to Mathias at a fixed rent; and the distress was therefore illegal. It is true that, if he had been tenant to the termor Lewis, the respondent, as Lewis's assignee, would have become entitled to the reversion without any attornment, by stat. 4 Ann. c. 16, s. 9. But the appellant was no more tenant to Lewis than a party, to whom a mortgagor after mortgage has demised, is tenant to

(a) April 24th. Before Lord Campbell, C. J., Erle and Crompton, Js.

the mortgagee or to a purchaser from the mortgagee. The attornment to the receiver has no effect beyond this, that it might perhaps, as between the receiver and the appellant, have entitled the receiver to distrain in his own name: but this would have been a personal right in the receiver, not a right accruing to him from his relation to any other party. The attornment was made only in obedience to the order of the Court of Chancery: it could have given Lewis no right to distrain. The appellant might have paid to the Accountant-General, and have taken his receipt. The attempt is to make the appellant tenant to a party whose right he disputes: the attornment, especially as it is worded, can have no such effect. [CROMPTON, J., referred to Doe dem. Marsack v. Read, 12 East, 57.] There the receiver had authority to let. *599] [ERLE, J.—Here he seems to have authority only to *receive the rent. Lord CAMPBELL, C. J.—The law does not know of such a thing as a hypothetical attornment to such person as may be shown to have title.] It might as well be said that the attornment made the appellant tenant to Jane Martha Jones, the mortgagee.

Horace Lloyd, contrà.—It must be assumed, for it was not disputed in the county court, that Lewis had good title to the term of one thousand years. [Lord CAMPBELL, C. J.—Assume that, and that the respondent has a good claim through him.] The right of the respondent does not rest simply on the attornment to the receiver. There was a payment to him, and also to the subsequent receiver. It seems, therefore, that the attornment was not to the individual, but to the party holding the character of receiver, as such. That must enure to the benefit of the party entitled to the legal estate. The Court of Chancery does not interfere with the legal titles of individuals, but directs the legal owners to do acts, as to convey. The attornment therefore, in this case, did not enure to the benefit of any party directly named by that Court, but to such party as the receiver might be found to represent. Thus, if an occupier of land be threatened with ejectment, he may attorn to the party so threatening, reserving the right to dispute the title, if it should turn out that there was a mistake. It cannot be held that a new attornment was necessary for every new receiver. Suppose the respondent had brought ejectment: could the appellant have set up the title of the receiver? [CROMPTON, J.—I am by no means sure that it is not a fallacy to treat this as, legally speaking, an attornment at all: it may be no more than an agreement to pay rent to the *600] *receiver.] If the receiver had authority to let, the legal owner could not have turned the lessee out. If a cestui que trust let a party into possession who pays him rent, that is evidence of the party being tenant to the trustee, the legal owner: Vallance v. Savage. 7 Bing. 595 (E. C. L. R. vol. 20).

Lush, in reply.—The object of the Court of Chancery, in appointing a receiver, is to make him landlord for the purpose of distraining in his own name. That appears from both equitable and legal authorities: Hughes *v.* Hughes, 1 Ves. Jun. 161, Bennett *v.* Robins, 5 C. & P. 379 (E. C. L. R. vol. 24), Dancer *v.* Hastings, 4 Bing. 2 (E. C. L. R. vol. 13).(*a*) [CROMPTON, J.—That case explains Doe dem. Marsack *v.* Read, 12 East, 57.] Evans *v.* Elliot, 9 A. & E. 342 (E. C. L. R. vol. 36), shows that a mortgagee cannot, by notice to the mortgagor's tenant, constitute the relation of landlord and tenant between himself and such tenant, and that an attornment to him by such tenant cannot relate to the notice, so as to make a tenancy from the time of the notice.(*b*)   *Cur. adv. vult.*

Lord CAMPBELL, C. J., now delivered the judgment of the Court.

This case entirely depends upon whether there was evidence, before the county court judge, that Evans, the appellant, held as tenant under the respondent Mathias, as alleged in the avowry. To establish the tenancy, reliance was placed on the attornment of 1st *December, 1853:(c)* and, if this operated as an attornment to Lewis, [*601 in whom the term created under the marriage settlement of 1818 was then vested, that term having been assigned to Mathias before the rent distrained for accrued, he would be entitled to our judgment. But there is no language in the attornment which naturally bears such a construction; and there certainly was no intention in any of the parties concerned to create or to procure an acknowledgment of a tenancy between Evans and Lewis. Evans attorns tenant "to Owen Davies, the receiver," and expressly provides that it shall be "without prejudice to my right to appeal against the decree." At this time, Evans denied the title of Lewis; and there was an uncertainty whether it would be recognised by the Court. The counsel for the respondents laid down the proposition that an attornment to a receiver appointed by the Court of Chancery enures to the benefit of the person who shall ultimately be found to have in him the legal estate. The Court of Chancery certainly does not assume to itself any title or power of conveying, directing its decrees only in personam, and requiring the parties in whom the legal or equitable interest may be to convey for the benefit of those found to be beneficially interested. But no authority was adduced to show that an attornment to a receiver appointed by the Court of Chancery hypothetically creates a tenancy under another person: and, if the party in whom the legal estate is vested were thus empowered to distrain, the object of the Court of Chancery in appointing the receiver would often be effectually defeated. The cases [*602 *cited by Mr. *Lush* in his reply seem clearly to show that the attornment to a receiver appointed by the Court of Chancery consti-

(*a*) See Chapman *v.* Beecham, 3 Q. B. 723 (E. C. L. R. vol. 43).
(*b*) See note, in 1 Smith's Leading Cases, 476 (4th ed.), to Moss *v.* Gallimore, 1 Dougl. 279; Cole's Law and Practice of Ejectment, pp. 39, 229, 476.
(*c*) That is, under the decree of that date: the actual instrument of attornment was dated 2d November, 1854.

tutes a tenancy by estoppel between the tenant and the receiver, which
the Court applies to the purpose of collecting and securing the rents
till a decree can be pronounced, taking care that the tenant shall be
protected, both while the receiver continues to act, and when by the
authority of the Court he is withdrawn. We must, therefore, hold
that Evans never became tenant to Lewis, either by the attornment or
by the subsequent payment of rent to the receiver; and that the relation of landlord and tenant, upon which the avowry is framed, was not
constituted by the subsequent assignment of the term to Mathias.

  The judgment of the Court below must therefore be reversed.

  We cannot conclude without animadverting on the manner in which
this case is drawn, setting out a bill and answer, and other proceedings
in Chancery, instead of the facts which they are supposed to prove;
whereby great perplexity is introduced, and the costs of the appeal
must be very improperly increased. There must be blame on the part
of the appellant; and we therefore order the judgment to be reversed
without costs.   Judgment reversed.

* * *

*603]   *WARDEN v. STONE. *April* 28.

Under the Absconding Debtors Arrest Act, 1851 (14 & 15 Vict. c. 52), the issuing of a warrant
  by a county court judge is not proceeding in the county court. Therefore, if the high bailiff
  of the county court act for the party applying for the warrant, he is not thereby liable to a
  penalty under stat. 9 & 10 Vict. c. 95, ss. 29, 30.
But, *per Curiam*, it is more fitting that he should not so act.

  THE declaration alleged that defendant, heretofore, to wit, 9th
July, 1855, then being high bailiff of the county court of Lancashire,
holden at Liverpool, in Lancashire, the same then being a county
court holden and established under the Act, &c. (9 & 10 Vict. c. 95),
was, by himself, directly or indirectly, concerned as attorney and agent
for George Rawlison and Robert Pagden in a proceeding in the said
court, to wit, an application to the deputy judge of the said court by
and on behalf of the said G. R. and R. P., by the defendant, as their
attorney and agent, for a warrant, under the Act of Parliament, &c.
(The Absconding Debtors Arrest Act, 1851, 14 & 15 Vict. c. 52),
against William Evans, and the obtaining such warrant from such
deputy judge, and the issuing of such warrant out of the said court by
the defendant, as such attorney and agent for the said G. R. and R.
P., contrary to the form of the statute in such case made. Whereby,
and by force of the said statute, defendant forfeited for his said offence
50l.: and an action accrued to plaintiff, to demand and have the same
of him. Yet defendant hath not as yet paid, &c.

  Plea: Non debet, by statute (21 Ja. 1, c. 4, s. 4). Issue thereon.
Also: Demurrer to declaration. Joinder.

On the trial of the issue in fact, before Martin B., at the last Liverpool Assizes, the facts appeared to be as *stated in the declaration; and it appeared that the cause, in which Evans was sued, [*604 was an action in the Court of Queen's Bench. For the defendant, it was objected that the action did not lie, on the grounds afterwards stated for the rule Nisi. The learned Baron directed a verdict for the plaintiff, giving leave to move to enter a verdict for the defendant.

In this Term, *C. Milward* obtained a rule Nisi, for entering a verdict for the defendant " on the grounds that the defendant's conducting the proceeding under The Absconding Debtors Act before the deputy judge of the county court is not a being engaged as attorney or agent for any party in any proceeding in the county court;" and on another ground which was not afterwards discussed.

The demurrer and the rule were now called on together.

C. Milward, for the defendant, in support of the demurrer and of the rule for entering a verdict for defendant, was not called upon.

Atkinson, Serjt., *Sowler* and *W. B. Brett*, contrà.—By sects. 29 and 30 of stat. 9 & 10 Vict. c. 95, a penalty of 50*l.* is imposed on any high bailiff, &c., for a county court who shall be directly or indirectly concerned as attorney or agent for any party in any proceeding in the said court. The defendant, being high bailiff of the county court of Lancashire holden at Liverpool, has been concerned for a party in a proceeding : the question is, whether this was a "proceeding in the said court." The proceeding is under stat. 14 & 15 Vict. c. 52, The *Absconding Debtors Arrest Act, 1851. Sect. 1 of that Act [*605 enables country commissioners of bankrupts and county court judges (except those acting in Middlesex and Surrey) to grant, on affidavit intituled in one of the Superior Courts, a warrant on which the debtor may be arrested ; and then a capias issues (preceded by a summons when there is no action), on which the debtor is deemed to have been arrested ; and, by sect. 8, the debtor, after the issuing of the warrant but before that of the capias, and before or after the arrest, may apply to have the warrant set aside, or to be discharged from arrest, to the commissioner or county court judge, or to a Judge of the Superior Courts, or to the Court mentioned in the affidavit. The obtaining such warrant appears to be a proceeding in the Court where it issues : Schedule B. gives a fee " to the clerk of the county court on the issuing of a warrant." The warrant, in the county court, is directed to the high bailiff and issued by him. In Pybus *v.* Gibb, 6 E. & B. 902 (E. C. L. R. vol. 88), the Court considered that this Act, among others, had the effect of so far altering the jurisdiction of the county court as to make a surety bond, given, before the passing of the Act, to the high bailiff for the due performance of the duties of his bailiff, unavailable, though the alleged breach of duty was in respect of a duty imposed before the passing of such Acts. The language of the Judges in that case shows that this additional jurisdiction was looked upon by them as an enlargement of the authority of the county court. If the proceedings were not in the county court, the warrant might issue in *606] one county court district, and *be executed in another, by the high bailiff of the former; which cannot be. It is true that the affidavit is entitled in a Superior Court: but that which ensues is not the less a proceeding in the county court. Stat. 10 & 11 Vict. c. 102, by sect. 10, transfers to the county courts the jurisdiction in cases of insolvency previously vested in the Commissioners of the Insolvent Debtors Court on their circuits; and all the proceedings in the county court, under this enactment, are entitled as of the Insolvent Debtors Court, including the petition, schedule, order for hearing, vesting order, &c. The county court judge appoints the assignees, the Insolvent Debtors Court having a concurrent jurisdiction. Yet surely all that, under this enactment, takes place in the county court is a proceeding in that court; and it cannot be said that the judge and clerk of the county court then act merely as officers of the Insolvent Debtors Court.

Lord CAMPBELL, C. J.—I think the defendant would have done better to have declined to be concerned in the proceeding. But we have to determine whether the case falls within sects. 29 and 30 of stat. 9 & 10 Vict. c. 95, which make it penal for the high bailiff, or any other officer of the county court, to be concerned as attorney or agent for any party "in any proceeding in the said court," that is, the county court. This is not a proceeding in the county court: for, though the judge of the county court was authorized to act, he acted as authorized by stat. 14 & 15 Vict. c. 52, and not as a county court judge. Looking at all the sections of that statute, it is clear that these proceedings are *607] only *ancillary to the Superior Court from which the process issues, of which Court, and not of the county court, he is in this respect the officer. The proceeding is in camerâ, not in curiâ, of the county court. It is suggested that the high bailiff could act only in his own district: but I think that, after the warrant, the proceedings are not at all confined to the particular court: I have no doubt that, under sect. 8, the debtor might apply to any commissioner of bankrupt or any county court judge, as well as to any Judge of the Superior Courts, or to the Court mentioned in the affidavit. My brother *Atkinson* has properly reminded us of some expressions which were used by the Bench in Pybus *v.* Gibb; from which, he suggested, it might appear that such proceedings were considered to be proceedings in the county court. But the principle of that decision was only that the perils of the surety were increased by enabling his principal, the bailiff, to receive more than he could receive before: the case goes no further. I think that this was not a proceeding in the county court, within the meaning of sect. 29 of stat. 9 & 10 Vict. c. 95.

WIGHTMAN, J.—I am of opinion that this is clearly not a case within sect. 29, and that the judge, in granting the warrant, was not acting in his court, but under the special authority of The Absconding Debtors Arrest Act, 1851.

ERLE, J.—I am also of opinion that the exercise of this authority was not a proceeding in the county court. *The words "the [*608 judge of any district county court" are only descriptio personæ, that is, of the person who, under sect. 3 of The Absconding Debtors Arrest Act, 1851, is to issue the warrant, which is to "be auxiliary only to the processes now in use." I think it clear, as my Lord has stated, that this authority may be exercised by the high bailiff of any district, at any rate within his own district.

CROMPTON, J.—Sect. 29 of stat. 9 & 10 Vict. c. 95, creates an offence if the high bailiff of a county court is concerned as attorney in a proceeding in that court: and we are to see it clearly made out, therefore, that the proceeding in question was a proceeding in the county court. I think that the proceeding is not in the county court, but in the Superior Court mentioned in the affidavit or warrant. Whilst it was necessary that affidavits for the purpose of arresting absconding debtors should come up to London, the debtors might have time to escape ; and therefore it became desirable that steps should be taken on the spot. I think that the intention of the framer of the Act was to provide officers to grant these warrants as delegates of the Superior Courts. The affidavit is to be intituled in the Superior Court; and the application under sect. 8, if made to a Superior Court, is to be made to the Court mentioned in the affidavit or warrant: and the warrant is, by sect. 3, to be merely auxiliary to the process of the Superior Court. I think, therefore, that the proceedings must be considered as taken in the Superior Court, and that the county court judge, or commissioner of bankrupts, is made a special officer of such Superior Court for the purpose of granting the *warrant. If the case were even doubt- [*609 ful, we should be bound, this being a penal enactment, to see that it was clearly made out. But I really do not see room for any doubt.

Lord CAMPBELL, C. J.—I think, however, we all agree that the high bailiff ought not to act in such a case, and that this ought not to be a precedent.

Judgment for defendant on the demurrer. Rule absolute to enter verdict for defendant.

The QUEEN *v.* EYRE, Clerk.   *April* 29.

A person rated under a rate for the relief of the poor in a parish gave to the churchwardens, in
due time, notice of appeal to the next Sessions, and in the same paper gave notice that he
should not then try the appeal, but only lodge, enter, and commence the same, and petition
for a respite to the next Sessions. The churchwardens gave him notice that they would oppose
such his petition. At the next Sessions both parties attended; the appellant applied to
enter and respite the appeal; the Sessions refused to do so, and required him to proceed, and
on his not doing so, dismissed the appeal. On a rule to quash their order dismissing the
appeal:
Held that, there being a notice in fact which the Sessions were justified in deciding to be a
reasonable notice, they were not bound to respite the appeal, and had jurisdiction to make the
order complained of.

DOWDESWELL, in last Hilary Term, obtained a rule Nisi to quash an
order of Sessions, made upon an appeal by the defendant, against a
rate for the relief of the poor of the parish of Dedham, in the county
of Essex, whereby the Quarter Sessions refused to respite such appeal,
and ordered that the same be dismissed with costs. The order had
been brought up by certiorari.

From the affidavits, on both sides, it appeared that the rate appealed
against was made on the 17th July, 1856, the next Sessions after which
were those holden in October, 1856.

*610]   *Mr. Eyre served on the churchwardens a notice in the fol-
lowing terms. "Essex, to wit. To the churchwardens and
overseers of the poor of the parish of Dedham, in the county of Essex:
To the overseers of the poor of the parish of Dedham: To William
Dawson of Dedham, in the same county: To Thomas Cole of Dedham,
in the same county; and to all others whom it may or doth concern:
Take notice, that I, the undersigned, the Rev. Charles Eyre, of Dedham, in the county of Essex, clerk, being, and having, at the time
when a certain rate and assessment hereinafter mentioned was made,
been, the occupier of a house, lands, and premises situate within the
said parish of Dedham, called the Upper Park Cottage, and being, and
having been, upon and in respect of such occupation, rated and assessed
in such hereinafter mentioned rate and assessment, which was made on
the 17th day of July now last past, for the relief of the poor of the
said parish of Dedham, and for the purposes chargeable thereon according to law, which said rate and assessment was and is entitled: 'Rate
made the 17th day of July, 1856. An assessment for the relief of the
poor of the parish of Dedham, in the county of Essex, and for other
purposes chargeable thereon according to law, made this 17th day of
July, 1856, after the rate of ten pence in the pound:' Take notice, I
repeat, each and every of you, that I, the said Charles Eyre, do intend,
at the next general Quarter Sessions of the peace, to be held in Chelms-
ford, in the county of Essex, in and for the said county, to enter, lodge,
and commence an appeal against the said rate and assessment, by which
rate and assessment I feel myself and am aggrieved and injured, and

to which I have material objection, by reason of you the said William *Dawson, and you the said Thomas Cole, being left out of, or [*611 not in the legal manner included in, the said rate and assess- ment: and take further notice, that the grounds and causes of my said appeal are as follows." The notice then set out the grounds, which it is unnecessary now to state, and proceeded: "And take further notice, each and every of you, that I shall not prosecute and try the said appeal at the next general Quarter Sessions of the peace, but only lodge and enter, and commence the same, and petition for a respite to the next following general Quarter Sessions of the peace, when I will try the same; and that the reason of my petition for a respite will be, and is, that the leading ground of appeal is the same in my present as in my last appeal: in regard to which last appeal I have obtained a writ of certiorari. And take notice that, at the trial of my said appeal, I shall rely on all or any one or more of the said grounds of appeal; and take further notice that, in the trial of my said appeal, you will be and you are hereby required to produce the rate and assessment above mentioned, and against which I intend to and do appeal as afore-said, and also each and every rate and assessment made for the relief of the poor of the said parish of Dedham, at any time during the five years now last past, and also the minute book or books of Dedham, containing the record of all the proceedings in vestry of the said parish of Dedham, during the year 1855. Given under my hand this 29th day of September, A. D. 1856. CHARLES EYRE."

The solicitor for the respondents served on Mr. Eyre the following notice: "The Rev. Charles Eyre, Appellant, and the Churchwardens and Overseers of the parish of Dedham, Essex, Respondents. As attorney *for and on behalf of the above-named respondents, [*612 I do hereby give you notice that I shall oppose any application that you may make for a respite of the appeal at the next general Quarter Sessions of the peace, to be held in and for the county of Essex, of which you have given the said respondents notice it is your intention to make. And take further notice that I do hereby call upon you and require you to prosecute at the next general Quarter Sessions of the peace, to be held in and for the county of Essex, the said appeal, of which you have given the respondents notice. Dated this 10th day of October, 1856. T. J. BARSTOW."

The Sessions were holden on the 14th October, 1856. Mr. Eyre in person, attended, and claimed as of right to enter and respite his appeal. The respondents opposed his claim. The Sessions made the order complained of, which was in the following terms: "Be it remembered that, at the general Quarter Sessions of the peace," holden 14th October, 1856, for the county of Essex, "application and complaint being made to this Court by the Rev. Charles Eyre, clerk, in person, setting forth that he is aggrieved by a certain rate or assessment made for the relief of the poor of the parish of Dedham, in the said county, on the 17th day of July now last past, at ten pence in the pound, first class, at seven pence half penny in the pound, second class, and at five pence in the pound, third class, and therefore appealing against the same; but praying that the hearing of the said appeal may be respited until the next general Quarter Sessions of the peace to be holden for the said county; and counsel appearing for and on behalf of the churchwardens and overseers of the poor of the said parish of Dedham, in support of *613] the said rate, and opposing such *respite: This Court doth refuse to respite such appeal; and the said Charles Eyre not being prepared to try the same at this Sessions, this Court doth order that the said appeal be dismissed, and that the said Charles Eyre shall and do forthwith pay to the churchwardens and overseers of the poor of the said parish of Dedham the sum of 50*l.* for their costs occasioned by the said appeal. By the Court."

T. Chambers and *Rodwell* now showed cause.—An appeal must be to the next practicable Sessions; and reasonable notice of appeal must be given. Here there was a notice of appeal in ample time for the October Sessions, accompanied by a statement that the appellant intended not to try the appeal at those Sessions, but to enter and respite it merely. The respondents gave a counter notice that they should oppose his claim to enter and respite, and insist upon a trial. This was done; and the Sessions have decided in favour of the respondents, and refused to enter and respite the appeal, and made the order complained of. The question is, whether the Sessions had jurisdiction to make this order; in other words, whether an appellant is entitled to enter and respite an appeal as a matter of right. It has been held that, by inveterate practice, a construction has been put upon stat. 9 G. 1, c. 7, s. 8, and stat. 17 G. 2, c. 38, s. 4, which must be adhered to; and that, when no notice of appeal has been given, the Sessions have no discretion, but must enter and respite. And the same construction applies to stat. 41 G. 3 (U. K.), c. 23, ss. 4, &c.; Regina *v.* Eyre, 6 E. & B. 992 (E. C. L. R. vol. 88). But, where a notice has been given in reasonable *614] *time, the application to enter and respite is an application to the discretion of the Court, like an application to postpone a trial at Nisi Prius: Rex *v.* The Justices of Wilts, 8 B. & C. 380 (E. C. L. R. vol. 15). The question whether there was a notice of appeal such as to give the justices jurisdiction to try the appeal, if it was proper to do so, and whether it was proper, under the circumstances, to do so, were facts to be determined by the Sessions; and their determination cannot be reviewed.

Pashley and *Dowdeswell,* in support of the rule.—"The question, what is such reasonable notice as gives" the sessions "jurisdiction to entertain an appeal, is a legal question, of which they are not the exclusive judges; and this Court will see that, in determining such a point, they act legally and according to the jurisdiction which they possess :" per Parke, J., in Rex *v.* The Justices of The West Riding, 5 B. & Ad. 667, 672 (E. C. L. R. vol. 27). In the present case there was no reasonable notice. [Lord CAMPBELL, C. J.—There was in fact a notice given, which the Sessions have decided to be reasonable. Can you show that it was such that, in point of law, it could not be a reasonable notice? CROMPTON, J.—It seems to be a very complete notice of appeal to the next Sessions, with an additional statement that the appellant will then petition for a respite. That petition he made ; and it was objected to, and not granted. Lord CAMPBELL, C. J.—Is not the question whether the Sessions had jurisdiction to hear an objection to his petition?] They had no jurisdiction if the Act gave the appellant a right to enter and respite the appeal, without notice; for then this notice *is reasonably to be read, not as a notice for the [*615 October Sessions, but for the next after it. If there had been no notice at all, the Sessions must have respited : Rex *v.* The Justices of Staffordshire, 7 East, 549, Regina *v.* Justices of London, 9 Q. B. 41 (E. C. L. R. vol. 58). This is a much stronger case than if there was no notice. If Mr. Eyre had gone on and tried the case at the October Sessions, the respondents would have had a right to set aside the judgment as tried without notice to them. The churchwardens, by their counter notice, have estopped themselves from doing so ; but Dawson and Cole might still make the objection. What is required is a notice that the appellant means to try at the Sessions. Here there was express notice that he meant not to try.

Lord CAMPBELL, C. J.—I am of opinion that the Sessions have not exceeded their jurisdiction, and that the order is valid. Under stat. 17 G. 2, c. 38, s. 4, if it appeared to the justices that reasonable notice had not been given, the justices were bound to respite : but it was for the justices to determine whether there had or had not been reasonable notice given. If there had been no evidence of a reasonable notice they would not have been justified in finding that there had been one ; and I believe it to be an established point of sessions law that, where there is no notice, it, in law, cannot be a reasonable notice. Whatever be the reason of the thing, I think that now an inveterate doctrine ; and I do not seek to break in upon it. But in this case there was a notice ; and in terms it was a notice of appeal ; and, had there been no addition to it, it would have been a reasonable notice *of appeal for the [*616 October Sessions : and I do not think it ceases to be one because of the addition. I construe it to be a notice that the appellant will appeal to the October Sessions, and then and there apply to the Court to enter and respite the appeal. There was a notice of appeal which the Sessions might consider reasonable. I attach some weight to the counter notice ; for after receiving it the appellant might have prepared himself for trial. My opinion is, that the Sessions had materials before them which justified them in finding that reasonable notice had been given, and that, if there was reasonable notice, it was at least not obligatory upon them to enter and respite the appeal.

WIGHTMAN, J.—The only question is, whether the justices had jurisdiction to exercise a discretion, or whether they were bound to adjourn the trial. This seems to me to depend on the words of stat. 17 G. 2, c. 38, s. 4. The next Sessions are "to receive such appeal, and to hear and finally determine the same;" if the enactment stopped there,. the right to try would be complete; but it goes on, "but if it shall appear to the said justices that reasonable notice was not given, then," and, it is to be observed, then only, "they shall adjourn the said appeal to the next Quarter Sessions." The contention now is that the notice in fact given in this case is in law equivalent to none. In the former case, Regina v. Eyre, there was no notice at all; and, that being so, there could not well be a reasonable notice: but in the present case there is a notice; and the only difficulty arises from the addition of superfluous words.

*617]   *ERLE, J.—I am of the same opinion. The Court of Sessions has power to enter and respite an appeal, if reasonable notice is not given; but in the present case notice of appeal was given, valid in every respect for trial at the October Sessions, save in adding that the appellant would not then try, but would petition for a respite. That means, I think, that he would not try unless the ̇Sessions compelled him to go on. It was the duty of the Sessions to compel him to go on unless there was a reason to the contrary. It has been urged that in all cases an appellant has a right to enter and respite his appeal at the first Sessions; and that he may secure this by giving no notice of appeal, though there is time for it. In Regina v. Justices of London, Lord Denman, C. J., says: "Many things have grown up in practice which we might wish to see altered: but the greatest confusion would ensue if we were to alter a course so well understood as the practice on this point. It has always been understood that no notice is the same as no reasonable notice; and that, if no notice has been given of trial at the first practicable sessions, and they are the sessions next after the order, and the appeal is then entered, the Court of Sessions is bound to adjourn it." That was an appeal against an order of removal; and for a time Mr. Pashley, who insisted on the respite, had his way: but the Legislature have intervened; and this is no longer the law on these appeals.(a) With respect to appeals against rates: in Rex v. The Justices of Wilts the appeal had been entered and respited as a matter of course; and the

*618]   objection was taken that the next Sessions had no *jurisdiction to hear it because the first had no jurisdiction to respite it. Lord Tenterden, in deciding in favour of the jurisdiction, does not put it on the ground that the appellant had a right to enter and respite, but that

(a) See stat. 11 & 12 Vict. c. 31, s. 9.

the Sessions had a discretion to permit him to do so, and that such was their practice. Bayley, J., says: "It was competent for the justices at the first sessions after the publishing of the rate, to refuse to receive the appeal unless there was proof that notice of appeal had been given." That is an authority in support of the practice of the Sessions at Essex to require such proof. I do not think that the statute was intended to enable the party to lie by for three months, if so much intervened, then enter the appeal, and try three months afterwards.

CROMPTON, J.—The appellant gave a notice of appeal for the October Sessions; he states his reason why he means not to try at that Sessions, and that he will submit it to the Sessions and petition for a respite; that is, will try to persuade them it is a matter fit to be adjourned. I put no stress on the counter notice, as far as the jurisdiction to refuse to adjourn goes; for, if the appellant had a legal right to adjourn it, no counter notice could vary his right; but it was a very material and important element for the Sessions when they were exercising their discretion as to whether it was proper to try then, or to adjourn.   Rule discharged.

---

*The QUEEN *v.* EYRE. *April* 29.   [*619

Notice of appeal was given against a poor-rate, stating, as one of the grounds of appeal, that certain parties enumerated in a schedule attached to the notice were improperly rated. These parties were not served with the notice; and the Sessions refused to respite the appeal for the purpose of such service, and dismissed the appeal with costs. The Court of Queen's Bench afterwards made absolute a rule commanding the Sessions to enter continuances and hear "the said appeal," on the ground that they were bound to respite for the purpose of notice being served on all the parties interested. Appellant then gave a second notice, in which the schedule, and the objections in respect of the parties named therein, were omitted. The Sessions, when the appeal came on for hearing, held that this was not a proper notice, and dismissed the appeal with costs.

Held, that they were right in so doing, inasmuch as, by the omission of the schedule and the objections in respect of the parties named therein, the character of the appeal was materially altered, so that it was not the " said" appeal which the Sessions were ordered to hear and determine.

DOWDESWELL, in this Term, obtained a rule calling on the prosecutor to show cause why an order of the Essex Court of Quarter Sessions, made on the 6th of January last, dismissing the appeal of the said Charles Eyre against a rate made for the relief of the poor of the parish of Dedham, on or about the 10th April, 1856, with costs, should not be quashed.

From the affidavits upon which the rule was obtained, it appeared that a rate was made on 10th April, 1856, under the provisions of The Small Tenements Act (13 & 14 Vict. c. 99), against which Mr. Eyre appealed. The notice of appeal was directed "to the churchwardens and overseers of the parish of Dedham, in the county of Essex, to W. D., of Dedham aforesaid, to T. C., of the same place, to each and all

person or persons, party or parties, named in one or more of the
columns of the following schedule of the rated or liable to be rated
for the relief of the poor of the parish of Dedham aforesaid, and for
other legal purposes, to," &c. (several other inhabitants of the parish),
" and to whoever may be the object or objects of the sixth section of
*620]   the twenty-third *chapter of the forty-first statute(*a*) of George
        the Third, whose name or names may or may not be found in
the foregoing schedule, that is to say, to all owners and occupiers of
rateable property in Dedham aforesaid, who in the hereinafter described
rate or assessment are rated or assessed, and ought not to be rated or
assessed, or who are omitted to be rated or assessed, but ought not to
be omitted, or who are rated or assessed at a greater or less sum or
sums of money than the sum or sums at which they ought to be rated
or assessed therein, or whose rate or assessment for any other cause
may require any alteration to be made therein." A schedule was
attached to the notice, containing the names of 434 persons. One of
the grounds of appeal stated in the notice was, " that you, the person
or persons, party or parties, named respectively in the before-mentioned
schedule, or numbered but not named therein, were, at the time the
said rate or assessment was made, owners or occupiers, or had recently
been occupiers, of property within the parish of Dedham aforesaid, in
the manner indicated by the said schedule, or in some other manner;
but that in the said rate or assessment you were and are rated or
assessed, or omitted to be rated or assessed, at amounts contrary to
law." There were other grounds of appeal not material here. The
affidavit of the appellant stated that he was induced to insert the said
names in the said schedule, and to address the notice to the persons
therein named, and to insert the above ground of appeal, in consequence of an objection made to a notice of appeal upon the same
grounds, entered by him against a previous rate; namely, that all the
*621] parishioners *were interested in the rate, and therefore, under
        stat. 41 G. 3, c. 23 (U. K.), should all have been named and
served with notice of appeal.

The churchwardens and overseers were served with a copy both of
the schedule and of the notice. A copy of the notice only was served
on the said W. D. and T. C. No other person was served with either.

On the hearing of the appeal it was objected, on behalf of the
respondents, that the notice should have been served on every one of
the persons mentioned in the schedule, and upon all the other persons
mentioned in the notice. The Sessions refused to allow the appeal to
be respited for this purpose, and dismissed it with costs, upon the
ground that the notice had not been properly served. The appellant
removed the order into the Court of Queen's Bench by certiorari, and
obtained a rule Nisi to quash the same. The Court held that the Ses-

sions were bound to adjourn the appeal to the next Sessions, in order that the notice might be properly served; and the rule was made absolute, the Sessions being ordered "to enter continuances upon the said appeal, and hear and determine the same upon the merits."(a) The appellant then, before the next Quarter Sessions, served a fresh notice of appeal, omitting the schedule altogether. The grounds of appeal were the same as those in the previous notice, except that the objection to the rating of the persons specified in the schedule was omitted. This notice was addressed only "to the churchwardens and overseers of the poor of the parish of Dedham," "to W. D., of the said parish of Dedham, and T. C., of the same parish" (as in the first part of the previous notice); and was *served on three of the parish officers, and on the said W. D. and T. C. [*622

On the hearing of the appeal it was contended, on behalf of the respondents, that the appellant was not at liberty to deliver a fresh notice, omitting one of the former grounds of appeal, but ought to have completed the service of the original notice, by serving it upon all the parties specified therein, who had not been served at the time of the last hearing; and the Sessions, on this ground, ordered the appeal to be dismissed with costs. Against this order the present rule was obtained.

T. Chambers and *Rodwell* now showed cause.—The appellant, by delivering a fresh notice, in which one of the former grounds of appeal is omitted, and which is not directed to the same parties as the former notice was, has, practically, brought forward a fresh appeal; and the Sessions were right in refusing to hear any but "the said appeal;" that is, the same appeal, both as to the grounds of appeal and as to the parties entitled to be served with notice, as that which the appellant had brought before the Sessions on the former occasion. The very ground upon which the rule for a hearing of the appeal was made absolute by this Court was, that the appellant had not had time, when the appeal came on for hearing before, to serve his notice upon all the parties specified. He has now had the opportunity of perfecting his original notice by so doing; and this is all that he was entitled to do. By the decision of this Court, the appellant was placed in the same position as if the Sessions had actually entered and respited the appeal, in which case he would not have been entitled to serve a fresh notice. In fact, if *he was not in Court upon the first notice, he could not be in Court at all. By stat. 17 G. 2, c. 38, s. 4, he was [*623 bound to give notice to the next General Quarter Sessions; he did so, and gave a notice which was good in form, and required nothing more to make it complete than a further service of it upon parties interested. He was not, therefore, entitled some six months after to serve a fresh notice, directed to different parties, and differing from the first one as to the grounds of appeal. [Lord CAMPBELL, C. J.—The grounds

(a) See Regina v. Eyre, 6 E. & B. 992 (E. C. L. R. vol. 88).

VOL. VII.—25

of appeal certainly could not be altered. That would destroy the identity of the appeal.] The mere omission of the schedule alone has that effect. [Lord CAMPBELL, C. J.—Suppose that no schedule had been attached to the first notice, would the appellant have been entitled to add a schedule to his second?] Clearly not; and that is one mode of testing the question. The addition or omission of the schedule entirely alters the whole character of the appeal. It is contended, by the appellant, that his grounds of objection are the same as before; if so, the second notice is nugatory; if the objections are not the same, the Sessions could not hear them, inasmuch as they were ordered to hear and determine "the *said* appeal" only.

Pashley and *Dowdeswell*, contrâ.—The second notice is good; and the Sessions were bound to hear and determine the appeal upon such notice. An appeal is for the purpose of enabling the Court to raise or otherwise alter the rating on the parties therein named; and the appellant is entitled to waive his right of requiring the Court to enter into the question of the rateability of any or none of the parties named.

*624] Suppose that, *when the appellant gave the first notice, he had also stated that it was not his intention to dispute the rating of the parties named in the schedule; the Sessions could not have objected to that course. [Lord CAMPBELL, C. J.—In that case the appeal would have remained "the said" appeal when it came before the Sessions a second time. Here the appellant does not make that statement in time to allow of its being incorporated with his first notice.] It is said that the second notice changes the character of the appeal. That is not so; the only change is in the omission of persons named in the schedule; and they were not parties to the original appeal. [Lord CAMPBELL, C. J.—They must be considered as parties: it was on that being proved that we held the Sessions ought to have respited the appeal.] The Court held that a fresh notice ought to be given. [Lord CAMPBELL, C. J.—No: we held that the original notice must be served upon certain fresh parties.] If the first notice was in any way insufficient, surely the appellant had a right to serve another.

Lord CAMPBELL, C. J.—I am of opinion that the Sessions acted rightly. They were ordered by this Court to enter continuances, and hear a certain appeal. That appeal had, at that time, acquired a certain character; the parties to it, and the grounds upon which the rating of the various persons named was disputed, being set out in the notice. Then the appellant, before the appeal comes again before the Sessions, delivers a fresh notice, which is, in effect, a notice of an appeal not the same as that which the Sessions were ordered to hear and determine: and the Sessions were therefore right in dismissing the appeal.

*625] *ERLE, J.(*a*)—The appeal which was originally entered by the appellant affected all the landlords in possession, all of whom

(*a*) Wightman, J., left the Court during the argument.

were before the Court as parties to the appeal, inasmuch as they were enumerated in the notice, which is a most essential document, as defining the character both of the appellant and of the parties whose rateability is to be determined by the Sessions. The second notice given by the appellant omitted the greater part of the parties to the first appeal, and thereby materially altered the character of the appeal; so that it was not the same appeal as that which the Sessions were ordered to hear. They were therefore right in dismissing it.

CROMPTON, J., concurred.   Rule discharged.(a)

(a) Reported by Francis Ellis, Esq.

IN THE EXCHEQUER CHAMBER.

HAINES, Appellant, v. ROBERTS and others, Respondents.
April 30.

An enclosure Act vested the surface of the land in allottees, and the mines in the lord of the manor, and prohibited the lord from working the mines within forty perpendicular yards of the foundation of buildings on the surface.

Held by the Exchequer Chamber, confirming the judgment of the Queen's Bench, that this prohibition did not affect the common law right of the owner of the surface to support, and that he might maintain an action against the lord for working the mines so as to cause the buildings on the surface, belonging to the owner of the surface, to give way, though the mines had been worked with ordinary care and not within forty perpendicular yards of the foundation of the buildings.

ACTION for injuring the plaintiff's reversion in certain messuages, which of right enjoyed the *support of certain foundations, by [*626 improperly removing the minerals under them. Plea 2 (the only one material) was a traverse of the right to the support.

On the trial, the plaintiff had a verdict, subject to leave to move to enter a nonsuit.

The Court of Queen's Bench having granted a rule to enter a non-suit, which was discharged,(a) the defendant appealed. The case for the appeal set out a private Act, the material part of which is stated in the report of the case below,(a) and the facts, in substance, as there stated.

Sir *F. Kelly*, for the appellant, defendant below, argued to the same effect as in the Court below.

Alexander, for the respondents, plaintiffs below, was not called upon to argue.

COCKBURN, C. J.—We are all of opinion that the decision of the Queen's Bench was right. The question arises on the second issue, which traverses the right to support. Now, looking to the provisions of the private Act, it appears that the effect is to place the parties in the same position as though the lord, originally owner in fee of the

(a) See Roberts v. Haines, 6 E. & B. 643 (E. C. L. R. vol. 88).

whole soil, had conveyed the surface to the allottees. I concur with the Queen's Bench in thinking that, under such circumstances, the owners of the surface have a right to support, which is the main question in this case. Our attention has been called very properly to the clauses at pages 56 and 57 of the Act. The clause at page 56 applies
*627]   to the case of the *lord entering on the surface and working there, which is not the case now before us. The clause at page 57 contains a prohibition against working the mines within the perpendicular distance of forty yards from the foundation of any houses. I am of opinion that this is an absolute prohibition against working within that distance, but that it does not confer a right to work beyond it, whatever damage may be done thereby. It is necessary only to say that, though the jury have found there was no negligence in the working, it does not interfere with the plaintiff's right to recover. The complaint in the declaration is that the defendant worked negligently, "and without leaving any proper or sufficient support." The finding of the jury does not negative this, but the contrary.

POLLOCK, C. B., and CRESSWELL, J., concurred.

MARTIN, B.—I will only add that I am inclined to think that the clause at page 56 applies to working the mines in any way; and that a good plea might probably be framed upon it. But on the pleadings the judgment is right.

CROWDER, J., WILLES, J., BRAMWELL, B., and CHANNELL, B., concurred.   Judgment affirmed.

———————

*628]   *KENRICK *v.* HORDER. *April* 30.

To declaration "for that the defendant debauched and carnally knew plaintiff's wife," the defendant pleaded not guilty.
Held that, under this issue, it was not necessary for the plaintiff to prove that a female shown to have been debauched by defendant was the wife of plaintiff.

FIRST count: for "that the defendant debauched and carnally knew plaintiff's wife."

Second count: for converting plaintiff's goods.

Third count: for false imprisonment.

Pleas: 1, to the whole declaration, Not guilty.

2, to the second count, that the said goods were not plaintiff's.

Issues on both pleas.

On the trial, before Lord Campbell, C. J., at the Middlesex Sittings after last Hilary Term, the plaintiff, in support of the first count, gave evidence to show the fact of a criminal intercourse between the defendant and a female who appeared to be treated by the plaintiff and others as the plaintiff's wife: but no further evidence was given of the marriage. As to this count, the counsel for the defendant insisted that the fact of the female being the wife of the plaintiff was put in issue by the plea of Not guilty. The Lord Chief Justice, as to this issue, directed the jury to say whether the criminal intercourse had taken place, and in that case to say what they considered the proper damages : and the jury found that the intercourse had taken place, and assessed the damages at 20*l*. His Lordship then directed a verdict to be entered on this issue for the defendant, reserving leave to move to enter a verdict for the plaintiff for 20*l*. On the issue on the second *plea [*629 the defendant had a verdict : on the issue on the third count the plaintiff had a verdict, with 5*l*. damages.

Edwin James, in last Term, obtained a rule to show cause why a verdict should not be entered for the plaintiff on the first issue for 20*l*. damages, "on the ground that the plaintiff was not bound to prove the marriage in the first count."

Petersdorff now showed cause.—The rule seems to have been obtained on the suggestion that the plea of Not guilty, under the General Rules of Hil. 4 W. 4, does not put in issue the marriage. Under the General Rules of Hil. 4 W. 4, the rule as to actions in Case is in IV. 1.(*a*) [Lord CAMPBELL, C. J.—The rule as to actions in Trespass would be applicable. CROMPTON, J.—I think the rules are the same in each instance ; the object was to distinguish the denial of the plaintiff's right from the denial of the doing of the wrong.] That is so. The rule as to actions in Trespass most applicable to the present case is V. 2,(*b*) where it is ordered that, " In actions of trespass quare clausum fregit, the plea of Not guilty shall operate as a denial that the defendant committed the trespass alleged in the place mentioned, but not as a denial of the plaintiff's possession or right of possession of that place, which, if intended to be denied, must be traversed specially :" or V. 3,(*b*) which orders that, " In actions of trespass de bonis asportatis, the plea of Not guilty shall operate as a denial of the defendant having committed the trespass alleged, by taking or damaging the goods mentioned, but not of the plaintiff's property therein." The rules are similar *in the [*630 Pleading Rules of Hil. 16 Vict.(*c*) The plea here denies the wrong only ; but, if the person debauched be not the wife of the plaintiff, no wrong is done to him. [CROMPTON, J.—It might as well be said that, if the horse converted be not the plaintiff's horse, no wrong is done to him.] The taking is in itself a wrongful act. [ERLE, J.— Not the taking of the goods of the party taking.] As the declaration is framed, a specific traverse could hardly be taken. [Lord CAMPBELL, C. J.—Why cannot the defendant plead that the said woman whom he debauched was not the plaintiff's wife ? CROMPTON, J.—Suppose there were an action for taking the plaintiff's horse.] The defendant might plead that the said horse was not the plaintiff's horse : but how can he

(*a*) 5 B. & Ad. ix. (E. C. L. R. vol. 27).
(*b*) 5 B. & Ad. x.
(*c*) Rules 16 to 20, 1 E. & B. lxxxi. (E. C. L. R. vol. 72).

plead that the said wife is not the plaintiff's wife? If there were a
formal inducement, alleging that one A. was the plaintiff's wife, and
that defendant debauched her, it might be otherwise. [CROMPTON, J.
—Can that make any difference?] It should seem so, from the language
to be found in the books.(a) The real question is, what constitutes the
wrong? In *Card v. Case*, 5 Com. B. 622 (E. C. L. R. vol. 57), the
declaration was in case, and averred that defendant knowingly kept a
ferocious dog, knowing that it was dangerous to let him go at large, yet
wrongfully suffered him to go at large, whereby the dog worried plaintiff's sheep: and it was held that Not guilty put in issue the ferocity
and the scienter. If the proof of the marriage was not necessary here,
the plaintiff would succeed by showing that the defendant had had
carnal *intercourse with any woman whatever. [CROMPTON, J.—
Some proof of identity must be given, certainly.(b)]

*631]

Edwin James and *Welsby*, contrà, were stopped by the Court.

Lord CAMPBELL, C. J.—I am of opinion that this rule must be made
absolute under the General Rules of Hil. 4 W. 4, and the Pleading
Rules of Hil. 16 Vict. In such actions as these (which I hope will not
exist much longer) it is much better that the real evidence should be
confined to that which is the question to be tried. It seems to me that
this case cannot be distinguished from that of an action for the conversion of goods. It does so happen here that the second count is for a
conversion; and there is a plea traversing the property. It seems to
be admitted, in the argument, that Not guilty, pleaded to such a count,
does not put in issue the fact that the goods were the goods of the
plaintiff, or in his possession, but merely denies the defendant's act.
So Not guilty pleaded to the first count puts in issue only the act of
debauching, but admits that the woman debauched is the plaintiff's wife.
It would be very easy to say that she was not so: but the plea of Not
guilty must be construed as in trover.

(WIGHTMAN, J., was absent.)

ERLE, J.—The purpose of the rules of Hil. 4 W. 4, was to narrow
the evidence. Among other things, they *provide that in the
case of an action for the violation of a private right the defendant shall consider whether he will deny both the right and the
violation of it, or only one of these. Here the plaintiff says, My
private right has been violated by you; the defendant might have
said, You have no such right, for the woman is not your wife: but all
he says is that he did not violate the right, did not do the act charged.
The only thing in dispute is, whether the plaintiff did the wrongful act
or not.

*632]

CROMPTON, J.—I cannot distinguish this from the analogous cases.

(a) See *Taverner v. Little*, 5 New Ca. 678 (E. C. L. R. vol. 32); *Hart v. Crowley*, 12 A. & E.
378 (E. C. L. R. vol. 40); *Grew v. Hill*, 3 Exch. 801.†
(b) See *Bond v. Downton*, 2 A. & E. 26 (E. C. L. R. vol. 29).

The defendant must show whether he means to dispute both the existence of the right and the commission of the wrong, or only one of these. The old rule was that the general traverse put in issue all that was material to the right of the plaintiff. But this is narrowed by The General Rules of Hil. 4 W. 4. It would be very strange if it made any difference whether you alleged, by way of inducement, that the woman was the plaintiff's wife, or alleged that the defendant debauched Ann the wife of the plaintiff, or, as here, simply alleged that the defendant debauched the plaintiff's wife. The plaintiff ought not to be put to proof of the marriage when the only question raised is the commission of the wrong. Rule absolute.

----

*HICKS v. SHIELD and GREY. *May* 1. [*633

By charter-party between defendant, owner of a ship, and plaintiff, it was agreed that the ship should proceed from London to B., and there load a cargo from plaintiff's factors, and therewith proceed to London, and deliver the same, on being paid freight at a specified rate: "cash for ship's disbursements, to be advanced to the extent of 300*l*., free of interest, but subject to insurance:" "the freight to be paid, on unloading and right delivery of the cargo, as follows: say, in cash, less two months' interest at," &c., "and, if required, 300*l*. to be paid in cash on arrival, less two months' interest." 300*l*. was advanced by plaintiff's agents at B. for ship's disbursements. Neither plaintiff nor defendants insured in respect of this 300*l*. The ship left B. with a cargo for London, but was lost before reaching London. Plaintiff claimed the payment of the 300*l*., as a loan made to defendants; defendants tendered the amount at which the 300*l*. might have been insured, but refused to pay more.

Held: that plaintiff's claim could not be supported, as it appeared from the charter-party that the advance was not a loan, but was an advance of freight.

In this case, a writ having issued, the following special case was stated, by consent of parties and order of Coleridge, J., under sect. 46 of The Common Law Procedure Act, 1852.

On 21st November, 1854, a charter-party was duly entered into between plaintiff, therein described as G. H. T. Hicks, of London, merchant, and the defendants, therein described as Messrs. Joseph Shield, Sons & Co., owners, &c., (as below): the material parts of the charter-party were as follows. "London, 21st November, 1854. Charter-party. It is this day mutually agreed, between Messrs. Joseph Shield, Sons & Co., owners of the good ship or vessel called the Orestes A. 1, of the burthen," &c., "whereof ———— is at present master, and now in London, and to be despatched from the 8th to 12th December next, and G. H. T. Hicks, Esq., of London, merchant, that the said ship, being tight," &c., "shall, with all convenient speed, sail and proceed to Rangoon and Bassein, or so near thereto as she may safely get, and there load from the factors of the said affreighters a full and complete cargo of rice, in bags, or other lawful produce, the same to be brought to or taken from alongside at *charterer's risk and expense, timber excluded," &c.: "and, being so loaded, shall therewith proceed to London direct, or so near thereunto as she may safely get and [*634 deliver the same, on being paid freight, as follows: 5*l.* 5*s.* per ton, of 20 cwt. net rice delivered; other goods, if any, in proportion, according to the customary scale of tonnage; 2*s.* 6*d.* per ton extra should the ship load at two ports. Cash, for ship's disbursements, to be advanced to the extent of 300*l.*, free of interest, but subject to insurance, and 2¼ per cent. commission, in full of all port charges and pilotages as customary (the act of God," &c., "excepted). The master is to sign bills of lading at any rate of freight required by charterer's agents, without prejudice to this agreement. The freight to be paid, on unloading and right delivery of the cargo, as follows: say, in cash, less two months' interest at 5*l.* per annum, and, if required, 300*l.* to be paid in cash on arrival, less two months' interest. Forty working days are to be allowed," &c.

The ship duly proceeded on her voyage, and reached Bassein, and. having taken in her cargo there, left that port on 19th July, 1855, on her voyage home to London. On 22d July, when off the coast of Bassein, on her voyage homeward, she struck, and became a total wreck. Whilst the ship was at, and before she left, the port of Bassein, Messrs. Berrell & Co., the agents of the plaintiff there, advanced to the master of the ship the cash necessary for the ship's disbursements, to the amount of 378*l.* 16*s.* 10*d.* Their commission for the advance of 300*l.* amounted to the sum of 7*l.* 10*s.*, and, on the advance of the remaining 78*l.* 16*s.* 10*d.*, to 3*l.* 18*s.* 9½*d.* On 18th July the master of the ship drew upon *defendants for 385*l.* 9*s.* 4½*d.*, by a bill of exchange, of which the following is a copy.

*635]

"No. 1. Exchange for 385*l.* 9*s.* 4½*d.* Bassein, 18th July, 1855. At ninety days after sight of this first of exchange (second and third of the same tenor and date unpaid), pay to Messrs. Berrell & Co., or order, the sum of 385*l.* 9*s.* 4½*d.* sterling, value received as cash for ship's disbursements: which place to account of owners of barque Orestes, with or without further advice.

"To Messrs. Joseph Shield, Sons & Co.   "T. B. DAY,
      Newcastle.   Master barque Orestes."

The reason why the Master only drew for 385*l.* 9*s.* 4½*d.* was that plaintiff's agents received 4*l.* 16*s.* 3*d.* on defendants' account at Bassein. This bill was endorsed and transmitted by Messrs. Berrell & Co. to the plaintiff, but not by the first post: and the plaintiff received notice of the loss of the vessel prior to receiving the bill on being informed of the advance of the money. But, had Messrs. Berrell & Co. transmitted the bill by the first post, or that by which the information of the loss of the ship was communicated (which occurred within three days of the vessel leaving the port of Bassein), notice of her loss would in ordinary course have been received some few days previously. as the fact of a wreck is always communicated to Lloyds by telegraph.

When the bill reached England, the plaintiff presented it for acceptance to the defendants. The defendants refused to accept, and wrote to the plaintiff as follows:

"Newcastle-upon-Tyne, 22d October, 1855.

"Sir, Your favour of 20th instant, handing account per Orestes, with Captain T. B. Day's draft for 385*l*. 9*s*. 4*d*., *is duly received. [*636 The draft we herewith return unaccepted, as, by the charter-party, you will doubtless have insured the amount. And, as you will receive the sum from your underwriters, there can be no claim upon your obedient servants, JOS. SHIELD, SONS & CO."

The plaintiff received advice in England of the loss of The Orestes on the 18th September, 1855, and of the advance on the 15th October, 1855. Defendants first knew of the loss of the ship on 22d September, 1855.

The plaintiff did insure part of the cargo by the Orestes; but no insurance of the said sum of 385*l*. 9*s*. 4*d*., or any part thereof, was effected by or on account either of plaintiff or defendants. Defendants insured freight to the extent of 3000*l*. on chartered freight, valued at 3500*l*. on the policy. The defendants have paid the plaintiff the sum of 85*l*. 9*s*. 4½*d*., and tendered him the sum of 12*l*. (being the amount which would have been paid for insuring the said advance of 300*l*. if it had been insured); which the plaintiff refused to receive.

The question for the opinion of the Court is, whether, under the circumstances stated in the case, the defendants are bound to repay to the plaintiff the whole or any part of the sum of 288*l*., being the residue of the said sum of 385*l*. 9*s*. 4½*d*. If the Court shall be of opinion that this question should be answered in the affirmative, then judgment is to be entered for the plaintiff for such sum as the Court shall direct, with costs of suit. And, if the Court shall be of opinion that the question should be answered in the negative, then judgment is to be entered for the defendants, with costs of defence.

Hugh Hill, for the plaintiff.—The plaintiff claims the money [*637 which he has in fact advanced, and which is in the nature of a mere loan: the defendants insist that this was in the nature of an advance of a part of the freight, and that they are therefore entitled to retain it, according to what is said in the Anonymous(a) case in Shower, where it is laid down that where part of the freight is advanced, though the ship be lost, wages must be paid, in proportion to the freight paid; and the reason given is that "the freighters cannot have their money." Reliance will probably be placed on De Silvale *v.* Kendall, 4 M. & S. 37 (E. C. L. R. vol. 30). There the freighter, by the charter-party, was to advance cash for freight and necessary ship's disbursements, "the residue of such freight to be paid on delivery of the cargo" in the port of delivery. The advances were made, and the cargo shipped; but the vessel was lost before arriving at the port of delivery.

(a) 2 Show. 283.

it was held that the freighter could not recover back the money advanced. There, however, the word "residue" was considered to explain the nature of the advance: no such expression occurs here And in Manfield v. Maitland, 4 B. & Ald. 582 (E. C. L. R. vol. 6), in consequence of the absence of words to suggest the same interpretation, it was held that the words in the memorandum of the charter-party, "the captain to be supplied with cash for the ship's use," showed no more than that the supply was a loan by the freighter to the ship-owner, so that the freighter had no insurable interest in that sum. The two cases of Stainbank v. Fenning, 11 Com. B. 51 (E. C. L. R. vol. 73), and Stainbank v. Shepard, 13 Com. B. 418 (E. C. L. R. vol. 76),
*638] illustrate the same principle. Then what is the most natural *interpretation here? The understanding of the parties appears from the form of the bill drawn, which is not for freight, but for "value received as cash for ship's disbursements." The charter-party contains distinct stipulations for payment of freight, without reference to the sum advanced, and indeed not consistent with the supposition that an advance of freight has taken place. [Lord CAMPBELL, C. J.—The advance is to be free of interest, but subject to insurance. CROMPTON, J.—Could the plaintiff insure his interest in a mere loan?] Perhaps not. [CROMPTON, J.—Who was to effect the insurance here?] The defendants, for whose benefit it was effected. [CROMPTON, J.—What insurable interest would they have? They would be exposed to no sea risk in respect of the 300l.] An argument might possibly be suggested, but no more, in favour of the defendants from the insertion of the stipulation as to insurance: but this cannot countervail the inference arising from the distinct stipulation as to the whole freight. [CROMP-TON, J.—That may mean, the freight which would remain due. Lord CAMPBELL, C. J.—Unless the 300l. were an advance in respect of freight, it would not be insurable at all.(a)]

Manisty, contrà, was stopped by the Court.

Lord CAMPBELL, C. J.—The only question is whether this was a mere loan or an advance of freight. We must make our construction from what appears on the face of the instrument. A sum of 300l. is
*639] to be advanced, subject to certain deductions, one of which *is for insurance. If it is to be insured, it must be for freight in advance; for a mere loan could not be insured: and, if it is not a mere loan, but advance of freight, the plaintiff cannot recover it back.

WIGHTMAN and ERLE, Js., concurred.

CROMPTON, J.—My opinion is that way. The clauses appear to be inconsistent; but I think they may be reconciled by this construction.
                                        Judgment for defendants.

(a) See Hall v. Janson, 4 E. & B. 500 (E. C. L. R. vol. 82).

TIGHE v. COOPER. *May* 1.

Declaration alleged that plaintiff was cashier to Q., and that defendant, in a letter addressed to Q., falsely and maliciously wrote and published of plaintiff the words "I conceive there is nothing too base for him to be guilty of."

Plea, in justification, alleged that plaintiff signed and delivered to defendant an I. O. U., and afterwards, on having sight thereof, falsely and fraudulently asserted that the signature was not his; and the plea averred that the libel was written and published solely in reference to this transaction.

Held: a sufficient justification, as the libel must be understood with reference to the subject-matter.

THE declaration alleged that, before and after the committing, &c., plaintiff was servant, to wit, cashier, to William Quinn and John Davison of Leeds, in, &c.: and the defendant falsely and maliciously wrote and published of the plaintiff, in a certain letter addressed to the said W. Quinn, the words following, that is to say: There is a duplicity about your bookkeeper (meaning the plaintiff) in serving your interest in this affair of ours, which is sadly too transparent. No doubt he would like to ascertain the date, and to have a look at the mem. I gratified him with the latter; the former, if he could have obtained, he would have used *greatly to advantage; for I conceive there is nothing too [*640 base for him (meaning the plaintiff) to be guilty of.

Plea (2). That, before defendant wrote and published of plaintiff, in the said letter addressed to the said W. Quinn, the words in the declaration in that behalf mentioned, defendant lent to W. Quinn the sum of 15*l.*, and on that occasion, and as a security to the defendant for the said sum of 15*l.*, plaintiff, at the request of W. Quinn, made and signed, with his own name and in his own handwriting, and delivered to defendant, a certain memorandum, commonly called an I. O. U., by which plaintiff acknowledged that he owed defendant the sum of 15*l.*; and that afterwards, and before defendant wrote and published of the plaintiff in the said letter addressed to W. Quinn the said words, defendant lent to W. Quinn a further sum of 15*l.*; and, on that occasion and as a security to defendant for the said last-mentioned sum of 15*l.*, plaintiff, at the request of W. Quinn, made and signed with his own name and in his own handwriting, and delivered to defendant, another memorandum, commonly called an I. O. U., by which plaintiff acknowledged that he owed defendant another sum of 15*l.*: which said memorandums were and are the same memorandums in the declaration mentioned and referred to, and not other or different memorandums. That, after defendant had lent the said two sums of 15*l.* each to W. Quinn, and the plaintiff had so made, signed, and delivered to defendant the said respective memorandums, and before defendant wrote and published of plaintiff, in the said letter addressed to W. Quinn, the said words, defendant applied to W. Quinn and to plaintiff for the repayment to him, defendant, of the said sums so by him lent as

*641] *aforesaid, but was unable to obtain the repayment thereof: and certain disputes and differences arose between the defendant and W. Quinn and plaintiff of and concerning the said loans: which said disputes and differences were and are the same affair as the affair in the declaration mentioned and therein described as this affair of ours. That afterwards, and before defendant wrote and published of plaintiff. in the said letter addressed to W. Quinn, the said words, plaintiff requested defendant to produce and show to plaintiff the said memorandums, upon which request defendant produced and showed to plaintiff the said first-mentioned memorandum. Whereupon plaintiff, upon being so shown the said first-mentioned memorandum, and upon his having sight thereof, falsely and fraudulently asserted that the signature of plaintiff to the same memorandum, so made and signed by plaintiff as aforesaid, was not the signature or handwriting of plaintiff. Whereupon defendant refused to produce or show to plaintiff the said memorandum secondly above mentioned, believing and suspecting, from and by reason of the plaintiff's said false and fraudulent denial of his signature and handwriting, that, if defendant showed to plaintiff the memorandum secondly above mentioned, plaintiff would take an unfair advantage thereof against defendant. Wherefore, and because plaintiff so falsely and fraudulently denied his said signature and handwriting, defendant afterwards wrote and sent to W. Quinn the said letter so addressed to W. Quinn of and concerning the said loans, and the said disputes and differences, and wrote and published therein the said words of plaintiff, the same being solely in reference to the said memorandums,

*642] disputes, and differences, and *the said false and fraudulent denial by the plaintiff of his said signature and handwriting as aforesaid.

Demurrer.   Joinder.

Unthank, for the plaintiff.—The plea does not state enough to justify the words in the declaration. A statement may be untrue, and yet the party making it not be capable of all possible baseness. [CROMPTON, J.—The plea alleges the assertion to be falsely and fraudulently made. ERLE, J.—Surely we need not take the words complained of in more than their common sense: they mean that the plaintiff is very base.] There are numerous authorities showing that the justification should strictly apply to the very words complained of. [ERLE, J.—The words mean that nothing in this particular line of transaction is too base for the plaintiff. CROMPTON, J.—I recollect being satisfied, early in my professional life, that I could justify the calling a man "a rugged Russian bear" by showing that his manners were rough.]

Joseph Addison, contrà, was stopped by the Court.

Lord CAMPBELL, C. J.—The plaintiff may vindicate his character by traversing the plea. But the plea, as it stands, is a justification.

WIGHTMAN, ERLE, and CROMPTON, Js., concurred.

Judgment for the defendant.

*The QUEEN *v.* The Justices of PETERBOROUGH. *May* 7. [*643

An order of removal made on 6th Sept., 1856, was duly served on 10th. On 21st September a letter, dated 20th, was received by the respondents from the clerk of the appellants, stating certain facts as to the paupers, and adding, "I shall on these grounds appeal against your order." On 29th September copies of depositions were applied for, and received on 30th. Notice of intention "to commence an appeal at the next general Quarter Sessions" was duly received on 8th October. At the next Quarter Sessions, held on 16th October, the appeal was not entered or respited; and the respondents applied for costs, which were, however, refused. On 20th October, the paupers were removed. On 23d December another notice of appeal, and grounds of appeal, were served. At the next Sessions, held 8th January, 1857, both parties appeared; but, after argument, the justices refused to hear the appeal.

Held that the justices acted rightly, and that the appellants ought to have entered and respited the appeal, even though they could not have tried it, at the October Sessions.

Held also that, in judging of the "practicability" of the next Sessions, the time of service of the order of removal was the proper time to reckon from.

HUDDLESTON, in last Hilary Term, obtained a rule Nisi for a mandamus commanding the justices for the liberty of Peterborough to enter continuances and hear an appeal by the trustees of the poor of the parish of Saint Leonard, Shoreditch, in the county of Middlesex, against an order for the removal of Eleanor Cockshaw and her four children from the parish of Peterborough, in the said liberty of Peterborough, to the said parish of St. Leonard, Shoreditch.

From the affidavits on which the rule was obtained the following facts appeared. The order of removal was made on the 6th September, 1856; and a copy thereof, with grounds of removal and notice of chargeability, was received by the appellants on the 10th September. On the 20th September the following letter was written by Henry Edwards, clerk to the appellants, and received by the respondents on the 21st.

"Shoreditch Workhouse, 20th September, 1856.
"Re Cockshaw and family.

"Gentlemen: Upon inquiring into this case I find *that these [*644 paupers are settled in St. Pancras, Middlesex, by parentage. Evan and Margaret Jones, he father and mother of the pauper Eleanor Cockshaw, were married at St. Pancras Church in December, 1817. They then went to live in Cromer Street, St. Pancras, where they occupied three unfurnished rooms, at five shillings per week rent, for six or seven months. The parents have not gained any subsequent settlement; and I shall, on these grounds, appeal against your order. This information is given to me by the pauper's mother, who is living in this parish, and is receiving relief simply on account of her irremovability by residence. If she had been removable, she would have been passed to St. Pancras long since. I shall be glad to hear from you respecting the matter at your earliest convenience. I am, Gentlemen, yours obediently, HENRY EDWARDS, clerk to the trustees of the poor of St. Leonard, Shoreditch. To the churchwardens and overseers of the parish of Peterborough."

Copies of the depositions, on which the order was made, were applied for by the appellants on the 29th September, and received on the 30th September.   On the 6th October the appellants sent, by post, to the respondents a notice, dated 26th September, that they did "intend, at the next general Quarter Sessions of the peace to be holden for the said liberty of Peterborough, to commence an appeal" against the order; and this notice was duly received on the 8th October.   The next general Quarter Sessions for the liberty of Peterborough com-, menced oṅ the 16th October.   No appeal was entered by the appellants; nor did they appear in any way at such Sessions: whereupon *645] the respondents applied for their costs; but the Court, *after considering the letter of the 20th September and the notice of appeal, declined to make an order for such costs, on the ground that the appeal had been abandoned, and that the paupers would now be sent to Shoreditch.   The paupers were removed on the 20th October; ·and, according to the affidavits on which cause was shown, such removal was made under the belief that the appeal had been abandoned.   On the 23d December another notice of appeal against the same order, together with grounds of appeal, was served on the respondents.   This notice stated that the appellants did "intend, at the next general Quarter Sessions of the peace to be holden in and for the said liberty of Peterborough, to commence and prosecute an appeal of which you have already had notice against an order," &c.   On the 8th January, 1857, the Epiphany Sessions (being the next general Quarter Sessions) were held: both parties attended; and, after hearing the arguments on both sides, the Court refused to hear the appeal.

Hugh Hill and *Cockle* now showed cause.—First, the appeal should have been entered and respited, even though it could not have been tried at the October Sessions; and, no steps having been taken by the appellants at those Sessions, the justices were right in refusing to let an appeal be entered at the Epiphany Sessions.   It is clear that next Sessions, in cases of appeal, mean next practicable Sessions; and the question will be, whether the October Sessions were, in this case, the next practicable Sessions.   If they were (and, upon a comparison of the dates, it will be found that this is the case), the appellants were *646] bound to go to those *Sessions and enter and respite their appeal; and no subsequent Sessions had jurisdiction to set right the omission: Regina *v.* Sevenoaks, 7 Q. B. 136 (E. C. L. R. vol. 53). In that case the appeal could not have been tried at the October Sessions owing to the notice of trial having been given too late.   Patteson, J., says: "The October Sessions were the next practicable Sessions, though it is now settled that the appellants were not compelled to try: but then, in order to keep the appeal, of which they served notice too late for trial, alive, they were bound to enter and respite it at those Sessions; for it is only when the next Sessions are so early as not to be practicable Sessions that the appellants are entitled to pass them by entirely." Wightman, J., says: "The October Sessions were the next practicable Sessions; but the appellants gave their notice so late that it became impracticable to go to trial at those Sessions: that being so, they were bound to enter and respite there; and, as that was not done, the Epiphany Sessions had no jurisdiction over the appeal." That case is a direct authority that, assuming that the appellants could not have tried the appeal at the October Sessions, still they were bound to enter and respite it, otherwise they would mislead the respondents, who, having received a notice in October of the intention to commence an appeal at the next Sessions, and not finding an entry of appeal, were led to treat it as abandoned, and remove the pauper.

But, in fact, in this case, the order of removal was served on 10th September; it was quite practicable to try any appeal against it at the October Sessions: and, if the appellants choose to lie by, and not apply for the *depositions, so as to secure the additional fourteen days granted under stat. 11 & 12 Vict. c. 31, s. 9, till too late to give [*647 effectual notice of trial, it did not render the Sessions impracticable. Besides, the letter of the 20th September was a good notice of appeal: Regina v. Recorder of Liverpool, 15 Q. B. 1070 (E. C. L. R. vol. 69). It contains the grounds of appeal, and is signed and sent by the proper party. There were therefore twenty-six days from the notice to the Sessions.

Huddleston, contrà.—The rule is this: if the Sessions in question are the next practicable Sessions, entry and respite is necessary; if they are not, no notice at all need be taken of those Sessions. [ERLE, J.—Regina v. Sevenoaks is an authority against that.] That was a case of a suspended order, where, by stat. 49 G. 8, c. 124, s. 2, the time of appealing is computed from the time of service of the order; and the October Sessions were therefore, in that case, the next practicable Sessions. [Lord CAMPBELL, C. J.—The practicability of the Sessions in the present case must be with reference to the service of notice of removal.] It was impossible for the appellants to try at the October Sessions. [WIGHTMAN, J.—I do not see the impossibility. They might have got the depositions earlier, though they were not perhaps bound to do so.] Unless the appeal could be tried at the October Sessions it was not necessary that it should be entered: Rex v. Justices of Devon, 8 B. & C. 640, n. (a) (E. C. L. R. vol. 15). There Lord Tenterden held that "the entry for the mere purpose of adjournment is an useless act, and only occasions unnecessary expense." In Regina v. *The Justices of Surrey, 8 D. & L. 843, it was said [*648 by Wightman, J., that appellants are not bound to enter and respite an appeal against an order of removal at the next Sessions after service of the order, unless the next Sessions are practicable *for all purposes*. [ERLE, J.—The appellants cannot, by lying by and not

serving notice of appeal, make the October Sessions, which were practicable when the order was served, impracticable. This is distinctly
held by my brother Wightman in Regina *v.* Sevenoaks.] As to the
respondents being misled: they need not and ought not to have gone
to the October Sessions, because no grounds of appeal had been delivered: there were none given till the 23d December. [Lord CAMPBELL,
C. J.—The respondents were right to go, because they coupled the
September letter with the October notice.]

Lord CAMPBELL, C. J.—I am of opinion that this rule should be
discharged. The Justices at the Epiphany Sessions were not bound to
receive and hear this appeal. It is clear that the Legislature has sim-
plified the removal of paupers with a view of lessening the expense
and uncertainty of such proceedings. They have restrained the right
of appeal, and anxiously tried to provide a time when the removing
parish might be safe in effecting the removal. Here the removal was
on the 20th October; and the respondents had good reason then to
believe that the appeal was abandoned. The notice of the 20th September is by no means to be kept out of sight; and, coupling it with
the subsequent notice of the 6th October, I think the respondents were
*649] perfectly justified in concluding *that the appeal was abandoned,
when they found that nothing was done at the October Sessions.
It would be most unjust if, after such conduct on the part of the appellants, and after all the expense of removal has been incurred, the respondents should be liable to have another appeal commenced against
them. What are "practicable Sessions" has been clearly pointed out
by my brother Wightman in the case referred to during the argument. They are the Sessions at which the parties desiring to appeal
might bring on such appeal by reasonable diligence; and it cannot be
that the appellants may lie by and delay, as has been contended in this
case.

WIGHTMAN, J., concurred.

ERLE, J.—I am clearly of the same opinion. The October Sessions
were the next practicable Sessions following upon an order served, as
in the present case, on the 10th September. The utmost limit of the
time for appealing sanctioned by the law is twenty-one days, and a
contingent fourteen days from the receipt of the deposition. And this
is in accordance with the decision of Regina *v.* Sevenoaks. The time
of service of the order of removal is, according to that case, the time
to be considered with reference to the practicability or impracticability
of the next Sessions; and I entirely concur in the decision. The
appellants here should have entered and respited the appeal at the
October Sessions as the next practicable Sessions. I think the notice
of September was a perfectly valid notice, and that the respondents
reasonably coupled it with the October notice; and that they were jus-

tified in considering that *the appeal was abandoned, when no [*650
steps were taken by the appellants at the October Sessions. I
agree with my Lord that the Legislature, seeing how great were the
expenses incurred, and how great was the annoyance caused to the
friends of the pauper, while the case was in suspense, made strenuous
efforts to force appellants to take definite steps within definite times.

CROMPTON, J., concurred.

Rule discharged with costs.(a)

(a) Reported by Henry T. Holland, Esq.

———◆———

ARABELLA MARSHALL THOMPSON HARDING v. RICHARD NOTT, Clerk.

The interest in the residue of a term of years in land was devised to R., his executors, &c.,
subject to a proviso that, if R. or his issue male should become actually entitled to land comprised in the will of N., the interest in the term should go over to another party.

By N.'s will, lands were devised to J. for life, remainder to trustees to preserve contingent
remainders, remainder to J.'s first and other sons in tail general, remainder to R., remainder
to trustees to preserve contingent remainders, remainder to R.'s first and other sons in tail
general.

On the death of the devisor of the term, R. became possessed of the land devised for the term.
He died; and his issue male entered into possession.

After R.'s death, J. died without issue, and the remainder to R.'s sons, under N.'s will, took
effect.

Held, that the interest of R.'s representative in the term was not defeated, the proviso being bad
for remoteness; for that, even if the proviso could be construed as contemplating independent
alternatives, namely, the devolution of the estates comprised in N.'s will either to R. or to his
issue male, still the alternative limitation under which alone, in the event, the proviso could
operate, was the devolution to R.'s issue male, which alternative limitation was originally bad
for remoteness.

And that it made no difference that in fact the devolution of the estate under N.'s will to R.'s
issue male occurred during lives in being at the time of R.'s will.

A WRIT of summons having issued in this case, a case was stated, by
consent, and order of Coleridge, J., for the opinion of this Court,
under sect. 46 *of The Common Law Procedure Act, 1852. The [*651
material statements in the case were as follows.

Richard Harding, hereinafter referred to as Richard Harding the
father, was, at the date of his will after mentioned, seised in fee simple
of a messuage or tenement called Beare ; and he was also possessed of
two messuages or tenements called respectively Higher Buzzacott and
Lower Buzzacott, for the residues of terms of 1500 and 2000 years,
computed respectively from 11th October, 1572, and 20th October, 1714,
or of some other long terms.

He duly made his will, dated 23d August, 1831, executed and attested
in manner then required by law for the devise of freehold estates. He
thereby devised Beare to trustees for 500 years, on certain trusts, and,
subject to the term, to his son Richard Harding (hereinafter referred

to as Richard Harding the son) in fee. He devised Higher **Buzzacott**
and Lower Buzzacott to Richard Harding the son, his executors, administrators, and assigns, for the residue of the testator's interest therein.
The will then contained the following proviso. "Provided always that,
if, by virtue of any of the limitations contained in the last will and
testament of my brother-in-law James Nott, late of Torr Down, in the
said county, Esquire, deceased, my said son Richard Harding, or the
issue male of his body, shall become actually entitled to the possession,
or to the receipt of the rents and profits, of the messuages, lands, and
tenements comprised in such will, and my said son John Nott Harding,
or any issue male of his body, shall be then living, then I do give, devise,
and bequeath the hereinbefore mentioned messuage and tenement, called
*652] Beare, and the said messuages and tenements called *Higher
Buzzacott and Lower Buzzacott, with their respective rights,
members, and appurtenances (subject as aforesaid), to the said John
Nott Harding, his heirs, executors, administrators, and assigns, for
and during all my right, term, and interest therein respectively, under
and subject to the same proviso and condition as I have given the said
messuages and tenements to my said son Richard. But, if my said son
John Nott Harding shall then happen to be dead, without having any
lawful issue male of his body, or shall become actually entitled to the
possession, or to the receipt of the rents and profits, of the messuages,
lands, and tenements late of the said James Nott, deceased, under and
by virtue of his said will, then I do give the said several messuages
and tenements called Beare and Higher Buzzacott and Lower Buzzacott (subject as aforesaid) to my said son Robert Harding, his heirs,
executors, administrators, and assigns, for and during all my right,
term, and interest therein respectively."

Richard Harding the father died 31st October, 1831 ; and, on 31st
December, 1831, his will was proved by the executors, who assented to
the bequest of Higher Buzzacott and Lower Buzzacott.

Richard Harding the son, after his father's death, entered into possession of Beare, Higher Buzzacott and Lower Buzzacott. By his will,
dated 8th April, 1836, he devised to his wife Higher and Lower Buzzacott, and The Floodgate Meadow (which is held and treated as part
of one of them), with their appurtenances, for life ; and, after her
decease, to his son the defendant, Richard Nott (therein called Richard
Harding), his executors, administrators, and assigns. He died on
10th March, 1841 ; and administration of his estate, with the will
*653] *annexed, was, on 12th February, 1844, granted to his wife,
who assented to the bequest of Higher Buzzacott and Lower
Buzzacott.

The wife died 10th April, 1855 : and the defendant Richard Nott
became possessed of Higher Buzzacott and Lower Buzzacott. He has
attained his age of twenty-one years ; and, by the Queen's license

dated 27th June, 1856, he assumed the name of Nott in lieu of Harding. He is in possession of Higher and Lower Buzzacott; and he has also. in the events hereinafter mentioned, become, by virtue of the limitations contained in the will of the said James Nott, actually entitled to the possession, or the receipt of the rents and profits, of the messuages, lands, and tenements comprised in such will.

The said will bears date 9th June, 1809; and the limitations contained therein, so far as it is necessary to state them, are as follows. James Nott devised his freehold messuages, lands, and tenements called Torr Down, in the parish of Swymbridge, Devonshire, to trustees in fee, in trust to permit his sister Susan to receive the rents and profits for her life; and upon further trust to convey the same, with certain other freeholds, messuages, lands, and tenements, to the use of his nephew John Nott, when he should attain the age of twenty-one years, for life, remainder to trustees to preserve contingent remainders, remainder to the first and other sons of the said John Nott in tail general; remainder to the use of the testator's nephew James Nott, when he should attain the age of twenty-one years, for life, remainder to trustees to preserve contingent remainders, remainder to the first and other sons of the nephew James Nott in tail general; remainder to testator's nephew Richard Harding the son for life, remainder to *trustees to preserve contingent remainders, remainder to the first and other sons of Richard Harding the son; remainder [*654 over. Other freehold property was similarly limited, except that, as to a part of it, the estates given to James Nott the nephew and his sons preceded the estates given to John Nott the nephew and his sons; both preceding the estates given to Richard Harding the son and his sons. There were also some other variations in the disposition of the different properties: but, in the events which happened, they did not vary the question now brought before the Court, the last of the interests prior to that of Richard Harding the son and his issue having expired after the death of Richard Harding the son; and therefore such variations are not further noticed in this report. There was a proviso that, when any of the testator's nephews, Richard Harding the son and others, not including John Nott and James Nott, should, by virtue of the limitations, become entitled in possession to the freehold messuages, lands, and tenements in Swymbridge, and receive the rents and profits thereof, they should take the surname of Nott only, and bear the arms of the testator's family, and use their utmost endeavours to procure His Majesty's license, &c.

The testator, James Nott, died on 9th August, 1809; and his will was duly proved.

By lease and release and assignment of 21st and 22d May, 1828, and 24th October, 1856, the freehold and leasehold hereditaments devised by the testator James Nott's will were conveyed, by the proper parties, to the uses directed by the will, to the defendant Richard Nott, his heirs, executors, administrators, and assigns.

*655]   *James Nott, the nephew, died many years since, under the age of twenty-one years, without having been married.

John Nott, the nephew, attained the age of twenty-one years, and died on 12th March, 1856, without having been married.

Robert Harding (named in the proviso of the will of Richard Harding, the father), by his will of 17th February, 1857, after certain bequests and devises not affecting Higher Buzzacott and Lower Buzzacott, devised the residue of his real and personal estate (including those tenements) to his wife, the plaintiff, Arabella Marshall Thomson Harding, her heirs, executors, administrators, and assigns, for her absolute use and benefit, and appointed her sole executrix. He died on 19th February, 1857 ; and the plaintiff has assented to the bequest in her favour.

The said plaintiff, A. M. T. Harding, alleges that, inasmuch as, by virtue of the limitations contained in the said will of the said testator, James Nott, the defendant, Richard Nott, has become actually entitled to the possession or to the receipt of the rents and profits of the said messuages, lands, and tenements comprised in the last-mentioned will, she, the said A. M. T. Harding (as such executrix and legatee as aforesaid), has become, and is, by virtue of the said will of the said Richard Harding, the father, absolutely entitled in possession to the said messuages and tenements called respectively Higher Buzzacott and Lower Buzzacott, for all the residue of the said several terms of 1500 and 2000 years, or of such other terms as aforesaid.

The said Richard Nott denies her to be so entitled.

*656]   *The question for the opinion of the Court is : Whether the said A. M. T. Harding is, in the events which have happened, entitled in possession to the messuages and tenements called respectively Higher Buzzacott and Lower Buzzacott, for the residue of the said several terms of 1500 and 2000 years, or of such other terms as aforesaid.

If the Court shall be of opinion in the affirmative, then it is agreed that the judgment of the Court shall be entered for the said A. M. T. Harding for the sum of 1s. without costs. But, if the Court shall be of opinion in the negative, then the judgment of the Court shall be entered for the said Richard Nott, for the sum of 1s. without costs.

The case was argued in this Term.(a)

Montague Smith, for the plaintiff.—The plaintiff is entitled to the leasehold lands as devisee of Robert Harding, who became entitled to them by virtue of the proviso in the will of Richard Harding, the father ; for the event there contemplated has occurred, Richard Nott, the issue male of the body of Richard Harding, the son, having become

(a) April 28th and 29th. Before Lord Campbell, C. J., Wightman, Erle, and Crompton, Js.

actually entitled to the possession and receipt of the rents and profits of the messuages, &c., comprised in the will of James Nott. It is objected, on behalf of the defendant, that this limitation is bad for remoteness. Now, by the will of James Nott, the first remainder, after Susan's life estate, is to John Nott and his sons in tail: had that estate tail taken effect, *it might at any time have been barred by the [*657 tenant in tail in possession: and so the contingency contemplated in the will of Richard Harding, the father, would not have occurred; and thus the limitation would have been capable of being defeated within the legal time: Nicolls v. Sheffield, 2 Br. Ch. Ca. 215. [CROMPTON, J.—The objection as to remoteness does not apply to an estate which can be barred; but the difficulty is as to the limitations in the will of Richard Harding, the father.] As to that, the limitations are on independent alternative contingencies; and the case may be considered to be within the rule in 1 Jarman on Wills, 231, &c. (2d ed.) One contingency, that of the devolution of the Nott estates in the lifetime of Richard Harding, would be within the life of Richard Harding; and so the proviso would take effect within the legal time; the limitation may therefore be supported: Leake v. Robinson, 2 Mer. 363. [CROMPTON, J.—Are the limitations alternative or successive?] The estates have in fact devolved within the time of lives in being at the time of the death of the devisor, Richard Harding, the father.

Butt, contrà.—That event cannot affect the question whether the limitation at its creation was too remote. [Lord CAMPBELL, C. J.— Certainly not.] The limitation under which the plaintiff claims clearly was too remote. The plaintiff claims because the issue male of Richard Harding, the son, has become entitled to the Nott estates: that event might have happened at any the most remote point of time. It is therefore unimportant that there *was an alternative under [*658 which, if it had occurred, the plaintiff might have claimed: Proctor v. Bishop of Bath and Wells, 2 H. Bl. 358, Lanesborough v. Fox, 3 Br. P. C. 130 (2d ed.), Grey v. Montagu, 2 Eden, 205.

Montague Smith was heard in reply.   *Cur. adv. vult.*

Lord CAMPBELL, C. J., in this Term (May 5th), delivered the judgment of the Court.

In this case Richard Harding, by will, dated the 23d August, 1831, bequeathed certain leaseholds called Buzzacott to his son, Richard Harding, his executors, administrators, and assigns, subject to an executory devise over if Richard Harding, the son, or the issue male of his body, should become entitled to certain lands under the will of one James Nott (dated 9th June, 1809), whereby a remainder was limited for life to Richard Harding, the son, with remainder in tail male to his first and other sons lawfully begotten. The defendant is the eldest son of Richard Harding, the son, and has succeeded to the estates devised by the will of James Nott. The plaintiff is entitled to the leaseholds if they went over on the other estates vesting in the defendant. And the question for our opinion is, Whether, on the defendant succeeding to the estate, under the will of James Nott, the leaseholds passed by the executory devise.

*659]   In our opinion they did not pass. The executory *devise over is to take effect on the succession of Richard Harding, the son, or the issue male of his body, to the property under the will of James Nott. Even supposing the limitation over in the event of Richard, the son, succeeding to the life estate in the lands devised by James Nott, could be considered as an independent and alternative limitation on an event which must take place in his lifetime, it would be of no avail to the plaintiff, whose claim is founded on that part of the proviso which directs the leaseholds to go over if *the issue male of Richard Harding. the son*, should become entitled to the lands devised by the will of James Nott. And this part of the proviso, whether coupled with the preceding part or standing alone, is most clearly bad for remoteness, as the issue male of Richard, the son, were only to take on an indefinite failure of the issue of the prior parties in the remainders under James Nott's will; and there is nothing to limit the time of their so taking to any time within the allowed period.

Our judgment therefore is for the defendant.

Judgment for defendant.

The rule against perpetuities—that an executory devise must be so limited as certainly to vest during a life or lives in being, and twenty-one years afterwards—has been fully recognised in the United States: Biscoe *v.* Biscoe, 6 Gill & Johns. 232; Guery *v.* Vernon, 1 Nott & McCord. 69; Adams *v.* Chaplin, 1 Hill Ch. 265; Booker *v.* Booker, 5 Humph. 505; Rapp *v.* Rapp, 6 Barr, 45; Bell *v.* Scammon, 15 New Hamp 381; St. Amour *v.* Rivard, 2 Mich. 294.

---

*660]   *In the Matter of W. C. PENNY and The SOUTH EASTERN RAILWAY COMPANY. *May* 7.

Compensation cannot be claimed under the Lands Clauses and Railways Clauses Consolidation Acts, 1845 (8 & 9 Vict. c. 18, and 8 & 9 Vict. c. 20), for deterioration in the value of property adjoining a railway, by reason of the premises being overlooked by persons on the railway and railway platform.

Actual injury to premises from the vibration caused by ballast trains, &c., on the railway. during the construction of the works, is a ground for compensation under these statutes: but. per Lord Campbell, C. J., not injury from that cause after the construction of the railway.

Where a jury, summoned under stat. 8 & 9 Vict. c. 18, s. 68, have taken into consideration, in awarding compensation, one claim, among others, as to which they had no jurisdiction. a certiorari lies, although such excess of jurisdiction does not appear upon the face of the proceedings.

Such excess of jurisdiction may be shown upon affidavit.

WILDE, in last Easter Term, obtained a rule calling on W. C. Penny to show cause why a certiorari should not issue to remove into this Court an inquisition taken before the sheriff of Kent, or his deputy, by virtue of a warrant under the seal of The South Eastern Railway Company to the said sheriff, directing him to summon a jury, under the provisions of The Lands Clauses Consolidation Act, 1845, to determine whether certain lands of the said W. C. Penny had been injuriously affected by the execution of the works of the said Company, and what compensation, if any, the said W. C. Penny was entitled to against the said Company; and the verdict and judgment given upon the said inquisition.

From the affidavits in support of the motion it appeared that, by stat. 9 & 10 Vict. c. cccv.,(a) The South Eastern Railway Company were empowered to construct a railway, called The North Kent Railway. *The special Act, by sect. 2, incorporated with it the [*661 "several provisions of" The Lands Clauses Consolidation Act, 1845, and The Railways Consolidation Act, 1845, "so far as the same may be applicable." The North Kent Railway was duly constructed by the Company, under the provisions of the said Acts, and was opened for public traffic in July, 1849. It passed near to certain lands and premises of W. C. Penny, at Lewisham; but no part of them was taken or used for the purposes of the railway. On 21st April, 1856, Penny served on the Company notice and particulars of his claim for compensation "for damage and injury done or caused to be done and which will hereafter arise and be occasioned to the property of the said W. C. Penny, by the exercise by the said Company of the powers conferred on the said Company by the several Acts of Parliament relating thereto, and by the execution by the said Company of the works connected with the said railway, and by the working of the said railway by the said Company, and consequential thereon." The particulars described the property, and Penny's interest therein, and stated that a deterioration to the amount of 19l. per annum had arisen in the value of the rentals, in addition to the necessity for repairs of the houses, "from the close approximation of the railway to the property, and the constant noise, and shaking, and annoyance by day and night caused by the passage of the trains, particularly the special luggage and ballast trains, and by or from the circumstance of the back windows and gardens being overlooked by the passengers on the railway and railway platform and by the servants and workmen employed by the Company, and the privacy of the said W. C. Penny and his family and of *his tenants being thereby invaded and disturbed; and also by [*662 the effluvium arising from the waste water which is frequently let out of the engines or boilers on the trains staying to take up and set down passengers at the railway station." The notice further

(a) Local and personal, public: "To enable The South Eastern Railway Company to make a railway from the London and Greenwich Railway to Woolwich and Gravesend."

required the Company to take the necessary steps for having the said claim for compensation, amounting to 475*l.*, settled by a jury. On 12th May, 1856, the Company issued their warrant to the sheriff, for a jury, under sect. 68 of The Lands Clauses Consolidation Act, 1845, "to determine and settle, by their verdict," "whether the said lands or property, or the interest of the said W. C. Penny therein, have or has been injuriously affected by the execution of the works authorised by the Acts relating to the said South Eastern Railway Company, or any of them; and, if the same have been so injuriously affected, what compensation, if any, the said W. C. Penny is entitled to as against the said Company in respect of the said lands or property, or his interest therein, having been so injuriously affected as aforesaid."

At the inquisition, which was held before the under-sheriff on 2d June, 1856, the counsel for the Company objected to any investigation of the claim, on the ground of want of jurisdiction; but the under-sheriff overruled the objection. The counsel for the Company then objected to the reception of any evidence of damage from the approximation of the railway, or from the user of it by the Company, as distinguished from the execution and construction of the works, and called upon the under-sheriff to direct the jury that Penny was not entitled to compensation in respect of any of the matters mentioned in his claim. The evidence was admitted. The under-sheriff, in summing

*663] up, told the *jury that they were, by the Act, the judges of both law and facts, but that it was probably his duty to guide them as to the law: that, in his opinion, damage occasioned by the ordinary noise of the trains was not a ground of compensation, and that there was no evidence of any other than ordinary noise; that he had also a strong opinion that the claim on account of the depreciation in the annual value of the property by the proximity of the railway was not a legal one; but that he was of opinion that the claim for compensation in respect of the overlooking of the premises by persons upon the railway platform near the same was matter for compensation, upon the ground that, by raising a higher fence, the Company might remove the ground of complaint. He further told the jury that, in his opinion, Penny was entitled to compensation for injury occasioned to his said premises by the vibration of the trains passing over the said railway; and directed the jury that they might, according to law, give the claimant compensation in respect of the said several matters as they thought fit. The jury found that the property of the plaintiff had been "injuriously affected by the execution of the works authorised by the Acts relating to" the Company, and assessed the compensation at 100 guineas, generally, without stating the particular item or items upon which they assessed it.

Joseph Brown now showed cause.—It will be contended that the under-sheriff ought not to have directed the jury to take into consideration the claim made in respect of the overlooking of the premises; that the jury consequently exceeded their jurisdiction; and that a certiorari ought therefore to issue. But, first, even if *the direction of [*664 the under-sheriff was wrong as to part, the Court cannot inter- fere if the proceedings are good upon the face of the record. Here is nothing upon the record to show that there was any excess of jurisdiction: the verdict is a general one; and the damages may have been assessed in respect of the vibration only, which is a proper item for compensation. The same principle was adopted by the Court in Rex v. The Justices of the West Riding of Yorkshire, 1 A. & E. 563, 573 (E. C. L. R. vol. 28). The decision of the jury here is made final by sect. 145 of the Lands Clauses Consolidation Act, 1845; and therefore no certiorari can issue, unless excess of jurisdiction appears on the face of the proceedings. Such excess cannot be shown by affidavits. [Lord CAMPBELL, C. J.—I do not see why it should not.] In Regina v. The Eastern Counties Railway Company, 2 Dowl. N. S. 945, where an application was made for a mandamus to the Company to issue a new precept to the sheriff, one ground being that he had, on the inquisition, improperly excluded one set of damages from the consideration of the jury, Coleridge, J., refused to grant the mandamus. [CROMPTON, J.— There the jury had jurisdiction for all that they actually did.] That case shows that the Court will not interfere on the ground of misdirection by the sheriff. [CROMPTON, J.—Unless the jury, under his direction, have done anything which amounts to an excess of jurisdiction.] Here is no evidence of any excess. [WIGHTMAN, J.—Have you seen Regina v. South Wales Railway Company, 13 Q. B. 988 (E. C. L. R. vol. 66)?] There the jury gave a verdict in writing, specifying the particular items and amounts of compensation, so that excess of *jurisdiction was shown upon the face of the proceedings. In [*665 the present case, if the Company were dissatisfied or doubtful as to the correctness of the verdict, they might have requested the under-sheriff to direct the jury to find separately upon each item. [Lord CAMPBELL, C. J.—But if the sheriff has not so directed them, we ought to interfere.] Caledonian Railway Company v. Ogilvy, 2 Macq. Sc. A. 229, will be relied on by the other side. But there, also, the excess of jurisdiction appeared upon the face of the proceedings.

Secondly, the direction of the under-sheriff was right. Sect. 6 of the Railways Clauses Consolidation Act, 1845 (8 & 9 Vict. c. 20), which is more explicit than sect. 68 of The Lands Clauses Consolidation Act, 1845 (8 & 9 Vict. c. 18), provides that "the Company shall make to the owners and occupiers of and all other parties interested in any lands taken or used for the purposes of the railway, or injuriously affected by the construction thereof, full compensation for the value of the lands so taken or used, and for all damage sustained by such owners, occupiers, and other parties, by reason of the exercise, as regards such lands, of

the powers by this or the special Act, or any Act incorporated there
with, vested in the Company." And sect. 16 of the same Act, in the
final proviso as to compensation, provides that it is to be made "to all
parties interested, for all damage by them sustained by reason of the
exercise of" the powers contained in that or the special Act. Under
these enactments, Penny is clearly entitled to compensation for the
injury caused by the vibration of the trains. It will probably be said
*666] that such injury is not *caused "by the execution of the works,"
within sect. 68 of The Lands Clauses Consolidation Act, 1845.
But, first, part of the injury was so caused, namely, by the ballast
trains, before the completion of the railway. Secondly (even setting
aside the much wider language of sect. 6 of The Railways Clauses Consolidation Act, 1845, before quoted), it has been frequently decided
that the words "by the execution of the works," in sect. 68 of The
Lands Clauses Consolidation Act, apply to injury caused by the user
of the railway, after the works have been actually completed. [Lord
CAMPBELL, C. J.—But before the inquisition.] Yes; that is the limit.
In The East and West India Docks and Birmingham Junction Railway
Company v. Gattke, 3 Macn. & G. 155, and The London and North
Western Railway Company v. Bradley, 3 Macn. & G. 336, this construction of sect. 68 was adopted; and, in the former of these two cases,
the Lord Chancellor observed that the jury had jurisdiction to inquire
into the question of the right to compensation. Penny was also, upon
this principle, entitled to compensation for the overlooking of his premises by the people on the railway. [Lord CAMPBELL, C. J.—Surely
that is not so. Where would you draw the line? Would the obstruction, by the railway, of a view from the windows of a house, entitle the
owner to compensation, on the ground that his property was "injuriously affected by the execution of the works?"] Perhaps not, if the
act had been done by a private individual; but sect. 68 is to be construed, not as if it related to the invasion of a jus, but in a popular
sense; and in that sense such an obstruction as is suggested, and still
*667] more the proximity complained *of here, does injuriously affect
the property, both in point of comfort and in a pecuniary sense.
Regina v. Great Northern Railway Company, 14 Q. B. 25 (E. C. L. R.
vol. 68), and Glover v. North Staffordshire Railway Company, 16 Q.
B. 912 (E. C. L. R. vol. 71), are in point. [WIGHTMAN, J.—In each
of those cases the owner of the property could have brought an action,
if the statutory powers had not been given to the Company.] No doubt
The London and North Western Railway Company v. Bradley is the
most direct authority in favour of the claimant here. [Lord CAMPBELL,
C. J.—But there, also, the owner of the property might have maintained an action but for the statutes.] It may be doubted whether that
is always a fair criterion. But the vibration, at all events, would have
been ground for an action, and is therefore a proper subject for com-

pensation. [WIGHTMAN, J., referred to Rex v. Pease, 4 B. & Ad. 80 (E. C. L. R. vol. 24).] Broadbent v. The Imperial Gaslight Company, 26 L. J. (N. S.) Ch. 276, will probably be relied on by the other side. But the decision there turned upon the construction of the Company's special Act.

Wilde, contrà.—Caledonian Railway Company v. Ogilvy is a direct authority upon both points. The Lord Chancellor there disposed of the objection that the judgment of the sheriff is final, and held that an excess of jurisdiction, with regard to particular items, on the part of the jury, under the direction of the sheriff, is a proper ground for overturning the verdict, although the particular amount assessed upon such item does not appear upon the face of such verdict. As to the question *of compensation : the Lord Chancellor laid down that the construction of the words " injuriously affected" (which are used in [*668 the Scotch (a) as well as the English Act) does not entitle a landowner to compensation for any act done by the Company which, supposing it not to have been done by authority of an Act of Parliament, would not have entitled him to bring an action. He further adds, " I am far from admitting that he would have a right of compensation in some cases in which, if the Act of Parliament had not passed, there might have been not only an indictment, but a right of action." [Lord CAMPBELL, C. J.—I think he would be entitled to compensation in such cases. ERLE, J.—Even where the damage was only a scintilla.] The Lord Chancellor certainly seems disinclined to go so far. But in Glover v. North Staffordshire Railway Company the Court held that the proper criterion was whether, but for the powers conferred on the Company by Parliament, the injury would have been actionable. [He was then stopped by the Court.]

Lord CAMPBELL, C. J.—As to the first point, we are clearly of opinion that a certiorari ought to issue. If the undersheriff has directed the jury to include in their verdict damages for an item which they ought not to have included, and there is reasonable evidence that they did include such an item in making their calculation, a certiorari clearly lies ; inasmuch as the jury have thus committed an excess of jurisdiction. Now, has there been such excess here ? As to the vibration, I am inclined *to think that Penny would be entitled to some [*669 amount of compensation. But it is unnecessary to go into that question, because I am clearly of opinion that he is not entitled to any compensation for the overlooking of his premises by the railway. It might as well be said that the owner of a house was entitled to compensation on account of the view from it, half a mile off, having been obstructed by the railway. Unless the particular injury would have been actionable before the Company had acquired their statutory powers, it is not an injury for which compensation can be claimed. Now we

(a) Stat. 8 & 9 Vict. c. 19, s. 20, "Injuriously affected by the execution of the undertaking."

are satisfied that the jury did take the overlooking of the premises into their consideration in giving the lump amount of damages; and that, consequently, there was an excess of jurisdiction as to this item. That is sufficient to enable us to interfere and grant a certiorari. Caledonian Railway Company *v.* Ogilvy is directly in point. In that case the Lord Chancellor and Lord St. Leonards entirely concur, a fact which gives the judgment additional weight.

WIGHTMAN, J.—I am also of opinion that there was an excess of jurisdiction. The claim for compensation was made on the ground that the premises were " injuriously affected" by the execution of the works, within the meaning of sect. 68 of The Lands Clauses Consolidation Act, 1845. One item of the claim was for injury to the property caused by its being overlooked by the railway. Is that a legitimate item for compensation? The line must be drawn somewhere. It is difficult to say that the most remote acts on the part of the *Company might not, in some sense, " injuriously affect" the property of landowners in the neighbourhood. But I think the true criterion was adopted in Caledonian Railway Company *v.* Ogilvy. Applying that criterion to the present case, it is clear that no action would have lain for such an injury before the existence of the statutory powers of the company, and that therefore it affords no ground for compensation now. And, as we are also satisfied that the jury included that item of claim in their calculation of the amount of compensation, their decision was an excess of jurisdiction. That being so, can a certiorari issue? It has been contended that it can issue only where the excess appears upon the face of the proceedings : but I am clearly of opinion that that is not so, and that the excess may be shown upon affidavit.

*670]

ERLE, J.—I am also of opinion that a certiorari ought to issue. It has been decided, in Caledonian Railway Company *v.* Ogilvy, that, if one item of compensation has been improperly taken into consideration, by the jury, their decision may be reviewed. Whether such excess of jurisdiction has been committed, I think may be properly determined from affidavits; and the affidavits here show that the jury included, in the items which they took into consideration, the claim in respect of the overlooking of the premises by the railway. That is not a proper ground for compensation, looking at the principle laid down in Caledonian Railway Company *v.* Ogilvy. The comfort and value of the property may have been diminished; but no action would have lain for the injury before the statutory authority was *conferred on the Company ; and therefore no claim for compensation can be made under the statute. With respect to the question of vibration, I think that, under section 68 of The Lands Clauses Consolidation Act, 1845, Penny would be entitled to compensation for damages arising from that cause during the construction of the works, but not for those arising after their completion; and, if the matter came again before the sheriff, we

*671]

might probably think it necessary to define where that claim for damage ought to end.

CROMPTON, J.—I am also of opinion that a certiorari ought to issue. The old rule, that this Court can grant a certiorari wherever it appears that an inferior tribunal has exceeded its jurisdiction, has not been taken away by the Lands Clauses and Railways Clauses Consolidation Acts, 1845. Then, are we satisfied that there has been an excess of jurisdiction here? I am clearly of opinion that we may look at affidavits in determining this: and I think the affidavits here show that there was such excess, looking at the rule laid down in Caledonian Railway Company v. Ogilvy. The overlooking of the premises by the railway is clearly no ground for compensation. It is impossible to say where such claims would end: it would be quite as reasonable, as has been already suggested, to claim compensation for the obstruction of a distant prospect. Perhaps, looking at the effect of the various statutes taken together, the damage arising from the vibration might be a proper ground for compensation, though I am inclined to think it not within the provisions of sect. 68 of the Lands Clauses Consolidation Act, 1845. But it is clear that one ground of *compensation has been improperly taken into consideration; and a certiorari ought therefore to issue. [*672

Lord CAMPBELL, C. J.—As it is our desire to assist the under-sheriff as much as possible in proceedings of this nature, I wish to add that I am of opinion that the injury arising from the vibration during the construction of the works was a proper ground for compensation, because an action could have been maintained before the Company had acquired their statutory authority; but that the damage arising from the vibration after the construction, and during the user, of the railway, is not a ground for compensation, at all events under this precept.

Rule absolute.   Inquisition quashed by consent.(a)

(a) Reported by Francis Ellis, Esq.

The QUEEN v. DAYMAN.   *May* 8.

A Metropolitan Police Magistrate, on a summons for an order, under the Metropolis Local Management Act (18 & 19 Vict. c. 120, ss. 105, 226), upon the proprietor of houses in D., alleged to be a "new street" within the metropolis, for his share of the expenses of paving it, after hearing the parties and their evidence, dismissed the summons on the ground that D. was not a "new street" within the meaning of the enactment, because it was an old highway. A rule, under stat. 11 & 12 Vict. c. 44, s. 5, calling on him to hear and adjudicate on the complaint, was obtained, with a view of obtaining the decision of this Court, that D. might be a "new street" within stat. 18 & 19 Vict. c. 120, s. 105, though it was an old highway.

Held, by Lord Campbell, C. J., Wightman and Crompton, Js., that this Court could not inquire whether the magistrate came to a right conclusion or not, but only whether he had adjudicated; and, they being of opinion that he had done so, the rule was discharged without any expression of opinion as to whether he was right or wrong in his construction of the Act.

Erle, J., dissentiente, and holding that, as the magistrate could not safely proceed unless D. was a new street, his decision, that it was not, was such as to give this Court jurisdiction under stat. 11 & 12 Vict. c. 44, s. 5, to determine whether he was right or wrong in that decision.

PRENTICE, in last Term, obtained a rule Nisi calling on Mr. Dayman, one of the Metropolitan Police Magistrates, "to hear and adjudicate" *673]   on a *complaint against William Carpmael: that he, being the owner of eight houses in a street called Dawson Place in Kensington, neglected to pay to the Kensington vestry his share of the expenses of paving that street.   From the affidavits on both sides, it appeared that a summons was taken out of the Hammersmith Police Court, addressed to Mr. Carpmael, reciting a complaint made before. Mr. Dayman, one of the magistrates of the Police Courts of the Metropolis, sitting at the Hammersmith Police Court, on behalf of the Kensington vestry in the parish of St. Mary Abbotts, Kensington, that he, being the owner of eight houses forming part of a street called Dawson Place, in that parish, neglected to pay 72l. 15s. 2d., being his share of the estimated expenses (as determined by the surveyor of the said vestry and demanded of Carpmael) of paving the said street, and commanding Carpmael's attendance to answer the complaint and show cause why an order for payment should not be made on him.   The summons was attended, and evidence given on both sides.   The magistrate took time to consider, and finally gave a judgment, in which he refused to make any order, giving, as his reasons, that, in his opinion, on the true construction of The Metropolis Local Management Act (18 & 19 Vict. c. 120), no street was "a new street," within the meaning of sect. 105, if, at the time of the passing of that Act, it had been given up to the use of the public so as to extinguish the right of the original owner to stop it up; and that it was proved before him that Dawson Place had been so dedicated to the public before the Act passed.   It was not disputed that there was evidence to justify this finding in fact.   After he *674]   had given these reasons, the magistrate *stated that the question on the construction of the Act was one of great importance, and that it was very desirable that his opinion should be reviewed by the Court of Queen's Bench.

Lush now showed cause.—The summons was taken out under stat. 18 & 19 Vict. c. 120, s. 105; and it was part of the duty of the magistrate to decide whether Dawson Place was or was not a new street within the meaning of that section.   He has decided that it is not; having done so, even if he was wrong, he has heard and adjudicated on the complaint.   This Court, in such a case, has no jurisdiction to inquire whether he was right or wrong: Regina v. Paynter, ante, p. 328.

Hugh Hill and *Prentice*, in support of the rule.—The magistrate's refusal proceeded on the ground that he had no jurisdiction if the street in question had been a highway before the Act passed.   If this was erroneous, he has declined to exercise jurisdiction which he really had: Regina v. Pilkington, 2 E. & B. 546 (E. C. L. R. vol. 75).   [WIGHTMAN, J.—There the justices refused to do a ministerial act, viz. to issue a warrant; and they were ordered to do so.   Here the rule is to com-

mand him "to hear and adjudicate."] He has in substance refused to
adjudicate, in order to raise the preliminary question for the Court, a
course sanctioned in Regina v. Charlesworth, 2 L. M. & P. 117. It is
a declining, on an erroneous ground, to exercise a jurisdiction. [ERLE,
J.—When the question whether there is jurisdiction or not depends
upon a cardinal fact, the inferior tribunal must decide in the first
instance how the fact is: but is *that decision conclusive? In [*675
Thompson v. Ingham, 14 Q. B. 710 (E. C. L. R. vol. 68), I had,
in the Bail Court, thought it conclusive; but the Queen's Bench put
the party to declare in prohibition; and he finally succeeded. CROMP-
TON, J.—In the county court, as soon as it appears that the title to
land bonâ fide comes in question, the jurisdiction ceases. But in this
case new street or old street is not a question preliminary to jurisdiction, but the very matter on which the decision is to be given.] If
the decision has been given on an objection which the Court can see to
be an erroneous decision in point of law, the mandamus to hear and
determine lies; otherwise if the error be in fact: Regina v. The Justices of Kesteven, 3 Q. B. 810 (E. C. L. R. vol. 43). If there is not
this mode of reviewing the decision of the Police Magistrate, there is
no way of correcting it; for the act gives no appeal, and the certiorari
is taken away.

Lord CAMPBELL, C. J.—This is an application to us to command a
Police Magistrate to hear and adjudicate upon a complaint. It is
resisted on the ground that he has already heard and adjudicated
upon it; and I think this answer completely established. By stat. 18
& 19 Vict. c. 120, s. 226, where any expenses are recoverable before
justices, a summons may issue calling the party before two justices;
and, upon his appearance, "it shall be lawful for such two justices to
hear and determine the matter, and for that purpose to examine such
parties, or any of them, and their witnesses, on oath, and make such
order, as well as to costs as otherwise, as to them may seem just." Mr.
Dayman, being a Police Magistrate in the Metropolitan District, has
the same powers *as two ordinary justices. The summons is [*676
before him on a complaint that the expenses alleged to be due
for paving what is said to be a new street within sect. 105 have not
been paid. He was bound to hear and to adjudicate upon this. I think
he did do so; the question was whether Dawson Place was or was not
a new street; on that issue was joined. He heard the parties and the
evidence, and gave a solemn judgment that it was not a new street.
Could we, supposing we should think that he was wrong in so determining, make an order that he shall give an opposite judgment? I
think that we cannot do so. We have no authority to do more than
order him to hear and adjudicate; such was the limit of our jurisdiction, under the prerogative writ of mandamus; and stat. 11 & 12 Vict.
c. 44, s. 5, does not extend our jurisdiction; it does no more than give

a cheaper and more summary remedy than the writ.   Then, having no jurisdiction, we should give no opinion.   We are not a court of advice, but of oyer and terminer ; we sit here, not to deliver opinions which out of respect to us might be generally followed, yet which might without impropriety be neglected, but to deliver judgments which may be enforced : we ought not to give an opinion except as a judgment.

WIGHTMAN, J.—The application is not, and could not be, to consider the propriety of the determination of the magistrate, but to order him to hear and determine ; still it is clear that it is made, not with a view to cause him to determine, but to obtain an opinion from us which may guide him and others as to what the determination should be.   If such an opinion from us would be binding I should gladly give it ; but, though *677] probably the *magistrate would, out of respect to our opinion, supposing it to be different from his own, yield, yet, if on consideration he retained his own opinion, he might very properly act upon it, treating ours as extrajudicial and not binding.

ERLE, J.—I have come to a different opinion : this case seems to me one within the purview of stat. 11 & 12 Vict. c. 44, s. 5.   When a justice has inquired into the cardinal fact on which it depends whether he has jurisdiction or not, and has come to the conclusion that he has not jurisdiction, he cannot safely proceed further ; but under stat. 11 & 12 Vict. c. 44, s. 5, if this Court is of opinion that he has jurisdiction, we may make an order on him to proceed, which will protect him. Our opinion given in such a case is not binding in any other matter, or on other parties, except as an authority.   This is the case with every decision.   No judgment ever binds any but parties and privies to it.

I take the facts in this case to be, that the Kensington Vestry have complied with all the requisites, and come with a complete primâ facie case under stat. 18 & 19 Vict. c. 120, s. 105, for an order on Mr. Carpmael, as owner of houses in Dawson Place, for the payment of his share of the expenses of paving it.   He answers, " You have no jurisdiction to cast any expense upon me, unless my houses were in a new street ; and Dawson Place is not a new street."   That was the cardinal fact on which the jurisdiction of the magistrate depended ; for unless it was a new street the magistrate could not safely act.   The magistrate gives a decision on this cardinal fact, that he had no jurisdiction: if we entertain the question and give an elaborate opinion either that he was mistaken and had jurisdiction, and therefore order him to proceed, *678] *or the other way, that he was right, and discharge the rule on that ground, it would be as binding as any judgment of this Court ever is ; that is, it would be binding on Mr. Dayman, in this case, in the sense that he must obey it, and binding on other parties, and in other cases, only in the sense that a decision of this Court is an authority for their guidance.

CROMPTON, J.—This is an application for a rule in the nature of a mandamus to order Mr. Dayman to hear and determine a matter, which, as it seems to me, he has already heard and determined. It is not a case in which the existence of a fact determines whether the inferior tribunal has jurisdiction or not, as when title to land comes into controversy in a county court. Had this Act said that, as soon as there was a dispute as to whether the place was a new street, the jurisdiction should cease, it might give rise to different considerations. But in every cause that comes before any court there are matters of law and fact, and matters of mixed law and fact, which the prosecutor must establish, or else he fails. On such matters, under this Act, the magistrate finally decides. If he were to step wholly out of his jurisdiction, then, though the certiorari is taken away, we could bring up and quash his order. But, even in a case where the magistrate stepped wholly out of his jurisdiction, there would be great difficulties in the way of the present form of proceeding. In the first place, the magistrate having dismissed the summons, that dismissal must be in some way got rid of before a further order can be made. But, besides that, the party has a right to insist upon having the judgment of the magistrate according to the Act. We have no power to substitute *our judgment [*679 for his. I go the full length of saying that, if we, four Judges sitting here, gave our opinions one way, and the magistrate deliberately and conscientiously formed his the other way, it would be his duty to disregard our opinions and determine the case according to his own. It is clear that a writ of mandamus never went to a justice, ordering him to decide in a particular way: if he has not heard and decided, it goes to order him to hear and determine according to his conscience and judgment, not according to that of this Court. But for the view thrown out by my brother Erle, I should have thought it quite clear that the rule under stat. 11 & 12 Vict. c. 44, s. 5, was only a substitution for the writ of mandamus.   Rule discharged.(a)

(a) See Regina v. Brown, post, p. 757. Also stat. 20 & 21 Vict. c. 43.

COPEMAN and Another v. ROSE. *May* 8.

Since stat. 19 & 20 Vict. c. 108, a debtor, discharged by the Insolvent Debtors Court, is not afterwards liable to committal by a county court judge, under stat. 9 & 10 Vict. c. 95, ss. 98, 99, in respect of any debt comprehended in the adjudication of the Insolvent Debtors Court.

N. PALMER, in this Term, obtained a rule calling upon the plaintiffs to show cause why a writ of prohibition should not issue to prohibit Thomas Jacob Birch, Esq., the judge of the county court of Norfolk holden at Norwich, the said court, the high bailiff, and other officers of the said court, from further proceeding in the plaint or action in that court between the plaintiffs and the defendant.

The rule was obtained upon the affidavit of the defendant, from which the following facts appeared.

On 27th June, 1856, the plaintiffs obtained judgment against the defendant, in the county court, for 18*l.* 4*s.* 6*d.* debt, and 4*l.* 8*s.* 6*d.* costs.

*680]   *On 9th July, 1856, defendant filed his petition in the Insolvent Debtors Court; and a vesting order was made, vesting the estate in the official assignee, on 10th July.   The names of the plaintiffs were inserted in the schedule for the debt and costs.   On 29th July, at the said county court, it was ordered that the defendant should be discharged from custody and be entitled to the benefit of stat. 1 & 2 Vict. c. 110, as to the debts or sums of money due or claimed to be due on 10th July, 1856, the time of making the vesting order, to the persons named in the schedule as creditors or claiming to be creditors.

The defendant was summoned, under sect. 98 of stat. 9 & 10 Vict. c. 95, to appear before the said county court at a court held on 20th March, 1857; and the judge of the said court thereupon made an order upon him for payment of the debt and costs by monthly instalments of 15*s.*; and, in case default were made in the payment of any such instalments, the judge made an order for the committal of defendant to the common jail of the court for forty days.

In this Term,(*a*)

Hugh Hill showed cause.—The defendant contends that the debt on the judgment in the county court is discharged by his discharge under stat. 1 & 2 Vict. c. 110.   That, however, does not take away the jurisdiction of the judge of the county court under sect. 98 of stat. 9 & 10 Vict. c. 95.   Upon a summons under that section, an order of commitment under sect. 99 and an imprisonment in any jail, &c., under *681]   sect. 102, the gaoler *is " bound to receive and keep the defendant therein until discharged under the provisions of this Act, or otherwise by due course of law; and no protection, order, or certificate granted by any court of bankruptcy, or for the relief of insolvent debtors, shall be available to discharge any defendant from any commitment under such last-mentioned order."   It has been held, in the Common Pleas, after time taken for consideration, that a previous order of discharge under the proceedings in the Insolvent Debtors Court does not prevent the county court judge, under stat. 9 & 10 Vict. c. 95, ss. 98, &c., from committing upon a summons in respect of a judgment in the county court, though such judgment is included in the schedule: Abley *v.* Dale, 11 Com. B. 378 (E. C. L. R. vol. 73).   That authority was acted upon in this Court in Ex parte Christie, 4 E. & B. 714 (E. C. L. R. vol. 82), in the Court of Common Pleas again in George *v.* Somers, 16 Com. B. 539 (E. C. L. R. vol. 81), and in the Court of Exchequer in George *v.* Somers, 11 Exch. 202.†   The only

(*a*) Wednesday, May 6th.   Before Lord Campbell, C. J., Wightman, Erle, and Crompton, Js

question, therefore, is whether the law is altered by stat. 19 & 20 Vict. c. 108. Sect. 2 of that Act repeals certain enactments, specified in schedule (A). Among these is "so much of section 102" of 9 & 10 Vict. c. 95, "as enacts that 'no protection order or certificate granted by any Court of Bankruptcy, or for the Relief of Insolvent Debtors, shall be available to discharge any defendant from any commitment' under the order of a judge." Sects. 98 & 99 of stat. 9 & 10 Vict. c. 95 are left untouched: and those are the sections under which the county court judge exercises his power. The repealed clause in sect. 102 applies only to the case where, the county court judge [*682 *having already committed on summons, an attempt might be made by a later order of the Bankruptcy or Insolvent Court to discharge the prisoner: such discharge was prohibited by the enactment in sect. 102; and that enactment is now repealed: that is all. It is to be observed that this enactment in sect. 102 was not the foundation of the decisions in the cases cited: it does not appear to have been referred to in the judgments; though it is noticed in the argument in Abley v. Dale. The decisions must therefore be understood to have proceeded on sects. 98, 99, which are still not repealed. In Abley v. Dale the judgment turned upon the word "unsatisfied" in sect. 98 of stat. 9 & 10 Vict. c. 95; and it was distinctly laid down that a discharge under the Insolvent Debtors Act does not satisfy the debt, and that, therefore, the discharged debtor might still be summoned under sect. 98 of stat. 9 & 10 Vict. c. 95. Nor is it easy to see how a commitment under sects. 98, 99, of stat. 9 & 10 Vict. c. 95, being for an offence, can be affected by provisions which merely relieve from liability to proceedings for debts. Sect. 90 of stat. 1 & 2 Vict. c. 110, is inapplicable here: that only relieves the prisoner from imprisonment for debts to which the adjudication extends: but it does not prevent the county court judge from committing for forty days in cases under sect. 98 of stat. 9 & 10 Vict. c. 95, toties quoties.(a)

N. Palmer, contrà.—The construction contended for on the other side would render the 98th and following *sections of stat. 9 & [*683 10 Vict. c. 95, a repeal of the Acts for the Relief of Insolvent Debtors. In what sense can a debtor be said to be discharged from a debt, when he may be committed for not paying it; and that, as put on the other side, toties quoties? The proceeding is rather in the nature of civil execution than of punishment.(b) In the cases which were decided on the authority of Abley v. Dale, that case is not spoken of, by the learned Judges, as entirely satisfactory. At any rate, if all were rightly decided, stat. 19 & 20 Vict. c. 108, s. 2, has altered the law. *Cur. adv. vult.*

(a) See Re Boyce, 2 E. & B. 521 (E. C. L. R. vol. 75).
(b) See, under stat. 8 & 9 Vict. c. 127, s. 1, Kinning's Case, 10 Q. B. 730 (E. C. L. R. vol. 59); Ex parte Kinning, 4 Com. B. 507 (E. C. L. R. vol. 56).

Lord CAMPBELL, C. J., now delivered the judgment of the Court.

In this case the question is, whether the judge of a county court has jurisdiction to commit a defendant to prison by warrant, upon a judgment summons issued under stat. 9 & 10 Vict. c. 95, s. 99, after the defendant has obtained a valid order of discharge under the Insolvent Debtors Act, comprising the judgment debt in respect of which the judgment summons was issued.

This question was first brought to a decision in Abley *v.* Dale, and answered in the affirmative, upon the express words of the statute, notwithstanding the manifest injustice of making a debtor liable to imprisonment for not paying a debt after the law has taken away from him all his property, and also of making him liable to be imprisoned in punishment for misconduct by the Insolvent Commissioner, and *684] liable to be again punished for *the same misconduct by the county court judge, or to be acquitted by the one, and found guilty by the other, upon the same evidence, in respect of the same charge. In Abley *v.* Dale, this injustice is recited in the judgment: but the Court act on what they considered the clear words of the statute. The decision in that case has been followed in Ex parte Christie, 4 E. & B. 714 (E. C. L. R. vol. 82), and in George *v.* Somers, 16 Com. B. 539 (E. C. L. R. vol. 81): but they both rest on Abley *v.* Dale.

Now the express words of stat. 9 & 10 Vict. c. 95, which led to the judgment in Abley *v.* Dale, are, in our opinion, the words in sect. 102, providing that no order granted by the Court for the relief of Insolvent Debtors shall be available to discharge any defendant from any commitment upon any order there mentioned, *i. e.* under sect. 99. In Abley *v.* Dale, the Court does not mention this section or any section in full: but the judgment is to be read with the argument on which it is given. The argument upon the question of jurisdiction was directed by the Court. Mr. *Lush*, who argued very ably against the jurisdiction, points out sect. 102, in the commencement of his argument, as a difficulty he has to contend with. Mr. *Hugh Hill*, who answered as ably, mentioned the same section at the close of his argument as the ground for a decision in his favour. We consider that the decision which followed was founded upon the section which had thus been a prominent point of contest on the argument. It also appears to us that the enactments in stat. 1 & 2 Vict. c. 110, and particularly sect. 79, would have discharged a defendant from commitment under a warrant, upon a judgment *summons, if the provision above stated *685] in sect. 102 of the first county court Act had been omitted.

The law, as thus declared in Abley *v.* Dale, 11 Com. 378 (E. C. L. R. vol. 73), being so manifestly unjust, and we may say absurd, the Legislature, by stat. 19 & 20 Vict. c. 108, s. 2, has repealed the very proviso in sect. 102 of the county court Act on which, as we consider, the decision in Abley *v.* Dale must have rested. It is clear to us that the Legislature intended to remedy an acknowledged evil which had been more than once judicially noticed: and we are of opinion that we give effect to the expressed intention of the Legislature in holding that an order for discharge, granted by a Court for relief of Insovent Debtors comprising a judgment debt in a county court, does take away from that court the power of committing to prison a defendant by warrant upon a judgment summons, issued for non-payment of that debt. Although such commitment may be, in some sense, a punishment for supposed misconduct, it is founded entirely upon a judgment debt; it is granted only at the instance of the judgment-creditor; and the sentence is for his sake; for, by stat. 9 & 10 Vict. c. 95, s. 110, the prisoner ought to be released as soon as the judgment-creditor is satisfied, although the period of imprisonment under the sentence has not expired.

We do not assume to overrule the decisions that have been already given upon the Acts as they formerly stood: but we take those Acts and decisions with stat. 19 & 20 Vict. c. 108, and consider that we decide consistently with them by now holding, in this case, that, as soon as *the order for discharge by the Insolvent Court was proved [*686 to the satisfaction of the county court judge, his jurisdiction to commit was at an end.

It follows that a prohibition should issue against such a commitment: and, accordingly, the rule is made absolute.

Rule absolute.

———◆———

CHOLLET v. HOFFMAN.

To a declaration for infringement of a patent, brought by an alleged assignee (by indenture) of the patent, the defendant pleaded, by denying the assignment modo et formâ. On the trial, it appeared that an instrument of assignment had been executed by the patentee, but that it had not been registered under The Patent Law Amendment Act, 1852 (15 & 16 Vict. c. 83). Held that, as, by sect. 35, the original patentee is, until the entry of the registration, to be deemed and taken to be the sole and exclusive proprietor of the patent, the defendant was entitled to a verdict.

Although the objection was not specified in the notice of objections delivered by him.

THE declaration alleged that Etienne Masson was the first and true inventor of a new manufacture, that is to say, &c.: and Her Majesty, by letters patent duly sealed, &c., granted E. M., his executors, &c., the sole privilege to make, use, exercise, and vend the said invention within England, for fourteen years from 12th November, 1850, subject to the condition of enrolling, within six months, in Chancery, an instrument particularly describing, &c.; which condition E. M. fulfilled: "and that, by an indenture bearing date the 20th day of March in the year of our Lord 1855, between the said E. M. of the first part, Charles Thutneyssen, Guillaume Schnapper, and Emile Antoine Crapelet, of the

second part, and the said plaintiff of the third part, for the considerations therein mentioned, the said letters patent, and all the liberties
*687] and privileges thereby *granted, were duly assigned to the said plaintiff. And the defendant, during the said term, did infringe the said patent right."

Plea 6. "That the said letters patent, liberties, and privileges were not assigned to the plaintiff as alleged." Issue thereon.

There were other issues of fact.

The notice of objections delivered with defendant's pleas commenced: "Take notice, that at the trial of this action the defendant will rely on the objections hereinafter mentioned, besides denying the several allegations contained in the declaration, and will object, contend, and insist." Then followed eight objections, which comprehended only objections to the patent itself, the novelty of the invention, and the specification : "and the defendant will rely on such objections respectively, as well by reason that the said letters patent are contrary to law, as also that the petition of the said Etienne Masson, or the recital thereof in the said letters patent, was false. Above are the particulars of the defendant's objections; in support of which he will avail himself of all and every or any of the pleas in this action applicable for that purpose."

On the trial, before Lord Campbell, C. J., at the London Sittings after last Hilary Term, the plaintiff put in a deed, duly executed by Etienne Masson, purporting to be an assignment to the plaintiff of the letters patent, agreeing with the description in the declaration; but it appeared that such deed had not been registered, pursuant to sect. 35 of The Patent Law Amendment Act, 1852 (15 & 16 Vict. c. 83). The counsel for the defendant contended that the plaintiff had failed to
*688] support his issue on plea 6 : and the Lord Chief Justice, *being of that opinion, directed a verdict for the 'defendant on that issue. The jury were discharged from giving a verdict on the other issues.

Sir *F. Thesiger*, in last Easter Term, obtained a rule Nisi for a new trial, " on the ground that the Lord Chief Justice ought not to have directed a verdict for the defendant on the issue raised by the 6th plea, and that the objection of the want of registration of the assignment could not avail the defendant under the plea and notice of objections." On an earlier day in this Term,(a)

Hindmarch and *Manisty* showed cause.—First : the assignment was not proved. By sect. 35 of stat. 15 & 16 Vict. c. 83, it is enacted that a book entitled " The Register of Proprietors" shall be kept at the office in Chancery, wherein shall be entered the assignment of any letters patent, or of any share or interest therein, any license under letters patent, and the district to which such license relates, with the

(a) April 30th. Before Lord Campbell, C. J., Erle and Crompton, Js.

names of persons having share or interest in such letters patent or
license, and the date of their acquiring the same, and any other matter or thing relating to or affecting the proprietorship in such letters
patent or license; and a copy of any entry, certified under the office
seal, is to be given to persons requiring it, which "shall be received
in evidence in all courts and in all proceedings, and shall be primâ facie
proof of the assignment of such letters patent, or share or interest
therein, or of the license or proprietorship, as therein expressed: provided always, that until such entry shall have been made *the [*689
grantee or grantees of the letters patent shall be deemed and
taken to be the sole and exclusive proprietor or proprietors of such
letters patent, and of all the licenses and privileges thereby given and
granted." There was therefore no effectual assignment proved, no
registration being proved. [Lord CAMPBELL, C. J.—The question is,
whether the want of registration should have been specially pleaded.
CROMPTON, J.—It would seem difficult to confess and avoid.] The
assignment alleged in the declaration must be understood to be an
assignment changing the proprietorship, or the declaration would be
bad in arrest of judgment: the plea traverses all that the declaration
alleges. The plea of Non demisit is analogous to this: and per Curiam
in Taylor v. Needham, 2 Taun. 278, 282, "in cases of a grant or feoffment, a stranger may plead, 'did not grant, or did not enfeoff,' and
that plea denies not only the existence, but the efficacy of the supposed
grant or feoffment. It brings in issue, therefore, the title of the grantor,
as well as the operation of the deed, and that plea would be a proper
plea to bring in issue the execution, construction, and efficacy of any
deed of demise." This principle also appears in Stephen's Treatise
on the Principles of Pleading, p. 528 (5th ed.), and from Baddeley v.
Leppingwell, 3 Burr. 1533, and Hynde's Case, 4 Rep. 70 b, 71 b. It
is true that, if there be two material allegations pleaded, and each is
essential to the deduction of the title of the party pleading, a traverse
of one admits the other, for the purpose of that issue: Cooke v. Blake,
1 Exch. 220 :† but here is only one allegation, that of an effectual
assignment. That case explains *Wallington v. Dale, 6 Exch. [*690
284,† where the plaintiff declared as assignee of a patent, and
alleged that the original grantee of the patent had, after the assignment, entered a disclaimer; and the plea took a special traverse, stating,
by way of inducement, that the grantee had assigned before the disclaimer, and was not capable of lawfully disclaiming, when the alleged
disclaimer was made, adding absque hoc that the grantee had entered
the disclaimer, modo et formâ; and it was held that this was merely a
denial that in fact a disclaimer had been entered by the grantee. The
case here stands as if the indenture of assignment had been signed but
not delivered. But, secondly, it will be contended, for the plaintiff,
that the defendant could not raise this question because it is not raised

by the notice of objections. But sect. 41 of stat. 15 & 16 Vict. c. 83 provides only that no evidence shall be allowed to be given "in support of any alleged infringement, or of any objection impeaching the validity of such letters patent which shall not be contained in the particulars delivered:" on this issue the defendant did not impeach the validity of the letters patent. Besides, the notice of objections comprehends a notice that the allegations of the declaration are denied. It cannot be requisite to explain the evidence by which the traverse of the assignment is to be supported. [Lord CAMPBELL, C. J.—You might as well be required to give notice that you denied the execution of the deed of assignment.]

Sir *F. Thesiger*, *Bovill*, and *Webster*, contrà.—The defendant was *691] confined to the notice of objections; and *this restriction was not applicable only to objections "impeaching the validity of such letters patent." The occurrence of these words in sect. 41 of stat. 15 & 16 Vict. c. 83, might indeed suggest such a restriction of the application; but by sect. 5 of stat. 5 & 6 W. 4, c. 83 (which is not repealed), the words are larger: the defendant, on pleading, is to give to the plaintiff "a notice of any objections on which he means to rely at the trial of such action, and no objection shall be allowed to be made on behalf of such defendant" "at such trial unless he prove the objections stated in such notice." The defence now insisted upon cannot be let in under the general words "besides denying the several allegations contained in the declaration;" the question is as to the necessity of specifying the particular ground of objection. But, supposing the objection open to the defendant, it cannot be sustained. The plea puts in issue, not the registration of the assignment, but the fact of the assignment. The two are treated, in sect. 35 of stat. 15 & 16 Vict. c. 83, as different things. The register is made primâ facie proof of the assignment; it is not itself the assignment. Till registration, the grantee of the patent is only to "be deemed and taken" to be proprietor: but he does not remain proprietor in fact. Had it been intended that the interest should not pass till the registration, words would have been used like those in stat. 27 H. 8, c. 16, s. 1, which enacts: "that no manors, lands, tenements, or' other hereditaments, shall pass, alter, or change from one to another, whereby any estate of inheritance or freehold shall be made or take effect in any person or persons, or any use thereof to be made, by reason only of any bargain and sale thereof, except the same bargain and sale be made by writing *692] indented, *sealed, and enrolled," &c. So the registration clauses in the old Shipping Acts distinctly prohibited the passing of the property till the registration.(a) It is to be observed that, under stat. 27 H. 8, c. 16, s. 1, if the enrolment be made within six months of

(a) See stat. 8 & 9 Vict. c. 89, s. 37. The scheme of legislation in this respect is changed: see The Merchant Shipping Act, 1854 (17 & 18 Vict. c. 104), Part 2, sects. 42, 43, 55, &c.

the date, the title relates back to the date: in the case of a patent, no
time for registration being assigned, the title must relate to the assignment whenever the registration is made. The original patentee, if he
made an assignment which was not registered, would surely not be capable of assigning to another person. [Lord CAMPBELL, C. J.—I incline
to think that such other assignee, if registered, would be in law the
assignee.] The object of the statute was that the owner might be
known: cases of complicated equitable titles had arisen, as Russell v.
Ledsam, 14 M. & W. 574.† [CROMPTON, J.—In the strongest case of
relation, that under stat. 27 H. 8, c. 16, s. 1, it could not be averred
during the interval between the execution and enrolment that any
freehold interest had passed. Here could the original patentee have
sued?] Not after assignment. [CROMPTON, J.—But yet he is to be
taken and deemed to be proprietor.] A license must be registered, as
well as an assignment: it will hardly be disputed that a license would
relate back after registration. Wallington v. Dale is an authority for
the plaintiff as to the pleading point: and that case is not met by the
interpretation put on Cooke v. Blake. [CROMPTON, J.—The traverse
of the assignment did not put in issue the allegation of the original
grant: Cowlishaw v. Cheslyn, 1 C. & J. 48,† *applies no fur- [*693
ther.] The decisions in the Exchequer go to the length of
establishing a distinction between the execution of the instrument in
fact and the collateral requisites of the deed. Taylor v. Needham, 2
Taun. 278, is inapplicable: the question here is not as to the title of
the party assigning. It is the assignment "by indenture" that is traversed: the registration is not by indenture. [Lord CAMPBELL, C. J.
—When the registration has been entered, there is an assignment by
indenture.] The traverse cannot have a wider effect than a traverse
of an allegation of the acceptance of a bill. *Cur. adv. vult.*

Lord CAMPBELL, C. J., in this Term (May 7th), delivered the judgment of the Court.

We are of opinion that the Judge at the trial of this cause properly
directed the jury to find for the defendant on the 6th plea.

The declaration averred that, by an indenture between Masson, the
grantee of the letters patent, and the plaintiff, "the said letters patent,
and all the liberties and privileges thereby granted, were duly assigned
to the said plaintiff." The 6th plea says "that the said letters patent,
liberties, and privileges were not assigned to the plaintiff as alleged."
We have therefore only to consider the meaning of the allegation in the
declaration. If it was, only, that an indenture was executed by which
Masson purported to assign the letters patent to the defendant, the
defendant ought either to have demurred to the declaration, or, con-
fessing and avoiding, to have *pleaded that no entry of the [*694
assignment had been made in the "Register of Proprietors."
But we think that the allegation in the declaration amounts to a state-

ment, not only that the indenture had been executed, but that all had been done which was necessary to give it operation, and that the letters patent had been duly assigned to the plaintiff so that he had a right to maintain the action as the sole and exclusive proprietor of the letters patent.   This is his title, and the only ground on which he can sue for the supposed infringement.   But stat. 15 & 16 Vict. c. 83, s. 35, provides that, till the entry of the assignment has been made in The Register of Proprietors, the grantee of the letters patent "shall be deemed and taken to be the sole and exclusive proprietor" thereof. Therefore, if Masson had sued for the alleged infringement, he must have been deemed and taken to be the sole person who had a right to sue ; and an issue upon any plea denying his title must have been found in his favour.   But the defendant could not be liable to be sued at the same time for the same infringement by the grantee and by the assignee of the letters patent.   We, at present, give no opinion upon the question whether and how far the entry of the assignment, when made, will refer back : but, supposing that it might refer back to the execution of the indenture, till the entry is made no legal interest passed by the indenture, and nothing beyond a right to have the title completed. The case of Wallington *v.* Dale, relied upon by the plaintiff's counsel, has no application, as the plea there was so framed by the absque hoc as to limit the traverse to the single fact that a disclaimer had been entered by the grantee.

*695]   *The only other point made by the plaintiff was that the defendant was precluded from insisting on the want of registration of the assignment, because it was not specifically mentioned in his notice of objections.   The requirements of the late statute as to the notices by the defendant are clearly confined to notices affecting the validity of the patent.   Although the words of the former Act are, as was suggested, more general, we ought to put upon both Acts the same construction, when we see that the later in pari materiâ is so carefully and clearly worded in this respect.   Even if the wider construction could be given in the former statute, the case might probably fall within the authority of Hull *v.* Bollard, 1 H. & N. 134,† in which the Court of Exchequer held that, where the objection to a patent is too general, the course of the plaintiff is to go before a Judge to require a better particular ; but that, if the notice comprehends the objection, it cannot be excepted to at the trial on account of its generality.

The consequence is that the verdict was rightly entered for the defendant on the 6th plea, and that this rule should be discharged.

Rule discharged.

END OF EASTER TERM.

The Court of Queen's Bench did not sit in banc in the Vacation following Easter Term.

CASES

ARGUED AND DETERMINED

IN

THE QUEEN'S BENCH,

Trinity Term,

XX. VICTORIA. 1857.

The Judges who usually sat in Banc in this Term were,—

Lord CAMPBELL, C. J.,   ERLE, J.,
COLERIDGE, J.,   CROMPTON, J.

MEMORANDUM.

In this Term, the Right Honourable James Stuart Wortley having resigned the office of Solicitor-General, Henry Singer Keating, of The Inner Temple, Esquire, one of Her Majesty's Counsel, was appointed to the office. He afterwards received the honour of Knighthood.

---

*Ex parte BAKER. *May 27.* [*697

Under stat. 4 G. 4, c. 34, s. 3, a potter was convicted and sentenced to imprisonment for leaving a service before the time of contract was expired. After the imprisonment had expired, but before the original time of contract had expired, he, not having returned to the service, was again convicted for absenting himself. Held: that the second conviction was good, as the contract continued, notwithstanding the first conviction and imprisonment.

The conviction did not expressly state that the servant had entered the service; but it found that he did "misconduct himself in his said service." Held: that this was a sufficient finding of his having entered into the service.

The conviction stated that it appeared to the magistrate, as well on the examination on oath of M., in presence of the party charged, "as otherwise," that the party had absented himself, &c. Held: that it was not to be inferred from this that the justice had proceeded upon evidence not given in the presence of the party.

The conviction stated that the party misconducted himself, &c., "by neglecting and absenting himself from his said masters' service." Held: that this was not a finding of two statutable offences, but only of the absenting.

SCOTLAND moved for a writ of habeas corpus to bring up the body of William Baker. From the affidavit of the said W. Baker the following facts appeared.

By an agreement in writing he was hired to serve Felix Hawley, John Hawley, and Robert Hawley, earthenware and china manufacturers, from 11th November, 1856, to 11th November, 1857. He entered into the service: but, in February, 1857, he gave a month's notice to determine the service (under a supposed custom in the trade); and, at the end of the month, he quitted the service, namely on 10th March, 1857; and, on 11th March, 1857, he entered into the service of William Barlow, manufacturer of china and earthenware. He was summoned before a magistrate for having unlawfully neglected and absented himself from the first service; and he appeared before Thomas Bailey Rose, Esq., a justice of the peace for Staffordshire, and was then convicted and committed under the following instrument.

"County of Stafford, to wit. To all constables and other Her *698] Majesty's officers of the peace in the said *county, and to the keeper of the House of Correction at Stafford, or his deputy. Whereas complaint upon oath hath been made unto me, T. B. Rose, Esq., one of Her Majesty's justices," &c., "by James Mayer, of Fenton, agent for Felix, John, and Robert Hawley, late of Fenton, in the said county, potters, that William Baker, late of Langton, in the said county, potter, did, on the 11th day of December last, contract, and agree with the said Felix, John, and Robert Hawley to serve them as a potter in their business of potters at the parish of Stoke upon Trent in the said county, under a written contract, for a certain time, to wit, until the 11th day of November next; and, having entered upon and worked under such agreement, and the term of his contract being unexpired, the said W. Baker did, on the 10th day of March last, unlawfully misdemean and misconduct himself in his said service by neglecting and absenting himself from his said masters' service without the leave of his said masters, without having given to his said masters any notice thereof, and without any sufficient reason for so doing, contrary to the provisions of the statute in such case made and provided: And whereas, the said W. Baker being now brought before me, the said justice, in pursuance of my warrant issued against him, to answer to the said complaint, and I, having duly examined into the nature thereof, do adjudge the said complaint to be true, it appearing to me, as well upon the examination on oath of the said J. Mayer in the presence of the said W. Baker as otherwise, that the said W. Baker, having contracted as aforesaid, to serve the said F., J., and R. Hawley, as a potter in their business of potters, and the term of his contract being *699] unexpired, did, on the 10th *day of March, misdemean and misconduct himself in his said service, by neglecting and absenting himself from his said masters' service, without the leave of his said masters, and without giving to his said masters any notice thereof, and without any sufficient reason for so doing: I do therefore convict him, the said W. Baker, of his said offence, and do order and adjudge that the said W. Baker, for his said offence, be committed to the House of Correction at Stafford aforesaid, there to remain and be held to hard labour for the space of one calendar month. These are therefore to command," &c. (order on the constables to take W. Baker to the House of Correction, and on the keeper to receive and detain him). " Given under my hand and seal, the 18th day of March, in the year of our Lord 1857, at Langton in the said county."

Baker was confined in the House of Correction till 17th April, when the term of his confinement expired, and he returned to the employment of William Barlow; and, while so employed, he was again summoned at the instance of Messrs. Hawley, and was, on 13th May, again convicted and committed by Mr. Rose for a calendar month, with hard labour, to the same House of Correction. The commitment and conviction were in the same form as the previous one, with a slight correction in the names, and an alteration of the date of the offence to 29th April. On the hearing, it was admitted that he had never in fact re-entered into the service of Messrs. Hawley, after first quitting it.

Scotland, in support of the application.—The conviction and commitment, which are in a single *instrument,(a) are bad. The justice professed to act under the Master and Servants' Act, 4 G. 4, c. [*700 34, s. 3, which includes " potters" by name.

First, the justice had no jurisdiction. After the first committal, Baker was no longer in the service of Messrs. Hawley. All that has taken place since is that he has not resumed the service. [Lord CAMP-BELL, C. J.—Did the conviction dissolve the contract?] It may be that it would not affect the civil rights: but there was no new offence: there was a single act of absenting, for which the prisoner was punished. [COLERIDGE, J.—Suppose he had gone back into the service of Messrs. Hawley, and had then absented himself again.] He could not then have said that he had not committed a fresh breach of the continuing contract. But absenting presupposes a presence. Surely the master cannot, by continually requiring the servant to return, create an infinite number of offences. [COLERIDGE, J.—Suppose the magistrate had dismissed the first complaint: could not the servant be again brought up on evidence of an absence, though he had not returned?]

Secondly, the adjudication is formally defective for not finding that the servant had entered into the service. The language of stat. 4 G. 4, c. 34, s. 3, is " shall not enter into or commence his or her service," " or having entered into such service shall absent himself:" and the conviction is on the latter clause. The evidence need not be set out; it is therefore the more important that the conviction should show pre-

(a) See Johnson v. Reid, 6 M. & W. 124.†

cisely what is charged and found to be true. [Lord CAMPBELL, C. J.—
*701] Certainly *it ought to be proved that he entered into the service.]
And it seems to follow that this should be alleged. [ERLE, J.—
It is alleged that he did "misconduct himself in his said service."] No
implication can be admitted to support a conviction except where the
words palpably admit of no other meaning.

Again: the conviction ought to show that the evidence on which the
justice proceeded was given in the presence of the party charged:.
Regina v. Tordoft, 5 Q. B. 933 (E. C. L. R. vol. 48). Here it appears
that the magistrate founded his view "as well upon the examination on
oath of the said James Mayer in the presence of the said William
Baker as otherwise." [ERLE, J.—In Rex v. Luffe, 8 East, 193, 203,
the case of non-access, Lord Ellenborough disallowed this objection.]
That was a case of filiation, not of a conviction.

Again: the conviction states two offences, "neglecting and absenting himself from his said masters' service:" the statute creates two
offences, absenting "or" neglecting. This is a valid objection: Rex
v. Salomons, 1 T. R. 249. In Paley's Law and Practice of Summary
Convictions, p. 202 (3d edit.), it is said, "Where two distinct offences
are charged in the information, judgment that the defendant is convicted of the said offence, is bad." [ERLE, J.—But there are not two
distinct offences alleged here : the statute makes it an offence to "neglect
to fulfil" the service: that is not here found.]

Lord CAMPBELL, C. J.—We must take care that no one is convicted
*702] except according to law: but another *duty is cast on us, namely,
to see that the law is not evaded by subtlety or by frivolous objections. Mr. Scotland has very properly brought before us the points on
which he seeks to impugn this conviction. As to the first point: I
think a fresh offence was committed when the prisoner, after being libe-
rated from imprisonment, did not return to the service, because the contract continued, and he absented himself: that is a distinct offence from
the offence of which he was before convicted; and he is liable to be
convicted for that, although he had not returned to the service in the
mean while. As to the second point, I was at first struck by the want
of an allegation that the prisoner had entered into the service; but I
think that, when the conviction states that he did "misconduct himself
in his said service," that is tantamount to an allegation that he had
entered into the service. As to the third point, we must suppose that
the magistrate did his duty, and was not guilty of what has been suggested by proceeding upon evidence in the absence of the party charged.
The meaning of "otherwise" must be that there were other grounds
by which the conviction was to be supported. As to the last point, I
think the conviction charges only one offence; and we may try it by
this test: if the words following "neglecting" had been omitted, the
conviction would have been bad; for it does not charge that the pri-

soner did "neglect to fulfil" the contract. We therefore ought not to interfere.

COLERIDGE, J.—I am of the same opinion. As to the points relating to the form of this particular conviction I have nothing to add. As to the general point, *I think the doctrine contended for most [*703 unreasonable. The servant absents himself; and, after the absence of a day or two, he is brought before the magistrate, who convicts him. He suffers his imprisonment. It was then his duty to return to the service : and, if he does not, he is liable to be again convicted, as much as if he had gone back to his master's premises and walked out, in which case Mr. *Scotland* admits the liability. We must recollect that this is a statute to be acted on by gentlemen residing in the country ; and it would be very wrong to construe it subtilly.

ERLE, J.—As to the last two points, the Court is called upon to support a subtle construction for the purpose of invalidating the conviction, whereas we ought rather to make an intendment for the purpose of supporting it. As to the second objection, the words "in his said service" imply that he had entered into the service. The other point is important. I think that, if a servant absents himself, is convicted, imprisoned, and discharged, and then does not return to the service, he absents himself as much as if he had returned and had afterwards absented himself. He could force the master to receive him into his service ; and it would be an intense grievance on the master if the servant, under such circumstances, could treat the contract as broken off. It clearly continues ; and it is perfectly clear that this was the intention of the Legislature. The justice may commit for any period not exceeding three months, and may abate a proportional part of the wages during imprisonment ; or he may, in lieu of imprisonment, punish by abating the whole or any part of the wages ; or he may discharge from the service. It is thus evident *that the Legislature has provided for [*704 temporary punishment : and, if after that the servant absent himself again, he is again liable to punishment.

(CROMPTON, J., was absent.)   Rule refused.(a)

(a) Subsequently, in this Term (May 29th), *Scotland* obtained a writ of habeas corpus in the Court of Exchequer ; and, on the prisoner being brought up, that Court (June 2d) ordered him to be discharged, the majority of the Court (Pollock, C. B., Martin and Bramwell, Bs., dissentiente Watson, B.), holding that the conviction was bad for not adjudicating any abatement of wages. Pollock, C. B., also held that the contract was put an end to by the first conviction, and that there could be no second conviction: dissentientibus Bramwell and Watson, Bs. ; dubitante Martin, B. Bramwell and Watson, Bs., held the objections, that there was no allegation of entering the service, and that conviction appeared to have been taken on evidence not given in the presence of the prisoner, invalid. In re Baker, 2 H. & N. 219.†

LEO SCHUSTER, SAMUEL SCHUSTER, and SIGISMUND
SCHUSTER, v. ALEXANDER McKELLAR and ROBERT
ANDERSON YOUNG. *May* 28.

Plaintiffs, merchants in London, purchased for C., but on their own credit, goods abroad, debiting
C. with the price and a commission. The goods were warehoused in London in plaintiffs'
name. C. in his own name engaged room for the goods in the ship E., which had been put
up as a general ship for Calcutta. Plaintiffs, at C.'s request, delivered the goods to a lighterman, but, with a view to preserve their lien, took the lighterman's engagement to give them
the mate's receipt. The goods were shipped on the E.; the mate's receipt in blank was
handed to the lighterman, who gave it to plaintiffs. C. promised plaintiffs to redeem the
mate's receipt, but never did so, and fraudulently induced the ship-brokers to get bills of
lading to C.'s order, to be signed by the master, though the mate's receipt was not produced.
C. fraudulently endorsed these bills of lading for value to a bonâ fide endorsee. Plaintiffs
had no communication with the ship-brokers or captain till after the ship had sailed, when, the
facts being discovered, they demanded the goods both in this country and on the arrival of
the ship at Calcutta. The goods were delivered by the captain at Calcutta to the holders
of the bills of lading. An action was brought for this conversion against the shipowner and
the captain. It appeared that the captain and crew were appointed by the shipowner, but the
ship was chartered for a lump sum to third parties, who put up the ship as a general ship. It
was proved that the refusal of the captain to deliver the goods at Calcutta was by the orders
of the shipowner. The only question left to the jury was, Whether, under the circumstances,
the master was justified in signing the bills of lading without the production of the mate's
receipt? The jury finding in the negative, the plaintiffs had the verdict against both defendants on the pleas of Not guilty and Not possessed.
Held : that the property in the goods remained the property of the plaintiffs, there never having
been any delivery animo transferendi to C.; and that the misdelivery at Calcutta was a conversion. And that the question whether the plaintiffs were precluded from relying on their
property or complaining of this conversion was in effect properly left to the jury and properly
found by them.
Held, also, that, the shipowner having authorized the detention at Calcutta, the verdict was
proper.
Semble : that under such a charter-party the shipowner, though perhaps not liable on the
contracts made for carriage of goods in the ship as a general ship, is still liable for the
misdelivery of the goods by the captain, who for many purposes remains his servant. *Sed
quære.*

FIRST count : That defendant McKellar was owner, and defendant
Young master, of the ship Emperor, *then lying in London, and
*705] bound for Calcutta, and received on board plaintiffs' goods in
exchange for the mate's receipt. Breach : that defendants signed bills
of lading to certain persons called Coles, Brothers, who never held the
mate's receipt, whereby the said persons were enabled to endorse the
bills of lading for value, and the plaintiffs lost their goods. Second
count : For not delivering goods received on board the defendants' ship
to be carried to Calcutta for plaintiffs. Third court : Trover for spelter.
Pleas to first count. 1. That defendants did not receive the plaintiffs' goods on board. 2. That they did not give the mate's receipt.
3. Not guilty. 4. That the goods were the property of Coles, Brothers,
and that Coles, Brothers, made the contract for the conveyance in
defendants' ship in their own name, and plaintiffs shipped the goods on
Coles, Brothers', order, without any knowledge, on defendants' part,
that the goods were not shipped by Coles, Brothers, and induced defend-

ants to believe that they were shipped by Coles, Brothers. 5. Leave and license.

Pleas to second count. 6. That plaintiffs did not ship, nor defendants receive, the goods to be carried as alleged. 7. A plea similar to plea 4.

*Pleas to the count in trover. 8. Not guilty. 9. That the goods were not the goods of the plaintiffs. [*706

Issue on these pleas respectively.

On the trial, before Lord Campbell, C. J., at the Guildhall Sittings after Hilary Term, 1857, it appeared that the plaintiffs formed the firm of Schuster & Co., merchants in London. Coles, Brothers, mentioned in the pleadings, were, in 1854, merchants in London. In February, 1854, Schuster & Co., by order of Coles, Brothers, and on their account, purchased on their own credit and in their own names, through their correspondents abroad, a large quantity of spelter. They accepted drafts for the price, and debited Coles, Brothers, with the amount of those drafts and a commission of one per cent. for purchasing. Schuster & Co., by order of Coles, Brothers, in April, caused the greater part of this spelter to be shipped from Hamburgh for New York : but it was shipped in the name of Schuster & Co. ; and the bills of lading were made deliverable to their order. The remainder, which consisted of two parcels forming together a little more than 100 tons, was, by order of Coles, Brothers, shipped from Hamburgh for London. This also was shipped in the name of Schuster & Co., and, on its arrival, was warehoused in Hay's wharf, in the name of Schuster & Co. Before this transaction Schuster & Co. had frequently made advances to Coles, Brothers, on the security of goods in warehouses, which were transferred into the name of Schuster & Co. When Coles, Brothers, wished to ship any goods so pledged, the course of business was for Schuster & Co. to give to the lightermen employed by Coles, Brothers, an order on the warehousemen for the delivery of the goods, taking, at the same time, the lighterman's undertaking to give the *mate's receipt to Schuster & Co. The lighterman then shipped the goods as [*707 directed by Coles, Brothers, taking the mate's receipt which he delivered to Schuster & Co. Coles, Brothers, in such cases, before they got the bills of lading signed, procured from Schuster & Co. the mate's receipt by paying off the advance upon the goods ; it was then attached to the bills of lading, which were delivered to the ship's broker ; and then the bills of lading were signed. There was evidence that this course of business was general in London, and that pledgees of goods allowed them to be shipped by the pledgers, relying for their security on the practice to refuse to sign bills of lading, where there was a mate's receipt, without having it produced. In this particular transaction, Coles, Brothers, informed Schuster & Co. that they intended to ship the spelter in question, part to Bombay part to Calcutta ; and Schuster

& Co., at their request, gave to Henbrey, a lighterman who ordinarily
acted for Coles, Brothers, the following delivery order.

All charges to be paid by us, S. & Co.

"No. 185.   London, 16th May.

"To the Superintendent of Hay's Wharf. Please to deliver
to Mr. Charles Henbrey's lighters the undermentioned goods,
entered by selves in the ship 'Thames' Captn.   @ Hamburgh.

	T.	C.		
"T. 3268 Plates Spelter N g	.	.	.	. 50 10 3 1
"S. 4855	. . .	.	.	. 50 14 1 26

"SCHUSTER & Co."

Schuster & Co. took from Henbrey an acknowledgment of which
the following is a copy.

*708]   *"London, 16th May, 1854.
"Received of Messrs. Schuster & Co. delivery order for

"T. 3268 Plates Spelter N g   .   50 10 3 1 to be shipped to
Calcutta.

"S. 4855 "   "   "   .   50 14 1 26 to be shipped to
Bombay.

"The mate's receipt for which to be handed over to them.
"C. HENBREY."

He brought back, in a day or two, two receipts which he delivered
to Schuster & Co. The following is a copy of the one relating to the
goods, the subject of this action.
"17th May, 1854.

"Received on board the Emperor, Captain Young, for Calcutta
from M.   No.   Packages.
                          3268   Plates Spelter.
"eight in dispute, if on board, will be delivered.
"JOHN FORREST, Chief officer.

"CHARLES HENBREY, licensed Lighterman, 18 Beer Lane, and
Brewer's Quay, Lower Thames Street."

It was admitted that the defendant McKellar was the owner, and the
defendant Young the master, of the Emperor, and that this receipt was
signed by the mate of that ship. In general, shippers of goods apply
to have the bills of lading signed within a day or two after the goods
are shipped. Schuster & Co., after receiving the mate's receipt, repeatedly applied to Coles, Brothers, to redeem it, and were informed
they would do so presently. Schuster & Co. made no application to
the ship-brokers, and made no further inquiries, till, on June 24th,
Coles, Brothers, failed. Schuster & Co. then learned, for the first
*709] time, that the Emperor had sailed on the 16th *June. They
wrote on June 30th to McKellar, at Glasgow, demanding to

have bills of lading given to them as holders of the mate's receipt; and at the same time, as unpaid vendors, giving him notice to stop in transitû. McKellar referred them to Messrs. Dawson & Arrow, shipbrokers in London. The following letters then passed between the parties.

Schuster & Co. to McKellar. "London, 12th July, 1854. Dear Sir, We duly received your letter of the 4th instant, and waited upon Messrs. Dawson & Arrow, who have informed you that bills of lading have been signed by Captain Young, and, to our great surprise, wrongfully delivered by the brokers to other parties, notwithstanding that we hold the mate's receipt. We think it advisable to inform you that the spelter can only rightfully be delivered to ourselves or our agents as holders of the mate's receipt, and that you are responsible to us, as we have intimated to Messrs. Dawson & Arrow, who promised to write to Captain Young by the mail on the 10th instant."—McKellar to Schuster & Co. "Glasgow, 14th July, 1854. Gentlemen, I beg to acknowledge the receipt of your letter of the 12th instant; and, in our communication with Messrs. Dawson & Arrow, they state that Messrs. Coles, Brothers, engaged and shipped the only spelter on board the ship Emperor, and that they received from them bills of lading duly signed. Messrs. D. & A. also state that you never engaged any spelter by the Emperor; nor had they heard of you in the transaction until we wrote them. I am also aware that parties shipping cargo by the Emperor were by public advertisement warned to call at Messrs. D. & A.'s office to get their bills of lading signed a week previous to the ship sailing. However, as I have *no interest in the spelter, but that the rightful owner should get it, I will write to my agent at Calcutta [*710 to discharge into store, if there are any disputed claims to it, when the ship arrives there." A letter from McKellar, to the defendant Young, was read, from which the following is an extract. Glasgow, 17th August, 1854. "As there is a dispute about the spelter you have on board, owing to the failure of the parties who shipped it, and as the sellers of the spelter hold the mate's receipt, which should have been given up when the bills of lading were signed, I would recommend you, if there are any other parties claim the spelter besides the holders of the bills of lading, to store it until they settle the dispute amongst themselves; or, if the mate's receipt is presented, do not give up the spelter till you get the receipt and the bills of lading." On the arrival of the ship at Calcutta the spelter was demanded from Young by the agents of the plaintiffs. Young had then received McKellar's letter, and refused to deliver the spelter. The price paid by Schuster & Co. for the spelter was within a trifle of 24l. per ton: and it was agreed that, if they were entitled to recover, the amount of damages should be taken at 1200l. This was the plaintiffs' case.

For the defence it was proved that McKellar had made an agreement

by way of charter-party of the Emperor for the voyage in question as
follows: "Charter-party.   London, 21st April, 1854.   It is this day
mutually agreed between Alexander McKellar, Esquire, owner of the
good ship or vessel called The Emperor, A. 1, Young, master, of the
measurement of 438/497 tons or thereabouts, now lying in London, and
Messrs. P. & C. Van Notten & Co., of London, merchants.   That the
said ship, being tight, staunch, and strong, and every way fitted for the
*711]   voyage, *shall, with all convenient speed, sail and proceed to a
loading berth in the St. Katherine's Docks, or so near thereunto
as she may safely get, and there load, from the factors of the said
merchants, a full and complete cargo of lawful merchandise, it being
understood that the charterers are to have the full and entire reach of
the ship's hold and tween decks, the freight; specie, and passengers
below to form part of the sum hereinafter guarantied as freight; gunpowder, if shipped, to be done on ship's passage to Gravesend, without
counting time as lay days, as customary, but not exceeding two days,
not exceeding what she can reasonably stow and carry over and above
her tackle, apparel, provisions, and furniture: and, being so loaded, shall
therewith proceed to Calcutta, or so near thereunto as she may safely
get, and deliver the same on being paid freight as follows, viz.: a lump
sum of 1800l. sterling; the ship to be subject to the usual and customary
terms of a vessel taking the berth to load outwards in London, the act
of God, the Queen's enemies, restraint of princes and rulers, fire, and
all and every other dangers and accidents of the seas, rivers, and navigation of whatever nature and kind soever, during the said voyage,
excepted.   The freight to be paid as customary at seventy days after
the vessel's clearance at Custom House in London, less freight payable
at Calcutta secured by bills of lading, not to exceed 300l.   The Captain
to sign bills of lading at any rate of freight without prejudice to this
charter; thirty-five running days are to be allowed the said master, if
the ship is not sooner despatched, for loading and unloading, to be computed from the time the master has given written notice that he is in
dock and ready to receive cargo, and ten days on demurrage over and
*712]   *above the said laying days at 7l. per day.   A commission of
5l. per cent. is due to Messrs. H. & C. Toulmin, Dawson &
Arrow, on this charter-party, ship lost or not lost; penalty for non-performance of this agreement, amount of freight.   The ship to be addressed at Calcutta to the charterers' agents on the usual and customary
terms; it being understood that the owner has the power of chartering
home on payment of a commission of 2½ per cent. on such chartered
homeward freight to charterers outwards.   The stevedore to be appointed by charterers and paid by owners; the vessel's draft of water
not to exceed 16 ft. 6 in., upon an even keel."   The following memorandum was written in the margin.   "If any passengers be taken for
the benefit of the charterers in the after tween decks, they are to pay

all expenses attendant thereon; if chartered home, notice to be given to the charterers outwards previous to ship's departure from London." Van Notten & Co., the charterers, put up The Emperor as a general ship, and employed Messrs. Dawson & Arrow as the ship-brokers, and also employed Mr. Ellis, another ship-broker, to obtain freight. Coles, Brothers, in the latter part of April, engaged with Ellis for room in The Emperor for 100 tons of metal. About the 16th May, Coles, Brothers, sent to Ellis for signature bills of lading bearing date 16th May for 3268 plates spelter, expressing that they were shipped by Coles, Brothers, deliverable at Calcutta to order. Ellis forwarded them to Dawson & Arrow. Coles, Brothers, repeatedly applied to Ellis to have the bills of lading delivered to them; but, for some days, they were refused because there was a dispute as to the quantity shipped on board. Ultimately a memorandum (similar to that contained in the mate's *receipt), "eight pieces in dispute, if on board, to be [*713 delivered," was added to the bills of lading; and, with this addition, they were signed and delivered to Coles, Brothers, it did not appear on what day, but it was before the 3d June, as, on that day, Coles, Brothers, endorsed the bills of lading to The Oriental Bank as security for an advance. The witnesses for the defence agreed that bills of lading ought to be given to the holder of the mate's receipt, and that, though sometimes they were signed without requiring its production, yet, if it was known that the mate's receipt existed, that was irregular. A mate's receipt is always given when goods are shipped from a lighter, but not when they are shipped from the quay; so that a mate's receipt does not necessarily accompany all bills of lading. Neither of the brokers remembered having heard of there being a mate's receipt in this instance, though they could not take upon themselves to say that they had not; and they admitted that it was very unusual to ship so large a quantity of metal as fifty tons from the quay. The goods were ultimately delivered at Calcutta to the holders of the bills of lading. After the 3d June, advertisements were published calling on all persons who held bills of lading to bring them in to be signed, as The Emperor was about to sail. Schuster & Co. were themselves shippers of goods by The Emperor; it appeared, however, that they never saw these advertisements, or were aware of the time of the sailing of The Emperor. The Lord Chief Justice ruled that, under such a charter-party as this, the owner, McKellar, was responsible for the acts of his captain to the same extent as if there had been no charter-party. He told the jury that, on the undisputed facts, the property in the goods was in Schuster & Co.; but that, if they had so conducted [*714 *themselves as to justify the defendants in becoming bound to deliver the goods to others, it would form a defence: and he directed the jury to consider all the circumstances of the case, and, if they thought that the plaintiffs had so conducted themselves as to justify the captain, under those peculiar circumstances, in signing bills of lading to Coles, Brothers, without requiring the production of the mate's receipt, to find for the defendants; if not, for the plaintiffs.   Verdict for the plaintiffs.

Bovill, in the ensuing Term, obtained a rule to show cause why the verdict should not be entered for the defendants, or a new trial had, "on the grounds that the verdict was against the evidence on the question left to the jury, and that the plaintiffs' case was not supported by the evidence; and that, if any parties were liable for a wrongful delivery of the bill of lading without the mate's receipt, it was the charterers Van Notten & Co. or their agents; and that the defendants were not liable, nor either of them, the vessel being under charter and put up by the charterers."

The case was argued on a former day in this Term (May 26th) and this day.(a)

Wilde and *Blackburn* showed cause.—The rule is misconceived.   No leave was or could be reserved to enter a verdict on the grounds stated in the rule; and it is obvious that the liability of the defendant Young is not affected by the existence of the charter-party: but it may be treated as a rule for a new trial moved for on behalf of McKellar alone. It is unnecessary to consider either the first or second counts, or the *pleadings arising on them; for the plaintiffs are entitled to retain their verdict on the count in trover both on the plea of Not guilty and on that denying the property.   When a merchant purchases on commission for another, but on his own credit, the property in the goods vests in him, and does not pass to his constituent till there is a delivery.   A shipment by order of the constituent is not such a delivery unless made with the intention of transferring the dominion of the goods: Wait v. Baker, 2 Exch. 1,† Turner v. Trustees of The Liverpool Docks, 6 Exch. 543.†   Where there is such an intention it is a delivery: Van Casteel v. Booker, 2 Exch. 691.†   The keeping of the mate's receipt, under such circumstances as those in the present case, is conclusive to show that the intention was to preserve the dominion: Abbott On Shipping (Part III., c. 9, s. 15, p. 378, 5th ed.; Part IV., c. 11, s. 8, p. 402, 10th ed.); Craven v. Ryder, 6 Taunt. 433 (E. C. L. R. vol. 1); Thompson v. Trail, 2 Car. & P. 334 (E. C. L. R. vol. 12), S. C. in banc, 6 B. & C. 36 (E. C. L. R. vol. 13); Ruck v. Halfield, 5 B. & Ald. 632 (E. C. L. R. vol. 7).   If the circumstances were such as to show that the retention of the receipt was with no such intention, and was a mere accident, it would be otherwise: Cowasjee v. Thompson, 5 Moore, P. C. 165: but there was no pretence for that here.   Then, it is true that the plaintiffs might have so conducted themselves as to be precluded from setting up their property at the time of the conversion

[*715]

(a) Before Lord Campbell, C. J., Coleridge and Erle, Js.   Crompton, J., heard part of the argument, but left the Court before it was completed.

relied on, that is when the goods were refused at Calcutta. The law on this subject is carefully laid down in Freeman v. Cook, 2 Exch. 654,† where the previous decision of Pickard v. Sears, 6 A. & E. 469 (E. C. L. R. vol. 33), is commented on and explained. To make *out a preclusion, it must be shown that the plaintiffs, either by [*716 actively doing something, or by neglecting a duty to do something, so conducted themselves as might lead the defendants, as reasonable men, to act so as to alter their position, and that the defendants were induced so to act. This exposition of the law was approved of and confirmed by this Court in Howard v. Hudson, 2 E. & B. 1 (E. C. L. R. vol. 75). The signing of the bills of lading to Coles, Brothers, altered the position of the defendants as soon as these bills came into the hands of The Oriental Bank; that is, on the 3d June. After that the whole mischief was done, and nothing occurred to alter the position of the parties. The question was left to the jury whether this alteration was induced by the conduct of the plaintiffs, and was found for the plaintiffs. It is said the finding is against evidence: but it is, in truth, very doubtful if, on this point, there was any evidence in favour of the defendant. No evidence was given of any mercantile usage making it the duty of the holder of the mate's receipt to communicate with the ship's brokers, or of anything to show that the ship's brokers were induced to believe that there was no mate's receipt. There was strong evidence that the brokers had notice that there was a mate's receipt; for, besides the improbability of so large a quantity of goods being delivered from the quay, the bills of lading were kept for some days whilst inquiries were made as to the quantity shipped. These inquiries ended in the brokers inserting in the bill of lading a precise copy of the memorandum in the mate's receipt, "eight pieces in dispute, if on board, will be delivered;" which was at least strong evidence that the brokers were informed of the circumstances of the shipment; *and, supposing that the brokers were ignorant, the mate was [*717 the agent of the defendants and his knowledge was theirs. It is enough, however, to say that the finding, that the defendants did not sign the bills of lading in consequence of being induced by the plaintiffs' conduct, is not against the weight of evidence. Lastly, the defendant McKellar was responsible for the conversion by Young in refusing to deliver the goods at Calcutta. It is true there was a charter-party: but it did not amount to a demise of the vessel. In such cases the possession of the vessel continues in the shipowner: Dean v. Hogg, 10 Bing. 345 (E. C. L. R. vol. 25). This is necessary, as otherwise the shipowner could have no lien for his freight: Belcher v. Capper, 4 M. & G. 502 (E. C. L. R. vol. 43). The captain and crew continue the servants of the shipowner, so that he is liable for their negligence: Fletcher v. Braddick, 2 N. R. 182; Fenton v. The City of Dublin Steam Packet Company, 8 A. & E. 835 (E. C. L. R. vol. 35);

Hodgkinson *v.* Fernie, 2 Com. B. N. S. 415 (E. C. L. R. vol. 89). The principle is explained by Abbott, C. J., in Laugher *v.* Pointer, 5 B. & C. 547, 578 (E. C. L. R. vol. 11). He says: "Let me put the case of a ship hired and chartered for a voyage on the ocean to carry such goods as the charterer may think fit to load, and such only. Many accidents have occurred from the negligent management of such vessels, and many actions have been brought against their owners, but I am not aware that any has ever been brought against the charterer, though he is to some purposes the dominus pro tempore, and the voyage is made not less under his employment, and for his benefit, whether he be on board or not, than the journey is made under the employment, *718] and for the *benefit of the hirer of the horses. Why, then, has the charterer of the ship, or the hirer of the wherry, or the hackney coach, never been thought answerable? I answer, because the shipmaster, the wherryman, and the hackney coachman, have never been deemed the servants of the hirer, although the hirer does contract with the wherryman and the coachman, and is bound to pay them, and the pay is not for the use of the boat, or horses, or carriage only, but also for the personal service of the man." For the same reason, where goods sold and not paid for are put on board a ship chartered by the vendee, they are still in transitu, because the possession of the captain is that of the shipowner, who is a carrier, and not of the charterer, who in such a case is vendee: Gurney *v.* Behrend, 3 E. & B. 622 (E. C. L. R. vol. 77). The general principle is that the shipowner has, in the ordinary charter-party, contracted with the charterer that the ship shall proceed with the cargo on the voyage to its destination, and there deliver the cargo, being paid the stipulated freight; and in all that is done by the captain to fulfil that contract, as in navigating the vessel, carrying and delivering the goods, he acts as servant of the shipowner. It is quite consistent with this that the master may, in other matters, act as agent for the charterer; and, where there is notice to the shipper of goods in a general ship that there is a charter-party such as the present, it may be that he has notice that the contract for shipment is made for the charterer and not for the shipowner: Marquand *v.* Banner, 6 E. & B. 232 (E. C. L. R. vol. 88); Major *v.* White, 7 C. & P. 41 (E. C. L. R. vol. 32). But in this case the conversion complained of was done by the captain in the delivering the *719] goods at their destination, the very *thing which the shipowner had contracted to do. For a misdelivery by the captain the shipowner is liable: Ewbank *v.* Nutting, 7 Com. B. 797 (E. C. L. R. vol. 62). However, in the present case, McKellar, by his letter of 17th August, directed Young to withhold the goods; and, even if the charterers were also liable for that conversion, McKellar, who was personally a party to it, is not thereby absolved.

Bovill and *Cleasby*, in support of the rule.—The plaintiffs had no

right to stop in transitû. [Lord CAMPBELL, C. J.—Though a notice
of stoppage in transitû was originally given, the plaintiff's counsel now
rest their case on their right to the property never having passed from
them.]   The particular goods were appropriated to Coles, Brothers,
by the assent of both parties; that passed the property: Rohde v.
Thwaites, 6 B. & C. 388 (E. C. L. R. vol. 13). Suppose a rise or fall in
price, Coles, Brothers, would have had the benefit or loss. [Lord
CAMPBELL, C. J.—They might have it, because it would be considered
in the damages in an action for not transferring the goods on payment
of the price and commission; but they could not have maintained an
action founded on the right of property. It may be that their right
was to have these particular goods, and these only; but that is by no
means conclusive as to the property. They might have jus ad rem;
they had not jus in re. ERLE, J.—On the bankruptcy of Barton, Irlam
& Higginson, some years ago at Liverpool, every variety of such cases
was considered, both in law and equity.(a) Do not the cases arising
*out of that bankruptcy (of which some have been cited for the   [*720
plaintiffs) establish that the property remains in the commission
merchant till there is a delivery by him; and that a shipment is not a
delivery unless made animo transferendi?] In this case Coles, Brothers,
were permitted by the plaintiffs to engage the freight room in their own
names, and to ship the goods in their own names. [ERLE, J.—On the
contrary, the shipment was made under a mate's receipt, in which the
name of Coles, Brothers, was not mentioned; and the object of doing
so was to preserve to the plaintiffs their control over the property.
Lord CAMPBELL, C. J.—And is it not to be taken, as established by
cases, that, by usage, the bills of lading ought not to be signed until
the mate's receipt is given up?] In all the cases on the subject, the
mate's receipt named the shipper. In the present case the mate's
receipt is in blank. [*Blackburn.*—In Craven v. Ryder, 6 Taunt. 433
(E. C. L. R. vol. 1), Gibbs, C. J., said that the particular form of the
receipt was not material.] The only question left to the jury was as
to the issuing of the bill of lading. That was the act of the ship's
brokers, over whom neither of the defendants had any control, and for
whose acts they are not responsible. The charter-party has the effect
of showing that the defendant McKellar, at all events, was not responsible for the issuing of the bill of lading: Marquand v. Banner, Colvin
v. Newberry, 1 Cl. & F. 283,(b) James v. Jones, 3 Esp. 27, Mackenzie
v. Rowe, 2 Camp. 482, Abbott on Shipping (Part I, ch. I, s. 12, &c.,
p. 19, 5th ed.; s. 8, p. 31, 10th ed.).   *Cur. adv. vult.*

(a) See Turner v. Trustees of the Liverpool Docks, 6 Exch. 543.† Van Casteel v. Booker, 2
Exch. 691.† Both of these actions were brought by orders from Chancery; but the suits in
equity, out of which they arose, do not appear to have been reported.
(b) In Dom. Proc., affirming the judgment of Exch. Ch., in Newberry v. Colvin, 7 Bing. 190
(E. C. L. R. vol. 20); S. C. 1 Cr. & J. 192;† which reversed the judgment of K. B. in Colvin v.
Newberry, 8 B. & C. 166 (E. C. L. R. vol. 15).

*721]
        *Lord CAMPBELL, C. J., on a later day in this Term (June
        2d), delivered the judgment of the Court.

We are of opinion that the verdict ought to stand for the plaintiffs
on the count which charges that their goods were unlawfully converted
by the defendants.   We are clearly of opinion that the property in the
spelter was in the plaintiffs, and was never transferred to Coles, Brothers.
They purchased the spelter from the merchant at Hamburgh, with the
view of transferring it to Coles, Brothers; and their profit was to be
a commission on the price paid for it: but they purchased it in their
own names; they paid for it with their own money; they received it
under a bill of landing making it deliverable to their own order; it was
warehoused in their own names in the port of London; and the intention of the parties was that it should remain the property of the plaintiffs till, according to the usual course of dealing, they received the
price of it from Coles, Brothers, by the redemption of the mate's
receipt.   They gave a delivery order to a lighterman employed by
Coles, Brothers, but with instructions that the lighterman should bring
back to them the mate's receipt, which represented the spelter; and
Coles, Brothers, knew full well that, until they redeemed the mate's
receipt, they had no property in the spelter, and no right to obtain a
bill of lading for it.   They were well aware that in obtaining a bill of
lading without the mate's receipt they committed a gross fraud.   They
thereby acquired the power of giving a right, as against the shipowner
or charterer, to a bonâ fide assignee of the bill of lading for value; but
they acquired no right as against the plaintiffs in whom the property
*722] was still vested.   The *property therefore remained in the
        plaintiffs when the spelter was stored at Calcutta, contrary to
their orders, and when it was delivered to The Oriental Company as
assignees of the bill of lading.   We have therefore to inquire whether
the plaintiffs have done, or omitted to do, anything to prevent them
from insisting upon their title.   This depends mainly upon the question
left to the jury, Whether, according to the usage of trade, under the
circumstances proved, the master of the ship was justified in signing
and delivering the bill of lading to Coles, Brothers, without the mate's
receipt.   If he was, the plaintiffs, having, by their improper conduct
or laches, induced the master, and, through him, the owner, or charterer
of the ship, to incur a liability to another, could not avail themselves
of their legal rights.   But the jury found that question in favour of
the plaintiffs, and we think on satisfactory evidence.   It was admitted
that, if the master and the brokers employed to superintend the loading of the ship had known that there was a mate's receipt, it would
have been their duty to have required the production of it, and to have
attached it to the bill of lading.   Their knowledge of it might well
have been presumed, and was not negatived by any evidence.   Again,
it is difficult to impute laches to the plaintiffs; for they made applica-

tion to Coles, Brothers, to redeem the mate's receipt; and, while this document remained in their possession, they had every reason to believe that they were secure. The bill of lading was dated the 16th of May, before the spelter was actually loaded in the ship. It would have been signed in a day or two after, but for a difficulty as to the number of the packages; and it must have been signed before the 3d *of June, [*723 the day when it was assigned to The Oriental Company. The subsequent delay in making the demand on the defendants could not in any respect prejudice them: and there is no ground whatever for the insinuation that the plaintiffs gave credit to Coles, Brothers, and were only induced to set up their claim upon the defendants by their failure.

We have therefore only further to consider whether the action has been brought against the proper parties. As far as Young the master is concerned, we were rather at a loss to understand on what his defence rested, assuming that there had been a wrongful conversion of the spelter, for which the plaintiffs were entitled to sue. We were told that the mere signing of the bill of lading operated nothing, and that it was delivered out to Coles, Brothers, by the brokers; but the master signed it that it might be delivered to Coles, Brothers; he actually had possession of the spelter on board his ships; and, after a demand of it from him by the plaintiffs, he delivered it to The Oriental Company at Calcutta. A more difficult question arises with respect to the liability of McKellar, the owner of the ship; and, if this had been a demand upon him by any one claiming under a bill of lading signed by the master, we should have been strongly inclined to hold that he was not liable. The ship had been chartered by him to Van Notten & Co. for the voyage from London to Calcutta for a lump sum of 1800l.; evidently to be put up by the charterers as a general ship, with a stipulation as to the master signing bills of lading for the benefit of the charterers. The master and crew were employed and paid by the owner: and this certainly cannot be considered locatio navis, a *demise [*724 of the ship itself with its furniture and apparel; it amounts to locatio navis et operarum magistri et nauticorum, a demise of the ship in a state fit for mercantile adventure, which is to be distinguished from the locatio operis vehendarum mercium, a contract for the carriage of the merchant's goods in the owner's ship and by his servants, where the owner has all the responsibility of a carrier of the goods. Notwithstanding some early conflicting decisions, it seems now settled by a numerous class of cases, from Newberry v. Colvin, 7 Bing. 190 (E. C. L. R. vol. 20),(a) to Marquand v. Banner, that, where there is a hiring of the ship according to the second form above specified, with the intention that the charterer shall employ the ship as a general ship for his own profit, when the master signs bills of lading he does so as the agent of the charterer, not of the owner. But still, the owner being in possession of the ship by his master and crew, he has rights in respect of this possession, as to claim a lien on goods on board for freight due to him ; and he is liable for the acts and negligence of the master as master, irrespective of the contracts entered into by the master with the shippers of goods, as agent for the charterer. Thus the owner, although the ship be so chartered, is clearly liable for a collision arising from the improper management of the ship, and for what the master does within the scope of his general authority as master, which cannot be ascribed to his agency for the charterer. Here the plaintiffs do not claim under any bill of lading; and they could not sue Van Notten & *725] Co., the charterers, for the act of the master in the *unlawful conversion of the spelter at Calcutta; for this act was in no respect for the benefit of the charterers, and can in no respect be considered authorized by them. But in the present case the liability of McKellar, the owner, appears to be placed beyond all doubt by his letter of 17th August, directing the master not to give up the spelter to the plaintiffs, who claimed it under the mate's receipt, but to store it at Calcutta. The conversion therefore was under his own express personal order.   Rule discharged.

GEORGE HINTON BOVILL *v.* THOMAS MICHAEL KEY-WORTH and CHARLES SEELY. *May* 28.

A patentee, in his specification, claimed, as his invention, exhausting from millstone cases the dusty air blown through between the grinding surfaces, by a blast of air ; being a combination of a blast and an exhaust applied to the working of a mill. The claim was not restricted to any particular mode of creating or applying the blast of air, nor to any particular mode of producing the exhaust; and both blast and exhaust had previously been used separately in working mills. Held : that the invention of this combination and application of a blast and an exhaust might be made the subject of a patent.

From the general description, it appeared that the upper stone was fixed and the lower stone was made to rotate ; and some advantages were pointed out as resulting from this arrangement. *Quære,* whether, according to the true construction of the specification, the claim should be limited to the application of a combination of a blast and an exhaust with a mill in which only the lower stone rotates?

But, Held that, if the claim be so limited, the use of a new part of the combination, viz. a combination of blast and exhaust, though in connexion with a mill in which the upper stone does rotate, may be an infringement of the patent.

THE declaration alleged : that the plaintiff was the first and true inventor of a new manufacture : that is to say, of "certain improvements in manufacturing wheat and other grain into meal and flour :" and that Her Majesty, by Her letters patent under the Great Seal, granted to the plaintiff and his assigns the sole privilege to make, use, exercise, *726] and vend the said *invention within England and Wales and Berwick upon Tweed, for the term of fourteen years from 5th June, 1849, subject to the usual condition requiring the enrolment of a specification of the invention. The declaration then averred that a specification had been enrolled, and that, pursuant to the statute, &c., a disclaimer and memorandum of alteration in writing had, by leave of the Attorney-General, been entered and enrolled; and that the defendants had afterwards infringed the patent right.

The defendants pleaded:

First; Not guilty.

Secondly; That the plaintiff was not the first and true inventor.

Thirdly; That the invention was not new at the date of the patent.

Fourthly; That the invention was not a new manufacture.

Fifthly; Non concessit.

Sixthly; That the plaintiff had not caused to be enrolled any instrument in writing, under his hand and seal, particularly describing the nature of his invention, and in what manner it was to be performed.

Seventhly; That the plaintiff did not enter such disclaimer and memorandum of alteration as alleged.

Issues on all the pleas.

On the trial, before Lord Campbell, C. J., at the London Sittings after Trinity Term, 1856, the plaintiff gave in evidence his specification, enrolled 5th December, 1849, and also a disclaimer and memorandum of alteration, entered, filed, and enrolled 1st May, 1855; by which latter he disclaimed the first part of the invention described and claimed in the specification, and altered *the specification so as to claim only the undisclaimed parts of the invention. [*727

The specification, as altered by the disclaimer and memorandum of alteration, described the invention as follows.(a)

"In compliance with the said proviso, I, the said George Hinton Bovill, do hereby declare the nature of my said invention, and the manner in which the same is to be performed, are particularly described and ascertained in and by the following statement thereof, reference being had to the drawings hereunto annexed, and to the figures and letters marked thereon, that is to say :—(a)

[" The first part of my Invention consists in making the bed or under stone rotate instead of the upper one, as heretofore practised. Secondly,] *Firstly*, in an arrangement for ventilating the grinding surfaces of millstones, and the introduction of air through the top stone (when fixed) either by blowing or exhaustion. [Thirdly,] *Secondly*, in exhausting the air from the cases of millstones, combined with the application of a blast to the grinding surfaces. [Fourthly,] *Thirdly*, in separating the stive or dust of flour from the air, when exhaustion or blast is employed to facilitate grinding, and preventing the dust and waste in the mill.

" And in order that my invention may be fully understood, I will proceed to describe the same. Drawing A is a transverse section of a pair of millstones, with the air blast applied, as formerly patented by

(a) The parts included in brackets in the following copy were disclaimed; and the words in italics were introduced by the disclaimer and memorandum of alteration.

mo, showing the top stone, A, a fixture, and the bottom stone, B, hung
*728] firmly in a cast-iron dish C to the driving spindle *D, which
works through a deep collar bearing in the cross stay E, fixed to
the hurst.   The spindle, with the bed stone hung upon it, is raised or
lowered in the ordinary manner.   F, air-tight covering to eye of stone,
through which the feed tube G works. H, air pipe from blowing machine,
from which the supply of air is regulated by the valve I.   When the
stones are set to work, it is first necessary to adjust the lower stone perfectly true and level, and then to lay the top stone down upon it face to
face ; the top one is then to be secured by the set screws, a, a, a, a, to
the hurst brackets b, b ; the miller then lowers the bed stone as required
for the operation of grinding ; the grinding surfaces being perfectly
true to each other, can never come in contact, when the bed stone has
been lowered in the slightest degree from the upper one ; and the injury
caused by the running stone rolling upon the other, and destroying
the grinding faces when short of feed on the old system, is entirely
avoided ; the delivery of the meal from between the stones by the cen-
trifugal action is much quicker ; the corn and meal being upon the
revolving stone are actuated outwards more rapidly than if rubbed outwards by the furrows of the top stone, as heretofore practised.

[" The Drawings show a combination of other parts of my Invention
hereafter described, but this part of my Invention may be applied to
stones worked with a current of air obtained by a blast or exhaustion,
or, when worked without wind, in the ordinary manner.   I may here
remark, that I am aware that it has before been tried to rotate the lower
as well as the upper stone for colour mills, but which I do not claim as
my Invention.]

*729] *" The [second] first part of my invention consists in intro-
ducing air-pipes into the top millstone, so as to more freely ven-
tilate the grinding surfaces when currents of air are forced or exhausted
through them.   In the top of stone A are placed the air-pipes c, c, c, c,
which open into the furrows on the face of the stone, and are led away
to the eye or back of the stone where the air is introduced.   These
pipes I prefer to have of about one inch in diameter, and as many in
number in the furrows in the stones, so as to give a free ventilation in
addition to the supply of air down the master line from the eye of the
stone.   I am aware that large holes have been cut out in the runner
stone and trumpet-mouthed pipes introduced into the back of the running stone with their ends terminating at the point of the master lines
in the eye of the stone, to induce air, if possible, so as to pass between
the stones ; but it will be seen these differ essentially from this part of
my invention, and have only been applied to the top stone when running;
air has also been exhausted down through the eye of the top stone when
running, and between the grinding surfaces.   I do not therefore claim

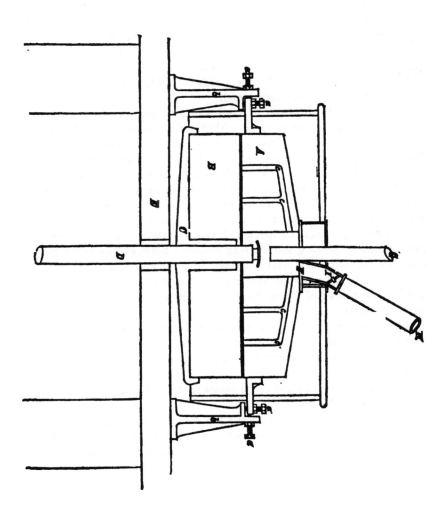

the principle except when worked in combination with a fixed upper stone.

" In carrying out the [third] *second* part of my invention when working millstones with a blast of air, I introduce a pipe to the millstone case from a fan or other exhausting machine, so as to carry off all the warm dusty air blown through between the stones to a chamber, as hereafter described, by which the dust in the mill is avoided, and the grinding improved. And this part of my invention relates only to sucking away the plenum of dusty air forced through the stones, and not to *730] *employing a sufficient exhausting power to induce a current of air between the millstones without a blast, this having before been practised, as above mentioned.

" The [fourth] *third* part of my invention consists in straining the stive or air, which is surcharged with fine flour through suitable porous fabrics, which retain the flour and allow the air to pass through; and this I accomplish by exhausting the air from the millstone case, or other closed chamber receiving the meal from the stones by means of a fan or other exhausting machinery, and blow the stive so exhausted into a chamber, having its sides and top formed of one or more thicknesses of suitable porous fabrics, to allow the air under pressure to pass out deprived of the flour by means of this filtration. I also obtain the same result by placing the filtering chamber between the stone case or chamber receiving the meal and dust from the stones and the exhausting machine. The stive or dusty air is then sucked through the filtering fabrics instead of being blown through, and the air passing away clean as before.

" Having now described the nature of my invention, and the manner in which the same is to be performed, I would remark, that I do not confine myself to the precise details, so long as the particular character of my invention be retained. But what I claim is,—

[" First, making the bed stone rotate instead of the top one, as heretofore practised.]

[" Secondly,] *Firstly*, fixing the top stone, and causing currents of air, either by exhaustion or pressure, to pass between the grinding surfaces of millstones when the top stone is so fixed, and in the introduction of the ventilating pipes in the stones, as herein described.

*731]   *" [Thirdly,] *Secondly*, in exhausting the dusty air when the same has been blown through the grinding surfaces of the millstones, from the stone cases or chambers receiving the meal, as herein described.

" And, lastly, I claim the passing of the dust or stive caused in the process of grinding through suitable porous fabrics, by which the flour is filtered from the air, as herein described.

" In witness whereof, I, the said George Hinton Bovill, have hereunto set my hand and seal, this fifth day of December, in the year of our Lord one thousand eight hundred and forty-nine.''

The plaintiff gave the usual primâ facie evidence in support of his case upon each of the issues. And, as to the infringement, it was proved that the defendants had made and used a flour-mill in which a blast of air was introduced into the centre of the millstones, so that the air was blown from the centre and between the grinding surfaces of the stones through to their peripheries. This mill also had an exhausting apparatus, by means of which the surplus air was exhausted from the interior of the case surrounding the millstones. The upper stone in the mill of the defendants rotated, the lower stone being fixed.

On the part of the defendants it was proved that the working of millstones with a blast of air, introduced in several ways, had been publicly used and known before the date of the plaintiff's patent : and the specifications of patents granted to the plaintiff and to Robert Gordon, for different modes of effecting that object, were given in evidence. The defendants also proved that exhausting the air from millstone cases, surrounding the peripheries of the stones, for the [*732 *purpose of drawing a current of air through and between the grinding surfaces of millstones from the eye or centre to the peripheries of the stones, had been published and used before the date of the plaintiff's patent : and the specification of a prior patent granted to A. B. Newton, for such an application of an exhausting apparatus, was given in evidence. There was also evidence given of a combination of a blast and an exhaust having been applied to a mill belonging to Mr. Muir at Glasgow ; upon which a question of fact for the jury arose, and was decided in favour of the plaintiff.

For the defendants it was contended that the second part of the invention claimed by the plaintiff's specification (as altered by the disclaimer) was claimed only as applicable to a mill with a fixed upper stone ; and that, as the mill of the defendants had not a fixed upper stone, they had not infringed the patent. That, if the specification was not to be construed so as to confine the second claim to a mill in which the upper stone was fixed, that claim would extend to a combination of every practicable mode of applying a blast and every practicable mode of applying an exhaust to a mill, if any one of such modes of applying a blast be used together with any one of such modes of applying an exhaust ; and that so large and indefinite a claim to such numerous combinations was not a claim for a new manufacture which could be made the subject of a patent within the meaning of the Statute of Monopolies : and, also, that the specification had not particularly described any manner of performing the second part of the invention, and had not described the manner of performing every combination to which the second claim extended, as *required by the proviso in [*733 the patent ; nor had it described any manner of new manufacture.

The Lord Chief Justice reserved these objections for the opinion of the Court of Queen's Bench; subject to which his Lordship left the case to the jury; and they gave their verdict for the plaintiff upon each of the issues.

In Michaelmas Term, 1856, Sir *A. J. E. Cockburn*, Attorney-General, obtained a rule Nisi to enter a verdict for the defendants, or for entering a nonsuit, or for a new trial, on the grounds: " That fixing the upper millstone, as mentioned in the plaintiff's specification, was an essential part of the invention; and that the defendant had not used a fixed millstone, and had not infringed.   That the second part of the invention, as described in the specification, could not be made the subject of a patent; and the specification does not describe the nature or manner of performing any new manufacture.   That the verdict was against evidence with respect to the prior use of the alleged invention." (And on another ground, not material to the points ultimately decided.)

In last Hilary Term,(a)

Knowles, Watson, and *Denman* showed cause, and *Atherton, Hindmarch,* and *Manisty* were heard in support of the rule.

The Court, at the close of the argument, declared their opinion that the rule could not be supported on the ground that the verdict was against the evidence.   On the other points, they took time for consideration; and *afterwards they directed that the case should be reargued by one counsel on each side, and called their attention to the recent judgment of this Court in Lister v. Leather.(b)   On an earlier day in the present Term,(c)

*734]

Knowles showed cause against the rule, and *Atherton* was heard in support of it.

The following authorities were referred to, besides Lister v. Leather: Kay v. Marshall, 8 Cl. & Fin. 245, Smith v. London and North Western Railway Company, 2 E. & B. 69 (E. C. L. R. vol. 75), Barber v. Grace, 1 Exch. 339,† Hornblower v. Boulton, 8 T. R. 95, Boulton v. Bull, 2 H. Bl. 463, Carpenter v. Smith, 9 M. & W. 300,† Neilson v. Harford, 8 M. & W. 806,† Sellers v. Dickinson, 5 Exch. 312,† Newton v. Grand Junction Railway Company, 5 Exch. 331 (note).†

The course of the arguments will be sufficiently collected from the statement of the points taken at Nisi Prius, the grounds of the rule, and the judgment of the Court.   *Cur. adv. vult.*

Lord CAMPBELL, C. J., now delivered the judgment of the Court.

(a) January 14th and 15th.   Before Lord Campbell, C. J., Coleridge, Wightman, and Erle, Js.   Coleridge, J., left the Court towards the close of the argument on the second day.

(b) April 27th, 1857.   The judgment having been given for discharging the rule obtained by the defendant, the defendant appealed to the Exchequer Chamber.   The judgment of the Queen's Bench was affirmed, 23d Feb., 1858.   The proceedings in both Courts will be reported together.   See post) Hilary Vacation, 1858.

(c) May 23d.   Before Lord Campbell, C. J., Coleridge, Wightman, and Erle, Js.

*We are of opinion that the objections to the validity of this [*735 patent cannot be supported.

The whole of the plaintiff's process, if the combination be new, is certainly the subject of a patent; and so would the part No. 2, if taken separately, for "exhausting the air from the cases of millstones, combined with the application of a blast to the grinding surfaces," as they introduce very important " improvements in manufacturing wheat and other grain into meal and flour." The combination of the *exhaust* with the *blast*, so as to carry off the warm dusty air blown through between the stones to a chamber above, while the pure flour, in a dry condition, without the stive, descends into a chamber below, added to the quantity and improved the quality of the flour produced in grinding: and its effect was highly favourable to the health and comfort of the men employed in the operation.

Still, if the specification does not point out the mode by which this part of the process (No. 2) is to be conducted, so as to accomplish the object in view, it would be the statement of a principle only, and the patent would be invalid. But we are of opinion that the specification of the face of it cannot (as contended) be pronounced, in point of law, to be bad in this respect: and we are of opinion that the evidence adduced at the trial shows it to be quite sufficient. The specification says: " In carrying out the second part of my invention when working millstones with a blast of air, I introduce a pipe to the millstone case from a fan or other exhausting machine, so as to carry off all the warm dusty air blown through between the stones to a chamber, as *here- [*736 after described." " And this part of my invention relates only to sucking away the plenum of dusty air forced through the stones, and not to employing a sufficient exhausting power to induce a current of air between the millstones without a blast." The *exhaust* produced by the pipe and fan is to be proportioned to the plenum caused by the *blast*, taking care not to produce the inconvenient current of air, against which a caution is given. How can a Judge take upon himself to say that this may not be enough to enable a workman of competent skill to construct the machinery? According to the evidence, the specification was abundantly sufficient for this purpose; and therefore it could be no more necessary in the specification to explain the details, by which the pipe and fan were to be employed to create and to regulate the *exhaust*, than to describe how the millstone case or the stones themselves were to be fashioned. The learned counsel for the defendants, after being familiarly acquainted with the manner in which this part of the process is conducted, being asked to suggest the fit language to be employed to instruct the workman how to adjust the *exhaust* so as properly to suck away the plenum, that the stive may be discharged into the chamber above, were unable to devise any improvement upon the specification.

Therefore, the plaintiff being now allowed to be the inventor, the jury being in our opinion fully justified in finding that the process had not been publicly practised at Glasgow before the date of the patent, and the specification being sufficient, the patent is valid: and we have only to consider whether there has been an actionable infringement of
*737] it by the defendants using *the exhaust and the blast in the manner described (No. 2), in a mill in which the upper stone rotated and the nether stone was fixed.

The plaintiff contends that his patent, as explained by the specification, was originally for four separate and independent inventions, and that No. 2, in the amended specification, must be considered a separate and independent invention, as if the patent had been granted for this alone.   The defendants contend, on the contrary, that the patent was granted for one process comprising several successive and connected parts, the use of fixed upper millstones being one of them. We do not think it necessary to try to reconcile the different parts of the specification (which are somewhat conflicting), or to give any positive opinion upon this question; for, supposing the patent to be for a combination, consisting of several parts of one process, we are of opinion that the defendants are liable in this action for having used a material part of the process which was new for the same purpose as that mentioned in the specification, although they did not at the same time use all the parts of the process as specified.   The defendants admit that they used the part of the process No. 2, as described in the amended specification; and they rest their defence upon the fact that they did so only in a mill with a rotating upper millstone.   But, if the fixed upper millstone were clearly described by the plaintiff, in the statement and diagram to be found in his specification, as part of the combination for which he took out his patent, as No. 2 is a material part of the combination and was new, we are of opinion that they cannot lawfully
*738] use No. 2 for the same purpose by substituting a *rotating upper millstone for a fixed upper millstone, or by resorting to any other equivalent for any other separate part of the process specified. This case seems to us to be governed by Lister *v.* Leather,(*a*) and the authorities which in that case we fully commented upon: and therefore that there ought to be judgment for the plaintiff.

Rule discharged.

(*a*) See note (*b*), ante, p. 734.

THOMAS DE LA RUE, WARREN DE LA RUE, JONAH
NATHAN and WILLIAM FREDERICK DE LA RUE v. JOHN
DICKENSON, CHARLES LONGMAN, FREDERICK WIL-
LIAM PRATT BARLOW, and JOHN EVANS. *May* 28.

In an action for the infringement of a patent, the question of infringement or not is for the
jury and not the Judge, although there be no question with respect to whether the defendant
has or has not used the particular machine or process which is alleged to be an infringement.

The specification of a patent for an invention of "improvements in the manufacture of envelopes"
described a machine in which a piece of paper was held upon a platform, whilst the flaps of
the envelope were folded, and concluded by claiming "the so arranging machinery that the
flaps of envelopes may be folded thereby as herein described." Held: that a machine in
which the flaps of an envelope were folded might be an infringement of the patent, although
the envelope was not held down during the operation of folding.

The specification of a patent for an invention with a similar title described and claimed "the
application of gum or cement to the flaps of envelopes by apparatus acting in the manner of
surface printing." Held: that an apparatus for applying the gum might be an infringement,
although it acted only in part in the manner of surface printing according to the description
contained in the specification.

THE declaration alleged that Edwin Hill and the plaintiff Warren
De la Rue were the true and first inventors of a new manufacture, that
is to say, "Improvements in the manufacture of envelopes;" and that
*Her Majesty, by Her letters patent under the Great Seal, [*739
granted unto the said Edwin Hill and Warren De la Rue, their
executors, administrators, and assigns, the sole privilege to make, use,
exercise, and vend their invention within England for the term of
fourteen years, from the 17th March, 1845, subject to a condition that
the patentees should, within six months, cause to be enrolled in Chancery an instrument in writing under their or one of their hands and
seals, particularly describing the nature of the invention, and in what
manner it was to be performed. The declaration then alleged the performance of this condition. The declaration further alleged that the
plaintiff Warren De la Rue was the true and first inventor of a certain
other new manufacture, that is to say, "Improvements in the manufacture of envelopes;" and that Her Majesty, by other letters patent
under the Great Seal, granted unto Warren De la Rue, his executors,
&c., the sole privilege to make, use, exercise, and vend his invention
within England for the term of fourteen years from the 19th day of
December, 1849, subject to a condition that the patentee should, within
six months, cause to be enrolled in Chancery an instrument in writing,
under his hand and seal, particularly describing and ascertaining the
nature of his invention and in what manner it was to be performed. The
declaration then alleged the performance of this condition by the
patentee. That afterwards, and before the committing of the grievances
by the defendants, by virtue of certain indentures of assignment, the
said letters patent firstly and secondly hereinbefore mentioned, and the
exclusive right and enjoyment of the inventions therein mentioned, and

*740]   all the benefits and advantages thereof, became and were, *and still are, vested in the plaintiffs and the defendants, during the said term of fourteen years by the said letters patent respectively granted.   And defendants, after the making of the said several indentures hereinbefore mentioned, and the exclusive privileges becoming vested in the plaintiffs, did infringe the said patent rights and exclusive privileges so vested in the plaintiffs.

Pleas by all the defendants.   1. Not guilty; 2. That Hill and W. De la Rue were not the true and first inventors of the invention in the declaration firstly mentioned; 3. That the same invention was not new; 4. That the same invention was not the working or making of any manner of manufacture for which letters patent could by law be granted; 5. That the patentees did not, within six months, cause to be enrolled in Chancery an instrument in writing under their hands and seals particularly describing and ascertaining the nature of their invention, and in what manner it was to be performed; 6. That W. De la Rue was not the true and first inventor of the invention in the declaration secondly mentioned; 7. That the same invention was not new; 8. That the same invention was not the working or making of any manner of manufacture for which letters patent could be granted; 9. That the patentee did not, within six months, cause to be enrolled in Chancery an instrument in writing under his hand and seal particularly describing the nature of his invention, and in what manner it was to be performed.   Issues on all the pleas.

On the trial, before Lord Campbell, C. J., at the London Sittings after Hilary Term, 1857, the assignments were admitted; and the two specifications were read in evidence.

*741]   *By the specification of the first patent, the patentees, after declaring that the nature of their invention and the manner in which it is to be performed were described and ascertained in and by the therein following statement thereof, reference being had to the drawings annexed, commenced the description of the invention as follows.

"Our invention relates: First, to improvements in machinery for cutting or shaping paper for the making of envelopes; And, secondly, to arranging machinery for folding over the flaps of envelopes.   And, in order that our invention may be fully understood and readily carried into effect, we will proceed to describe the means pursued by us.

" In making envelopes, as heretofore practised, the paper has been cut into suitable shapes by various means.   Now the object of the first part of our invention is to improve the machinery employed for cutting or shaping paper for making envelopes; and of the second part in making up envelopes for folding the flaps of properly-shaped paper by machinery.   The flaps have been generally folded by hand, without preparation by machinery; but in some cases the paper, having been

cut or shaped thus, has been creased by machinery, so as to aid the.
persons when folding: but in all cases the folding over of the flaps of
envelopes has been done by hand.   Now, accordingly, the second part
of our invention is so to arrange the machinery that, properly-shaped
paper being introduced into it, the flaps shall be folded by the working
of the machinery.   And in order that our invention may be most fully
understood and readily carried into effect, we will proceed to describe
the drawings hereunto annexed."

*The specification then described the drawings of the ma- [*742
chinery which the patentees had invented for cutting or shaping
pieces of paper intended to be converted into envelopes, and which
constituted the first part of the invention; and as to which no question
was raised.

The specification also described the second part of the invention,
consisting of "machinery for folding over the flaps of envelopes, the
properly-cut paper being fed into the machine by hand."

This machinery consisted of a shallow open box, the top of which
was of the size and shape of an envelope; and the box was furnished
with a movable bottom or platform, placed within it, so as to be capable of being elevated to the top of the box,· when the flaps of an
envelope were to be folded down upon it.   The machine was also furnished with a hollow plunger, mounted above the box.   The lower end
of the plunger was of the same shape, and nearly the same size, as the
opening in the top of the box, and of the same shape and size as the
envelopes to be made.   It was attached to mechanism actuated by a
cam, by which it was, during the operation of the machine, depressed
into the interior of the open box, and again raised out of it.   Each of
the four sides of the box was furnished with a folding instrument or
folder, the folders being of nearly the same shape as the flaps of an
envelope, but somewhat less.   These folders were hinged upon the
upper edges of the box, and attached to mechanism by which they could
all be turned over, so as to cover the open top of the box, and fold
down the flaps of a piece of paper or blank placed within the box, and
convert it into an envelope by pressing it upon the movable bottom or
platform within *the box; after which the folders were, by the [*743
action of the mechanism, turned back to allow the folded envelope to be withdrawn from the top of the box.   When an envelope was
to be made by this machinery, a piece of paper of the proper size and
shape for forming an envelope (usually called a blank) was placed upon
the top of the box, with that part of it which was to form the face of
the envelope immediately over the square open top of the box; and
the parts of the paper which were to form the four flaps of the envelope were placed immediately above the hinged folders attached to the
four sides of the box, as they lay horizontally outside the box.   The
plunger then descended into the box a short distance, carrying down

under it that part of the paper blank which was above the opening of
the box, and causing the flaps to rise up between the sides of the
plunger and the sides of the box; and in this way were *creased* the
parts of the paper blank at which the flaps of the envelope were to be
folded down.   Two sides of the hollow plunger (which was called an
inverted box) were then elevated, so as to allow two of the folders to
fold down two of the flaps of the envelope, during which operation the
paper was held down by the other sides of the plunger.   This being
done, the paper was held down by those two folders, and the remainder
of the plunger was removed; and then the other two folding instruments folded down the two remaining flaps of the envelope.

The specification described the general nature of the machine as
follows.   " This machine is so arranged that, a piece of paper of the
proper figure or shape for an envelope being placed in the machine upon
a movable platform, what we call an inverted box, of the size of the
*744]   envelope when folded, descends and creases the *paper and raises
the flaps of the envelope out of the horizontal position; and
thus far the general character of the machine is not new.   But in this
machine the inverted box (having performed its office of creasing and
raising the flaps of the envelope out of the horizontal) is so arranged
that two of its sides go away, leaving the paper held down by the other
two sides of the box, and then angular flaps, or folding instruments,
fold the flaps of the envelope at those sides where the sides of the box
have moved away; and the paper, being held down at those sides by
the folding instruments, allows of the other sides of the inverted box
going away, when two other folding instruments will fold the other two
flaps of the envelope, the folding instruments working in such manner,
slightly in advance one of the other, that the angles or ends of the
flaps of the envelopes will be successively folded over the preceding one
in the same manner as if each of the four flaps of an envelope had
been folded by hand one after the other.   The envelope having been
folded by the machine, it is removed by suitable apparatus, and a fresh
piece of paper of the proper form for an envelope is fed into the machine."

After describing another machine for folding the flaps of envelopes,
the specification concluded by declaring that the patentees made no
claim to the mechanical parts separately which were used in construction.   And, as to the second part of the invention, they made the following claim: " Secondly, we claim the so arranging machinery that
the flaps of envelopes may be folded thereby as herein described.'

In the specification of the second patent, the patentee commenced
the description of the invention by stating that it consisted: " First,
*745]   of means of applying gum or *adhesive cement to the flaps of
envelopes during the process of folding, so as to cause flaps of
each envelope to adhere together according to the order or succession

in which they are folded: Secondly, my invention consists of means of
subjecting envelopes (after the flaps have been gummed) to pressure
between surfaces, so as more certainly to insure the holding of the
cement; and, Thirdly, my invention consists of the means hereinafter
described, for causing what I call 'the seal flaps' of envelope paper to
be coated with gum or cement, and then to be transmitted to and
through drying apparatus." The specification, then, with the aid of
drawings, described the first part of the invention, which consisted of
apparatus for applying to the flaps of an envelope, during the course
of its manufacture in a machine, the gum or cement necessary for
causing three of the four flaps of the envelope to adhere together.
The essential parts of the apparatus consisted of a reservoir containing
the gum or cement in a liquid state; and of an endless apron mounted
upon rollers, one of which was below the surface of the liquid gum in
the reservoir, so that the apron, during the action of the machine, was
continually passing through the liquid gum, and, upon rising up from
the surface of the liquid, carried with it, and adhering to its surface,
sufficient gum to yield the necessary quantity to the surface of an
instrument, by means of which the gum was taken from the apron and
deposited upon the flaps of the paper to be folded into an envelope.
An instrument, having projecting surfaces (like type) of the sizes and
shapes of the parts of the flaps to be covered with gum, had alternating
motions given to it in such a way as, first, to cause the projecting surfaces to come in contact with the endless apron, from which *they [*746
took a portion of the liquid gum; and then, by another motion,
the same surfaces were brought into contact with three of the flaps of
an envelope (before being folded) in a folding machine, and deposited
a portion of the gum upon the flaps in the required places; so that,
when the flaps were all folded, three of them adhered together, leaving
the other one open, so as to permit the introduction of a letter or other
enclosure.

In the drawings, this gumming apparatus was shown as connected
with a machine such as described in the specification of the first-mentioned patent: but it was stated that the apparatus might be used in
conjunction with any other machine for making envelopes.

In the description of this part of the invention, it was stated that
the peculiar character of the gumming consisted "in having the gum
or cementing material on a suitable surface, and employing apparatus
to take or receive such gum or cement, and transmit a quantity thereof
to the flaps of an envelope, so as to imprint the surfaces of the flaps
of an envelope, in contradistinction to what has been heretofore proposed to be done, wherein the paper has been pressed down on the surface of a fountain, or wherein a fountain has been proposed to be
brought down on to the flaps; in both cases the flaps of the envelopes
receiving the gum or cement from the fountain or vessel containing such

cementing matter." At the end of the description of this part of the
invention the patentee stated : " I would remark, in respect to this part
of my invention, that, although I have been particular in describing
the details as practised by me, that the same may be varied in form,
and also in the instruments, and yet remain substantially the same apparatus as that described, the peculiar character of *the same being
the applying of gum or cement to the flaps of envelopes by im-
printing the same thereon by suitable surfaces, caused to take or receive
gum or cement from a suitable surface or source, and to convey or im-
part the same on to the flaps of envelopes."

*747]

After describing the second and third parts of the invention (which
are not now material), the specification contained the following claims.

" Having thus described the nature of my invention, and the manner
in which the same is to be performed, I would have it understood that
I do not confine myself to the details as herein shown and described,
so long as the peculiar character of any part of my improvements be
retained. But what I claim is : First, the applying gum or cement to
the flaps of envelopes which are folded by machinery on to each other
in such manner that part of the process of folding of the flaps is performed before and part after the application of the gum or cement. I
also claim the application of gum or cement to the flaps of envelopes by
apparatus acting in the manner of surface printing, in contradistinction
to the application of gum or cement direct from a fountain or vessel
containing the fluid gum or cement."

The specification then contained claims respecting the other parts of
the invention, which are not now material.

It was admitted that the mode of creasing the flaps of a blank to be
made into an envelope by pressing the middle of the blank which is to
form the face of the envelope into a square box of an appropriate shape
and size, and by means of a plunger or instrument of the same shape
and size as the front of an envelope, had been invented, by a person
of the name of Addenbrook, *before the date of the plaintiffs'
first patent, and was not new at that date.

*748]

The plaintiffs gave primâ facie evidence of the novelty of each of the
inventions, and of the sufficiency of the specifications.

In order to establish the infringement of the first patent by the
defendants, the plaintiffs proved that the defendants had made and
used a machine in which the blanks or pieces of paper to be folded into
envelopes were first creased, so as to raise each of the flaps up into a
vertical position, by a hollow plunger pressing a blank or piece of paper
into a box in the same way as in the machine of the plaintiffs. But
that part of the process performed by the machine of the plaintiffs, not
being new, was disclaimed by the specification. Instead of folding
down the flaps of an envelope by means of hinged folding instruments,
such as used by the plaintiffs, the machine of the defendants was so

arranged that, as soon as the hollow plunger had creased and turned
·up the four flaps of the paper against its four sides, it was raised up
from within the flaps, and four jets of air were caused to act upon the
flaps, so as to blow them inwards. The interior of the plunger was
furnished with four inclined planes, placed immediatoly within the bottom edges of the plunger : they were somewhat smaller in size than the
flaps of the envelopes; and they were placed at different angles to a
horizontal line across the bottom of the plunger, so as to act in the
required succession for the folding of the flaps of an envelope. The
plunger having been raised up after creasing and turning up the flaps
of the paper to be made into an envelope, and the flaps being inclined
*inwards by the action of jets of air as already mentioned, the [*749
plunger again descended ; and, the points of the flaps being sufficiently inclined inwards, they passed into the interior of the plunger ;
and the inclined planes in succession acted upon the flaps as the plunger
descended, so as to fold them down in their proper order, and so complete the folding : after which the envelope was discharged at the bottom of the box in which it had been formed, instead of the top as in the
machine of the plaintiffs.

The case against the defendants with respect to the infringement of
the second patent was, that they had made and used apparatus for
applying gum to the flaps of envelopes, in which the instrument for
applying the gum to the flaps obtained a supply of gum direct from the
reservoir, by being dipped into it, instead of taking a supply from the
surface of an endless apron passing through the gum in the reservoir,.
as in the machine of the plaintiffs. The surface of the instrument of
the defendants for applying the gum pressed it upon the proper parts
of the envelope flaps.

The plaintiffs called witnesses who gave evidence that the implements
of the defendants for folding the flaps of the envelopes were substantially the same as those of the plaintiffs, producing the same effect, and
being nearly the same in shape as the folding instruments of the plaintiffs, having an up and down motion with the plunger, instead of being
turned over upon hinges and having the effect produced by means of a
cam action, as in the machine of the plaintiffs. The witnesses of the
plaintiffs also stated that, in the gumming apparatus of the defendants,
the instrument for applying the gum printed or pressed the gum upon
the flaps of the *envelope "after the manner of surface print- [*750
ing," and in that respect was substantially the same as the apparatus of the plaintiffs.

The defendants gave in evidence the specification of a patent granted
to A. F. Remond, on 28th February, 1849, which described the
folding apparatus used by the defendants (alleged to be an infringement of the plaintiffs' first patent), and also described a gumming
apparatus. Remond's gumming apparatus consisted of a fountain

which kept two small reservoirs continually full with a slight over-flow: the upper parts of these reservoirs were of the same dimensions as the parts of the flaps to be gummed; and those parts received a portion of gum by being pressed down upon the surfaces of the gum in the reservoirs.

For the defendants it was objected that there was no evidence that they had infringed either of the patents.

As to the first patent, it was contended that the claim in the specification of the plaintiffs was either too general, or confined to the particular mode or machine. If confined to the particular machine, the claim was for an apparatus which held down the paper whilst the flaps were folded; and the holding was essential to make a machine come within the meaning of the description in the specification of the plaintiffs; and, as the machine of the defendants did not hold down the paper during the process of folding, they did not infringe the first patent of the plaintiffs.

With respect to the second patent, the defendants contended that the claim was either confined to the particular kind of apparatus described, or the claim of invention was too large, and extended to all modes of *applying gum to envelope flaps, and therefore included

*751]

the gumming apparatus described in Remond's prior specification. That, if the plaintiffs' claim extended only to the particular gumming apparatus, the defendants had not infringed; for the instrument which applied the gum to the flaps did not take it from another surface (the endless apron) as was done in the plaintiffs' machine, but directly from the reservoir.

The defendants called witnesses in support of their case, who gave evidence respecting the differences between the machines of the defendants and those of the plaintiffs; and they stated (with respect to the infringement of the second patent) that the placing of a supply of ink upon the surface of type *by means of another surface* covered with the ink was essential to that description of printing called surface printing; and that in this way the plaintiffs' gumming process resembled surface printing, and the process of the defendants did not.

The counsel for the defendants also contended that, there being no dispute with respect to what apparatus the defendants had made and used, the questions to be determined respecting the infringements of the patents were for the Court and not for the jury.

The Lord Chief Justice overruled the objections, and held that each of the specifications claimed only the particular modes or apparatus described; that there might an infringement of the first patent by an apparatus for folding the flaps of envelopes, although the paper was not held down during the operation. Also, that a mode of applying gum to the flaps of envelopes after the manner of surface printing

might *be an infringement of the second patent, although the [*752
printing instrument took the gum directly from the reservoir.
His Lordship also held that the questions respecting the infringement
of the patents were for the jury; and that there was evidence sufficient
to go to the jury.

The jury, in answer to questions from his Lordship, stated that, in
their opinion, the folding machine and gumming apparatus of the defendants were imitations of the plaintiffs' two inventions: and they found a
verdict for the plaintiffs. The Lord Chief Justice, at the request of
the counsel of the defendants, reserved for the opinion of the Court the
objections which were taken for the defendants.

In last Easter Term, *Byles*, Serjt., moved in pursuance of the leave
reserved, and obtained a rule Nisi to enter a verdict for the defendants
or for a new trial, on the grounds: " First, that, if the plaintiffs' specifications are to be read as embracing the defendants' or Remond's processes, the patents and specifications are respectively too wide, and the
patents cannot be supported. Second; that, if the patents are for the
specific machinery described, there was no evidence of infringement.
Third; that the verdict was against the weight of evidence."

In an earlier part of this Term,(a)

Sir *F. Thesiger*, *Grove*, *Hindmarch*, and *Lush* showed cause, and
Byles, Serjt., *Hugh Hill*, *Bovill*, and *T. Webster* were heard in support
of the rule.

*The following authorities were referred to: Jupe *v.* Pratt, [*753
Webster's Reports, &c., on Letters Patent, 144, Smith *v.* London
and North Western Railway Company, 2 E. & B. 69 (E. C. L. R. vol.
75), Unwin *v.* Heath, 5 H. L. Ca. 505,(b) Bush *v.* Fox, 5 H. L. Ca.
707.(c) It does not appear necessary to state the arguments more
fully.   *Cur. adv. vult.*

Lord CAMPBELL, C. J., now delivered the judgment of the Court.

We are of opinion that the rule obtained by the defendants in this
case ought to be discharged.

It is admitted that the inventions for which the two patents sued
upon were granted were new and useful: and the only objection to the
specifications is, that the claims in them are too wide and vague. The
usual dilemma, however, is propounded: that, upon this objection, the

---

(a) May 25th and 26th. Before Lord Campbell, C. J., Coleridge and Erle, Js. Crompton,
J., was also present during a part of the argument on each day.

(b) In Dom. Proc., reversing the judgment in Heath *v.* Unwin, 12 Com. B. 522 (E. C. L. R.
vol. 74), in the Exchequer Chamber, which Court had, upon a bill of exceptions in an action
brought in the Court of Common Pleas, pronounced a judgment differing from that given by
the Court of Exchequer in a former action there brought, of Heath *v.* Unwin, 13 M. & W.
583.† See also Heath *v.* Unwin, 15 Sim. 552; Heath *v.* Smith, 3 E. & B. 256 (E. C. L. R.
vol. 77).

(c) In Dom. Proc., affirming the judgment given in the Court of Exchequer Chamber, on a
bill of exceptions in an action brought in the Court of Exchequer, Bush *v.* Fox, 9 Exch. 651.†

patents are void, or that, if the claims are construed to be within legal limits, there has been no infringement of them by the defendants.

After carefully considering the specifications, we think that the claim in each is for described means of conducting a useful process, resulting *754]   in a valuable *manufacture; and that the specifications distinctly show what portions of those means are claimed as new, and what portions are allowed to be old.

We therefore have only to determine whether the alleged infringement of them has been established.

The defendants contend that there was no evidence of infringement to be left to the jury, and that the Judge, at the close of the plaintiffs' case, was bound either to have directed a nonsuit, or to have ordered a verdict to be entered for the defendants upon the plea of Not guilty. We were told that, evidence being given of what the defendants actually did in the process alleged to be the infringement, it is always the province of the Judge to say whether there has been an infringement or not; and that, in the present case, the Judge, without calling upon the defendants for any answer, ought to have determined by his own authority that there had been no infringement. We consider, however, that the doctrine contended for is contrary to principle, would render it impossible to administer the law of patents, and is by no means to be deduced from Unwin *v.* Heath, 5 H. L. Ca. 505, or any of the other decisions referred to. There may well be a case where the Judge may and ought to take upon himself to say that the plaintiff has offered no evidence to be left to the jury to prove infringement, as if there were a patent for a chemical composition, and the evidence was that the defendant had constructed and used a machine for combing wool. But, if the evidence has a tendency to show that the defendant has used sub-
*755]   stantially the same means to *obtain the same result as specified by the plaintiff, and scientific witnesses have sworn that the defendant actually has used such means, the question becomes one of fact, or of fact mixed with law, which the Judge is bound to submit to the jury. There can be no doubt that such evidence was adduced by the plaintiffs, both with respect to the patent of 1848 and the patent of 1849.

The defendants, therefore, are confined to the contention that the verdict was against the evidence.

. With respect to the patent of 1845, they are clearly so far right, when they insist that nothing which they did in their mode of conducting the process of making envelopes, prior to the stage of the process when they had got the flaps of the blank in a fit state for the second descent of the plunger to fold them, could be construed to be an infringement; for the plaintiffs had disclaimed the "*creasing*" accomplished by Addenbrook's machine, and admitted that the defendants' "*air jets*" must be considered a discovery, which would be the subject of a patent. But at this stage the plaintiffs' claim begins; and there was evidence of resemblance between the manner in which the plaintiffs and the defendants completed the process and produced the perfect envelopes, from which we are of opinion that the jury were justified in coming to the conclusion that the defendants' process was an imitation of, and was substantially the same as, the plaintiffs. The folding of the flaps now commences; and the plaintiffs fold the flaps in succession by the folding instruments most ingeniously actuated by cams. The defendants likewise use folding instruments, inserted in the inverted box of the plunger; and the stroke of the descending plunger, [*756 *making these folding instruments, called *projections*, touch the different flaps in succession, folds them finally in the same manner, although not in the same order. Whether the two modes of folding by the *cams* and by the *plunger* be essentially different or substantially the same, we think was a pure question of fact for the jury; and we cannot say that the jury were wrong in the conclusion at which they arrived. Great stress was laid by the defendants upon the fact that, according to their process, there was no contrivance for holding the blank while the folding was going on: but we think that the Judge was right in telling the jury that there might be an infringement without a contrivance to hold the flap, if, without such a contrivance, the two modes of folding were substantially the same.

The folding being a material part of the plaintiffs' process of manufacturing envelopes, it is not necessary to determine whether their claim extended to the rest of the process, and whether the two modes of delivery of the perfect envelopes *above* and *below* be essentially different, or be substantially the same: but we would observe that, generally speaking, as the *manufacture* which is the result of the process invented and patented is the ultimate object in view, the purpose of the patent laws is to protect all that is new in this process, if it be described, although not expressly claimed.

With respect to the patent of 1849, for *gumming* the envelopes, the jury at the trial, after attentively examining the two models, and seeing them work, expressed a clear opinion that the defendants' was a colourable imitation of the plaintiffs'; and we think that this conclusion was fully warranted by the evidence. The great argument of the defendants was, that they did *not take the gum from *an inter-* [*757 *mediary surface*, and that their process of gumming could not properly be called "surface printing." But we are of opinion that they might be guilty of an infringement without using an intermediary surface, and that, without what is strictly called "surface printing," they might apply gum to the flaps of envelopes by operations acting *in the manner of surface printing*, in contradistinction to the application of gum direct from a fountain containing the gum.

For these reasons, we think that the verdict ought not to be disturbed: and we pronounce judgment for the plaintiffs. Rule discharged.

The QUEEN v. BROWN and Others. *May* 27.

A party was summoned before Justices upon an information, under sect. 11 of stat. 18 & 19 Vict. c. 108, charging that he, "being one of the owners and manager" of a colliery, had worked the colliery without providing the boiler with a proper steam gauge, as required by sect. 4. In defence, he contended that, as there were other owners, they ought to be charged together with him: but he did not deny that he was resident owner and took an active part in the management.

The justices, upon this objection alone, dismissed the complaint, considering the information to be bad on the face of it, because it showed that there were other owners.

Mandamus granted, commanding them to hear and determine the information: For that

(1) The objection was invalid.

(2) The justices had not excercised jurisdiction, but had declined it, the objection being preliminary, though taken in defence and not at the outset. *Haesitante* Crompton, J.

WELSBY, in last Term, obtained a rule calling on Thomas Brown, Esq., Frederick Levick, Esq., George Parker Hubbuck, Esq., and The Rev. Daniel Rees, four justices of Monmouthshire, to show cause why a mandamus should not issue, commanding them to hear and determine an information against Crawshay Bailey, Esq., exhibited by Herbert Mackworth, Esq., one of Her Majesty's Inspectors of coal mines, before *the said George Parker Hubbuck, one of the said *758] justices, on the 16th day of March last, for an offence against an Act, &c. (stat. 18 & 19 Vict. c. 108, " To amend the law for the inspection of Coal Mines in Great Britain").

The rule was obtained on the affidavit of Mr. Mackworth, which stated the following facts. On 16th March, 1857, Mr. Mackworth, as inspector, &c., exhibited before Mr. Hubbuck, a justice of Monmouthshire, an information against Crawshay Bailey, Esq., one of the owners of, and who then and still took an active part in the management of, a colliery called the Deep Pit Colliery, in the parish of Aberystwith in Monmouthshire, within the district of which Mr. Mackworth was inspector, for an offence against stat. 18 & 19 Vict. c. 108. " For that he, the said Crawshay Bailey, being one of the owners and manager of the said colliery for the working and management thereof, within the space of three calendar months last past, to wit, on the 23d day of January, in the year of our Lord 1857, did work and cause to be worked the said colliery without having provided the boiler of the pumping engine then and there in use with a proper steam gauge and safety valve, and contrary to the form of the said statute." Mr. Bailey was thereupon duly summoned to appear before two justices of Monmouthshire. Mr. Mackworth at the same time exhibited before Mr. Hubbuck informations against Mr. Bailey for other alleged offences against the said Act. The informations came on to be heard on 20th March, 1857, before the four justices named in the rule. Of these Mr. Brown was then and still one of the managing owners of the Ebbw Vale Company's collieries; Mr. Levick was then and still the managing owner of the Blaina and Coal Brook Vale collieries; and Mr. Hubbuck was

then and still *the principal manager of the Rhymney collieries : [*759
all in Monmouthshire. Upon the hearing of the first-mentioned
information, Mr. Bailey's attorney objected that there were several
other owners, besides Mr. Bailey of the Deep Pit colliery, and that the
information ought to have been against all ; the attorney, however,
admitting that Mr. Bailey was the resident owner and took an active
part in the management. The attorney who appeared in support of the
information called the attention of the justices especially to sects. 4, 11,
and 17 of the Act. The justices " dismissed the said information, on
the ground, as then stated by the said Thomas Brown, who sat as
chairman of the said Bench of justices, that the Bench were of opinion
that, as the charge was against one of the owners only, the same was
defective."

In answer, the four justices deposed that the objection was, as they
believed and understood, that the Act " did not authorize such information to be laid against one only of several owners of a coal mine ; and
that the said information, being laid against Crawshay Bailey, in the
said information named, as one of the owners and manager of the
colliery therein mentioned, was therefore bad on the face of it as
unauthorized by the Act." They further deposed that, " in so dismissing the said information, we acted· unanimously, and under the
sincere and conscientious belief that the said objection taken by Mr.
Secretan Woodhouse" (Mr. Bailey's attorney) " was a good and valid
objection."

J. *Gray* now showed cause.—The first question is, whether the
objection, which the justices sustained, was valid. Sect. 4 of stat. 18
& 19 Vict. c. 108, by the 7th rule, directs that the gauges shall be
provided : *those rules are to be observed " by the owner and [*760
agent" of the colliery : a part owner is not *the* owner. So sect.
11 speaks of " the default of the owner." [COLERIDGE, J.—Suppose
a mine, having two owners, is in proper order, and one owner goes to
France ; and, after that, the mine gets out of order : is the absent
owner liable for " the default of the owner ?" Lord CAMPBELL, C. J.
—Suppose only one owner can be found. CROMPTON, J.—The language
of sect. 11,—if " any of such general rules or special rules which ought
to be observed by the owner and principal agent or viewer of such coal
mine or colliery, be neglected or wilfully violated by any such owner,
agent, or viewer, such person shall be liable to a penalty,"—clearly
points to personal responsibility. Lord CAMPBELL, C. J.—Did it appear
that the other partners had been in any way parties to the violation of
the Act?] It did not. [COLERIDGE, J.—Suppose all the owners had been
brought before the justices, and it had appeared that one only had been
wilfully violating the Act : could all be convicted ?] It must be admitted
that the arguments suggested from the Bench furnish very strong
grounds for believing that the justices have put an erroneous interpre-

tation on the Act. But, secondly, they have interpreted it in fact, in the exercise of their undoubted jurisdiction. [Lord CAMPBELL, C. J. —Have they not declined jurisdiction?] No: they heard the case, and, upon the objection being raised in defence, they decided in favour of the objection. [ERLE, J.—But the decision was that the case was out of their jurisdiction.] No doubt the decision was not that Mr. Bailey was Not guilty: it must be taken that the justices refused to inflict the penalty, even on the assumption of his guilt.

*761]   * *Welsby*, contrà, was not called on to support the rule.

Lord CAMPBELL, C. J.—I am clearly of opinion that this rule must be made absolute. The justices swear that they acted conscientiously; and we are bound to believe them. But there is no pretence for saying that the party charged with personal neglect was not separately liable: the notion that it was necessary to charge all the partners is, I might almost say, absurd: at any rate it is wrong, beyond the slightest doubt. Then comes the question, whether, the justices having said this, they can be held to have adjudicated so as to preclude us from compelling them to proceed. I am not prepared to lay down a general rule: but in this case there is no difficulty. The objection taken was a preliminary objection, that the proper parties were not before the Court. To uphold that objection is not to exercise jurisdiction, but to decline it. The mandamus therefore should go. I cannot help adding that, considering what consequences may follow from a neglect of the regulations prescribed by the statute, it is peculiarly incumbent on magistrates to enforce the observance of these regulations.

COLERIDGE, J.—It appears to me that the duty of adjudging has been declined. I agree that there is a difficulty in laying down a rule. But certainly the case cannot depend upon the time at which the objection is raised: if it could, a party would only have to lie by, and turn a preliminary objection into an objection on the merits, upon the ground that the jurisdiction had been recognised. But we may apply this test.

*762]   If the *magistrates say that, whatever they think as to the merits, they are not at liberty to give a judgment, because they are unable, for want of right parties or any similar objection, to enter into the question, that is a declining of jurisdiction.

ERLE, J.—I agree: and I take the view which I lately expressed in Regina *v.* Dayman, ante, p. 672. I will now only add that it is most important that we should have a decision, after an argument by able advocates, as to what is a question of jurisdiction and what of merits. I do not think that this can depend upon the time at which the objection is taken. When the magistrates say that, because only one of several parties is brought before them, they will dismiss the complaint, they are determining as to that on which their jurisdiction depends. The case seems to me much like what we had in Regina *v.* Dayman, where the magistrate held a place not to be a new street, within the meaning of a statute, because it was an old highway. I mention this for the purpose of saying that my own mind conceives that to be a fact on which the jurisdiction hinges.

CROMPTON, J.—On the first point, it is quite clear that the magistrates were as wrong as they could possibly be. If I agreed with my brother Erle, that the question here is the same as that in Regina v. Dayman, I should decide for discharging this rule; for there I agreed with the decision of the Court: and it appeared to me that what the magistrate had adjudged on was part of that which was to be proved before him. *If the present case were like that, I should adhere to the decision: but in this case I am not prepared to disagree [*763 with the rest of the Court; I rather agree with them. The objection seems to be in the nature of a plea of abatement: the magistrates held that the complainant could not go on when it appeared that the person charged had partners. The point is a nice one. But I am by no means disposed to doubt the correctness of our former decision.

Rule absolute.

ANDREA ESPOSITO v. SAMUEL WILSON BOWDEN. *May 29.*

Error from the Court of Queen's Bench.

Declaration charged that, by a memorandum for charter, it was agreed between plaintiff, owner of a ship then in a British port, and defendant, that the ship should proceed to Odessa, and there load from the freighter's factors a complete cargo of specified goods, and proceed there with to a port of discharge, the act of the Queen's enemies and all accidents of the seas, navigation, &c., excepted; thirty-five running days to be allowed for loading and unloading, to commence at the port of loading, and 4l. per day for demurrage above the running days. Breach: (1). That, although a reasonable time for loading the cargo had elapsed, defendant made default in loading the agreed cargo; (2). That defendant detained the ship on demurrage ten days above the laying days, and did not pay for such demurrage.

Plea: that defendant was always a subject of the Queen, and Odessa was a port within the dominions of the Emperor of Russia; and that, after the making of the charter-party, and before the ship arrived at Odessa, and before the defendant provided a cargo, the Queen declared war against the Emperor; since which time war had existed between them, and Odessa had been a hostile port in the possession of the Queen's enemies. That, from the time war was so declared, it became impossible for defendant to perform his agreement without dealing and trading with the Queen's enemies, of which plaintiff had notice before the expiration of the laying days: and the charter-party, by reason of the premises, was wholly rescinded.

Replication: that the Queen, by order of council, waived (except in the case of contraband of war) the seizure of confiscation of enemies' property on board neutral ships and of neutral property on board enemies' ships; and, by a second order in council, allowed a certain time for Russian ships to load their ships in British ports, and allowed Russian merchant vessels, which should have sailed before the date of the order for any British port, to discharge at such port; and, by a third order, made before the expiration of the running days, and while there was time to load the cargo, ordered that neutral or friendly vessels might import into any British port all goods (not being contraband of war or requiring a special permission) to whomsoever belonging, and that the subjects of the Queen or of any neutral or friendly state might trade with all ports not blockaded (except that British vessels might not enter enemies' ports). That the ship was a neutral vessel, and plaintiff the subject of a neutral state: that Odessa was not blockaded during any part of the time during which the cargo ought to have been loaded; and no part of the agreed cargo was contraband of war or requiring special permission for importation; and the cargo might have been loaded notwithstanding the hostilities. On demurrer:

Held, by the Court of Exchequer Chamber, reversing the judgment of the Court of Queen's Bench, that the plea was good, as showing a dissolution of the contract before the time for performance had expired, and an impossibility of legally performing the contract, as the shipment of a cargo from an enemy's port, even in a neutral vessel, was an act, primâ facie at least, involving a trading and dealing with the enemy, and therefore forbidden by law to a British subject; and that, if such a shipment could under peculiar facts be legal, it lay on the plaintiff to show the facts, which on this record he had not done.

Held, by both Courts, that the replication did not answer the plea; for that the first order in council related only to neutral or hostile goods or ships; the second only to Russian ships: and the third was not shown to have come into operation till after the alleged dissolution of the contract.

THE first count stated that, on 16th September, 1853, by a certain
*764] memorandum for charter, it was that *day mutually agreed
between the plaintiff, therein described as of Naples, master of
the ship called The Maria Christina, of Naples, of the burden, &c.,
whereof the plaintiff was master, then in Hull, and the defendant, that
the said ship, being tight, &c., should with all convenient speed take an
outward cargo from the Tyne to Naples, and, after discharging same,
sail and proceed to Odessa, or so near thereto as she might safely get,
and there load from the factors of the said freighter a full and complete
cargo of wheat, seed, or other grain, not exceeding what she could reasonably stow and carry, over and above the tackle, apparel, provisions,
and furniture: and, being so loaded therewith, proceed to Falmouth,
&c. (stipulations as to the places of discharge, and payment of freight
thereon). The freighter engaged to provide the necessary dunnage
mats, which the ship would take out free of charge; ship free from
risk and expense of lighterage, but her boats and crew to render all
necessary assistance in towing the lighters, &c. The act of God, the
Queen's enemies, fire, and all and every other dangers and accidents
of the seas, rivers, and navigation, of what nature or kind soever,
*765] during the said voyage, always excepted. (Then followed *stipu-
lations as to mode of payment of freight.) Cash for ship's
use, not exceeding 50*l.*, to be advanced the master at his loading port,
free of interest and commission, on account of freighters having liberty
to insure same at ship's expense. Thirty-five running days were to be
allowed the said merchants (if the ship were not sooner despatched) for
loading and unloading, to commence at her port of loading on her being
ready to load; laying days at port of discharge to commence, &c.
And, for demurrage over and above the said laying days, the said
freighter agreed to pay 4*l.* per day, detention by frost or quarantine
not to be reckoned as lay days. The ship to be addressed at the within
foreign loading ports to the charterer's agents, free of commission.
Captain and owners to have an absolute lien on the cargo for freight,
dead freight, and demurrage: and charterer's responsibility to cease
on shipment of cargo. Penalty for non-performance of that agreement,
850*l.* The words " demurrage, 4*l.* per day," to be inserted in bills of

lading; 80l. to be advanced the master by charterers before sailing from Hull, on account of freight subject to insurance. Averment of the performance of all conditions precedent, and that all things have been done and happened that ought to have been done and happened, and that the plaintiff was ready and willing to do all things that it was necessary for him to be ready and willing to do, to entitle him to have the agreed cargo loaded on board the said ship at Odessa aforesaid, and the payment of the demurrage hereafter in this count mentioned. That, although a reasonable and proper time for loading the agreed cargo had elapsed before the commencement of this suit, nevertheless defendant made default in loading the agreed cargo; *and, before this suit, [*766 kept and detained the said ship on demurrage at Odessa afore- said for divers, to wit, ten days over and above the said laying days in the said memorandum of charter mentioned. Yet defendant did not nor would pay the 4l. per day, due and payable for such demurrage, as aforesaid.

Plea (1) to the first count. That defendant is and always has been a subject of our Lady the Queen; and that Odessa, the port where the said ship was to load her said cargo, is a port of Russia, and within the dominions of the Emperor of Russia. And that, after the making of the charter-party, and before the ship arrived at Odessa, and before defendant provided or purchased any cargo to be loaded on board the ship, to wit, on 29th March, 1854, our Lady the Queen declared war against the Emperor of Russia; and from that time war has existed between our Lady the Queen and the Emperor of Russia; and Odessa has been a hostile port, in the possession of the Queen's enemies. That, from the time war was so declared as aforesaid, it became and was impossible for him the defendant to perform his said agreement, and fulfil the terms of the said memorandum of charter, without deal- ing and trading with the Queen's enemies: of which plaintiff, before the expiration of the said laying days in the said charter-party men- tioned, had notice. And the said charter-party, by reason of the pre- mises, then became and was wholly rescinded.

Replication. That, by an order or declaration of Her Majesty the now Queen, bearing date and made on the same day and at the same time on which war was so declared as aforesaid, to wit, on 28th March, 1854, Her Majesty the now Queen declared herself to be *desi- [*767 rous of rendering the war as little onerous as possible to the persons with whom she remained at peace: and that, to preserve the commerce of neutrals from all unnecessary obstruction, Her said Majesty was willing, for the present, to waive a part of the belligerent rights appertaining to the law of nations: Her said Majesty declared that she would waive the right of seizing enemy's property laden on board a neutral vessel, unless it should be contraband of war, and that it was not Her said Majesty's intention to claim the confiscation of

neutral property not being contraband of war found on board of enemies' ships.   That, by an order in council bearing date 29th March,
1854, Her said Majesty ordered that Russian merchant vessels in any
port or places within Her said Majesty's dominions should be allowed
until the 10th May then next, six weeks from the date thereof, for
loading their cargoes and departing from such ports or places ; and that
any Russian merchant vessel, which, prior to the date of that order,
should have sailed from any foreign port bound for any port or place
in Her said Majesty's dominions, should be permitted to enter such port
or place, and to discharge her cargo, and afterwards forthwith to depart
without molestation ; and that any such vessel, if met at sea by any
of Her said Majesty's ships, should be permitted to continue her voyage
to any port not blockaded.   And, by a certain other order in council,
made long before the expiration of the said thirty-five running days,
and whilst there was yet time to load the said cargo within the said
running days, to wit, on 15th April, 1854, after reciting, amongst
other things, that Her Majesty was desirous of rendering the war as
*768] little onerous as possible to the powers with whom she *remained
         at peace, and, to preserve the commerce of neutrals from all
unnecessary obstruction, was willing for the present to waive a part of
the belligerent rights appertaining to the law of nations, and that Her
Majesty would waive the right of seizing enemies' property laden on
board a neutral vessel unless it should be contraband of war, and that
it was not Her Majesty's intention to claim the confiscation of neutral
property, not being contraband of war, found on board enemies' ships :
it was ordered, by and with the advice of Her Majesty's Privy Council,
that all vessels under a neutral or friendly flag, being neutral or friendly
property, should be permitted to import into any port or place in Her
Majesty's dominions all goods and merchandise whatsoever, to whomsoever the same might belong, and to export from any port or place in
Her Majesty's dominions to any port not blockaded any cargo or goods
not being contraband of war, or not requiring a special permission, to
whomsoever the same might belong : and it was thereby further ordered
that, save and except as thereinbefore excepted, all the subjects of
Her Majesty, and the subjects or citizens of any neutral or friendly
state, should and might, during and notwithstanding the said hostilities
with Russia, freely trade with all ports and places, wheresoever situate, which should not be in a state of blockade : save and except that
no British vessel should under any circumstances be permitted or
empowered to enter or communicate with any port or place which
should belong to or be in the possession or occupation of Her said
Majesty's enemies.   Averment : that the said ship Maria Christina
was, at the time of the making of the said charter-party, and so continued to be, and still is, a neutral vessel, and neutral and friendly

property, and sailing under a neutral and *friendly flag: and [*769 that the plaintiff was, during all the time aforesaid; and still is, the subject of a neutral state, and friendly with Her said Majesty: and that the said port of Odessa was not in a state of blockade at any part of the time during which the said cargo could and might and ought to have been loaded, pursuant to the said charter-party: and that the said cargo, so agreed to be loaded, was not, nor was any part thereof, contraband of war, nor requiring a special permission to be imported into any port or place in Her now Majesty's dominions: and that the said cargo might and could and ought to have been loaded, pursuant to the said charter-party, in the said neutral ship, notwith-standing the said hostilities.

Demurrer. Joinder.

In the Court of Queen's Bench, judgment was given for the plaintiff on the demurrer in Easter Term, 1855.(a)

Issue was taken on the plea, which was found for the defendant. There were other issues in fact on pleas to other counts of the declaration; all which issues were found for the defendant. The final judgment in the Queen's Bench was for the plaintiff on the replication to the above plea to the first count.

The defendant suggested error, in the Exchequer Chamber; which the plaintiff denied.

The case was argued in Easter Term 1856.(b)

Mellish, for the party suggesting error (defendant below).

The Court below, and the plaintiff's counsel, treated *the repli- [*770 cation as bad; but the Court below has held the plea also to be bad.

First: as to the plea. If the declaration of war made the perform-ance of the contract illegal, the contract was dissolved by such decla-ration: Abbott on Shipping, Part III., c. 11, s. 3, p. 427, 5th ed. (Part IV., c. 12, s. 2, p. 426, 10th ed.); Atkinson *v.* Ritchie, 10 East, 530. This proposition will probably not be disputed. The question then is as to the effect of the declaration of war. Was the defendant, finding war declared before the arrival of the ship at Odessa and before the time for performance according to the contract had arrived, bound to procure a cargo? The plea is that, from the time of the declaration of war, it was impossible for the defendant to perform his agreement without dealing and trading with the Queen's enemies. The Court below say, in effect, that they see from the record that this averment is untrue. They suggest two modes in which the defendant might have performed the contract: by purchasing the corn from any one, friend or foe, before the declaration of war, or by purchasing it, after the

(a) Esposito *v.* Bowden, 4 E. & B. 963 (E. C. L. R. vol. 82).
(b) May 1st. Before Jervis, C. J., Pollock, C. B., Cresswell, Crowder, and Willes, Js., and Alderson, B.

declaration of war, from English subjects or allies.   Now, as to the first, there clearly was no breach from the non-performance in this mode; for the possibility of doing so had ceased before the time for performing the contract had expired.   [ALDERSON, B.—Suppose war had not occurred, would not a performance on the last day but one of the time allowed by the contract have been good?]   It can scarcely be questioned that it would; and Reid v. Hoskins, 4 E. & B. 979 (E. C. L. R. vol. 82), is to that effect, and indeed goes somewhat further, inasmuch as in that case the ship arrived at the port of loading before declaration of war.

*771]   It is true that there both the parties were British *subjects, and here the defendant only is a British subject and the plaintiff a neutral: but how can that affect the principle now under discussion? [WILLES, J.—The averment here is that the defendant could not perform the contract "without dealing and trading with the Queen's enemies:" in Reid v. Hoskins it was that the defendant could not do so " without trading and corresponding" with the enemy.   " Corresponding" may refer to the necessity of applying to the custom house before quitting the enemy's port.]   The essence of the averment in each case is the impossibility of performing without dealing with the enemy.   Supposing (a supposition which appeared, on the trial of the issues in fact in this case, to be true) that duties were payable on all exports, and that, by the rules of the port, the ships shipping cargoes were compelled to employ Russian lightermen, it is manifest that the averment would be supported.   In fact the general rule of law goes further than appears to have been allowed by the Court below.   Not only all trading with an enemy is forbidden, but all intercourse.   If the British ship do not depart from the enemy's port immediately on the declaration of war, or if, after the declaration of war, she goes into the enemy's port for the purpose of bringing away property, she is liable to be taken as a prize of war.   A British subject cannot, after declaration of war, sell property which he has in an enemy's country and buy other property there.   If a vessel be loaded for an enemy's port, the owner must use his utmost diligence to prevent her going thither.   Every one domiciled in an enemy's country is, for the purpose of these questions, an enemy.

*772]   The English Courts would not recognise the obligation of *Bowden to pay an export duty in the Russian port.   If a contract be made and broken before the war, a plea, in an action brought after war begins, that the defendant is an alien enemy is in abatement: but, if the breach took place during the war, such a plea would be in bar. The defendant, therefore, in the present case, could not, after the declaration of war, take a step towards performance which would not be illegal.   Numerous authorities in the Admiralty Courts are collected in The Hoop (Cornelis), 1 Rob. Rep. Adm. 196, in which Sir W. Scott pronounced a judgment fully affirming the general principle for which the present defendant contends.   In The Lady Jane, 1 Rob. Rep. Adm.

202, and The Eenigheid, 1 Rob. Rep. Adm. 210, the goods were shipped before the war broke out ; in The Elizabeth, 1 Rob. Rep. Adm. 202,(a) it merely appeared that the ship came from an enemy's port; in The Juffrouw Louisa Margaretha, 1 Rob. Rep. Adm. 203, the ship was neutral; and so it was in The St. Louis, 1 Rob. Rep. Adm. 204, where it appeared that there were no other means of getting the goods away but by sending them into an enemy's port and there selling them ; and the same circumstances existed in The Bella Guidita, 1 Rob. Rep. Adm. 207. Sir William Scott, 1 Rob. Rep. Adm. 216, says that this law " has been enforced, where strong claim, not merely of convenience, but almost of necessity, excused it on behalf of the individual; that it has been enforced where cargoes have been laden before the war, but where the parties have not used all possible diligence to countermand the voyage after the first notice of hostilities ; and that· it has been enforced not only against the subjects of the Crown, but likewise against those of its allies in the war, upon the supposition *that the rule was founded on a strong and universal princi- [*773 ple, which allied states in war had a right to notice and apply, mutually, to each other's subjects." And he refers to Gist v. Mason, 1 T. R. 88, as showing that such is the maritime law of England. The leading common law case is Potts v. Bell, 8 T. R. 548, where Sir John Nicholl, in argument, 8 T. R. 556, cited the case of The St. Philip, in which the Privy Council refused to give the claimants liberty to prove that the goods condemned as prize had been bought before the war. Potts v. Bell shows that, if the defendant had in Odessa purchased goods from any one after the declaration of war, and had brought them from Odessa, they would not have been insurable. In The Jonge Pieter (Musterdt), 4 Rob. Rep. Adm. 79, 83, Sir William Scott says : "Without the license of Government, no communication direct or indirect can be carried on with the enemy:" yet the Court below appears to have considered that such communication might have been " meritorious."(b) Willison v. Patteson, 7 Taunt. 439, is a case which shows how very strictly the law of not dealing in any way with an enemy is enforced in English Courts. The same law is laid down by American writers. In 2 Wheaton's Elements of International Law, p. 25, it is said : " One of the immediate consequences of the commencement of hostilities is the interdiction of all commercial intercouse between the subjects of the states at war, without the license of their respective governments." And the writer then gives extracts from the judgment of Sir W. Scott in The Hoop (Cornelis), 1 Rob. Rep. Adm. 196 ; and he adds, p. 32 : " The same principles were *applied by the [*774 American courts of justice to the intercourse of their citizens with the enemy on the breaking out of the war between The United

(a) See 8 T. R. 556.
(b) 4 E. & B. 977 (E. C. L. R. vol. 82).

States and Great Britain." He illustrates this by a very strong case of condemnation, where the condemned goods were purchased by an American citizen within the British territory, long before the declaration of war, deposited on an island near the frontier, and, after the commencement of the war, brought away by a ship hired by the purchaser's agents. That is the course of conduct which the Court below treats as meritorious.(a) The law is laid down in conformity with what has been cited from Wheaton in 1 Kent's Com., Part I., Lect. 3; and, in a note at p. 66 (4th ed.), it is said: "The doctrine goes to the extent of holding it unlawful, after the commencement of war, except under the special license of the Government, to send a vessel to the enemy's country to bring home, with their permission, one's own property which was there when the war broke out. It would be liable to seizure in transitu, as enemy's property." He cites The Rapid (Perry), 8 Cranch (Sup. Ct. U. S.), 155.(b) In Duer's Law and Practice of Marine Insurance, Lect. VI., s. 6, &c., the general law is laid down similarly; but, in sect. 9, a less strict view appears to be taken of the case "of a subject, who, finding himself in an enemy's country, on the breaking out of a war, immediately withdraws himself, with his property, and returns to his native country." That, however, is not the present case. In the judgment below, Touteng v. Hubbard, 3 B. & P. 291, is referred to.

*775] Lord *Alvanley there in effect says that, when the British government lays an embargo on the ships of another state, a British Court must act upon the presumption that the British government is in the right, and the other state in the wrong; and that, in a British court of justice, nothing which is in contravention of the embargo can be enforced. The case, as far as it applies, which is only very remotely, is in favour of the defendant.

Then, as to the replication. [JERVIS, C. J.—The Court wishes first to hear the argument against the plea.]

Manisty, for the party denying the error (plaintiff below).

It appears that the defendant detained the vessel beyond the laying days: there is therefore a clear breach, unless the declaration of war of itself dissolved the whole contract. But that is not so. It is true that in general it is illegal to trade with an enemy; and that no one can be sued for non-performance of a contract when the performance has become illegal. But there is no illegality in trading with an enemy if the Queen's license is obtained for the purpose. Here it is not averred, as was averred in Reid v. Hoskins, that no license could be obtained. The case is as if a statute prohibited a trading without the Queen's license: in order to show a violation of such a statute, an averment would be necessary that no Queen's license was obtained. [POLLOCK, C. B.—In the present case, the effect of the Queen's license

(a) 4 E. & B. 977 (E. C. L. R. vol. 82).

(b) This appears to be the case referred to by Dr. Wheaton, as cited in the text above.

would be to supersede the general law: it should seem to be no more necessary to aver that *such a license could not be obtained than to aver that it was not practicable to obtain a repeal of an [*776 Act of Parliament.] The illegality here shown is set up as an excuse for non-performance. But the defendant, by deferring the performance, took upon himself the risk of its becoming impossible. Nor was it absolutely impossible. The ship was a neutral vessel, and might have safely left Odessa. In Reid v. Hoskins there never was a possibility of legally performing the agreement. If there be several ways of performing a contract, one of which becomes illegal, that is no excuse for not performing it by some of the other ways. [CRESSWELL, J.—The Court below appears to admit that the contract was dissolved: you seem not to do so.] It was dissolved only in a particular sense. [CRESSWELL, J.—That proposition I cannot deal with. POLLOCK, C. B.—The case of war is an exception implied in the contract, as the termination of life is an exception implied in many other contracts.] Could it be implied in a contract that, if war were proclaimed and a peace followed almost immediately, the contract should not be performed? The exception can be no more than this: that, if war should be proclaimed under circumstances making it impossible legally to perform the contract, there should be no performance.

As to the replication. The first order in council allowed a neutral to leave an enemy's port with enemy's goods. The second allowed an enemy's ship to bring enemy's goods. No doubt a license would have been given extending the same privilege to British goods; and it may be contended that what was allowed in the *case of enemy's [*777 goods would be allowed in the case of British goods. The last order, issued while there was yet time to perform the contract, clearly would have legalized the performance of the contract. That was decided in Clemontson v. Blessig, 11 Exch. 135.† Indeed the remarks of Martin, B., in that case would appear to extend to justifying the performance, even without the order in council, and thus to show the plea absolutely bad. [WILLES, J.—Suppose the charterer's agent at Odessa had had the corn in his hands, but was unable to get it on board without employing Russian lightermen, and entering the corn at the Russian custom house, and paying Russian duties. Do you say that the charterer would have been excused?] On that supposition, the performance would be illegal, but for the Queen's license.

Mellish, in reply.—If there had been a license, it was for the party insisting on that fact to show it. That would be so as to the burthen of proof: Holland v. Hall, 1 B. & Ald. 58: and the rule as to the burthen of averment must be the same. The question on the plea is really whether the declaration of war dissolved the contract: that is shown to be so on the authorities already cited, to which may be added the language of Lord Ellenborough in Barker v. Hodgson, 3 M. & S.

267, 270 (E. C. L. R. vol. 80).   The greatest inconvenience would arise from any other view.   How long is the party to wait?

Then, as to the replication.   The first two orders in council had no application to British property or ships.   It seems to be urged that these would extend, in spirit *at least, to British property in a ⸺*778] neutral or British ship.   But that this was not so is clear from the issuing of the third order in council, which would, on that view, have been unnecessary.   The effect of the third order depends upon the same question as the validity of the plea; for, if the war dissolved the contract, there was no contract at the time when the third order issued.

Cur. adv. vult.

WILLES, J., now delivered the judgment of the Court.

This case was argued before our lamented colleagues the late Lord Chief Justice Jervis and Baron Alderson, together with the Lord Chief Baron, my brothers Cresswell and Crowder, and myself.

Upon the argument, all the members of the Court were unanimous as to the result of the judgment we ought to pronounce: but, in consequence of the importance of the case, we took time to consider and state our reasons for that judgment.

We agree in the opinion of the Court of Queen's Bench that, if the plea be sufficient, the replication furnishes no answer to it, and in their reasons for that opinion, which we need not repeat.

The principal question in the case is as to the validity of the plea. It is, in effect, whether a charter-party, made before the late Russian war between an English merchant and a neutral shipowner, whereby it was agreed that the neutral vessel should proceed to Odessa, a port of Russia, and there load from the freighter's factors a complete cargo of wheat, seed, or other grain, and proceed therewith to Falmouth, with usual provisions as to laying days and demurrage, was dissolved by the war between England and Russia, alleged by the *charterer, in ⸺*779] his plea, which is to be taken as true for the purpose of the present discussion, to have broken out before the vessel arrived at Odessa, and to have continued up to and during the time when the loading was to have taken place; it being further alleged in the plea that, from the time war was declared, it became and was impossible for the charterer to perform his agreement without dealing and trading with the Queen's enemies.

It is now fully established that, the presumed object of war being as much to cripple the enemy's commerce as to capture his property, a declaration of war imports a prohibition of commercial intercourse and correspondence with the inhabitants of the enemy's country, and that such intercourse, except with the license of the Crown, is illegal.

Doubt was thrown upon the law on this subject by the case of Bell *v.* Gilson, 1 B. & P. 345 (1798), where Buller and Heath, Js. (Rooke, J., dissentiente), held that an insurance of goods purchased in Holland during hostilities between England and Holland, on board a neutral ship, was lawful. That case, however, was, in the year 1800, overruled, Lord Kenyon being Chief Justice, by the Court of King's Bench, in Potts *v.* Bell, 8 T. R. 548; which, together with the great case of The Hoop (Cornelis), 1 Rob. Rep. Adm. 196 (1799), before Lord Stowell, then Sir William Scott, upon the authority of which Potts *v.* Bell was decided, has restored and finally established the rule already mentioned, that one of the consequences of war is the absolute interdiction of all commercial intercourse or correspondence between the subjects of *the hostile countries except by the permission of their respec- [*780 tive sovereigns.

The cases of The Hoop (Cornelis) and Potts *v.* Bell further established that it is illegal for a subject in time of war, without license, to bring from an enemy's port, even in a neutral ship, goods purchased in the enemy's country after the commencement of hostilities, although not appearing to have been purchased from an enemy; in effect, that trading with the inhabitants of an enemy's country is trading with the enemy. And, in the case of The Hoop (Cornelis), Lord Stowell, after laying down the rule that trading with the enemy, except under a royal license, subjects the property to confiscation, and citing numerous cases in support of that rule proceeds to say :(a) " The cases which I have produced prove that the rule has been rigidly enforced,—where Acts of Parliament have on different occasions been made to relax the navigation law and other revenue acts; where the government has authorized, under the sanction of an Act of Parliament, a homeward trade from the enemy's possessions, but has not specifically protected an outward trade to the same, though intimately connected with that homeward trade, and almost necessary to its existence; that it has been enforced, where strong claim not merely of convenience, but almost of necessity, excused it on behalf of the individual; that it has been enforced where cargoes have been laden before the war, but where the parties have not used all possible diligence to countermand the voyage after the first notice of hostilities; and that it *has been enforced [*781 not only against the subjects of the Crown, but likewise against those of its allies in the war, upon the supposition that the rule was founded on a strong and universal principle, which allied states in war had a right to notice and apply, mutually, to each other's subjects. Indeed it is the less necessary to produce these cases, because it is expressly laid down by Lord Mansfield, as I understand him" (see Gist *v.* Mason, 1 T. R. 88), " that such is the maritime law of England; and he who for so long a time assisted at the decisions of that Court" (prize appeals), " and at that period, could hardly have been ignorant of the rule of decision on this important subject; though none of the instances which I happen to possess prove him to have been personally present

(a) 1 Rob. Rep. Adm. 216.

at those particular judgments. What is meant by the addition 'but this does not extend to a neutral vessel,' it is extremely difficult to conjecture, because no man was more perfectly apprised that the neutral bottom gives, in no case, any sort of protection to a cargo that is otherwise liable to confiscation, unless under the express stipulations of particular treaties ; and therefore I cannot but conclude, that the words of that great person must have been received with some slight degree of misapprehension."

The force of a declaration of war is equal to that of an Act of Parliament prohibiting intercourse with the enemy except by the Queen's license. As an Act of State, done by virtue of the prerogative exclusively belonging to the Crown, such a declaration carries with it all the force of law. It is founded upon the jus belli which Lord Coke (Co.

*782] Lit. 11 b) states to *be a portion of the law of England, adding, " in republicâ maximè conservanda sunt jura belli." This force has been attributed to it, amongst other cases, in Furtado *v.* Rodgers, 3 B. & P. 191, 198, where Lord Alvanley, C. J., said : " We are all of opinion that on the principles of the English law it is not competent to any subject to enter into a contract to do anything which may be detrimental to the interests of his own country ; and that such a contract is as much prohibited as if it had been expressly forbidden by Act of Parliament. It is admitted that if a man contracts to do a thing which is afterwards prohibited by Act of Parliament, he is not bound by his contract." " And on the same principle, where hostilities commence between the country of the underwriter and the assured, the former is forbidden to fulfil his contract." Accordingly, in that case it was held that an insurance effected in Great Britain on a French ship, though before the commencement of hostilities between Great Britain and France, did not bind the insurer to indemnify the assured against a loss by British capture in the subsequent war, although the policy contained general words of insurance against all captures and detentions of princes, without any exception of the acts of the insurers' own government. These remarks as to the force of a declaration of war furnish a complete answer to the dictum attributed to one of the learned Judges in the report of Clemontson *v.* Blessig, 11 Exch. 135,† relied upon by Mr. *Manisty* in his able argument for the plaintiff. That case itself was decided upon the ground that, by the terms of the declaration of war, the performance of the contract there in question

*783] was *permitted ; and therefore it does not affect the present discussion : and we need not give any opinion upon the point there decided.

As to the mode of operation of war upon contracts of affreightment, made before, but which remain unexecuted at, the time it is declared, and of which it makes the further execution unlawful or impossible, the authorities establish that the effect is to dissolve the contract, and to absolve both parties from further performance of it. Such was the opinion of Lord Ellenborough, at a time when the question must recently have often occurred and been well considered and understood, in Barker v. Hodgson, 3 M. & S. 267, 270 (E. C. L. R. vol. 30) (1814); where it was held that the prevalence of an infectious disorder at the port of loading, and consequent prohibition of intercourse by the law of the port, were not sufficient to excuse the charterer from loading; and Lord Ellenborough, in delivering judgment, said: "The question here is, on which side the burthen is to fall. If indeed the performance of this covenant had been rendered unlawful by the government of this country, the contract would have been dissolved on both sides, and this defendant, inasmuch as he had been thus compelled to abandon his contract, would have been excused for the non-performance of it, and not liable to damages. But if in consequence of events which happen at a foreign port, the freighter is prevented from furnishing a loading there, which he has contracted to furnish, the contract is neither dissolved, nor is he excused for not performing it, but must answer in damages." A similar opinion was expressed by the *same eminent judge in Atkinson v. Ritchie, 10 East, 530. Lord Tenterden also, in his work on Shipping (10th ed. by Serjeant Shee, p. 426; 5th ed., p. 427), states the law thus. "Another general rule of law furnishes a dissolution of these contracts" (i. e. for the carriage of goods in merchant ships) "by matter extrinsic. If an agreement be made to do an act lawful at the time of such agreement, but afterwards, and before the performance of the act, the performance be rendered unlawful by the government of the country, the agreement is absolutely dissolved. If, therefore, before the commencement of a voyage, war or hostilities should take place between the state to which the ship or cargo belongs, and that to which they are destined, or commerce between them be wholly prohibited, the contract for conveyance is at an end, the merchant must unlade his goods, and the owners find another employment for their ship. And probably the same principles would apply to the same events happening after the commencement and before the completion of the voyage, although a different rule is laid down in this case by the French Ordinance." It may be added that the cases above put by Lord Tenterden cannot be treated as isolated propositions, but as instances of the general principle of law with which they are prefaced. Chancellor Kent also, in his Commentaries, 3d vol., p. 248 (4th ed.), after stating that "the contract of affreightment may be dissolved without execution, not only by the act of the parties, but in many cases by the act of the law," proceeds to state that inter alia, war making performance unlawful or impossible, either before or after its commencement, dissolves the contract. The same distinguished person *held, in the Court of Errors in New York, that a contract of partnership with a foreigner was absolutely dissolved [*785

by the breaking out of war between the two countries.   (See Griswold
v. Waddington, 16 Johnson, 488.(a))

Further, there is very high authority for saying that the removal of
merchandise, even though acquired before the war from the enemy's
country, after knowledge of the war, without a royal license, is generally illegal.   This was laid down at the Cockpit in 1747, in the case
of the St. Philip (referred to and stated by Sir John Nicholl in his
learned argument in Potts v. Bell, 8 T. R. 556), where the Lords Commissioners of Appeal, present Willes, C. J., refused to give the claimants liberty to prove that their goods were bought before the war.   The
same law was laid down by Mr. Justice Story in The St. Lawrence, 1
Gallison (U. S.), 467, and the Joseph (Sargent), 1 Gallison (U. S.),
545.   See also Willard Phillips's very able work On the Law of Insurance, 3d ed., 1 vol. p. 137, et seq.   The cases before Lord Stowell of
The Juffrow Catherina (Hansen), 5 Rob. Rep. Adm. 140, and The
Madonna delle Gracie (Copenzia), 4 Rob. Rep. Adm. 195, in which that
great Judge fastened upon peculiar circumstances to exempt the claimants from the operation of the general rule, tend strongly to confirm
its applicability in all cases in which trade or intercourse with the enemy
after knowledge of the war is involved in the shipment.   And in such
cases the circumstance of previous purchase seems, as a general rule,
to be matter for the consideration of the Crown in its clemency alone.

*786]   *The law as to trading with the enemy was considered and
          acted upon by the Court of Queen's Bench in Reid v. Hoskins,
4 E. & B. 979 (E. C. L. R. vol. 82), a case identical in its facts with
the present, except that the shipowners in that case were British subjects.   It was there decided that the contract was dissolved and the
parties absolved from its performance, amongst other reasons stated,
because, without any previous default on the charterer's part, performance had become illegal by the declaration of war and its consequences.
But it was also in that case stated, in the judgment of the Court, to be
material that the owners of the ship were British subjects, because it
was, by reason of that circumstance, the duty of the captain, " as soon
as he heard of the declaration of war, to make his escape, and to seek
a place of safety, instead of lingering at Odessa in the hope of obtaining a cargo, although he might safely have done so if he had not been
a British subject, and the ship had been neutral property."   (See the
result of that case in the Queen's Bench(b) and Exchequer Chamber ;(c)
also Avery v. Bowden.(d))

We entirely concur in the decision in Reid v. Hoskins, and in the
reasons advanced in the judgment ; either of which, however, would, in

(a) See the case below, 15 Johnson, 57.
(b) Reid v. Hoskins, 5 E. & B. 729 (E. C. L. R. vol. 85).
(c) Reid v. Hoskins, 6 E. & B. 953.
(d) In Q. B. 5 E. & B. 714 (E. C. L. R. vol. 85); and in Exch. Ch. 6 E. & B. 953 (E. C. L. R.
vol. 88).

our opinion, have been sufficient. The fact that it was the duty of the master in that case to leave Odessa, and that he could not have received a cargo without dealing and trading with the enemy, was a sufficient ground for the decision that his owners could not recover against the charterer *for not loading a cargo which he could not lawfully [*787 have received. But that was not the only reason, stated in the judgment, by which it could have been supported. The argument, which was again urged in this case, that, apart from any considerations affecting the shipowner only, the defence was valid by reason of the law also forbidding the charterer to load a cargo, and, as a consequence of that prohibition, dissolving the charter-party and absolving both parties from further performance, remains to be considered.

In order to escape the application of this latter argument, founded upon the principles above stated, it is necessary for the shipowner to establish that the plea of the charterer cannot be true in alleging an impossibility of performance without dealing and trading with the enemy, or, in other words, that the charterer could, but for some default of his own, and notwithstanding the war, have fulfilled his contract in a lawful manner.

We proceed to consider the arguments advanced for that purpose.

In the first place, it is said that the contract admitted of being fulfilled after the war by purchasing the cargo from Her Majesty's subjects, or those of her allies at Odessa, who may have had wheat, seed, or other grain which they were willing to dispose of, and may have been about to leave the enemy's country: and it is assumed that the charterer might lawfully have purchased the cargo from such persons, and lawfully have shipped it when so purchased.

Assuming, for argument's sake, that this assumption is correct in point of law (which, independently of express authority, we should have doubted, inasmuch as persons inhabiting an enemy's country are primâ *facie enemies: The Bernon, Dunn, 1 Rob. Rep. Adm. [*788 102, 104; and even the Queen's subjects become enemies if they remain and trade in the enemy's country after they know of the breaking out of war: see O'Mealey v. Wilson, 1 Camp. 482), still it should seem a harsh and inequitable position that the charterer, by no wrongful act or default of his own, but by the unquestionably rightful act of his sovereign in declaring war in the exercise of her undoubted prerogative against a public enemy, should be reduced to the necessity of seeking out, at his peril, in an enemy's country, persons who had themselves acquired the goods before war, and were possessed of them under circumstances which established a right to remove them from the enemy's country without a license.

What if it had happened that there were no British or French subjects in the enemy's country having such property in their possession to sell, or, if there were, that the charterers had purchased from one profess-

ing at the time of the sale that he was about to depart, but who afterwards remained so as to acquire the character of an alien enemy?
Without, however, resorting to that supposition, it is enough to refer
to Potts v. Bell, 1 T. R. 88, already cited, where it was expressly
decided that goods purchased in the enemy's country after the war broke
out, though not from enemies, could not without a license lawfully be
shipped thence during the war even in a neutral vessel.

Moreover, it is not correct to say that the charterer, even if he could
have succeeded in lawfully acquiring the goods, could have lawfully
shipped them, if doing so involved dealing or trading with the enemy.
*789] It is *more than likely that the cargo could not have been put
on board without passing through the enemy's custom house and
paying export duties. The passing it through the custom house and
obtaining a Russian permit for its shipment might have been but a slight
case ; still it would have been a case of dealing with the enemy. The
payment of export duties would have supplied him directly with the
means of carrying on the war. If that were proved to be necessary in
point of fact, it would sustain the defence raised by the plea. That it
is not a far-fetched supposition appears by the fact mentioned in
Abbott on Shipping, by Shee, 10th ed., p. 437, that in this very case
it was proved at the trial at York, before Platt, B., that the cargo could
not have been shipped without payment of export duties to the Russian
government, a fact which, though not directly admissible into the argument, suggests a case capable of proof under this plea, and in which
the charterer would, according to the principles already stated, be
absolved.

Another case may be put, to illustrate the extreme hardship and
injustice of forcing a British subject into such straits as those suggested
in the argument for the plaintiff, viz., that of one who had chartered
several neutral ships for which, after the war, he had purchased cargoes
as they arrived, through himself or any other British subject remaining in Odessa for that purpose. Whatever British subjects so remained
and traded in the enemy's country would be in imminent danger of
acquiring a hostile character.

In our opinion, therefore, the first argument on behalf of the shipowner is not maintainable.

It was, however, further argued that the breach of contract in ques-
*790] tion was brought about, not *altogether by the war, but partly
by the default of the charterer himself in not providing a cargo
before the war and keeping it until the war, and thereafter until the
arrival of the neutral vessel, then to be lawfully loaded in pursuance
of the charter-party.

But, assuming again, for the sake of argument, that this result would
follow in point of law if the charterer had provided a cargo before the

war, is it true that he has been guilty of default? A default, to affect
him with injurious consequences, ought to be either a breach of contract
with the person who claims to benefit by it or a breach of some duty
imposed by law. Not buying the corn was not the former, because it
was expressly stipulated by the charterer that he should have all the
laying days within which to provide and ship a cargo; and no breach
of that contract had been committed when the war took place. And
so far from its being a wrong or default in point of duty, apart from
contract, not to have so provided a cargo, it might have been a prudent
and rightful act for the charterer, anticipating the war, to abstain from
trading with the inhabitants of the enemy's country, and to remove
himself and his property before the war began.

To impose upon the charterer the necessity of providing a cargo
before the war, and of keeping that cargo until the war, and afterwards
until the arrival of the vessel, apart from any difficulty as to dealing
with the enemy in shipping it, would be to compel one of Her Majesty's subjects to do what he has not contracted to do, in order to save
himself from being unable to perform his contract by reason of the
possible event of a declaration of war, intended to injure the Queen's
enemies, not her own subjects nor those of her ally.

*The dictum of Lord Alvanley in Touteng v. Hubbard, 3 B. [*791
& P. 291, 302, cited, on behalf of the shipowner, in support of
this argument, was applied by that learned Judge to a totally different
state of facts. There a Swedish vessel had been chartered by a British
subject to proceed to a port abroad, and take in a cargo. An embargo
of a hostile character was laid by the British government upon Swedish
vessels, which prevented the chartered vessel from proceeding to her
destination for, such a period as would, by reason of delay, in the
absence of excuse, have disentitled her to receive a cargo at the port
of loading. She proceeded thither, nevertheless, after the embargo,
but did not receive a cargo from the charterer. And, in an action subsequently brought by the Swedish shipowner against the British charterer for not loading, it was held that the former could not recover by
reason of his delay, and that he could not set up the British embargo
as a justification for such default. That dictum, explained by the subject-matter, is therefore inapplicable.

In this case, again supposing that the charterer had obtained the
property before the war, and kept it in the enemy's country with the
intention of fulfilling his contract when the vessel arrived, were there
war or were there not, the same difficulty as is before pointed out would
arise as to its shipment without passing through the enemy's custom
house, and possibly paying export duties to the hostile government.

It is clear that the charterer could maintain no action against the
shipowner for refusing to take on board a cargo which the charterer

*792] could load only by dealing *and trading with the enemy: and, on the other hand, neither ought the shipowner to maintain an action against the charterer for not doing so.

This is not an unequal law, because, if war had broken out between the Czar and the King of the Two Sicilies, instead of Her Majesty, the vessel would, according to the principles stated above, have been absolved from going to Odessa, and might forthwith have proceeded upon another voyage. Even the common principle of reciprocity, therefore, points out that a similar indulgence ought to be allowed to the merchant, when, in consequence of war declared by his sovereign, he is involved in like difficulties. Under such circumstances, in all ordinary cases, the more convenient course for both parties seems to be that both should be at once absolved, so that each, on becoming aware of the fact of a war, the end of which cannot be foreseen, making the voyage or the shipment presumably illegal for an indefinite period, may at once be at liberty to engage in another adventure without waiting for the bare possibility of the war coming to an end in sufficient time to allow of the contract being fulfilled, or some other opportunity of lawfully performing the contract perchance arising. The law upon this subject was doubtless made, according to the well-known rule, to meet cases of ordinary occurrence, and in times when to permit trading with the enemy even through neutrals was the exception, not the rule. These considerations may explain the origin of the rule authoritatively laid down in the books as to war at once working an absolute dissolution.

A distinction was suggested between the first alleged breach of contract, in not loading the vessel, and the *second breach for *793] demurrage. Inasmuch, however, as the second breach would be proved by showing that the vessel remained in the loading port without being loaded during the demurrage days, no one being there to act on the part of the charterer, we think that that breach amounts to nothing more than an averment that the vessel was not loaded during those days; and so it stands upon the same footing as the first alleged breach for not loading the vessel during the laying days.

We are of opinion that for a British subject (not domiciled in a neutral country, which the defendant cannot be presumed to have been) to ship a cargo from an enemy's port even in a neutral vessel, without license, is an act primâ facie and under all ordinary circumstances a dealing and trading with the enemy, and therefore forbidden by law; that it lies on the person alleging it to be lawful in the particular instance to establish the circumstances which make it so ; and that, in the absence of proof that it was lawful, neither a British subject nor an alien friend can found any action upon the fact of its not having been performed.

. The sovereign of this country has the right to proclaim war, with all its consequences, enforcing or mitigating them either generally or in particular instances as may be thought best by the Government.' One of those consequences, not removed or dispensed with by any treaty, order in council, or license, or by any special circumstance of necessity in the particular case, is that trade and dealing with the enemy, unless expressly permitted, are forbidden.

The plea alleges that the contract could not have been fulfilled without such dealing and trade. That, as we have already shown, upon grounds not considered in *the judgment of the Court of Queen's Bench, may be true. If it may, then, inasmuch as the law justifies what it commands, and effects that purpose, in cases like the present, by dissolving contracts which presumably cannot be executed without dealing and trading with the enemy, the plea is sufficient. [*794

We therefore reverse the judgment of the Court below, and give judgment for the defendant. Judgment reversed.

It is a well settled doctrine in the English courts, and with the English jurists, that there cannot exist at the same time, a war for arms and a peace for commerce. The war puts an end at once to all dealing and all communication with each other, and places every individual of the respective governments as well as the governments themselves, in a state of hostility. This is equally the doctrine of all the authoritative writers on the law of nations and of the maritime ordinances of all the great powers of Europe. It is equally the received law of this country, and was so decided frequently by the Congress of the United States during the revolutionary war, and again by the Supreme Court of the United States during the course of the last war; and it is difficult to conceive of a point of doctrine more deeply or extensively rooted in the general maritime law of Europe and in the universal and immemorial usage of the whole community of the civilized world : 1 Kent's Com. 67. See, besides the American cases cited in the text, The Rapid, 8 Cranch, 155; Amory v. M'Gregor, 15 Johns. 24; Griswold v. Waddington, Ibid. 57, 16 Ibid. 438; Scholefield v. Eichelberger, 7 Peters, 586. "To say that the rule is without exception, would be assuming too great a latitude. The question has never yet been examined, whether a contract for necessaries or even for money to enable the individual to get home, would not be enforced; and analogies familiar to the law as well as the influence of the general rule in international law, that the severities of war are to be diminished by all safe and practical means, might be appealed to in support of such an exception. But at present, it may be safely affirmed that there is no recognised exception but permission of a state to its own citizen, which is also implied in any treaty stipulation to that effect, entered into by the belligerents." Per Johnson, J., Ibid.

The QUEEN v. The Inhabitants of the Township of HUDDERS-
FIELD. *May* 30.

On appeal against an order of removal, the Sessions stated for the opinion of the Court a case
by which it appeared that the pauper was an able-bodied single woman, who, while in service,
became pregnant, and was dismissed from the service; and, by reason of her advanced state
of pregnancy, was unable to take a situation and maintain herself. The removing justices had
not found that she was chargeable in respect of relief made necessary by sickness, but only
that she "has become and now is actually chargeable."
Held that, upon this statement, it was not to be inferred that she had become chargeable in
respect of any sickness; and that the order of removal was not therefore objectionable under
stat. 9 & 10 Vict. c. 66, s. 4, pregnancy not being necessarily sickness within the meaning of
that section.

ON appeal against an order of two justices, whereby Mary Ann Littlewood, single woman, was removed from the township of Huddersfield
to the township of Fulstone, both in the West Riding of Yorkshire, the
order stating that "she has become and now is actually chargeable,"
but not further explaining the chargeability: the Sessions quashed the
order, subject to the opinion of this Court upon the following case.

*795]   *The said Mary Ann Littlewood's settlement was admitted by
the appellants to be in their township of Fulstone. The said
pauper was, in April, 1856, in service in the respondent township as
domestic servant, and, being, whilst in such service, found to be pregnant with a bastard child, was dismissed from the said service: and,
being then unable from her advanced state of pregnancy to take a
situation and maintain herself, she was, on 21st of the said month of
April, admitted into the Huddersfield Union Workhouse as chargeable
to the township of Huddersfield, and entered upon the books of the
said workhouse as "an able-bodied woman;" the cause of relief being
specified in the said book as "pregnancy." And she continued to be
relieved therein at the cost of the township of Huddersfield until delivered of a child on 27th July, and thenceforward until the hearing of
the appeal.

Upon these facts, the appellants objected that the relief to the said
pauper had been made necessary by sickness or accident, which would
not produce permanent disability; and therefore that, under the fourth
section of stat. 9 & 10 Vict. c. 66, no warrant should have been granted
for her removal: and that, in the said order appealed against, the justices granting the same had not stated that she had become chargeable
in respect of relief made necessary by sickness or accident, and that
they were satisfied such sickness or accident would produce a permanent
disability.

The Court of Quarter Sessions held the above objection to be good
in law, and quashed the order of removal.

The question for the Court of Queen's Bench is: Whether the said
*796]   pauper Mary Ann Littlewood was, at *the date of the order, in
consequence of her pregnancy, though "an able-bodied woman,"

removable from the respondent township. If the Court shall decide that she was not so removable, the order of Quarter Sessions is to be confirmed, and the order of removal to be quashed: but, if the Court shall decide she was removable, then the order of Quarter Sessions is to be quashed, and the order of removal to be confirmed.

Pashley and *Needham*, in support of the order of Sessions.—By stat. 9 & 10 Vict. c. 66, s. 4, "no warrant shall be granted for the removal of any person becoming chargeable in respect of relief made necessary by sickness or accident, unless the justices granting the warrant shall state in such warrant that they are satisfied that the sickness or accident will produce permanent disability." No such certificate has been here granted; nor indeed could it; for there is no ground for supposing permanent disability. Regina *v.* Prior's Hardwick, 12 Q. B. 168 (E. C. L. R. vol. 64), shows that, where the chargeability in fact arises from sickness, the order of removal is bad if it does not state the sickness and that such sickness was not permanent. The question therefore is, whether the pregnancy was "sickness" within the meaning of the section. Now any bodily infirmity producing helplessness is sickness: thus blindness is sickness; and an order of removal is bad which states that the pauper has not become chargeable in respect of relief made necessary by sickness if the chargeability was in fact produced by the blindness.(a) Here the case shows a bodily inability produced by the pregnancy: the word "sick" is ordinarily applied *to such inability: the declaration in actions of seduc- [*797 tion used to aver that the party seduced "became pregnant and sick with child." In Richardson's New Dictionary of the English Language, "sick" is defined as "weak, ailing, diseased, disordered; nauseating (as if affected with a *sick* stomach), disgusted." Nausea is an ordinary symptom of pregnancy. In Bouvier's Law Dictionary (Philadelphia, 1856) "sickness" is thus explained: "By sickness is understood any affection of the body which deprives it temporarily of the power to fulfil its usual functions." [ERLE, J.—At one time, pregnancy constituted actual chargeability; but that is not so now.] The statute now under consideration appears to have been framed with the intention of legislating in respect of every species of bodily incapacity, permanent or temporary. [Lord CAMPBELL, C. J.—What would you say of the case of a married woman pregnant by her husband?] If the pregnancy disabled her, so as to render her chargeable, she would, unless stat. 9 & 10 Vict. c. 66, s. 4, applies, be removable, but for the law which prevents the separation. [Lord CAMPBELL, C. J.— The husband would, on that view, be chargeable in respect of the wife. COLERIDGE, J.—He would be removed, and his wife with him.]

Maule (with whom was *H. W. West*), contrà.—The pauper is found to be able-bodied. It is not said that she was even so far incapacitated

(a) See Regina *v.* Bucknell, 3 E. & B. 587 (E. C. L. R. vol. 77).

by pregnancy as to be unable to work. She was discharged on account of her loss of character; and that may be the only cause of her inability "to take" a situation. But, supposing the pregnancy to have produced a bodily disability resulting in chargeability, that is not sickness within the *definitions cited on the other side. It is not a

*798]   morbid state of body, nor one which deprives it of the power to fulfil its functions: on the contrary, the body, at the time of pregnancy, is performing perhaps the very highest corporeal function, and is in the state most opposed to a state of disease or disorder. [He was then stopped by the Court.]

Lord CAMPBELL, C. J.—We all agree with the respondents: we might perhaps have done so yet more strongly if we had allowed their counsel to continue his able argument. It is impossible to say that pregnancy, per se, shows disease: and I think that by "sickness," in the statute, is meant "disease." There is nothing to show that the pauper was unable to work: the question proposed for the Court states her to be able-bodied. So that we are asked, whether an able-bodied woman who is pregnant is sick within the meaning of the section. It cannot be said that she is.

COLERIDGE, J.—I am entirely of the same opinion. In carrying out the Act, we must be careful not to go beyond it. It may be, though I do not go quite so far as Mr. *Pashley*, that incapacity produced by pregnancy is chargeability by reason of sickness. But we find "sickness" joined with "accident." We cannot say that an able-bodied person, who is under any derangement organic or physical, is necessarily in a state of sickness. It does not follow that, because pregnancy may produce illness, it must produce it. And, if the statement be consistent with both suppositions of fact, it lies upon those who insist upon the application of the section to show which supposition is the true one.

*799]   *ERLE, J.—I think that the justices who made the order were right and the Sessions wrong. The cases excepted in the section are sickness and accident, that is, a morbid state arising from external accident or from a diseased body. Unless you can call pregnancy a morbid state of body, the exception does not apply: and we have no right to go beyond it.

(CROMPTON, J., had left the Court.)

                                        Order of Sessions quashed.

The QUEEN *v.* ALLDAY. *May* 30.

Under stat. 6 & 7 Vict. c. 18, s. 48, the town clerk of a borough is bound, incidentally to his office, to cause the lists of voters to be copied and printed, and to have the names arranged and numbered : and, if he hires a person to do this for him, to make copies for the printer, and to superintend the printing, he is not entitled to be reimbursed the expense by the parish officers under sect. 55, unless he cannot, by the reasonable labour of himself and his ordinary assistants, perform the duty without extra aid.
But he is entitled to be reimbursed for the expense of printing.

FIELD, in last Term, obtained a rule to show cause why the disallowance by James Hunt, auditor of the Oxfordshire and Worcestershire Audit District, on 13th December last, in the accounts of the Guardians of the Poor of the parish of Birmingham for the half year ending 29th September last, of the sum of 25*l.* 1*s.* 6*d.*, part of a sum of 35*l.* 15*s.*, purporting to be a charge of Allen Preston for arranging lists alphabetically, and making copy register, &c., as a payment illegally made out of the funds of the said parish, and his surcharge of Joseph Allday, George Harrison, Thomas Ridley Jackson, William Aldington, and James Smith, five of the Guardians of the Poor of the said parish, jointly and severally, with the same, should not be quashed.

*The disallowance and surcharge had been brought up by cer- [*800 tiorari. They were as follows.

" Expenses incurred in carrying into effect the provisions of the Act of the 6 Vict. cap. 18, entitled ' An Act to amend the law for the registration of persons entitled to vote, and to define certain rights of voting, and to regulate certain proceedings in the election of members to serve in Parliament for England and Wales.'

"James Upton : Printing 250 copies of Register as per contract	26	2	6
" Allen Preston : Arranging lists alphabetically, and making copy register, &c.	85	15	0
" Disallowed £25 : 1 : 6			
" J. HUNT.			
" Martin Billing : Printing notices, &c., of Revision Court	0	14	0
" John Burton : Posting and watching same .	2	2	0
	£64	13	6

" I do hereby certify that, in the account of the Guardians of the Poor. of the Parish of Birmingham for the half year ended at Michaelmas last, I have disallowed, at folio 92 of the treasurer's account in this ledger, the sum of 25*l.* 1*s.* 6*d.*, as a payment illegally made out of the funds of the said parish. And I find that Mr. Alderman Joseph Allday," &c. (the parties named in the rule), " Guardians of the Poor of the said Parish, authorized the making of such illegal payment.

And I do hereby charge them the said Joseph Allday," &c., "jointly and severally, with the same. As witness my hand this 13th day of December, 1856."

"Auditor's reasons. I disallowed, in the accounts of the Guardians *801] of the Poor of the Parish of Birmingham *for the half year which ended at Michaelmas, 1856, the sum of 25l. 1s. 6d. part of a payment made to the town clerk of the Borough of Birmingham, purporting to be a charge of Allen Preston for arranging lists alphabetically and making copy of register, &c. : because the sum so disallowed was not a legal charge upon the rates made for the relief of the poor of the said parish, inasmuch as it was the duty of the town clerk of the said borough, in virtue of his office, to have performed the work for which the said sum of 25l. 1s. 6d. was charged, without any extra remuneration whatever. Dated this 23d day of December, 1856. JAMES HUNT, auditor," &c.

Hayes, Serjt., and *Bittleston* now showed cause.—The duty for the performance of which the town clerk has made a charge is one which he was bound to perform as town clerk : his salary is his remuneration for all such duties. Sect. 55 of stat. 6 & 7 Vict. c. 18, authorizes the defraying from the poor-rate "all the expenses incurred by any town clerk or returning officer of any city or borough in carrying into effect the provisions of this Act." These words apply only to moneys properly expended by him, not to remuneration for his labour, or to money paid for doing his work to another party. This was decided in Regina v. Governors of Poor in Hull, 2 E. & B. 182 (E. C. L. R. vol. 75). The same point came again before this Court in another case between the *802] same parties :(a) *and there the Court stated that they would adhere to the principle they had laid down, leaving the parties

(a) The Queen v. The Governor, Deputy Governor, Assistants, and Guardians of the Poor of the Poor of the Town of Hull. Mandamus, commanding the defendants to pay to the town clerk of Hull the amount allowed by the town council for his expenses in preparing the register of voters. The money was stated, on the record, to have been paid by the town clerk to another party for correcting, arranging, and numbering in strict alphabetical order, as required by stat. 6 & 7 Vict. c. 18, a list of voters for the borough, in order that the same might be formed into a register, making copies for the printer and town clerk, attending and instructing the printer, and examining the proof. The defendants having made a return, the prosecutor having pleaded to the return, and the defendants having replied, the prosecutor demurred to the replication. The case was argued on Wednesday, June 6th, 1855, before Lord Campbell, C. J., Coleridge, Erle, and Crompton, Js., by *Phipson* for the prosecutor and *Bovill* for the defendants. Reference was made to Regina v. Governors of Poor in Hull, 2 E. & B. 182 (E. C. L. R. vol. 75), Regina v. Prest, 16 Q. B. 32 (E. C. L. R. vol. 71), Regina v. Saunders, 3 E. & B. 763 (E. C. L. R. vol. 77), Jones v. Mayor of Carmarthen, 8 M. & W. 605.† Lord Campbell, C. J., at the close of the argument, suggested that the pleadings should be amended, in order to raise the question more distinctly, and to enable the parties to bring error. The case stood over ; and, on Saturday, June 9th, 1855, it was again mentioned, before the same Judges. The counsel then jointly applied to the Court to lay down the general principle, without reference to the pleadings, it being agreed that error should not be brought. To this the Court assented : and, on Tuesday, June 12th, 1855, Lord Campbell, C. J., delivered the judgment of the Court as follows. In this case we are asked to give our opinion as to the principle on which the town clerk is to be paid the expenses incurred by him in carrying out the provisions of stat. 6 & 7 Vict. c. 18. We are ready to do so. The question is in the long run not important ; for the salary of the town clerk will be adjusted

to *apply it to the particular facts. Here the expense of print-[*803 ing has not been disallowed: nothing has been disallowed except that of which the performance is imposed on the town clerk by sect. 48.

Pashley and *Field*, contrà.—The second Hull case carries the principle no further than the first: the question really is as to the application. What the town clerk cannot reasonably be expected to do without calling in extraordinary assistance, that he may pay for, and may claim repayment. He cannot be called upon, as part of his ordinary duty, to copy out lists for the printer and to superintend the printing, any more than he could be called on to print; and it is allowed that he is to be repaid the expense of printing. He is, by sect. 48, to "cause the said lists to be copied and printed:" he can no more be required personally to copy than to print. His duty as to the list of freemen is not so described: he is to "make out" that; sect. 14.

Lord CAMPBELL, C. J.—It is quite clear that this rule must be discharged. According to the principle which we laid down in the second Hull case, there is no ground for saying that the town clerk has laid out money in doing anything which he was not bound to do, anything which might not reasonably have been done in his own office. If he had done so, whether by manuscript or printing, the expense would have been fit to be allowed. Here the printing has been allowed; and so are all disbursements save those in respect of what he might have done in his own office. I must again repeat that there is no danger of the town clerk *going without reasonable remuneration: he [*804 should be remunerated reasonably and liberally, but not by paying others for performing duties which he ought to perform himself.

COLERIDGE, J.—I am of the same opinion. I was not present when the first Hull case was decided; but the principle has been most reasonably laid down. There is not the slightest hardship on the town clerk. He has or has not an adequate salary: but this duty is well known to exist, and to recur year by year.

ERLE, J.—There is no question of law here. The principle has been laid down in the Hull cases. The Act of Parliament has imposed certain duties on officers; in some cases the officers are without remuneration; in some they are salaried: all that the Legislature provides for is expense out of pocket. But, as to personal services, whether by

at less or more according as he has more or less recourse to the different parishes for repayment; and this will seldom make any difference to the ratepayers of those parishes, as they will generally be burgesses. We adhere to the principle which we laid down in the former case between the same parties: that the town clerk cannot make a charge for his own time or trouble, or for that of his ordinary clerks: that would not be comprehended under "expenses." But, if he is not able, by the reasonable exertions of himself and his ordinary clerks, to do the work, and is obliged to pay for extra labour, he is entitled to repayment for that. He must not employ himself solely on other matters, and hire a person specially to do this work: but, if he is fully employed on this work and yet cannot get it done without hiring the assistance of others, he may claim repayment. And the town council should adjust the salary on this principle.   :⁴

overseers or by the town clerk and his ordinary assistants, there is no charge allowed.

(CROMPTON, J., had left the Court.)   Rule discharged.

———◆———

*805]   *The QUEEN *v.* The Justices of GLOUCESTERSHIRE.
June 1.

A coroner is not entitled to the fee of 20*s.* mentioned in stat. 25 G. 2, c. 29, for holding an inquest, unless in the judgment of the Court of Quarter Sessions it was proper that such inquest should have been held: and the Court of Queen's Bench will not review the judgment of the Sessions on this point.
And this Court refused to grant a mandamus to the Sessions to pay such fees.
But the Court made absolute a rule for a mandamus to pay the fee of 6*s.* 8*d.* on inquests which the Sessions had held not to be duly holden, that the question might be discussed on the record whether, under stat. 7 W. 4 & 1 Vict. c. 68, the coroner is entitled as of right to the fees and disbursements mentioned in that Act.

SIR F. THESIGER, in last Easter Term, obtained a rule calling upon the justices of Gloucestershire to show cause why a writ of mandamus should not issue, commanding them to order payment to the coroner of Gloucestershire of the several sums of 20*s.* and 6*s.* 8*d.* in respect of an inquisition on the body of one Mary Bryant, and the like sums in respect of an inquisition on the body of Charles Ball.   In the affidavit in support of the rule it was stated that the coroner, on, &c., received notice from the parish constable that Mary Bryant, a female of the age of sixty years, was, on, &c., found lying dead on the floor of her room, near the outer door, which was open, and that the cause of her death was unknown; and that he was requested by the constable to hold an inquest on her; that, upon inquiry, he, the coroner, found that she was not subject to any known disease, had not been for many years attended by any medical man, and had been left in the morning in good health: that he thereupon went seventeen miles and held an inquest; and the jury found that she died in a natural way, by the visitation of God: that, on, &c., he received notice from the police that Charles Ball, a child sixteen months old, had then recently died a violent, and not a natural, death, the said child having been scalded by

*806]   *hot water, which was the cause of death: that he thereupon went eleven miles and held an inquest; and that the jury found that the child died of an accidental scald: that he considered it necessary to hold the inquests: that afterwards he sent in his accounts to the justices in Quarter Sessions, and attended personally to be examined as to the correctness of the accounts; and that the justices ordered the county treasurer to pay him his disbursements and mileage in respect of the said inquests, but refused to make an order for the payment of his fees of 20*s.* and 6*s.* 8*d.* on either of the inquests, alleging, as the ground of such refusal, that the inquests were unnecessary.   The affidavits in answer stated that the justices, after consideration, came to the conclusion that the inquests in question had been unduly taken, and that they had therefore, in obedience to the decision in the case of Regina *v.* Justices of Carmarthenshire, 10 Q. B. 796 (E. C. L. R. vol. 59), disallowed the fees of 20*s.* and 6*s.* 8*d.* in both cases; and that the said coroner, in answer to questions put to him by the justices, had said that no suspicious circumstances were stated to him respecting either death as a reason for holding either inquest.

Byles, Serjt., and *A. M. Skinner*, now showed cause.—A coroner is not entitled to either of the fees in question unless the inquest be duly taken; the justices are the judges whether the inquest was duly taken; their decision as to that fact cannot be reviewed. By the statute of Westminster the First (3 Ed. 1), c. 10, it is provided that "no coroner demand nor take anything of any man to do his office, upon pain of great forfeiture to the King." By stat. 3 H. 7, c. 1, s. 4, "upon every inquisition taken upon the view of the body slain," the coroner *shall have for his fee 13*s.* 4*d.* of the goods, &c., "of him that [*807 is the slayer and murderer, if he have any goods, and if he have no goods," out of any amerciaments: and by stat. 25 G. 2, c. 29, s. 1, it is enacted, after reciting stat. 3 H. 7, c. 1, and that such fee so to be taken is not an adequate reward for the general execution of the office, that "for every inquisition, not taken upon the view of a body dying in a gaol or prison," which "shall be duly taken" in England in any place contributory to county rates, the sum of twenty shillings, and for every mile which the coroner is compelled to travel the further sum of nine pence, over and above the said sum of twenty shillings, shall be paid to him "by order of the justices" in Quarter Sessions. Sect. 2 enacts that for every inquisition, which "shall be duly taken upon the view of a body dying in any gaol or prison" in England by a coroner, so much money not exceeding twenty shillings shall be paid to him as the justices in Quarter Sessions "shall think fit to allow as a recompense for his" labour and charges, "to be paid in like manner by order of the said justices," &c. Sect. 3 provides "that over and above the recompense hereby limited and appointed for inquisitions taken as aforesaid, the coroner or coroners, who shall take an inquisition upon the view of a body slain or murdered, shall also have the fee of 18*s.* 4*d.*, payable by virtue of the said Act" of H. 7. Stat. 7 W. 4 & 1 Vict. c. 68, s. 3, enacts that every coroner shall, "within four months after holding any inquest, cause a full and true account of all sums paid by him under the provisions of this Act, including all sums paid to any medical witness," "to be laid before the justices," &c., and such justices "may, if they shall think fit, examine the said coroner on oath as to such account, and on being *satisfied of the correctness thereof, [*808 such justices" shall make an order on the treasurer, &c., "for payment to the said coroner not only of the sum due to him on such account, but also of a sum of 6s. 8d. for every inquest holden by him as aforesaid, over and above all other fees and allowances to which he is now by law entitled." These statutes have received a judicial construction. In Rex v. The Justices of Kent, 11 East, 229, this Court refused a mandamus to the justices to allow a coroner his fee. In that case the verdict of the coroner's jury was that the deceased died by the visitation of God: but it appeared that the death had been sudden, and that the coroner had been called upon by respectable inhabitants to execute his office: and the Court exculpated the coroner from any improper practice, as the taking of the inquisition seemed to have been suggested to him by others; " but the Court still thought that there was no sufficient ground for the present application; for the statute had directed that the fees should be allowed to the coroner for all inquisitions *duly taken;* and the justices were to judge whether the inquisition in question had been duly taken; and there was no reason for imputing to them that they had exercised their judgment with any undue bias; and the Court did not see any occasion to interfere with that judgment in this instance." [Lord CAMPBELL, C. J.—The Court seems to have considered that an inquest was not duly taken, if there was no apparent necessity for taking it, and that the justices were the judges whether there was such necessity.] Yes: and that view was

*809]   adopted in Regina v. Justices of Carmarthenshire, in *which case a rule for a mandamus to justices to pay a coroner his fees and disbursements, which they had disallowed, was made absolute as to the disbursements, but discharged as to the fees. In that case, which was after stat. 7 W. 4 & 1 Vict. c. 68, both the 20s. fee and the 6s. 8d. fee were before the Court, and the decision was the same as to both. [COLERIDGE, J.—The distinction, if there be one, between the two fees was not presented to the Court. CROMPTON, J.—Is the case satisfactory as to the fee of 6s. 8d. given by the last statute? It decides that the statute is applicable to an inquest, which is assumed in the case to have been improperly holden: and it decides that the coroner was entitled by virtue of the statute, as of right, to repayment of his disbursements in such a case. But, if he was as of right entitled to repayment of his disbursements, was he not equally entitled as of right to the payment of his fee of 6s. 8d.? Is not that fee, according to the statute, a fee for the trouble, thrown upon the coroner by the statute, of making the disbursements and making out the account? Lord CAMPBELL, C. J.—What do you say is the consideration for which the further fee of 6s. 8d. is given?] The holding of the inquest. [Lord CAMPBELL, C. J.—Then, according to you, it is a mere increase of fee from 20s. to 26s. 8d. COLERIDGE, J.—Though the inquest be properly held, this fee is not due until the coroner has rendered an account, and the justices are satisfied of its correctness. The condition of the order for payment of this fee is "on being satisfied of the correctness" of the account.] But still the occasion of the making of the order is to be the holding of an inquest duly taken.

Sir *F. Thesiger* and *W. Payne*, in support of the rule.—The correct proposition is, that the coroner is bound to *execute his office, [*810 if he be required so to do, and is, in such case, entitled as of right to the fees in question. This proposition is supported both by a review of the older statutes, and by the interpretation of them contained in modern Acts upon similar matters. By 2 stat. 4 Ed. 1, s. 1, de officio coronatoris, the coroner, when commanded by the King's bailiffs, *or by honest men, shall* go to the place where any be slain or suddenly died or wounded, and shall forthwith inquire, &c.: and, by stat. 1 H. 8, c. 7, "*upon a request* made to a coroner to come and inquire upon the view of any person slain, drowned, or otherwise dead by misadventure, the said coroner diligently shall do his office," &c., upon pain of 40*s.* Therefore, by these statutes, the coroner is bound to hold an inquest, if required so to do and informed that any be slain or suddenly dead. Stat. 25 G. 2, c. 29, s. 1, then enacts that a fee of 20*s.* shall be paid to the coroner for every inquest duly taken, which, having regard to the statute last mentioned, must signify that he shall be paid such fee for every inquest taken upon request and information of a sudden death. The meaning of the word "duly" cannot be that attributed to it by the other side; for it is again used in the second section of the Act, which applies to the cases of inquest holden on persons dead in prison, and which, it will not be denied, are inquests which must of necessity be holden. By stat. 13 & 14 Vict. c. 115, s. 8, no sum shall be paid by the trustees of any friendly society insured and payable on the death of a child, &c., unless the party applying for the same shall produce and deliver a certificate signed by a physician, &c., *or coroner,* in the form (D.) in the schedule; and the form is: "I hereby certify that I have held an inquest on the body," &c., "who *was found dead,*" &c.; which does not *suggest any other circumstance authorizing [*811 the holding of the inquest than that the person was found dead. The Legislature assumes that the coroner is bound to hold an inquest in such case, if required; and, if he is so bound, he must in justice be entitled to his fees. [CROMPTON, J.—Would it not be a dangerous precedent if we were to review a decision forty years old, on a point on which there has a recent solemn decision confirming the other, and when there has been legislation on the subject, since the earlier decision, and whilst the Legislature must have supposed it properly to declare the law? ERLE, J.—In assuming that the coroner must necessarily hold an inquest when required, you seem to make the discretion of the constable supreme as to whether it should be holden.] If there be a discretion at all, it is to be exercised subject to the review of this

Court: Regina v. Justices of Devonshire.(a) There a mandamus went to the justices to enter continuances and allow expenses to a coroner, which they had disallowed; so that they must have thought the decision might be reversed. In Rex v. The Justices of Kent, 11 East, 229, the rule Nisi was refused: there was no argument on a return.

Lord CAMPBELL, C. J.—I am of opinion that there is sufficient doubt *812] as to the construction of the statute *with regard to the fee of 6s. 8d. to justify the Court in directing a mandamus to issue: but as to the fee of 20s. I think there is no doubt, and that the mandamus should be refused. I am of opinion, as to that fee, that by stat. 25 G. 2, c. 29, the Legislature has made it payable only when the inquest was duly taken, and has made the justices in Quarter Sessions the judges to determine whether the inquest was duly taken; and I am of opinion that, by the word " duly," the Legislature did not mean to raise the question whether the inquest was taken with due solemnity or formality, but whether it was proper that an inquest should be held; and that it is not proper that an inquest should be held unless there were grounds laid before the coroner which made it proper that there should be an inquiry; and that the justices are to exercise their discretion in determining whether it was proper that the inquest should be held. The justices are called upon to exercise a solemn duty: on the one hand to see that the coroner be paid his fees, if he was right in holding the inquest; but, on the other hand, to guard the ratepayers against any improper act of the coroner. I should have so construed the Act at first; but now still more so, after the solemn decision of this Court forty years ago. That decision is indeed impugned on the ground that the argument was not taken upon the return, but upon the rule. The rule for a mandamus however was refused because the Court thought that the statute was clear; and the Court long afterwards reconsidered the point in the case of Regina v. Justices of Carmarthenshire, and, after solemn argument, confirmed the former decision. Though we did not entirely concur with those decisions, it would be *813] contrary to all the rules by which the Court is guided if *we were now to overrule them after they have so long formed the law of the land. If the law as explained by them be inexpedient, it must be altered by the Legislature. But I concur in the propriety and expediency of those decisions. No doubt justices, in considering whether there was reasonable ground for the holding of an inquest, should do so with a leaning in favour of the coroner; but, if there was no reason-

(a) This case was heard in Trinity Term (June 9th), 1846, before Lord Denman, C. J., Patteson and Williams, Js. Crowder and Montague Smith showed cause; and Sir Fitzroy Kelly. Solicitor-General, and John Greenwood argued in support of the rule for the mandamus. Lord Denman, C. J., said that there was so much doubt as to the mode in which the order was made, and the general principle on which the jurisdiction ought to be exercised, that the writ should go. Patteson and Williams, Js., concurred. Rule absolute. (From the notes of Messrs. Adolphus and Ellis.)

able ground, they ought to disallow the fee; and, in my judgment, they are the proper persons to decide such a case.

COLERIDGE, J.—The point which we now decide was solemnly determined forty years ago, and again in the case of Regina v. Justices of Carmarthenshire. The strength of those decisions is not weakened as to the fee of 20s. because in the latter case no distinction was pointed out between that fee and the fee of 6s. 8d.; and we now allow the case of the second fee to be discussed upon a return. The law having been administered in accordance with those cases during so long a time, the very strongest grounds should be shown for saying that they were wrongly decided, before the Court should send the case for rediscussion; but, so far from being of opinion that the decisions are wrong, I think they are perfectly right. They are right unless the word "duly" in the statute means with due solemnity; but I am clearly of opinion that it does not. I think that the statute leaves a discretion in the justices to determine whether the inquest ought to have been held, and that the discretion, if fairly exercised, ought not to be subject to appeal. The argument derived from the assumed meaning of the word "duly" in the section *relating to the deaths of prisoners in gaol does not [*814 seem to me to be well founded; for, though, in the case of the death of a prisoner, I should think that an inquest ought to be held, and that it would be wrong in justices to disallow the fee, yet the words of the section are equally applicable to the case of a visitor dying within the precincts of the gaol without any colour given for the holding of an inquest, in which case I should think the holding of an inquest was not imperative, that it ought not to be held, and that the justices might properly decline to allow the fee.

ERLE, J.—I am of opinion that the rule ought to be discharged with regard to the fee of 20s. Stat. 25 G. 2, c. 29, gives that fee when an inquest has been duly taken, and enacts that the fee is to be allowed by the justices in Quarter Sessions. The question raised before us is, who is finally to decide whether the inquest was duly taken. If an inquest is to be pronounced duly held whenever it is held with due formality, the coroner is supreme as to the propriety of holding it. If the coroner is bound to hold an inquest whenever he is called upon to do so by the constable, that person is supreme. Lord Ellenborough, however, held that the justices are supreme. It is now desired that we should review his decision; and, if I understand the argument which has been offered, that we should declare that this Court will review the exercise of the discretion by the justices. But it seems to me that the justices are the proper supreme tribunal in the matter. They form a Court collected from the neighbourhood; and the subject-matter is one which ought to be decided by local knowledge. In a case in which violence is suggested, the *magistrates of the neighbourhood will be strongly [*815 disposed in favour of inquiry. I agree that, wherever a coroner is bound to hold an inquest, it would be almost a contradiction to say that he ought not to have his fee; and, if his fee were refused in such case, I think there would almost be ground for a criminal information against the justices: but such a case can hardly arise. Most cases are proper for the exercise of a discretion; and the justices seem to me to be a thoroughly satisfactory tribunal for the purpose.

CROMPTON, J.—It is most important that decisions deliberately given should not be questioned after a long lapse of time. In this case there was one solemnly made half a century ago, and another lately; and, what is always of great weight with me, there have been enactments by the Legislature upon the subject-matter since those decisions were published. If those decisions had been considered open to reversal, the Legislature might have made a positive enactment. Such decisions should not be questioned but on the strongest grounds. I, however, am of opinion that they were strictly correct. It seems to me that the fee of 6s. 8d. is on a very different footing, because the question was not discussed in Regina v. Justices of Carmarthenshire, no distinction being pointed out to the Court as between it and the fee of 20s. I think, therefore, that the question raised with regard to it may properly be now discussed, and that the question as to the allowance of the disbursements may be considered at the same time.

Rule absolute for a mandamus as to the fees of 6s. 8d. only.(a)

(a) Reported by W. B. Brett, Esq.

*816]   *MARTHA SHARP and JOSHUA SHARP v. THOMAS WATERHOUSE and WILLIAM CALVERT. June 2.

By indenture between S. and W., it was recited that S. was seised and possessed of closes L. and W., and that W. was proprietor of a mill from which was produced a quantity of refuse: that W. had, by S.'s license, made a reservoir on L. for the reception of the refuse, in order to filter it, and drains for conveying it away from the reservoir; and had agreed with S. for license to convey the refuse down the drains on to W.: and, in consideration of such license, W. agreed to give to S. the "liberties and privileges" after mentioned, and to supply him with pure water, and indemnify him as after mentioned. And it was witnessed that S., in consideration of being supplied with pure water, and of receiving for his own use the refuse "which may from time to time be found" in the reservoir and drains, and of the privilege of using it for manuring his land, and of the covenants and agreements by W., covenanted, for himself, his heirs, executors, and administrators, to license W. to use the reservoir and drains for the purposes aforesaid, and that S., his heirs, &c., would scour and cleanse the reservoir and drains when necessary; W. to indemnify S. against actions brought against him for conveying away the refuse (except in a specified direction). And W., for himself, his heirs, executors, and administrators, covenanted to supply S. with pure water, sufficient to supply his cattle on certain closes, including L. and W., and convey it to a reservoir made by S. for the purpose: but W. was not to be compellable to convey it further; and that it should be "lawful" for S., his heirs and assigns, to cleanse and scour the reservoir and drains made by W., "and to take" the refuse "away therefrom, to and for his and their own use and benefit."

Admitted: That the covenant to supply S. with pure water ran with the closes the cattle on which were to be supplied with water, and that L.'s devisee of such closes might maintain an action against W. for neglecting to supply the water.

But held, by Lord Campbell, C. J., Erle and Crompton, Js., dissentiente Coleridge, J., that there was no covenant, express or implied, compelling W. to send the refuse to the first-mentioned reservoir or drains.

THE last count of the declaration alleged that, before and at the time of making the deed after mentioned, Samuel Sharp was seised in his demesne as of fee of and in the land at Pudsey, in the county of York, in the deed mentioned: and, being so seised, on 23d December, 1835, a deed was made between the said Samuel Sharp and defendants, which was in the words following.

"Articles of agreement indented, made, and entered into this 23d day of December, in the year of our Lord 1835 : between Samuel Sharp, of," &c., "of the first part, William Musgrave, of," &c., "Samuel Moss the elder, Joseph Rayner, James Waterhouse, and William Calvert, all of," &c., *"Samuel Farren, of," &c., "and Abraham Gibson [*817 and John Crowther, both of," &c., "of the second part, and Joshua Shoesmith," &c., naming forty-one others, among whom was Thomas Waterhouse, "of the third part, as follows. Whereas the said Samuel Sharp is seised of three closes of land, called Proctor Close, Lister Close, and Walker Low Close, now in his possession, situated in Pudsey," &c. ; "and whereas the said parties hereto of the 2d and 3d parts are the proprietors of a scribbling and fulling mill, dyehouse and other buildings, situate at Pudsey," &c., "from which is produced a considerable quantity of dyewater, and also a considerable quantity of suds and refuse commonly called soar or sake; and whereas the said parties hereto of the 2d and 3d parts sometime agreed with the said Samuel Sharp for leave and license to make, and they have made, a reservoir on the west side of the said close of land called Lister Close for the reception of such dyewater and soar or sake, in order to filter or clarify the same; and the said parties hereto of the 2d and 3d parts at the same time agreed with the said Samuel Sharp for leave and license to make, and they have all since made, in the said close of land called Lister Close, a sough or drain for the purpose of carrying away the said dyewater and soar or sake from the said reservoir; and the said parties hereto of the 2d and 3d parts at the same time also agreed with the said Samuel Sharp for leave and license to convey down the present sough or drain on the south side of the said close of land called Walker Low Close the said dyewater and soar or sake : and, in consideration of such leave and license, they the said parties hereto of the 2d and 3d parts at the same time agreed to give unto the said Samuel Sharp the liberties and privileges hereinafter *mentioned, and to supply [*818 him with pure water and indemnify him as hereinafter mentioned: and, in order the better to carry such agreements into effect, they, the said parties hereto, have mutually agreed that these presents shall contain the covenants, provisions, declaration, and agreements herein-

after expressed : Now these presents witness that, in consideration of
being supplied by the said parties hereto of the 2d and 3d parts with
pure water as hereinafter mentioned, and of receiving for his own use
the sediment or sludge which may from time to time be found in the
said reservoir and soughs, and of the privilege of using such dyewater
and soar or sake for tilling or manuring, not only the three closes of
land hereinbefore mentioned, but also all other the lands of the said
Samuel Sharp, and also in consideration of the covenants and agreements hereinafter contained by and on the part and behalf of the said
parties hereto of the 2d and 3d parts, their heirs, executors, and administrators, to be observed, performed, and kept, he, the said Samuel
Sharp, for himself, his heirs, executors, and administrators, doth hereby
covenant, promise, and agree to and with the said parties hereto of the
2d and 3d parts, their heirs, executors, administrators, and assigns, that
it shall and may be lawful to and for, and he the said Samuel Sharp
doth hereby give leave and license unto, the said parties of the 2d and
3d parts, their heirs, executors, administrators, and assigns, at all times
for ever hereafter to use the .said reservoirs and soughs for the purposes
aforesaid; and also that he, the said Samuel Sharp, his heirs and
assigns, shall and will, at all times hereafter, at his and their own
expense, scour and cleanse the said reservoir and soughs or drains whenever it may be necessary to scour and cleanse the *same.   Pro-
*819]   vided always, and it is hereby declared and agreed by and
between the said parties to these presents, that, if the said Samuel
Sharp, his heirs or assigns, shall at any time hereafter think fit to carry
or convey the said dyewater and soar or sake over or upon the said
closes of land called Proctor Close, Lister Close, and Walker Low
Close, or any of them, or any part thereof, or over or upon any other
of the lands or grounds, or any part thereof, for the purpose of tilling
or manuring the same lands or any of them, it shall and may be lawful
to and for him and them to carry and convey the same accordingly;
but, unless he or they shall eventually carry or convey away such dyewater and soar or sake at and out of the south east corner of the
said close of land called Walker Low Close, it is hereby expressly
declared and agreed by and between the said parties hereto that the
said parties hereto of the 2d and 3d parts, their executors, administrators, or assigns, shall not be liable or compellable to indemnify the said
Samuel Sharp," &c., pursuant to the covenant after contained : covenant by Sharp that, if the owner of land through which the dyewater,
&c., should pass shall commence an action or suit against him, he should
deliver the process served upon him to a party named, and authorize
such party to defend, as his attorney. at the costs of the parties of
the 2d and 3d parts, or, if that party would not so defend, would not
suffer judgment by default, but would, at such costs, defend by some
other attorney.   " And these presents further witness that, for the con-

siderations aforesaid, and for and in consideration of the covenants and agreements hereinafter contained by and on the part and behalf of the said Samuel Sharp, his heirs, executors, administrators, and assigns, they, the *said parties hereto of the 2d and 3d parts, do hereby, [*820 for themselves, their heirs, executors, and administrators, jointly, and any two, any three, any four, and any greater number than four, of them, apart from the others of them, do hereby, for themselves, their heirs, executors, and administrators, jointly, and each of them, separately and apart from the others and other of them, do hereby, for himself, his heirs, executors, and administrators, severally, covenant, promise and agree to and with the said Samuel Sharp, his heirs and assigns, that they, the said parties hereto of the 2d and 3d parts, their heirs, executors, administrators, or assigns, shall and will, at all times hereafter, at their own expense, supply from their said dam or reservoir, or from some other source, pure and unadulterated water, sufficient for the consumption of the horses, cows, and other cattle of the owners and occupiers for the time being of the said closes of land called Proctor Close, Lister Close, Walker Low Close, and another close belonging to the said Samuel Sharp, called Great Three Days Work, and, at the like expense, convey the same pure unadulterated water into the reservoir already made for the same by the said Samuel Sharp in the said close of land called Lister Close, by or through the sough or drain already made by the said parties hereto of the 2d and 3d parts for that purpose: but the said parties hereto of the 2d and 3d parts, their heirs, executors, administrators, or assigns, shall not be compellable to convey such pure and unadulterated water further than the reservoir last mentioned: and, further, that it shall and may be lawful to and for the said Samuel Sharp, his heirs and assigns, at all times hereafter, at his and their own expense, to cleanse and scour the said reservoir which has been *made by the said parties hereto of the [*821 2d and 3d parts for the reception of the said dyewater and soar or sake, and also all the soughs or drains hereinbefore mentioned, and to take the sediment and sludge away therefrom to and for his and their own use and benefit." Covenant for indemnification of Sharp by the parties of the 2d and 3d parts in the event of such action, &c., as before specified, and of his acting as stipulated; and other provisions for such event.

Averment: that the defendants then duly executed the said deed, as parties thereto of the 2d(a) part; and that the said Samuel Sharp then duly executed the same as party thereto of the 1st part; and that the recitals in the said deed were and are true. And that the said Samuel Sharp afterwards duly made and published his last will and testament in writing, duly executed," &c., " and thereby devised the said land, of which he was seised as aforesaid, to the plaintiffs in fee, and after-

(a) Sic.

wards died without altering his said will.   And that everything has
been done and happened, on the part of the said Samuel Sharp, and
of the plaintiffs, to entitle the plaintiffs to the continuance of the several
last-mentioned benefits and privileges by the said deed granted to the
said Samuel Sharp, his heirs and assigns, and to sue the defendants in
respect of the several grievances and breaches of covenant hereinafter
mentioned.   And that the plaintiffs have been from the death of the
said Samuel Sharp, and still are, in possession of the said land of which
the said Samuel Sharp was seised as aforesaid, and were in possession
thereof at the times of the grievances and breaches of covenant hereinafter *mentioned.   Yet the defendants, after the death of the
said Samuel Sharp, wrongfully and improperly and in breach of
their said covenant and agreement in that behalf, diverted divers large
quantities of the dyewater, soar or sake produced at the said mill, dyehouse, and buildings, which, according to the true intent and meaning
of the said deed, ought to have flowed through and into the said sough
and reservoir, from flowing through and into the same, and otherwise
disposed of the same, and wrongfully and improperly prevented from
coming into the said sough or drain and reservoir divers quantities of
sediment, and the dye, which, according to the true intent and meaning
of the said deed, ought to have come into the same, and wrongfully and
improperly sent through and into the said sough and reservoir, dyewater,
soar or sake of a different description from those mentioned and intended
by the said deed, and from which the profitable part had been extracted,
and which were useless and noxious to the plaintiffs; and the plaintiffs
were thereby deprived of the use and benefit which they otherwise
would have derived from the dyewater, soar or sake which ought to
have flowed through and into the said sough and reservoir, and were put
to expense in obtaining other manure for their said land.   And the
defendants, after the death of the said Samuel Sharp, wrongfully
neglected to supply from their said dam or reservoir, or from any other
source, pure and unadulterated water sufficient for the consumption of
the horses, cows, and other cattle of the plaintiffs, as occupiers of the
said closes in the declaration in that behalf mentioned; and wrongfully
and improperly neglected to convey any such pure and unadulterated
*823]   water into the said reservoir in the said deed in that behalf *men-
tioned through the sough or drain in the said deed in that behalf
mentioned; and wrongfully and improperly conveyed, through the said
sough or drain, into the said reservoir, impure and adulterated water
which was unfit for the consumption of horses, cows, or cattle.

The defendants demurred to this count so far as regards the breach
that defendants wrongfully, &c., diverted large quantities of the dyewater, soar, or sake, &c., and also so far as regards the breach that
defendants wrongfully neglected to supply from their dam, &c., pure
and unadulterated water sufficient, &c., neglected to convey, &c.

Joinder on both demurrers.

Hugh Hill, for the defendants.—The demurrer to the breach respecting the water cannot be sustained. It was proposed to raise the question whether the covenant, in respect of which that breach is complained of, runs with the land. But the authorities seem conclusive in the affirmative: Spencer's Case, 5 Rep. 16 a, and Mr. Smith's note to that case,(a) where the case in 42 Ed. 3,(b) commonly called The Prior's Case, is referred to; Jourdain *v.* Wilson, 4 B. & Ald. 266 (E. C. L. R. vol. 6). In the learned note to Bythewood & Jarman's Selection of Precedents, &c., vol. 9, p. 356 (3d ed. by Sweet), there is a reference to a passage in the 10th edition of Sugden's Practical Treatise of the Law of Vendors and Purchasers, vol. 2, p. 472,(c) from which a contrary inference might be suggested: but the law seems now to be settled that such a covenant runs with the land.

*As to the other breach, the defendants contend that there is no covenant shown which is broken by the conduct complained [*824 of. In consideration of the license given by the devisor Samuel Sharp to the defendants to make on his land, Lister Close, a reservoir for receiving the dyewater, soar, and sake, and a drain for carrying it away therefrom, and to convey down the drain that dyewater, soar, and sake, the defendants agree to give him the liberties and privileges after mentioned, and to supply him with pure water: and he, in consideration of being supplied with pure water, "and of receiving for his own use the sediment or sludge which may from time to time be found in the said reservoir and soughs, and of the privilege of using such dyewater and soar or sake for tilling or manuring," covenants with them to license the use of the reservoirs and soughs for the purposes aforesaid and that he will scour and cleanse them, he reserving power to carry away the dyewater, &c., over lands specified, and to be indemnified against actions brought for his use of this power (except in one mode): and, in consideration of the above, and of the devisor's covenants and agreements after mentioned, the defendants covenant to supply the pure water, and that it shall be lawful for the devisor to cleanse the reservoir and all the soughs, "and to take the sediment and sludge away therefrom" for his own use and benefit. This covenant does not oblige the defendants to send any of the dyewater, &c., into the reservoirs or soughs, but only authorizes the devisor to use what does come thither. It does not give him any right to the refuse before it comes thither.

Atherton, contrà.—The interpretation with the *defendants [*825 put on the covenant is too restricted, and would fail to carry into effect the intention of the parties. It is evident that they contemplate reciprocal benefits: the millowners are enabled to get rid of their

(a) 1 Smith's Lea. Ca. 43, 50 (ed. 4).
(b) Yearb. H. 42 Ed. 3, pl. 14, fol. 3 A.
(c) See 13th edition, p. 474.

refuse; the landowner is to have the use of the refuse: each benefit is conferred in consideration of the other. But as the defendants seek to interpret the deed, the landowner would really get nothing by the covenant; for, without any covenant at all, he would be entitled to use all the refuse which he might find on his land.

Hugh Hill, in reply.—No such covenant can be implied; and it is not pretended that there is any express covenant to the effect. In Aspdin *v.* Austin, 5 Q. B. 671, 683 (E. C. L. R. vol. 48), this Court laid down and limited the principle upon which, on the authority of decided cases, covenants not expressed may be implied from what appears to be the general intent of the parties to the deed. "It will be found in those cases that, where words of recital or reference manifested a clear intention that the parties should do certain acts, the Courts have from these inferred a covenant to do such acts, and sustained actions of covenant for the non-performance, as if the instruments had contained express covenants to perform them. But it is a manifest extension of that principle to hold that, where parties have expressly covenanted to perform certain acts, they must be held to have impliedly covenanted for every act convenient or even necessary for the perfect performance of their express covenant. Where parties have entered into written *826] engagements with expressed stipulations, it is manifestly *not desirable to extend them by any implications: the presumption is that, having expressed some, they have expressed all the conditions by which they intend to be bound under that instrument." Now here is an express covenant for the supply of pure water by the defendants; and there are also permissive words which give them a certain license; and that is all: they covenant to supply the water; in return they are allowed the means of getting rid of their refuse.

Lord CAMPBELL, C. J.—It is admitted that the covenant as to the water will run with the land; and our attention has been most properly drawn to the question, whether there is also a covenant to send the refuse into the sough or reservoir. I certainly was of opinion, looking merely at the recital, that the intention of the parties was that, while the mill was there and produced the dyewater, &c., Sharp should have it in the state in which it was produced by the mill, without alteration; that whatever refuse there was should flow into Sharp's reservoir. But, on looking at the whole of the deed, it seems to me that we are not entitled to put such a construction upon it: that may have been in the contemplation of the parties; but I cannot say that it was. The deed appears to have two objects, the supply of the pure water, and the benefit to each party in respect of the refuse. Now, as to the pure water, the covenant is express: it is to be supplied at all times at the expense of the millowners: that is expressed in the most clear terms. But, when we come to the dyewater, we find no covenant at all. If it was meant that the millowners should be obliged to send the dyewater

to the reservoir, one is at a loss to see why there is not a covenant of
the *same kind; but there is not. The deed rather seems to [*827
intimate a perpetual and positive obligation to supply pure
water, but that the dyewater was to be sent down only as long as it
suited the millowner. Had there been no covenant with regard to the
one or the other, we might have implied one as to both: but, finding
an express covenant as to the one, we cannot imply it as to the other.
I think, therefore, that there is no covenant to support this assignment
of breach.

COLERIDGE, J.—I am very sorry to say that I cannot at present concur with the judgment which has been just delivered. With more
deliberation I might change my view: and that I say seriously, in order
that I may not encourage parties to go to another Court. It has
always been held that we are not to tie ourselves to the words of the
supposed covenant, but to examine the whole instrument, and to ascertain from its language the intention of the parties; and, if possible, to
put upon it such a construction, as will effectuate that intention. Now,
applying that, let us see what is the state of things here disclosed, what
each party had done and intended to do. I collect, on the one hand,
that the millowners were to have the benefit of the easement on Samuel
Sharp's land, and he was to keep the reservoir and drains in repair;
and this was for the benefit of the millowners; for I suppose that without the use of the reservoir and drains they could not have a convenient
outflow for the refuse, which would become a nuisance either to themselves or to occupiers lower down. This was the benefit which the millowners were to have. On the other hand, the landowner was to have
two things: first, a supply of pure water; secondly, the *refuse [*828
water which was beneficial to him. That was the state of things
when the deed was executed: and I cannot suppose but that each party
had these benefits in contemplation. I think, therefore, it was meant
that the landowner should have both benefits; and I cannot but think
that the taking away of one benefit is as unwarranted as the taking
away of both. If the construction which my Lord and Brothers put
upon this instrument be correct, a great, and not perhaps the least
valuable, benefit will be taken from the landowner; and, more, the
burthensome part will still be imposed on him: he will still have to bear
the burthen without having the whole of the profitable part. I am
slow to believe that the deed ought to be construed so as to produce
that inequality. I may be wrong: but at present I am not prepared
to concur with the rest of the Bench.

ERLE, J.—I agree with my Lord. The question is, whether the
defendants covenanted to send any refuse down to the reservoir and
soughs. The landowner wanted to get pure water; the defendants to
get rid of the foul water which, it was calculated, would be produced
by the mill: they therefore obtained permission to discharge it on the

land of the landowner, he being permitted to take for his own use and
benefit all found on the land; and the millowners also covenant to
supply him with pure water. The question comes to be, whether permitting the landowner to use all the refuse that he should find on
cleansing raises a covenant, on the part of the millowners, to send the
refuse water down to the land. There is a marked difference in the
*829] language of the two stipulations. The defendants *covenant, as
        to the refuse water, that the landowner may use whatever he
finds on the land, without binding themselves to send any down. Suppose the fact to be that the landowner has subjected his land to a dis-
agreeable servitude by allowing the foul water to pass through it, I can
only say that the terms of the deed are all I can look at. The
material part of the contract may have been the supply of the pure
water; but of this I do not feel competent to judge. I am at a loss to
imply from this instrument such a covenant as the plaintiff suggests.
Probably the landowner thought there would be no change in the mode
of discharging the refuse water, and that he should thus get the full
benefit; the millowners probably thought that a restriction on this
point would be burthensome: and therefore no covenant as to this was
inserted.

CROMPTON, J.—I think the defendants are entitled to judgment on
this plea. The real question is, whether we can imply a covenant, on
the part of the defendants, to send down the refuse water to the land
of the landowner. I am of opinion that we cannot. What covenant
could be intended? Is it to be a perpetual easement, to last for ever,
or as long as the mill is worked, or as long as the landowner finds it
desirable to get the refuse? I really do not know what the limit would
be. Yet it is allowed that there is some limit: and I think some would
have been expressed, had such a covenant been intended. Upon looking at the deed, I can see no more than a right on the one side to get
rid of the refuse, and a right on the other to use what is got rid of:
*830] cross easements, in fact. The defendants undertake *to supply
        the landowner with pure water; and their object is to pass away
their refuse water. In doing this without the landowner's license they
would be committing a nuisance; but the correlative easement which
the plaintiffs claim by no means arises. If the intention had been that
the defendants should have the easement of getting rid of the refuse
but not be bound to send it, I do not see how fitter words for that
purpose than those which are here used could have been found. They
say, they covenant that they will at their own expense supply pure
water, and convey it to the reservoir; and then they stipulate that they
shall not be compellable to convey it further: they therefore had in
their minds the mode of creating a right without being bound beyond a
certain point. Then follows a remarkable change of words: it is not
said that they shall be bound to send down the refuse, but that it shall

be lawful to the landowner to cleanse the reservoir and drains, and take the sediment and sludge away therefrom for his own use. We should be merely guessing, if we implied from this a covenant compelling the defendants to send down the refuse.

Judgment for defendants.

---

*The QUEEN v. WILLIAM OGLE DICKENSON. *June* 3. [*831

By sect. 90 of stat. 5 & 6 W. 4, c. 76 (The Municipal Corporation Act), councils of corporate boroughs are empowered to make by-laws. By sect. 91 offences against such by-laws may be punished by summary conviction. By sect. 132 the writ of certiorari is taken away. The Recorder, upon an appeal against such a conviction for an offence against a by-law, having, with the consent of the parties, stated a case and referred, as the only question for this Court to determine, the question whether the facts amounted to an offence within the by-law, and the Court having granted a writ of certiorari to bring up the case:

Held that, by virtue of the consent of the parties, the Court might receive the case, and determine the question, although the writ of certiorari was taken away.

LIDDELL had obtained a rule calling upon the prosecutors to show cause why an order of Sessions, made upon an appeal against a conviction by two justices of the borough and county of Newcastle-upon Tyne, should not be quashed. The appeal was heard at the Quarter Sessions held in October, 1856, before the Recorder, who confirmed the conviction, subject to the opinion of the Court of Queen's Bench upon a case. The case first set out the conviction, which stated that the appellant, William Ogle Dickenson, was convicted before two justices, &c., for that he, on, &c., did cause an obstruction in a certain street and public highway within the said borough, by then and there erecting and placing a certain wooden frame or shop-front in and upon the said street and public highway, and by continuing the same so erected and placed in and upon the said street, &c., for divers, to wit, six hours; whereby the said street and public highway was greatly obstructed and straitened: contrary to a certain by-law, made and passed, &c., by virtue of the statutes in that behalf, &c. The case then stated that, after the passing of The Municipal Corporation Act (5 & 6 W. 4, c. 76), and of stat. 7 W. 4 & 1 Vict. c. lxxii.,(a) the town council made *certain by-laws, the ninth of which was as follows: " that if any [*832 person shall within the said borough carry a sedan chair, not having any person in it, on any public footway, or shake or dust after eight o'clock in the morning any carpet, mat, or furniture in any of the streets," &c., " or roll, drive, drag, or carry on any public footway, any wagon, cart, dray, wheelbarrow," &c., " or project over or upon any public footway any awning which shall impede the passengers, or hang out goods for sale or exhibition, so as to project over any public foot-

(a) Local and personal, public: " For regulating and improving the borough of Newcastle upon Tyne."

way and obstruct the passengers:" The by-law then enumerated many other similar offences, such as rolling casks, flying kites in the streets, and then continued: " or shall cause or commit any other obstruction, nuisance, or annoyance in any of the streets," &c., and then imposed a penalty.   In the month of May, 1852, W. O. Dickenson, a tobacconist, became the owner in fee of the house mentioned in the conviction, which, up to the time of his becoming possessed of it, had been used as a private residence; and in front of the said house and abutting on the foot pavement of the street, except for a distance of about four feet at each end thereof, which was occupied by the doors and steps, was an area protected by iron railings set into a stone coping.   In October, 1855, Mr. Dickenson, being desirous of converting the ground floor into a shop, commenced the construction of a new shop front, extending the whole length of the house, and projecting in front of the walls of the said house to the foot pavement of the street.   The projection was substantially built, and formed the front of the appellant's house, and contained a door and shop front, supported by wooden pilasters, with large glass windows; and the floor inside was brought up to the new outside

*833] wall, and so covered the *area and steps which had previously existed; but the plinths of the pilasters extended one inch and a half over the footway; and the shop front covered a space of two feet by seven inches not previously covered in any way whatever.   For making this projection the appellant was summoned and convicted as above; and against such conviction he appealed, on the ground, amongst others, that the by-law did not authorize the conviction.   On the hearing of the appeal, witnesses were called on both sides as to the facts; and it was objected, on behalf of the appellant, that the obstruction alleged was not within the by-law.   The Recorder confirmed the conviction, subject to the opinion of the Court of Queen's Bench, as to whether the erection of the shop front, as above described, constituted an offence within the ninth by-law.   The question left was thus stated: " If the Court shall be of opinion that the projection over the footway, or the extension of the shop front, was an offence within the said by-law, the conviction is to stand confirmed; if the Court should be of the contrary opinion, the conviction is to be quashed." The special case and the conviction had been brought up by certiorari.

Overend and *Davison* now showed cause.—The certiorari to bring up the order of Sessions and the case has been improvidently issued, and must be quashed.   The conviction is for an alleged offence against a by-law passed by virtue of stat. 5 & 6 W. 4, c. 76, s. 90.   The appeal was entertained by the Recorder under sects. 91, 131; and the writ of certiorari is taken away by sect. 132.   The only mode of bringing a case before this Court by way of appeal is by means of a writ of cer-

*834] tiorari.   When *the writ is taken away, this Court cannot receive a statement of a case: Rex *v.* The Justices of Middlesex, 8 D.

& R. 117 (E. C. L. R. vol. 16). Neither can the statement of the case be looked at to show that the justices had no jurisdiction. To do that, the conviction itself may be brought up, or affidavits may be filed. But, in the present instance, the conviction is good upon the face of it, and there are no affidavits. If the Court, on the question of jurisdiction, do refer to the statement of the case, it shows that the Recorder had jurisdiction and exercised it. The question of jurisdiction arises before a Court in two ways, either upon the complaint itself, or upon alleged facts proffered at the hearing. If it arise upon the complaint, the Court can determine at once; if otherwise, the Court must hear and determine the facts on which the question turns before it can determine the question of jurisdiction; and sometimes all the facts in the case must be determined before the question of jurisdiction can be decided. Such was the case in the present instance; and the Recorder heard and determined all the facts. The question whether he had or had not jurisdiction depends upon whether the shop front was a temporary or permanent obstruction. He had jurisdiction to try that question, and exercised it. If there was any evidence on which he might properly determine the facts, and if he has decided them, this Court cannot interfere: Brittain v. Kinnaird, 1 B. & B. 432 (E. C. L. R. vol. 5);(a) Regina v. Bolton, 1 Q. B. 66 (E. C. L. R. vol. 41); the judgment of Coleridge, J. in Regina v. Dunn, antè, p. 270. [COLERIDGE, J.—In 2 Nolan's Poor Laws, p. 558, *(4th ed.), it is said: " If the Ses- [*835 sions entertain any doubt upon a point of law, they may refer the matter to the judge of assize for his opinion, or state a case for the determination of the Court of King's Bench, and this without the consent of the parties." CROMPTON, J.—So in Paley on Convictions, p. 301 (3d ed.). " This, however, must not be understood, as applying to a special case reserved by the Sessions, and returned with the conviction for the consideration of the Court of King's Bench. Such cases have frequently been reserved upon convictions, which have been brought by appeal before the Sessions, and removed from thence into the King's Bench."] The cases cited in support of the proposition do not warrant the text. Moreover, the powers of a Recorder depend entirely upon stat. 5 & 6 W. 4, c. 76; and that gives him no power to state a case. That is pointed out in note (b) to 1 Chitty's Statutes (2d ed., by Welsby and Beavan, p. 863).

Hugh Hill and *Liddell*, contrà.—The Court may properly look at the statement of a case returned by the Sessions for the consideration of the Court. Such a statement is in the nature of a special verdict, and part of the confirmation by the Sessions of the conviction. The confirmation is conditional, and made dependent upon the decision of this Court upon the case. At all events, the Court may look at the statement for the purpose of seeing whether the Sessions had jurisdic-

(a) See Regina v. Dayman, ante, p. 672; Regina v. Brown, ante, p. 757.

tion. It is admitted that the Court might receive affidavits; and a statement of the facts by the Court below is of equal authority. If the case be looked at, it shows that the facts were wrongly interpreted as *836] bringing the case within the by-law; and therefore *that the decision was wrong upon the point of jurisdiction: for, upon a true interpretation, the case was not within the by-law, and neither the justices nor the Recorder had jurisdiction. The question is not whether there was any evidence of the facts; this Court will review the decision of the Court below upon the facts which determine the question of jurisdiction: Thompson v. Ingham, 14 Q. B. 710 (E. C. L. R. vol. 68). There is no distinction between the powers of a Recorder and of the Sessions. If there were, the Recorder in the present instance stated the case by consent of the parties.(a) [CROMPTON, J.—If we can take cognisance of the statement of the case by virtue of the consent of the parties, the question of jurisdiction need not be determined. There is another question reserved, which is the only one submitted to the Court.]

Lord CAMPBELL, C. J.—This is a case in which the conviction is good upon the face of it. It is made under a statute by which the writ of certiorari is taken away. According to the general rule in such cases, this Court could not entertain the question which has been referred to it. But the parties have agreed that the Recorder should state the facts in the nature of a special verdict, and that we should answer the question referred to us. That question being submitted to us by consent, we will, by virtue of that consent, take cognisance of and answer it. If parties will consent that a Recorder or Justices shall state the facts, and submit the question in dispute to this Court, and that this Court shall determine it, it may be a very salutary practice. It seems *837] to me *to be a much more convenient course than the one now in use of bringing before the Court a mass of conflicting affidavits, from which the Court is to gather the facts and determine whether the case was or was not within the jurisdiction of the Court below. Looking to the facts stated in this case, I am clearly of opinion, in answer to the question submitted to us, that the case as proved was not an offence within the by-law.

COLERIDGE, J.—I never doubted that, if we were at liberty to look at the statement of facts for that purpose, we should determine that the conviction was wrong. The difficulty I felt all along in the case, and which I should have felt to the end but for the consent of the parties, was how we could take cognisance of the facts. The conviction is good on the face of it; and the writ of certiorari is taken away. But, by virtue of the consent, I think we may determine the question submitted to us. We might have inquired upon affidavit whether the case was within the jurisdiction of the Court below; and therefore, upon its being shown to us that, in consideration of the appellant giving up his

(a) This was admitted by the other side, and confirmed by the Recorder, who was in Court.

right to make such affidavits, the other party agreed to admit a statement of the facts by the Recorder as equivalent, I should have seen no objection to the Court recognising such a proceeding, which is undoubtedly much more convenient than the course of bringing the case up on conflicting affidavits. Further, I see no objection to our allowing the parties to waive the question of jurisdiction, and to state the question which they wish the Court to determine. If the question of jurisdiction had not been waived, I should have felt great difficulty in saying that there was not such a dispute and doubt as to the facts *as gave the Recorder jurisdiction to determine what they were : [*838 but by the consent of the parties that difficulty is avoided ; and the only question to be determined is whether the conviction was correct. Upon that question I have no doubt. The conviction was clearly wrong.

ERLE, J.—I join with much satisfaction in the judgment, because I think that such a question, namely, the exposition of a statute, may very often in important cases be usefully raised in this way. The Legislature took away the writ of certiorari in many cases, because it had been used for the purpose of enforcing objections to mere informality in the proceedings below : but, if the use of it were restored for the purpose of raising questions of substance for the opinion of the Superior Courts, it would be a salutary addition to the laws. The course pursued by the consent of the parties in the present instance seems to me entirely satisfactory.

CROMPTON, J.—I will not go into the difficult question which has been raised as to the power of this Court to review the decision upon the facts determining the jurisdiction of an inferior tribunal. I can quite understand where to draw the line in the cases in which the jurisdiction below is to cease upon a question of title arising ; but, where the inferior Court must decide the facts, in order rightly to determine whether the case is within its jurisdiction or not, I feel great difficulty in saying how far this Court can review the decision of the Court below. It is, however, unnecessary to decide the point. I am of opinion that the Recorder could not, without the consent of the parties, have referred for the *consideration of this Court the question which is now [*839 to be determined ; but I see no objection to his having done so with the consent of the parties. The case is now, by consent, before the Court in the way of a special verdict ; and there is a particular question stated for the opinion of the Court. The Court cannot entertain any other. In answer to that, I agree that the conviction should be quashed.(a) Conviction quashed.(b)

(a) The arguments on the construction of the by-law have been omitted.
(b) Reported by W. B. Brett, Esq.

The QUEEN v. HENRY JOSEPH LANCASHIRE. *June* 3.

By stat. 9 G. 4, c. 61, s. 18, a penalty is imposed on every person who shall, without a license, sell any excisable liquor by retail to be drunk on the premises; and by sect. 37 "excisable liquor" is to include sweets or wine, which now are or hereafter may be charged with duty either by customs or excise.

By stat. 4 & 5 W. 4, c. 77, s. 9, the excise duty on sweets or made wines is repealed; but, by sect. 10, the duty on licenses to be taken out by retailers thereof is continued, and all such licenses shall still be taken out.

Held that a person who, since the stat. 4 & 5 W. 4, c. 77, sold sweets or made wines by retail, &c., without a license could not be convicted under sect. 18 of stat. 9 G. 4, c. 61, sweets and made wines being no longer excisable liquors within the meaning of that Act. Dissentiente Erle, J.

THIS was an appeal against a conviction by two justices of the county of Stafford under stat. 9 G. 4, c. 61, s. 18, whereby the appellant was convicted for permitting and suffering to be sold by retail for value in a certain house and premises of him, &c., a certain quantity of wine, to be then drunk and consumed in the said house and premises, the said wine being an excisable liquor, in respect of which a duty of excise was then and there by law charged: and he (the appellant) not being *840] then *and there duly licensed so to do, &c.   The appeal came on to be heard at the Sessions, and was respited; and, by consent, and by order of Wightman, J., the following case was stated for the opinion of this Court.   The appellant was a British wine merchant, and retailer of sweets or made wines, and, at the time of the sale alleged in the conviction, carried on the said trade in a shop and premises at Bilston, in the county of Stafford.   He had, at the time, an excise license for his shop and premises, as a retailer of sweets or made wines, in the ordinary form taken out by retailers of sweets or made wines under The Excise Act, 6 G. 4, c. 81, for which 1l. 1s. and 1s. additional was paid; but he had not obtained any license of justices under stat. 9 G. 4, c. 61.   The appellant was in the habit of selling and sending out by retail British made port, sherry, cowslip, ginger, and other made wines in quantities less than a cask containing 15 gallons, and sometimes as small as a glass, and of allowing the same to be consumed on the said premises, across the counter.   He did not sell foreign wines, and therefore did not take out a foreign wine license.   On the 28th of July, 1856, the appellant, for the sum of three pence, sold a glass of sweets or made wine of English manufacture, being a quantity less than a quarter of a pint, to be then drunk and consumed on the said premises; and the same then was drunk and consumed on the said premises of the appellant by the person to whom it was sold and supplied.   For this act of selling the appellant was summoned and convicted.   By stat. 6 G. 4, c. 37, s. 2, "from and after the 5th day of January, 1826, the following duties of excise shall be raised, levied, collected, and paid:" "For and upon every 100 gallons, imperial gallon standard measure, of liquor *which shall be made in any [*841 part of the United Kingdom of Great Britain and Ireland, for sale, by infusion, fermentation, or otherwise, from fruit or sugar, or from fruit and sugar mixed with any other ingredients or materials whatsoever, commonly called sweets or made wines, to be paid by the maker thereof, the sum of 2*l.* 10*s.*" On the passing of stat. 9 G. 4, c. 61, the above statute was unrepealed: and, by stat. 9 G. 4, c. 61, s. 18. a penalty not exceeding 20*l.*, and not less than 5*l.*, is imposed on every person who shall sell, barter, exchange, or for valuable consideration otherwise dispose of, any excisable liquor by retail, to be drunk or consumed in his house or premises, or shall permit or suffer any excisable liquors to be drunk or consumed in his house or premises without being duly licensed so to do : and, by the interpretation clause (sect. 37), the words "'excisable liquor' shall be deemed to include any ale, beer, or other fermented malt liquor, sweets, cider, perry, wine, or other spirituous liquor which now is or hereafter may be charged with duty either by customs or excise." By The Excise Act, 4 & 5 W. 4, c. 77, s. 9, "all the duties and drawbacks of excise on sweets or made wines," "and all duties upon licenses required to be taken out by any maker of sweets or made wines," are repealed : but it is provided, by sect. 10, "that nothing herein contained shall extend or be deemed or construed to extend to repeal or affect any duty on licenses to be taken out by retailers of sweets or made wines," "but all such licenses shall continue to be taken out as if the Act had not been passed:" and, by sect. 11, "every person who shall sell or send out any liquor made by infusion, fermentation, or otherwise, from fruit or sugar, or from fruit or sugar mixed with other materials, commonly called sweets or made wines," "in any less quantity than *in a whole cask containing [*842 15 gallons, shall be deemed and taken to be a retailer of sweets, and shall take out a license accordingly." The appellant contends that sweets or made wines are no longer excisable liquors within the meaning of stat. 9 G. 4, c. 61; that the payment for a license to sell sweets under stat. 6 G. 4, c. 81, cannot be said to make the liquor sold chargeable with duty within the meaning of stat. 9 G. 4, c. 61, and that therefore the sale of the glass of sweets or made wine on the day in question was not the sale of excisable liquor in respect of which a duty of excise was then and there by law charged. The respondents contend that sweets and made wines, when retailed in less quantities than a cask of fifteen gallons, shall continue liable to an excise duty under stat. 6 G. 4, c. 81, and that the appellant was properly convicted. If the Court shall be of opinion that sweets or made wines are not excisable liquors within the meaning of stat. 9 G. 4, c. 61, the conviction is to be quashed ; otherwise it is to be confirmed.

Scotland, in support of the conviction.—The conviction is founded on stat. 9 G. 4, c. 61, by sect. 18 of which every person who shall sell any excisable liquor by retail to be drunk or consumed in his house or premises, without being duly licensed so to do, is subject to a penalty; and, by sect. 87, the words "excisable liquor" shall be deemed to include any sweets, wine, &c., which now is or hereafter may be charged with duty either by customs or excise. The question therefore is, whether the wine sold by the appellant, under the circumstances stated in the case, was, at the time of such sale, excisable liquor within the meaning of the statute. · At the time of the passing of the statute, such wine was *clearly excisable liquor, because at that time stat. 6 G. 4, c. 87, by which an excise duty is imposed on the manufacture of sweet wines, and stat. 6 G. 4, c. 81, by sect. 2 of which an excise duty is imposed on licenses to retail sweet wines, were both in force as to such wine. But at the time of the sale stat. 4 & 5 W. 4, c. 77, had been passed. By sect. 9 of that Act all the duties of excise on sweets or made wines, and all duties upon licenses required to be taken out by any maker of sweets or made wines, are repealed. By sect. 10, however, nothing herein contained shall extend to repeal or affect any duty on licenses to be taken out by retailers of sweets or made wines ; but all such licenses shall continue to be taken out ; and, by sect. 11, any person who shall sell any liquor commonly called sweets or made wines in any less quantity than in a whole cask containing 15 gallons shall be deemed and taken to be a retailer of sweets, and shall take out a license accordingly. The appellant, therefore, in selling the wine as stated, was selling a liquor for which, as so sold, he was liable to pay an excise duty, and which was therefore an excisable liquor. The intention of stat. 4 & 5 W. 4, c. 77, clearly is to leave retailers of made wines in the same position as they were in before the passing of the Act. If stat. 9 G. 4, c. 61, is not applicable to the sale of made wines under the circumstances stated in the case, there is no police or other regulation applicable to such sales, although the sale of beer, cider, and perry is subject to very stringent supervision ; for stat. 11 G. 4 & 1 W. 4, c. 64, and stat. 3 & 4 Vict. c. 61, by which the sale of the latter liquors is regulated, are not applicable to the sale of made wines, which are expressly excluded from them by sect. 2 of *the former and by sect. 10 of the latter Act. In stats. 6 & 7 W. 4, c. 72 (Schedule), 5 & 6 Vict. c. 25 (Schedule), and 17 & 18 Vict. c. 27 (Schedule), the Legislature has assumed that sweets and made wines in England are still excisable liquors.

*843]

*844]

J. W. Huddleston, contrà.—The conviction is for selling by retail sweets or made wines without being duly licensed so to do. The case states that the appellant had an excise license in the ordinary form, but that he had not a license of justices under stat. 9 G. 4, c. 61· The question is, whether a conviction under that Act can be legally founded upon such circumstances. This depends upon whether sweets or made wines are now excisable liquor within the meaning of sect.

18 of that Act as interpreted by sect. 37. They are not so, if they are not now charged with duty either by custom or excise. They were charged with an excise duty by stat. 6 G. 4, c. 37, s. 2 ; and that was the only statute by which they were charged with duty. The duty charged by stat. 6 G. 4, c. 81, was not a duty charged upon the liquor, but upon an excise license to be taken out by every maker and every retailer of such liquor. By stat. 4 & 5 W. 4, c. 77, s. 9, the duty charged on sweets or made wines by stat. 6 G. 4, c. 37, is repealed. , It follows, from that enactment alone, that sweets and made wines are no longer charged with duty, and are therefore no longer excisable liquor within stat. 9 G. 4, c. 61, s. 18, as interpreted by sect. 37. This result is not affected by the further enactment, in stat. 4 & 5 W. 4, c. 77, s. 9, that the duty on the excise license to be taken out by the maker of sweets and made wines under stat. 6 G. 4, c. 81, is also repealed, nor by the enactments in sects. 10 *and 11, that the [*845 duty on licenses to be taken out by retailers of sweets or made wines is to be retained, and that such licenses shall continue to be taken out : those enactments refer to the excise license under stat. 6 G. 4, c. 81. The fact remains that the liquors called sweets or made wines are no longer charged with an excise duty, and are no longer excisable liquors.

Scotland was heard in reply.

Lord CAMPBELL, C. J.—The only question submitted to the Court is, whether sweets or made wines are excisable liquors within the meaning of sect. 18 of 9 G. 4, c. 61. If they are, the conviction is to stand; if they are not, it is to be quashed. In my opinion they are not excisable liquors within the meaning of that statute. They are not excisable liquors unless they are liable, as liquor, to pay an excise duty. They were formerly liable to such a duty; but now they are not. That duty is repealed by stat. 4 & 5 W. 4, c. 77. Sweets and made wines are now no more excisable liquors than is water.

COLERIDGE, J.—But for the fact that my brother Erle differs from the rest of the Court, I should have said there was no difficulty in the case. The clause to be interpreted is a penal clause, and to be construed according to the ordinary applicable rule. The question is, whether sweets or made wines are now excisable liquors within the meaning of that clause. It is not disputed that they were so when stat. 9 G. 4, c. 61, was passed; but the question is whether they are so now since the passing of stat. 4 & 5 W. 4, c. 77. By the [*846 *interpretation clause in stat. 9 G. 4, c. 61, the phrase " excisable liquor" is made expansive according to the circumstances which may arise in the future. In stat. 4 & 5 W. 4, c. 77, there is a distinction carefully made in sects. 9 and 10 between a duty on the liquors and on the licenses to sell them. By sect. 9, those which were before excisable liquors are made to be so no longer ; but by sect. 10 it is declared that, although the liquors are no longer excisable liquors, no person shall sell them by retail without taking out the same license as before. That seems to me to show distinctly that the liquors in question are no longer excisable liquors : and, if so, I am clearly of opinion that sect. 18 of stat. 9 G. 4, c. 61, is not applicable.

ERLE, J.—In my opinion, reading stat. 4 & 5 W. 4, c. 77, with stat. 9 G. 4, c. 61, the liquors in question are, for the purposes of this case, still excisable liquors. If stat. 4 & 5 W. 4, c. 77, had not been passed, this person would have been clearly liable to the penalty which has been imposed on him by the conviction. It is true that, by stat. 4 & 5 W. 4, c. 77, in one sense sweet wines are no longer excisable liquors ; but, as to persons selling them by retail to be consumed on their premises, they are left in the same state as they were under stat. 9 G. 4, c. 61. If stat. 4 & 5 W. 4, c. 77, had not been passed, the appellant could not lawfully have sold sweet wines on his premises by retail without a license ; he has now so sold them, and says he may lawfully do so. But by the express words of the statute, and for reasons which seem to me most important, the statute enacts that he may not do so, and that, if he do, he shall be liable to the same penalty *847] as before. *Therefore it seems to me that sweet wines are, upon the true exposition of the latter statute, still to be considered as excisable liquors within the meaning of the former statute as to all persons who sell them by retail to be consumed on their premises.

CROMPTON, J.—I cannot see that that part of the conviction is made out in fact which alleges that the said wine is "an excisable liquor, in respect of which a duty of excise was then and there by law charged." Throughout the Acts there are two different duties imposed, one on certain liquors, and another on the licenses to sell them. In the first Act (6 G. 4, c. 37), a duty of excise was imposed on the liquors, which thereby became excisable liquors. In the same year, by stat. 6 G. 4, c. 81, another duty was imposed on another thing, though relating to the same liquors, which duty was a duty upon the licenses to sell the liquors, which licenses were to be granted by the excise. By stat. 9 G. 4, c. 61, another license was to be taken out, namely, a license to be granted by justices to any person keeping or about to keep inns, &c., to sell excisable liquors by retail to be drunk or consumed on the premises. By stat. 4 & 5 W. 4, c. 77, the duty on the liquors in question is repealed, but the necessity of taking out the excise license mentioned in 6 G. 4, c. 81, is preserved, and so is the duty on such license. The license to be granted by justices is not mentioned : and I should suppose designedly so ; because such license is no longer necessary or applicable, the liquors in question being no longer excisable liquors. If sects. 10 & 11 be confined to excise licenses, the whole Act is *848] sensible. If I had agreed with my brother Erle as to his view of *the present state of the law, I should have thought this con viction wrong in form; that a new form was necessary, or that there should have been an indictment. I am of opinion that the conviction cannot be supported. Conviction quashed.(a)

(a) Reported by W. B. Brett, Esq.

The QUEEN v. WILLIAM BAKEWELL. *June 3.*

By stat. 4 & 5 W. 4, c. 85, s. 2, every person applying for a license to sell beer or cider by retail to be drunk on the premises must annually deposit with the excise a certificate of good character, signed by six householders. By sect. 8 a penalty is imposed upon summary conviction on any person who shall in such certificate certify any matter as true, knowing the same to be false. Other sections of the statute impose a duty on excise licenses for selling beer, &c., and relate to the revenue of excise. By stat. 11 & 12 Vict. c. 43, s. 17, summary convictions may be drawn up in a short form given in the schedule. But, by sect. 35, "nothing in the Act shall extend to any proceedings under or by virtue of any of the statutes relating to Her Majesty's revenue of excise."

Upon a rule to quash a conviction under sect. 8 of stat. 4 & 5 W. 4, c. 85, for an offence against sect. 2, which was drawn up in the form given in the schedule as authorized by sect. 17 of stat. 11 & 12 Vict. c. 43:

Held, that the conviction, which was for an offence against a police regulation in sect. 2, was sufficient, although there were in the statute other sections relating to the revenue of excise. The word "statutes" in sect. 35 is to be read as if it were "enactments."

PASHLEY, in last Term, obtained a rule calling upon the prosecutors to show cause why the conviction and order of Sessions confirming the same, which had been brought up by certiorari, should not be quashed. From the affidavits filed upon the motion for the certiorari it appeared that the conviction was before three justices of the county of Stafford against the defendant: For that he did sign a certificate in writing, required by one Daniel Craddock to obtain a license for the sale of beer to be consumed in the house of the said D. C., in pursuance of the statute (4 & 5 W. 4, c. 85, s. 2), and did in and by such certificate certify, as true, that the said D. C. was a person of good character, he well knowing that the said D. C. was not a person of good *character; and adjudging the defendant to pay the mitigated [*849 penalty of 2*l.*, one moiety to the prosecutor and the remainder to the treasurer of the county, to be applied by him according to law, and also to the prosecutor the sum of 12*s.* 6*d.* for costs; and, if the said several sums should not be paid on, &c., the same to be levied by distress, and in default of a sufficient distress, the said W. B. to be imprisoned for one month, unless the said sums and all costs, &c., should be sooner paid. This conviction had been confirmed upon appeal by the Sessions, with costs. The defendant's points for argument were, that the conviction was bad on the face of it, as showing that the justices had no jurisdiction; that, if it was made under any statute, such statute related to Her Majesty's revenue of excise, and therefore that stat. 11 & 12 Vict. c. 43 had no application; that the conviction was defective in not setting out the evidence on which it proceeded; and that the justices had no jurisdiction to adjudge the defendant to pay the costs. The chief point in support of the conviction was that it was good under stats. 11 G. 4 & 1 W. 4, c. 64, 4 & 5 W. 4, c. 85, and 3 & 4 Vict. c. 61, or under those statutes combined with stat. 11 & 12 Vict. c. 43.

J. E. Davis and *Scotland* now showed cause.—The conviction is in the form (I. 1.) given in the schedule to stat. 11 & 12 Vict. c. 43, and referred to by sect. 17. The costs are allowed by virtue of sect. 18. If that statute is applicable, there can be no doubt that the conviction is sufficient. It is true that, by sect. 35, "nothing in this Act shall extend or be construed to extend" "to any information or complaint or other proceeding under or by virtue of any of the *statutes relating to Her Majesty's revenue of excise or customs." The question therefore is, whether the complaint, which was under stat. 4 & 5 W. 4, c. 85, s. 8, was a complaint under or by virtue of any statute relating to the revenue of excise within the meaning of that section. The complaint was for making a false statement in a certificate under stat. 4 & 5 W. 4, c. 85, s. 2: and although there are undoubtedly sections in that Act which do relate to revenue of excise, yet sect. 2 is entirely a police regulation. The Act is partly a Police Act, though partly an Excise Act. It professes in the recital to remedy evils which had arisen under stat. 11 G. 4 & 1 W. 4, c. 64, which is purely a Police Act for the regulation of the sale of beer and cider. The license, in order to obtain which the certificate in question was given, is similar to that required by stat. 9 G. 4, c. 61, s. 1, which is another pure Police Act with regard to the sale of liquors. The regulations are so far from being revenue regulations that they injure the revenue by interfering with a free sale of liquors. The Legislature, in the Act itself (4 & 5 W. 4, c. 85, s. 16), recognises a distinction between the enactments in it which refer to revenue and those which refer to police; for it enacts that, if any person licensed under it to sell beer or cider shall permit or suffer any wine or spirits, &c., to be drunk or consumed in his house, "such person shall, *over and above any excise penalty or penalties* to which he may be subject, forfeit 20l., to be recovered," &c., "in the same manner as other penalties (*not being excise penalties*) are by the Act to be recovered." The same distinction is taken between different enactments in one Act, in stat. 3 & 4 Vict. c. 61, s. 16. In Bateman's Laws of Excise, p. 401, note (z), it is stated, *in the note, that stats. 11 G. 4 & 1 W. 4, c. 64, 4 & 5 W. 4, c. 85, and 3 & 4 Vict. c. 61, are partly Excise Acts and partly regulations of police.

Pashley, contrà.—The case is clearly within the words of stat. 11 & 12 Vict. c. 43, s. 35. It is admitted that there are in stat. 4 & 5 W. 4, c. 85, enactments relating to the revenue of excise; and it follows that it is a statute relating to that revenue. The words are clear. If the Legislature has omitted the particular case, there is no remedy. *Quod voluit, non dixit.*

\[*850\]

\[*851\]

Lord CAMPBELL, C. J.—I am of opinion that this conviction is properly drawn in the form given by stat. 11 & 12 Vict. c. 43. The statute undoubtedly contains in sect. 35 an exception, that it shall not extend to any proceedings under or by virtue of any statutes relating to Her Majesty's revenue of excise. But I am of opinion that this conviction does not proceed upon any statute relating to the revenue of excise within the meaning of the exception. I read the word "statute," in the section, as if it were written "enactment." The word "statute" has several meanings. It may mean what is popularly called an Act of Parliament, or a code such as the stat. of West. 1, or all the Acts passed in one session, which was the original meaning of the word. But the question is, what is the meaning of it in sect. 35 of stat. 11 & 12 Vict. c. 43. I think it means that the form given by the Act shall not be used where the complaint is one relating to the revenue of excise. The conviction proceeds on stat. 4 & 5 W. 4, c. 85, s. 8, which, as referred to sect. 2, does not in any way relate to revenue objects, but to an offence wholly irrespective *of revenue considerations. [*852 The character of the person holding the house is quite irrespective of any revenue consideration, though very material as a police regulation. The sensible interpretation of sect. 35 is, that it leaves the revenue officers to follow their ancient mode of conducting proceedings which are to be instituted and pursued by them, but that all other proceedings before magistrates may be conducted in the new and useful form.

COLERIDGE, J.—Giving a reasonable construction to the words of sect. 35, which are very large, I am of opinion that this conviction is not within the exception. I am not sure that stat. 4 & 5 W. 4, c. 85, is a statute the governing object of which is one relating to the revenue of excise. Though some clauses relate to that revenue, I doubt whether it can fairly be called a revenue statute. But I am of opinion that the true construction of sect. 35 is, that it applies only when the proceeding is in a matter relating to the revenue of excise. If the proceedings had been on any of the revenue clauses in stat. 4 & 5 W. 4, c. 85, I should have thought they were within the exception; but these proceedings are clearly not under such clauses.

ERLE, J.—I am of opinion that the conviction was not based upon any enactment relating to the revenue of excise, and therefore that it was not within the exception.

CROMPTON, J., concurred.   Rule discharged.(a)

(a) Reported by W. B. Brett, Esq.

*853]   *The QUEEN v. JOHN CRIDLAND and Others.
               June 3 and 6.

A conviction under stat. 1 & 2 W. 4, c. 32, s. 30, and stat. 11 & 12 Vict. c. 43, s. 23, against four
  defendants for trespass in pursuit of game, contained an order that, "if the said several
  sums" (being the penalty and costs of conviction before awarded to be paid by each defendant)
  "be not paid on or before the 10th November instant, we adjudge each of them the said"
  (names of the defendants) "to be imprisoned" "for the space of one month, unless the said
  several sums and the costs and charges of conveying each of them, the said" (names of the
  defendants), "so making default, to the said common gaol, shall be sooner paid."
By stat. 1 & 2 W. 4, c. 32, s. 30, it is provided "that any person charged with any such trespass
  shall be at liberty to prove, by way of defence, any matter which would have been a defence
  to an action at law for such trespass."
At the hearing before the justices, a bonâ fide claim of title to the land was set up on behalf
  of the defendants; but no evidence was offered of the actual existence of any dispute, or of
  any title in the person under whom the defendants claimed.
Held, that the conviction was bad; for that it adjudicated each defendant to be imprisoned for
  one month, unless the costs and charges of conveying all to gaol should be sooner paid, and
  it was not in the form authorized by stat. 11 & 12 Vict. c. 43, s. 17, or to the like effect.
Semble : that the jurisdiction to convict summarily was ousted; that the general rule is that, in
  case of summary convictions, justices have jurisdiction to determine whether the claim to title
  to real property is set up bonâ fide; but, if it is bonâ fide set up, they have no jurisdiction
  to proceed further in the matter: that the proviso in stat. 1 & 2 W. 4, c. 32, s. 30, does not
  give justices jurisdiction, upon a charge of trespass in pursuit of game, to determine a claim
  of title to land against the wish of the defendants.

PASHLEY, in last Easter Term, obtained a rule calling upon the prosecutors and the convicting justices to show cause why the conviction,
which had been brought up by certiorari, should not be quashed, on
the grounds that the conviction was bad on the face of it, for not disclosing any offence, or showing any jurisdiction either to convict or to
order any such imprisonment as is ordered by the conviction, and that
the justices had refused to hear evidence that the defendants were
licensed by the real owner of the land to kill game on the land in the
conviction mentioned.   In the affidavits filed in support of the rule it
was alleged that the defendant and four others were shooting game, on
the 13th of October, 1856, on the Swinfen estates, by invitation of
Thomas Bacon: that the defendant, on the 11th of November, was
served with a summons, for that he, in company with four others, within
*854]   three months then last *past, did unlawfully commit a trespass,
        by entering and being in the daytime upon land in the posses-
sion of Patience Swinfen in search of game, without the license or consent of the owner, &c. : that the defendant attended the summons on
the 5th of November before twó justices : that the attorney of the
defendant at the hearing proposed to the justices to put in evidence an
authority in writing from Frederick Hay Swinfen to the said Thomas
Bacon, whereby the said F. H. Swinfen authorized the said Thomas
Bacon, or any of his friends, to shoot over his (F. H. Swinfen's) estate
of Swinfen, and to prove that the land was not in the possession of
Patience Swinfen, and that the defendants were not guilty of trespass;
but that the justices refused to receive the evidence, and said that they

should decide the case without any reference to the title; that they sat there to adjust the penalties; and that they could not hear any objection as to questions of title : and that the justices convicted the defendant Cridland and three others, the charge against a fifth defendant being abandoned. The affidavits then set out the conviction as follows : "County of Stafford, to wit. Be it remembered that, on the 3d day of November, A. D. 1856, at the Guildhall in the city of Litchfield, John Cridland, John Bannister, William Whilton, and Jonathan Sanders are convicted before the undersigned, two of the justices," &c., "for that they, the said" J. C., &c., "on the 13th day of October last, at the parish," &c., "did unlawfully commit a certain trespass by entering and being, in the daytime of the same day, upon a certain piece of land, called Swinfen Wood, in the possession and occupation of Patience Swinfen, there in search and pursuit of game, there without the license or consent of the owner of the land so trespassed upon, or of any person having the *right of killing the game upon such land, or of [*855 any other person having any right to authorize the said John Cridland," &c., "to enter or be upon the said land for the purpose aforesaid, contrary to the statute," &c. : "And we adjudge each of them, the said John Cridland, John Bannister, William Whilton, and Jonathan Sanders, for their said offence, to forfeit and pay the sum of 2l. each, to be paid and applied according to law, and also to pay the prosecutor, namely Robert Lester," &c., "the sum of four shillings and one penny halfpenny, each, for his costs in this behalf; and, if the said several sums be not paid on or before the 10th day of November instant, we adjudge each of them, the said J. C., J. B., W. W., and J. S., so making default, to be imprisoned in the common gaol of Stafford," &c., "for the space of one month, unless the said several sums and the costs and charges of conveying each of them, the said J. C.," &c., "so making default, to the said common gaol, shall be sooner paid. Given under our hands," &c. The affidavits further alleged that, upon a similar summons against another person, named Meanley, as being a party to the same alleged trespass of the 13th of October, and which was heard before the same justices on the 12th of November, the attorney for the defendant produced an office copy of a rule of Court in an action of Patience Swinfen v. Frederick Hay Swinfen, by which, after reciting that a cause was pending, it was ordered, by the consent of the parties, that the jury should be discharged, upon the terms, among others, that the Swinfen estates should be conveyed by the plaintiff to the defendant as from the 29th of September, 1855, and a writing, proved to be by Frederick Hay Swinfen, in the following terms: "September 29th, 1856. I authorize Mr. Bacon, or any of his friends, to shoot *over my estate at Swinfen until I make further arrangements [*856 relative to the shooting;" and that the defendant had been invited by Bacon to shoot by virtue of the said authority; whereupon

the justices dismissed the information, on the ground that, as the title
to the Swinfen estate was bonâ fide in dispute, they had no jurisdiction.
The affidavits then stated that the above order had been made by the
consent of counsel at the trial of the cause, but that Patience Swinfen
afterwards and still contested its validity; and that the declarants
believed that Frederick Hay Swinfen was legally entitled to the Swin-
en estates, and that the prosecution in question was really instituted
by Patience Swinfen.   The affidavits in answer stated that, on the hearing of the summons on the 5th of November, the attorney for the
defendants applied for an adjournment in order to enable him to communicate with the London attorneys of Frederick Hay Swinfen, and
on the ground that the defendants had not had reasonable notice, and
that the proceeding was part of a larger system of litigation respecting
the Swinfen estate: that the application was opposed; and that the
justices decided that the case should proceed, stating that the case
before them was easy, and that they had nothing to do with litigation
elsewhere: that the said attorney did not specify any evidence which
he intended to bring forward, but said, generally, that, if an adjournment were granted, he should be able to produce such evidence as, in
his opinion, would entitle the defendants to a verdict: that the evidence for the prosecution was then given: that the attorney for the
defendants addressed the Bench on behalf of his clients, but did not
call any witness or give any evidence: and that it was not true that
*857] he proposed to prove that the land was not in the *possession
       of Patience Swinfen, and that the defendants were not guilty of
trespass, and that the justices refused to hear such evidence; nor was
it true that the attorney for the defendants proposed to put in evidence
the authority in writing from F. H. Swinfen, mentioned in the affidavits in support of the rule; but that he did hand such writing to the
justices, who said that it could not be read or taken as evidence until
proved, whereupon he did not propose or attempt to prove it, but said
he thought an advocate ought to be believed when he stated, as he had
done, that he could produce evidence.

   C. R. Kennedy and J. Gray now showed cause.—By stat. 1 & 2 W.
4, c. 32, s. 30, "If any person whatsoever shall commit any trespass
by entering or being, in the daytime, upon any land in search or pursuit of game," &c., "such persons shall, on conviction thereof before a
justice of the peace, forfeit and pay such sum of money, not exceeding
2l., as to the justice shall seem meet, together with the costs of the
conviction; and that if any persons to the number of five or more
together, shall commit any trespass, by entering or being, in the daytime, upon any land in search or pursuit of game," &c., "each of such
persons shall, on conviction thereof before a justice of the peace, forfeit
and pay such sum of money, not exceeding 5l., as to the said justice
shall seem meet, together with the costs of the conviction: Provided

always, that any person charged with any such trespass shall be at liberty to prove, by way of defence, any matter which would have been a defence to an action ·at law for such trespass." By sect. 45 the certiorari is taken away in case of any summary conviction under the Act. By stat. 11 & 12 Vict. c. 43, s. 17, justices *may draw up [*858 their convictions and orders in forms given in schedules to the Act. By sect. 23, in all cases where the statute, by virtue of which a conviction for a penalty, &c., is made, makes no provision for levying the penalty by distress, but directs imprisonment for a certain time unless such penalty be sooner paid, in every such case, if the defendant do not pay, &c., it shall be lawful for the justice, &c., to issue his warrant of commitment (O. 1, 2,) under his hand, &c., requiring the constable, &c., to take and convey such defendant to the common gaol, &c., and there to imprison him for such time as the statute on which such conviction, &c., is founded shall direct, unless the sum or sums adjudged to be paid, and also the costs and charges of taking and conveying the defendant to prison, if such justice shall think fit so to order, shall be sooner paid. By sect. 28, in all cases in which any person shall be imprisoned as aforesaid for non-payment of any penalty or other sum, he may pay or cause to be paid to the keeper of the prison, &c., the sum in the warrant of commitment mentioned, together with the amount of the costs, charges, and expenses, if any, therein also mentioned, and the said keeper shall receive the same, and shall thereupon discharge such person, if he be in his custody for no other matter. By sect. 32, "the several forms in the schedule," "or forms to the like effect, shall be deemed good, valid, and sufficient in law." The conviction in the present case was made under the first clause of sect. 30 of stat. 1 & 2 W. 4, c. 32, imposing a penalty and costs: and there is inserted in it, or made part of it, the order under sect. 23 of stat. 11 & 12 Vict. c. 43, for the payment of the costs of conveying the defendants to gaol in default of payment of the penalty *and costs: and the convic- [*859 tion is in one of the forms authorized by sect. 19 of the latter statute. If that be so, the conviction is good upon the face of it by virtue of sect. 32: Regina v. Hyde.(a) It will be argued *that [*860 the conviction is bad for imposing a penalty upon each of the

(a) REGINA v. JOHN HYDE. Jan. 21, 1852.

A conviction for killing a pheasant, contrary to sect. 2 of stat. 1 & 2 W. 4, c. 32, following the form given in Schedule (L. 2) to stat. 11 & 12 Vict. c. 43, adjudged the offender to forfeit and pay a penalty, "to be paid and applied according to law." By sect. 37 of stat. 1 & 2 W. 4, c. 32, and sect. 31 of stat. 3 & 6 W. 4, c. 20, the penalty is directed to be paid, one half to the informer, and one half to some one of the overseers of the poor, or to some other officer (as the convicting justice or justices may direct) of the parish, &c., in which the offence shall have been committed. Held: that the conviction was sufficient by virtue of sects. 17 and 22 of stat. 11 & 12 Vict. c. 43, being in the form given by the Schedule to that Act referred to in sect. 17, though it did not in terms distribute the penalty, nor name the informer or the overseer to whom the penalty was to be paid.

H. HAWKINS, in Hilary Term, 1852, had obtained a rule calling upon the prosecutors to show

*861] defendants; but the penalty in the first *clause of sect. 30 of stat. 1 & 2 W. 4, c. 32, may be properly imposed upon each person guilty of the offence therein described, because the offence is in

cause why the conviction, and an order of Sessions confirming it, which had been brought up by certiorari, should not be severally quashed: on the grounds that the conviction did not disclose any jurisdiction in the justices to make it; that the adjudication was defective; that it did not duly adjudge to whom the penalty was to be paid; and that the offender could not tell how to absolve himself from the imprisonment adjudged. The conviction was in the following terms.

"Kent, to wit." "That, on," &c., "at," &c., John Hyde "is convicted before the undersigned, two" justices, &c., "for that he" "did between the first day of February, last past, and the first day of October, last past, to wit, on," &c., "at," &c., "kill one pheasant, contrary to the statute in such case made and provided. And we adjudge the said John Hyde, for his said offence, to forfeit and pay the sum of 5*s.*, to be paid and applied according to law; and also to pay to George Turner, who prosecuteth in this case, the sum of 1*l.* 2*s.* for his costs in this behalf: and, if the said several sums be not paid forthwith, we adjudge the said John Hyde to be imprisoned in the House of Correction at Maidstone, in the said county, for the space of one calendar month, unless the said several sums shall be sooner paid. Given under our hands," &c.

Archbold, in the same Term (January 21st), showed cause.—The conviction is for an offence against sect. 3 of stat. 1 & 2 W. 4, c. 32. By sect. 37, the penalty incurred under sect. 3 shall be paid to some one of the overseers of the poor, or to some other officer (as the convicting justice or justices may direct) of the parish, &c., in which the offence shall have been committed, to be by such overseer or officer paid over to the use of the general rate of the county, &c. By sect. 21 of stat. 5 & 6 W. 4, c. 20, one moiety of all such penalties as by the said last recited Act, 1 & 2 W. 4, c. 32, are directed to be paid and applied as aforesaid shall go and be paid to the person who shall inform and prosecute for the same; and the other moiety thereof only shall go and be paid to such overseer or officer as aforesaid, and be by him applied in the manner by the said last recited Act directed; and the form of conviction set forth in the last recited Act shall, so far as relates to the distribution of the penalty for which judgment shall be given, be made according to the fact and conformably with the direction given by stat. 5 & 6 W. 4, c. 20, as to such distribution. It is objected: first, that the conviction does not in terms distribute the penalty as directed by the last-mentioned statute; secondly, that it does not name the parties to whom the penalty is to be paid. But, first, no such objections can properly be entertained, because, by sect. 45 of stat. 1 & 2 W. 4, c. 32, the writ of certiorari is taken away. Secondly, the objections are invalid; for, first, the penalty is distributed by the statute itself; so that the justices had no discretion as to the distribution, and therefore need not have set out the mode of it more than they have done, even if the conviction had been drawn up under the stats. 1 & 2 W. 4, c. 32, and 5 & 6 W. 4, c. 20, In re Boothroyd, 15 M. & W. 1; and, secondly, the conviction is drawn up in the form given in Schedule (I. 2) to stat. 11 & 12 Vict. c. 43; so that it is sufficient by virtue of sect. 32 of that statute, if otherwise it would be informal. The cases of Griffith *v.* Harries, 2 M. & W. 335, and Chaddcok *v.* Wilbraham, 5 Com. B. 645, are distinguishable: in both the penalty was directed by the conviction to be paid to a particular person, who was the wrong person according to the Act.

H. Hawkins, contrà.—The objections can be properly entertained upon the present rule, because the conviction is before the Court upon the writ of certiorari. If that writ issued improvidently, there should have been a motion to quash it. The conviction is bad on the face of it. Every conviction should show an adjudication of an offence and an award of a penalty, and that both are adjudged according to law; but this conviction does not show that the penalty was adjudged according to law, because it does not show that half was adjudged to be paid to the informer and half to the overseer; and, if that be unnecessary, as alleged, still the conviction does not show who is the informer to whom the law distributes the one moiety, or who is the overseer to whom it assigns the other; so that the offender cannot tell to whom the payments are to be made which are to free him from imprisonment. Stat. 11 & 12 Vict. c. 43, does not cure these defects, because the forms given in the schedule are wholly inapplicable; and, by sect. 17, they are made available only when applicable to the case. This case therefore is governed by the decisions in Griffith *v.* Harries and Chaddock *v.* Wilbraham.

Lord CAMPBELL, C. J.—I am very doubtful whether this Court has jurisdiction to entertain the objections, the writ of certiorari being taken away. I am strongly inclined to think that the writ issued improvidently: and, if it did, I doubt whether the fact of its having issued can authorize us to entertain the objections. I also feel very serious doubts whether the conviction would have been sufficient if drawn up under stats. 1 & 2 W. 4, c. 32, and 5 & 6 W. 4, c.

its nature several. In Rex *v.* Clark, 2 Cowp. 610, upon an information against several for assaulting and resisting custom house officers in the execution of their duty, by reason whereof the defendants had severally forfeited the sum of 40*l.* apiece, it was moved, in arrest of judgment, that there was only one offence, though there were several parties, and therefore that there should have been only one penalty of 40*l.* imposed. But Lord Mansfield, C. J., said: "Where the offence is in its nature single, and cannot be severed, there the penalty shall be only single; because, though several persons may join in committing it, it still constitutes but one offence. But where the offence is in its nature several, and where every person concerned may be separately guilty of it, there, each offender is separately liable to the penalty; because the crime of each is distinct from *the offence of the [*862 others, and each is punishable for his own crime." If the penalty may not properly be imposed on each person, the Act is absurd; for the greater the number of trespassers in pursuit of game, the greater must be the offence, and yet the penalty on each offender would be less. In Rex *v.* Hube, 5 T. R. 542, there was an indictment against several for disturbing a dissenting congregation assembled for religious worship. The indictment was under stat. 1 W. & M. c. 18, s. 18, by which, if any person or persons shall disquiet, &c., such person or persons shall find two sureties, &c., and, in default, shall be committed to prison, there to remain till the next General or Quarter Sessions, and, upon conviction at the said Sessions, shall suffer the pain and penalty of 20*l.* Upon a question as to the punishment to be awarded, and as to the construction of the conviction, it was held that the penalty was intended to be levied on each offender; that otherwise the construction of the Act would be absurd; for, if the penalty were single, then, if there were but one offender, he would pay 20*l.*, and, if there were twenty offenders, in which case the offence would be much increased, each would only pay 20*s.*, which could never be intended. In Regina *v.* Dean, 12 M. & W. 39,† upon an information under stat. 3 & 4 W. 4, c. 53, s. 44, for smuggling, a rule was moved for to stay proceedings until the result should be ascertained of a writ of error upon a similar information for the same transaction against the defendant's partner. The rule was refused. Alderson, B., said: "We must

20; but it is drawn up in one of the forms authorized by sect. 17 of stat. 11 & 12 Vict. c. 43; and I have no doubt that that statute is applicable, and that therefore the conviction is sufficient.

PATTESON, J.—I am of opinion that the conviction is sufficient by virtue of sect. 17 of stat. 11 & 12 Vict. c. 43.

COLERIDGE, J.—The form in Schedule (I. 2) to stat. 11 & 12 Vict. c. 43, is in terms made applicable to the case of a conviction for a penalty, and, in default of payment, imprisonment. That is an exact description of the present case; and therefore it seems to me that the conviction, which accurately follows the form, is sufficient.

(WIGHTMAN, J., was absent.) Rule discharged.

From the notes of Mr. Adolphus and Mr. Blackburn.

look at the statute to see whether it was intended that every person offending should be punished, or merely that every offence should be punished." In Morgan *v.* Brown, 4 A. & E. 515 (E. C. L. R. vol. 31),

*863] *a conviction against two defendants for an assault was held to be bad, because a single fine was imposed on both, an assault being in its very nature a several offence by each party assaulting. It will be said that, if this argument used in support of the conviction be correct, there ought to have been separate informations and separate convictions. But that is merely an objection of form; or, at all events, it is not an objection valid as against the jurisdiction, which is the only objection which can be now maintained, the writ of certiorari being taken away. The only question being whether the justices had jurisdiction to try each offender, if they had, it is no objection to their jurisdiction to say that they tried and convicted them under one indictment. If the objection be only one of form, it is made too late; if made at the trial, the information might have been amended. And, if it be not too late, the Court can amend the conviction now under sect. 7 of stat. 12 & 13 Vict. c. 45. It will be argued that the conviction adjudicates each defendant to be imprisoned, unless the costs of taking and conveying all to gaol be sooner paid, and that such adjudication is an excess of jurisdiction; but the necessary inference of the language used, which is strengthened by the use of the word "several," is that each should be imprisoned unless the costs of conveying him to gaol be sooner paid. It will be said that the justices were ousted of their jurisdiction by a bonâ fide claim of title. But no evidence which was admissible was offered on behalf of the defendants of any claim of title. There was no fact proved which could properly lead the justices to the conclusion that there was a bonâ fide claim of title. In the case now under discussion, the existence of the cause of Swinfen *v.* Swinfen was not put in evidence. Besides, by the proviso in sect. 30, the

*864] *defendants ought to have shown the title in answer to the information, as it would have been a defence in an action of trespass; so that the justices had jurisdiction.

Pashley, contrà.—The summons was for a joint offence by five persons contrary to the second clause of 1 & 2 W. 4, c. 32, s. 30; and therefore, when the case against one was given up, there was no legal case under that summons against the others; and they were entitled to have the summons dismissed. [Lord CAMPBELL, C. J.—That does not necessarily follow. The offence may have been committed by four of the persons summoned, and a fifth not summoned. CROMPTON, J.—The summons would be bad under the second clause of sect. 30. It does not say that the five were on the land "together." Are not both summons and conviction, if they are good at all, good under the first clause?] The conviction is bad under the first clause. It states merely that the parties were on the land in the daytime, without defining that time to be between the beginning of the last hour before sunrise and the expiration of the first hour after sunset, which is the limit of time given in section 34. [Lord CAMPBELL, C. J.—May we not assume that daytime in the conviction means the statutable period in the Act?] The conviction is bad for joining all the defendants in one conviction and imposing on them separate penalties; for, if the offence be joint, there should be only one penalty; and, if it be separate, there should be several convictions. By stat. 11 & 12 Vict. c. 43, s. 10, every complaint upon which a justice may make an order, and every information on which he may adjudicate a summary conviction, shall be for one matter or offence only, and not for two or more matters or offences. [Lord CAMPBELL, C. J.—Does not *that apply to [*865 the laying of a charge of two offences against one person, and not to the charging of several persons with one offence or similar offences?] If that were so, sect. 5 would be useless. The conviction is bad for ordering each defendant to be kept in prison until the costs of taking and conveying all to prison are paid. Such an order is in its nature unjust; and it is clearly contrary to the intention of sect. 23 of stat. 11 & 12 Vict. c. 43, which says that the defendant shall be imprisoned unless the costs and charges of conveying the defendant to prison shall be sooner paid. It is contrary to the form (I. 2) in the schedule, which is: "I adjudge the said A. B. to be imprisoned," &c., "unless the" "costs and charges of conveying the said A. B. to the said house of correction shall be sooner paid." The same form is used in (K. 1) and (O. 1). In 3 Burn's Justice, 296 (*Game*, § 22),(a) the form is very carefully drawn. These words are added: "but not that as either of them, the said A. O. or T. O., shall be imprisoned or kept in prison for the default of the other of them." The Court will not now amend the conviction if it is bad. Though the conviction were good on the face of it, the affidavits show that the justices were ousted of jurisdiction to make it. It is clear that in the case of this defendant a bonâ fide claim of title was set up, though no evidence of it was actually offered: for, in a subsequent case, the evidence which was mentioned in this case was given, and the justices at once decided that there was a dispute of title which ousted their jurisdiction. It is sufficient to oust the jurisdiction of justices that a claim of title should be bonâ fide made: it is not necessary that evidence *of such title [*866 should be laid before them. The justices were not entitled to try a disputed claim of right by virtue of the provision in sect. 30 of stat. 1 & 2 W. 4, c. 32, against the will of the defendant. That is a privilege given to the defendant to be exercised at his option.

Lord CAMPBELL, C. J.—I am of opinion that the conviction is bad upon the face of it, and that it should be quashed. After imposing the penalty and costs, it proceeds to adjudge, "if the said several sums

(a) 29th ed. by Bere and Chitty.

be not paid on or before the 10th of November instant," "the said John Cridland, John Bannister, William Whilton, and Jonathan Sanders, so making default, to be imprisoned in the common gaol of Stafford," &c., "for the space of one month, unless the said several sums and the costs and charges of conveying each of them, the said J. C.," &c., "so making default, to the said common gaol, shall be sooner paid." It is said that the conviction follows the form (I. 2) given in the schedule to stat. 11 & 12 Vict. c. 43, referred to in sect. 17. If it had done so, the position might have been sustained that it should be taken to express what the law justified. But it does not follow the form. It makes by its language each of the persons convicted to be imprisoned for one month unless the costs and charges of conveying all of them to the common gaol be sooner paid. Although one paid his own penalty and costs, and the costs and charges of conveying him to gaol, yet, if the terms of this conviction were followed, he would still be kept in prison until the costs and charges of conveying each of the others to gaol should be paid. The forms of commitment (O. 1) and (O. 2), given in the schedule to stat. 11 & 12 Vict. c. 43, provide

*867] anxiously against *this; for they ascertain the amount of the costs and charges of conveying the defendant to gaol. If it had been intended that each should be kept in gaol until the costs and charges of conveying all to gaol had been paid, the conviction must have been in the form in which it is now drawn. But that is not the intention of the Act; and therefore this conviction is wrong. Such being the judgment of the Court, it is unnecessary to determine the other questions which have been argued. But my present impression is, that the justices were wrong in proceeding to adjudicate upon the case at all. Though no evidence of title was actually offered, it was quite clear that a bonâ fide claim of title was set up: and, when such a claim is so set up, it seems to me that justices have no longer jurisdiction to proceed to a summary conviction.

COLERIDGE, J.—The primary punishment in this case was not the imprisonment, but the penalty and costs under stat. 1 & 2 W. 4, c. 32. s. 30. The imprisonment was partly awarded under sect. 28 of that statute. It is quite clear that under that section it should only continue until the penalty and costs to be paid by the person upon whom they are imposed under sect. 30 be paid. The imprisonment was partly awarded under stat. 11 & 12 Vict. c. 43, s. 23; and it is equally clear that under that section it should only continue until the costs and charges of taking to gaol the person upon whom the penalty and former costs were imposed under sect. 30 of the former statute be paid. The natural meaning of the words of the statutes is clear. It is, that every person, adjudged to imprisonment in order to enforce the payment

*868] by him of a penalty and the *costs of imprisoning him, is to be released from prison upon payment of those sums. The statute,

however, might, in the case of a joint offence, have made the imprisonment of each depend upon the payment of the cost of taking all to
gaol. The question therefore is, whether this conviction points out with
reasonable clearness the legal liability of the defendant. If it is so
worded that a gaoler might reasonably construe it as imposing the larger
obligation, which might have been imposed, and so as imposing a greater
punishment than is authorized by the Act, it is not sufficiently certain.
I should say that a gaoler might reasonably read this conviction as a
requirement to him to keep each defendant in gaol during the whole
allotted time, unless the costs of taking and conveying all of them to
gaol were sooner paid. Therefore I am of opinion that the conviction
is bad. I agree that it is unnecessary to decide the graver question
which has been argued. But I entirely agree that, as a general rule,
the jurisdiction of justices to convict summarily ceases as soon as a
claim of title is bonâ fide made. If not, magistrates might, against
the will of a defendant, determine upon his title to a large property.
In the present case, the magistrates could not fairly doubt that a claim
to title was bonâ fide made. But then it is said that jurisdiction is
given in the case of a trespass in pursuit of game by virtue of the proviso in sect. 30 of stat. 1 & 2 W. 4, c. 32, which provides "that any
person charged with any such trespass shall be at liberty to prove, by
way of defence, any matter which would have been a defence to an
action at law for such trespass." It may be that a defendant might,
by virtue of that provision, compel justices to try a question of title
*to property; but it by no means follows that the justices, of [*869
their own inclination, and against the will of a defendant, may
determine on his title to estates. If they are not so compelled by him,
the ordinary rule which existed before the statute must prevail, that,
upon a bonâ fide claim of title being made, the jurisdiction of the
justices ceases.

ERLE, J.—I am of opinion that the conviction ought to be quashed
for excess of jurisdiction. The power given to the justices in such a
case is to imprison each defendant until the penalty and the cost of
conveying him to prison have been paid. There is no power given to
punish any defendant beyond that. But this conviction goes further.
It makes each defendant a surety for all the others if they be defaulters,
and imposes a duty on the gaoler to hold each in prison unless the costs
of all are paid. The conviction might be amended by guessing that the
justices could not have intended any such consequence; but the power
of amendment is discretionary, and I think ought not to be exercised
in this case. As to the other question, I think, if the point had been
further gone into, it would have appeared that the justices are not
called upon by sect. 30 of stat. 1 & 2 W. 4, c. 32, to try the title to
the land therein mentioned: I strongly incline to the opinion that the
true meaning of the statute is, that the justices ought to try whether

the defendant entertained an honest belief that he had a title; and, if he had such belief, he ought not to be convicted; I think that in a criminal statute trespass means an intended trespass. In Regina *v.*

*870] Burnaby, 2 Ld. Raym. 900, it seems to have been held *that in matters of summary proceeding, when a party charged makes an honest claim of title, the proper course is at once to dismiss the information. The question in that case arose in a curious way. A conviction for robbing orchards and cutting trees was removed by certiorari into this Court; and it was proposed to put in a plea to the conviction, suggesting a title in the defendant. Powell, J., refused to allow the plea, in these terms: "If they had not jurisdiction, as I take it they have not where property is in question, then an action lies against the maker, and him that executes the conviction; and that is the party's proper remedy, and the proper method to bring this matter into question." Powys and Gould agreed: and those were Judges who weighed carefully their words. Holt, C. J., would have allowed the plea, but agreed that without doubt, if the defendant had but a colour of title, the justices had no jurisdiction in the cause. All therefore agreed that justices ought to dismiss a summons, which is to result in a summary conviction, immediately on being convinced that the case involves a bonâ fide claim of title to real estate.

CROMPTON, J.—I wish it to be understood that I do not agree to the proposition that, consistently with sect. 10 of stat. 11 & 12 Vict. c. 43, several defendants can be convicted in one conviction on one information for an offence which is separate in its nature, and which is therefore a separate offence by each of them. But this conviction is bad on another ground. No one reading this conviction can fail to see that each defendant is to be kept in prison for the full period, unless the costs of conveying all to prison are sooner paid. That is

*871] clearly *an imprisonment of each for a longer period than the justices had power to imprison him. It is an excess of jurisdiction in a most important part of the conviction. It is said that the Court can amend. But it seems to me that we cannot guess what was the intention of the justices. They may have intended to order precisely what they have expressed. If they did they were clearly wrong. Upon the second and more important question, whether, when there is a bonâ fide claim of title, the magistrates have jurisdiction to go on against the will of the defendant and inquire into the title and determine it, I am at present strongly of opinion that they cannot. The general rule of law is that, upon such a claim bonâ fide arising, justices are ousted of their jurisdiction to convict summarily. In Paley's Law and Practice of Summary Convictions, 3d ed., p. 28, it is said, "Where property or title is in question, the jurisdiction of justices of the peace to hear and determine in a summary manner is ousted, and their hands tied from interfering, though the facts be such as they have otherwise authority to take cognisance of." The editor mentions this rule as not arising from any legislative enactment, but as the old legal maxim applicable to summary trials in general. Being an old maxim of law, which has been so generally applied for ages, we must assume that it is still intended to be applied by every Act relating to such matters, though not specifically mentioned. I cannot think that the provision in sect. 30 of 1 & 2 W. 4, c. 32, is intended to abrogate that great principle of law in the case of trespasses in pursuit of game. It may mean that, if the defendant so insists, the justices must try and determine his title to the land: but it can mean no more. It *struck me however, [*872 during the argument, that it was only applicable to such defences as, in a civil suit for a trespass on lands, are pleaded by way of excuse, such for instance as leave and license. It would be very difficult to try a title to land before such a tribunal. I cannot think that it was intended to abrogate the old rule against the will of a defendant. According to the old and general rule, it seems to me that justices have jurisdiction to try the fact whether the claim is bonâ fide made; but, if it is, they have no jurisdiction to inquire into any further fact. In this case it was clear that there was a bonâ fide claim of title. The jurisdiction was thereupon ousted; and the conviction must be quashed.

Conviction quashed.(a)

(a) Reported by W. B. Brett, Esq.

HARTLEY v. PONSONBY. *June* 4.

A vessel, in consequence of the desertion of some of the seamen, was left short of hands in harbour, before the voyage was completed. The master, to induce the remaining seamen to perform the rest of the voyage, promised to pay them a sum of money in addition to their wages. They accordingly performed the rest of the voyage with the diminished number of hands.

On an action by one of the seamen against the master for the sum promised, the jury found that he made the agreement without coercion, for the best interests of the owners; that he could not have obtained additional hands at a reasonable price; and that it was unreasonable for so large a ship to proceed on the completion of the voyage with the diminished number of hands.

Held, that on this finding, which the Court understood to mean that it was unsafe so to proceed, the plaintiff was entitled to recover, as the seamen were not bound, by their original contract of service, to proceed with the diminished number of hands; and their undertaking to do so was therefore a good consideration for the master's promise.

THE first count of the declaration alleged that defendant promised plaintiff to pay to plaintiff in Liverpool 40*l*., provided plaintiff would assist in *taking the ship Mobile from the port of Port Philip in [*873 Australia to Bombay in the East Indies, with a crew of nineteen hands. Averment: that, before this suit, he performed all things on his part to be performed to entitle him to the payment of the said sum of 40*l*., according to the terms and true intent and meaning of the said promise of defendant; of which defendant had notice: and a reasonable time for the payment thereof elapsed before this suit. Breach: that defendant had not paid the same or any part thereof.

Pleas. 1. Non assumpsit. 2. To first count: That, by virtue of certain ship's articles made and entered into between plaintiff and defendant, and signed by plaintiff, and which were in force at the times in the first count mentioned, plaintiff, at the times aforesaid, was bound, if required by defendant to perform, and defendant, at the said times, had a right to require plaintiff to perform, the matter mentioned or referred to in the said first count as the consideration for the supposed promise: and there was no consideration for defendant's making or performing the supposed promise.

Issues on these pleas.

On the trial, before Erle, J., at the London Sittings after last Hilary Term, it appeared that the defendant was captain of The Mobile, a ship of 1045 tons register. The plaintiff was a mariner in the ship. The mariners, by their articles, agreed to serve on board the ship "on a voyage from Liverpool to Port Philip, from thence (if required) to any ports and places in the Pacific Ocean, Indian or China Seas, or wherein freight may offer, with liberty to call at a port for orders, and until her return to a final port of discharge in the United Kingdom: or for a term not to exceed three years." The wages *of the plaintiff were to be 3*l.* per month. The proper complement of men was thirty-six. The three years would expire in July, 1855. The ship left Liverpool, and reached Port Philip in Australia on 9th October, 1852. While she was at Port Philip, seventeen of the crew refused to work, and were sent to prison. Among the remaining nineteen, there were only four or five able seamen. The master proposed to sail for Bombay: and, to induce the remaining crew to take the ship to Bombay, he promised to pay to some of them a sum in addition to their wages: and he gave to the plaintiff a written promise, which was as follows.

*874]

"Port Philip, 18 October, 1852.

"I promise to pay, in Liverpool, to Robert Hartley the sum of forty pounds sterling, provided he assist in taking ship Mobile from this port to Bombay with a crew of nineteen hands.

"As witness my hand."

(Signed)   "HENRY PONSONBY."

A similar note was given to eight other seamen. Contradictory evidence was given as to what passed between the defendant and the seamen at the time of this agreement being made, and as to the facility of hiring fresh seamen at Port Philip. The ship set sail for Bombay, where she arrived on 31st December, 1852. She encountered much rough weather on the voyage, in consequence of which, and of the shortness of hands, extraordinary labour fell upon the crew. At

Bombay additional hands were taken on board. The Mobile sailed for Liverpool on 14th February, 1853, and arrived there on 14th June, 1853. The owners and the master refused to pay the seamen more than the wages originally contracted for: and this action was brought against the *master for the 40l. Evidence was given as to the [*875 unfitness of so small a crew as nineteen to navigate the ship. The learned Judge put three questions to the jury. First: Whether the defendant made the agreement voluntarily: to which the jury answered that he did so, and not by coercion; and that this was for the best interests of the owners. Secondly: whether the defendant could, by reasonable exertions, obtain more hands at Port Philip: to which the jury answered that he could not have done so at a reasonable price. Thirdly: whether it was unreasonable or unsafe to proceed on the voyage to Bombay with so few hands: to which the jury answered that they considered it unreasonable for a vessel of 1045 tons to proceed on that voyage with only nineteen hands. His Lordship then directed a verdict for the plaintiff, reserving leave to move to enter a verdict for the defendant.

Knowles, in last Easter Term, obtained a rule to show cause why a verdict should not be entered for the defendant, "on the ground that the finding of the jury amounted to a verdict for the defendant; or why a new trial should not be had between the parties, on the ground that the evidence given at the trial showed that the plaintiff was not entitled to recover."

Hugh Hill and *C. Milward* now showed cause.—It appears that the captain, at the time when he made the contract, was striving to persuade the crew to undertake a risk which they were not bound to undertake: a sufficient consideration therefore arises from their undertaking it. It is undoubtedly true that, if an irremediable emergency arises in the course of a voyage, as, for instance, if a large part of the crew are washed *overboard, the crew on board are bound to [*876 perform so much more of their ordinary duty as may have become necessary for the completion of the voyage; and a promise to pay them for the performance of such extraordinary duty would be without consideration, or contrary to the policy of the law. But that rule is inapplicable to a case when a British ship is in a British harbour, and, for want of a sufficient number of hands, is in fact unseaworthy. A refusal to put to sea in an unseaworthy ship is no desertion of the ship; that was ruled at Nisi Prius by Crowder, J., in a case of Davidson *v.* Todhunter, Liverpool Summer Assizes, 1855. So, if a master, by unwarrantable severity, compel a seaman to quit the ship: Limland *v.* Stephens, 3 Esp. 269, Edward *v.* Trevellick, 4 E. & B. 59 (E. C. L. R. vol. 82). So, if the master do not supply the seamen with provisions; The Castilia (Stewart), 1 Hag. Rep. Adm. 59; or if he alter the mariners' contract in respect of the voyage to be performed; The Eliza (Ireland)

1 Hag. Rep. Adm. 182. The only question here is whether there was an irremediable emergency. Now there is nothing to show that, by waiting a reasonable time, a sufficiency of hands might not have been procured. The captain himself proposed the extra pay; which at any rate shows his view of the obligation of the seamen.

Knowles and *Aspland*, contrà.—The agreement of the captain cannot be considered to have been voluntary: the jury have indeed found that it was; which may be true in a vague and popular sense of the word: but, legally speaking, the refusal of the crew to proceed was a compul-

877] sion. [COLERIDGE, J.—It should seem that, if *the circumstances excused the crew from going to sea, they also excused the captain from going.] The case is like Harris v. Carter, 3 E. & B. 559 (E. C. L. R. vol. 77),(a) where it was held that a seaman was not relieved from his duty, so as to enable him to make a fresh contract, by the desertion or discharge of some of the hands. [*C. Milward.*—There the plaintiff failed because it could not be shown that the ship had become unseaworthy.] Here no more appears than that the desertion imposed additional labour on those who remained. Harris v. Watson, 1 Peake's N. P. C. 72, is an authority for the defendant; there the action was against the captain, as here. In The Eliza (Ireland), 1 Hag. Rep. Adm. 182, the original contract was put an end to by the master. But in The Araminta (Feran), 1 Spinks' Ecc. & Adm. Rep. 224, where, upon some of the crew deserting at Geelong in Australia, the captain proposed to the remaining crew that they should take the ship on, she being then short-handed, for additional wages, to which they assented, it was held that such additional wages could not be contracted for, and that, if they were paid, they might be deducted from the wages due on the original contract.

Lord CAMPBELL, C. J.—I think that this verdict should stand. The answer given by the jury to the third question imports to my mind that for the ship to go to sea with so few hands was dangerous to life. If so, it was not incumbent on the plaintiff to perform the work; and he was in the condition of a free man. There was therefore a consideration for the contract; and the captain made it without coercion. This is

878] *therefore a voluntary agreement upon sufficient consideration. This decision will not conflict with any former decisions. In The Araminta (Feran), Dr. Lushington says: "I do not wish it to be inferred from anything I now say, that mariners, having completed the voyage outwards, are compellable to make the return voyage when the number of the crew is so small that risk of life may be incurred." In Harris v. Carter there was no such risk. As to the weight of evidence, the evidence was conflicting: but my brother Erle is not dissatisfied with the verdict.

COLERIDGE, J.—I am of the same opinion, and for the same reasons.

(a) See Stilk v. Meyrick, 2 Campb. 317.

I understand the finding of the jury to be, that the ship was unseaworthy; and that, owing to the excessive labour which would be imposed, it was not reasonable to require the mariners to go to sea. If they were not bound to go, they were free to make a new contract: and the master was justified in hiring them on the best terms he could make. It may be that the plaintiff took advantage of his position to make a hard bargain; but there was no duress.

ERLE, J.—I am of the same opinion. I was deeply impressed with the consequence of not holding the plaintiff liable to perform his original engagement. But there is a point of danger at which it becomes unreasonable for mariners to be required to go on. That is a question for a jury. The mariners, not being bound to go on, were to all intents and purposes free, and might make the best contract they could.

*CROMPTON, J.—The jury have found that this was a free [*879 bargain. As regards public policy, it would be very dangerous to lay down that, under all circumstances and at any risk of life, seamen are bound to proceed on a voyage. The jury have found in this case (and, I think, upon the evidence, correctly) that it was not reasonable to require the seamen to go on. Where, from a ship being shorthanded, it would be unsafe for the seamen to go to sea, they become free to make any new contract that they like.   Rule discharged.

SUMMERS v. SAMUEL SOLOMON. *June 4.*

Defendant had a jeweller's shop at Lewes, he residing near London; the business at Lewes was managed by A., who, by defendant's authority, was in the habit of giving orders at Lewes, verbally and by letter, for goods to be sent to the shop: and A. had given such orders to plaintiff, who resided in London, and who had, in compliance with them, sent goods to the shop, which defendant had accepted. A. absconded from the shop, came to London, verbally ordered goods, consisting of jewellery, of plaintiff, as for defendant, and took them away, saying that he was going to Lewes.

Held that, upon these facts, a jury might find that defendant had so conducted himself as to make plaintiff believe that A., whilst in defendant's employment, had authority to order goods as he did; and, on such finding, plaintiff, not having had notice of the termination of the authority, would be entitled to recover the price from defendant.

DECLARATION for money payable by defendant to plaintiff for goods sold and delivered, goods bargained and sold, and for money found due on accounts stated.

Pleas: 1, except as to 2*l.* 7*s.*, Never indebted; 2, as to 2*l.* 7*s.*, tender and payment into Court. Issues on these pleas.

On the trial before Erle, J., at the London sittings after last Hilary Term, the tender was admitted by the plaintiff; and the following facts were admitted, by both parties, as to the issue on the first plea. The defendant lived at Maida Vale, near London. He also had a [*880 *jeweller's shop at Lewes in Sussex, which was managed by his nephew, Abraham Solomon. The plaintiff was a jeweller carrying on business in Hatton Garden, London. He had formerly been traveller for some wholesale jewellers in London, and, as such traveller, had, at Lewes, received orders by Abraham Solomon for articles which were to be sent on defendant's credit to the shop at Lewes; and which were so sent accordingly. In November, 1856, the plaintiff, being in business on his own account, received two orders by letter written from Lewes by Abraham Solomon for goods to be sent on defendant's credit to the shop at Lewes; and which were so sent accordingly. In all the above transactions Abraham Solomon acted by the defendant's authority. The second plea related to the goods furnished in compliance with the two orders last-mentioned. Defendant used to attend at the shop at Lewes once a month, to check the goods with the invoices and take stock. On 7th March, Abraham Solomon absconded from Lewes and came to London. On 10th March he obtained from plaintiff the goods which were the subject of the first count, stating that they were for the defendant, and that he himself was going back that afternoon to Lewes; and these goods, which consisted of jewellery, he then took into his possession and afterwards appropriated. They were never delivered to the defendant, who was never informed of the transaction until payment was demanded by the plaintiff. On these admissions, the learned Judge was requested by the parties to draw the inference of fact; and he directed a verdict on the first issue, with leave to move as after mentioned, it being understood that the Court should have the same power as a jury to draw inferences of fact. On the second issue, verdict for defendant.

*881]   *H. Hawkins, in last Term, obtained a rule to show cause why a verdict should not be entered on the first issue for defendant, "or why a nonsuit should not be entered, on the ground that there was no sale or delivery of the goods in question by the plaintiff to defendant, and no account stated, or other cause of action; that Abraham Solomon was not the agent of defendant to order or receive the goods in question, and there was no sufficient evidence of such agency to warrant the verdict."

M. Chambers and Manisty now showed cause.—There was reasonable evidence for a jury that the plaintiff was justified in assuming that Abraham Solomon had authority from the defendant to make the purchase. Plaintiff, by defendant's authority, had dealt with defendant through the nephew, exclusively; and, as the defendant lived at Maida Hill, plaintiff had no reason to expect any personal intervention on the part of the defendant. [Lord CAMPBELL, C. J.—A banker's clerk has authority to act for his employer at the office; but, if he acted elsewhere, would that bind the employer?] The question in all cases depends much on the particular business. If the servant of a livery stable keeper warrants a horse at the livery stable, contrary to his master's orders, the master is nevertheless bound. In the present case the authority could not be limited to orders given in the shop : it could not be contended, for instance, that, if the nephew had met the defendant in an hotel at Lewes, and had there given him the order, that would not have bound the defendant. Where, then, is the line to be drawn? Would not an order given at Brighton be binding? The plaintiff was led, by the defendant's conduct, to believe *that the nephew had [*882 all the authority which the defendant himself had ; and that might be exercised anywhere. Nor was there any reason for suspecting a determination of the authority from the circumstance that the goods were to be given to the nephew and not sent to Lewes. It was quite in the natural course of business that either the defendant or his agent, in purchasing an article of small bulk, might prefer taking personal charge of it to trusting it to a carrier. The case is not like that of a cook or other servant living under the domestic control of a master.

H. Hawkins and *F. H. Lewis*, contrà.—There was no evidence of any authority given to the nephew to order goods elsewhere than at Lewes, nor to receive them except at Lewes. Suppose a cook had been authorized to give orders to a butcher, calling at her master's house, for meat to be sent to the house : that would not warrant the butcher in supplying the cook, calling at the butcher's shop, with meat to be then taken away by the cook. It is said that such a case is different from the present, because the cook is under the domestic control of the master : that circumstance, however, is of no importance except as constituting the evidence of the holding out of authority. The butcher knows the relation of the master to this particular servant : the plaintiff knew that the nephew had authority to act in respect of articles ordered from Lewes and sent thither ; but he knew no more. And the distinction is perfectly reasonable ; for an employer has much greater security when the article is delivered at his shop than when it is delivered elsewhere. [Lord CAMPBELL, C. J.—Could the nephew have bound the defendant by giving in London *an order for the goods to be [*883 sent to Lewes?] That is very questionable : the plaintiff should have been put on his guard by the departure from the usual course. But the case here is much stronger : a delivery at the defendant's house is a delivery to the defendant himself. There would be much danger in allowing the authority to be extended further : a man may have many shopmen ; and the place of delivery may in effect be his main security. It is asked where the line is to be drawn : but that difficulty rather presses upon the plaintiff. Would the defendant be bound by the nephew giving an order in Bristol or in Spitzbergen? The defendant had no means of giving notice of the termination of the agency which ensued upon the absconding ; for he did not know of it. Then it is said that it was natural to suppose that the goods were taken in the ordinary course of business : but in the instance of jewellery, where so much value lies in so small a space, the caution ought to have been greater. If there be a balance of presumption, potior est conditio defendentis.

Lord CAMPBELL, C. J.—The question put to us is whether there is reasonable evidence on which a jury might find for the plaintiff. The plaintiff had dealt with the defendant through the nephew, and had, I presume, seen the nephew left to manage the shop and to do all that should be necessary for procuring a stock of goods. The nephew had ordered goods to be sent to Lewes, which the defendant had received and paid for. That was evidence upon which a jury might well suppose the nephew to be the defendant's general agent for conducting the business; and the nephew, within the scope of such general authority, *884] might procure *goods in London to be taken by him to Lewes: and the plaintiff had every reason to infer such general authority, and to deliver goods which were required as for an old customer. If the nephew had in London ordered the goods to be sent to Lewes by a carrier, the defendant would beyond question have been liable: and why should not the nephew be supposed to be himself the carrier? The defendant clearly acted bonâ fide.

COLERIDGE, J.—I am of the same opinion. The question is, not what was the actual relation between the defendant and his nephew, but whether the defendant had not so conducted himself as to make the plaintiff suppose the nephew to be the defendant's general agent. What passes between the defendant and his nephew cannot limit the defendant's liability to the plaintiff.

ERLE, J.—I am of the same opinion, and precisely on the same grounds.

CROMPTON, J.—I am of the same opinion. I think the evidence sufficient to warrant a verdict. It was laid down in very early times that one instance of authorizing an agent to pledge the employer's credit was enough to justify a party dealing with the employer in assuming that the authority continued. It is no answer, that the employer here would find it difficult to give notice of withdrawing the agency. As soon as you have given the agent authority to pledge your credit, you render yourself liable to parties who have acted upon notice of such authority until you find the means of giving them notice that the authority is *determined. And, on the first occasion of the authority *885] being exercised, it must always be at a particular place and for the delivery of goods at a particular place. Here the representation was that the goods were to be used in the shop: that was evidence for a jury; and this is the only question before us.

Rule discharged.

Where it is sought to bind a principal by an instrument executed by an agent acting without express authority, on the ground of a previous recognition of similar acts, it is necessary to show that the instrument in question was taken on the faith of such previous recognition: St. John v. Redmond, 9 Porter, 428.

JAMES WILSHER ALDRIDGE v. PATRICK JOHNSON.
June 5.

Plaintiff agreed with K. to purchase from K. 100 out of 200 quarters of barley which plaintiff
had seen in bulk and approved of; and he paid part of the price. It was agreed that plaintiff should send sacks for the barley, and that K. should fill the sacks with the barley, take
them to a railway, place them upon trucks free of charge, and send them to plaintiff. Plaintiff sent sacks enough for a part only of the 100 quarters: these K. filled; and K. also
endeavoured to find trucks for them, but was unable to do so. Plaintiff repeatedly sent to K.
demanding the barley. K. finally detained it, and emptied the barley from the sacks back
into the bulk.

Held, that the property in so much of the barley as was not put into the sacks did not pass to
plaintiff.

But, per Lord Campbell, C. J., Coleridge and Erle, Js., that the portion put into the sacks
passed to the plaintiff: hæsitante Crompton, J., on the ground that it did not appear quite
clearly that, at the time when plaintiff demanded the barley, he knew that any portion had
been put into the sacks, and that, therefore, his assent to the particular appropriation was
doubtful.

K. having become bankrupt after he had emptied the barley from the sacks into the bulk, and
the defendant, his assignee, having removed the whole together: Held, by the whole Court,
that this was a conversion, by the assignee, of all the barley (if any) which, by the putting it
into the sacks, had become plaintiff's property.

THIS was an action brought by the plaintiff to recover certain goods
alleged to be his property, and to have been detained by the defendant;
or the value of such goods, and damages for their detention; and also
to recover damages for the wrongful conversion of the same goods by
the defendant.

The defendant pleaded to the whole declaration: 1st. Not guilty;
and, 2dly, that the goods were not the plaintiff's property.

*On the trial, before Erle, J., at the Sittings in London in [*886
last Hilary Term, a verdict was found for the plaintiff, by consent, for the whole amount of his claim, and costs 40s., subject to the
opinion of the Court upon the following case.

The plaintiff is a corn merchant at Witham in Essex; and the defendant is the official assignee of the estate and effects of one James Watling Knights, a bankrupt, who, up to the time of his bankruptcy as
hereinafter mentioned, carried on business at Ipswich in Suffolk as an
auctioneer and seed merchant.

On 12th September, 1856, the plaintiff took 34 bullocks to Ipswich
for the purpose of having them sold by auction by the said J. W.
Knights, and instructed Knights to sell them if they should fetch a certain price. They did not, however, fetch that price; and consequently
were bought in by the plaintiff. Knights then informed the plaintiff
that he had a quantity of barley in his granary, and proposed to
exchange a portion of it for the plaintiff's bullocks. The plaintiff went,
and looked at the barley, which consisted at that time of one large heap
containing between 200 and 300 quarters. He weighed a bushel of it
for the purpose of ascertaining its quality, and took a sample away with
him; but no bargain was made on that day; and the bullocks were sent

to Colchester the same evening.   On the following day (13th September) the plaintiff and Knights were at Colchester market ; and the plaintiff sold two of his bullocks there : after which a conversation took place, between the plaintiff and Knights, upon the subject of the exchange proposed on the previous day, which resulted in the following arrangement between them.

*887]   It was agreed that Knights should have the remaining *32 bullocks at the price of 6l. apiece, and that the plaintiff should take in exchange 100 quarters of the barley which he had seen at Ipswich the day before, at the price of 2l. 3s. a quarter.   The difference between the value of the barley and of the bullocks, viz., 23l., was to be paid in cash by the plaintiff to Knights.   It was further agreed that the plaintiff should send his own sacks to Ipswich on the following Monday (15th), and that Knights should fill the sacks with the barley, take them to the railway, and place them upon trucks, free of charge, to be conveyed to the plaintiff at Witham.   Something was also said about a sum of 20l. 7s., which the plaintiff owed Knights for some goods which he had previously purchased : but it was agreed that this transaction should not interfere with the arrangement which was then being made.

As soon as this arrangement was effected, the plaintiff made the following note of it in his pocket-book.

"Septr. 13.   J. W. Knights exchange
32 beasts at 6l. 0s. 0d. for barley.
J. W. Knights,
100 barley 43/
£ 215 barley

"less b^t.

£ 192 beasts
£ 23 money to pay."

And the 32 bullocks were then and there delivered by the plaintiff to Knights.   •

On the following Monday, pursuant to the above arrangement, the plaintiff sent to Ipswich 200 sacks (being a sufficient number to contain the whole 100 quarters of barley).   Some of these sacks were marked in the plaintiff's name ; and they were all duly received by Knights:

*888]   but the barley was not delivered or *forwarded to the plaintiff.
On 16th September the plaintiff wrote to Knights for a sample of the barley, which was accordingly sent.   On 17th September, Knights sent one of his men, named Abel Smith, to fill 155 out of the 200 sacks with barley from the above-mentioned heap : and accordingly Smith proceeded to the granary, and, with the assistance of other persons, filled 155 of the sacks with barley from the heap (each sack containing one coomb, or half a quarter).   After the sacks had been filled, there was left in the heap some 70 or 80 quarters; so that the quantity put into the sacks was only about half the bulk.   By the fur-

ther direction of Knights, Smith applied, the same day, at the railway station at Ipswich for some trucks, to convey the 155 sacks to the plaintiff at Witham, but was not able to obtain any. On the following Saturday (20th), the plaintiff again saw Knights at Colchester market, and complained to him of the non-delivery of the barley. He said he was sorry that he had not sent it ; but that he had been very busy, and unable to get trucks ; and that it should be sent on the Monday following without fail. On the following Monday morning (22d) Knights gave directions to a clerk in his employ, named Mulley, to get some trucks, and have the 155 full sacks, which were then standing in the granary, put upon them to be sent to the plaintiff. Mulley accordingly applied for the trucks, without success. After giving these directions, Knights himself went up to London, saw the plaintiff in Mark Lane, and told him that the barley would be put upon the rail that day.

In the course of the same morning, the plaintiff had sent to Ipswich a person in his employ, named Church, to demand of Knights the 100 quarters of barley. *Accordingly, Church called at Knights' [*889 about noon, and found that he was away from home, but saw Mulley, and demanded the barley of him. Mulley said that he could get no trucks to put it upon, and that Church had better try himself to get some: that, if he could procure any, the barley should be put upon the rail that afternoon ; but that, at any rate, it should be forwarded the first thing the next morning. After this, Church returned to Witham.

While the above communication was passing between Mulley and Church, the former received from Knights a telegraphic despatch in the following terms.

" The following message forwarded from Mark Lane station, and received at Ipswich town station, Septr. 22, 1856.

From		To	
Name and Address. }	J. W. Knights.	Name and Address. }	G. Mulley, Quay House, Ipswich.

" If you have not put oats on rail, do not, nor allow more barley to go, if applied for. Private."

The barley mentioned in the said despatch was the same barley in respect of which Knights had given Mulley directions in the morning: but Mulley did not mention to Church the contents of the despatch, nor the fact that he had received any communication from Knights.

The barley was not forwarded to the plaintiff the next day, but remained in the sacks till the following Wednesday; when Abel Smith, by Knights' directions, turned it all out of the sacks again on to the heap from which it was taken, so as to be undistinguishable from the rest of the heap.

*On Thursday, 25th September, in consequence of informa- [*890 tion which the plaintiff had received, he went himself to Ipswich and saw Knights at his own house. He remonstrated with him for not sending the barley; and, after some conversation, Knights stated that he was sorry to say he was in trouble, and had a notice of bankruptcy served upon him.   On 29th September, Knights filed a petition for arrangement under the 211th section of The Bankrupt Law Consolidation Act, 1849.(a)   And, at the first sitting which was held in the matter of that petition, on the 4th November following, Knights was adjudicated a bankrupt; and the defendant was then named and made the official assignee of his estate and effects.

The plaintiff had, previously to this, taken out a summons against Knights before the borough magistrates at Colchester; which was heard on the 30th October, and dismissed.   After the hearing, the plaintiff, and his attorney's managing clerk, Mr. Beaumont, went to Ipswich: when the latter served a copy of the following notice, signed by the plaintiff, upon Lewis Bloomfield, the messenger of the Court of Bankruptcy, who was then in possession of all Knights' property.

"Notice.

"Without prejudice to the notice or demand made by me on my behalf on or about the 22d day of September, 1856.

"To James Watling Knights, of Ipswich, in the county of Suffolk, auctioneer, or whom else it may concern.

*891]   "I hereby demand the delivery by you of 100 *quarters of barley, my property, now being in or upon your warehouse or premises at Ipswich in the county of Suffolk, and sold by you, the said Jas. Watling Knights, to me, on or about the 13th day of September last.

"Dated the 30th day of October, 1856.

"J. W. ALDRIDGE."

At the time of the service of this notice, Mr. Beaumont tendered to the messenger 23*l.* in cash, as the money balance due from the plaintiff to Knights for the barley.   The messenger received the notice, but refused to take the 23*l.*   This was the first occasion on which any tender of the 23*l.* had been made by or on behalf of the plaintiff.

On 11th November the following demand, signed by the plaintiff, was served upon the defendant.

"To Patrick Johnson, Esq.,
Official Assignee,
Basinghall St., London.

"In the matter of James Watling Knights, of Ipswich in the county of Suffolk, corn merchant, dealer, and chapman, a bankrupt.

"Sir, I hereby demand the delivery of 100 quarters of barley, agreed by the above-named bankrupt, on the 13th day of September last, to be delivered to me in exchange for 32 bullocks then sold and delivered by me to him: and I now tender you (although I protest

(a) Stat. 12 & 13 Vict. c. 106.

against it being considered that I am liable so to do) the sum of 23*l*., being the difference between the agreed price of the said barley and the agreed price of the said bullocks.

"I am, Sir, Your most obedt. Servt.,

"JAMES WILSHER ALDRIDGE."

"Witham, 10 November, 1856."

*And, at the time of the service of this demand, 23*l*. in cash was duly tendered to the defendant, as being the balance due [*892 from the plaintiff as aforesaid.

The demand was not complied with; and the money was not accepted. On 18th November, this action was commenced.

The said 200 sacks remained upon Knights' premises until the bankruptcy, when they were taken possession of by the assignees. On 24th December, an order was made in this action by Coleridge, J., in the following terms.

"Upon hearing the counsel on both sides, I do order that, upon the defendant's delivering up or tendering to the plaintiff 200 sacks, being the sacks in the declaration mentioned, and paying nominal damages and costs, the proceedings herein be stayed.

"Or, if the plaintiff will not consent thereto, that he be subject to the costs of the action, unless he obtain a verdict for some of the other goods in the declaration mentioned, or damages beyond nominal damages for the detention of the sacks in question. And I order that the plaintiff be at liberty to amend the declaration, by inserting a claim for special damages as to the detention of the sacks. I certify for a counsel.

"Dated the 24th day of December, 1856.

"J. T. COLERIDGE."

On 29th December, 1856, Louis Blomfield, the said messenger, went to the plaintiff's house and made a tender, on behalf of the defendant, to Mrs. Aldridge, the plaintiff's wife, in his absence, of the 200 sacks, and damages for the detention thereof, in accordance with the above order. At first she refused to take them; but afterwards, having seen the plaintiff's attorney, she *received back the sacks, but would not take the 1*s*. damages. [*893

It is agreed that the defendant would at any time have given up the sacks to the plaintiff, had he been requested so to do.

The barley remained at Knights' granary until Christmas last, when it was removed: and the value of it remained the same, viz. 2*l*. 3*s*. per quarter, from the time of the above-mentioned assignment until after the commencement of this action.

The damage sustained by the plaintiff being deprived of his sacks was at the rate of one penny per week for every sack.

The action was commenced originally against both the assignees of Knights' estate: but, on the 21st of January last, the name of one of the defendants was struck out of the proceedings by an order of Mr. Justice Crompton.

The pleadings in this action are to form part of this case; and the questions for the opinion of the Court are:

1. Whether the issues joined in the said action respectively should be found for the plaintiff or for the defendant.

2. If the plaintiff is entitled to maintain the action, for what goods or moneys the verdict found for him is to stand.

Bittleston, for the plaintiff.—The first question is, whether, before the bankruptcy, the property in the barley passed to the plaintiff; secondly, whether, if so, there was a conversion by the defendant. There is no question as to apparent possession, the bankrupt not having had possession by the consent of the plaintiff.

*894]   *As to the first question, the plaintiff contends that all the hundred quarters passed. The principal part of the consideration, the bullocks, was received by the bankrupt: and barley was delivered into the plaintiff's sacks in pursuance of the bargain. It is true that all the barley was not so delivered: but what was delivered was taken from a specific heap; and that sufficiently defined the identity. [CROMPTON, J.—Which hundred quarters was the plaintiff to have? Whatever hundred the bankrupt might put into the plaintiff's sacks. [CROMPTON, J.—That might be any hundred. Lord CAMPBELL, C. J.—Really your proposition as to the whole is not tenable.] The plaintiff then insists only on the portion put into the 155 sacks. By the arrangement, the plaintiff was to send his own sacks: he does send them; and the bankrupt delivers the barley into them, and does all that is in his power to send them off. That trucks could not be found at the time, to despatch the sacks, does not render this the less a delivery. [Lord CAMPBELL, C. J.—Suppose the plaintiff had been present, and had, after the barley was put into the sacks, sealed up the sacks, without taking them away.] No doubt the property would then have passed: and what actually took place was quite as effectual. [Lord CAMPBELL, C. J.—Certainly the property may be in the vendee though it is in the manual possession of the vendor.] That is so. In Rohde v. Thwaites, 6 B. & C. 388 (E. C. L. R. vol. 13), a vendor sold twenty hogsheads of sugar out of a larger quantity: he delivered four, and filled up and appropriated other sixteen, desiring the vendee to take them away: the vendee said that he would take

*895]   them as soon as he could: and, in an action *by the vendor for goods bargained and sold, it was held that the property in the sixteen passed, though they were not removed from the premises of the vendor. [ERLE, J.—That case would be exactly in point if there it appeared that there remained a duty, on the part of the vendor, to forward. CROMPTON, J.—You will say that the sacks were in the bankrupt's hands in order that he might perform a certain duty, not that he might otherwise meddle with them.] Yes. [Lord CAMPBELL, C. J.—You say that his doing more was a wrongful conversion.] It was so. There was no question as to the bankrupt's original intention to appropriate; for he gave orders to send the sacks away by the railway. It is immaterial that there was no tender before the bankruptcy. But, indeed, no tender was necessary at all: there was no lien. Nor did the bankrupt or defendant profess to hold the barley on the ground that it might be retained till the money was paid. The assignee can be in no better position than the bankrupt.

Then as to the conversion. [CROMPTON, J.—When you demanded the barley of the assignee, what was he to do? How could he separate your barley from the rest? You have a case against the bankrupt: but how could the assignee deliver?] The bankrupt could not, by having mixed up the plaintiff's property with his own, gain the right of retaining it: nor can his assignee be in a better position. [CROMPTON, J.—The assignee is not liable for the tortious act of the bankrupt. ERLE, J.—Where a party mixes up another man's property inseparably with his own, the consequence is that he loses his own. Lord CAMPBELL, C. J.—Yes, unless the portion mixed up be quite insignificant. ERLE, J.—Then, if the *plaintiff was entitled to [*896 take the whole from the bankrupt, he would be entitled to take it from the assignee.] Those consequences would follow. [CROMPTON, J.—I find it stated that the whole was removed: that must mean, a removal by the assignees.] That is enough to constitute a conversion.

But, further, there is at any rate no defence as to the sacks. [CROMPTON, J.—Surely that point is disposed of by my brother Coleridge's order.] Then that is not insisted on.

Prentice, contrà.—The barley placed in the sacks was taken from the bulk, of which an unascertained hundred quarters had been sold: the particular portion placed in the sacks was not sold. [CROMPTON, J.—The property would not pass if anything remained to be done by the vendor.] In order that the separation of the particular quantity may effect a transfer of the property there must be an assent by the vendee; the reason of which is, that the vendee is entitled to see that the portion separated corresponds with the bulk. [ERLE, J.—If the portion is separated in conformity with the contract, surely the property in that passes.] The vendor might have substituted another portion before the sacks arrived at the railway: till then the property did not pass, by the agreement. In Blackburn's Treatise On the Effect of the Contract of Sale, p. 126, the law is thus stated: "the specific goods must be agreed upon; that is, both parties must be pledged, the one to give and the other to accept those specific goods." Here, though the vendee did assent to the goods being placed in his sacks, the property did not pass till he had inspected the barley.

*897] Holroyd, J., *in Rohde *v.* Thwaites, 6 B. & C. 393 (E. C. L. R. vol. 13), makes not only the selection by the vendor essential, but also the "adoption of that act" by the vendee. Suppose the goods had been burnt. [ERLE, J.—That was the test in my mind: I think the plaintiff would have had to bear the loss, according to the principles laid down in Rugg *v.* Minett, 11 East, 210.] In p. 123 of Mr. Blackburn's Treatise, the final appropriation which transfers the property is stated to take place when the party who is to do the first act makes the election, the property being made certain by such election; for which Sir Rowland Heyward's Case, 2 Rep. 35 a, is cited. Here the act to be done was despatching the barley. [ERLE, J.—Mr. Blackburn has expressed himself with perfect accuracy. He says: "where from the terms of an executory agreement to sell unspecified goods, the vendor is to despatch the goods, *or* to do anything to them that cannot be done till the goods are appropriated, he has the right to choose what the goods shall be; and the property is transferred the moment the despatch *or other act* has commenced, for then an appropriation is made, finally and conclusively, by the authority conferred in the agreement."] In the case of goods sent by a carrier, the delivery to the carrier is the transfer. The necessity of commencing the act agreed upon, in order to fix the appropriation, appears by the two cases cited by Mr. Blackburn, Fragano *v.* Long, 4 B. & C. 219 (E. C. L. R. vol. 10), and Atkinson *v.* Bell, 8 B. & C. 277 (E. C. L. R. vol. 15). Here the act agreed upon was the sending: nothing short of that fixed the property. Wallace *v.* Breeds, 13 East, 522, illustrates this. Further, the contract was indivisible: putting a portion into the sack

*898] *could not transfer the goods sold. [Lord CAMPBELL, C. J.— Do you say none passed?] Yes: the plaintiff might have refused to receive a part. [CROMPTON, J.—Is there not evidence that the plaintiff assented to the appropriation? Did he not know of it? Lord CAMPBELL, C. J.—May there not be an anticipative assent—"I will take to what you put into the sacks—"?]

Then, next, there was no conversion by the assignee. If there was any conversion, it was completed by the bankrupt: after that, his assignee could not convert. [Lord CAMPBELL, C. J.—That is not so. If a man takes my horse he converts it: if he hands it over to another, who refuses to give it up to me on demand, that other converts also. If the bankrupt had divested the property from the plaintiff it would be otherwise: but he has only done a wrongful act. Here the assignee denies the plaintiff's claim to any part; and he is right in claiming all, if the former part of your argument be correct.] No distinct act of conversion by the assignee is shown.

Bittleston, in reply, was stopped by the Court.

Lord CAMPBELL, C. J.—In cases of this sort there often is great doubt and great difficulty; but the present case seems to me, on both points, free from all doubt and difficulty. I think that no portion of what remained in bulk ever vested in the plaintiff. We cannot tell what part of that is to vest. No rule of the law of vendor and purchaser is more clear than this: that, until the appropriation and separation of a particular quantity, or signification of assent to the particular quantity, the property is not transferred. Therefore, *except as to what was put into the 155 sacks, there must be judgment [*899 for the defendant. It is equally clear that, as to what was put into those sacks, there must be judgment for the plaintiff. Looking to all that was done, when the bankrupt put the barley into the sacks eo instanti the property in each sackful vested in the plaintiff. I consider that here was a priorian assent by the plaintiff. He had inspected and approved of the barley in bulk. He sent his sacks to be filled out of that bulk. There can be no doubt of his assent to the appropriation of such bulk as should have been put into the sacks. There was also evidence of his subsequent appropriation, by his order that it should be sent on. There remained nothing to be done by the vendor, who had appropriated a part by the direction of the vendee. It is the same as if boxes had been filled and sent on by the bankrupt, in which case it cannot be disputed that the property would pass: and it can make no difference that the plaintiff ordered the sacks to be forwarded by the vendor. As to the question of conversion, the pro er y being in the plaintiff, he has done nothing to divest himself of it.p It is not like the case of confusion of goods, where the owner of such articles as oil or wine mixes them with similar articles belonging to another. That is a wrongful act by the owner, for which he is punished by losing his property. Here the plaintiff has done nothing wrong. It was wrong of the bankrupt to mix what had been put into the sacks with the rest of the barley; but no wrong has been done by the plaintiff. That being so, the plaintiff's property comes into the hands of the defendant as the bankrupt's assignee. If the defendant had a lien, he does not detain the barley on that ground. He denies the plaintiff's *property altogether, and cannot therefore claim a lien. He claims all the barley, and claims all of it as being the property [*900 of the bankrupt. He therefore has converted the plaintiff's property.

COLERIDGE, J.—I am of the same opinion. I think the property in that portion which was put into the plaintiff's sacks passed to the plaintiff. That portion was subtracted by the vendor from the bulk, in part performance of the contract; and there is abundant evidence of appropriation, as far as the bankrupt could appropriate. There is also abundant evidence of assent by the plaintiff. He had before assented to the quality of the bulk; and, after the portion was put into the sacks, he desired that they should be sent to him. There is thus evidence of the completion of the act of appropriation. Atkinson v. Bell, 8 B. & C. 277 (E. C. L. R. vol. 15), is a very different case. There the goods were in the course of being made; and many alterations had taken place; and the purchaser had never done any act by which he adopted the particular thing made. Here is a complete appropriation. As to the conversion, nothing that either the bankrupt or the assignee could do without the plaintiff's consent could divest the plaintiff's property: and the removal is abundant proof of the conversion.

ERLE, J.—I also am clearly of opinion that the property in what was put into the sacks passed to the plaintiff. It is clear that, where there is an agreement for the sale and purchase of a particular chattel, the chattel passes at once. If the thing sold is not ascertained, and *something is to be done before it is ascertained, *901] it does not pass till it is ascertained. Sometimes the right of ascertainment rests with the vendee, sometimes solely with the vendor. Here it is vested in the vendor only, the bankrupt. When he had done the outward act which showed which part was to be the vendee's property, his election was made and the property passed. That might be shown by sending the goods by the railway: and in such case the property would not pass till the goods were despatched. But it might also be shown by other acts. Here was an ascertained bulk, of which the plaintiff agreed to buy about half. It was left to the bankrupt to decide what portion should be delivered under that contract. As soon as he does that, his election has been indicated; the decisive act was putting the portion into the sacks. If it were necessary to rest the decision on the assent of the vendee in addition to this, I am of opinion that there is abundant evidence of such assent; for the vendee demanded, over and over again, the portion which had been put into the sacks. I think Mr. Blackburn has expressed the law with great clearness and accuracy. He first takes the case where one party appropriates and the other assents; and then the case where, by virtue of the original agreement, the authority to appropriate is in one party only. As to the question of conversion, I am of opinion, on the grounds which have already been stated, that the assignee has converted the plaintiff's property.

CROMPTON, J.—As to the first point, respecting the part not put into the sacks, I never felt any doubt. As to the second point, I do not feel so clear as the other members of the Court, though I do not say that I *disagree with them. It is suggested that the plaintiff *902] said to the bankrupt, in effect, I will buy what you will put into the sacks. After that was done, I much doubt whether the bankrupt could meddle with the sacks and turn out what had been put in. It may be that the bargain was as my Lord and my brother Erle put it, that the plaintiff would take what the vendor should put in. On that view, when the barley was put into the sacks it was just as if it had been sent by a carrier. Also I agree that, if the plaintiff sent for the barley after it was in the sacks, that would be an assent to the appropriation. But I doubt whether, as the case is stated, it is quite clear that the plaintiff knew that the barley had been put into the sacks : if he did, there was clear evidence of assent. Then it is argued, on behalf of the defendant, that the contract was entire, and that either all or none of the barley must pass. I do not agree to that. There was an appropriation of so much; and so much passed. As to the conversion, the law is, beyond question, as my Lord puts it: a prior conversion does not prevent a subsequent conversion; the true owner may waive the first conversion. It is difficult to say what the assignee was to do. But I think that, if he remove all, it is a conversion of the part which belongs to the plaintiff: if he sells all, an action for money had and received may be brought in respect of that part. I think therefore that, as he has removed all, he has been guilty of a conversion.

Judgment for plaintiff, as to the part put into the sacks: as to the residue, judgment for defendant.

---

*JAMES DIXON, Executor of ALEXANDER DIXON, *v.* [*903
HOLDROYD. *June 5.*

By deed between D. and H., D. sold to H. beds of coal, and H. covenanted to pay to D. a sum named for the purchase-money, "in manner and at the times following," that is to say, part in cash on the day of the date of the deed, and the remainder by five promissory notes under H.'s hand, bearing even date with the deed, payable to D. or order on the 1st of July in every year till the whole purchase-money should be paid, with interest, until the notes should be paid.

D. declared against H. on this deed, alleging that, though H. gave D. two notes, &c. (according to the language of the covenant), and afterwards paid a part of the principal and interest mentioned in those notes, yet he did not pay the residue of the principal and interest mentioned in those notes, but, except as to the part so paid, those notes and so much of the purchase-money and interest as was therein mentioned remained wholly unpaid to D.

Held a good breach, the covenant extending to the payment of the money named in the notes, and not being satisfied by the mere delivery of the notes.

And that it was a bad plea, that the causes of action did not accrue within six years before the suit.

THE first count of the declaration, which was dated 19th February, 1857, alleged that the testator, Alexander Dixon, in his lifetime, by deed made the 12th day of July, A. D. 1834, between the said Alexander Dixon of the one part, and the defendant of the other part, sold and conveyed to the defendant certain seams and beds of coal and minerals : And the defendant, in and by the said deed, did covenant with the said Alexander Dixon that the defendant, his heirs, executors, or administrators, should and would well and truly pay or cause to be paid to the said Alexander Dixon, his executors or administrators, the sum of 213*l.* 15*s.*, as and for the purchase-money for the said seams and beds of coal and minerals, in manner and at the times following : that is to say, the sum of 21*l.* 7*s.* 6*d.* on the day of the date thereof,

and the remaining sum of 192*l*. 7*s*. 6*d*. by four several promissory
notes under the hand of the said David Holdroyd, bearing even date
*904]   with *the said deed, payable to the said Alexander Dixon or
order, respectively, on the first day of July in every year until
the whole of the said purchase-money should be fully paid, together
with interest thereon after the rate of 5*l*. per centum per annum, until
the same promissory notes should be severally paid, without any deduction thereout on any account whatsoever.   Averment: that though
defendant, in part performance of his said covenant, did make and
deliver to the said A. Dixon in his lifetime a certain promissory note
bearing even date with the said deed, and did thereby promise to pay
to the said A. Dixon, or his order, the sum of 50*l*., with interest from
the 1st day of July then instant, on the 1st day of July, 1837, and also
a certain other promissory note, bearing even date with the said deed,
and did thereby promise to pay to the said A. Dixon, or his order, the
sum of 50*l*., with interest from the 1st day of July then instant, on the
1st day of July, 1838; and did afterwards pay to the said A. Dixon,
in his lifetime, the sum of 15*l*. 5*s*., parcel of the principal money and
interest mentioned in the said promissory notes: Nevertheless the
defendant hath not at any time paid or caused to be paid the residue
of the principal moneys and interest mentioned in the said promissory
notes, or either of them, or any part thereof, to the said A. Dixon in his
lifetime, or to the plaintiff as executor as aforesaid, since the decease
of the said A. Dixon; but, except as to the said sum of 15*l*. 5*s*., the said
promissory notes respectively, and so much of the said purchase-money
and interest as is therein mentioned, remains wholly unpaid to the said
A. Dixon in his lifetime.

*905]   *Plea to the first count: that the alleged causes of action did
not, nor did any or either of them, accrue within six years before
this suit.

The defendant also demurred to the first count.

The plaintiff demurred to the plea; and joined in demurrer as to the
first count.

The defendant joined in demurrer as to the plea.

T. F. Ellis, for the plaintiff.—The argument on the part of the
defendant appears to be that, if the covenant is to give the promissory
notes, the record shows that this has been done, and there is no breach;
but, if the action be for non-payment of the promissory notes, that is
for a breach of a simple contract, and the Statute of Limitations is a
bar.   But neither of those suppositions represents the real cause of
action.   The covenant is, not simply to give promissory notes, but to
pay a portion of the purchase-money by promissory notes which are to
be payable annually till the purchase-money be fully paid: and the
question therefore is as to the meaning of a covenant to pay by a promissory note.   This is not satisfied by giving the note: a note is not

payment of even a simple contract debt, till it is honoured: it only suspends the remedy, being in the nature of an agreement to give credit. In the case of a covenant, the giving of the note does not even suspend the remedy. Therefore the action for the breach of the covenant to pay the notes still lies; and the plea that the causes of action did not accrue within six years is bad. And it is plain that this view of the deed carries out the intention of the parties, and that the deed can be explained in no other way. The *promissory notes [*906 are to be of even date with the deed of covenant; and they are handed over at once with the cash. If, therefore, the parties had meant merely to contract for the giving the notes, the whole intention would have been carried out by this being done at the time; and the deed of covenant would have been merely superfluous. [CROMPTON, J.—The covenantee got the benefit of a security which he might negotiate.] He would get that without the covenant. [CROMPTON, J.—He gets the covenant also.] But that, on the defendant's view, gives him no additional benefit. Suppose, in answer to a declaration in debt, the defendant were to plead that he had paid the debt by a promissory note, and issue were taken on that plea: it is clear that the defendant would not support his plea by mere proof that he had handed over a note which had been dishonoured, or even which was outstanding.

Manisty, contrà.—The covenant is to pay partly by notes "in manner and at the times following." If the defendant had not given the notes, that would have constituted a breach of covenant. It could not be intended to give two remedies, one on the notes, the other by covenant to pay them. [ERLE, J.—Suppose the covenant had been to pay 50l. on a particular day in each year, to be secured by promissory notes. CROMPTON, J.—That would be a case of collateral security; and there would be two remedies. ERLE, J.—Is not this covenant the same in effect?] A payment by a note suspends the action for the debt. [CROMPTON, J.—It is a conditional payment, but not a payment if the note *is dishonoured. COLERIDGE, J.—Here interest is [*907 payable till the whole principal is paid.] The declaration shows that the defendant has given the security which he covenanted to give: the covenantee has not availed himself of that security in time.

T. F. Ellis, in reply.—The argument on the other side assumes that a covenant to pay by a note is the same thing as a covenant to give a note. There is nothing unreasonable in supposing that the covenantee was to have two remedies.

Lord CAMPBELL, C. J.—I am of opinion that the plaintiff is entitled to judgment. The covenant is, not only to give promissory notes, but that those promissory notes should produce payment of the purchase-money. The defendant has given notes which are dishonoured: that is not to pay by notes but only to give notes. He covenants to pay "in manner and at the times following:" that is to say, part in cash immediately and the remainder by four several promissory notes: that is a covenant to pay the purchase-money as the notes should become due. Here the notes, when due, are not paid. Is not that a breach of the covenant? Had the covenant been to deliver promissory notes on a given day, that would have been performed by what has been done: but such a covenant would have been useless, since the notes are to be of an even date with the covenant. The deed would be mere waste paper if the covenant could be performed by merely giving the notes. It is true that our construction gives a double remedy: but that was the intention of the parties: the covenantee *was to have the negotiable security immediately, and also a remedy by covenant.

*908]

COLERIDGE, J.—I am of the same opinion. The declaration clearly shows what is the contract between the parties. A mode of payment is provided. It is to be by instalments: but the interest is to be paid until all the principal is paid off. The mode of doing this is by giving promissory notes. If that is payment at once, in the sense in which the covenantor covenants to pay, and the only thing stipulated for was to give the notes which are to bear an even date with the deed of covenant, the covenant, as was pointed out in argument, would have been absurd, and might have been put into the fire. If you say that the payment is the substance of the covenant, and that the giving the notes is merely the mode of payment, the plaintiff, it is true, secures to himself two remedies: but it comes only to this; that the mode of securing payment is to be by notes bearing interest. The meaning is that the covenantor should pay by promissory notes.

ERLE, J.—I also am clearly of opinion that the defendant covenanted with the defendant to pay the purchase-money: all that follows relates to the mode of payment; although the words, at first sight, might look as if the covenant would be satisfied by merely giving the notes, the meaning clearly was that the covenantor should pay the sum of money, giving the security of the notes. On reading the deed, it is clear to me that the covenant extends beyond the giving of the promissory notes for securing the whole *purchase-money and interest. My brother Coleridge says what is quite true: that on the opposite construction, the deed might just as well have been burnt the moment it was given.

*909]

CROMPTON, J.—I am of opinion that the deed bears the construction which the plaintiff seeks to put upon it. The argument urged from the circumstance that the notes are to bear even date with the deed is very strong. The covenant is for payment; and the mode is, to pay in this particular way. A covenant to pay need not be express. A covenant to account means, to account and pay. When there is an agreement to pay half the freight of a cargo by good bills, if the bills are given and dishonoured the shipowner may bring an action for non-payment of the whole freight, declaring upon the whole agreement. We must, therefore, read this as a covenant including in it the payment of the notes. It occurred to me that a difficulty might arise from the notes being payable to order, so that they might be outstanding in the hands of third parties. But the breach alleges that the notes remain unpaid to the said Alexander Dixon, the covenantee.

Judgment for the plaintiff.

---

*The QUEEN v. The Mayor and Assessors of ROCHESTER. [*910
(In the matter of the Parish of STROOD.)

The QUEEN v. The Mayor and Assessors of ROCHESTER.
(In the matter of the Parish of ST. NICHOLAS.)

The QUEEN v. The Mayor and Assessors of ROCHESTER.
(In the matter of the Parish of STROOD.

Mandamus directed to the mayor and assessors of R., a borough within the Municipal Corporation Reform Act, 5 & 6 W. 4, c. 76, comprising several parishes. Suggestions: that, at the Court holden in October, 1856, before the mayor and assessors for the revision of the burgess lists of that year, the mayor and assessors refused to revise the burgess list of the parish of S. on the ground that the list had not been affixed in some public place in the borough for a week. Mandatory part of the mayor and assessors to hold a Court and revise the list for this parish. The writ was tested in January, 1857. Return by the mayor, that the mayor who presided in October, 1856, went out of office in November, 1856; that the present mayor was not the same person, but would obey if he could. Demurrer to this return, and to an insufficient return by one of the assessors.

Another mandamus, directed and tested in the same way, contained suggestions that, at the Court in October, 1856, the mayor and assessors refused to hear and consider the list of objections for the parish of St. N., on the ground that the list of objections had not been personally delivered to the town clerk, though it had been given to his servant and came to his hands. Mandatory part to the mayor and assessors to hold a court and revise the burgess list so far as related to the names contained in the list of objections. Similar returns. Demurrer.

Held: that the provisions of the Municipal Corporation Reform Act (sects. 15 to 22), as to the time at which the burgess lists were to be revised, were directory only; and that this Court could grand a mandamus to revise them, after the 15th October.

That the mayor and assessors, though not a corporation, were in the nature of a standing tribunal, to whom the writ was well directed, and who could obey it though the individual members were changed.

That the grounds on which the mayor and assessors refused to revise the burgess list in the one case, and hear the objections in the other, were untenable, and amounted, not to an erroneous exercise of jurisdiction, but to a refusal to adjudicate.

That there was no objection to the form of the writ in the St. N. case, as it commanded the performance of the whole of that part of the duty which appeared to be unperformed.

Peremptory mandamus awarded in both cases.

MANDAMUS directed to the mayor and assessors of the city and borough of Rochester. The suggestions of the writ were: that the city and borough of *Rochester is one of the boroughs in Schedule A. to stat. 5 & 6 W. 4, c. 76; that the parish of Strood is [*911 partly within the said city and borough; and that, after stats. 7 W. 4

& 1 Vict. c. 78, and 16 & 17 Vict. c. 79, to wit, on the 5th of September, 1856, the overseers of the parish of Strood did duly make out an alphabetical list of all persons who were entitled to be enrolled in the burgess roll of that year in respect of property within that part of the parish, &c. ; that the said list was duly signed by the overseers and delivered to the town clerk ; that a Court was duly holden on the 13th of October, 1856, for the purpose of revising the burgess lists before the mayor and assessors ; that the said burgess list for the said portion of the parish of Strood contained the names of John Cobb and 167 other persons, as persons entitled to be enrolled in the burgess roll; that at the said Court the said burgess list was produced by the town clerk ; that, at the time of the production of the said list, it was objected that a copy thereof had not been by the said town clerk caused to be fixed in or near the outer door of the town hall, or in some public and conspicuous place within the city and borough, on every day during the week next preceding the 15th of September, 1856; and that it was thereupon proved that such copy had been caused to be fixed on the outer door of the town hall on the 9th of September, 1856; and that, on hearing the said objection and proof, the mayor and assessors wholly refused to revise the said list, and the said list was thereupon wholly rejected; by means whereof the names of John Cobb and the others have not been enrolled in the burgess roll. The writ then commanded the mayor and assessors of the city and borough of *Rochester
*912] immediately to hold a Court and revise the said list of the parish of Strood made on the 5th of September, 1856, or to show cause to the contrary. The writ was tested on the 26th of January, 1857.

Return of the mayor : that he was not mayor at the time when the said Court in the writ mentioned was holden, nor was the same holden before him, but that he was first elected and appointed and first became mayor on the 10th of November, 1856; and that he was willing and desirous, if he could by law do so, to hold a court and revise the said list, &c., as by the writ commanded. Demurrer. Joinder.

Return of Thomas French, one of the assessors : that his power and duties as assessor were conferred and imposed on him by the Acts of Parliament in the writ mentioned, and that he was advised and did submit that he was not bound by the common law of the land, or by the said or any other Acts of Parliament, to hold a court and revise the said list as by the said writ commanded ; and that the other assessor, to whom the writ was directed, refused to, and would not, concur or join with him in this answer, although requested. Demurrer. Joinder.

The case was argued on a previous day in this Term.(a)

Hugh Hill, for the Crown.—The real question is whether the mandamus is sufficient. By The Municipal Corporation Act (stat. 5 & 6 W. 4, c. 76, s. 15), on the 5th of September in every year the overseers of the poor of every parish wholly or in part within any borough shall make out an alphabetical *list, to be called "The Burgess [*913 List," of all persons entitled to be enrolled in "The Burgess Roll" of that year in respect of property within such parish; and the overseers shall sign such burgess lists, and deliver the same to the town clerk on the said 5th of September in every year, and shall keep a true copy of such lists, to be perused by any person, without payment of any fee, at all reasonable hours between the 5th and 15th days of September in every year; and the town clerk shall cause copies to be printed, and shall cause a copy of all such lists to be fixed on or near the outer door of the town hall, or in some public and conspicuous situation within the borough, on every day during the week next preceding the 15th day of September in every year. By sect. 17, every person whose name shall have been omitted in any such burgess list, and who shall claim to have his name inserted therein, shall, on or before the 15th day of September in every year, give notice thereof to the town clerk in writing; and every town clerk shall include the names of all persons so claiming to be inserted on the burgess list in a list, and shall cause copies of such lists, and also lists of persons objected to, to be fixed on or near the outer door of the town hall, or in some public and conspicuous situation within such borough, during the eight days next preceding the 1st day of October in every year. By sect. 18, the mayor and two assessors shall hold an open court within such borough for the purpose of revising the said burgess lists at some time between the 1st day of October inclusive and the 15th day of October inclusive in every year; and the town clerk shall, at the opening of the court, produce the said lists, and a copy of the lists of the persons claiming, and of the persons objected to, so made out *as aforesaid; and [*914 the overseers, &c., shall attend, and shall answer on oath all such questions as the Court may put to them touching the burgess lists; and he mayor shall insert in such lists the name of every person who shall be proved to be entitled to be inserted therein. By sect. 19, every mayor holding any court under that Act for the revision of the said lists shall have power to adjourn the same from time to time, so that no such adjourned court shall be held after the 15th day of October in any year. By sect. 22, the burgess lists, revised and signed, shall be delivered by the mayor to the town clerk, who shall keep the same, and shall cause the said burgess lists to be fairly and truly copied into one general alphabetical list in a book, and shall cause such books to be completed on or before the 22d day of October in every year; and every such book, in which the said burgess lists shall have been copied, shall be the burgess roll of the burgesses of such borough at any election which may take place in such borough between the 1st day of November inclusive in the year wherein such burgess roll shall have been made and the 1st day of November in the succeeding year.

By sect. 48, if any mayor or assessor, who shall be in office at the time herein appointed for the revision by them of the burgess list under this Act, shall neglect or refuse to revise such burgess list, every such mayor, &c., shall forfeit and pay 100l. The intention of the Legislature is that these enactments should be directory, and not imperative. The language is affirmative only; there is no enactment that any of the proceedings shall be void, if not carried out according to the provisions; and there is a penalty imposed for disobedience of the directions. *915] According to the ordinary canons of *construction, these are reasons for holding enactments to be only directory. There is also a reason more peculiar to this class of cases, which has been styled ex necessitate, founded on the inconvenience and injustice of any other interpretation to persons affected by negligence over which they have no control. If the enactments were not held to be directory only, and the present remedy were held to be inapplicable, the voters would be disfranchised without redress. For a mandamus to insert the name could not be granted under stat. 5 & 6 W. 4, c. 76; In the matter of The Mayor of Hythe, 5 A. & E. 832 (E. C. L. R. vol. 31); nor under stat. 7 W. 4 & 1 Vict. c. 78, s. 24, because here no person's claim was rejected, nor any name expunged at the revision of the burgess roll, but the mayor and assessors refused to revise the burgess list for the parish. These grounds of construction have been recognised in many cases. By stat. 43 Eliz. c. 2, s. 1, the churchwardens and four, three, or two substantial householders, "to be nominated yearly in Easter week, or within one month after Easter, under the hand and seal of two or more justices," shall be called overseers; and, by sect. 10, if there happen to be no such nomination, then every justice dwelling within the division, where such default of nomination shall happen, shall forfeit 5l. In Rex v. Sparrow, 2 Str. 1123, S. C. 7 Mod. 393, it was held that a mandamus to justices to appoint overseers, according to stat. 43 Eliz. c. 2, tested in June, in a year in which Easter was on the 22d of April, was good. The Court held that the statute was only directory, on the grounds that the Legislature, by imposing a penalty for default, recognised the probability of *it, and yet only *916] awarded a punishment; and that the parish was intended to have overseers, and ought not to suffer for the justices' neglect. In Rex v. Birmingham, 8 B. & C. 29 (E. C. L. R. vol. 15), it was held that stat. 4 G. 4, c. 76, s. 16, is directory only; although it in terms enacts that the consent of certain parties to a marriage is thereby required for the marriage. In Rex v. The Mayor of Norwich, 1 B. & Ad. 310 (E. C. L. R. vol. 20), a local Act (7 & 8 G. 4, c. xxix.) provided that the mayor, &c., at an assembly to be held within three calendar months before the 4th of May in each succeeding year, should elect twenty persons to be guardians of the poor; and on the Monday in Easter week in every succeeding year there should be elected for each parish an additional number of persons to be guardians of the poor, amounting in the whole to forty-eight; and the several persons so elected should enter upon the office of guardian on the 4th of May: proviso that, in case of default of such election, the other guardians might proceed as if the elections had taken place: it was held that the clause fixing the time of election was directory only; and that, the mayor, &c., having neglected to elect within the three months, a mandamus should issue to compel them to elect. The ground of the judgment was, that the main intention of the Legislature clearly was that there should be a certain number of guardians. In Regina v. Mayor of Harwich, 1 E. & B. 617 (E. C. L. R. vol. 72), a mandamus, by virtue of the ordinary jurisdiction of the Court, was issued in Michaelmas Term, 1852, commanding the then mayor and assessors to revise the list of burgesses so far as regarded the vote of one person, on the ground that the mayor and assessors at the previous registration *had wrongly held that a notice of objection was bad, and had [*917 therefore refused to entertain the objection. The cases of Pearse v. Morrice, 2 A. & E. 84, 96 (E. C. L. R. vol. 29), Cole v. Green, 6 M. & Gr. 872, 890 (E. C. L. R. vol. 43), Morgan v. Parry, 17 Com. B. 834 (E. C. L. R. vol. 84), are also in point. In them the principle was recognised that such enactments are directory only, unless there be a clause enacting that, in case of disobedience, the transaction should be null and void. The case of Regina v. The Mayor of Lichfield, 1 Q. B. 458 (E. C. L. R. vol. 41), will be relied on, to show that the proper remedy in this case was to proceed under stat. 7 W. 4 & 1 Vict. c. 78, s. 24: but the judgment of the Court in that case was made to depend upon the assumption that the claim of the applicant had been rejected at the revision, whereas here the mayor and assessors refused to entertain the subject at all at the revision. The case of Regina v. Deputies of Freemen of Leicester, 15 Q. B. 671 (E. C. L. R. vol. 69), is an authority in favour of the propriety of the mandamus in this case. In Regina v. Mayor of Dartmouth(a) the powers of the *Court, which are now claimed, were exercised without objec- [*918 tion. It cannot be successfully argued that the mandamus is directed to the wrong mayor; for the former person who held the office

(a) The mayor and assessors of Dartmouth refused to revise the burgess lists for the parish of Tounstal in that borough for the year 1853, on grounds which appear in Seale v. The Queen, in error (Trinity Vacation, June 17, 1857, 8 E. & B.). This Court, in Hilary Term, 1854, awarded a mandamus in terms similar to that in the principal case. The mayor and one assessor made a return that they were unable to obey the writ because the other assessor refused to concur with them in holding a Court. No return was made by the other assessor. Kinglake, Serjt., in Easter Term, 1854, obtained a rule Nisi to set aside this return as frivolous and a contempt of Court. In Trinity Term, 1854 (June 8th), Butt showed cause on affidavits, by which it appeared that the now mayor and the assessor who joined in the return were of the party opposed to the late mayor Sir Henry Seale and the other assessor, and bonâ fide wished the Court to be held. Per Curiam (Lord Campbell, C. J., Wightman and Crompton, Js.): A peremptory mandamus to the mayor and assessors must be awarded. No further mention of the case was made in Court.

is functus officio; but the office is in the nature of a corporation sole, and has a continuous existence.

Sir *F. Thesiger*, for the assessor, contrà.—The enactments are imperative. The intention is clear, that the whole revision should be completed within the given period. The object of all the enactments is that there should be a complete register ready for use from the 1st of November in the year of the registration to the 1st of November in the succeeding year. In order to accomplish that object, there is a time specified for each step in the process of registration, and then a time stated, after which it is expressly enacted that no court shall be held. Thus, by sect. 22 of stat. 5 & 6 W. 4, c. 76, the burgess roll is to be made up complete on or before the 22d of October, in order that it may be used as the register of voters at every election from and after the 1st of November. By sects. 15 and 17 the preliminary steps are to be taken by specified days. By sect. 18, the mayor and assessors are to hold the Courts of revision between the 1st and the 15th of October. By sect. 19, the mayor is prohibited from adjourning any such Court beyond the 15th of October. The multiplicity of Acts to be done, each at a specified time, excludes the supposition that time is not of the essence of the enactments. There is further a negative and prohibitory clause, which is decisive that the enactments are imperative as to time. There was another remedy for the claimants. They should have applied for the *mandamus given by stat. 7 W. 4 & 1 Vict. c. 78, s. 24. The claims were in fact rejected. They were preferred at the revision: and the mayor and assessors, having heard evidence as to them, refused to insert the names in the burgess list. They exercised jurisdiction: Regina v. Sneyd, 9 Dowl. P. C. 1001. The case, therefore, was one in which there was no remedy before the late statute: In re The Mayor of Hythe, 5 A. & E. 882 (E. C. L. R. vol. 31). But it is the case remedied by the statute: Regina v. The Mayor of Lichfield, 1 Q. B. 453 (E. C. L. R. vol. 41). This Court has acted on the assumption that persons in the position of the claimants were entitled to redress under the stat. 7 W. 4 & 1 Vict. c. 78, s. 24, as being persons whose names had been rejected from the burgess roll: Regina v. The Mayor of Rochester.(a) The cases relied on by the other side are not authorities in this case; because the point, which is now taken, that the

*919]

(a) In Michaelmas Term, 1856, *Macnamara* obtained a rule nisi for a mandamus commanding the mayor of Rochester to insert on the burgess roll the names of ninety-seven persons, whose names were included in the lists of the parishes of Strood, St. Nicholas, and Fridsbury; which lists had been rejected by the mayor and assessors at the revision.

In Hilary Term, 1857 (January 30th), *J. W. Huddleston*, for the mayor then in office, showed cause on an affidavit stating that on inquiry he was satisfied that ninety-four of the ninety-seven claimants were entitled, and that three were not; and that he was desirous to do what the Court thought right. [Lord CAMPBELL, C. J.—No cause is shown as to the ninety-four; the rule must be absolute as to them.] *Macnamara* did not press his rule as to the other three.

Per Curiam. (Lord Campbell, C. J., Coleridge, Wightman, and Crompton, Js.)—Rule absolute as to all but three.

proper remedy is under stat. 7 W. 4 & 1 Vict. c. 78, s. 24, was not in them brought before the Court. The present mayor has no authority or jurisdiction to hold a revision Court for the purpose required. The Court will not order him by mandamus to do that which he has no legal power to do.

J. W. Huddleston, for the mayor, stated that that officer desired to submit to the judgment of the Court. [*920

Hugh Hill was heard in reply.　　　　　　　　*Cur. adv. vult.*(a)

(a) Reported by W. B. Brett, Esq.

The QUEEN v. The Mayor and Assessors of ROCHESTER.

(In the matter of the Parish of ST. NICHOLAS.)

For syllabus, see ante, p. 910.

MANDAMUS tested 26th January, 1857. Suggestions that the parish of St. Nicholas was a parish within the borough of Rochester: that, on 15th September, 1856, one William Lucas was inserted in a burgess list for the city and borough: that twenty persons named were persons whose names were included in the burgess list for the parish of St. Nicholas, which had been duly made out according to stat. 5 & 6 W. 4, c. 76. That Lucas objected to those persons; and, after 5th September, and before 15th September, 1856; "gave to the town clerk of the said borough notices of such his several objections in writing according to the form No. 3, in Schedule (D.) to" (stat. 5 & 6 W. 4, c. 76), "or to the like effect, by leaving the same with the man servant of the said town clerk at his, the town clerk's, then residence situate in the said borough," and gave notice to each of the parties objected to. That a court was duly holden by the mayor and assessors for revising the list for the parish of St. Nicholas. That the list was produced by the town clerk; and, at the *same time, the written notices of objection by Lucas were produced by the town clerk: and that it [*921 was objected "that the said notices of objection were bad and invalid because they had not been delivered personally to the said town clerk:" that therefore the mayor and assessors "then wholly refused to hear or consider the objections of the said William Lucas:" by means whereof the names objected to remained on the list and got on the burgess roll. The mandatory part of the writ was, that "you do, without delay, hold a court and revise the list of the burgesses of the said city and borough, so far as relates to the names and votes of" (the several names were set out), "being persons objected to as not being entitled to be enrolled on the list of burgesses of the said city and borough for the parish of St. Nicholas." Return by the mayor: that he was not mayor at the time the Court was holden, but first became so on 9th November, 1856; and was willing and desirous, if by law he could do so, to hold a court and revise the list.(*a*) Demurrer. Joinder. Return by Thomas French, one of the assessors: that he had not by law power to hold the Court.(*a*) Demurrer. Joinder.

Hugh Hill, in this Term,(*b*) argued for the prosecution.—The mandatory part of the writ follows the same form as that adopted in *Regina v. Mayor of Harwich*, 1 E. & B. 617 (E. C. L. R. vol. 72). The objection made before the mayor and assessors was untenable; there is

*922] nothing to require personal service *on the town clerk. (Sir *F. Thesiger*, contrà, admitted this to be so.) Then the other points are precisely the same as those in the case of *Regina v. Mayor of Rochester* (Parish of Strood), ante, p. 910.

Sir *F. Thesiger*, for the assessor.—It is impossible to obey the writ. The lists have long since ceased to be of any value; the names have been placed on a burgess roll, over which the mayor and assessors have no control. The remedy is by mandamus under stat. 7 W. 4 & 1 Vict. c. 78, s. 24. The mayor and assessors are not a body corporate: but, even if they are considered a standing tribunal, the time when they could act with effect is long past. [Lord CAMPBELL, C. J. —I have, in my experience, before The Municipal Corporation Reform Act, known frequent instances in which litigation as to the right to an annual corporate office has been protracted till after the term of the office had expired. The real question is only whether time is of the essence of the provisions of the statute.] Then, there is another objection: here the mayor and assessors had, under 5 & 6 W. 4, c. 76, s. 18, to hear objections where the name "shall have been duly objected to." That gives jurisdiction to inquire whether the objections were duly made. They have bonâ fide, though erroneously, decided that the name has not been duly objected to. The mandamus is to compel them to decide the other way.

J. W. Huddleston, for the mayor, expressed his desire to submit to the judgment of the Court.

*923] *Hugh Hill*, in reply.—There is no remedy here under *stat. 7 W. 4 & 1 Vict. c. 78, s. 24; for no name has been expunged. This refusal to hear was a declining to exercise the jurisdiction, under the erroneous supposition that the preliminary form was required, when it was not. That is not an erroneous exercise of jurisdiction, but a refusal to exercise it: *Regina v. Deputies of Freemen of Leicester*, 15 Q. B. 671 (E. C. L. C. vol. 69). *Cur. adv. vult.*

Lord CAMPBELL, C. J., on a subsequent day in this Term (June 12th), delivered judgment in both cases.

(*a*) The returns were identical in form with those in *Regina v. The Mayor and Assessors of Rochester* (Parish of Strood), in the report of which case they are set out more fully, ante, p. 912.

(*b*) June 8th. Before Lord Campbell, C. J., Coleridge, Wightman, and Crompton, Js.

The QUEEN *v.* The Mayor and Assessors of ROCHESTER.

(In the matter of the Parish of STROOD.)

The question which we have to decide upon this demurrer is, whether the writ of mandamus is sufficient in point of law; for the mayor and the assessor, who have made a return, traverse none of the allegations in the writ; and they aver nothing beyond what we must have judicially taken notice of.

The defendants' counsel admits that the mayor and assessors, who were in office in October, 1856, were guilty of a default in not revising the burgess list; the objection made by them that it had not been fixed on the outer door of the town hall, or in some public and conspicuous place within the city, on every day during the week next preceding 15th September, being untenable; but he contends that the writ is bad because it is tested on the *26th day of January, 1857, and requires a revision to take place after the 15th day of October, 1856.   [*924

The first question which arises is, whether, by stat. 5 & 6 W. 4, c. 76, the enactment upon this subject is directory only? There are no annulling words in the statute, and no words alleged to be negative except in sect. 18, which says that the court for the revision of the lists shall be held " at some time between the 1st day of October inclusive and the 15th day of October inclusive in every year." But, where such an act is required to be done for the public good, and there has been a wrongful omission to do it, a serious inconvenience will arise from its not being done, this Court has been considered to have the power of ordering it to be done, under the prerogative writ of mandamus, while practically it may be done for the benefit of the public. Of this we have a well known instance in Rex *v.* Sparrow, 2 Str. 1123, where, overseers of the poor not having been appointed for a parish, as the statute requires, "in Easter week, or within one month after Easter," a mandamus was granted after the expiration of that time to justices to appoint overseers for that parish: and the appointment, having been made, was solemnly adjudged to be valid. This decision has been frequently recognised and acted upon.

There can be no doubt that for the public good, and to effectuate the intention of the Legislature, the revision of the list, if practicable, ought still to take place; otherwise all who are entitled to be on the burgess roll within a large section of the city of Rochester must be disfranchised for a whole year; a councillor cannot be lawfully elected for a particular ward; and *the administration of the affairs of the city may be thrown into confusion. There is no other mode,   [*925 besides that prescribed by the mandamus, in which the names of those who were in the overseers' list, handed to the town clerk, can be put

upon the burgess roll.   Before stat. 7 W. 4 & 1 Vict. c. 78, this Court
had no power whatever to order by mandamus the name of the person
entitled to be upon the burgess roll to be put upon it; In re The Mayor
of Hythe, 5 A. & E. 832 (E. C. L. R. vol. 31); and that statute gives
us the power only in favour of " a person whose claim shall have been
rejected, or name expunged, at the revision of the burgess roll," i. e. a
person whose claim to be upon the burgess roll has been examined and
adjudicated upon, and, being on the list of claims, has been rejected;
or, being in the overseers' list, has been expunged.   But, at the Court
held on the 13th of October, the mayor and assessors refused to examine
or to adjudge upon the claims of any individual in the overseers' list,
on the ground that they had no jurisdiction to do so, the list not having
been fixed every day for a week on some public place within the city
of Rochester.

The further objection is made that the mandatory part of the present
writ cannot now be obeyed, because the mayor, who made default, is no
longer in office.   But the mandamus is directed to the mayor and
assessors for the city of Rochester; and there always are such functionaries: although not a corporation, they constitute a standing and
perpetual tribunal within the city as much as the town council; and
they are now competent to do what ought to have been done by the
mayor and assessors on the 13th of October last.

*926]   *Next, a difficulty is raised by observing that the revision of
         the list is one of a series of proceedings for which particular
times are appointed in the Act of Parliament.   But, although some
inconvenience might have been experienced in conducting the revision
in January, 1857, when the writ issued, no impossibility was pointed
out to completing the revision nunc pro tunc, and adjusting the burgess
roll according to the rights of the claimants.   The inconvenience which
may be experienced, in doing the act after the time specified in an Act
of Parliament, must be weighed against the detriment which may arise
to individuals and to the public from the act not being done at all; and
an inference may be drawn from that comparison with regard to the
intention of the Legislature to permit the act to be done after the time
has expired.

This Court has exercised, without question, the same power with
respect to other Acts of Parliament, as the election of guardians of the
poor for the city of Norwich under a local Act of Parliament: Rex *v.*
The Mayor of Norwich, 1 B. & Ad. 310 (E. C. L. R. vol. 20).

In Regina *v.* Mayor of Harwich, 1 E. & B. 617 (E. C. L. R. vol.
72), this Court, under the Municipal Corporation Act, 5 & 6 W. 4, c.
76, after the time mentioned in the Act for the revision of the burgess
list by the mayor and assessors had expired, directed a mandamus to
the mayor and assessors to revise the list of burgesses, so far as
regarded the name of a particular individual to whom objection had

been made, and on whose case they had, on insufficient grounds, refused to adjudicate. That writ issued and was obeyed. The counsel who there resisted the *mandamus certainly did not rely upon want [*927 of jurisdiction in the Court to award it; but he was a gentleman of great learning and experience: and the understanding seems to have generally prevailed in Westminster Hall that, if, for any insufficient reason, the mayor and assessors have refused to revise the overseers' list, or to adjudicate upon any claim or objection to a name being on the burgess roll, they may, after the time for the regular revision, be compelled by mandamus to do so. Accordingly, in a very much contested case similar writs of mandamus were directed to the mayor and assessors of the borough of Dartmouth, without the jurisdiction of the Court to grant them being questioned.

In the present case the application was made for the mandamus as soon as well could be after the default of the mayor and assessors. The Court ought not to expose any of the Queen's subjects to an attachment by ordering them by mandamus to do that which is impossible: but, as we are of opinion that this mandamus may be, and ought to have been, obeyed, we consider ourselves bound to give

Judgment for the Crown.

The QUEEN v. The Mayor and Assessors of ROCHESTER.

(In the matter of the Parish of ST. NICHOLAS.)

This case differs from that of which we have just disposed, in commanding the mayor and assessors to hold a Court and revise the list of the burgesses of the city of Rochester, so far as relates to the names of certain persons objected to as not having been entitled to be *re- [*928 tained on the list of burgesses for the parish of St. Nicholas in the said city, made by the overseers of the said parish. The mayor and assessors had refused to consider any of the objections to the persons in the overseers' list, because the list of objections which had been left with a servant of the town clerk at the town clerk's house, and which was produced to them at the revision by the town clerk, had not been personally served upon the town clerk. On the part of the present mayor and assessors, the defendants, it was admitted that this objection could not be supported; but it was contended that the impossibility of obeying the mandamus is here more striking than in the former case, where an addition was to be made to the burgess roll; whereas here, on giving effect to well founded objections, names may be taken from the burgess roll. But still the mayor and assessors may well do what they are commanded to do; and therefore they can be in no danger of an attachment. If we saw that public mischief would be the consequence, still we should think that the proceeding ought not to be commanded : but we think, on the contrary, that, if this long list of names for the parish of St. Nicholas objected to, or any of them, are improperly upon the burgess roll, right will be done by now removing them from it, instead of allowing them to usurp the franchise for the remainder of the current year.   It will be recollected that this is the very same form of mandamus as in Regina *v.* Mayor of Harwich : and whethèr the list is to be revised with respect to one name only, or to fifty, if the mayor and assessors have, upon a frivolous preliminary objection, *refused to adjudicate, must be wholly immaterial. It

*929]   would indeed be lamentable if there were not an equal remedy by commanding the mayor and assessors to do their duty for the purpose of preventing names being improperly put upon the burgess roll as to procure the insertion in the burgess roll of names improperly excluded from it.   But, if the resistance to these writs of mandamus were to succeed, a temptation would be held out to the mayor and assessors in every borough to insure a majority for their party during the ensuing year, by refusing to revise the overseers' list, or by refusing to consider the list of objections, on such a pretext as that the names are, or are not, arranged alphabetically ; which would not be more frivolous than the pretext that the list of objections had not been personally served upon the town clerk.   Judgment for the Crown.

WILLIAMS *v.* LEWIS and Others.   *June 8.*

A cause stood for trial at Nisi Prius. The action was for rent in arrear. One issue was on a plea of an eviction by P. by title paramount to that of plaintiff. P. was not a party to the cause, but claimed the reversion in the premises held by defendant. P. became, by parol, party to an arrangement, by which the matter was to be settled by a reference of the cause to an arbitrator, who was to determine, inter alia, on what terms the plaintiff's interest in the premises should be purchased, and in what proportion P. should contribute to the payment, and to the amount of the damages. An order of Nisi Prius was drawn up, incorporating these terms, and containing a provision that P. should become a party to the reference : it was not expressed to be drawn up by his consent ; but it was shown by other evidence that it was in fact by his consent. P. afterwards refused to be bound by this order.

Held that, having submitted to the order in fact, he was bound by it, and could not retract ; and that the Court had jurisdiction to enforce obedience in a summary manner.

HUGH HILL, in Easter Term, on behalf of the plaintiff, obtained a rule calling on the defendants and John Powell to show cause why it should not be referred to one of the Masters of this Court to settle the terms on which a Judge's order should be drawn up, *pursuant

*930]   to an order of Nisi Prius made in this cause, and why a Judge's order should not be drawn up accordingly.

From the affidavits on both sides it appeared, in substance, that the action was by the plaintiff, as executrix of a deceased termor, against the defendants as testator's sublessees, to recover rent in arrear. The pleas raised, as a defence, an eviction by John Powell, by title paramount to that of the testator; which title was put in issue: and the cause was entered for trial at the Shrewsbury Spring Assizes, 1856. A similar action was pending for subsequent rent, but had not been entered for trial. At the assizes, Mr. Powell, accompanied by the attorney for the defendants, called on the plaintiff's attorney, and proposed an arrangement on the terms, amongst others, that the interest of the plaintiff, who claimed under a lease dated in 1838, should be given up for a fair price to be ascertained by an arbitrator. The plaintiff's counsel were consulted by the plaintiff's attorney; and, by their advice, he accepted the proposal, and agreed that the cause should be referred by order of Nisi Prius. Mr. Powell subsequently came to the plaintiff's attorney, accompanied by Powell's own solicitor, and requested that some alterations should be made in the order proposed, which were made at his request; and, finally, an order of Nisi Prius was drawn up as follows.

" Shropshire, to wit. At the Assizes," &c.

" Williams	It is ordered by the Court, by and with the
v.	consent of the parties, their counsel and attor-
Lewis and another.	neys, that a verdict be entered for the plaintiff.

Damages 405*l.* Costs 40*s.*

*" It is likewise ordered, with the like consent, that the other [*931 action between the said parties, and all other matters in differ- ence between them, be referred to Thomas Bros, Esquire, Barrister at Law, who shall determine what sum shall be paid by the defendants to the plaintiff for the value of the lease of 1838, so far as regards the premises, for the rent of which this action is brought. The lease by Martin Williams and John Williams to be given up. Such order of reference to contain all usual terms. John Powell, Esquire, of Brecon, to be a party to the reference; and the arbitrator to determine in what proportions the defendants and the said John Powell, Esquire, shall contribute, as well to the amount of the verdict as to the sum awarded to be paid and the costs of the actions; and, in so doing, the arbitrator is to consider the effect of the leases granted by the said John Powell, Esquire, to the defendants Richard Lewis and Messrs. Chafers. For the purpose of this reference, but not further or otherwise, the lease of 1838 to be taken to be a valid and subsisting lease. It is likewise ordered, with the like consent, that a Judge's order shall be drawn up. And, lastly, it is ordered, with the like consent, that either of the said parties shall be at liberty to move Her Majesty's Court of Queen's Bench that this order may be made a rule of the said Court. By the Court. E. A. WILDE; Associate."

After this, the defendants and Powell refused to concur in settling a Judge's order of reference; and, on a summons being taken out calling on them to settle it, they opposed it before Bramwell, B., on the ground that Powell was taken by surprise when he assented to the order of

Nisi Prius, and that the lease of 1838, which, by the terms of that
order, was to be taken as valid, had *in fact, as he alleged, been
forfeited, of which at the time he was ignorant.   It was not
alleged that any fraud had been practised to induce him to enter into
the order of Nisi Prius; but it was deposed that Powell's solicitor had
advised him not to become a party to the submission without further
inquiry as to the facts; but then Powell disregarded his advice.   The
learned Baron refused to make any order, without prejudice to an
application to the Court.   On the affidavits, the testimony differed as
to the extent to which Mr. Powell was interested in the action, the
plaintiffs representing him as substantially defendant, whilst his statement was that he attended the assizes merely as a witness, and under a
moral obligation to assist one of the actual defendants who had attorned
to him; but it was not at all in dispute that he claimed an interest in
the property.   On the affidavits enough of the title was disclosed to
show that the validity of the lease of 1838 to the plaintiff's testator
was bonâ fide in controversy between the plaintiff and Powell, who had
purchased the interest of the person who was alleged to have created
that term.   The order of Nisi Prius had been made a rule of Court;
and this rule was drawn up on reading that rule.

*932]

. *Knowles, Dowdeswell,* and *R. V. Williams,* showed cause for Powell.—
The lease of 1838, it sufficiently appears, was not valid.   [Lord CAMP-
BELL, C. J.—On this rule we are not to inquire as to that.   All that
we need to determine is whether Powell is bound by the order of Nisi
Prius.]   It is an application to the equitable jurisdiction of the Court,
in the nature of an application to enforce a specific performance.
Equity will not enforce an agreement made under a mistake.   Besides,
*Powell was not bound by the order of Nisi Prius; he was not
a party to the cause; and the order is not his submission in
writing so as to be irrevocable under stat. 3 & 4 W. 4, c. 42, s. 39.   It
is doubtful if it is, for this purpose, the submission even of the parties
in the action: Anderson *v.* Coxeter, 1 Str. 301, Regina *v.* Hardey,
14 Q. B. 529 (E. C. L. R. vol. 68).

*933]

Hugh Hill and *J. Gray* were not called upon to support the rule.

Lord CAMPBELL, C. J.—I am of opinion that this rule must be made
absolute.   It calls upon this Court to enforce specific performance
of an agreement entered into by Powell and incorporated in an order
at Nisi Prius.   If a person, not a party to a cause, deliberately enters
into such an agreement, and becomes a party to an order of Nisi Prius,
the Court will, unless he shows cause to the contrary, enforce the order
of Nisi Prius in the manner now pursued.   Such has always been the
practice since I have known anything about the practice of these Courts.
Then, in this case, it appears that Mr. Powell advisedly and deliberately
entered into this agreement, even against the remonstrance of his

attorney. He supposed the agreement was for his advantage; if it was not so, that is not a mistake such as to entitle him to relief.

COLERIDGE, J.—It would be very dangerous to do anything that might raise a doubt whether a third party deliberately coming in and submitting to an order at Nisi Prius is bound thereby. I never before heard it *questioned: and every one must be aware that the practice is common and beneficial. Still I am far from saying [*934 that, if it appeared that advantage had been taken of the party, it might not be a ground on which the Court would refuse to enforce the order; but no such case is made out here. All that appears is, that on consideration Mr. Powell thinks that he might have made a more advantageous arrangement.

ERLE, J.—Mr. Powell assented to come in under an order of Nisi Prius; and I am of opinion that he thereby became bound by what is in that order. He has submitted to the jurisdiction of the Court; and his obedience may be enforced by attachment. His position is like that of a party coming in to show cause against a rule, and so submitting to the jurisdiction of the Court. And, if we can enforce this order, no reason is shown why we should not do so.

CROMPTON, J.—I am of the same opinion. The question is in effect whether an order of Nisi Prius to which a third party has submitted may, against him, be made a rule of Court. The general rule is correctly laid down in Watson on Awards, p. 3 (3d ed.) " In referring a cause by rule of Court, or order of a Judge, or at Nisi Prius, other matters than the subject-matter of the action may be included in the reference; so, in like manner, strangers to the suit who are interested may be made, with their consent, parties to the rule or order; and such persons, so made parties to the submission, as to all matters contained in the submission, will be bound by the award, in the same manner as the parties to the action." In the present case the order would have been *more formally drawn up had it stated the consent of Powell as well as of the parties; but that is not material, as we have [*935 evidence enough that he did in fact consent. Then, the Court having jurisdiction to enforce the submission, is there any reason why it should not be enforced? I agree that, if there were a strong case of mistake made out, the Court might refuse to exercise its summary jurisdiction to enforce the order; though I think we hardly should do so if the facts were short of those under which, if money had passed, it might be recovered back as money had and received. Nothing approaching to such a case is shown here.   Rule absolute.

The QUEEN *v.* The Justices of STAFFORDSHIRE.   *June* 10.

On appeal the Quarter Sessions made an order confirming an order of justices subject to a case. The order of Sessions was silent as to costs. The appellants abandoned the case; the respondents applied to a subsequent Sessions, who made an order, stating that the original order was confirmed, and giving the respondents costs.

Held, that the subsequent Sessions had no jurisdiction to deal with the order made by the prior Sessions : and a rule was made absolute to bring up the second order, on certiorari, to be quashed.

J. W. HUDDLESTON, in this Term, obtained a rule to show cause why a certiorari should not issue to bring up an order of Quarter Sessions, made at the January Quarter Sessions, 1857, for the county of Stafford, for the purpose of quashing it.

The order recited that, in an appeal against an order of two justices, dated 27th April, 1856, adjudging the settlement of a lunatic, sent to an asylum from the parish of Wednesbury, to be in the parish of Monmouth, and ordering the appellants to pay the expenses, in which appeal the guardians of the Monmouth Union and the churchwardens and *936] overseers of Monmouth Parish *were appellants, and the guardians of the Bromwich Union and the churchwardens and overseers of Wednesbury were respondents, the Quarter Sessions of June, 1856, after hearing the merits, ordered that the order of justices appealed against "should be, and the same was then and there, confirmed; but subject to the opinion of Her Majesty's Court of Queen's Bench" upon a special case to be afterwards stated; the order for the special case being granted upon the special application of the counsel for the appellants. The order then proceeded to recite that, on the information of counsel for the appellants, it had been made to appear, to the justices assembled in the Epiphany Sessions, "that the said special case had not been stated or agreed upon; and that the appellants, the said guardians of the poor of the said Monmouth Union and the said churchwardens and overseers of the poor of the said parish of Monmouth, have abandoned their intention of stating or agreeing to the said special case, and of further proceeding in the said appeal;' and that notice of the same had been given by the said appellants to the respondents, the said guardians of the poor of the said West Bromwich Union, and the said churchwardens and overseers of the poor of the said parish of Wednesbury, on the 8th December, 1856. Now, therefore, upon the motion of counsel for the said respondents, and upon proof of notice of the present application having been given by the said respondents to the said appellants, and of the hereinbefore recited order of the said Court of Quarter Sessions holden on the 30th of June, 1856, and after hearing counsel for the said appellants, it was ordered that the said order and adjudication so made by the said justices, and *987] bearing date the 27th of April, 1856, *be, and the same is hereby, absolutely confirmed:" and it ordered the appellants to pay 46*l.*

16*s*., the costs of the appeal. The rule was obtained on the ground that the Sessions of January, 1857, had no jurisdiction to order the payment of costs of the appeal heard before the Sessions of June, 1856.

Scotland now showed cause.—The appellants ought in justice to pay the costs of the appeal; and, as the writ of certiorari is discretionary, the Court will not grant it for the purpose of frustrating justice, even if the order of January was beyond the jurisdiction of the Sessions. But it was not beyond their jurisdiction. The confirmation by the Sessions of June was subject to a case. In Kendall *v.* Wilkinson, 4 E. & B. 680, 690 (E. C. L. R. vol. 82), Lord Campbell, C. J., says: " Rex *v.* The Justices of Pembrokeshire, 2 B. & Ad. 391 (E. C. L. R. vol. 22), shows that the confirmation of an order by Sessions subject to a case leaves the order exactly as it was before the confirmation." If the order is merely interlocutory, requiring a subsequent confirmation after the case is disposed of, the order of January Sessions was required. [CROMPTON, J.—Do you go so far as to say that, even if the first order had confirmed the order of justices with costs, but subject to a case, it would be necessary, on the case not being taken up, to get a fresh order for costs?] It would seem so: the decision subject to a case is, in such circumstances, not a decision: Rex *v.* The Justices of Suffolk, 1 Dowl. P. C. 163. The Sessions are a permanent tribunal: Keen *v.* The Queen, 10 Q. B. 928 (E. C. L. R. vol. 59). [CROMPTON, J.—Is not your position new? There must have been many cases in which a *case has been granted but abandoned; yet I never heard of this proceeding before. It should seem that the confirmation [*938 of an order subject to a case is analogous to a verdict subject to leave to move to enter the verdict otherwise. If no motion is made, the verdict stands. COLERIDGE, J.—According to this practice, the justices hear the case at one Sessions, and the justices at another Sessions, who are not the same individuals, decide as to the costs. They must either decide in ignorance of the merits, or have a fresh trial to determine them.]

J. W. Huddleston was not called upon to argue in support of his rule.

Lord CAMPBELL, C. J.—There is in this case a seeming hardship that the respondents should not have costs; but they lose them by their own default. They should at the June Sessions have asked for the costs; and, if that Sessions in their discretion thought it a fit case for costs, they would have then been awarded in the order confirming the order of justices, subject to the case. But they did not ask for costs; and the order was silent as to them. Had the case been proceeded with, and that order brought up with the case, we could not have confirmed that order with costs of the appeal, but only as it was, that is, silent as to costs. So the respondents have not lost these costs in consequence of the abandonment of the case by the appellants. Then it seems to me that when that order was made the Sessions were *functi officio*. The order was subject to a case; but the Sessions then, as far as they were concerned, confirmed or quashed the order of justices according to what the opinion of this Court might turn out to be. I *989] think *the observation I made in Kendall *v.* Wilkinson, 4 E. & B. 690 (E. C. L. R. vol. 82), as to the effect of Rex *v.* The Justices of Pembrokeshire, 2 B. & Ad. 391 (E. C. L. R. vol. 22), carries that case too far. I think the order subject to a case is in the nature of a judgment Nisi; and, if the order is not brought up with a case by certiorari, it becomes absolute at the end of six months; and, that being so, I think the Sessions had no further jurisdiction as to costs. If the Sessions who hear on the merits and grant the case think it a fit case for costs they should give them; but, if it were necessary, for the purpose of getting costs, to go before a subsequent Sessions and ask for them from justices who do not know what happened before, it would be productive of much expense, and probably of much injustice. Such a course is not required.

COLERIDGE, J.—I am also of opinion that this rule should be absolute. On principle, the subsequent Sessions can have no jurisdiction in this matter. The appeal came before the Sessions in June, who heard it and determined it, and came to no decision as to costs. But their order was subject to the opinion of this Court on some points. Now, if the case had been drawn up, and came before us as it ought, we could not have made a new order giving the costs, but could only have confirmed it as it was; and, in common sense, the order made subject to a case for our opinion, on the case being abandoned, is absolute. It is said, however, that the order ought to go back to Sessions, not to let them exercise any judicial functions as to the order itself, for it is conceded that the order itself is not to be varied, but to exer- *940] cise a *judicial discretion as to whether costs should be given or not. Could anything be devised more inconvenient than to sever the decisions on the merits and as to costs, so as necessarily to have the question as to whether there should be costs decided by persons ignorant whether they ought to be granted or not, or else to have all the expense and inconvenience of a new trial? The first Act giving power to the Sessions to grant costs was I think stat. 8 & 9 W. 3, c. 30, s. 3; and it carefully confines the power to grant costs to the justices at the same Sessions; and many subsequent acts giving costs refer back to this, so as to tie up the power in the same way. The Act giving power to award costs in the present case is stat. 12 & 13 Vict. c. 45, s. 5: this enacts that upon every appeal to the Sessions " the Court before whom the same shall be brought may, if it think fit, order and direct" the unsuccessful party to pay costs. The words of the Act restrict the power to that Court; which is accordant with principle and convenience.

ERLE, J.—I also am of opinion that the subsequent Sessions had no jurisdiction over this order. No doubt the Quarter Sessions is for many purposes a permanent tribunal: but still there are many things that can be done only by a particular Sessions, as the specific tribunal for that thing. Here the Sessions who heard the appeal confirmed the order, and were silent as to costs. That was in legal effect the same as if they had confirmed it expressly without costs. The confirmation was subject to a case; but, so far as this Court did not interfere, it was absolute. That being so, it seems to me that the application to the Epiphany Sessions clearly was an application to them to alter the judgment *of the former Sessions, by rectifying the error which they had [*941 committed in omitting to give costs in a fit case. But the Epiphany Sessions had no jurisdiction to do this.

CROMPTON, J.—It was first said that this was a discretionary writ. That is true: but, when it appears clearly that an order is without jurisdiction, our discretion must be to let the certiorari go. Then I think that it would be very mischievous if parties under such circumstances as these were entitled to go before a subsequent Sessions to ask for costs. I think that they would be equally entitled to go and ask for them if the first Sessions had on deliberation refused them. Lord Tenterden, in Rex v. The Justices of Pembrokeshire, 2 B. & Ad. 391 (E. C. L. R. vol. 22), was speaking in a case where a negotiation about a case was still pending, and where, as I infer, the writ of certiorari had been sued out within the six months, but the case could not be settled. There he throws out that they might enter continuances and hear the appeal: but he cannot have meant that, where one Sessions had heard and decided the appeal, it was to be heard over again by another. It is clear to my mind that, where an order is confirmed subject to a case, if the case is not got the confirmation becomes absolute.   Rule absolute.

---

*PARKER v. WINLOW. *June* 10.   [*942

A memorandum of charter-party was expressed to be made "between P., of the good ship C., and W., agent for E. W. & Son," to whom the ship was to be addressed. It was signed by W. without any restriction.
Held, that W. was personally liable as charterer.
By the charter-party the ship was to proceed "to Plymouth, not higher than T. or N., or as near thereunto as she can safely get, and deliver" her cargo, with certain lay days and demurrage days. The port of Plymouth is a tidal estuary. On the ship's arrival in Plymouth the consignees ordered her to discharge at B., an ordinary landing place in the port of Plymouth, lower than T. or N. At this time the tides were neap: the vessel went as near to B. as she could in that state of the tide, and lay on the sand for some days, till, the tides being higher, she got to B. In an action for demurrage:
Held, that the consignee had the option of naming any ordinary loading place in the port of Plymouth within the limits assigned, and that the lay days did not commence till the vessel reached the place so named. The delay in getting to it being occasioned only in the ordinary course of navigation in a tidal harbour.

ACTION for demurrage of a ship. Plea: Never indebted. Issue thereon.

On the trial, before Martin, B., at the Newcastle Spring Assizes, 1857, it appeared that a memorandum for charter was made and signed by the plaintiff and defendant. It was an ordinary printed form filled up. The material parts are stated below. It bore date at Newcastle, and commenced: " It is this day mutually agreed between Captain W. Parker, of the good ship Celerity, himself master, now lying in the Tyne, and G. W. Winlow, agent for E. Winlow & Son, of Devonport, merchants, that the said ship" should load from the freighters a cargo of coals, " and, being so loaded, shall therewith proceed to Plymouth, not higher than Torpoint or New Passage, or so near thereunto as she may safely get, and deliver the same" on being paid freight. " A keel a day to be allowed for the said merchant (if the ship is not sooner despatched) for delivery. Demurrage over and above the said laying days at 3*l.* per day." " The ship to be addressed to E. Winlow & Son, of Devonport. G. W. WINLOW." G. W. Winlow, whose signature was
*943] attached, *was the defendant; E. Winlow & Son in the memorandum mentioned were persons, distinct from G. W. Winlow, carrying on business at Devonport. The ship took her cargo on board, and arrived in the port of Plymouth, and anchored in the Tamar on the 21st of June; and, on the 22d, the plaintiff reported to E. Winlow & Son, of Devonport, his arrival and readiness to discharge. They ordered the ship to the Brunswick Wharf, Stenhouse, there to discharge. The port of Plymouth includes the tidal estuary of the Tamar, in which, besides the harbour of Plymouth and Devonport, there are several usual landing places, one of which is the Brunswick Wharf, which is below Torpoint and New Passage. In order to reach the Brunswick Wharf it is necessary to cross a mud bank in the Tamar. At the time when the order to discharge at the Brunswick Wharf was given, the tides were neap; and the plaintiff's vessel drew too much water to be able to pass the bank even at high water during those tides. The captain requested E. Winlow & Son to send lighters to take part of the cargo out, so as to enable him to cross the bank: they did not do so. It was not however contended that there was any custom of the port requiring the consignees to furnish lighters: and nothing further appeared to have taken place at this time. The vessel proceeded towards the Brunswick Wharf, and grounded upon the mud bank, where she was fixed and lay till the high tides, when she got to the Brunswick Wharf; and notice was given that she was there ready to discharge on Monday, July 2d. After this there was some delay; but it appeared to. be from the default of the plaintiff. The plaintiff's counsel contended that the lay days commenced on the notice of the arrival of the ship
*944] in the Tamar on 22d June; in which case there *were nine days occupied beyond the lay days. The defendant, besides denying this, contended that the defendant was not the contracting party, and that the action should have been brought against E. Winlow & Son.

The learned Judge directed a verdict for the plaintiff for 27*l*., with leave to move to enter a verdict for the defendant on both grounds : the Court to have power to draw inferences of fact.

Udall, in Easter Term, obtained a rule Nisi accordingly. In this Term,(a)

Temple and *Manisty* showed cause.—The contract is expressly made between the plaintiff and G. W. Winlow; and he signs the contract in his own name without restriction. It is true that he states, on the face of the contract, that he is agent for E. Winlow & Son; but that is quite consistent with his contracting personally. The question always is, Who is the contractor: and, primâ facie, he who says he agrees is the contractor: Cooke *v.* Wilson, 1 Com. B. N. S. 153 (E. C. L. R. vol. 87); Tanner *v.* Christian, 4 E. & B. 591 (E. C. L. R. vol. 82); Lennard *v.* Robinson, 5 E. & B. 125 (E. C. L. R. vol. 85). The second point raises the question of the relative rights of the freighter and shipowner under such a memorandum of charter as the present. The shipowner has bound himself to cause his vessel " to proceed to Plymouth, not higher than Torpoint or New Passage, or so near thereunto as she may safely get, and deliver" the cargo. He did arrive safely in Plymouth, and notified his arrival to the consignees. [Lord CAMPBELL, C. J.— But under this charter-party the place of discharge in Plymouth was to be ascertained. Surely *the persons who were to discharge the cargo had the option of naming any place within the limits [*945 specified in the charter-party.] The right must be subject to some restriction. [Lord CAMPBELL, C. J.—When the order was given to go to the Brunswick Wharf, no objection was taken to it by the master on the ground that the Brunswick Wharf was an improper discharging place. Must it not be taken to be in fact a proper one?] The consignees were not entitled to name a place to which the vessel could not go till the next spring tides: if they were entitled to require the vessel to remain till then, they were equally entitled to name a place to which the vessel could not go till the equinoctial spring tides, and so detain the vessel for months. [CROMPTON, J.—If the charter-party, instead of leaving it to the consignees to select a discharging place in Plymouth, had named the Brunswick Wharf, would the lay days commence before the vessel got there?] They would commence as soon as the vessel got as near to it as she safely could. The contract is not absolute to go to the discharging place; if causes over which the shipowner has no control prevent it, he has complied with his contract: Shield *v.* Wilkins, 5 Exch. 304.† If, having arrived, the commencement of the discharge is prevented without default of the shipowner, the lay days continue to run: Randall *v.* Lynch, 2 Campb. 352, Brown *v.* Johnson, 10 M. & W. 331.† At all events, the lay days commenced when the ship got fixed on the

(a) On June 4th, before Lord Campbell, C. J., Coleridge, Erle, and Crompton, Js.; and on this day, before the same Judges.

mud bank ; she could not then get nearer to Brunswick Wharf : and, if they began then, there is a sum due for demurrage, though the damages should be reduced.

*946] *Udall, in support of the rule.—The contract expressly states that the now defendant is agent for E. Winlow & Son. When the principal is named, the agent is not liable. This is the rule laid down in Story on Agency, sect. 263, citing Lord Erskine, C., in Ex parte Hartop, 12 Ves. 349, 352. [Lord CAMPBELL, C. J.—It is per-. fectly accurate with the qualification which Lord Erskine attaches. He says : "But, for the application of that rule, the agent must name his principal as the person to be responsible."] Then, on the other ground. The shipowner in general binds himself to bring his ship as near as it can safely get to the place of discharge ; and the lay days do not commence till he has done so. A mere arrival at the port is not enough : Brereton v. Chapman, 7 Bing. 559 (E. C. L. R. vol. 20). And he has not arrived as near as he may safely get to the place of discharge as long as he may in the ordinary course of navigation get nearer. If a ship arrives off a bar harbour at low water, she cannot safely get nearer till the tide makes, and must wait for high water ; or, if it be a tidal harbour, and she arrives when it is dry, she must wait till there is water to float her : yet in neither case has she arrived. And it is precisely the same in principle whether he has to wait for high water in an ordinary tide, or for the spring tides. [Lord CAMPBELL, C. J.—That would be so if the discharging place was fixed in the charter-party. But, when the place is to be selected, is it not a reasonable construction of the contract to say that an accessible place must be selected ?] It must be one of the ordinary proper discharging places, no doubt ; and, if the Brunswick Wharf had not been such a place, a remonstrance on
*947] that ground should have been made *at the time when it was named. But it was not even suggested at the trial that it was not such a place.

Lord CAMPBELL, C. J.—Though it is not necessary, in the view which I take of this case, to decide the question whether the defendant bound himself personally by this contract, we ought not to allow any doubt to exist as to our opinion on the construction of such a contract. I can have no doubt myself that the defendant is personally liable. He makes the contract, using apt words to show that he contracts ; and the only ground suggested for rebutting his personal liability is that he says he is agent for another : but he may well contract and pledge his personal liability, though he is agent for another. If he had signed the contract as by procuration for E. Winlow & Son, he might have exempted himself from liability ; but on principle, and on the authorities cited, an agent is liable personally if he is the contracting party ; and he may be so though he names his principal. On this charter-party I think that the contracting parties are the plaintiff and the defendant.

But then, though he is personally liable for the fulfilment of the contract, I think, as the facts are now explained, that there is no claim for demurrage. If, when the ship got fixed on the mud bank, the master had given notice that he was ready to discharge there, it might have been open to him to show that it was the duty of the other party to take the cargo there; and, if he could have shown such to be their duty, the lay days would have commenced. But no such notice was given; there was no suggestion of any custom requiring the consignees to procure lighters; and both sides acted as if they did not contemplate any unloading till the vessel *got up to the wharf. And I think, when [*948 Brunswick Wharf was named as a proper and usual discharging place, the objection to it, if there was any, ought to have been made. It appears to me that the whole was an after thought.

COLERIDGE, J.—I perfectly agree that the defendant is personally liable on this contract; on that point I add nothing. And I think, under the circumstances, that, as Brunswick Wharf was named as the place to which the ship was to proceed and there discharge, and no objection was made, it is a fair inference that the parties understood each other. But, without relying on that, I think that, as by the contract the vessel was to proceed " to Plymouth, not higher than Torpoint or New Passage, or as near thereunto as she may safely get," the freighter had a right to name any proper place of discharge within those limits. As Plymouth is a tidal harbour, the words must bear the meaning of parties contracting with reference to a tidal harbour, who know that, in the ordinary course of navigation, the state of the tide may delay the possibility of getting safely to the destination. The risk of that ordinary delay the shipowner undertakes to bear.

ERLE, J.—I agree that the defendant has bound himself. He says that he is agent for E. Winlow & Sons; but that is not enough to rebut the inference of personal liability arising from the rest of the contract. Then I think that the plaintiff contracted that the ship should go to such place, within the limits, as should be named, provided it was a proper place. It now appears that in fact Brunswick Wharf, which was named, was a *proper place. The plaintiff therefore contracted [*949 to take the ship to that place; and the lay days did not commence till it got there.

CROMPTON, J.—Mere words of description attached to the name of a contractor, such as are used here, saying he is agent for another, cannot limit his liability as contractor. A man, though agent, may very well intend to bind himself; and he does bind himself if he contracts without restrictive words to show that he does not do so personally. It is important that mercantile men should understand that, if they mean to exclude personal recourse against themselves on contracts which they sign, they must use restrictive words, as if they sign per procuration, or use some other words to express that they are not to be personally liable. Then, on the other point, I think that the lay days commenced just as they would have done if the charter-party had expressed from the first that the vessel was to proceed to Brunswick Wharf, or so near thereunto as she could safely get. The ship is to go to Plymouth, a tidal harbour; for the security of the shipowner two points are named; and the vessel is not to be required to go higher than those; but below those points she is to go to some discharging place. I take it that place is to be selected by those who are to discharge her, with this restriction on their choice, that it is to be one of the regular usual discharging places in the port. I do not think that the freighters could require the ship to go to some discharging place not in the regular course of navigation, and only accessible at rare intervals. Then it appears that Brunswick Wharf is a regular place, and is selected, and *950] the ship is to go there. It is a tidal *harbour; and in all tidal harbours a ship is liable to be delayed by the state of the tide. If such a misfortune happens, it is in the regular course of navigation. The ship here, when she lay on the mud bank, was not as near to Brunswick Wharf as she could safely get, and that the event shows; for, in the ordinary and regular course of navigation, she might and did safely get to Brunswick Wharf and there discharge her cargo.

Rule absolute.(a)

(a) See Schilizzi *v.* Derry, 4 E. & B. 873 (E. C. L. R. vol. 82).

In contracts not under seal, if the agent intend to bind his principal and not himself, it will be sufficient if it appear in such contract that he acts *as agent*: Andrews *v.* Estes et al., 2 Fairfield, 267; Shotwell *v.* M'Kown, 2 Southard, 828. It is not sufficient to charge the principal or protect the agent from personal responsibility, merely to describe himself as agent, if the language of the instrument imports a personal contract on his part: Ponts *v.* Stanton, 10 Wendell, 271. See Byles on Bills, note to 4th American edition.

◆

The QUEEN *v.* JAMES LINFORD and three Justices of the County of NORFOLK. *June* 11.

When a relieving officer is surcharged by the auditor of an audit district, and application is made to justices to issue a distress warrant, if the statutable proof of the surcharge be complete, the justices have no power to inquire into the grounds of the surcharge, but must issue the warrant. If they refuse to do so, the Court will compel them by a rule or a *mandamus.*

TOMLINSON, in last Term, obtained a rule calling on James Linford and three justices of the county of Norfolk to show cause why the justices, or two of them, should not issue a distress warrant to levy the sum of 28*l.* 11*s.* 6*d.*, certified by Robert Rising, auditor of the East Norfolk Audit District, to have been disallowed in the accounts of

James Linford, relieving officer of the incorporation of East and West Flegg district, with which he was surcharged, on Linford's goods.

From the affidavits it appeared that the sum in question was disallowed by the auditor; and that, a summons having been taken out before the justices, the certificate of disallowance was produced and proved. The justices determined not to issue the distress warrant, but without assigning any reasons for the refusal. From *what passed before they came to this determination, it was surmised [*951 that they refused because similar payments had been allowed on former audits, and they thought it was hard on the relieving officer to disallow them now.

Hugh Hill and *N. Palmer* now showed cause.—[Lord CAMPBELL, C. J.—It seems to me impossible to contend that the justices have any jurisdiction to review what has been regularly done by the auditor, if it has been properly brought before them. The remedy is given by stat. 7 & 8 Vict. c. 101, ss. 85, 86.] In Regina *v.* Justices of Brecknockshire (a) the Court is understood to have refused a mandamus to the justices, it appearing that the sums were improperly disallowed. [CROMPTON, J.—If it can be shown that the conduct of the justices was occasioned by any improper conduct on the part of the auditor, perhaps we may have a discretion to refuse a mandamus on the ground that it was required only from the improper conduct of the applicant.]

Tomlinson, contrà.—The relieving officer and the justices [*952 have all along been perfectly aware of the grounds on which the auditor has proceeded. If the officer has not appealed it is not the auditor's fault. If the disallowance, though legal, was harsh, there is a remedy under stat. 11 & 12 Vict. c. 91, s. 4: but it is important that there should be no doubt that the justices have no power to inquire into the propriety of the disallowance. [Lord CAMPBELL, C. J.—We are not competent, in this proceeding, any more than the justices, to inquire into the propriety of the disallowance. Is there any objection on the part of the auditor to state the reasons and enable the relieving officer to have the matter investigated? If he is willing to do so, it seems a reasonable course that he should give his reasons in writing

(a) Regina *v.* Two Justices of Brecknockshire, Easter Term, May 8th, 1857. *C. Milward* had obtained a rule calling on two justices of Brecknockshire to show cause why they should not issue a distress warrant to levy from the relieving officer a sum with which he had been surcharged. *Lush* showed cause on affidavits disclosing a case of great apparent harshness on the part of the auditor; it being stated that the disallowance was on the ground that the relieving officer had not on the audit produced vouchers, which he had subsequently found, and produced before the two justices. It appeared that the justices had on this ground refused to issue the warrant; but *Lush* also pointed out that it did not appear on the affidavits in support of the rule that the statutable proof of the certificate was complete. *C. Milward.*—That is merely a slip in the technical part of the affidavits.

Lord CAMPBELL, C. J.—You, coming to us to command the justices to act in a case of such hardship, should be aware that the other side are justified in taking every objection, however technical. You were bound to show that all was correctly done before the justices.

WIGHTMAN, ERLE, and CROMPTON, Js., concurred.   Rule discharged, with costs.

immediately, and that the rule, which must be made absolute, should not be acted on till there has been an opportunity to apply under the statute.]   No objection will be made to this course.

Per CURIAM.(a)

Rule absolute, to lie in the office for a month.

(a) Lord Campbell, C. J., Coleridge, Erle, and Crompton, Js.

The QUEEN v. HENRY MOORE GRIFFITHS.   *June* 11.

The high sheriff of a county, in August, 1854, appointed G. election auditor for the county, under The Corrupt Practices Prevention Act, 1854 (17 & 18 Vict. c. 102, s. 15), to act at any elections for and during the year then next ensuing, and until another appointment should be made. No fresh appointment was made in 1855. In March, 1856, the then high sheriff appointed W. election auditor for the current year.

On a rule for a quo warranto against G.:

Held, that it was not necessary that the appointment for 1855–1856 should be made during the month of August: that W. was well appointed; and that, on his appointment, G. ceased to be election auditor: and the rule was made absolute.

C. MILWARD, in this Term, obtained a rule Nisi for an information *953] in the nature of Quo warranto *against Mr. Griffiths for usurping the office of election auditor of Warwickshire.   From the affidavits it appeared that, in August, 1854, the high sheriff of Warwickshire appointed Mr. Griffiths, under The Corrupt Practices Prevention Act, 1854 (17 & 18 Vict. c. 102), sect. 15, election auditor for the county.   No fresh appointment was made till the month of March, 1856, when the high sheriff for that year appointed Mr. West.   Both these gentlemen claimed to be entitled to act from March, 1856, till August, 1856.

Phipson now showed cause.—Stat. 17 & 18 Vict. c. 102, s. 15, enacts that " once in every year, in the month of August," the returning officer shall appoint an election auditor to act " for and during the year then next ensuing, and until another appointment of election auditor shall be made."   It cannot be contended that an appointment made after the month of August would be bad; but the high sheriff cannot make his appointment before that month.

C. Milward was not called on to support the rule.

Lord CAMPBELL, C. J.—The high sheriff appoints in March, 1856, because no appointment was made in August, 1855, not in anticipation of August, 1856.   Mr. Griffiths, after August, 1855, held over till another appointment should be made: it has been made; and he has ceased to be auditor.

COLERIDGE, ERLE, and CROMPTON, Js., concurred.

Rule absolute.

*The QUEEN *v.* The Inspectors of Votes for No. 5 Ward of   [*954
the Parish of ST. PANCRAS.   *June* 11.

At a vestry election, holden under the provisions of stat. 18 & 19 Vict. c. 120, R., a person not
duly qualified, had more votes for the office of vestryman than a person duly qualified. The
inspectors of votes returned in their list the latter. This Court refused a rule Nisi for a
mandamus to the inspectors to return the name of R.

TAPPIN moved for a rule Nisi for a mandamus commanding the
inspectors of votes of No. 5 ward of the parish of St. Pancras to
return Thomas Ross as vestryman, on affidavits disclosing that he had
a large majority of votes, but that he was not duly qualified as he was
not rated; and that the inspectors had, on that account, returned a
candidate who had fewer votes. The duty of the inspectors under stat.
18 & 19 Vict. c. 120, s. 22, is to return those chosen by the parishioners.
It is merely ministerial.

Lord CAMPBELL, C. J.—Under stat. 18 & 19 Vict. c. 120, the vestrymen are those who have been chosen by a majority of votes given for
persons duly qualified according to the Act.(*a*)   There will be no rule.

COLERIDGE, ERLE, and CROMPTON, Js., concurred.

                                                         Rule refused.

        (*a*) See sect. 18.

———◆———

*Ex parte COBBETT.   *June* 12.   [*955

A person who attends before justices at petty sessions in order to obtain a summons with a view
to recover a penalty, and gives evidence before them for the purpose, is not privileged from
arrest either in going there with a view to give the evidence and obtain the summons, or on
his return after having done so.

STURGEON moved for a rule to discharge William Cobbett out of custody. From his statement, it appeared that Mr. Cobbett, as representative of a mortgagee on a turnpike road, brought ejectment against
the trustees. He was nonsuited; and, to procure information as to
the state of the trust so as to avoid a nonsuit in future, he wished to
inspect the accounts of the trustees. With a view to procure this
information, he left his home at Battersea and went down to Winchester, to attend a petty sessions there, for the purpose of procuring a
summons against the clerk of the turnpike trustees for a penalty of
5*l.*, incurred under stat. 12 & 13 Vict. c. 87, s. 5, for not having transmitted a copy of the accounts to the Secretary of State; the annual
meeting of the trustees not having been held. Mr. Cobbett gave evidence before the justices that such meeting had not been held, and
such copy not transmitted, and obtained the summons. He was arrested,
under a ca. sa. for the costs of the nonsuit, when :n his direct road
home.

Sturgeon, in support of the motion.—The applicant is entitled to be discharged out of custody, as he was returning from giving that evidence which was necessary to procure the summons. The protection which is given to a person attending a legal proceeding is given to facilitate the administration of the law: and, if the *proceeding is in a court having jurisdiction, it is immaterial whether it is of much or little dignity; nor is it any objection that Mr. Cobbett's attendance was voluntary. A person attending to prove before commissioners in bankruptcy is privileged: Ex parte King, 7 Ves. 312. So is a witness coming from abroad without any subpœna: Walpole *v.* Alexander, 3 Doug. 45. So is the husband of a petitioner in bankruptcy, attending with her: Ex parte Britten, 4 Jurist, 943. [Lord CAMPBELL, C. J.—But here Mr. Cobbett goes down when there is no suit pending. Is there any authority that a person is privileged when going to take out a writ?] He was perhaps not privileged going; but he was, at all events, privileged when returning after the suit had been instituted.

Lord CAMPBELL, C. J.—I hope that this Court will ever be tender of the liberty of the subject, and take care that no one is improperly arrested, when having a privilege because engaged in assisting in the administration of justice. But it is equally bound to take care that the privilege against arrest is not abused, or carried so far as, instead of furthering the administration of justice, to enable a party to defy justice. Mr. *Sturgeon* in this case is obliged to rest his motion on this proposition, that, though a common informer going to obtain a summons is not privileged from arrest, he is privileged when he is on his return, having obtained the summons. For this he has cited no authority. Hitherto, in every case where there has been held to be a privilege redeundo, there has been a privilege eundo. It is so in the case of a witness coming from abroad; his privilege *commences when he first starts. It was properly admitted that Mr. Cobbett had no privilege when going; it would be monstrous if he had. The privilege is in favour of those attending in furtherance of the administration of justice: but this is the case of a person going voluntarily with a view of commencing a proceeding as a common informer; and he is in no better position than any other subject. It was suggested that the clerk to the trustees had incurred a penalty by not complying with stat. 12 & 13 Vict. c. 87, s. 5. Mr. Cobbett correctly says he has a right to apply for this penalty. But, in doing so, he was not a witness either in going, staying, or returning: he was a voluntary prosecutor. Now, to say that every person may acquire a privilege against his creditors, by merely suing out a summons before a justice, is a novelty; and, if it were permitted, it would enable any one to set his creditors at defiance. But for this doctrine there is neither authority nor principle. No case has been brought to our notice having any tendency to support it. Privilege in

analogous cases has often been claimed at Chambers, and as often disallowed. This is the first case, I believe, in which it has been brought
before a Court in banc.

COLERIDGE, J.—I am of the same opinion. It is clear on principle,
and indeed it is admitted, that Mr. Cobbett had no privilege when going
down to Winchester with a view to lay an information before the justices. And, that being so, he had not a privilege in the terms ordinarily used, eundo, morando et redeundo. But I think that a test of
whether he had privilege at all. When a person goes to attend a court
of justice, under such circumstances as to protect him from arrest when
*going, the privilege would be ineffectual unless it also protected [*958
him whilst staying there, and on his return. The two latter privileges are ancillary to the first. The object of all three is, not to
benefit the party, but to protect the administration of justice: and, if
the object with which he sets out is not such as to render it proper to
protect him when going, neither will it protect him whilst staying or
returning.

ERLE, J.—I am of the same opinion. Mr. Cobbett is a person
against whom a ca. sa. has been issued to enforce a judgment. It is
the duty of the Court to endeavour to enforce the law and facilitate
the obtaining satisfaction of a judgment; and therefore, generally, it
is our duty to support the execution of a ca. sa. There is an exception where legal proceedings are going on, and the presence of the
debtor is required to assist in those, either as a witness or as a legal
adviser. When attending for that purpose, he has a privilege from
arrest whilst going, staying, and returning. So far the privilege is
recognised; but further no decision has hitherto gone. In the present
case, Mr. Cobbett went down to Winchester to lay an information. I
am aware, from what had passed before, that he did not go as a common informer in the odious sense of the words, but with a view to
other matters than the penalty: but still he went to do that which any
common informer had as much right to do as he; and the question is
whether a person, going to lay an information qui tam, is a person
attending to assist in legal proceedings in such a way that, to facilitate
the administration of justice, he should be privileged from arrest. It
would seem ludicrous to say he could claim such a privilege when
going; and I never *heard before of any privilege that was not [*959
equally in going, as in staying and returning; and I see no
occasion for extending the privilege in this case. Any other person
might have ascertained whether the returns had been made as well as
Mr. Cobbett, and might have gone down to give all the evidence
required to obtain the summons. I think it would be very prejudicial
if we were to extend the privilege to such a case; and, as there is
neither authority nor principle for it, I think that there should be no
rule.

CROMPTON, J.—There is no colour here for saying that Mr. Cobbett went as a witness. He went with a view to take out process. And, as soon as it is ascertained that the privilege does not exist when going to attend a court for such a purpose, it follows that it does not exist when staying or returning. All I think depends on the nature of the attendance. I agree with what is stated in Taylor on Evidence, vol. 2, p. 1033, sect. 1202 (2d ed.), that, however inferior the tribunal may be, if it be a lawful tribunal, the privilege on principle exists; though that point has never been yet decided. My judgment proceeds on this ground: that a person, going for his own purposes to sue out process to institute a proceeding, is not privileged ; though I think that, after it was instituted, witnesses attending at the trial would be.   No rule.

---

*960] *WILLIAM WALKER, one of the Public Officers of THE NEWCASTLE COMMERCIAL BANKING COMPANY, v. FREDERICK GOODYERE. *June* 12.

Judgment was obtained in a Court of record at Dublin against the official manager of an Irish Joint Stock Banking Company for a large sum. The amount due was reduced by subsequent payments in the name of the defendant. The plaintiff executed a warrant of attorney (under stat. 6 G. 4, c. 42, s. 12) to confess judgment for the sum remaining due ; and judgment was signed in this Court. Subsequently the plaintiff executed a fresh warrant to confess judgment for the sum for which judgment had been signed in the Irish Court ; and judgment was signed accordingly. On this latter judgment a sci. fa. issued against a shareholder. On his motion to set it aside :

Held, that the provisions in stat. 6 G. 4, c. 42, s. 12, for enforcing judgments against the public officers of Banking Companies in Ireland, were, by stat. 11 & 12 Vict. c. 45, made applicable to judgments against official managers : and that the judgment on which this sci. fa. proceeded was regular.

THIS was a sci. fa. against a shareholder in The Tipperary Joint Stock Bank, to obtain execution on a judgment in this Court for 25,627*l*. 9*s*. 11*d*. and 3*l*. 10*s*. costs, signed on 4th June, 1857, in an action by Walker, as nominal plaintiff for The Newcastle Commercial Banking Company against George McDowell, the official manager, under the Winding-up Act, of the Tipperary Joint Stock Banking Company, as nominal defendant for that corporation.

C. Milward, in this Term (June 10th), on behalf of the defendant in the sci. fa., moved for a rule to show cause why the warrant of attorney, dated 29th May, 1857, on which the judgment against the Company was founded, and the judgment itself, should not be set aside. The rule was obtained on affidavits, by which it appeared that judgment was obtained in the Queen's Bench in Ireland, by Walker, as nominal plaintiff, against McDowell, as nominal defendant, for 25,000*l*., and 627*l*. 9*s*. 11*d*. costs, making together 25,627*l*. 9*s*. 11*d*. The plaintiff Walker, intending to act under stat. 6 G. 4, *c. 42, s. 12, executed a warrant of attorney, dated 13th April, 1857, reciting the judgment in the Irish Queen's Bench as being for 25,000*l*. debt

*961]

and 627*l.* 9*s.* 5*d.* for costs, "making together the sum of 25,127*l.* 9*s.* 5*d.*," reciting some payments on account, and authorizing his attorney to appear for the official manager in an action in the Queen's Bench in England by Walker, and confess judgment for 23,064*l.* 14*s.* 5*d.*, the balance remaining due. Judgment was accordingly signed on 9th May for that sum. No proceedings appeared to have been taken on that judgment. The plaintiff Walker then executed, on 29th May, 1857, a second warrant of attorney correctly reciting the Irish judgment as for 25,627*l.* 9*s.* 11*d.*, taking no notice of the payments on account, and authorizing the attorney to appear and confess judgment for 25,627*l.* 9*s.* 11*d.* On this warrant of attorney judgment was signed, on 4th June, 1847, for 25,627*l.* 9*s.* 11*d.*; and on this latter judgment the sci. fa. was founded. *Milward* obtained his rule on two grounds. First: that stat. 6 G. 4, c. 42, s. 12, applied only to judgments against a public officer of an Irish joint stock bank, and not to actions against an official manager. Second: that Walker's authority, if he had any, was exhausted when the first judgment was signed. The Court, when granting the rule, ordered that cause should be shown peremptorily, in this Term.

Bovill and *Kemplay* now showed cause.—The Irish Bank Act (6 G. 4, c. 42), sect. 12, enacts: "that it shall and may be lawful for any person or persons obtaining a judgment in any of His Majesty's Courts of Record in Dublin, against any such public officer for the time being of any such society or copartnership; and such *person or persons is and are hereby empowered, by warrant, under hand and [*962 seal, reciting the effect of such judgment, to authorize any attorney or attorneys in Great Britain to appear for such public officer in an action for debt to be brought in any Court of record in Great Britain against such public officer, at the suit of the person or persons obtaining such judgment in Ireland, and thereupon to confess judgment forthwith in such action for a sum equal to the sum for which judgment shall have been so obtained in Ireland, together with the costs of such proceeding; and such judgment shall be thereupon entered up of record in the said Court in Great Britain against such public officer, and shall have the like effect in Great Britain against the members of such society or copartnership as the original judgment so obtained in Ireland." In the present case the judgment in Ireland was not against a public officer of The Tipperary Joint Stock Banking Company, but against the Official Manager; and therefore it is said that the provisions of stat. 6 G. 4, c. 42, s. 12, do not apply to this Act. But The Joint Stock Companies Winding-up Act, 1848 (11 & 12 Vict. c. 45), extends to Ireland; and, by sect. 50, as soon as an official manager of a company is appointed, all suits on behalf of the company shall be in the name of the official manager as nominal plaintiff; and all suits against such company shall and may be prosecuted " against the official manager of such company (by such style and designation as aforesaid), as the nominal defendant for and on behalf of such company." And, by sect. 57, " all judgments which shall be entered up in any action at law against the official manager of any such company shall have the like effect and operation upon and against the property of such company, and upon *and against the persons and property of the contributories [*963] thereof, and shall be enforced in like manner, as if such judgments had been entered up against such company, or against any person duly authorized to be sued on behalf of the same." The intention clearly was to substitute the official manager for the public officer in every way; and the words are quite large enough to effectuate that intention. Then it is true that a warrant of attorney was executed, and a judgment signed before the present judgment; but the first warrant did not recite " the effect" of the Irish judgment: it misrecited it: and the judgment which the attorney was authorized by it to confess was not " for a sum equal to the sum for which judgment" had been obtained in Ireland, together with the costs; but a different one. That first warrant therefore did not pursue the statutable authority, and was a mere nullity; and the plaintiff was entitled to proceed as if it had never been.

C. Milward, in support of his rule.—The first warrant was no nullity; it authorized the signing of judgment for what remained due on the Irish judgment, and was right. [Lord CAMPBELL, C. J.—The object of the Act was not to cause the party to commence a new suit in England, but to make the Irish judgment, such as it was, equivalent to an English judgment; and therefore it provides that the English judgment shall be, not for the sum due on the Irish judgment, but for the sum for which the Irish judgment was " obtained."] Then this mode of enforcing the judgment is only given on judgments against the public officer. [CROMPTON, J.—I see no reason for saying that this is not within the words " proceedings, at law," in stat. 11 & 12 Vict. c. 45, s. 50.]

[*964] *Lord CAMPBELL, C. J.—I am glad that the rule was made returnable this Term; for it seems to have been applied for merely as a means of throwing the plaintiff over the long Vacation.

Per CURIAM.(*a*)   Rule discharged, with costs.

(*a*) Lord Campbell, C. J., Coleridge, Erle, and Crompton, Js.

The METROPOLITAN BOARD OF WORKS *v.* The VAUX-
HALL BRIDGE COMPANY. *June* 12.

A sewers' rate, laid on an occupier by the Metropolitan Commissioners of Sewers under stat. 11
& 12 Vict. c. 112, could be impeached only by appeal to the Commissioners, under sects. 95, 96.
Therefore, in an action to recover for such a rate, brought by The Metropolitan Board of Works,
under stat. 18 & 19 Vict. c. 120, s. 147, against the party rated, it is not competent to such
party to object that the property in respect of which he is rated derives no benefit from the
sewers.

The Court (Lord Campbell, C. J., Coleridge, Erle, and Crompton, Js.), at the request of the
parties, stated extrajudicially their opinion that, since stat. 11 & 12 Vict. c. 112, the sewers'
rate should be made, taking into account the benefit which the property derived from the
sewers, as under the previous law of sewers.

THIS was an action to recover 233*l.* 14*s.* for sewers rates claimed to
be due from the defendants to the late Metropolitan Commissioners of
Sewers, and recoverable by the plaintiffs as successors to such Commissioners under stat. 18 & 19 Vict. c. 120, s. 147, "For the better local
management of the metropolis."

The defendants pleaded, Never indebted.

On the trial, before Pollock, C. B., at the last Summer assizes for
Surrey, a verdict was entered by consent for 233*l.* 14*s.*, costs 40*s.*, subject to a case; which, so far as material to the points decided, was as
follows.

The plaintiffs were constituted a corporation under the stat. 18 & 19
Vict. c. 120, s. 43; and, by sect. 147, they are empowered to levy all
rates made by the Metropolitan *Commissioners of Sewers pre- [*965
viously to the commencement of that Act.

The amount now in dispute, and sought to be recovered, arises from
rates made by the late Surrey and Kent Commissioners of Sewers in
the years 1845 and 1848 respectively; and which rates, under and by
virtue of The Metropolitan Sewers Act, 1848, 11 & 12 Vict. c. 112, s.
9, became payable to the late Metropolitan Commissioners of Sewers;
and also from rates made by the said Metropolitan Commissioners of
Sewers between the years 1849 and 1855, both inclusive, in pursuance
of the powers vested in them by the said stat. 11 & 12 Vict. c. 112.

The particulars of the said rates, as far as relates to the dates, the
description of the persons' assessed, the rateable annual value, the
amount, and the proportion in the pound of the said rates, were set out
in the case.

"Western Division of Westminster Sewers. St. Margaret and St.
John, Westminster."

This included rates for 1849, 1851, 1852, 1853, and 1855, "The
Vauxhill Bridge Company" being assessed to each.

"Surrey and Kent District. St. Mary, Lambeth."

This included rates for 1845, 1848, 1849, 1851, 1853, 1854, and
1855, "The Vauxhill Bridge Company" being assessed to each.

The defendants are incorporated by 49 G. 3, c. cxlii., local and personal, public, " For building a bridge across the river Thames, from or near Vauxhall turnpike, in the parish of Saint Mary Lambeth, in the *966] county of Surrey, to the o os. e shore, in the parish of Saint pp. it *John, in the city and liberty of Westminster, and county of Middlesex, and for making convenient roads thereto."

By sect. 42 of the same Act the defendants were empowered to build the bridge, and to execute all other things requisite and necessary, useful or convenient, for erecting and building, maintaining and supporting the same. By the 46th section, the defendants were empowered, in order to have a proper access to the said bridge, to make certain roads on each side of the bridge, and were required to keep such roads, when made, in repair. And, by the 54th section, they were empowered to take and hold lands for these purposes. By the 89th section, the defendants were empowered to erect one or more gate or gates, turnpike or turnpikes, in, upon, or across the said bridge, and to take for each and every time of passing over the said bridge, for horses, cattle, carriages, vehicles, and foot passengers, the tolls respectively mentioned in such section, subject to certain provisions and exemptions. By the 120th section, it was enacted that one-half of the bridge should be deemed to be in and part of the parish of St. John, Westminster, in the county of Middlesex, and the other half to be in the parish of St. Mary, Lambeth, in the county of Surrey. By the 123d section the tolls are directed to be applied, first, in paying the expenses of carrying the Act into execution and of keeping the bridge, roads, and accesses in repair, and of lighting and watching the same, and in payment of any yearly rents which might be charged upon or reserved or made payable for or in respect of any of the lands or hereditaments to be purchased or taken under or for the purposes of the said Act, and, in the next place, in paying to the mortgagees and annuitants under *967] the *said Act the interest and annuities to which they should be respectively entitled ; and the surplus was to be divided among the proprietors. By sect. 125, if the Company should fail to keep the said bridge and roads in repair, they were made subject to indictment. By the 127th and 128th sections, the rights, powers, and authorities of the Commissioners of Sewers for the city and liberty of Westminster, and part of the county of Middlesex, and of the Commissioners of sewers for parts of the counties of Surrey and Kent, were respectively saved.

Before and at the time of the passing of the last-mentioned Act, and thence continually until the determination, by stat. 18 & 19 Vict. c. 120, of the powers of the said Commissioners of Sewers respectively, the River Thames and the parishes of St. John, Westminster, since called St. Margaret and St. John, and the parish of St. Mary, Lambeth, including the Bridge and the property of the defendants held therewith, as hereinafter mentioned, were for sewerage purposes within the juris-diction of the said Commissioners of Sewers for Westminster and part of Middlesex, and for Surrey and Kent, respectively.

The defendants, under the powers of their said Act, made the bridge and approaches thereto: and the bridge was opened for public use in the year 1816: and it has ever since been kept open. And the defendants have, ever since, taken the tolls authorized to be taken by them under the said Act as aforesaid, in respect of the use of the same bridge by the public.

A plan was annexed to and formed part of the case, representing the portion of the bridge and approaches, and the sewers near them. Sewers shown upon this *plan were constructed by the Metro- [*968 politan Commissioners of Sewers, or their predecessors, prior to the making of the first sewers' rate sought to be recovered, but not until after the bridge was opened to the public.

The case set out several particulars respecting the position of the sewers, the way in which they were connected together, the property of the defendants, and the inclination of the ground; and pointed out what sewers had been maintained by the late Commissioners and their predecessors.

All the sewers have always, since their construction, been flushed, repaired, and maintained by the Metropolitan Commissioners of Sewers and their predecessors.

The case also described the direction taken by the drainage for the buildings and other property of the defendants.

By stat. 6 G. 4, c. xxxi., local and personal, public, " To enable The Vauxhall Bridge Company to raise a further sum of money, and to alter and amend the Acts relating to the said Bridge," sect. 27, a penalty was imposed on the defendants, or any body or persons, who should suffer washings or waste liquids, which should arise from gas, to run or flow into the river Thames, or any sewer or ditch connected therewith, or do any annoyance, act, or thing to the water therein, whereby the water might be soiled, fouled, or corrupted.

For the years 1825 and 1827 the defendants were rated, by the Commissioners of Sewers for the city and liberty of Westminster and part of the county of Middlesex, for such parts of their said property and tolls as were situate and taken within the jurisdiction of the said Commissioners, on an assessment of 250l. per annum, for a sewers' rate at 6d. in the pound; and for *each of those years the defend- [*969 ants paid the sums of 6l. 5s. for each sewers' rate. For the year 1829, and down to the end of the year 1846, as often as the sewers' rate was required, the defendants were assessed, by the said Commis-sioners for Westminster and part of the county of Middlesex, for such parts of their said property and tolls as were situate and taken within the jurisdiction of the said Commissioners, at 290l. per annum, 40l.

thereof being separately assessed in respect of the secretary's house and office. And, up to the year 1846, the defendants paid the said sewers' rate to the said Commissioners.

From the year 1830 to the end of the year 1839, the defendants were assessed by the Surrey and Kent Commissioners of sewers five times, on an assessment of 250*l.*, for such parts of their said property and tolls as were situate and taken within the jurisdiction of such Commissioners. And the sum of 12*l.* 10*s.* for each such assessment was paid by the said defendants. In the years 1841 and 1843 the said Commissioners for Surrey and Kent assessed the defendants, for such parts of the said property and tolls as were taken and situate in the said parish of St. Mary, Lambeth, in the sum of 600*l.*, at the rate of 1*s.* in the pound. These two rates were duly demanded; and the payment was disputed; and they have never been paid.

By stat. 52 G. 3, c. xlviii., local and personal, public, " For empowering the Commissioners of Sewers for the city and liberty of Westminster, and part of the county of Middlesex, to purchase a messuage and premises for holding their meetings; and for enlarging the powers of the said Commissioners," the said Commissioners of Sewers for Westminster and part of Middlesex were *empowered to inspect and take copies of the poor-rates of all the parishes within the limits of their jurisdiction, in order to enable them to lay an equal rate upon the inhabitants within their limits. Down to the year 1847 the said Commissioners of Sewers for Westminster and part of Middlesex made their sewers' rate by means of a jury under the Commissioners of Sewers, grounded upon the stat. 23 H. 8, c. 5,(*a*) commonly known as the Bill of Sewers, aided by the powers of inspecting the poor-rates derived from the stat. 52 G. 3, c. xlviii.

970]

By the statute 50 G. 3, c. cxliv., local and personal, public, " For amending, enlarging, and extending the powers of an Act passed in the last session of Parliament, relating to the execution of the Commission of Sewers for the limits from East Moulsey in Surrey, to Ravensborne in Kent," sect. 6, the said Commissioners of Sewers for Surrey and Kent were empowered to make rates in manner therein provided: and the rate mentioned in the particulars before set forth for the parish of St. Mary, Lambeth, in 1845, was made by the then Commissioners of Sewers for Kent and Surrey, acting under the provisions of that statute, and without the intervention of a jury. By the last-mentioned statute, powers were given to appeal against and to amend any rates made in pursuance thereof.

The second rate for the parish of St. Mary, Lambeth, mentioned in the said particulars, dated 1848, was made by the then Commissioners for Surrey and Kent, acting under the powers conferred upon them by stat. 10 & 11 Vict. c. ccxvii., local and personal, public, " To facilitate

(*a*) Made perpetual by stat. 3 & 4 Ed. 6, c. 8, s. 1.

*the effectual drainage of certain districts within the Commis- [*971
sion of Sewers for the limits extending from East Moulsey in
Surrey to Ravensbourne in Kent."

In the year 1848 the several Metropolitan Commissioners of Sewers
were consolidated by virtue of The Metropolitan Sewers Act, 1848
(11 & 12 Vict. c. 112).

By the 18th section of The Metropolitan Sewers Amendment Act,
1849 (12 & 13 Vict. c. 93), it was enacted that The Metropolitan
Sewers Act, 1848, as amended, and that Act, should be one Act, and
should be put in execution accordingly.

After the passing of The Metropolitan Sewers Act, 1848, The Metropolitan Commissioners of Sewers, in making sewers' rates upon persons
within their jurisdiction, followed the poor-rate assessment precisely.
They called for the poor-rate books for the parishes of St. Margaret
and St. John, Westminster, and St. Mary, Lambeth (which they were
empowered to do by the said Acts of 1848 and 1849); and, finding
The Vauxhall Bridge Company rated in the former parish in the year
1849 at 290l. for their said property and tolls, The Metropolitan Commissioners rated the defendants accordingly; and the rate was paid by
the defendants.

In the year 1849 the defendants were rated to the poor in the said
parish of St. Margaret and St. John, Westminster, in 2000l., for their
said property and tolls.   The Metropolitan Commissioners of Sewers,
accordingly, rated the defendants in 2000l. in a district rate then made.
But, the defendants having got the assessment reduced by the poor-rate
authorities to 1000l., The Metropolitan Commissioners of Sewers, upon
a representation of this alteration being made to them by the defendants, ordered the assessment of the Bridge *Company to the [*972
district sewers' rate to be reduced to 1000l.   The defendants
refused to pay the rate; and The Metropolitan Commissioners of
Sewers, in the years 1851, 1852, and 1853, assessed the defendants in
1000l. for their said property and tolls, at the rate of 6d. in the pound.
In the year 1854, the defendants refusing to pay the sum of 87l. 10s.
then due for arrears of rates in the parish of St. Margaret and St. John,
Westminster, The Metropolitan Commissioners of Sewers issued a warrant, under their common seal, for the sum of 87l. 10s. due for arrears.
Their officers levied on the property of the defendants : but the distress
only produced the sum of 1l. 6s.   The defendants never replevied, and
never appealed to the Commissioners against any sewers' rate; and
the defendants always paid the poor-rate on 1000l. from the year 1849
to the time of this action, without appeal.

As regards the parish of St. Mary, Lambeth, the defendants were,
in the year 1849, rated to the poor in 600l. in respect of their said
property and tolls: and the sewers' rate made on the 16th November,
1849, was made by the said Metropolitan Commissioners of Sewers

according to the said assessment of the Bridge Company to the poor-rate in that parish; and the sewers' rates in the years 1851, 1853, 1854, and 1855, in the same parish, were made according to the said poor-rate assessment of the said Company in the like sum to this parish. The defendants never appealed against the poor-rate nor the sewer-rate. The poor-rate was paid by the defendants as demanded; but the defendants have not paid sewers' rates for this parish, although such rates have been duly demanded since 1845: and the various rates, mentioned in the particulars for the parishes of St. Margaret and *St. John, Westminster, and St. Mary, Lambeth, less the said *973] sum of 1*l.* 6*s.* paid as aforesaid, are due.

The Court are to be at liberty to draw its inferences, from the facts above stated, which a jury might have drawn.

If the Court should be of opinion that the plaintiffs are entitled to recover, the verdict for them is to stand for such sum as the Court shall direct. If the Court should be of a contrary opinion, a verdict is to be entered for the defendants.

The case was argued on an earlier day in this Term.(*a*)

M. Chambers, for the plaintiffs.—It will be sufficient, for the present, to confine the argument to the ten rates which have been levied since the passing of The Metropolitan Sewers Act, 1848, 11 & 12 Vict. c. 112. That Act gives large power for sanatory purposes, as well as for drainage; and the jurisdiction conferred upon the Commissioners is wider than that given by the old Sewers Act, 23 H. 8, c. 5. Sect. 1 of stat. 11 & 12 Vict. c. 112, recites former Acts, gives power to issue the new commission within the limits set forth, and enacts that "no place or part comprised within such limits shall be exempt from the jurisdiction of the Commissioners by reason of the same being extra-parochial, or being beyond the ebb or flow of the tide, or by reason of any other exemption or supposed exemption from the general law of sewers previously to the passing of this Act." It will be contended, for the defendants, that they are without the jurisdiction, not from any exemption from the general law of sewers, but under *the *974] general law of sewers itself, as not deriving benefit from the drainage in question; and Callis on Sewers, pp. 222, 223, may be relied on. But that test, which was correct under stat. 23 H. 8, c. 5, is not applicable to the recent statute. Sect. 32 directs that the Commissioners shall have the area within their district surveyed, and such maps as they shall think proper published: which are to be open "to the inspection of the owners or occupiers of any lands within the limits of their commission:" and these expenses, as appears by sect. 76, are to be defrayed out of the sewers' rate of the district: which shows that the rate is to be borne by the whole district. By sect. 34, the sewage districts are to be formed by the Commissioners, who are to divide the area within the limits of their commission, "having regard in such division or formation to the nature of the ground, to the main lines of sewers by which such separate districts are or shall be drained, or to the main lines of sewers which it may appear to the Commissioners expedient to form for the drainage of such sewerage districts, and to the equal benefit, as far as may be, of all lands and buildings comprised in such districts." From this it appears that the discretion is lodged in the Commissioners. Sect. 36 shows that the jurisdiction of the Commissioners, as to the exercise of their jurisdiction within the limits, is restricted solely by their discretion; for it enacts "that the Commissioners may, if they think fit, forbear to exercise their jurisdiction, either wholly or in part, over any place within the limits of their commission chiefly used for agricultural purposes, or which, in the judgment of the Commissioners, shall be in such a state as not to require the exercise of all or any of the powers vested *in the [*975 Commissioners, until such time, under such circumstances, and in such manner as they shall think fit." Sect. 37 enacts that all sewers, &c., within the limits of the commission shall be subject to the Commissioners: and sect. 38 enacts that the Commissioners shall make "such sewers and works, or such diversions or alterations of sewers and works, as may be necessary for effectually draining the area within the limits of the commission, and shall cause any banks or defences abutting on any river, stream, canal, or watercourse to be raised, strengthened, or altered, where it may be necessary so to do, for effectually draining or protecting from floods or inundation such area." From these sections it is clear that the Legislature assumed the drainage of any part of the area to be beneficial to the whole area. Sects. 48, 49, 50, 51, 52, and 53 are directed to sanatory purposes, showing the object of the Act to be more extensive than that of stat. 23 H. 8, c. 5. [Lord CAMPBELL, C. J.—Certainly water closets were not thought of in the time of Henry the 8th.] But the rate under the present Act is to cover all these expenses, including compensation to parties. The rating clause, sect. 76, enacts: "That it shall be lawful for the Commissioners, from time to time, as occasion shall require, to levy and raise on each separate sewerage district within the limits of the commission a separate rate, to be called 'The district sewers rate,' in respect of such portion as in the judgment of the Commissioners should be borne by such separate sewerage district of the expenses of repairing, cleansing, and maintaining in effective action the sewers already made and completed, and which from time to time shall be made and completed within the limits of the commission, and the payments to and *general expenses of the Commissioners and their [*976 officers and servants, and the expense of making and completing the said map and survey, and such other expenses authorized by this Act as shall in the opinion of the Commissioners be incurred for or on account of or enure to the common benefit of all the sewerage districts, or shall not be defrayed out of any other rate or rates hereby authorized to be made, and in respect of any expenses or portion of expenses of making, or of enlarging, contracting, or otherwise improving, or altering, discontinuing, closing, or destroying, any sewer, or of any other works of a permanent nature, where such expenses or portion of expenses, in the judgment of the Commissioners, shall be incurred for the special benefit of such separate sewerage district, or ought to be charged thereon under this Act, and also in respect of any mortgages or other debts or liabilities which would have been paid or answered out of rates raised in such district in case this Act had not been passed; and such district sewers' rate shall in each case be levied on the persons and in respect of the property within such district by law rateable to the relief of the poor," or by precepts. This would appear to give the Commissioners unlimited discretion. But then follows the proviso on which the defendants rely: " Provided also, that where in any separate sewerage district any property is by law or by the practice of the existing commissions or Commissioners of Sewers entitled to exemption, wholly or partially, from, or to any reduction or allowance in respect of the sewers' rate, the Commissioners shall in making the district sewers' rate observe and allow such exemption, reduction, or allowance." Now it is clear that the defendants are rateable to the poor in

*977] respect *of this property: Rex *v.* Barnes, 1 B. & Ad. 113 (E. C. L. R. vol. 20), Regina *v.* The Blackfriars Bridge Company, 9 A. & E. 828 (E. C. L. R. vol. 36). [Lord CAMPBELL, C. J.—Is it disputed that the defendants are rateable to the poor? *Shee*, Serjt., for the defendants.—No.] Then the question is, only, whether the property of the defendants is entitled to exemption, within the meaning of the proviso of sect. 76, as being " entitled to exemption, wholly or partially," "by law or by the practice of the existing commissions or Commissioners of Sewers." But the exemption there pointed to cannot be an exemption arising from parties not being within the enactments of stat. 23 H. 8, c. 5: the reference is rather to special exemptions, such as that by prescription, mentioned in Callis on Sewers, p. 223, or by particular provisions in Acts of Parliament. By sect. 77, rates for permanent works may be spread over thirty years, showing that more than the immediate drainage of particular parts was looked to: and a similar inference arises from the powers given, by sect. 66, for purchasing land, contracting for supplies of water, &c. The power given by sect. 87 to the Commissioners to inspect the poor-rates is quite general. Next, assuming that the Court is here to inquire whether the property in question derives a benefit from the drainage, the inference arising from the facts of the case is that such benefit is derived. The amount of benefit is not now open to discussion. It is for the defendants to show the absence of such benefit. [He then referred to

Stafford *v.* Hamston, 2 B. & B. 691 (E. C. L. R. vol. 6), Dore *v.* Gray, 2 T. R. 358, Soady *v.* Wilson, 8 A. & E. 248 (E. C. L. R. vol. 30); and he *contended that, as, under the local Act 49 G. 3, c. cxlii., [*978 sects. 127, 128, the powers of the Commissioners are saved, the Company could not, by the mode in which they constructed their works, create an exemption. The remainder of the argument on this point is omitted.] The defendants also rely on some objections on points of form. [On these he was stopped by the Court.] As to any objection supposed to arise from the assessment being too extensive, that is merely matter of appeal to the Commissioners, who may correct, if necessary: stat. 11 & 12 Vict. c. 112, s. 96. [Lord CAMPBELL, C. J.—That is clearly so, unless the rate can be shown to be an absolute nullity.]

Shee, Serjt., contrà.—The Metropolitan Sewers Act, 1848, does not alter the old law of sewers. There is now a sanatory purpose; but so there always was; and it is only by the instrumentality of the sewage that the sanatory purpose is to be effected; indeed the main provisions for the health of the Metropolis are those of The Public Health Act, 1848 (11 & 12 Vict. c. 63). Now, under the old law of sewers, no property could be rated to the sewers' rate which was not benefited: Masters *v.* Scroggs, 3 M. & S. 447 (E. C. L. R. vol. 30), Stafford *v.* Hamston, 2 B. & B. 691 (E. C. L. R. vol. 6), Rex *v.* Commissioners of Sewers for the Tower Hamlets, 9 B. & C. 517 (E. C. L. R. vol. 17), Soady *v.* Wilson, 3 A. & E. 248 (E. C. L. R. vol. 30), Callis on Sewers, p. 135: and here there is no benefit in fact. [The argument as to the fact of benefit is omitted.] It lies upon the plaintiffs to show that stat. 11 & 12 Vict. c. 112, alters the law in this respect. Had the Legislature *so intended, the intention would have been clearly ex- [*979 pressed. The language of sect. 1 furnishes no argument against the defendants: they do not contend that the Commissioners have no jurisdiction; but the Commissioners can exercise it only by forming the districts according to the benefit derived, in pursuance of the directions of sect. 34: Rex *v.* Commissioners of Sewers for the Tower Hamlets. Sect. 37 does not affect the present question. Then the proviso in sect. 76 is express: the framers of the Act knew that by the existing law property not benefited was exempted from sewers' rates. [CROMPTON, J.—Perhaps the Legislature expressly preserved the exemptions lest the enlarged application to sanatory purposes should raise an inference that the law in this respect was altered.] That is highly probable. Sect. 80, were it not for the proviso in sect. 76, might appear to favour the argument for the plaintiffs; for it directs that the rate, when not imposed in gross on parishes, is to be assessed on the net annual value ascertained by the poor-rate. But that is merely for furnishing the amount, according to the argument on a similar provision, urged by Sir W. W. Follett in Tracey *v.* Taylor, 3 Q. B. 966, 978 (E. C. L. R. vol. 43). And this purpose is carried out in sect. 102, where the Commissioners are directed to specify in their precept the part subject to the rate, and the exemptions "where in any parish or place any property shall be entitled to any exemption." [COLERIDGE, J.—Suppose a property did derive benefit from the sewer, but happened from some particular circumstance to be exempt from the poor-rate: would it be

*980] exempt from the sewers' rate?] It would not: the *liability to the poor-rate is the test, not of the rateability, but only of the amount. Next, if the objection be good, the rate is wholly bad: Rex *v.* Cunningham, 5 East, 478, Neave *v.* Weather, 3 Q. B. 984 (E. C. L. R. vol. 43). The argument that the only remedy is by appeal rests on sects. 95 and 96. Sect. 95 enacts: "That whenever any district sewers' rate shall be made under this Act, and shall not be imposed in gross, and in every case where a special sewers' rate or an improvement rate shall be made under this Act, it shall be lawful for any occupier or for any owner or person interested in or rated to such rate, who shall consider himself aggrieved thereby, within one month after the making of any such rate, to appeal against the same or the apportionment thereof on him, on the ground of non-liability to pay the same, or of unfairness or incorrectness in the appointment or assessment thereof:" and sect. 94 contains an analogous provision for the case where rates are laid in gross. Sect. 96 enacts that, on the appeal, "the decision of the Commissioners shall be final;" "and in case no complaint shall be made against such rate or the apportionment thereof within one month after the making of such rate, the same shall be final and conclusive on all parties and places whatsoever." That seems to assume the rateability of the property, and to give the appeal only in the case of the wrong party being rated, as where a servant is rated instead of his master. [ERLE, J.—You would rely on Milward *v.* Caffin, 2 W. Bl. 1330, and that class of cases. CROMPTON, J.—The Legislature may have thought the Commissioners the very persons best capable of making the proper

*981] *exemptions or deductions.] If this objection to the case for the defendants prevails, it is very desirable that the Court should also, for the direction of the Commissioners, lay down a rule on the general question. [He then referred to the questions on the points of form.]

M. Chambers, in reply.—The plaintiffs concur in asking for a decision on the general question. But the appeal clauses are fatal to the defendants. As to the argument that a rate, if laid at all on property not rateable, is wholly bad, Crease *v.* Sawle, 2 Q. B. 862 (E. C. L. R. vol. 42), is a decision, in the Exchequer Chamber, to the contrary.

Cur. adv. vult.

Lord CAMPBELL, C. J., now delivered the judgment of the Court.

We are of opinion that the plaintiffs are entitled to recover, on the ground that the defendants have not appealed against the rates nor made any complaint against any of such rates, or the apportionment thereof, within one month from the making thereof.

The defendants were the occupiers of property which was occupied by them within the district, and which may be liable to be rated. There is reason for holding therefore that, without any special enactment for that purpose, the defendants could not in this action have contested their liability: Churchwardens of Birmingham *v.* Shaw, 10 Q. B. 868 (E. C. L. R. vol. 59). But sects. 90, 94, 95, 96, of stat. 11 & 12 Vict. c. 112, respecting rates made under that statute, appear to us to be quite conclusive as to the liability of the defendants.

*We therefore cannot judicially determine the great question [*982 meant to be submitted to us, whether, under stat. 11 & 12 Vict. c. 112, property is to be rated according to the old established principle of the law of sewers, having regard to the benefit derived from the sewers by the property to be rated, or all property within the district is to be assessed uniformly as for a poor-rate or highway-rate. However, we have been strongly solicited by both parties to give our opinion upon this question, after the expense they have incurred in this litigation; and, under these peculiar circumstances, we think that we may, without impropriety, intimate our opinion, although we are aware that it is not binding.

Primâ facie, assessment under a sewers' rate must have regard to the benefit which the property derives from the sewers; and property which derives no benefit from the sewers is not liable to be assessed. The onus therefore lies upon the party who alleges that a different principle of rating has been adopted by the Legislature. The plaintiffs therefore, who contend for a uniform rating over all the area within the jurisdiction of the Commissioners, rely upon some clauses in the Act, introduced with a view to the sanatory condition of the district, and the application of the fund raised by the rate to some purposes which would not be authorized under an ordinary commission of sewers. But all these clauses have reference to sewers: and, although it might be considered fair to distribute equally over the district all expenses incurred with a view to the general health of the district, we must see whether there be any enactment in the statute to justify such an equal distribution. The plaintiffs rely upon the concluding part of sect. 1: that "no place or part" within the defined limits "shall *be [*983 exempt from the jurisdiction of the Commissioners by reason of the same being extraparochial," &c.: but we consider this to apply only to the general jurisdiction of the Commissioners, without affecting the rateability of property irrespective of benefit derived from the sewers. The plaintiff's counsel then relied upon sect. 76, which regulates the mode of rating. But, having regard to the whole of this clause, we think it carefully preserves the ancient principle of rating for sewers: and the last proviso, instead of sanctioning a uniform rate over the whole district, anxiously directs "that where in any separate sewerage district any property is by law or by the practice of the existing Commissions or Commissioners of Sewers entitled to exemption, wholly or partially, from, or to any reduction or allowance in respect of the sewers' rate, the Commissioners shall, in making the district sewers' rate, observe and allow such exemption, reduction, or allowance." This seems clearly to intimate that, in rating, the benefit derived from the sewers by the property rated shall still be regarded. Further, the powers given to the Commissioners with respect to district rates seem to have a special reference to the well known rules of law respecting rates by Commissioners of Sewers, whereby property is to be assessed according to the benefit which it derives from the sewers.

We are, therefore, of opinion that the Commissioners, in considering whether the Vauxhall Bridge Company were liable to be rated and to what amount, ought not to have considered merely the value of the property of the Company, as in making a poor-rate, but should have been guided by the benefit which they considered that this property derived from the sewers.

*984]   *Having said so much respecting the construction of the Act of Parliament, we must refrain from giving any opinion as to whether benefit was derived from the sewers to any or what part of the property, which the Commissioners must be fully competent to determine.

And we now conclude by giving judgment for the plaintiffs.

Judgment for plaintiffs.

END OF TRINITY TERM.

INDEX

TO

THE PRINCIPAL MATTERS.

Gillespie

(985)

III. Proceedings at trial.

1. Evidence. See EVIDENCE.

2. Verdict: defendant beginning, plaintiff, after leave to move for a verdict on the ground of there being no evidence for defendant, calls evidence proving defendant's case. Plaintiff cannot afterwards move.

On a trial, where the issue was on defendant who accordingly began, plaintiff, at the end of defendant's case, claimed a verdict on the ground that there was not evidence to support the issue for defendant. The Judge refused to direct a verdict, but gave plaintiff leave to move to enter one. The plaintiff then called evidence; and, on the evidence which followed, the issue for the defendant was proved.

Held: that the plaintiff was not entitled to enter a verdict on the ground that there was no proof for the defendant at the close of the defendant's original case. *Allen* v. *Carey*,   463

IV. Proceedings after trial.

1. Motion to enter verdict for plaintiff, upon leave reserved at trial; not allowable where plaintiff elected to continue case after leave reserved, and defendant, having begun, obtained the verdict, 463. Supra, III. 2.

2. Judgment and execution. See JUDGMENT.

V. Costs. See COSTS.

ADMINISTRATORS.

See EXECUTORS AND ADMINISTRATORS.

AFFILIATION.

See BASTARDY.

AGENT.

See PRINCIPAL AND AGENT.

AGREEMENT.

See CONTRACT.

AMENDMENT.

I. Of writ of summons before service, by altering name of defendant, and resealing: date of original teste may be retained, 49. ACTION, II. 2.

II. Of an affiliation order, by Court of Queen's Bench, under stat. 12 & 13 Vict. c. 45, s. 7. What omissions and errors are amendable, 557. JUSTICES, I.

APPEAL.

I. Right of, in particular cases.

1. Separate right of overseers, under stat. 16 & 17 Vict. c. 97, s. 100, to appeal against an order of adjudication of the settlement of a pauper lunatic, addressed to them and the guardians of the Union, 14. POOR, II. 2.

2. Appeal under Church Discipline Act. Where Archbishop acts for Bishop, appeal lies to the Court of Appeal for the province, 315. CHURCH DISCIPLINE ACT.

3. Appeal to Commissioners of Sewers, under sects. 95 & 96, of stat. 11 & 12 Vict. c. 112, the only method of contesting the validity of a sewers' rate imposed by them under that Act, 964. RATE, V.

II. Notice of.

1. Appellant against a poor-rate having, with his notice of appeal, given notice that he should, at the next Sessions, apply for a respite, Sessions have jurisdiction to dismiss altogether.

A person rated under a rate for the relief of the poor in a parish gave to the churchwardens, in due time, notice of appeal to the next Sessions, and in the same paper gave notice that he should not then try the appeal, but only lodge, enter, and commence the same, and petition for a respite to the next Sessions. The churchwardens gave him notice that they would oppose such his petition. At the next Sessions both parties attended; the appellant applied to enter and respite the appeal; the Sessions refused to do so, and required him to proceed, and on his not doing so, dismissed the appeal. On a rule to quash their order dismissing the appeal:

Held that, there being a notice in fact which the Sessions were justified in deciding to be a reasonable notice, they were not bound to respite the appeal, and had jurisdiction to make the order complained of. *Regina* v. *Eyre*,   609

2. Respite of appeal against a poor-rate, to allow appellant to complete service of notice on all parties interested. Service of a second notice, omitting some of the parties and some of the objections in the first, not a proper service; and appeal dismissible.

Notice of appeal was given against a poor-rate, stating, as one of the grounds of appeal, that certain parties enumerated in a schedule attached to the notice were improperly rated. These parties were not served with the notice; and the Sessions refused to respite the appeal for the purpose of such service, and dismissed the appeal with costs. The Court of Queen's Bench afterwards made absolute a rule commanding the Sessions to enter continuances and hear "the said appeal," on the ground that they were bound to respite for the purpose of notice being served on all the parties interested. Appellant then gave a second notice, in which the schedule, and the objections in respect of the parties named therein, were omitted. The Sessions, when the appeal came on for hearing, held that this was not a proper notice, and dismissed the appeal with costs.

Held, that they were right in so doing, inasmuch as, by the omission of the schedule and the objections in respect of the parties named therein, the character of the appeal was materially altered, so that it was not the "said" appeal which the Sessions were ordered to hear and determine. *Regina* v. *Eyre,* 619

3. Constructive abandonment of an appeal against a poor-rate, by not entering it for the next General Quarter Sessions, after notice to that effect. What are "the next practicable Quarter Sessions?"

An order of removal made on 6th September, 1856, was duly served on 10th. On 21st September a letter, dated 20th, was received by the respondents from the clerk of the appellants, stating certain facts as to the paupers, and adding, "I shall on these grounds appeal against your order." On 29th September copies of depositions were applied for, and received on 30th. Notice of intention "to commence an appeal at the next general Quarter Sessions" was duly received on 8th October. At the next Quarter Sessions, held on 16th October, the appeal was not entered or respited; and the respondents applied for costs, which were, however, refused. On 20th October, the paupers were removed. On 23d December another notice of appeal, and grounds of appeal, were served. At the next Sessions, held 8th January, 1857, both parties appeared; but, after argument, the justices refused to hear the appeal.

Held that the justices acted rightly, and that the appellants ought to have entered and respited the appeal, even though they could not have tried it, at the October Sessions.

Held also that, in judging of the "practicability" of the next Sessions, the time of service of the order of removal was the proper time to reckon from. *Regina* v. *Justices of Peterborough,* 643

III. Proceedings on the hearing at Quarter Sessions.

Sessions may hear together the separate appeals of the overseers of a parish and the guardians of the union, against an order of adjudication of the settlement of a pauper lunatic, addressed to both parties, 14. Poor, II. 2.

IV. Appeals brought up to Court of Queen's Bench.

Confirmation, by Sessions, of a conviction for obstructing a highway, subject to a case. Court of Queen's Bench cannot take notice of any objection to the conviction not stated in the case, 399. Highway, I.

V. Costs. See Costs, III.

ARBITRATION.

I. Submission.

Agreement to become a party to a reference at Nisi Prius. Consent need not appear upon face of order. When Court of Queen's Bench may enforce summarily.

A cause stood for trial at Nisi Prius. The action was for rent in arrear. One issue was on a plea of an eviction by P. by title paramount to that of plaintiff. P. was not a party to the cause, but claimed the reversion in the premises held by defendant. P. became, by parol, party to an arrangement, by which the matter was to be settled by a reference of the cause to an arbitrator, who was to determine, inter alia, on what terms the plaintiff's interest in the premises should be purchased, and in what proportion P. should contribute to the payment, and to the amount of the damages. An order of Nisi Prius was drawn up, incorporating these terms, and containing a provision that P. should become a party to the reference: it was not expressed to be drawn up by his consent; but it was shown by other evidence that it was in fact by his consent. P. afterwards refused to be bound by this order.

Held that, having submitted to the order in fact, he was bound by it, and could not retract; and that the Court had jurisdiction to enforce obedience in a summary manner. *Williams* v. *Lewis,* 929

II. Award.

Judgment upon an award confirming verdict taken, in Vacation, subject to such award. Within what time it may be enforced.

A verdict was taken in Vacation, subject to the award of an arbitrator, to whom the cause and all matters in difference were referred. The award was made directing a verdict in favour of the plaintiff. Before next Term, but more than fourteen days after the publication of the award, the plaintiff signed judgment. A summons having been obtained to set aside the judgment, the matter was referred to the Court.

Held, that the judgment was regular, and that it was not necessary, before signing judgment, to wait till the time for moving to set aside the award had elapsed. *O'Toole* v. *Pott,* 102

ARCHBISHOP.

His jurisdiction under Church Discipline Act, 315. Church Discipline Act.

ARREST.

Extent of privilege from, while assisting the furtherance of legal proceedings.

A person who attends before justices at petty sessions in order to obtain a summons with a view to recover a penalty, and gives evidence before them for the purpose, is not privileged from arrest either in going there with a view to give the evidence and obtain the summons, or on his return after having done so. *Ex Parte Cobbett,*   955

ARTIFICER.

Within the meaning of the Truck Act, 115. TRUCK ACT.

ASSIGNMENT.

Of patents. See PATENT, I.

ASYLUM.

Pauper lunatic. See POOR.

ATTORNEY.

1. Purchase by an attorney, from his client, of the interest in a verdict already obtained, but upon which judgment had not been signed: void as against policy of law, 84. CONTRACT, III. 2.

II. Signed bill delivered under stat. 6 & 7 Vict. c. 73. What is sufficient particularity. Items properly described may be sued upon by themselves.

Action by a solicitor to recover the amount in his bill. Plea, No signed bill delivered. A signed bill was proved to have been delivered. It contained items for business done in a cause, without any statement as to what Court the cause was in. The nature of the business was not such as to show conclusively whether the action was in one of the Superior Courts at Westminster or not. The bill contained other items admitted to be unobjectionably described. On a rule to enter a nonsuit, on the ground that this was not a compliance with the statute:

Held that, the description of the business being such as was reasonably sufficient, when coupled with what must have been known to the client, to give information as to the charges, none of the items were objectionable, and the solicitor might recover his whole bill.

Held also that, even if some items had been badly described, the solicitor might, notwithstanding, recover for the items in his bill sufficiently described. *Haigh v. Ousey,* 878

AUDITOR.

Election. See CORRUPT PRACTICES PREVENTION ACT.

AUDITOR.

Poor Law. See POOR.

AVERAGE.

See INSURANCE, II.

BAILMENT.

Action against depositee of title deeds as security for a loan, by the party interested under the deeds, and contemporaneous demand of the deeds by the heir of the depositor, having paid off the loan. Interpleader proceedings.

A., being in possession of a house, deposited the title deeds with a bank as a security for a loan. Amongst them was what purported to be a grant to B., deceased, in fee. A. died. B.'s heir demanded the grant from the bank, claiming it as his property. A.'s heir, who was in possession of the house, paid off the advance, and demanded the deeds deposited. The bank gave up all but the grant claimed by B.'s heir, which they refused to give to either party. B.'s heir brought trover against the bank; A.'s heir threatened to sue the bank. On a rule under the Interpleader Act, this court relieved the bank, though in the relation of bailee to the person represented by the claimant: Crompton, J., hesitante. *Roberts v. Bell,* 323

BANKER.

Check on one branch of a bank, presented at and paid by another, but dishonoured on being forwarded by the latter to the former. Bank may sue payee.

A joint stock banking Company carried on business by means of branches, at various places; amongst others, at G. and B. The Company was one; but each branch kept separate accounts, had separate customers, and in all respects transacted business like a separate bank. Defendant, holder of a check drawn on the G. branch, by a person who kept an account there, got cash for it at the B. branch. The check was without laches forwarded by the B. branch to the G. branch. When it was cashed the balance in the G. branch to the credit of the drawer exceeded the amount of the check; but when it arrived at G. that balance had been paid away, and the check was dishonoured.

The Company having sued for money had and received, on the ground of failure of consideration,

Held: that they were entitled to recover, as the B. branch could not, under the circumstances, be considered as honouring the check, nor as purchasing it, but as taking it from defendant on his credit, as they might have done a check drawn on any other bank:

the circumstance that the banks at G. and B. were branches of the same Company being, for this purpose, immaterial. *Woodland* v. *Fear*, 519

Liabilities of Joint Stock Banks. See COMPANY, II.

BANKRUPT AND INSOLVENT.

I. Rights of creditors against Bankrupt.

A judgment against husband and wife, for debts of wife dum sola, the wife only having been taken into custody, the husband having obtained final protection. Discretion of Court of Q. B. as to discharging her, 159. HUSBAND AND WIFE, II.

II. Rights of creditors against assignees.

Action against assignee for conversion of property which had, by a specific appropriation, vested in the purchaser under a contract of sale by the bankrupt before bankruptcy, 885. VENDOR AND VENDEE, I. 2.

III. Rights of assignees.

1. To the interest in a contract by bankrupt, before bankruptcy, to pay a sum of money on a contingency still unarrived, 58. CONTRACT, III. 1.

2. Judgment against an incumbent, but suspension of execution, before his insolvency : subsequent vesting order by Insolvent Court. Sequestration on petition of assignee, when entitled to priority.

D. recovered judgment against a beneficed clergyman, and issued a levari facias, which he lodged with the deputy registrar of the Ecclesiastical Court, directing that the execution should be suspended till further orders. Afterwards the clergyman petitioned the Court of Insolvent Debtors; and a vesting order was made by that Court. The assignee, under stat. 1 & 2 Vict. c. 110, s. 55, petitioned the bishop for a sequestration. On the day following, and before anything had been done, or, according to the Ecclesiastical practice, could have been done, upon the petition, D., for the first time, applied to the deputy registrar to issue sequestration. Held, that the sequestration of the assignee was entitled to priority. *Sturgis* v. *Bishop of London*, 542

IV. Proceedings in Insolvent Court.

1. Order by, under stat. 1 & 2 Vict. c. 110, s. 92, vesting surplus assets in insolvent, his heirs, executors, &c. : a judicial, and not merely a ministerial act, 366. JURISDICTION, IX.

2. Order of discharge, comprising a county court judgment debt. County court cannot afterwards commit for such debt, 679. COUNTY COURT, IV.

BARON AND FEME.

See HUSBAND AND WIFE.

BASTARDY.

Amendment, by Court of Q. B., of affiliation order. What omissions and errors are amendable, 557. JUSTICES, I.

BENEFICE.

See INCUMBENT.

BILL OF SALE.

I. Filing of, under stat. 17 & 18 Vict. c. 36, s. 1.

Under stat. 17 & 18 Vict. c. 36, s. 1, a bill of sale is void against creditors unless a description of the residence and occupation of the person granting it be filed along with the bill of sale. It is not sufficient that the bill of sale, which is filed, itself contains a description of his residence and occupation. *Hatton* v. *English*, 94

II. Interpleader issue between two creditors claiming under separate bills of sale by the same party, one not being duly filed. Substance of issue, 564. INTERPLEADER, II.

BOARD OF HEALTH.

See PUBLIC HEALTH ACT.

BOARD OF WORKS.

See METROPOLIS LOCAL MANAGEMENT ACT.

BOND.

Under Municipal Corporation Reform Act, by sureties of the treasurer of a borough : their present liability, 97. MUNICIPAL CORPORATION REFORM ACT., II.

BOROUGH.

I. Treasurer.

Bond by, under Municipal Corporation Reform Act : present liability of sureties, 97. MUNICIPAL CORPORATION REFORM ACT, II.

II. Clerk of the peace.

The creation of a clerk of the peace for a borough, created by charter, after the passing of stat. 5 & 6 Vict. c. 111, and the area of which was formerly part of the county, does not entitle the clerk of the peace for such county to compensation, under 5 & 6 W. 4, c. 76, 249. MUNICIPAL CORPORATION REFORM ACT, III.

III. Town clerk.

To what extent he may be reimbursed for causing the lists of Parliamentary voters to be copied, &c., under stat. 6 & 7 Vict. c. 18, s. 48.

Under stat. 6 & 7 Vict. c. 18, s. 48, the town clerk of a borough is bound, incidentally to his office, to cause the lists of voters to be copied and printed, and to have the names arranged and numbered : and, if he hires a person to do this for him, to make copies for the printer, and to superintend the printing, he is not entitled to be reimbursed the expense by the parish officers under sect. 55, unless he cannot, by the reasonable labour of himself and his ordinary assistants, perform the duty without extra aid.

But he is entitled to be reimbursed for the expense of printing. *Regina* v. *Allday*,   799

BRANCH BANK.

See BANKER.

BURIAL ACTS.

(15 & 16 VICT. C. 85, AND 16 & 17 VICT. C. 134.)

By whom the members of a Burial Board are to be elected, where there is a select vestry for the parish under a local Act, as well as a general vestry.

In the parish of L., under a local Act, a body called The Select Vestry of L. have the functions of a Board of Guardians. There is also a general Vestry, having the management of the general parochial affairs of L.

Held, that the members of a Burial Board for L., under stats. 16 & 17 Vict. c. 134, s. 7, 15 & 16 Vict. c. 85, ss. 10, 11, 52, were to be elected by the General Vestry having the management of the general parochial affairs, and not by the body created by the local Act. *Regina* v. *Gladstone*,   575

BURIAL BOARD.

See BURIAL ACTS.

CALLS.

The provisions in stat. 7 & 8 Vict. c. 110, s. 23, as to power to make calls, not applicable to a demand by a Company on a subscriber to the parliamentary contract, for the payment of his share of the preliminary expenses, 164. COMPANY, I. 1.

CARGO.

See SHIP, INSURANCE.

CERTIORARI.

I. Removal of inquisition, &c., by sheriff to assess compensation.

Excess of jurisdiction, as to a particular item, by a jury summoned to assess compensation, under sect. 68 of Lands Clauses Consolidation Act. Certiorari lies, though such excess not on face of proceedings, 669 LANDS CLAUSES CONSOLIDATION ACT.

II. Jurisdiction of Queen's Bench, when exercisable, where certiorari is taken away by statute.

Special case, stated by Recorder, with consent of parties, on appeal against a conviction under Municipal Corporation Reform Act.

By sect. 90 of stat. 5 & 6 W. 4, c. 76 (The Municipal Corporation Act), councils of corporate boroughs are empowered to make by-laws. By sect. 91 offences against such by-laws may be punished by summary conviction. By sect. 132 the writ of certiorari is taken away. The Recorder, upon an appeal against such a conviction for an offence against a by-law, having, with the consent of the parties, stated a case and referred, as the only question for this Court to determine, the question whether the facts amounted to an offence within the by-law, and the Court having granted a writ of certiorari to bring up the case :

Held that, by virtue of the consent of the parties, the Court might receive the case, and determine the question, although the writ of certiorari was taken away. *Regina* v. *Dickenson*,   831

III. Removal of indictments. Stat. 16 & 17 Vict. c. 30.

1. Recognisance by prosecutor not necessary when indictment is against a corporation.

An indictment against a corporation, found at Quarter Sessions, may be removed by certiorari into this Court, at the instance of the prosecutor, without the prosecutor entering into the recognisance required by sect. 5 of stat. 16 & 17 Vict. c. 30. *Regina* v. *Mayor of Manchester*,   453

2. Discretion of Judge, on granting certiorari, to order conditional payment of costs, where there are two defendants.

Two defendants being indicted jointly in the Central Criminal Court for conspiracy, one of them applied to a Judge for a certiorari, who granted it on such defendant entering into a recognisance for the payment of prosecutor's costs in case either defendant should be convicted.

Held, that such terms were reasonable, and within the discretion of the Judge;

and that stat. 16 & 17 Vict. c. 30, s. 5, made no difference in this respect. *Regina* v. *Jewell*, 140

CHAMPERTY.
See CONTRACT, III. 1, 2.

CHARTER-PARTY.
See SHIP.

CHECK.
See BANKER.

CHURCH DISCIPLINE ACT.
(3 & 4 VICT. c. 86.)

Appeal under sect. 15, against a decision of the Archbishop of the Province, lies to Court of Appeal of such Province.

In a proceeding under the Church Discipline Act (3 & 4 Vict. c. 86), the accused party holding preferment in the gift of the Bishop of the Diocese, the Archbishop of the Province (under sect. 24) sat and heard the cause in the diocese, and there pronounced judgment of deprivation. The accused appealed to the Court of Appeal of the Province. The Judge of that court refused to hear the appeal, on the ground that he had no jurisdiction to entertain an appeal from the Archbishop. On a rule for a mandamus to hear the appeal,

Held : that the proceeding was in a court of the nature of a Diocesan Court, in which the Archbishop sat as representing the Bishop; and that the appeal under sect. 15 of the Act lay to the Court of Appeal of the Province. Rule absolute. *Regina* v. *Judge of Arches Court*, 315

CHURCHWARDEN.

Action against, for rejecting a vote at an election of vestrymen and auditors, under Metropolis Local Management Act. Necessary to allege and prove malice, 377. ELECTION, III. 2.

CLERK OF THE PEACE.

For a county, not entitled to compensation under stat. 5 & 6 W. 4, c. 76, by reason of the creation of a clerk of the peace for a borough, the area of which was part of the county, incorporated after stat. 5 & 6 Vict. c. 111, 249. MUNICIPAL CORPORATION REFORM ACT, III.

COLLIERY.

Information against owner of mine, under stat. 18 & 19 Vict. c. 109. Dismissal of in-

formation by justices; when it amounts to a declining of jurisdiction, 757. JURISDICTION, XVI.

COLLISION.
Insurance against. See INSURANCE, I. 1.

COMMON LAW PROCEDURE ACT, 1852.
(15 & 16 VICT. c. 76.)

Sect. 120. Execution upon an award, confirming verdict taken in vacation subject to such award. When judgment may be signed, 102. ARBITRATION, II.

COMPANY.

I. Railway Company.

1. Power to sue for payment of preliminary expenses of undertaking abandoned before complete incorporation.

Covenant by the trustees named in a deed, being the ordinary Parliamentary subscription contract required before applying for an Act to make a railway. The contract contained a clause that the provisional directors might abandon the application. Averment that the provisional directors called upon the defendant, who had executed the deed, to pay money in pursuance of a covenant so to do. Breach, non-payment. Plea 2, on equitable grounds, that the scheme was abandoned. Plea 4, that the plaintiffs sued as trustees for the Company, which was not provisionally registered at the time of the suit. Plea 5, that the Company was not completely registered, and that the action was for the purpose of enforcing payment of a call. On demurrer : Held, that all the pleas were bad : the object of the Parliamentary subscription contract being to provide means for paying preliminary expenses in case the scheme should be abandoned, and such object not being rendered illegal by any enactment. *Aldham* v. *Brown*, 164

2. Compensation by, under Lands Clauses Consolidation Act. See LANDS CLAUSES CONSOLIDATION ACT.

II. Joint Stock Bank.

1. Action against, under stat. 7 & 8 Vict. c. 113.

A creditor of a banking Company, incorporated under stat. 7 & 8 Vict. c. 113, cannot maintain an action against a shareholder for the debt. His remedy is by action against the corporation, and execution in the statutable mode. *Fell* v. *Burchett*, 537

2. Judgment against official manager.

The provisions of stat. 6 G. 4, c. 42, s. 12, as to public officers of Irish Banks applicable, under stat. 11 & 12 Vict. c. 45, to judgments against official managers.

Judgment was obtained in a Court of record at Dublin against the official manager of an Irish Joint Stock Banking Company for a large sum. The amount due was remaining due; and judgment was signed in this Court. Subsequently the plaintiff executed a fresh warrant to confess judgment for the sum for which judgment had been signed in the Irish Court; and judgment was signed accordingly. On this latter judgment a sci. fa. issued against a shareholder. On his motion to set it aside:

Held, that the provisions in stat. 6 G. 4, c. 42, s. 12, for enforcing judgments against the public officers of Banking Companies in Ireland, were, by stat. 11 & 12 Vict. c. 45, made applicable to judgments against official managers: and that the judgment on which this sci. fa. proceeded was regular. *Walker v. Goodyere,*   960

3. Judgment against bank by innocent creditor: execution against shareholder: plea of fraud, when bad.

Under stat. 7 & 8 Vict. c. 113, s. 10, if judgment has been obtained against a joint stock bank, and, execution against them being ineffectual, it is sought to charge a shareholder, such shareholder cannot resist the claim on the ground that he was induced to become a shareholder by fraud on the part of the bank, and repudiated the shares after the bank had become bankrupt but as soon as he discovered the fraud, the judgment-creditor being no party to the fraud.

The fact that the party charged is a shareholder is (at any rate primâ facie) sufficiently shown by his name appearing on the registered memorial at the time of the judgment being recovered. Although such memorial varies in some particulars from the register prescribed in stat. 7 & 8 Vict. c. 113, s. 16, and Schedules (A.), (B.); as in referring to a wrong Act of Parliament at the head of the memorial, and in signatures not having been affixed at the proper times. *Henderson v. Royal British Bank,*   356

COMPENSATION.

I. Under Lands Clauses Consolidation Act. See LANDS CLAUSES CONSOLIDATION ACT.

II. To clerk of the peace for a county, for abolition of office, 249. MUNICIPAL CORPORATION REFORM ACT, III.

CONTRACT.

(By charter-party.) See SHIP.

(Of Insurance.) See INSURANCE.

FIRST: Statutory contracts by corporations.

I. Railway Company. Parliamentary subscription contract, for preliminary expenses. Right of Company to sue for payment of such expenses, though undertaking abandoned before complete registration, 164. COMPANY, I. 1.

II. Local Board of Health. Contract for works by: when an estimate and report is necessary, under s. 85 of Public Health Act, 107. PUBLIC HEALTH ACT.

SECONDLY: Common law contracts by private individuals.

III. Void and voidable contracts.

1. Contract to supply evidence for the purpose of proving a title to property: what amounts to maintenance.

The first count of a declaration stated that plaintiff was in possession of documents and information which would prove defendant entitled to property not then in defendant's possession, and of which the defendant was not aware: that, by written agreement, after reciting as above, and that plaintiff proposed to give defendant all the documents in plaintiff's possession on defendant agreeing to pay plaintiff one-fifth of the value of the property if it should come into his possession, to which defendant agreed, defendant, in consideration of the premises, agreed that, if by the documents and information defendant should become possessed of any property not then in his possession or that he did not know of, he would pay to plaintiff one-fifth of the value of the said property "to be recovered and possessed by the defendant as aforesaid;" and it was agreed that "defendant should not be compelled, for the purposes of that agreement, to take any proceedings at law or in equity to recover the said property or any part thereof;" provided that, if defendant did not become possessed of any property, he should not be called upon to pay any money whatever, and that, if he "did not think proper to proceed to recover the property," he would return the papers, and the agreement should be cancelled. Averment that plaintiff gave defendant the documents and information; and defendant, upon the documents and information, took "proceedings in equity and law to recover, and did proceed to recover, and by the said documents and information did actually recover, and did actually become possessed of," property which at the time of the agreement was not in his possession and which he then did not know of. Breach, that defendant had not paid the fifth of the value.

On demurrer to plea, held that the agreement as stated in this count did not disclose champerty or maintenance, and that the count was good.

Plea, that T. died a bachelor and intestate, possessed of personal property, without any known relation, and administration was granted to the solicitor of the Treasury as nominee of the Queen. That, at the time of the unlawful agreement after mentioned, defendant had no knowledge that he was next of kin to T. or entitled to the property: and plaintiff represented to defendant that plaintiff would give such information and evidence, if it became necessary for defendant to institute proceedings in law or equity for the recovery of the property, that by means of such information and evidence defendant should recover the property, provided he would enter into an agreement with plaintiff to pay plaintiff one-fifth of the property which defendant should so recover. That thereupon it was unlawfully agreed by plaintiff and defendant that plaintiff should give such information and evidence, &c. (as before), and that, if by means of such information and evidence defendant should recover the property, defendant should pay plaintiff one-fifth of the property so to be recovered. That, in and for the purpose of carrying out the agreement, and in order to secure to plaintiff one-fifth of the property so to be recovered, defendant entered into the agreement mentioned in the first count. That proceedings were taken in Chancery and Q. B. by defendant for recovering the property; and information and evidence was given by plaintiff in pursuance of the agreement, and defendant recovered the property as next of kin to T., which was the property mentioned in the first count. That plaintiff was not interested in any of the property save under the agreement. And so the agreement was void.

Held, on demurrer, that the plea showed maintenance and was good.

There were also counts for work and labour, for the price of documents delivered by plaintiff to defendant, for money paid, and on accounts stated.

Plea to these counts, stating the facts and the agreement as in the preceding plea, and that the claim of defendant was for work and labour performed, for documents delivered and for money paid, in carrying the agreement into effect, and for accounts stated in respect of documents delivered and money paid in so doing.

Held, on demurrer, a good plea, as showing maintenance.

Plea to 1st count, and to so much of the claim in the other counts as related to any matter happening before the vesting order after mentioned, imprisonment of plaintiff for debt, and petition by him to the Insolvent Court, after the promise in the first count, and after the accruing of the causes of action in the other counts pleaded to, and a vesting order by that Court before the commencement of the suit. There was no allegation that the assignee had interfered.

On demurrer, held that the interest in the contract stated in the first count was part of the insolvent's estate and vested in the assignee, and that the plea to the first count was good: it was admitted to be a good plea as to the rest of the claim pleaded to. *Sprye* v. *Porter*, 58

2. Purchase by an attorney, from his client, of the benefit of a verdict already obtained, but upon which judgment had not been signed: void as against the policy of the law.

An attorney conducting a cause for the plaintiff, though not the attorney on the record, after verdict, but before judgment, bonâ fide purchased from his client the benefit of his verdict, and gave notice of this to the defendant. Afterwards the same plaintiff became nonsuited in another action against the same defendants. A rule having been obtained to set off the one judgment against the other:

Held, that the set-off was subject not only to the lien for costs, but to any equitable rights acquired in the judgment.

Held, also, that the transaction, being a purchase of the subject-matter of a suit by the attorney, was void as against the policy of the law, and that it made no difference that the purchaser was not attorney on the record. *Semble*, that such a purchase by a stranger to the suit would have been valid. *Simpson* v. *Lamb*, 84

3. Contract by seamen with master, for additional remuneration for completing the voyage; when good.

A vessel, in consequence of the desertion of some of the seamen, was left short of hands in harbour, before the voyage was completed. The master, to induce the remaining seamen to perform the rest of the voyage, promised to pay them a sum of money in addition to their wages. They accordingly performed the rest of the voyage with the diminished number of hands.

On an action by one of the seamen against the master for the sum promised, the jury found that he made the agreement without coercion, for the best interests of the owners; that he could not have obtained additional hands at a reasonable price; and that it was unreasonable for so large a ship to proceed on the completion of the voyage with the diminished number of hands.

Held, that on this finding, which the Court understood to mean that it was unsafe so to proceed, the plaintiff was entitled to recover, as the seamen were not bound, by their original contract of service, to proceed with the diminished number of hands; and their undertaking to do so was therefore a good consideration for the master's promise. *Hartley* v. *Ponsonby,* 872

4. Statute of Frauds. Agreement relating to the sale of interest in land, not in writing: when that part of the contract not so relating may be severed, and sued upon, 503. STATUTE OF FRAUDS.

5. Agreement by owner of ship, that she should proceed to and load at a foreign port: when it is avoided by the breaking out of war between the two countries after such agreement and before her arrival, 763. SHIP, I. 4.

IV. Qualified contracts.

Oral evidence of custom in trade, qualifying written contract.

Defendant, a broker, being employed by S. to purchase oil, signed a note as follows: "Sold this day, for Messrs. T." plaintiff's broker, "to our principals, ten tons of linseed oil," &c.; "quarter per cent. brokerage to" defendant. This note defendant delivered to Messrs. T. Defendant did not disclose the name of his principal, S., who became insolvent and did not accept the oil. Plaintiff then sued defendant for not accepting the oil, laying the sale as by himself to defendant. Defendant denied the contract.

On the trial, plaintiff proved a custom in the trade that, when a broker purchased without disclosing the name of his principal, he was liable to be looked to as purchaser.

Held: that evidence of the custom was admissible, as not contradicting the written instrument but explaining its terms, or adding a tacitly implied incident; and that the action lay. *Humfrey* v. *Dale,* 266

V. Rights and liabilities upon particular contracts.

1. When one of several joint contractors is barred by his own act from claiming under the contract, he cannot recover for a breach of it by joining the other co-contractors, 234. PLEADING, I. 1.

2. Covenant to pay by a promissory note, not satisfied by a mere delivery of such note: action for non-payment of such note not barred in six years, 903. PROMISSORY NOTE, I.

3. Contract by a party bonâ fide, but in mistake, representing himself as agent. Alleged principal having repudiated, action lies against agent for breach of implied promise that he had authority, 301. PRINCIPAL AND AGENT, III. 1.

4. Contract between owner of land and mill owner, having a reservoir constructed by license on such land. Covenants running with land: express and implied covenants.

By indenture between S. and W., it was recited that S. was seised and possessed of closes L. and W., and that W. was proprietor of a mill from which was produced a quantity of refuse: that W. had, by S.'s license, made a reservoir on L. for the reception of the refuse, in order to filter it, and drains for conveying it away from the reservoir; and had agreed with S. for license to convey the refuse down the drains on to W.: and, in consideration of such license, W. agreed to give to S. the "liberties and privileges" after mentioned, and to supply him with pure water, and indemnify him as after mentioned. And it was witnessed that S., in consideration of being supplied with pure water, and of receiving for his own use the refuse "which may from time to time be found" in the reservoir and drains, and of the privilege of using it for manuring his land, and of the covenants and agreements by W., covenanted, for himself, his heirs, executors, and administrators, to license W. to use the reservoir and drains for the purposes aforesaid, and that S., his heirs, &c., would scour and cleanse the reservoir and drains when necessary; W. to indemnify S. against actions brought against him for conveying away the refuse (except in a specified direction). And W., for himself, his heirs, executors, and administrators, covenanted to supply S. with pure water, sufficient to supply his cattle on certain closes, including L. and W., and convey it to a reservoir made by S. for the purpose: but W. was not to be compellable to convey it further; and that it should be "lawful" for S., his heirs and assigns, to cleanse and scour the reservoir and drains and made by W., "and to take" the refuse "away therefrom, to and for his and their own use and benefit."

Admitted: That the covenant to supply S. with pure water ran with the closes the cattle on which were to be supplied with water, and that L.'s devisee of such closes might maintain an action against W. for neglecting to supply the water.

But held, by Lord Campbell, C. J., Erle and Crompton, Js., dissentiente Coleridge, J., that there was no covenant, express or implied, compelling W. to send the refuse to the first-mentioned reservoir or drains. *Sharp* v. *Waterhouse,* 816

5. Contract by a labourer, must, in order to make him an artificer within the meaning of the Truck Act, bind him to perform

some part of the work personally, 115. TRUCK ACT.

6. Conviction and imprisonment of a workman, under stat. 4 G. 4, c. 34, s. 3, for leaving service before time of contract has expired, does not destroy the contract, 697. MASTER AND SERVANT, I.

VI. Measure of damages for breach of contract. See DAMAGES.

CONVICTION.

Summary. See JUSTICES, II.

CORONER.

Not entitled to the fee of 20s. mentioned in stat. 25 G. 2, c. 29, unless Sessions think inquest was properly held.

A coroner is not entitled to the fee of 20s. mentioned in stat. 25 G. 2, c. 29, for holding an inquest unless in the judgment of the Court of Quarter Sessions it was proper that such inquest should have been held; and the Court of Queen's Bench will not review the judgment of the Sessions on this point.

And this Court refused to grant a mandamus to the Sessions to pay such fees.

But the Court made absolute a rule for a mandamus to pay the fee of 6s. 8d. on inquests which the Sessions had held not to be duly holden, that the question might be discussed on the record whether, under stat. 7 W. 4 & 1 Vict. c. 68, the coroner is entitled as of right to the fees and disbursements mentioned in that Act. *Regina* v. *Justices of Gloucestershire*, 805

CORPORATION.

Removal of indictment against, by certiorari. No recognisance of prosecutor, under stat. 16 & 17 Vict. c. 30, necessary, 453. CERTIORARI, III. 1.

CORRUPT PRACTICES PREVENTION ACT.

(17 & 18 VICT. c. 102.)

Sect. 15. Appointment of election auditor, how to be made, when more than a year has elapsed since the last appointment.

The high sheriff of a county, in August, 1854, appointed G. election auditor for the county, under The Corrupt Practices Prevention Act, 1854 (17 & 18 Vict. c. 102, s. 15), to act at any elections for and during the year then next ensuing, and until another appointment should be made. No fresh appointment was made in 1855. In March, 1856, the then high sheriff appointed W. election auditor for the current year.

On a rule for a quo warranto against G. :

Held, that it was not necessary that the appointment for 1855–1856 should be made during the month of August: that W. was well appointed; and that, on his appointment, G. ceased to be election auditor: and the rule was made absolute. *Regina* v. *Griffiths*, 952

COSTS.

I. Of case sent up from County Court, 590. LANDLORD AND TENANT, II.

II. On removal of indictment by certiorari. Recognisance for costs by one of two joint defendants, to pay in the event of either being convicted, 140. CERTIORARI, III. 2.

III. On appeal to Quarter Sessions.

1. Dismissal, by Quarter Sessions, of an appeal against an information under the Excise Acts. Costs cannot be awarded against the Crown.

An officer of the excise having, on behalf of Her Majesty, sued before two justices for a penalty imposed by one of the Excise Acts, and the information being dismissed, appealed on behalf of Her Majesty to the Quarter Sessions, where the Sessions made an order, by which his appeal was dismissed with costs. This Court quashed the order of Quarter Sessions, on the ground that they had no jurisdiction to award costs against the Crown. The provisions of stat. 18 & 19 Vict. c. 95, ss. 1, 2, do not apply to such a case. *Regina* v. *Beadle*, 492

2. Where an order of Sessions, confirming an order of justices, is silent as to costs, subsequent Sessions cannot give costs by a fresh order.

On appeal the Quarter Sessions made an order confirming an order of justices subject to a case. The order of Sessions was silent as to costs. The appellants abandoned the case; the respondents applied to a subsequent Sessions, who made an order, stating that the original order was confirmed, and giving the respondents costs.

Held, that the subsequent Sessions had no jurisdiction to deal with the order made by the prior Sessions: and a rule was made absolute to bring up the second order, on certiorari, to be quashed. *Regina* v. *Justices of Staffordshire*, 935

III. On a conviction by justices.

For a trespass in search of game, under stat. 1 & 2 W. 4, c. 32. Bad for adjudicating that *each* of the defendants should be imprisoned till the costs of conveying *all* to gaol had been paid, 853. JURISDICTION, XIX.

IV. Lien for, as between attorney and client. Set-off of one judgment against another.

Lien for costs, where one judgment, before signing and after verdict, purchased by the attorney from the client, 84. CONTRACT, III. 2.

V. Taxation of.

Allowance to plaintiff, on taxation, of conduct money paid to a witness on subpœna, the cause having been settled and witness not having attended, not a defence, under Nunq. indeb., in an action to recover it from him by plaintiff, 1. ACTION, I. 1.

VI. Lien for, on a judgment, by the attorney, 84. CONTRACT, III. 2.

COUNTY COURT.

I. Jurisdiction of, in disputes of Friendly Societies.

The rules of a Friendly Society had not been enrolled previous to the passing of stat. 18 & 19 Vict. c. 63. Subsequently, a copy of the rules was deposited with the registrar. After this deposit, but before any certificate was obtained, application was made to the judge of the county court to settle a dispute which had arisen before the deposit.

Held, that the county court had no jurisdiction; and a prohibition was awarded. *Smith v. Pryse,*   339

II. Costs of special case sent up from county court, 590. LANDLORD AND TENANT, II.

III. Warrant by county court judge, under Absconding Debtors Arrest Act; high bailiff not liable to penalty for acting for the party applying.

Under the Absconding Debtors Arrest Act, 1851 (14 & 15 Vict. c. 52), the issuing of a warrant by a county court judge is not a proceeding in the county court. Therefore, if the high bailiff of the county court act for the party applying for the warrant, he is not thereby liable to a penalty under stat. 9 & 10 Vict. c. 95, ss. 29, 30.

But, *per Curiam,* it is more fitting that he should not so act. *Warden v. Stone,*   603

IV. Order of discharge by Insolvent Court, comprising a county court judgment debt. Effect as to power of commitment by county court judge for such debt.

Since stat. 19 & 20 Vict. c. 108, a debtor, discharged by the Insolvent Debtors Court, is not afterwards liable to committal by a county court judge, under stat. 9 & 10 Vict. c. 95, ss. 98, 99, in respect of any debt comprehended in the adjudication of the Insolvent Debtors Court. *Copeman v. Rose,* 679

CRIMINAL CONVERSATION.

Action for. Effect of plea of Not Guilty, 628. PLEADING, II. 3.

CUSTOM.

I. Prescriptive right in inhabitants of township to take water from a well for domestic purposes, not extinguished by the enclosure of the locus in quo under the General Enclosure Act.

Action for breaking a close. Plea that, by custom, the inhabitants of a township had a right to take water for domestic purposes from a well in the close; that plaintiff choked it up, and justifying the acts complained of as done by inhabitants of the township to clear out the well. Issue thereon.

On the trial it appeared that the inhabitants had, from time immemorial, taken the water from the well. About fifty years before the action the locus in quo was enclosed under a special enclosure Act, incorporating the general Enclosure Act then in force (41 G. 3, c. 109). Neither in the special Act, nor in the award of the Commissioners, was any mention made of this well, or of any access to it. Verdict for defendants, with leave to move.

Held, on a rule to enter the verdict for the plaintiff, that the right to take water from the well was not extinguished by the enclosure; and that, whether the ancient right of access to the well for that purpose was or was not extinguished (and *semble* it was not extinguished), the inhabitants might in other modes legally get access to the well, so that the fifty years' enjoyment de facto since the enclosure might have a legal origin; and the verdict for defendants stood. *Race v. Ward,*   384

II. Oral evidence of custom in trade, qualifying written contract, 266. CONTRACT, IV.

CUSTOMS.

See EXCISE.

DAMAGES.

Measure of.

I. Proceedings in Chancery for specific performance, dismissed on the ground that the alleged agent by whom the contract was made had in mistake, bonâ fide, represented himself as having authority. Measure of damages in action against agent, for breach of promise that he had such authority, 391. PRINCIPAL AND AGENT, III. 1.

II. Action for breach of implied warranty that defendant had authority to purchase a ship on behalf of another party. Resale of ship: measure of damages.

Action for a breach of implied warranty that the defendant, purchasing a ship in the name of R. from plaintiff, had authority to make the contract for R. It appeared at the trial that, R. having refused to adopt defendant's contract, plaintiff resold the ship at a less price than the contract price. The re-sale was taken to be reasonably made for the best price that could be obtained : and it was taken that R. was perfectly solvent. A ver-dict for the plaintiff being taken for the dif-ference between the contract price and that obtained on the resale,

Held, that the damages were properly as-sessed. *Simons* v. *Patchett,* 568

DEBTOR.

Insolvent. See BANKRUPT AND INSOLVENT.

DECLARATION.

On oath, of a deceased relative, before a master in Chancery, as to who was heir at law, ad-missible, as being ante litem motam, in a subsequent action on the question of heir-ship, 509. EVIDENCE, I. 1.

DECLARATION.

·In Pleading. See PLEADING, I.

DEDICATION.

See HIGHWAY, I.

DEMURRAGE.

See SHIP, I. 4; II. 5.

DEVISE.

See WILL.

DILAPIDATION.

What structures, erected by an incumbent upon the glebe, may be removed by him or his executors, 237. INCUMBENT, I.

DIOCESE.

When, under Church Discipline Act, the Arch-bishop of the province sits for the bishop of the diocese, the Court is in the nature of a diocesan court, and an appeal lies to the Court of Appeal of the province, 815. CHURCH DISCIPLINE ACT.

DISTRESS.

I. By landlord, for rent. See LANDLORD AND TENANT.

II. Under a warrant of justices, for poor law expenses. Jurisdiction of justices, 144. POOR, III. 2, 3.

EASEMENT.

I. Prescriptive right of inhabitants of a town-ship to take water from a well for domestic

purposes, not extinguished by the enclosure of the locus in quo under the General En-closure Act, 384. CUSTOM, I.

II. Covenants with owner of land, by mill-owner having a reservoir constructed, by license, on such land, for the supply of water to, and use of the refuse in the reservoir by, such landowner. Covenant as to supply of water runs with the land,·816. CONTRACT, V. 4.

III. Mine : qualified right of owner of surface to support as against owner of mine, 625. MINE.

IV. Action for obstructing watercourse. Plea, justifying under twenty years right of user. Proper form of plea.

Count by the owner of a mill on the river C., which mill of right ought to be supplied with a flow of water from a mill pool on the C. against the owner of works higher up the stream, for placing cinders, &c., at his works, so as to fall into the stream of the C., whence they were carried down into plaintiff's mill pool and filled it up, to the obstruction of his right to water.

Plea : that the occupiers of defendant's works had, for more than twenty years, of right placed cinders, &c., the refuse of their works, on the banks of the stream and in its channel; and that the cinders, &c., com-plained of were such refuse, so placed. The issue on this plea having been found for the defendant :

Held, that the plea was bad, non obstante veredicto, as not showing that defendant had, during twenty years, of right caused the refuse to go into the plaintiff's pond ; as, till the occupiers of the mill sustained some damage from the defendant's user, no right as against them began to be acquired. *Mur-gatroyd* v. *Robinson,* 391

ELECTION.

I. Parliamentary.

1. Appointment of election auditor, under Corrupt Practices Prevention Act; how to be made, when more than a year has elapsed since the last appointment, 952. CORRUPT PRACTICES PREVENTION ACT.

2. Copying, printing, &c., of lists of parlia-mentary voters in a borough, by town clerk, under stat. 6 & 7 Vict. c. 18. To what extent he may be reimbursed, 799. BOROUGH, III.

II. Municipal.

Revision of burgess lists, by mayor and as-sessors, under stat. 5 & 6 W. 4, c. 76. Mandamus lies commanding them to re-vise, 910. MUNICIPAL CORPORATION RE-FORM ACT, I.

EXCISE.

I. "Sweets" and "made wines" no longer excisable liquors within the meaning of stat. 9 G. 4, c. 61, s. 18.

By stat. 9 G. 4, c. 61, s. 18, a penalty is imposed on every person who shall, without a license, sell any excisable liquor by retail to be drunk on the premises; and by sect. 37 "excisable liquor" is to include sweets or wine, which now are or hereafter may be charged with duty either by customs or excise.

By stat. 4 & 5 W. 4, c. 77, s. 9, the excise duty on sweets or made wines is repealed; but, by sect. 10, the duty on licenses to be taken out by retailers thereof is continued, and all such licenses shall still be taken out.

Held that a person who, since the stat. 4 & 5 W. 4, c. 77, sold sweets or made wines by retail, &c., without a license could not be convicted under sect. 18 of stat. 9 G. 4, c. 61, sweets and made wines being no longer excisable liquors within the meaning of that Act. Dissentiente Erle, J. *Regina* v. *Lancashire,*   839

II. Information under Excise Acts dismissed, and appeal against such dismissal. Sessions cannot, on discussing such appeal, award costs against Crown, 492. COSTS, III. 1.

III. Summary conviction under stat. 4 & 5 W. 4, c. 85, ss. 2, 8, not within the exception in stat. 11 & 12 Vict. c. 43, s. 17, as to proceedings within the Excise Acts.

By stat. 4 & 5 W. 4, c. 85, s. 2, every person applying for a license to sell beer or cider by retail to be drunk on the premises must annually deposit with the excise a certificate of good character, signed by six householders. By sect. 8 a penalty is imposed upon summary conviction on any person who shall in such certificate certify any matter as true, knowing the same to be false. Other sections of the statute impose a duty on excise licenses for selling beer, &c., and relate to the revenue of excise. By stat. 11 & 12 Vict. c. 43, s. 17, summary convictions may be drawn up in a short form given in the schedule. But, by sect. 35, "nothing in the Act shall extend to any proceedings under or by virtue of any of the statutes relating to Her Majesty's revenue of excise."

Upon a rule to quash a conviction under sect. 8 of stat. 4 & 5 W. 4, c. 85, for an offence against sect. 2, which was drawn up in the form given in the schedule as authorized by sect. 17 of stat. 11 & 12 Vict. c. 43:

Held, that the conviction, which was for an offence against a police regulation in sect. 2, was sufficient, although there were in the statute other sections relating to the revenue of excise. The word "statutes" in sect. 35 is to be read as if it were "enactments." *Regina* v. *Bakewell,*   843

EXECUTION.

See JUDGMENT.

EXECUTORS AND ADMINISTRATORS.

I. What structures, erected by an incumbent on the glebe, his executors may remove, 237. INCUMBENT, I.

II. Bonâ fide payment and delivery to a feme covert, appointed co-executrix, but whose husband never assented to her acting, and to whom probate has in consequence been refused: when good, as a defence to action by co-executor.

Payment, by a debtor of a testator, and delivery of chattels bailed by the testator, by the bailee, to a feme covert who is appointed executrix, are valid as against the co-executor, though the husband of the executrix never assented to his wife acting as executrix, and, subsequently to the payment, refused to allow her to act, and although on that ground probate was refused to her; if the payment and delivery were made bonâ fide at the request of the executrix as such, without knowledge of the dissent of the husband, though with knowledge that she was a feme covert. *Pemberton* v. *Chapman,*   210

III. Action by administrator, original action by intestate having abated under the Statute of Limitations. Within what time he may sue, 283. STATUTE OF LIMITATIONS, II.

FEES.

I. To coroner.
Fee of 20s. for holding an inquest, under stat. 25 G. 2, c. 29: coroner not entitled unless Sessions think inquest properly held, 805. CORONER.

II. To clerk of justices. When he is liable to penalty for receiving too much: revision of fees by Sessions, 26. SESSIONS, VII.

FEME SOLE.—FEME COVERT.

See HUSBAND AND WIFE.

FRAUD.

Judgment against joint stock bank; execution against a shareholder, under stat. 7 & 8 Vict. c. 113, s. 10. No defence, that he was induced to become a shareholder by the fraud of the bank, 356. COMPANY, II. 3.

See also CONTRACT.

GAME LAWS.

See JUSTICES, II. 1, 2.

GENERAL AVERAGE.

See INSURANCE, II.

GUARDIAN.

See INFANT.

HABEAS CORPUS.

To restore a child between seven and fourteen to the custody of its legal guardian for nurture, 186. INFANT.

HIGH BAILIFF.

See COUNTY COURT, III.

HIGHWAY.

I. Compulsory repair by parish. Evidence of dedication.

On appeal against a conviction for obstructing a highway, the Sessions confirmed the conviction subject to a case; and it was brought before this Court by certiorari.

Held that this Court could not take notice of any objections to the conviction not stated in the case.

The case showed that the road in question was made by turnpike trustees, under a temporary Turnpike Act, which expired in 1848; but the whole line of turnpike road authorised by the Act was never completed. That the road as made had been used by the public, and had been repaired by the parish, both before and since the expiration of the Act: and the question for the Court was, if there was any evidence that it was a highway compulsorily repairable by the parish.

Held : that there was evidence of a dedication, and of an adoption by the public, and that, though the fact that the road was originally made under the Turnpike Act might explain away such evidence in fact, it did not conclusively in law rebut it.

Held, also, that the General Highway Act (5 & 6 W. 4, c. 50), sect. 23, did not apply to a road made by turnpike trustees; and that, consequently, the absence of a certificate by two justices, &c., as required by that section, did not prevent the road becoming compulsorily repairable by the parish, on a dedication by the owners of the soil in 1848. *Regina* v. *Thomas,*   399

II. Exemption from turnpike tolls under stat. 3 G. 4, c. 126, s. 32.

A parish road crossed a turnpike road from P. to W., at a place where there was a toll bar, and then met another turnpike road from P. to C. under the same trust as the first, but not being the same road. A carriage passing along the parish road, crossed the turnpike road from P. to W. at the turnpike, and then, without proceeding farther on that turnpike road, followed the parish road, and then went more than one hundred yards on the road from P. to C.

Held, that it was exempted from toll by stat. 3 G. 4, c. 126, s. 32, not having passed over one hundred yards on the same turnpike road, though it had passed more than that distance on one in the same trust. *Gerrard* v. *Parker,*   493

III. General Highway Act. (5 & 6 W. 4, c. 50.)

1. Does not apply to a road made by turnpike trustees, 399. Supra, I.

2. Arrears of rate under the Act, to whom payable, after the passing of the Metropolis Local Management Act, 5. METROPOLIS LOCAL MANAGEMENT ACT, II.

HUSBAND AND WIFE.

I. Payment and delivery to co-executrix, a feme covert, whose husband has not assented to her acting, and to whom probate has in consequence been refused: when a good defence to action by co-executor, 216. EXECUTORS AND ADMINISTRATORS, II.

II. Judgment against husband and wife, and execution against wife, for debt of wife dum sola. Discretion of Court as to discharging her from custody.

Where judgment is obtained against a husband and wife for the debt of the wife dum sola, and the wife is taken in execution, the Court, in its discretion, will discharge the wife from custody, unless it is shown that she has separate property which may be applied to the satisfaction of the debt.

Although the husband has not been and cannot be taken, he having obtained final protection from the Court of Insolvent Debtors.

It is not sufficient, in order to prevent this exercise of the discretion of the Court, that the wife's property was, before her marriage, assigned to trustees for her creditors, and the trustees had power, if they thought fit, to make her an allowance, and were to make over to her any surplus which might remain after the creditors should be satisfied. *Ison* v. *Butler,*   159

INCUMBENT.

I. What structures, erected by an incumbent on the glebe, may be removed by him or his executors.

A rector erected in the garden of the rectory, apart from the rectory house, hothouses about 70 feet long and between 10 and 20 feet high. They consisted of a frame and glass work, resting on brick walls about 2 feet high, and embedded in mortar on these walls.

Held that he, or his executors in a reasonable time after his death, were entitled to remove them, without incurring any liability as for either dilapidations or waste. *Martin v. Roe,* 237

II. Judgment against an incumbent, with suspension of execution, before his insolvency : subsequent vesting order by Insolvent Court. Sequestration on petition of assignee, when entitled to priority, 542. BANKRUPT AND INSOLVENT, III. 2.

INDICTMENT.

Removal of, by certiorari. CERTIORARI, III.

INFANT.

Right of custody of child between seven and fourteen, in the legal guardian for nurture ; when not affected by the wishes of the ward.

An infant of the age of ten years being brought up from a school, on habeas corpus, at the instance of the mother, who was guardian for nurture, the father being dead, and there being no testamentary guardian, although it was deposed that the child was of intelligence and wished on religious grounds to remain in the school, this Court refused to examine the child and ascertain its intelligence, holding that a guardian for nurture has a legal right to the custody of the ward, irrespective of the wishes of the ward, unless it be shown that the custody is sought for improper objects, or that the application is not bonâ fide, or that the guardian making the application is grossly immoral. And, in this case, no more appearing than that the father had been a Protestant, and that the mother was a Catholic, and intended to educate the child in her own persuasion, the Court ordered the child to be given to its mother. *Regina v. Clarke,* 186

INFORMATION.

Dismissal, by Sessions, of appeal against an information under the Excise Acts. Costs cannot be awarded against the Crown, 492. COSTS, III.

INFRINGEMENT.

Of patent. See PATENT.

INQUEST.

See CORONER.

INSOLVENT COURT.—INSOLVENT DEBTOR.

See BANKRUPT AND INSOLVENT.

INSPECTORS OF VOTES.

Under Metropolis Local Management Act. See ELECTION, III.

INSURANCE (MARINE).

I. Construction of policy.

1. Insurance against collision.

A ship, the M., was insured, "including the risk of running down or doing damage to any other vessel, the same as the Indemnity Company's policy," valued at 3000l. The Indemnity Company's running down clause is, that, if the ship, by negligence, shall run down any other vessel, "and the assured shall thereby become liable to pay, and shall pay, any sum not exceeding the value of the ship or vessel" (assured) "and her freight, by or in pursuance of the judgment of any Court of law or equity," the insurers shall pay "such proportion of three-fourths of the sum so paid as aforesaid as the sum" "hereby assured shall bear to the value of the said ship or vessel hereby assured and her freight."

The M., through negligence, ran down another vessel. The M. was sold under a decree of the Court of Admiralty, and the proceeds paid over for satisfying the damage. On a demurrer, upon pleadings in which it was admitted that the insured lost his ship, which was of the value of 3000l. and upwards, it being sold aginast his will, but that the proceeds which were paid over were only 2110l. :

Held, that the underwriters were bound to make good three-fourths of the proceeds actually paid, viz. 2110l., and not three-fourths of the value of the ship. *Thompson v. Reynolds,* 172

2. Time policy on cargo. When only maritime risks protected.

A time policy was made on the G. B. "on 15,000l. on cargo, valued at 15,000l. with liberty to increase the value on the homeward voyage." The body of the policy was in the ordinary printed form, expressing the risk on the goods to be from the loading thereof aboard the ship, including risk of craft, and to endure until discharged and safely landed. On the margin was a memorandum, "with liberty to load, reload, exchange, sell, or barter, all or either, goods or property on the coast of Africa and African islands, and with any vessels, boats, factories, canoes ; and to transfer interest from the vessel to any other vessel, or from any other vessels to this vessel, in port and at sea, and in any ports or places she may call at or proceed without being deemed a deviation."

The G. B. sailed to Africa with a cargo, part of which was landed in a factory for the purposes of barter, and was lying at anchor loading from the factory native produce, when the factory with its contents were destroyed by fire.

Held: that the policy embraced only maritime risks, and did not protect either the goods which had been part of the cargo of the G. B., but had been landed in the factory, nor the produce intended to be her cargo, but still on shore; whether that produce had been obtained by barter of the G. B.'s cargo or otherwise. *Harrison* v. *Ellis*, 465

II. General average.

Policy on chartered freight. Expenses of getting ship off shore, after cargo rescued, chargeable on ship, freight, and cargo.

A case without pleadings, between the insured and the underwriters on a policy on chartered freight, was stated, on which the following facts appeared.

The ship was chartered to proceed from Liverpool to a foreign port and there load a return cargo, for freight payable on delivery of the home cargo. She took on board an outward cargo and sailed. She was driven on a bank by a storm near Liverpool; and the cargo was rescued from her, and carried to Liverpool, and there warehoused; the ship still remaining ashore in a situation of peril. Some days afterwards the ship was got off and taken to Liverpool, where she was repaired, and again took the cargo on board and proceeded on her voyage.

It was agreed between the parties in the case that the freight was to be taken as liable to contribute to general average; and the question for the Court was, only, whether the expenses, incurred after the goods were in Liverpool, in getting the ship off, without which she could not have proceeded on her voyage or earned the chartered freight, were general average to which ship, freight, and cargo were to contribute; or were chargeable to ship alone; or were chargeable on any other principle.

Held: that, as the ship and freight were both in peril and both saved, the freight must contribute as well as the ship, supposing the cargo not to contribute.

But the Court drew the inference of fact that the whole saving of the cargo and ship was one continued transaction: and, on that hypothesis,

Held: that the expenses were general average to which ship, freight, and cargo must contribute. *Moran* v. *Jones*, 523

INTERPLEADER ACT.

(1 & 2 W. 4, c. 58.)

I. Action against depositee of title deeds (as security for a loan) by the party intrusted under the deeds, and contemporaneous demand by the heir of the bailor, having paid off the loan. Interplead. proceedings, 322. BAILMENT.

II. Interpleader issue between two creditors, claiming under separate bills of sale by the same party, one not being duly filed. Substance of issue.

A bill of sale of goods was bonâ fide made by J. H. to F. H. by way of security, and was filed, but with an affidavit which turned out to be defective. A subsequent bill of sale of the same goods, subject to that to F. H., was bonâ fide made by J. H. to E. by way of security, and was properly filed. A creditor of J. H. suing out execution against him required the sheriff to seize the goods as those of J. H. Two interpleader issues were directed, in which F. H. and E. respectively were plaintiffs, and the creditor defendant; in each of which the issue was whether the goods were the goods of the plaintiff.

In F. H.'s issue defendant had a verdict, on the ground that the bill of sale to F. H. was void as against defendant, a creditor, because not duly filed. In E.'s issue it was urged that, though void against defendant, F. H.'s bill of sale was valid as against E., and that therefore the goods were not the goods of E., and the defendant was entitled to the verdict in that issue.

Held, that the substance of the issue was to inform the Court whether the goods were seizable by the sheriff as against E.; that they were not so seizable, and that therefore the plaintiff was entitled to the verdict. *Edwards* v. *English*, 564

JUDGMENT.

FIRST: Against public companies.

I. Against a joint stock bank, and execution against a shareholder, under stat. 7 & 8 Vict. c. 113, s. 10. No defence, that he was induced to become a shareholder by fraud of the bank, &c., 356. COMPANY, II. 3.

II. Against official manager of an Irish Bank. The provisions of stat. 6 G. 4, c. 42, s. 12, as to judgments against public officers, applicable, under stat. 11 & 12 Vict. c. 45, to judgments against official managers, 960. COMPANY, II. 2.

SECONDLY: Against individuals.

III. Upon an award, confirming verdict taken in Vacation, subject to such award. When it may be signed, 102. ARBITRATION, II.

IV. Against husband and wife, and execution against wife for debt of wife dum sola. Discretion of Court as to discharging her out of custody, 159. HUSBAND AND WIFE, II.

V. Against an incumbent, with suspension of execution, before his insolvency. Subsequent vesting order by Insolvent Court: sequestration on petition of assignee, when entitled to priority, 542. BANKRUPT AND INSOLVENT, III. 2.

VI. Set-off of one judgment against another, in two actions by the same party. Lien for costs, 84. CONTRACT, III. 2.

JURISDICTION.

FIRST: Of the Superior Courts.

I. Mandamus, in particular cases.

1. Lies to mayor and assessors of a borough, under 5 & 6 W. 4, c. 76, to revise the burgess lists. What is a refusal by them of adjudication. Form and direction of writ, 916. MUNICIPAL CORPORATION REFORM ACT, I.

2. Lies to justices to issue a distress warrant to levy a sum disallowed in the accounts of the relieving officer by the poor law auditor, the statutable proof of surcharge being complete, 950. POOR, III. 3.

3. Lies to justices to hear and determine an information, dismissed by them on grounds amounting to a refusal to adjudicate, 757. Infra, XVI.

4. Does not lie to Insolvent Court to make an order vesting surplus assets in assignee, instead of insolvent, 366. Infra, IX.

II. Rule, under stat. 11 & 12 Vict. c. 44, s. 5, to justices, to hear and determine. See JUSTICES, infra, XVI., &c.

III. Enforcement of rule of Court.

Agreement to become a party to a reference at Nisi Prius. Consent need not appear upon the face of the order. When Court has jurisdiction to enforce order summarily, 929. ARBITRATION, I.

IV. Jurisdiction as to proceedings brought up from inferior tribunals.

1. Confirmation, by Sessions, subject to a case, of appeal against conviction for obstructing a highway. Court cannot take notice of objections to the conviction not stated in the case, 399. HIGHWAY, I.

2. Decision of magistrate, on a summons under Metropolis Local Management Act, that a certain street was not a "new street" within the Act, cannot be inquired into, as to its correctness, by the Court of Q. B., 672. Infra, XX.

3. On an appeal against a conviction for infringing a by-law of the town council, under Municipal Corporation Reform Act, Court of Q. B. may receive a special case stated by the Recorder by consent of the parties, though no certiorari lies, 831. CERTIORARI, II.

SECONDLY: Of a Judge at Chambers.

V. Making of order, upon granting a certiorari to remove an indictment, for payment of prosecutor's costs by one of two joint defendants, in the event of either being convicted, 140. CERTIORARI, III. 2.

THIRDLY: Of County Courts.

VI. Issuing of warrant, under Absconding Debtors Arrest Act, not a proceeding in the county court. Therefore high bailiff not liable to penalty for acting for party applying, 803. COUNTY COURT, III.

VII. Order of discharge by Insolvent Court, comprising a county court judgment debt. County court cannot afterwards commit for such debt, 679. COUNTY COURT, IV.

VIII. County court has no jurisdiction, under stat. 18 & 19 Vict. c. 63, to settle a dispute of a Friendly Society of which the rules were not enrolled before, but have been deposited after the passing of the Act, and which has not obtained a certificate, 339. COUNTY COURT, I.

FOURTHLY: Of Bankruptcy and Insolvent Courts.

IX. Jurisdiction of Insolvent Court, as to making an order vesting surplus assets in the insolvent, his heirs, executors, &c.

Under stat. 1 & 2 Vict. c. 110, s. 92, which directs that it shall be lawful for the Insolvent Debtors' Court, if there be a surplus after satisfaction of the debts, to make an order vesting such surplus in the insolvent, his heirs, executors, administrators, and assigns, that Court acts judicially and not merely ministerially.

Therefore, where a party claimed such order under an alleged assignment from the insolvent, and that Court, upon inquiry, held the assignment invalid as against other claimants; this Court refused to issue a mandamus commanding the Insolvent Debtors' Court to make an order vesting the property in the alleged assignee. *Regina v. Law*, 366.

FIFTHLY: Of Quarter Sessions.

X. Discretion of Sessions as to dismissing an appeal against a poor-rate, appellant having previously, with his notice of appeal, given notice that he should apply for a respite, 609. APPEAL, II. ?.

XI. Rule absolute to Sessions to enter continuances and hear an appeal, notice not having been served on all parties interested.

Service of a second notice, omitting some of the parties and some of the objections in the first, not a proper service, and appeal dismissable, 619. APPEAL, II. 2.

XII. Sessions cannot award costs against the Crown, on dismissing an appeal against the dismissal of an information under the Excise Acts, 492. COSTS, III. 1.

XIII. Where an order of Sessions, confirming an order of justices, is silent as to costs, Sessions cannot make a second order confirming their first order and giving costs, 935. COSTS, III. 2.

XIV. Sessions have no power to adjourn approval of table of fees, made under stat. 26 G. 2, c. 14, 26. SESSIONS, VII.

XV. Jurisdiction of Sessions as to disallowance to coroner of the fee of 20s., payable under stat. 25 G. 2, c. 29, 805. CORONER.

SIXTHLY: Of justices.

XVI. Dismissal, by justices, of an information. What objections amount to a declining of jurisdiction.

A party was summoned before justices upon an information, under sect. 11 of stat. 18 & 19 Vict. c. 108, charging that he, "being one of the owners and manager" of a colliery, had worked the colliery without providing the boiler with a proper steam gauge, as required by sect. 4. In defence, he contended that, as there were other owners, they ought to be charged together with him: but he did not deny that he was resident owner and took an active part in the management.

The justices, upon this objection alone, dismissed the complaint, considering the information to be bad on the face of it, because it showed that there were other owners.

Mandamus granted, commanding them to hear and determine the information: For that

(1) The objection was invalid.

(2) The justices had not exercised jurisdiction, but had declined it, the objection being preliminary, though taken in defence and not at the outset. Hawitante Crompton, J. . Regina v. Brown, 757

XVII. Jurisdiction of justices on an application for a distress warrant to levy a sum disallowed to the relieving officer by the poor law auditor, 950. POOR, III. 3.

XVIII. Jurisdiction of justices as to order upon a parish for arrears of expenses of maintenance of a pauper lunatic. Effect of stat. 16 & 17 Vict. c. 97, on previous orders of maintenance, 144. POOR, III. 2.

XIX. General rule (semble) as to jurisdiction of justices, where a bonâ fide claim of title to land is set up by way of defence.

A conviction under stat. 1 & 2 W. 4, c. 32, s. 30, and stat. 11 & 12 Vict. c. 43, s. 22, against four defendants for trespass in pursuit of game, contained an order that, "if the said several sums" (being the penalty and costs of conviction before awarded to be paid by each defendant) "be not paid on or before the 10th November instant, we adjudge each of them the said" (names of the defendants) "to be imprisoned" "for the space of one month, unless the said several sums and the costs and charges of conveying each of them, the said" (names of the defendants), "so making default, to the said common gaol, shall be sooner paid."

By stat. 1 & 2 W. 4, c. 32, s. 30, it is provided "that any person charged with any such trespass shall be at liberty to prove, by way of defence, any matter which would have been a defence to an action at law for such trespass."

At the hearing before the justices, a bonâ fide claim of title to the land was set up on behalf of the defendants; but no evidence was offered of the actual existence of any dispute, or of any title in the person under whom the defendants claimed.

Held, that the conviction was bad; for that it adjudicated each defendant to be imprisoned for one month, unless the costs and charges of conveying all to gaol should be sooner paid, and it was not in the form authorised by stat. 11 & 12 Vict. c. 43, s. 17, or to the like effect.

Semble: that the jurisdiction to convict summarily was ousted; that the general rule is that, in case of summary convictions, justices have jurisdiction to determine whether the claim to title to real property is set up bonâ fide; but, if it is bonâ fide set up, they have no jurisdiction to proceed further in the matter: that the proviso in stat. 1 & 2 W. 4, c. 32, s. 30, does not give justices jurisdiction, upon a charge of trespass in pursuit of game, to determine a claim of title to land against the wish of the defendants. Regina v. Cridland, 853

XX. Jurisdiction of a magistrate, on a summons under Metropolis Local Management Act, to decide whether a certain street was a "new street" within the Act.

A Metropolitan Police Magistrate, on a summons for an order, under the Metropolis Local Management Act (18 & 19 Vict. c. 120, ss. 105, 226), upon the proprietor of houses in D., alleged to be a "new street" within the metropolis, for his share of the expenses of paving it, after hearing the parties and their evidence, dismissed the summons on the ground that D. was not a "new street" within the meaning of the enactment, because it was an old highway. A rule, under stat. 11 & 12 Vict. c. 44, s. 5, calling on him to hear and adjudicate on the complaint, was obtained, with a view of obtaining the decision of this Court, that D. might be a "new street" within stat. 18 & 19 Vict. c. 120, s. 105, though it was an old highway.

. Held, by Lord Campbell, C. J., Wightman and Crompton, Js., that this Court could not inquire whether the magistrate came to a right conclusion or not, but only whether he had adjudicated ; and, they being of opinion that he had done so, the rule was discharged without any expression of opinion as to whether he was right or wrong in his construction of the Act.

Erle, J., dissentiente, and holding that, as the magistrate could not safely proceed unless D. was a new street, his decision, that it was not, was such as to give this Court jurisdiction under stat. 11 & 12 Vict. c. 44, s. 5, to determine whether he was right or wrong in that decision. *Regina* v. *Dayman*,   672

XXI. Jurisdiction of a magistrate to decide, upon a summons to pay a lighting rate, whether two meetings, held at different times by the rate-payers, for levying rates, were substantially the same meeting.

Under stat. 3 & 4 W. 4, c. 90, a meeting of the rated inhabitants of the parish of H. was held, to determine whether the provisions of the Act should be applied to the parish. The assent of as much as two-thirds of the voters was not given. Within a year, a meeting was held of the rated inhabitants of a district of the parish, to determine whether the Act should be applied to that district ; when two-thirds of the voters assented. A rate was laid upon the district in conformity with this.

S., one of the parties so rated, having refused to pay the rate, was summoned before the justices, when he objected that, the latter meeting having been held within a year of the former, the proceedings were void by sect. 16, and the rate invalid. The parties agreed that the question was whether the two meetings were substantially the same. The justices decided in the affirmative, and refused a warrant for levying.

Held, that the question was properly put before the magistrates, and that, they having determined it, the Court could not, on a rule to order the justices to issue a distress warrant, review their decision.

Although S. had, before he was aware of the objection, paid a rate. *Regina* v. *Dunn*,   220

XXII. Discretion of a justice as to adjudicating, upon a summons, under Metropolis Local Management Act, of a gas company by a district board of works, for opening ground without their consent.

A district board of works, under sects. 109 and 227 of The Metropolis Local Management Act (18 & 19 Vict. c. 120), and stat. 11 & 12 Vict. c. 43, summoned a gas company before a justice for opening ground without the consent of the Board. The Company defended the proceeding on the ground that, under their charter and certain Local Acts, they were justified. The justice stated that he considered the answer valid, and that the summons ought to be dismissed ; but, at the request of the Board, he refused to adjudicate, stating that he did so in order that the opinion of this Court might be obtained. The Company insisted on his dismissing the summons.

A rule having been obtained by the Board for an order directing the justice to adjudicate and convict, this Court discharged the rule, refusing to give any opinion upon the question, holding that the justice must act upon his own view, and could not by this proceeding obtain the opinion of the Court ; and that the Board, having requested him to refuse to adjudicate, were not entitled to an order compelling him to do so.

Stat. 11 & 12 Vict. c. 44, s. 5, is inapplicable to such a case. *Regina* v. *Paynter*,   328

XXIII. Summary conviction, under stat. 4 & 5 W. 4, c. 85, ss. 2, 8, not within the exception as to excise proceedings in stat. 11 & 12 Vict. c. 43, s. 17, 848. Excise, III.

SEVENTHLY : Of municipal officers.

XXIV. Of inspectors of votes, under Metropolis Local Management Act, 954. Election, III. 1.

EIGHTHLY : Of a jury.

XXV. In an action for infringement of a patent, 738. Patent, III.

XXVI. Under sect. 68 of Lands Clauses Consolidation Act. Certiorari lies for excess of jurisdiction as to a particular item of compensation, though such excess not upon the face of the proceedings, 660. Lands Clauses Consolidation Act.

JUSTICES.

Jurisdiction of, generally. See Jurisdiction, XVI.

I. Orders of.

Amendment by Court of Q. B., under stat. 12 & 13 Vict. c. 45, s. 7. General rule.

An affiliation summons against H. was served at the house of H.'s father. An attorney appeared to the summons before the justices for the petty sessional division of B. in the county of N., representing himself to be authorized to appear for H. In fact he was retained and paid by H.'s father. He examined and cross-examined witnesses. An order was drawn up purporting to be made on the complaint of the mother "residing at M. within the county," and to be made as on a contested summons, the defendant appearing by attorney. In fact M. was not only in the county, but in the petty sessional division of B., as was well known to every one; but nothing was said about it. H. deposed that, a few days before the summons was served, he, anticipating annoyance from the woman, left his father's house, which had up to that time been his abode, without any intention to return, and was not informed of the proceedings before the justices. A rule to quash the order having been obtained, on the grounds that the attorney was not authorised to appear and that the order did not mention that M. was within the division,

Held: that the Court would infer in fact that H., leaving his abode avowedly for a temporary motive, did intend to return when the, motive ceased, notwithstanding his deposition to the contrary; and that, such being taken to be the fact, the summons was duly served; and that, all proper to be proved in an unopposed summons having in fact appeared before the justices, and the state of proof being such as would justify them in drawing up an order stating M. to be in the division of B., the omissions and mistakes were amendable by this Court under stat. 12 & 13 Vict. c. 45, s. 7. *Regina* v. *Higham*, 557

II. Summary convictions. Decisions as to sufficiency, in particular cases.

1. Conviction for killing a pheasant; adjudication, that the penalty be "paid and applied according to law," held sufficient.

A conviction for killing a pheasant, contrary to sect. 3 of stat. 1 & 2 W. 4, c. 32, following the form given in Schedule (I. 2) to stat. 11 & 12 Vict. c. 43, adjudged the offender to forfeit and pay a penalty, "to be paid and applied according to law." By sect. 37 of stat. 1 & 2 W. 4, c. 32, and sect. 21 of stat. 5 & 6 W. 4, c. 20, the penalty is directed to be paid, one half to the informer, and one half to some one of the overseers of the poor, or to some other officer (as the convicting justice or justices may direct) of the parish, &c., in which the offence shall have been committed. Held: that the conviction was sufficient by virtue of sects. 17 and 32 of stat. 11 & 12 Vict. c. 43, being in the form given by the Schedule to that Act referred to in sect. 17, though it did not in terms distribute the penalty, nor name the informer or the overseer to whom the penalty was to be paid. *Regina* v. *Hyde*,   559, note

2. Conviction of several defendants, for trespass in pursuit of game. Held bad for adjudicating that *each* should be imprisoned until the costs of conveying *all* to gaol had been paid, 853. JURISDICTION, XIX.

3. Conviction and imprisonment of a workman, under stat. 4 G. 4, c. 34, s. 3, for leaving service before time of contract had expired. Wording of conviction, 697. MASTER AND SERVANT.

4. Conviction under Sale of Beer, &c., Act, for false certificate, not within the exception as to excise proceedings in stat. 11 & 12 Vict. c. 42, s. 17, 848. EXCISE, III.

III. Clerk.

When liable to penalty, under stat. 26 G. 2, c. 14, s. 2, for taking too large a fee, 26. SESSIONS, VII.

LAND.

I. Agreement relating to sale of interest in. See STATUTE OF FRAUDS.

II. Covenants running with. See CONTRACT, V. 4.

LANDS CLAUSES CONSOLIDATION ACT.

(8 & 9 VICT. c. 18.)

I. Compensation, under sects. 68, &c. Meaning of "injuriously affected."

Compensation cannot be claimed under the Lands Clauses and Railways Clauses Consolidation Acts, 1845 (8 & 9 Vict. c. 18, and 8 & 9 Vict. c. 20), for deterioration in the value of property adjoining a railway, by reason of the premises being overlooked by persons on the railway and railway platform.

Actual injury to premises from the vibration caused by ballast trains, &c., on the railway, during the construction of the works, is a ground for compensation under these statutes; but, per Lord Campbell, C. J., not injury from that cause after the construction of the railway.

Where a jury, summoned under stat. 8 & 9 Vict. c. 18, s. 68, have taken into consideration, in awarding compensation, one claim, among others, as to which they had no jurisdiction, a certiorari lies, although such excess of jurisdiction does not appear upon the face of the proceedings.

Such excess of jurisdiction may be shewn upon affidavit. *Re Penny*,   660

II. Excess of jurisdiction by jury, as to a particular item of compensation, under sect. 68. Certiorari lies, though such excess does not appear upon the face of the proceedings, 660. Supra, I.

LANDLORD AND TENANT.

I. Mortgage, by tenant, afterwards bankrupt, of his goods. Mortgagee not protected against distress for rent due from mortgagor.

The goods of a trader on premises of which he was tenant were mortgaged for more than their value. The mortgagee entered and took possession. Then the tenant became bankrupt, owing more than a year's rent. Held, that the landlord might make his distress upon those goods available for the whole rent due; sect. 129, of the Bankrupt Law Consolidation Act, 1849, protecting only the interest of the assignees of the bankrupt, and not that of his mortgagee.

The assignees of the bankrupt, being ordered to elect whether they would accept or decline the tenancy, declined it. No formal notice was given to the bankrupt; and nothing was done. Then, a fresh quarter having elapsed: Held, that the tenancy continued, and that the landlord might distrain on the goods of the mortgagee for the quarter's rent thus accruing. *Brocklehurst* v. *Lawe*,　　176

II. Attornment and payment of rent to a receiver in Chancery under a decree: subsequent sale of term by receiver: relation of landlord does not enure to purchaser.

In an action of replevin, brought by E. against M., M. avowed for rent arrear in respect of a farm V., and E. pleaded in bar denying the tenancy.

M., in support of the avowry, proved that C. had filed a bill against E. and others, in which C. claimed to be entitled to V. as tenant for life, subject to a term of 1000 years and a later mortgage for 500 years, and prayed for an account of what was due on the trusts of the term of 1000 years and the mortgage; and that directions might be given to raise the sums required for the trusts of the term; that C. might be permitted to redeem the mortgage; that E. and the mortgagee might be decreed to deliver V. to C.; that the money which ·C. should pay for the redemption might be raised by sale of V.; and that a receiver might be appointed of the rents of V.

M. further proved that the Court of Chancery decreed that V. should be sold, and that out of the proceeds the sum required for the trusts of the term should be first paid, then the mortgage debt; that a receiver should be appointed, and that E., who was in possession of V., should attorn to him for V.

That a receiver was appointed; and E. attorned to him, adding, "such attornment being without prejudice to my right to appeal against the decree."

That E. paid the rent to the receiver, and afterwards to another receiver appointed on the death of the first.

That the term of one thousand years was sold to M., and the termor in trust conveyed to M.

Held: that on this evidence, and assuming M. to have a good title under the term, the relation of landlord and tenant was still not proved to exist between M. and E.

Where a case from a county court was stated by the parties at unnecessary length, the judge signing it in obedience to the county court rule, this Court, in reversing the judgment of the county court, refused costs. *Evans* v. *Mathias*,　　599

LAY DAYS.

See SHIP, II. 5.

LIBEL.

I. Publication of defamatory matter. Newspaper report.

The publication of matter defamatory of an individual is not privileged because the libel is contained in a fair report in a newspaper of what passed at a public meeting. *Davison* v. *Duncan*,　　229

II. Action for libel; justification, setting out a particular transaction, and averring that the libel was written and published solely with reference to that.

Declaration alleged that plaintiff was cashier to Q., and that defendant, in a letter addressed to Q., falsely and maliciously wrote and published of plaintiff the words " I conceive there is nothing too base for him to be guilty of."

Plea, in justification, alleged that plaintiff signed and delivered to defendant an I. O. U., and afterwards, on having sight thereof, falsely and fraudulently asserted that the signature was not his; and the plea averred that the libel was written and published solely in reference to this transaction.

Held: a sufficient justification, as the libel must be understood with reference to the subject-matter. *Tighe* v. *Cooper*,　　639

LIEN.

For costs. See CONTRACT, III. 2.

LIMITATION.

Of actions. See STATUTE OF LIMITATIONS.

Of estates. See WILL.

LIS MOTA.—LIS PENDENS.

See EVIDENCE, I. 1.

LOCAL AUTHORITY.

Under Nuisances Removal Act. See NUISANCES REMOVAL ACT.

LOCAL BOARD OF HEALTH.

See PUBLIC HEALTH ACT.

LUNATIC.—LUNATIC ASYLUM.

See POOR.

MAINTENANCE.

Of actions. See CONTRACT, III. 1.
Of poor. See POOR.

MALICE.

Allegation and proof of, necessary in an action against a churchwarden for rejecting a vote at an election of vestrymen and auditors, under Metropolis Local Management Act, 377. ELECTION, III. 2.

MANDAMUS.

See JURISDICTION, I.

MASTER AND SERVANT.

I. Conviction and imprisonment of a workman, under stat. 4 G. 4, c. 34, s. 3, for leaving service before time of contract had expired. Such conviction and imprisonment does not destroy the contract.

Under stat. 4 G. 4, c. 34, s. 3, a potter was convicted and sentenced to imprisonment for leaving a service before the time of contract was expired. After the imprisonment had expired, but before the original time of contract had expired, he, not having returned to the service, was again convicted for absenting himself. Held: that the second conviction was good, as the contract continued, notwithstanding the first conviction and imprisonment.

The conviction did not expressly state that the servant had entered the service; but it found that he did "misconduct himself in his said service." Held: that this was a sufficient finding of his having entered into the service.

The conviction stated that it appeared to the magistrate, as well on the examination on oath of M., in presence of the party charged, "as otherwise," that the party had absented himself, &c. Held: that it was not to be inferred from this that the justice had proceeded upon evidence not given in the presence of the party.

The conviction stated that the party misconducted himself, &c., "by neglecting and

absenting himself from his said masters' service." Held: that this was not a finding of two statutable offences, but only of the absenting. *Ex parte Baker*,   697

II. Meaning of "artificer" within the Truck Act, 115. TRUCK ACT.

MEMORANDA.

Hilary Term, 375.
Hilary Vacation, 376.
Trinity Term, 696.

MEMORANDUM.

Of insurance. See INSURANCE.

METROPOLIS LOCAL MANAGEMENT ACT.
(18 & 19 VICT. c. 120.)

I. Sect. 16. Election of vestrymen and auditors.

1. Action against churchwarden, for refusing a vote. Necessary to allege and prove malice, 377. ELECTION, III. 2.

2. Jurisdiction of inspectors of votes, 954. ELECTION, III. 1.

II. Sect. 97. By whom, after the passing of the Act, are to be collected arrears of a rate made under the General Highway Act.

Under the General Highway Act, 5 & 6 W. 4, c. 50, s. 18, a board was elected, on 26th March, 1855, to serve the office of surveyors of the highways in a parish for the year ensuing. On 23d November, 1855, they made a highway-rate. In August, 1855, The Metropolis Local Management Act (18 & 19 Vict. c. 120) passed; and, by sect. 251, it came into operation on 1st January, 1856. On 28th November, 1855, under sects. 31, 32, a District Board of Works was elected for the district comprehending the parish, which was included in Part I. of Schedule (B).

After 25th March, 1856, application was made, on the part of the late Highway Board, to a party rated to the said highway-rate, for payment of arrears of the rate, under sect. 97 of stat. 18 & 19 Vict. c. 120. Payment not having been made, a summons was taken out against the party; but the magistrate refused to issue a warrant for levying. Afterwards the party paid the arrear to the District Board of Works.

A rule having been obtained for an order directing the magistrate to issue the warrant, this Court discharged the rule, on the ground that the collection of such arrears was not, under sect. 97, to be made by the late Highway Board. *Regina v. Ingham*,   5

III. Sects. 105, 226. Decision of magistrate, on

a summons for an order, that a certain street was not a "new street" within the Act, cannot be inquired into, as to its correctness, by the Court of Q. B., 672. JURISDICTION, XX.

IV. Sects. 109, 227. Summons of a Gas Company, by District Board of Works, for opening ground without their consent. Discretion of justice as to adjudicating, 328. JURISDICTION, XXII.

V. Sect. 147. Action by Board of Works, to recover for a sewers' rate under stat. 11 & 12 Vict. c. 112. The question of rateability cannot be raised in such action, but only by appeal to Commissioners of Sewers, 964. RATE, V.

MINE.

Right of owner of surface to support, as against owner of mine.

An enclosure Act vested the surface of the land in allottees, and the mines in the lord of the manor, and prohibited the lord from working the mines within forty perpendicular yards of the foundation of buildings on the surface.

Held by the Exchequer Chamber, confirming the judgment of the Queen's Bench, that this prohibition did not affect the common law right of the owner of the surface to support, and that he might maintain an action against the lord for working the mines so as to cause the buildings on the surface, belonging to the owner of the surface, to give way, though the mines had been worked with ordinary care and not within forty perpendicular yards of the foundation of the buildings. *Haines v. Roberts,* 625

MISREPRESENTATION.

I. By a party, bonâ fide, but under a mistake, that he had authority to act as agent: action lies against him, the contract being repudiated by the alleged principal, for breach of his promise that he had authority, 301. PRINCIPAL AND AGENT, III. 1.

II. Action for breach of implied warranty that defendant had authority to purchase a ship on behalf of another party. Resale of ship: measure of damages, 568. DAMAGES, II.

MONEY HAD AND RECEIVED.
See ACTION, I.

MORTGAGE.

Of goods, &c., by a trader, afterwards bankrupt. Mortgagee not protected from distress for rent due from mortgagor, 176. LANDLORD AND TENANT, I.

MUNICIPAL CORPORATION REFORM ACT.
(5 & 6 W. 4, c. 76.)

I. Sects. 15-22. Revision of burgess lists.

Mandamus to mayor and assessors, to revise. What grounds of objection by them amount to a refusal to adjudicate. Form and direction of writ.

Mandamus directed to the mayor and assessors of R., a borough within the Municipal Corporation Reform Act, 5 & 6 W. 4, c. 76, comprising several parishes. Suggestions: that, at the Court holden in October, 1856, before the mayor and assessors for the revision of the burgess lists of that year, the mayor and assessors refused to revise the burgess list of the parish of S. on the ground that the list had not been affixed in some public place in the borough for a week. Mandatory part to the mayor and assessors to hold a Court and revise the list for this parish. The writ was tested in January, 1857. Return by the mayor, that the mayor who presided in October, 1856, went out of office in November, 1856; that the present mayor was not the same person, but would obey if he could. Demurrer to this return, and to an insufficient return by one of the assessors.

Another mandamus, directed and tested in the same way, contained suggestions that, at the Court in October, 1856, the mayor and assessors refused to hear and consider the list of objections for the parish of St. N., on the ground that the list of objections had not been personally delivered to the town clerk, though it had been given to his servant and came to his hands. Mandatory part to the mayor and assessors to hold a court and revise the burgess list so far as related to the names contained in the list of objections. Similar returns. Demurrer.

Held: that the provisions of the Municipal Corporation Reform Act (sects. 15 to 22), as to the time at which the burgess lists were to be revised, were directory only; and that this Court could grant a mandamus to revise them, after the 15th October.

That the mayor and assessors, though not a corporation, were in the nature of a standing tribunal, to whom the writ was well directed, and who could obey it though the individual members were changed.

That the grounds on which the mayor and assessors refused to revise the burgess list in the one case, and hear the objections in the other, were untenable, and amounted, not to an erroneous exercise of jurisdiction, but to a refusal to adjudicate.

That there was no objection to the form of the writ in the St. N. case, as it commanded the performance of the whole of that part of the duty which appeared to be unperformed. Peremptory mandamus awarded in both cases. *Regina* v. *Mayor of Rochester*, 910

II. Sect 58. Bond by treasurer of borough. Present liability of sureties.

A bond executed before the passing of stat. 6 & 7 Vict. c. 89, by the sureties of P., treasurer of a borough, was subject to a condition by which, after reciting that P. had been elected treasurer under stat. 5 & 6 W. 4, c. 76, it was provided that the bond should be void if P. should account for moneys that might come to his hands as treasurer "(whether by virtue of his present or any subsequent appointment to the said office), according to the directions and true intent and meaning of the said statute, and in every other respect act in strict conformance with the same, and all other laws and regulations now or hereafter to be in force touching the said office of treasurer, or the person or persons performing or liable to perform the duties thereof."

Held, that the sureties were liable for misconduct of P. after the tenure of the office had been altered by stat. 6 & 7 Vict. c. 89, from an annual office to an office held during pleasure. *Mayor of Dartmouth* v. *Silly*, 97

III. Sect. 66. Compensation to officers for removal, or abolition of office.

After the passing of stat. 5 & 6 Vict. c. 111, the corporate borough of B. was created by charter, not containing a non-intromittant clause. Its area was a part of the county of S. A grant of a Court of Quarter Sessions was made, and the council appointed a clerk of the peace for the borough.

Held, that the clerk of the peace of the county of S. was not entitled to compensation under sect. 66 of stat. 5 & 6 W. 4, c. 76, he not having been removed nor his office abolished, although the profits were diminished. *Regina* v. *Council of Brighton*, 249

IV. Sects. 90, 91, 132.

By-laws of town council. On appeal against a conviction for infringing them, Court of Q. B. will receive a special case stated by Recorder with consent of parties, though sect. 132 takes away certiorari, 831. CERTIORARI, II.

V. Sects. 84, 92. Local Acts. Levying of rates by town council.

Where part of the land comprehended within a municipal borough has, previously to the coming into operation of stat. 5 & 6 W. 4, c. 76, ss. 84, 92, been subject, under a local Act, to a rate including the expense of watching, and part expressly exempted, the town council, under those sections, may rate so much of the exempt part, for the purposes

of watching, as is not more than 200 yards distant from any street or continuous line of houses regularly watched; but they cannot rate parts more distant, if exempt under the local Act.

And, though the council does not lay a watch-rate, but defrays the expenses of watching out of the borough fund of which part is raised by a general borough-rate to be paid by the parish officers out of the poor-rate, parties cannot be indirectly made to contribute to the expense of watching, in respect of parts so exempt and so distant, by being rated to a poor-rate partly applicable to the borough fund; but such poor-rate, so far as applicable to such expenses, cannot be sustained as against such parties. *Hallett* v. *Overseers of Brighton*, 342

NEWSPAPER.

Report of proceedings at a public meeting. Publication of defamatory matter not privileged, 229. LIBEL, I.

NEGLIGENCE.

Contractors acting bonâ fide under the authority of the Metropolitan Commissioners of Sewers, not liable for negligence, 426. SEWERS.

NOT GUILTY.

See PLEADING, II. 3.

NUISANCES REMOVAL ACT.
(18 & 19 VICT. c. 121.)

Sects. 10, 12, 14. Notice to Local Authority by party aggrieved by nuisance. Discretion of Local Authority as to enforcing order.

Under The Nuisances Removal Act for England, 1855 (18 & 19 Vict. c. 121), the sanitary inspector for The Local Authority of a district obtained an order of justices for the abatement of a nuisance. The Local Authority were requested by the party aggrieved by the nuisance to take steps for enforcing the order, but did not do so. This court refused an application by the party aggrieved, for a mandamus to compel the Local Authority to enforce the order. *Ex parte Bassett*, 238

OCCUPATION.

Rateability by reason of. See RATE, I. 1, 1.

OFFICIAL MANAGER.

See COMPANY, II. 2.

ORDER.

Of reference. See ARBITRATION.

Vesting order. See BANKRUPT AND INSOLVENT, III. 2 : IV. 1.

Order of discharge by Insolvent Court. See BANKRUPT AND INSOLVENT, IV. 2.

Orders of Justices. See JUSTICES, I.

PATENT.

I. Action for infringement, brought by assignee of patent. Plea, denying the assignment, held good, upon evidence of non-registration under Patent Law Amendment Act.

To a declaration for infringement of a patent, brought by an alleged assignee (by indenture) of the patent, the defendant pleaded, by denying the assignment modo et formâ. On the trial, it appeared that an instrument of assignment had been executed by the patentee, but that it had not been registered under The Patent Law Amendment Act, 1852 (15 & 16 Vict. c. 83). Held that, as, by sect. 35, the original patentee is, until the entry of the registration, to be deemed and taken to be the sole and exclusive proprietor of the patent, the defendant was entitled to a verdict.

Although the objection was not specified in the notice of objections delivered by him. *Chollet* v. *Hoffman*, 686

II. Patent for working flour mills. Construction of specification. What would amount to an infringement.

A patentee, in his specification, claimed, as his invention, exhausting from millstone cases the dusty air blown through between the grinding surfaces, by a blast of air; being a combination of a blast and an exhaust applied to the working of a mill. The claim was not restricted to any particular mode of creating or applying the blast of air, nor to any particular mode of producing the exhaust; and both blast and exhaust had previously been used separately in working mills. Held: that the invention of this combination and application of a blast and an exhaust might be made the subject of a patent.

From the general description, it appeared that the upper stone was fixed and the lower stone was made to rotate; and some advantages were pointed out as resulting from this arrangement. *Quære*, whether, according to the true construction of the specification, the claim should be limited to the application of a combination of a blast and an exhaust with a mill in which only the lower stone rotates?

But, Held that, if the claim be so limited, the use of a new part of the combination, viz. a combination of blast and exhaust, though in connexion with a mill in which the upper stone does rotate, may be an in-

fringement of the patent. *Sevill* v. *Keyworth*, 725

III. Patent for making envelopes. What would be an infringement of the particular patent. Question of infringement for the jury.

In an action for the infringement of a patent, the question of infringement or not is for the jury and not the Judge, although there be no question with respect to whether the defendant has or has not used the particular machine or process which is alleged to be an infringement.

The specification of a patent for an invention of "improvements in the manufacture of envelopes" described a machine in which a piece of paper was held upon a platform, whilst the flaps of the envelope were folded, and concluded by claiming " the so arranging machinery that the flaps of envelopes may be folded thereby as herein described." Held : that a machine in which the flaps of an envelope were folded might be an infringement of the patent, although the envelope was not held down during the operation of folding.

The specification of a patent for an invention with a similar title described and claimed " the application of gum or cement to the flaps of envelopes by apparatus acting in the manner of surface printing." Held : that an apparatus for applying the gum might be an infringement, although it acted only in part in the manner of surface printing according to the description contained in the specification. *De La Rue* v. *Dickenson*, 728

PATENT LAW AMENDMENT ACT.

(15 & 16 VICT. c. 83.)

See PATENT, I.

PAYMENT INTO COURT.

See PLEADING, II. 2.

PENALTY.

I. For reception of too large a fee, by clerk of justices : when payable, 26. SESSIONS, VII.

II. High bailiff of county court, not liable to penalty for acting for a party applying to the county court for a warrant under the Absconding Debtors Arrest Act, 603. COUNTY COURT, III.

III. Information for penalty under the Excise Acts : dismissal. Sessions cannot, on dismissing an appeal against such dismissal, award costs against the Crown, 492. COSTS, III. 1.

IV. Penalty upon conviction for killing a pheasant, under stat. 1 & 2 W. 4, c. 32. Adjudication, that it be " paid and applied according to law," held sufficient, 859, note. JUSTICES, II. 1.

PLEA.

See PLEADING, II.

PLEADING.

I. Declaration.

1. Joinder of plaintiffs. One of several co-contractors, barred by his own act from claiming under the contract, cannot recover for a breach of it by joining the others.

Action by J. and two other plaintiffs on a contract, on the deposit of goods by the three plaintiffs with defendant, not to give them up without the joint order of the three plaintiffs. Breach, that they were given up without the joint order. Plea, that they were given up to J., one of the present plaintiffs, at his request. On demurrer:

Held a good plea; for J., being disabled from suing for what he himself procured, could not at law sue, though joining other plaintiffs with him. *Brandon v. Scott*, 234

1. Declaration against churchwarden, for refusing a vote at an election of vestrymen and auditors, under Metropolis Local Management Act. Necessary to allege malice, 377. ELECTION, III. 2.

II. Plea.

1. Nunquam indebitatus, in an action to recover back conduct money paid to a witness, when cause is settled and he does not attend, does not raise the question whether plaintiff has had the money allowed on taxation of costs, 1. ACTION, I. 1.

2. Payment into Court, not pleadable together with pleas denying or justifying whole cause of action.

A plea of payment of money into Court will not be allowed together with pleas denying or justifying the whole cause of action in respect of which the payment is pleaded.

Even on the terms of the defendant consenting, if plaintiff accept the money, to withdraw the other pleas and suffer judgment.

Although the complaint in the declaration appear to be oppressively multifarious. *Gales v. Lord Holland*, 336

3. Not Guilty. Effect of, in an action for debauching plaintiff's wife.

To declaration "for that the defendant debauched and carnally knew plaintiff's wife," the defendant pleaded not guilty.

Held that, under this issue, it was not necessary for the plaintiff to prove that a female shown to have been debauched by defendant was the wife of plaintiff. *Kenrick v. Horder*, 628

4. Justification, alleging 20 years user, to an action for obstructing plaintiff's use of a watercourse. Bad, for not alleging that such user had actually obstructed, 391. EASEMENT, IV.

5. Justification, to action for libel, setting out a particular transaction, and alleging that the libel was written and published solely with reference to that, 639. LIBEL, II.

6. Equitable plea, to action on promissory note, that it was made by defendant, as surety only, jointly with another, as principal, and that plaintiff gave time to the latter, held good, 431. PROMISSORY NOTE, II.

POLICY.

Of insurance. See INSURANCE.

POOR.

I. Settlement.

1. Under stat. 3 W. & M. c. 11, s. 6, by paying rates for one year. Effect of Reform Act (2 & 3 W. 4, c. 45, s. 3), as to rating of occupiers, upon previous local Acts.

By a local Act (11 G. 4 & 1 W. 4, c. x.), the landlords of houses in the parish of G., instead of the occupiers, are to be rated to the relief of the poor if the assessable value of the house be assessed at less than 30l. per annum. G. is within a borough. The occupier of a house in G., assessed at less than 30l., claimed under the Reform Act to be rated, and was rated, and paid the rates for three successive years; he did not during that period occupy the entire house.

Held, that he had acquired a settlement, under stat. 3 W. & M. c. 11, s. 6, by being charged with the rates and paying them. *Regina v. Inhabitants of St. Giles in the Fields*, 295

2. Under stats. 3 W. & M. c. 11, s. 6, and 6 G. 4, c. 57, s. 2, by payment of parochial taxes. The tenement, if not the property of the party paying, must have been occupied by him for a year.

Under stats. 3 & 4 W. & M. c. 11, s. 6, and 6 G. 4, c. 57, s. 2, a settlement cannot be gained by payment of parochial taxes for a tenement not being the property of the party paying, without an occupation of the tenement by him for a year. *Regina v. The Inhabitants of Westbury on Trym*, 444

II. Order of removal.

1. Stat. 9 & 10 Vict. c. 66. Pregnancy not necessarily "sickness" within sect. 4.

On an appeal against an order of removal, the Sessions stated for the opinion of the Court a case: by which it appeared that the pauper was an able-bodied single woman, who, while in service, became pregnant, and was dismissed from the service; and, by reason of her advanced state of pregnancy, was unable to take a situation and maintain herself. The removing justices had not found that she was chargeable in respect of relief made necessary by sickness, but only that she "has become and now is actually chargeable."

Held that, upon this statement, it was not to be inferred that she had become chargeable in respect of any sickness; and that the order of removal was not therefore objectionable under stat. 9 & 10 Vict. c. 66, s. 4, pregnancy not being necessarily sickness within the meaning of that section. *Regina v. The Inhabitants of Huddersfield,* 794

2. Appeal against order of adjudication, under stat. 16 & 17 Vict. c. 97, s. 108: where it is addressed to the overseers of a parish and the guardians of the union, overseers may appeal separately.

Two justices made an order, adjudging the settlement of a lunatic, who had been sent to an asylum, to be in the township of H. in the union of H., addressed to the overseers of the township and the guardians of the union, and ordering the guardians to pay the expenses. The overseers and the guardians separately appealed. At the first Sessions the appeal of the guardians was entered and respited, that of the overseers was called on. The Sessions refused to hear it on the ground that the overseers had no locus standi.

Held: that the Sessions might in their discretion regulate the time of hearing the two appeals so as to secure that they should be heard together and justice done; but that they were bound, under stat. 16 & 17 Vict. c. 97, s. 108, to hear the appeal of the overseers of the township, to whom at all events the statute gave an appeal. And a rule for a mandamus to enter continuances and hear the appeal was made absolute. *Regina v. Justices of West Riding,* 14

III. Expenses of maintenance.

1. Expenses of maintenance of pauper lunatics, by whom payable, in particular cases, under stat. 16 & 17 Vict. c. 97.

i. Pauper having resided five years in A., a parish in an union, was removed without an order to the workhouse of the union, where he remained twelve months. A. paid the Union a small sum; afterwards M., another parish in the Union, paid the Union for the maintenance, by consent of the guardians for M. at the board of the Union, on the supposition that pauper was settled in M. Pauper became lunatic, and was removed to an asylum by an order describing him to be from A.; it did not appear that either A. or M. interfered in this removal. Afterwards stat. 9 &

10 Vict. c. 66, passed. M. paid for pauper's maintenance in the asylum for many years after his removal thither, and after the passing of that statute, and of stat. 16 & 17 Vict. c. 97.

Held that, under stat. 16 & 17 Vict. c. 97, s. 102, the Union was properly chargeable for the expenses in the lunatic asylum, as the pauper, at the time of his removal thither, would, but for such removal, have been exempt from removal from A. under stat. 9 & 10 Vict. c. 66, inasmuch as neither the removal to the workhouse without an order, nor the removal to the lunatic asylum, interrupted the residence in A., by stat. 12 & 13 Vict. c. 103, s. 4 (though the time spent in the workhouse and lunatic asylum was excluded from the computation of time of residence).

Stat. 7 & 8 Vict. c. 101, passed before the removal to the workhouse. Held that, so far as regarded irremovability under stat. 9 & 10 Vict. c. 66, sect. 56 of stat. 7 & 8 Vict. c. 101, did not (though it made the workhouse part of the parish of settlement, and though M. had made payments on the supposition of the settlement being in M.) break the residence in A.

And, further, that the payment by M., if evidence of settlement there, was such evidence as might be rebutted. *Regina v. West Ward Union,* 21

ii. A pauper, having the status of irremovability in L. by virtue of stat. 9 & 10 Vict. c. 66, while she was in W. for a temporary purpose not such as to break the status, became lunatic, and was removed by a justice's order to a lunatic asylum. She was settled in T.

Held that, under The Lunatic Asylums Act, 1853 (16 & 17 Vict. c. 97), sect. 102, justices had power to make an order on L. for payment of expenses incurred since 29th September, 1853, in the examination, removal, maintenance, &c. *Guardians of Leeds v. Guardians of Wakefield,* 258

2. Distress warrant to levy arrears of expenses of maintenance. Jurisdiction of justices. Effect of stat. 16 & 17 Vict. c. 97, on previous orders of maintenance.

A lunatic having a settlement in I., but having the status of irremovability from M., was, in 1851, sent to an asylum from M., which was not comprised in any union; and an order for the expenses was made on I. Stat. 16 & 17 Vict. c. 97, having afterwards passed, I. refused to pay any expenses incurred subsequently to 29th September, 1853. Two justices issued a distress warrant to levy the arrears, under which the goods of one of the overseers of I. were seized. A writ being issued by him, against the justices, a case was stated for the Queen's Bench.

Held, by the Exchequer Chamber, reversing the judgment of the Queen's Bench, that the justices. had no jurisdiction to issue the warrant; the order on I. being by implication annulled by stat. 16 & 17 Vict. c. 97, and there being no obligation on I. to take any steps to get rid of it. *Knowles* v. *Trafford*,   144

3. Relieving officer. Surcharge of, by poor law auditor. Application to justices for a distress warrant: their jurisdiction.

When a relieving officer is surcharged by the auditor of an audit district, and application is made to justices to issue a distress warrant, if the statutable proof of the surcharge be complete, the justices have no power to inquire into the grounds of the surcharge, but must issue the warrant. If they refuse to do so, the Court will compel them by a rule or a mandamus. *Regina* v. *Linford*,   950

IV. Poor-rate. See RATE, I.

POST OFFICE.

Public. Non-rateability of premises leased and occupied for that purpose, 483. RATE, I. 1, i.

PRINCIPAL AND AGENT.

FIRST: Liability of principal for acts of agent.

I. Of shipowner for acts of the master, when the ship is chartered for a lump sum, and put up by the charterer as a general ship, 704. Infra, V.

SECONDLY: Liability of agent.

II. As principal, in particular cases.

1. Charter-party made "between" owner and "W., as agent for" certain parties, to whom the ship was to be addressed. W. personally liable as charterer, 942. SHIP, II. 5.

2. Contract to purchase by agent, stating it was on behalf of his principal, but not disclosing his name. Evidence admissible, in action against agent for not accepting, of a custom that, under such a contract, agent was liable to be treated as principal, 266. CONTRACT, IV.

III. As agent, for breach of promise that he had authority to contract.

1. Grant of lease by supposed agent, bonâ fide, in mistake.

W. signed a written agreement, describing himself in the signature as agent to G., whereby he agreed with C. that a lease should be granted to C. of a farm belonging to G. C. and W. both believed that W. had authority from G. to make the agreement; in fact W. had no such authority. G. refusing to grant the lease, C. filed a bill

against G. for specific performances; and, after G. had put in his answer, denying W.'s authority, C. gave notice to W. of the suit and ground of defence, and that C. would proceed with the suit at W.'s expense, unless W. gave him notice not further to proceed; and that C. would bring an action against W. for damages in the event, either of the bill being dismissed on the ground of defence set up, or of W. requiring C. not further to proceed. W. answered, repudiating his liability to C. The bill was dismissed on the ground of defence set up.

On a case, stating the above circumstances, with liberty to the court to draw inferences of fact: Held:

1. That C. was entitled to maintain an action against W. as for breach of a promise that W. had the authority.

2. That C. might recover in such action damages for the expense of the Chancery proceedings, it not appearing that he had instituted them incautiously, and they being therefore damages naturally resulting from the misrepresentation made by W. *Collen* v. *Wright*,   391

2. Purchase of ship by alleged agent. Resale of ship: measure of damages, 568. DAMAGES.

IV. As agent, upon contract entered into by him as such.

Evidence of general authority to agent to order goods, so as to give vendor the right of action against such agent, in the absence of notice that his authority had expired.

Defendant had a jeweller's shop at Lewes, he residing near London; the business at Lewes was managed by A., who, by defendant's authority, was in the habit of giving orders at Lewes, verbally and by letter, for goods to be sent to the shop: and A. had given such orders to plaintiff, who resided in London, and who had, in compliance with them, sent goods to the shop, which defendant had accepted. A. absconded from the shop, came to London, verbally ordered goods, consisting of jewellery, of plaintiff, as for defendant, and took them away, saying that he was going to Lewes.

Held that, upon these facts, a jury might find that defendant had so conducted himself as to make plaintiff believe that A., whilst in defendant's employment, had authority to order goods as he did; and, on such finding, plaintiff, not having had notice of the termination of the authority, would be entitled to recover the price from defendant. *Summer* v. *Solomon*,   879

V. Rights of agent.

Purchase of goods abroad, by order and on account of a correspondent. Shipment of

goods in exchange for mate's receipt, &c.
Vesting of property.

Plaintiffs, merchants in London, purchased for C., but on their own credit, goods abroad, debiting C. with the price and a commission. The goods were warehoused in London in plaintiffs' name. C. in his own name engaged room for the goods in the ship E., which had been put up as a general ship for Calcutta. Plaintiffs, at C.'s request, delivered the goods to a lighterman, but, with a view to preserve their lien, took the lighterman's engagement to give them the mate's receipt. The goods were shipped on the E.; the mate's receipt in blank was handed to the lighterman, who gave it to plaintiffs. C. promised plaintiffs to redeem the mate's receipt, but never did so, and fraudulently induced the ship-brokers to get bills of lading to C.'s order, to be signed by the master, though the mate's receipt was not produced. C. fraudulently endorsed these bills of lading for value to a bonâ fide endorsee. Plaintiffs had no communication with the ship-brokers or captain till after the ship had sailed, when, the facts being discovered, they demanded the goods both in this country and on the arrival of the ship at Calcutta. The goods were delivered by the captain at Calcutta to the holders of the bills of lading. An action was brought for this conversion against the shipowner and the captain. It appeared that the captain and crew were appointed by the shipowner, but the ship was chartered for a lump sum to third parties, who put up the ship as a general ship. It was proved that the refusal of the captain to deliver the goods at Calcutta was by the orders of the shipowner. The only question left to the jury was, Whether, under the circumstances, the master was justified in signing the bills of lading without the production of the mate's receipt? The jury finding in the negative, the plaintiffs had the verdict against both defendants on the pleas of Not guilty and Not possessed.

Held: that the property in the goods remained the property of the plaintiffs, there never having been any delivery animo transferendi to C.; and that the misdelivery at Calcutta was a conversion. And that the question whether the plaintiffs were precluded from relying on their property or complaining of this conversion was in effect properly left to the jury and properly found by them.

Held, also, that, the shipowner having authorized the detention at Calcutta, the verdict was proper.

Semble: that under such a charter-party the shipowner, though perhaps not liable on the contracts made for carriage of goods in the ship as a general ship, is still liable for the misdelivery of the goods by the captain, who for many purposes remains his servant. Sed quære. Schuster v. McKellar,
704

PRINCIPAL AND SURETY.

I. Rights of surety, as against a third party.

Constructive relation of principal and surety, between two joint makers of a promissory note for the accommodation of one: equitable plea setting up such relation, 431. - PROMISSORY NOTE, II.

II. Liability of surety, to a third party.

Under a bond by treasurer of a borough, under Municipal Corporation Reform Act, 97. MUNICIPAL CORPORATION REFORM ACT, II.

PRIVILEGE.

I. From arrest. See ARREST.

II. As to publication of defamatory matter, 229. LIBEL, I.

PROBATE.

See EXECUTORS AND ADMINISTRATORS.

PROMISSORY NOTE.

I. Covenant to pay by a promissory note. Not satisfied by the mere delivery of such promissory note. Action for non-payment of a note so delivered not barred in six years.

By deed between D. and H., D. sold to H. beds of coal, and H. covenanted to pay to D. a sum named for the purchase-money, " in manner and at the times following," that is to say, part in cash on the day of the date of the deed, and the remainder by five promissory notes under H.'s hand, bearing even date with the deed, payable to D. or order on the 1st of July in every year till the whole purchase-money should be paid, with interest until the notes should be paid.

D. declared against H. on this deed, alleging that, though H. gave D. two notes, &c. (according to the language of the covenant), and afterwards paid a part of the principal and interest mentioned in those notes, yet he did not pay the residue of the principal and interest mentioned in those notes, but, except as to the part so paid, those notes and so much of the purchase-money and interest as was therein mentioned remained wholly unpaid to D.

Held a good breach, the covenant extending to the payment of the money named in the notes, and not being satisfied by the mere delivery of the notes.

And that it was a bad plea, that the causes of action did not accrue within six years before the suit. Dixon v. Holdroyd,   903

II. Action on promissory note. Equitable

plea, alleging that note was made by defendant, as surety only, jointly with another, as principal, and that holder gave time to the latter.

Action on a promissory note. Plea on equitable grounds, that defendant made the notes jointly with J. for J.'s accommodation, and as surety for J.; and that the notes were delivered to plaintiff and taken by him on an agreement between them that defendant should be liable as surety only, and with notice that he was surety only; and that afterwards plaintiff, without defendant's consent, gave time to J., but for which he might have obtained payment. On demurrer,

Held: that, though the absolute written contract between defendant and plaintiff contained in the note could not be varied by parol in equity any more than at law, yet an equity arose from the relation of surety and principal between defendant and J., and the notice thereof to plaintiff at the time he took the note; and therefore that the plea was good.

Quære, whether the equity would have existed if the notice had been after the taking of the notes, but before the giving of time. *Pooley v. Harradine,* 431

PROTECTION.
See BANKRUPT AND INSOLVENT.

PUBLICATION.
Of libel. See LIBEL.

PUBLIC HEALTH ACT, 1848.
(11 & 12 VICT. c. 63.)

Sect. 85. Estimate and report of expense of works, when necessary.

A local Board of Health required the owners of property adjoining a street, not being a highway, to level it; and, they having made default, the Local Board caused the work to be done by contract. Before making the contract, no estimate was made of the annual expense of repairing the work when done; nor was any report obtained as to whether it would be more advantageous to contract only for the execution of the work, or for the execution and maintenance thereof. In other respects the directions of sect. 85 of the Public Health Act, 1848 (11 & 12 Vict. c. 63), were followed. On a special case:

Held, that, as the work when complete would not be repaired and maintained under the Act, or out of the rates, no such estimate or report was required; and that the Local Board might enforce payment of the expenses from the owners, notwithstanding the absence of the estimate and report. *Cunningham v. Local Board of Wolverhampton,* 107

PUBLIC OFFICER.
See COMPANY, II. 2.

QUARTER SESSIONS.
See SESSIONS.

RAILWAY COMPANY.
See COMPANY, I.

RAILWAYS CLAUSES CONSOLIDATION ACT.
(8 & 9 VICT. c. 20.)

Compensation under sect. 6. Meaning of "injuriously affected." Remedy for excess of jurisdiction by jury, 660. LANDS CLAUSES CONSOLIDATION ACT.

RATE.
I. Poor-rate.

1. Rateability to.

i. By occupation: exception of Public Post Office, leased and occupied as such.

Houses, the property of a subject, were taken on lease by the Postmaster-General, and occupied as a post office, for the purposes of the post office revenue.

Held, that, the premises being occupied by the servants of the Crown for public purposes, no one was rateable in respect of the occupation of them. *Smith v. Guardians of Birmingham,* 483

ii. Settlement by payment of rates for one year.

Effect of Reform Act (2 & 3 W. 4, c. 45), s. 30, as to rating of *occupiers,* upon previous local Acts, 205. POOR.

iii. Crediting of excess paid.

Crediting, by parish officers, of excess of rate, paid during an appeal, upon the assessment appealed against, and afterwards reduced.

Under stat. 41 G. 3, c. 23, if a rate be appealed against and reduced, but the party rated has during the appeal paid on the unreduced assessment, the parish officers may, in subsequent rates, credit him for the excess paid, without an order of Sessions. *Regina v. Parker,* 155

2. Appeal against. See APPEAL.

II. Highway-rate.

Arrears of, under General Highway Act, to whom payable, after the passing of the Metropolis Local Management Act, 5. METROPOLIS LOCAL MANAGEMENT ACT, II.

III. Paving-rate, under Public Health Act (11 & 12 Vict. c. 63).

When estimate, &c., of expense of works is necessary to enable Local Board to enforce the rate for their construction, 107. PUBLIC HEALTH ACT.

IV. Lighting and watching rates.

1. Under stat. 3 & 4 W. 4, c. 90.

Jurisdiction of magistrate to decide whether two meetings, held at different times under the Act by the ratepayers, were substantially one and the same meeting, 220. JURISDICTION, XXI.

2. Under 5 & 6 W. 4, c. 76.

Extent of powers of town council as to levying a watch-rate upon a part of the borough previously exempted by a local Act: who are to contribute, 342. MUNICIPAL CORPORATION REFORM ACT, V.

V. Sewers' rate.

Question of rateability, where rate is imposed by the Commissioners of Sewers, how to be raised: on what principle such rate should be made.

A sewers' rate, laid on an occupier by the Metropolitan Commissioners of Sewers under stat. 11 & 12 Vict. c. 112, could be impeached only by appeal to the Commissioners, under sects. 95, 96.

Therefore, in an action to recover for such a rate, brought by The Metropolitan Board of Works, under stat. 18 & 19 Vict. c. 120, s. 147, against the party rated, it is not competent to such party to object that the property in respect of which he is rated derives no benefit from the sewers.

The Court (Lord Campbell, C. J., Coleridge, Erle, and Crompton, Js.), at the request of the parties, stated extrajudicially their opinion that, since stat. 11 & 12 Vict. c. 112, the sewers' rate should be made, taking into account the benefit which the property derived from the sewers, as under the previous law of sewers. *Metropolitan Board of Works* v. *Vauxhall Bridge Company*, 964. III. 1.

RECOGNISANCE.

I. By prosecutor, upon removal of an indictment by certiorari, not necessary where it is against a corporation, 453. CERTIORARI, III. 1.

II. By one of two joint defendants, upon removal of an indictment by certiorari, for payment of prosecutor's costs in the event of either being convicted, 140. CERTIORARI, III. 2.

III. Taking of, by clerk of justices. Penalty for receiving too large a fee, under what circumstances payable, 26. SESSIONS, VII.

RECTOR.
See INCUMBENT.

REFORM ACT.
(2 & 3 W. 4, c. 45.)

Right of *occupiers* to be rated (sect. 30) controls operation of local Acts providing that the *landlords* are to be rated, 205. POOR, I. 1.

REGISTRATION.
Of Joint Stock Companies. See COMPANY, I. 1.
Of assignments of patents. See PATENT, I.

REGULÆ GENERALES.
Hilary Term, 536.

RELIEVING OFFICER.
See POOR, III. 3.

REMOVAL.
See POOR.

REPORT.
In a newspaper, of proceedings at a public meeting. Publication of defamatory matter not privileged, 229. LIBEL, I.

RETURNING OFFICER.
See ELECTION, III.

RISK.
Maritime. See INSURANCE.

SALE.
See VENDOR AND VENDEE.

SALE.
Bill of. See BILL OF SALE.

SEQUESTRATION.
On petition of assignee, under stat. 1 & 2 Vict. c. 110, s. 55, when entitled to priority, 542. BANKRUPT AND INSOLVENT, III. 2.

SERVANT.
See MASTER AND SERVANT.

SESSIONS.
I. What is the meaning of the next "practicable" quarter sessions with respect to an appeal against an order of removal, 643. APPEAL, II. 3.

II. Discretion of sessions as to dismissing an appeal, where appellant has, with his notice of appeal, given notice that he should apply for a respite, 609. APPEAL, II. 1.

III. Rule absolute to sessions to enter continuances and hear an appeal, notice not having been served on all the parties interested. Service of a second notice, omitting some of the parties and some of the objections in the first, not a proper service, and appeal dismissable, 619. APPEAL, II. 2.

IV. Express order of sessions unnecessary to enable parish officers to credit, in future rates, a party who has appealed against a former rate, and, during the appeal, has paid upon such assessment, which was afterwards reduced, 155. RATE, I. 1, iii.

V. When an order of sessions, confirming an order of justices, is silent as to costs, a subsequent sessions cannot make an order confirming the first order of Sessions, and giving costs, 935. COSTS, III. 2.

VI. Sessions cannot award costs against the Crown, on dismissing an appeal against the dismissal of an information under the Excise Acts, 492. COSTS, III. 1.

VII. Reception, by clerk to justices, of too large a fee. Jurisdiction of Sessions as to approving the table of fees.

If a clerk to justices demands and receives a fee for the taking of recognisances, as for a principal and two sureties, there being in fact only one surety, he is not guilty of an offence or liable to a forfeiture under stat. 26 G. 2, c. 14, s. 2, if he actually believed that there were two sureties. By the Court of Q. B.

A table of fees to be taken by the clerks of justices was made at the June Quarter Sessions, and submitted for approval to the next October Quarter Sessions; when the further consideration thereof was adjourned to the next Epiphany Sessions; and at these last-mentioned Sessions the table (with some alterations) was approved of; and the same was afterwards ratified and confirmed by the Judges at the next following Assizes. Held: that the table was not duly approved, ratified, and confirmed, under stat. 26 G. 2, c. 14, s. 1, as the approval ought to have been given at the October Sessions, and such Sessions had no power to adjourn the consideration thereof. By the Court of Exch. Ch., affirming the judgment of the Court of Q. B. *Bowman* v. *Blyth*, 26

SET-OFF.

Of one judgment against another, in two actions between the same parties, 84. CONTRACT, III. 2.

SETTLEMENT.

Of paupers. See POOR.

Of estates. See WILL.

SEWERS.

Metropolitan Commissioners of. Contractors acting bonâ fide under their authority not liable for negligence.

Defendants, being contractors acting under the authority of the Metropolitan Commissioners of Sewers, and bonâ fide acting for the purpose of executing stat. 11 & 12 Vict. c. 112, by negligence injured the plaintiff's premises.

Held that, under sect. 128, they were exempted from all liability; and a verdict was entered for the defendants on a plea of Not guilty by statute. *Ward* v. *Lee*, 426

SEWERS' RATE.

See RATE, V.

SHAREHOLDER.

See COMPANY.

SHIP.

I. The chartering.

1. Charter-party made "between" owner and "W., as agent for" certain parties, to whom the ship was to be addressed. W. personally liable as charterer, 942. Infra, II. 5.

2. Advance of freight by charterer to owner. Construction of charter-party.

By charter-party between defendant, owner of a ship, and plaintiff, it was agreed that the ship should proceed from London to B., and there load a cargo from plaintiff's factors, and therewith proceed to London, and deliver the same, on being paid freight at a specified rate: "cash for ship's disbursements, to be advanced to the extent of 300l., free of interest, but subject to insurance:" "the freight to be paid, on unloading and right delivery of the cargo, as follows: say, in cash, less two months' interest at," &c., "and, if required, 300l. to be paid in cash on arrival, less two months' interest."

300l. was advanced by plaintiff's agents at B. for ship's disbursements. Neither plaintiff nor defendants insured in respect of this 300l. The ship left B. with a cargo for London, but was lost before reaching London. Plaintiff claimed the payment of the 300l., as a loan made to defendants; defendants tendered the amount at which the 300l. might have been insured, but refused to pay more.

Held: that plaintiff's claim could not be supported, as it appeared from the charter-party that the advance was not a loan, but was an advance of freight. *Hicks* v. *Shield*, 633

3. Liability of shipowner for conversion of cargo by the master, where the ship is chartered for a lump sum and put up by the charterer as a general ship, 704. PRINCIPAL AND AGENT, V.

4. Contract by owner of a ship, that she should proceed to and load at a foreign port: when it is avoided by the breaking out of war between the two countries after such agreement and before her arrival : plea to that effect.

Declaration charged that, by a memorandum for charter, it was agreed between plaintiff, owner of a ship then in a British port, and defendant, that the ship should proceed to Odessa, and there load from the freighter's factors a complete cargo of specified goods, and proceed therewith to a port of discharge, the act of the Queen's enemies and all accidents of the seas, navigation, &c., excepted ; thirty-five running days to be allowed for loading and unloading, to commence at the port of loading, and 4*l*. per day for demurrage above the running days. Breach : (1). That, although a reasonable time for loading the cargo had elapsed, defendant made default in loading the agreed cargo ; (2). That defendant detained the ship on demurrage ten days above the laying days, and did not pay for such demurrage.

Plea : that defendant was always a subject of the Queen, and Odessa was a port within the dominions of the Emperor of Russia ; and that, after the making of the charter-party, and before the ship arrived at Odessa, and before the defendant provided a cargo, the Queen declared war against the Emperor; since which time war had existed between them, and Odessa had been a hostile port in the possession of the Queen's enemies. That, from the time war was so declared, it became impossible for defendant to perform his agreement without dealing and trading with the Queen's enemies, of which plaintiff had notice before the expiration of the laying days : and the charter-party, by reason of the premises, was wholly rescinded.

Replication : that the Queen, by order of council, waived (except in the case of contraband of war) the seizure or confiscation of enemies' property on board neutral ships and of neutral property on board enemies' ships; and, by a second order in council, allowed a certain time for Russian ships to load their ships in British ports, and allowed Russian merchant vessels, which should have sailed before the date of the order for any British port, to discharge at such port; and, by a third order, made before the expiration of the

running days, and while there was time to load the cargo, ordered that neutral or friendly vessels might import into any British port all goods (not being contraband of war or requiring a special permission) to whomsoever belonging, and that the subjects of the Queen or of any neutral or friendly state might trade with all ports not blockaded (except that British vessels might not enter enemies' ports). That the ship was a neutral vessel, and plaintiff the subject of a neutral state : that Odessa was not blockaded during any part of the time during which the cargo ought to have been loaded; and no part of the agreed cargo was contraband of war or requiring special permission for importation ; and the cargo might have been loaded notwithstanding the hostilities. On demurrer :

Held, by the Court of Exchequer Chamber, reversing the judgment of the Court of Queen's Bench, that the plea was good, as showing a dissolution of the contract before the time for performance had expired, and an impossibility of legally performing the contract, as the shipment of a cargo from an enemy's port, even in a neutral vessel, was an act, primâ facie at least, involving a trading and dealing with the enemy, and therefore forbidden by law to a British subject ; and that, if such a shipment could under peculiar facts be legal, it lay on the plaintiff to shew the facts, which on this record he had not done.

Held, by both Courts, that the replication did not answer the plea; for that the first order in council related only to neutral or hostile goods or ships; the second only to Russian ships; and the third was not shewn to have come into operation till after the alleged dissolution of the contract. *Esposito* v. *Bowden*, 763

5. Lay days. See infra, II. 5.

II. The voyage.

Time policy on cargo : construction of policy : when only maritime risks protected, 465. INSURANCE, I. 2.

2. Insurance against collision : construction of policy, 172. INSURANCE, I. 1.

3. Policy on chartered freight. Expenses of getting ship off shore, after cargo in safety, how chargeable, 523. INSURANCE, II.

4. Contract by master with the seamen, for additional remuneration to them to complete the voyage, under what circumstances good, 872. CONTRACT, III. 3.

5. Lay days. What are ordinary delays of navigation.

A memorandum of charter-party was expressed to be made "between P., of the good ship C., and W., agent for E. W. & Son," to whom the ship was to be addressed. It was signed by W. without any restriction.

Held, that W. was personally liable as charterer.

By the charter-party the ship was to proceed "to Plymouth, not higher than T. or N., or as near thereunto as she can safely get, and deliver" her cargo, with certain lay days and demurrage days. The port of Plymouth is a tidal estuary. On the ship's arrival in Plymouth the consignees ordered her to discharge at B., an ordinary landing place in the port of Plymouth, lower than T. or N. At this time the tides were neap: the vessel went as near to B. as she could in that state of the tide, and lay on the sand for some days, till, the tides being higher, she got to B. In an action for demurrage:

Held, that the consignee had the option of naming any ordinary loading place in the port of Plymouth within the limits assigned, and that the lay days did not commence till the vessel reached the place so named. The delay in getting to it being occasioned only in the ordinary course of navigation in a tidal harbour. *Parker* v. *Winlow,*   942

SHIPMENT.

See SHIP.

SHIPOWNER.

See SHIP.

SPECIFICATION.

See PATENT.

STATUTES.

FIRST: General Public Acts.

I. 3 Ed. 1, c. 25. (Champerty.) 58. CONTRACT, III. 1.

II. 28 Ed. 1, stat. 3, c. 11. (Maintenance.) 58. CONTRACT, III. 1.

III. 33 Ed. 1, stat. 3. (Champerty.) 58. CONTRACT, III. 1.

IV. 32 H. 8, c. 9. (Buying of titles.) 58. CONTRACT, III. 1.

V. 5 Eliz. c. 9. (Punishment of Perjury, &c.) Sect. 12. Attendance of witnesses, 1. ACTION, I. 1.

VI. 21 Ja. 1, c. 66. (Limitation of Actions.) Sect. 4. Fresh actions by executors or administrators, 283. STATUTE OF LIMITATIONS, II. Sect. 4. Actions on simple contracts barred in six years, 903. PROMISSORY NOTE, I.

VII. 29 C. 2, c. 3. (Statute of Frauds.) Sect. 4. Agreements for sale of interest in land, 503. STATUTE OF FRAUDS.

VIII. 3 W. & M. c. 11. (Poor.) Sect. 6. Settlement by payment of rates for one year, 205, 444. POOR, I. 2.

IX. 17 G. 2, c. 38. (Poor.) Sect. 4. Notice of Appeal, 609, 619, 642. APPEAL, II.

X. 25 G. 2, c. 29. (Remuneration to Coroners.) 805. CORONER.

XI. 26 G. 2, c. 14. (Fees of clerks to justices.) Sect. 1. Approval by justices of table of fees, 26. SESSIONS, VII. Sect. 2. Penalty for taking too large a fee, 26. SESSIONS, VII.

XII. 41 G. 3, c. 23. (Collection of Poor Rates.) Crediting of payments on appeal, 155. RATE, I. 1. iii.

XIII. 41 G. 3, c. 109. (General Enclosure.) Sects. 10, 11, 14. Extinguishment of roads, &c., 384. CUSTOM, I.

XIV. 3 G. 4, c. 126. (Turnpike Amendment.) Sect. 32. Exemptions from tolls, 498. HIGHWAY, II.

XV. 4 G. 4, c. 34. (Disputes between masters and workmen.) Sect. 3. Conviction for leaving service before contract expired, 697. MASTER AND SERVANT.

XVI. 6 G. 4, c. 42. (Irish Joint Stock Banks.) Sect. 12. Judgments against public officers, 960. COMPANY, II. 2.

XVII. 6 G. 4, c. 57. (Poor.) Sect. 2. Settlement by payment of taxes, 444. POOR, I. 2.

XVIII. 9 G. 4, c. 61. (Excise.) Sect. 18. Definition of excisable liquors, 839. EXCISE, I.

XIX. 1 & 2 W. 4, c. 32. (Game Laws Amendment.) Sect. 30. Title to land set up as a defence, 853. JURISDICTION, XIX.

XX. 1 & 2 W. 4, c. 37. (Truck Act.) Interpretation of "artificer," 115. TRUCK ACT.

XXI. 1 & 2 W. 4, c. 58. (Interpleader.) 323 BAILMENT. 564. INTERPLEADER.

XXII. 2 & 3 W. 4, c. 45. (Reform Act.) Sect. 30. Rating of occupiers, 205. POOR, I. 1.

XXIII. 3 & 4 W. 4, c. 90. (Lighting and Watching.) Sects. 5, 16, 73. Meeting of ratepayers for adoption of Act, 220. JURISDICTION, XXI.

XXIV. 4 & 5 W. 4, c. 77. (Excise.) Sect. 9. Repeal of duty, 839. EXCISE, I.

XXV. 4 & 5 W. 4, c. 85. (Sale of beer, &c., amendment.)

Sects. 2, 8. License and certificate : penalty : 848. EXCISE, III.

XXVI. 5 & 6 W. 4, c. 20. (Stamps.)

Sect. 21. Application of penalties under stat. 1 & 2 W. 4, c. 32 : 859 n. (a.) JUSTICES, II. 1.

XXVII. 5 & 6 W. 4, c. 50. (General Highway Act.)

Collection of arrears of rate, 5. METROPOLIS LOCAL MANAGEMENT ACT, II.

Sect. 23. What is to constitute a highway, 399. HIGHWAY, I.

XVIII. 5 & 6 W. 4, c. 76. (Municipal Corporations Reform Act.)

Sects. 15, 22. Revision of burgess lists, 90. MUNICIPAL CORPORATION REFORM ACT, I.

Sect. 58. Appointment of treasurer to borough : bond by sureties, 97. MUNICIPAL CORPORATION REFORM ACT, II.

Sect. 66. Compensation to officers for removal, or abolition of office, 249. MUNICIPAL CORPORATION REFORM ACT, III.

Sects. 76, 91, 132. By-laws : conviction for infringement : abolition of certiorari, 831. CERTIORARI, II.

Sects. 84, 92. Local Acts : town council to levy rates, 342. MUNICIPAL CORPORATION REFORM ACT, V.

XXIX. 7 W. 4 & 1 Vict. c. 4, s. 68. (Expenses of Inquests.) 805. CORONER.

XXX. 1 & 2 Vict. c. 110. (Insolvent Debtors.)

Sect. 55. Sequestration on petition of assignee, 542. BANKRUPT AND INSOLVENT, III. 2.

Sect. 92. Vesting of surplus assets, 366. JURISDICTION, IX.

XXXI. 3 & 4 Vict. c. 86. (Church Discipline.)

Sects. 15, 24. Jurisdiction of archbishop : appeal, 315. CHURCH DISCIPLINE ACT.

XXXII. 6 & 7 Vict. c. 18. (Registration of Parliamentary Voters.)

Sects. 48, 55. Copying, &c., lists by town clerk, 799. BOROUGH, III.

XXXIII. 6 & 7 Vict. c. 73. (Attorneys Amendment.)

Sect. 37. Signed bill, 578. ATTORNEY, II.

XXXIV. 6 & 7 Vict. c. 89. (Municipal Corporations Amendment.)

Sect. 6. Tenure of office of treasurer of borough, 97. MUNICIPAL CORPORATION REFORM ACT, II.

XXXV. 7 & 8 Vict. c. 101. (Poor.)

Sect. 56. Workhouse to be considered in parish, 21. POOR, III. 1.

XXXVI. 7 & 8 Vict. c. 110. (Joint Stock Companies.)

Sect. 23. Powers of Company provisionally registered, 164. COMPANY, I. 1.

XXXVII. 7 & 8 Vict. c. 113. (Regulation of Joint Stock Banks.)

Sect. 7. Liability of shareholders upon transactions of Company, 537. COMPANY, II. 1.

Sect. 10. Execution against individual shareholders, 356. COMPANY, II. 3.

XXXVIII. 8 & 9 Vict. c. 18. (Lands Clauses Consolidation.)

Sect. 68. Assessment of compensation, 660. LANDS CLAUSES CONSOLIDATION ACT.

XXXIX. 8 & 9 Vict. c. 20. (Railways Clauses Consolidation.)

Sect. 6. Assessment of compensation, 660. LANDS CLAUSES CONSOLIDATION ACT.

XL. 9 & 10 Vict. c. 66. (Poor.)

Sect. 1. Computation of time of residence, 21. POOR, III. 1.

Sect. 4. Sickness or accident, as affecting removability, 794. POOR, II. 1.

XLI. 9 & 10 Vict. c. 95. (County Courts.)

Sects. 29, 30. Officers not to act as attorneys : penalty, 603. COUNTY COURT, III.

Sects. 98, 99. Commitment by Judge for debt discharged by Insolvency Court, 679. COUNTY COURT, IV.

XLII. 11 & 12 Vict. c. 43. (Summary Convictions.)

Sect. 17. Exception of excise proceedings, 848. EXCISE III.

Sects. 17, 23. Form of conviction, 853. JURISDICTION, XIX.

XLIII. 11 & 12 Vict. c. 44. (To protect Justices from vexatious Actions.)

Sect. 5. Rule of Q. B., to compel justices to act, 672. JURISDICTION, XX.

XLIV. 11 & 12 Vict. c. 45. (Winding-up Acts Amendment), 960. COMPANY, II. 2.

XLV. 11 & 12 Vict. c. 63. (Public Health.)

Sect. 85. Contracts for works : estimate, 107. PUBLIC HEALTH ACT.

XLVI. 11 & 12 Vict. c. 112. Metropolitan Commissioners of Sewers.

Sects. 95, 96. Appeal to Commissioners, 964. RATE, V.

Sect. 128. Non-liability of parties acting under authority of Commissioners, 426. SEWERS.

XLVII. 12 & 13 Vict. c. 45. (Quarter Session Procedure Amendment.)

Sect. 7. Amendment of orders of justices by Court of Q. B., 557. JUSTICES, I.

STATUTE OF FRAUDS.

(29 C. 2, c. 3.)

Sect. 4. Agreement for the sale of an interest in land. Divisibility of contract.

Plaintiff and defendant agreed, by word of mouth, that plaintiff should pay 37l. for the interest of the defendant in premises occupied by him as a slaughter-house, and for the fixtures; defendant to return 10l. if plaintiff were refused a license to use the premises as a slaughter-house. The premises and fixtures were transferred to plaintiff; and defendant received the 37l. Subsequently, this action was brought to recover 10l., on an allegation that the license to use the premises had been refused to plaintiff. A nonsuit was directed, on the ground that the contract was for an interest in land, and was void under sect. 4 of the Statute of Frauds. On a rule to set aside the nonsuit:

Held, by Wightman and Erle, Js. (Crompton, J., not concurring), that, the contract being executed as far as regarded the land, and the promise sued on relating wholly to money, the plaintiff might recover, though the contract was not in writing. *Green* v. *Saddington,*　　　503

STATUTE OF LIMITATIONS.

(21 JA. 1, c. 16.)

I. Covenant to pay by a promissory note, not satisfied by a mere delivery of such note. Right of action for non-payment not barred in six years, 903. PROMISSORY NOTE, I.

II. Sect. 4. Fresh action by administrator, original action by intestate having abated. Within what time he may sue.

Plaintiff sued defendant, administrator of W., for money due from intestate in his lifetime.

Plea: that the cause of action did not accrue within six years before the suit.

Replication: that plaintiff, in the lifetime of W., commenced an action against W. within six years after the cause of action against W. accrued and W. was never served or appeared to the writ, and plaintiff never appeared for him, and no declaration was filed or delivered, and no proceedings to outlawry taken; and the suit was continued up to the death of W., which occurred on a day named, within six years before the commencement of the present suit; whereby the first action abated: that W. died intestate; and defendant became his administrator; and thereupon plaintiff commenced the present suit against defendant within a reasonable time after the death of W., and within a reasonable time after defendant became administrator, and within one year after defendant became administrator, and within one year next after the time when it first became possible to issue any writ against any personal representative of W.

Rejoinder: that, after the death of W., at the time mentioned, plaintiff, as a creditor of W., on a day named (more than four years after W.'s death), no administration having been granted, caused defendant, as sole next of kin of W., to be served with a citation to accept or refuse administration, or show cause why administration should not be granted to plaintiff as creditor; and, in consequence, on a day named (between two and three months from service of citation), administration was granted to W., and the suit was not commenced until a day named (more than four years from the death).

On demurrer to the rejoinder:

Held, that the plaintiff was entitled to judgment, no laches appearing on his part, and he having a reasonable time (not necessarily limited to a year) for bringing his action, within the equity of sect. 4 of stat. 21 Ja. 1, c. 16. *Curlewis* v. *Lord Mornington,*　　283

SUMMONS.

I. Writ of. Amendment and resealing, before service: date of original teste may be retained, 49. ACTION, II. 2.

II. Under Metropolis Local Management Act, of a Gas Company, by the District Board of Works, for opening ground without their consent. Discretion of justice as to adjudicating, 328. JURISDICTION, XXII.

SUPPORT.

Right of owner of surface to. See MINE.

SURETY.

See PRINCIPAL AND SURETY.

SURFACE.

Right of owner to support. See MINE.

TAXES.

Settlement by payment of. See POOR.

TOLLS.

Turnpike. See HIGHWAY.

TOWN CLERK.

Of a borough, bound, under stat. 6 & 7 Vict. c. 18, s. 48, to cause the lists of parliamentary voters to be copied, printed, &c. To what extent he may be reimbursed under sect. 55, 799. BOROUGH, III.

TREASURER.

Of a borough. Bond by, under Municipal Corporation Reform Act. Present liability of sureties, 97. MUNICIPAL CORPORATION REFORM ACT, II.

TRIAL.

Expenses of witness, paid in advance upon subpœna, when and how recoverable back, 1. ACTION, I. 1.

TRUCK ACT.
(1 & 2 W. 4, c. 37.)

Who is an "artificer" within the Act.

The plaintiff, an illiterate labouring man, attached his mark to a written contract with defendant, by which he engaged to make as many bricks as defendant required in defendant's brick field, finding all labour, the defendant finding the materials. Payment to be 10s. 6d. per thousand for the bricks when complete. Plaintiff, assisted by others, made bricks, having worked at them personally; in payment he accepted tickets for goods. Afterwards he sued for the full price, contending that he was an artificer within the Truck Act (1 & 2 W. 4, c. 37), and that, consequently, the payment by tickets was void.

Held, by Lord Campbell, C. J., and Coleridge, J., in the Queen's Bench, that, though if the matter were res integra they might have come to a contrary conclusion, they were concluded by authority from holding him an artificer, as he was not bound by the contract to do any part of the work personally. Erle, J., dissentiente.

Held, by Cockburn, C. J., Cresswell, Williams, and Willes, Js., Martin, Bramwell, and Channell, Bs., in the Exchequer Chamber, affirming the judgment of the Queen's Bench, that the plaintiff, not being bound by his contract to do any part of the work personally, was not an artificer within the Truck Act.

And quære, per Cockburn, C. J., and Bramwell, B., whether, if the plaintiff had been bound to labour personally, but was at liberty to hire labourers to assist him, he would have been within the Act. *Ingram v. Barnes*, 115

TURNPIKE.
See HIGHWAY.

UNDERWRITER.
See INSURANCE.

USAGE.
See CUSTOM, II.

USER.
See EASEMENT.

VENDOR AND VENDEE.

I. Vesting of the property.

1. Purchase of goods abroad by order and on account of a correspondent. Shipment of goods in exchange for mate's receipt, &c. Vesting of the property, 704. PRINCIPAL AND AGENT, V.

2. Agreement for purchase of corn in bulk, to be packed in sacks sent by purchaser. Vesting of the property.

Plaintiff agreed with K. to purchase from K. 100 out of 200 quarters of barley which plaintiff had seen in bulk and approved of; and he paid part of the price. It was agreed that plaintiff should send sacks for the barley, and that K. should fill the sacks with the barley, take them to a railway, place them upon trucks free of charge, and send them to plaintiff. Plaintiff sent sacks enough for a part only of the 100 quarters: these K. filled; and K. also endeavoured to find trucks for them, but was unable to do so. Plaintiff repeatedly sent to K. demanding the barley. K. finally detained it, and emptied the barley from the sacks back into the bulk.

Held, that the property in so much of the barley as was not put into the sacks did not pass to plaintiff.

But, per Lord Campbell, C. J., Coleridge and Erle, Js., that the portion put into the sacks passed to the plaintiff: hæsitante Crompton, J., on the ground that it did not appear quite clearly that, at the time when plaintiff demanded the barley, he knew that any portion had been put into the sacks, and that, therefore, his assent to the particular appropriation was doubtful.

K. having become bankrupt after he had emptied the barley from the sacks into the bulk, and the defendant, his assignee, having removed the whole together: Held, by the whole Court, that this was a conversion, by the assignee, of all the barley (if any) which, by the putting it into the sacks, had become plaintiff's property. *Aldridge v. Johnson*, 885

II. Liability of vendee as agent.

1. Contract to buy, by agent, stating it was on behalf of his principal, but not disclosing him. Evidence admissible, in action against agent for not accepting, of a custom that under such circumstances agent was liable to be treated as principal, 266. CONTRACT, IV.

2. Evidence of general authority to agent to order goods, so as to give vendor a right of action against such agent, in the absence of notice that his authority had terminated, 879. PRINCIPAL AND AGENT, IV.

III. Form of payment.

Covenant to pay by a promissory note, not satisfied by a mere delivery of such note: action for non-payment of such note not barred in six years, 963. PROMISSORY NOTE, I.

IV. Statute of Frauds.

Sect. 4. Agreement for the sale of an interest in land. Divisibility of contract, 543. STATUTE OF FRAUDS.

VESTING ORDER.

See Bankrupt and Insolvent, III., IV.

VESTRY.

I. Election of, under Metropolis Local Management Act.

1. Action against churchwarden, for refusing a vote. Allegation and proof of malice necessary, 877. Election, III. 2.

2. Jurisdiction of inspectors of votes, 954. Election, III. 1.

II. Election of Burial Board by vestry, under Burial Acts. See Burial Acts.

III. Vestries under certain local Acts.

What is a "majority" of the vestry, under stats. 2 G. 2, c. 10, and 18 G. 3, c. 74.

By a local Act, the management of the affairs of a parish was confided to a select vestry, consisting of an indefinite body. The Act provided that the vestry at their meetings, " or the major part of such of them as shall be assembled at such meetings," might do whatever could be done by an ordinary vestry. By a subsequent Act, power was given to the vestry, " or the major part of them," to appoint and dismiss collectors of the poor-rate. B. was appointed a collector of the poor-rate. A charge being brought against him, a meeting of the vestry was duly convened to consider. The vestry then consisted of eighty persons; thirty-five attended the meeting. A motion being made to dismiss B., sixteen voted for it, and eleven voted against it. It was declared to be carried; and B. was dismissed.

Held, by the Court of Exchequer Chamber, affirming the judgment of the Queen's Bench, that though the motion was carried by a majority of those voting, yet, not being carried by a majority of those present, it was not carried by a majority of those assembled; the vestrymen declining to vote not being considered in point of law absent. Consequently, that the dismissal was not effectual. *Regina v. Overseers of Christchurch,*   409

VOTE.

See Election.

WAR.

greement by owner of ship, that she should proceed to and load at a foreign port: when it is avoided by the breaking out of war between the two countries after such agreement and before her arrival, 769. Ship, I. 4.

WARD.

See Infant.

WARRANT.

Under Absconding Debtors Arrest Act. See County Court, III.

WARRANTY.

Action for breach of implied warranty that defendant had authority to purchase a ship on behalf of another party. Resale of ship: measure of damages, 568. Damages, II.

WASTE.

What structures, erected upon the glebe by an incumbent, may be removed by him or his executors, 237. Incumbent, I.

WATERCOURSE.

See Easement.

WILL.

I. Rights and liabilities of executors and administrators. See Executors and Administrators.

II. Construction of.

1. Devise "to G., his heirs lawfully begotten, for ever," subject to legacies out of the land.

Devise of land to G., his heirs lawfully begotten, for ever, gives G. an estate tail.

Although there is no limitation over.

And although the devise is made subject to G.'s making payments of specific pecuniary legacies out of the land. *Good v. Good,* 295

2. Devise of residue of a term to R., his executors, &c. Proviso, devesting it if R. or his issue male should become entitled to land comprised in the will of N. &c.: bad for remoteness.

The interest in the residue of a term of years in land was devised to R., his executors, &c., subject to a proviso that, if R. or his issue male should become actually entitled to land comprised in the will of N., the interest in the term should go over to another party.

By N.'s will, lands were devised to J. for life, remainder to trustees to preserve contingent remainders, remainder to J.'s first and other sons in tail general, remainder to R., remainder to trustees to preserve contingent remainders, remainder to R.'s first and other sons in tail general.

On the death of the devisor of the term, R. became possessed of the land devised for the term. He died; and his issue male entered into possession.

After R.'s death, J. died without issue, and the remainder to R.'s sons, under N.'s will, took effect.

Held, that the interest of R.'s representative in the term was not defeated, the proviso being bad for remoteness; for that, even if the proviso could be construed as contemplating independent alternatives, namely, the devolution of the estates comprised in N.'s will either to R. or to his issue male, still the alternative limitation under which alone, in the event, the proviso could operate, was the devolution to R.'s issue male, which alternative limitation was originally bad for remoteness.

And that it made no difference that in fact the devolution of the estate under N.'s will to R.'s issue male occurred during lives in being at the time of R.'s will. *Harding* v. *Nott*,   650

WITNESS

Conduct money, paid on subpœna, when and how recoverable back, 1.   ACTION, I. 1.

WRIT OF SUMMONS.

Amendment of.   See ACTION, II. 2.

END OF VOL. VII.